The Registers of St. Bene't and St. Peter, Paul's Wharf, London

THE

Publications

OF

The Harleian Society.

ESTABLISHED A.D. MDCCCLXIX.

Registers—Volume XL.

FOR THE YEAR MDCCCCXI.

The Registers of St. Bene't and St. Peter, Paul's Wharf, London.

EDITED BY

WILLOUGHBY A. LITTLEDALE, M.A., F.S.A.

Vol. III.—Marriages.

ST. BENE'T, 1731 TO 1837—ST. PETER, 1607 TO 1834.

LONDON:
1911.

YE WARDOVR PRESS
ESTABLISHED, 1797
140, WARDOVR STREET, LONDON, W.

The Registers

OF

St. Bene't, Paul's Wharf.

MARRIAGES.

1731.

Mar. 25 John Stevens of Whitechappel, Midx., B., and Elisabeth Wade of St Dunstan, Stepny, Midx., S.; by L. C.
*THO. COOKE, Rector.

April 1 Abraham Abell of Greenwich, Kent, B., and Elisabeth Hawkins of St Margaret, Westminster, Midx., W. L. C.

1 Emanuel Hicks of St Martin in the fields, Midx., W., and Alie [*sic*] Haydon of the same, W.; by Mr Phipps

3 Robert Towell of St James, Westminster, Midx., B., and Sarah Ronsom of the same, S.; by L. C.

4 John Stevens of St George, Midx., W., and Sarah Wooley of St Dunstan, Stepny, Midx., S.; by L. C.

4 Lewis Roussell of St Gyles in the fields, Midx., B., and Susanna Bishop of St Ann, Westminster, W.; by Dr Watkinson

5 William Withers of St Gyles, Cripplegate, Midx., W., and Elisabeth Roe of St John, Hackny, Midx., S.; by Mr Crank, Rector, Hatford

6 Thomas Reed of Stoke Newington, Midx., B., and Catherine Mark of the same, S.; by L. C.

7 William Millington of St Gyles in the fields, Midx., B., and Jemima Coy of the same, S.; by L. C.

8 Richard Chicheley of Chatham, Kent, W., and Abigail Hartop of Deptford, Kent, W.; by L. C.

10 Samuel Turner of St Paul, Covent Garden, Midx., B., and Elisabeth Fox of St Dunstan in the East, Lond., S.; by L. C.

11 Edward Colleton of St George, Hanover Square, Midx., Esq., B., and the Honourable Lady Ann Cowper of the same, S.; by Corn: Ford, A.M.

11 Edward Blackett of St Nicholas, Deptford, Kent, B., and Margarett Sherwell of the same, S.; by L. C.

11 John Bowman of St Andrew, Holborn, Midx., B., and Susanna Mantle of the same, S.; by L. C.

12 Robert Leper of Fincheley, Midx., W., and Elisabeth Woodward of Aldenham, Hertford, W.; by L. C.

17 John Horton of St Mary Aldermary, Lond., W., and Mary Atwell of this Parish, W.; by L. C.

17 James Parker of St Dunstan in the East, Lond., B., and Ann Yatman of Westham, Essex, S.; by L. C.

18 John Crawley of St James, Westminster, Midx., B., and Barbara Shuttleworth of the same, S.; by L. C.

* This is the last page signed by Tho. Cooke, the Rector, or by any succeeding Rector. The entries, however, continue to be made in apparently the same handwriting up to 22 Mar. 1731.—ED.

1731

April 18 Henry Shaw of St Andrew, Holborn, Midx., B., and Mary Weight of the same, S.; by L. C.

19 Henry Wilson of Northaw, Hertford, B., and Sarah Povey of Hampton, Midx., S.; by L. C.

19 Samuel Colebrook of St James, Westminster, Midx., B., and Ann Phillips of the same, S.; by L. C.

19 John Littleford of St Giles's, Cripplegate, Midx., B., and Ann Younger of St Martin in the Fields, Midx., W.; by L. C.

19 Isaac Greentree of Harrow on the Hill, Midx., B., and Elisabeth Peaton of Ealing, Midx., S.; by L. C.

20 John Pettener, Clerk, Rector of Wainfleet, Lincoln, B., and Sarah Carter of Worplesdon, Surry, S.; by L. C.

20 Thomas Palmer of Wingham, Kent, B., and Sarah How of Bexley, Kent, S.; by L. C.

20 Thomas Armstrong of St Martin in the Fields, Midx., B., and Jane Henderson of the same, W.; by L. C.

20 John Edmonds of Deptford, Kent, B., and Elisabeth Pedder of Battersea, Surry, S.; by L. C.

20 Caleb Simmonds of St Dunstan, Stepny, Midx., B., and Judith Goodchild of the same, S.; by L. C.

20 James Leaver of North Hull, Hertford, B., and Sarah Brown of St Margaret Pattons, Lond., S.; by L. C.

20 John Weir of St Margaret, Westminster, Midx., W., and Agnes Christy of the same, S.; by L. C.

21 James Pilkington of St Mary Magdalene, Milk Street, Lond., W., and Mary Robins of the Precinct of Norton Folgate, Midx., W.; by L. C.

22 Thomas Moggeridge of St Peter le Poor, Lond., B., and Rose Newman of the same, S.; by L. C.

22 Charles Day of Wincanton, Somerset, B., and Elisabeth Cheney of the Isle of Whight in the County of Southampton, W.; by L. C.

22 James Jackson of Edmington, Midx., B., and Elisabeth Smite of St Mary Aldermary, Lond., S.; by L. C.

22 Richard Granger of St Ann, Blackfryers, Lond., B., and Mary Mills of the same, S.; by L. C.

22 Thomas Bromley of St Martin in the Fields, Midx., B., and Alice Wilkins of the same, S.; by L. C.

22 Samuel Hurst of St John, Wapping, Midx., B., and Alice Lunt of St Paul, Shadwell, Midx., W.; by L. C.

23 Thomas Wyat of Witham, Essex, B., and Susanna Read of the same, S.; by L. C.

23 Hugh Boulton of St Albans, Hertford, B., and Mary Smith of Barnett, Midx., S.; by L. C.

24 John Winfeild of Aldenham, Hertford, B., and Sarah Wharton of Otterspool, Hert., S.; by L. C.

25 Robert Stacey of St George the Martyr, Midx., B., and Philippa Adson of St Clement, Eastcheap, Lond., S.; by L. C.

25 William Potton of St Mary, White Chappell, Midx., B., and Jane Sherrer of St Leonard, Eastcheap, Lond., S.; by L. C.

25 Charles Smith of St Pancras, Midx., B., and Jane Terrel of St Andrew, Holborn, Midx., S.; by L. C.

26 James Roberts of Allhallows, Bread S^t, Lond., W., and Catherine Rauthmall of the same, W.; by L. C.

26 Gabriel Everard of St Clement Danes, Midx., B., and Triphana Cowdell of St Giles's in the Fields, Midx., W.; by L. C.

27 Edmund Favill of St Martin in the Fields, Midx., B., and Cœlia Woolley of Allhallows the Great, Lond., S.; by L. C.

1731

April 27 John Wellbeloved of Thorpe, Surry, B., and Ann Chapman of Chessey, Surry, S.; by L. C.

27 John Grover of Uxbridge, Midx., B., and Silence Hills of Christ Church, Midx., S.; by L. C.

27 Griffith Jones of Richmond, Surry, B., and Elisabeth Turner of the same, S.; by L. C.

28 John Nossiter of St George, Hanover Square, Midx., B., and Mary Clarke of St Brides, Lond., S.; by L. C.

29 Henry Juer of Battersea, Surry, B., and Sarah Berry of the same, S.; by L. C.

29 John Douglas of St James, Westminster, Midx., B., and Mary Gardner of Croydon, Surry, S.; by L. C.

29 Richard Gimber of St George, Southwark, Surry, W., and Judith Webb of the same, W.; by L. C.

29 Bartholomew Watson of Great Boughton, York, B., and Dorothea Baynes of Bentham in the same County, S.; by L. C.

30 Peter Echus of Disley in the county of Chester, B., and Esther Davis of Landislea, Carmarthen, S.; by L. C.

30 Thomas Stevens of Banstead, Surry, B., and Elisabeth Kingham of Hattfordbury, Herts, S.; by L. C.

30 John Pescot of St Botolph, Bishopsgate, Lond., W., and Elisabeth Cooke of the same, W.; by L. C.

May 3 John Nott of Brayden Forrest, Wilts, B., and Elisabeth Neale of Allesley, Warwick, S.; by L. C.

4 William Martyr of St George, Hanover Square, Midx., B., and Elisabeth Cooper of St James, Westminster, Midx., S.; by L. C.

4 John Brown of St James, Westminster, Midx., B., and Elisabeth Newport of the same, W.; by L. C.

5 William Norton of Aylesbury, Bucks, W., and Susanna Winfield of Rickmansworth, Hertford, S.; by L. C.

5 Gabriel Moore of Kingston, Surry, B., and Ann Smith of the same, S.; by L. C.

5 Scroop Lyon of St Margaret, Westminster, Midx., B., and Francis Meredith of St Martin in the Fields, Midx., S.; by L. C.

5 Thomas Whitehead of Marybone, Mx., B., and Jane Goat of St James, Westminster, Mx., S.; by L. C.

5 John Watson of St James, Westminster, Mx., B., and Elisabeth Bridge of St Martin in the Fields, Mx., W.; by L. C.

6 Joseph Beach of St Nicholas, Deptford, Kent, W., and Martha Simons of the same, W.; by L. C.

6 George Townsend of St James, Westminster, Mx., B., and Ann Dowthat of St George, Hanover Square, Mx., S.; by L. C.

6 Richard Honyman of St George, Hannover Square, Midx., B., and Mary Palmer of the same, S.; by L. C.

6 Mark Jackson of St James, Westminster, Mx., B., and Sarah Foulston of St George, Hannover Square, Mx., S.; by L. C.

6 George Atterberry of Chalgrave, Bedfordshire, W., and Elisabeth Osborn of the same, S.; by L. C.

6 Robert Porter of West Drayton, Midx., B., and Alice Bagnall of the same, S.; by L. C.

6 William Hardistey of St James, Westminster, Midx., W., and Mary Bannister of the same, S.; by Mr Turner

7 Thomas Johns of One Ash, Surry, B., and Mary Griffith of Horseley in the same County, S.; by L. C.

8 John Owen of St Andrew, Holborn, Midx., B., and Jane Scates of St James, Westminster, Midx., S.; by L. C.

1731

May 8 Thomas Hudspe of St Andrew, Holborn, Lond., B., and Susanna Weston of the same, S.; by L. C.

8 Robert Davidson of St Stephen, Coleman St., Lond., B., and Mary Ward of the same, S.; by L. C.

10 Robert Oliver of Stockton in the County of Durham, B., and Jane Elstob of Greatham in the same county, S.; by Dr Watkinson

10 John Kaye of St Mary, Islington, Midx., B., and Ann Stevens of St Albans, Hertford, S.; by Dr Watkinson

11 Ezekiel Varrenne of St Ann, Westminster, Midx., W., and Antonia Brugnier of St Martin in the Fields, Midx., S.; by L. C.

11 Abraham Miller of Rumford in the Parish of Hornchurch, Essex, B., and Sarah Coumbers of North Weal in the same County, S; by L. C.

11 Marcellus Green of Basingstoke, Southampton, W., and Catherine Fisher of St Margaret, Westminster, Midx., S.; by L. C.

11 Martin Arundell of St Giles's, Cripplegate, Midx., B., and Ann Darbyshire of the same, S.; by L. C.

12 John Nickolls of Fish Field, Essex, B., and Elisabeth Oram of the same, W.; by L. C.

12 John Bellman of St Mary, Rotherhith, Surry, B., and Judith Hutton of the same, S.; by L. C.

13 Peter Crayford of the City of Canterbury, W., and Mary Didier of the same, S.; by L. C.

13 Richard Faulkner of Harmonsworth, Midx., W., and Sarah Blunt of the same, S.; by L. C.

13 Stephen Stanly of St John Zachary, Lond., B., and Ester Cord of the same, S.; by L. C.

13 Joel Season of St James, Westminster, Midx., B., and Ann Radmore of the same, S.; by L. C.

13 William Cockerill of St John, Wapping, Midx., B., and Jane Oxley of the same, S.; by L. C.

15 Charles Port of St Pancras in the Fields, Midx., B., and Jane Bromley of the Precinct of St Catherine, Lond., S.; by L. C.

16 John Coulthurst of St Clement Danes, Midx., B., and Martha Forrest of the same, S.; by L. C.

18 Thomas Jones of St Giles's in the fields, Midx., W., and Sarah Jackson of the same, S.; by L. C.

20 Thomas Woodward of Aldenham, Herts, B., and Mary Winfield of the same, S.; by L. C.

22 John Perry of St Olave, Southwark, Surry, W., and Ann Bartterworth of the same, S.; by Mr Turner

24 Francis Wilson of Whitby, Yorkshire, B., and Isabella Crow of the same, S.; by Dr Watkinson

25 Isaac Rideout of St Leonard, Foster Lane, Lond., B., and Elisabeth Scarlett of the same Parish, S.; by L. C.

26 William Petit of St Martin in the Fields, Midx., B., and Mary Howard of the same, S.; by L. C.

27 George Hawkins of St Botolph, Bishopsgate, Lond., B., and Sarah Handwine of St Dunstan, Stepney, Midx., S.; by L. C.

27 Clement Dawson of St John, Wapping, Midx., W., and Mary Ray alias Holdsworth of St George in the East, Midx., W.; by L. C.

27 William Penn of St Margaret, Westminster, Midx., W., and Sarah Adams of Richmond, Surry, W.; by Dr Watkinson

31 Roger Russell of St Dunstan in the West, Lond., B., and Jemima Jones of the same, S.; by L. C.

June 1 William Lyster of Quatford, Shropshire, B., and Elisabeth Owen of Dukhill in the same County, S.; by L. C.

1731

June 3 John Benson of Richmond, Surry, W., and Catherine Withell of the same, S.; by L. C.

3 Isaac Woolley of S[t] Gyles, Cripplegate, Midx., B., and Mary Kirk of the same, W.; by L. C.

3 Richard Harrin of Lambeth, Surry, B., and Elisabeth Perry of the same, S.; by L. C.

3 William Clisbee of S[t] Giles's, Cripplegate, Lond., B., and Elisabeth Williams of S[t] Ann, Aldersgate, Lond., S.; by L. C.

3 Jonathan Stanton of Ebisham, Surry, B., and Ann Wright of the same, S.; by L. C.

4 William Copley of S[t] Andrew, Holborn, Midx., W., and Mary Kentish of S[t] Giles's in the Fields, Midx., S.; by L. C.

5 Richard Giver of Kelshall, Hertford, B., and Susanna Rassell of the same, S.; by L. C.

5 John Lodge of S[t] Catherine Cree-Church, Lond., B., and Margaret Hollman of S[t] Catherine Coleman, Lond., W.; by L. C.

7 Edward Ives of S[t] George the Martyr, Midx., B., and Elisabeth Bateman of S[t] Pancras, Midx., S.; by L. C.

7 Clement Plum of Albury, Hertford, B., and Mary Some of S[t] Giles's, Cripplegate, Lond., S.; by L. C.

7 Robert Gardner of Barnes, Surry, B., and Ruth Maybank of the same, S.; by L. C.

7 James Dunn of Fulham, Midx., W., and Eleanor Gray of the same, S.; by L. C.

8 Thomas Pratt of the Middle Temple, Lond., B., and Margaret Hubbard of S[t] George's, Surry, S.; by L. C.

8 Richard Burch of S[t] Catherine Coleman, Lond., B., and Honour Hunt of the same, S.; by L. C.

8 Charles Woodd of S[t] Helen's, Lond., B., and Elisabeth Burtwell of the same, S.; by L. C.

8 William Oldham of S[t] Margaret, Westminster, Midx., B., and Susanna Keep of Grays, Oxon, S.; by L. C.

9 Thomas Hebert of S[t] Bennett Fink, Lond., B., and Martha Susanna De Meausee Dauteuil of this Parish, S.; by L. C.

10 John Smith of S[t] Lawrence in the Old Jewry, Lond., B., and Ann Mason of the same, S.; by L. C.

11 Edward Willis of S[t] Clement Danes, Midx., B., and Mary Austin of the same, S.; by L. C.

11 Thomas Jones of S[t] John, Wapping, Midx., W., and Ann Puleston of the same, S.; by L. C.

12 Ralph Blackbourn of Wandsworth, Surry, B., and Esther Blackbourn of the same, S.; by L. C.

13 John Cox of S[t] Sepulchre's, Lond., B., and Elisabeth Dickinson* of the same, S.; by L. C.

13 William Willis of S[t] Andrew, Holborn, Midx., W., and Mary Griffith of the same, S.; by L. C.

15 William Wardroper of Battersea, Surry, B., and Ann Grumein of the same, S.; by L. C.

15 John Spencer of S[t] John, Clerkenwell, Midx., B., and Isabella Clarkson of the same, W.; by L. C.

15 Matthew Totterdell of S[t] John the Evangelist, Midx., B., and Mary Shugg of the same, S.; by L. C.

15 William Anderson of S[t] Michael Bassishaw, Lond., B., and Ann Burwash of the same, S.; by L. C.

15 Samuel Ogburn of S[t] Vedast alias Foster Lane, Lond., B., and Mary Browne of S[t] Leonard, Shoreditch, S.; by L. C.

* Altered from "Dickenson."—Ed.

1731

June 16 John Didelsfold of St Giles in the Fields, Midx., B., and Grace Sparrow of Cooledge, Camb., S.; by L. C.

17 William Scott of Christ-Church, Lond., B., and Ann Roswell of St Mary, Islington, Midx., S.; by L. C.

17 Edward Sanderson of St Giles's in the Fields, Midx., B., and Selenia Herriott of the same Parish, W.; by L. C.

20 George Buckeridge of St Andrew, Holborn, Midx., B., and Ann Martin of the same, S.; by L. C.

22 John Charlton of Chigwell, Essex, B., and Jane Masters of Christ Church, Midx., S.; by L. C.

23 Benjamin Mitchell of St Alban's, Hertford, B., and Abigail Jeffs of the same place, S.; by L. C.

24 Samuel Godfrey of St George's, Bloomsbury, Midx., B., and Dorothy Ecton of the same, S.; by L. C.

24 John Wilson of Whitechappel, Midx., B., and Elisabeth Allright of the same, W.; by L. C.

26 Jervis Rawson of Stepny, Midx., B., and Amy Kendrick of the same, S.; by L. C.

28 Richard Darlington of St Stephen, Coleman Street, Lond., B., and Rachael Jordan of the same, W.; by L. C.

29 Richard Ward of St James, Westminster, Midx., W., and Olive Loyd of the same, S.; by L. C.

29 Thomas Jackson of Beckenham, Kent, B., and Ann Elphick of the same, S.; by L. C.

29 Thomas Miller of Epping, Essex, B., and Ann Palmer of Stanstead Mountfitchet in the same County, S.; by L. C.

30 John Williamson of Christ Church, Spittlefields, Midx., W., and Elisabeth Butler of St Giles's, Cripplegate, Midx., W.; by L. C.

30 John Hanscomb of Clapham, Surry, B., and Elisabeth Hunter of the same, S.; by L. C.

30 Nathanael Reed of Wilsdon, Midx., W., and Dinah Ward of Fulmore, Bucks, S.; by L. C.

July 1 Rice Lewelyn of St Andrew, Holborn, Lond., B., and Elisabeth Creed of St Dunstan in the West, Lond., S.; by Mr Turner

1 Daniel Weeden of Heston, Midx., W., and Ann Darley of the same Parish, W.; by Mr Turner

1 John White of Bromley, Midx., B., and Elisabeth Hatt of St Mary, Stratford le Bow, Midx., W.; by Mr Turner

1 Henry Bishop of St Botolph, Bishopsgate, Lond., W., and Mary Day of St Mary Athill, Lond., S.; by Mr Turner

2 John Bowman of St Dunstan, Stepny, Midx., W., and Christian Hard of the same, W.; by L. C.

3 Nathanael Weeden of St Dunstan in the East, Lond., B., and Elisabeth Heacock of St Giles's, Cripplegate, Midx., S.; by L. C.

8 Thomas Oswin of All Saints in the Town of Leicester, B., and Elisabeth Lingard of St Martins in the same Town, S.; by L. C.

8 Linstead Reeves of St Giles's, Cripplegate, Lond., B., and Jane Hill of St Bridgett, Lond., S.; by L. C.

8 John Graham of Rocliff, Cambridgeshire, B., and Hannah Irwing of Farnborow, Hants, S.; by L. C.

10 Thomas Simmonds of St George, Hanover Square, Midx., B., and Margarett Johnson of the same, S.; by L. C.

10 John Fasson of St Botolph, Aldersgate, Lond., B., and Mary Willis of St George, Bloomsbury, Midx., S.; by L. C.

10 John Wright of the City of Coventry, B., and Ann Monk of the same city, S.; by L. C.

11 Richard Mugridge of Horton, Kent, B., and Elisabeth Lane of the same, S.; by L. C.

1731

July 11 John Austin of Richmond, Surry, B., and Mary Taylor of the same, S.; by L. C.

13 Robert Owen of St Michael, Queenhith, Lond., B., and Elisabeth Oldberry of the same, W.; by L. C.

13 Thomas Fallowfield of Birmingham, Warwickshire, B., and Savilia Hyde of St Martin in the Fields, Midx., S.; by L. C.

14 William Martin of Plumstead, Kent, B., and Francis [*sic*] Moore of Deptford, Kent, S.; by L. C.

14 Felix Wilson of St James, Clerkenwell, Midx., B., and Mary Stevens of St Dunstan in the West, Lond., S.; by L. C.

15 William Quelch of St Magnus the Martyr, Lond., W., and Mary Scott of St Margaret, Westminster, Midx., W.; by L. C.

15 Richard Symes of Lewisham, Kent, Esqr, B., and Mary Austen of Bexley, Kent, S.; by L. C.

17 William Knight of St George, Bloomsbury, Midx., B., and Jane Stumps of St Margaret, Westminster, Midx., S.; by L. C.

20 James Rous of St Paul, Deptford, Kent, B., and Elisabeth Rowley of the same Parish, S.; by L. C.

20 Robert Raitt of St George's, Midx., B., and Alice Thomson of the same, W.; by L. C.

23 Thomas Foster of St Nicholas, Deptford, Kent, B., and Elisabeth Bowen of Christ Church, Lond., S.; by L. C.

25 Bridger Lambe of St Bartholomew by Exchange, Lond., B., and Elisabeth Gitton of St Stephen, Coleman Street, Lond., S.; by L. C.

26 William Burch of Acton, Midx., B., and Sarah Baker of Bromley, Kent, S.; by L. C.

28 John Dighton of Deptford, Kent, B., and Elisabeth Sanders of St Brides, Lond., S.; by L. C.

30 Henry Hemrick of St Catherine's by the Tower, Lond., W., and Rebecca Gratwick of St Dunstan, Stepny, Midx., W.; by L. C.

30 John Phillips of St Olave, Southwark, Surry, B., and Sarah Wheatland of the same, S.; by L. C.

30 William Wind of this Parish, B., and Bridgett Fidler of St Martin, Ludgate, Lond., S.; by L. C.

Aug. 1 Samuel Gill of St Clement Danes, Midx., B., and Ann Savill of the same, S.; by L. C.

1 John Skerry of St Leonard, Shoreditch, Midx., B., and Elisabeth Le Brumen of the same, S.; by L. C.

1 John Turnbull of St Martin in the Fields, Midx., B., and Elisabeth Erving of St Margaret, Westminster, Midx., S.; by L. C.

2 Henry Butler Pacey of Clements Inn, Midx., B., and Margaret Wallington of St Botolph, Bishopsgate, Lond., S.; by L. C.

3 Robert Bell of St Ann, Westminster, Midx., W., and Martha Gale of the same, S.; by L. C.

6 Isaac Bourne of Edmonton, Midx., B., and Ann Barnes of St Hellen's, Lond., S.; by L. C.

7 Francis Withers of St Ethelburgh, Lond., W., and Ruth Clarke of St Botolph, Aldgate, Lond., W.; by L. C.

7 Davie Steward of Barnett, Hertford, W., and Susanna Ireland of the same, S.; by L. C.

8 James Oldis of St Saviour's, Southwark, Surry, B., and Mary Bowen of the same, S.; by L. C.

9 Thomas Green of St Margaret, Westminster, Midx., B., and Mary Bird of the same, W.; by L. C.

9 William Buckland of Greenwich, Kent, B., and Susanna Wood of the same, S.; by L. C.

1731

Aug. 10 Jonathan Bushnell of St Lawrence, Jewry, Lond., B., and Elisabeth Blissett of the same, S.; by L. C.

10 Samuel Toft of St Botolph, Aldgate, Lond., B., and Margaret Wilkins of the same, W.; by L. C.

10 John Saywell of Mile End Old Town, Midx., B., and Mary Cooper of the same, S.; by L. C.

10 Robert Crucefix of St Ann, Westminster, Midx., B., and Ann Purquot of St John the Evangelist, Midx., S.; by L. C.

12 Robert Silk of St Mary Athill, Lond., B., and Elisabeth Ottey of the same, S.; by L. C.

13 Thomas Haines of St Leonard, Shoreditch, Midx., B., and Salome Clarke of Bocking, Essex, W.; by L. C.

13 Thomas Champnes of Epping, Essex, B., and Mary Weldon of St John the Evangelist, Midx., S.; by L. C.

14 Isaac Kimpton of St Austin's, Lond., W., and Lydia Winter of Christ Church, Lond., S.; by L. C.

14 Daniel Davis of Bromley, Kent, B., and Elisabeth Kiffin of the same, W.; by L. C.

14 James Straddan of Thames Ditton, Midx., B., and Sarah Talker of the same Parish, S.; by L. C.

17 Henry Sell of St Mary Athill, Lond., B., and Frances Hearn of St Lawrence Pountney, Lond., S.; by L. C.

17 Thomas Ward of this Parish, Lond., W., and Mary Clarke of St Mary, Islington, Midx., W.; by L. C.

19 The Revd Henry Bache, Clerk, of Doddington, Kent, B., and Lucy Whitfield of St Margaret, Westminster, Midx., S.; by L. C.

20 Richard Hughes of St Ann, Limehouse, Midx., B., and Catherine Heater of the same, W.; by L. C.

20 Jacob Massy of St Ann, Westminster, Midx., W., and Magdalen Bent of the same Parish, S.; by L. C.

22 John Bradley of Christ Church, Midx., B., and Ann Coxeter of St Gyles's, Cripplegate, Lond., S.; by L. C.

24 Richard Frizzell of St James, Clerkenwell, Midx., W., and Susanna Walker of St Sepulchres, Midx., W.; by L. C.

24 Nehemiah Barnett of St Faith's, Lond., B., and Dorothy Nash of St Martin's in the Fields, Midx., S.; by L. C.

26 Thomas Harris of St Andrew, Holborn, Midx., W., and Elisabeth Lewis of the same, S.; by L. C.

26 Henry Mountfort of St Buttolph, Aldgate, Midx., B., and Rebecca Jones of St Paul, Shadwell, in the same County, S.; by L. C.

27 Nelson Bigsby of Welton, Suffolk, B., and Abigail Vertue of Debbish, Suffolk, S.; by L. C.

30 William Turner of Christ Church, Surry, B., and Elisabeth Oates of Lambeth, Surry, W.; by L. C.

31 David Pike of Christ Church, Surry, B., and Elisabeth Throsley of the same, W.; by L. C.

31 John Nehring of St Giles's in the Fields, Midx., B., and Frances Gunthorpe of St James, Westminster, Midx., S.; by L. C.

31 Robert Kirk of Hammersmith in the Parish of Fulham, Midx., B., and Elisabeth Morley of the same, W.; by L. C.

Sept. 1 John Chrutchley of St Botolph, Bishopsgate, Lond., B., and Martha Sadler of Bromley, Midx., S.; by L. C.

3 Thomas Rippon of Fulham, Midx., B., and Elisabeth Brassett of the same, S.; by L. C.

3 George Leicester of St Mary Magdalen, Bermondsey, Surry, W., and Elisabeth Bell of the same, W.; by L. C.

1731

Sept. 3 John Moore of St Giles's in the Fields, Midx., W., and Jane De Berdt of the same Parish, W.; by L. C.

5 William Mandevill of St Stephen, Coleman Street, Lond., W., and Isabella Bunnis of the same, S.; by L. C.

5 Robert Streames of Allhallows the Great, Lond., B., and Mary Richards of the same, W.; by L. C.

5 John Hulme of St Clement Danes, Midx., B., and Mary Pearce of the same S.; by L. C.

7 John Smith of St Olave, Southwark, Surry, B., and Mary Johnson of Hearne, Kent, S.; by L. C.

7 Henry James of St Margaret, Westminster, Midx., B., and Ann Barlow of the same, S.; by L. C.

8 Earl Newland of Deptford, Kent, B., and Susanna Newman of the same, S.; by L. C.

8 William Chapman of Acton, Midx., B., and Rachael Beck of the same Parish, S.; by L. C.

9 William Bathe of St George, Hanover Square, Midx., B., and Francis Andrews of the same, S.; by L. C.

9 Robert Jennings of St Margaret, Westminster, Midx., B., and Mary Webb of the same, S.; by L. C.

9 John Dawson of Isleworth, Midx., B., and Ann Sharp of the same Parish, S.; by L. C.

9 Michael Martin of St Paul, Shadwell, Midx., B., and Elisabeth Baxendin of the same, W.; by L. C.

10 Samuel Finch of Woodbridge, Suffolk, W., and Ann Upton of the same, S.; by L. C.

11 Robert Todd of St Clement Danes, Midx., B., and Ann Parker of St Andrew, Holborn, Midx., W.; by L. C.

12 Richard Randell of New Brentford, Midx., W., and Elisabeth Fluse of Staines,* Midx., S.; by L. C.

13 John Braiser of Lambeth, Surry, B., and Ann Karby of the same Parish, S.; by L. C.

13 Robert Harris of Hammersmith in the Parish of Fulham, Midx., W., and Susanna Beazer of the City of Bristol, W.; by L. C.

14 Robert Long of the Parish of St Laurence in the Isle of Thanett, Kent, B., and Sarah Goatley of the same Parish, S.; by L. C.

14 Robert Cook Babington of South Weald, Essex, B., and Jane Ramsden of the same, S.; by L. C.

14 Edward Dennis of St Gyles's, Cripplegate, Midx., B., and Sarah Saunders of St Leonard, Shoreditch, Mx., S.; by L. C.

16 John Allin of Linfield, Sussex, B., and Mary Mitchell of Horstead, Sussex, S.; by L. C.

16 James Willson of St Saviour's, Southwark, Surry, B., and Ann Wright of Farnborough, Kent, S.; by L. C.

17 Henry Rasor of St Saviour's, Southwark, Surry, B., and Elisabeth Cooke of the same, S.; by L. C.

18 John King of All Saints in Hertford, Herts, B., and Alice Nash of Cheshunt, Hert., S.; by L. C.

18 Jeffery Taylor of St George's, Southwark, Surry, B., and Mary Martin of the same, S.; by L. C.

19 Oliver Luddington of St Martin's in the Fields, Midx., B., and Sarah Jones of the same Parish, W.; by L. C.

19 William Farra of St Nicholas, Deptford, Kent, B., and Ann Browne of the same, S.; by L. C.

19 John Reid of St Clement Danes, Midx., B., and Rachael Dale of St Martin in the Fields, Midx., S.; by L. C.

* "Staines" written over an erasure.—ED.

1731

Sept. 19 John Barnes of St Olave, Southwark, Surry, W., and Eleanor Humphrys of St Gyles's in the Fields, Midx., S.; by L. C.

20 Richard Burrell of St Paul, Deptford, Kent, W., and Mary Budge of the same, S.; by L. C.

20 William Baker of Weston Turvil, Bucks, B., and Jane Goodson of the same, S.; by L. C.

21 Thomas Welling of Alhallows on London Wall, Lond., B., and Sarah Hance of the same, S.; by L. C.

28 Edward Warwick of Rickmansworth, Hertford, B., and Martha Aldwin of the same, S.; by L. C.

28 James Gilbert of St Paul, Covent Garden, Midx., B., and Mary Vandenan of St Martin in the Fields, Midx., S.; by L. C.

29 Abraham Cock of St George the Martyr, Midx., B., and Ann Batcheler of the same, W.; by L. C.

29 John Scrogham of St Ann and Agnes, Aldersgate, Lond., B., and Ann Stanley of Woodford, Essex, W.; by Dr Watkinson

30 George Merrick of East Greenwich, Kent, B., and Jane Wagstaff of the same, S.; by L. C.

30 Thomas Vaughan of St Stephen, Coleman Street, Lond., B., and Mehetabell Twelves of the same, W.; by L. C.

30 Moses Cottrill of Hanworth, Midx., B., and Hannah Smith of the same, S.; by L. C.

30 John Merrill of St Botolph, Bishopsgate, Lond., B., and Elisabeth Maynard of the same, S.; by L. C.

30 John Parr of St Vedast alias Foster, Lond., B., and Mary Fendall of St Mary Magdalen, Bermondsey, Surry, S.; by Wm Browning, Rector of Bermondsey

Oct. 1 Thomas Roberts of Feversham, Kent, B., and Rachael Durin of the same, S.; by L. C.

3 George Colins of St Paul, Covent Garden, Midx., B., and Mary Brice of the same, S.; by L. C.

3 John Jarrett of Limehouse, Midx., B., and Mary Dennis of the same, S.; by L. C.

3 Benjamin Ayers of St Clement Danes, Midx., B., and Ann Sisson of the same, S.; by L. C.

4 George Douglass of St Clement Danes, Midx., B., and Margaret Colless of the same, S.; by L. C.

4 William Wettnal of Burley, Kent, B., and Mary Figg of the same, S.; by L. C.

4 John Moore of Hatfield, Hertfordshire, B., and Martha Acton of Fulham, Midx., S.; by L. C.

6 John Hart of Hackney, Midx., B., and Mary May of the same, S.; by L. C.

6 John Burles of Butsbury, Essex, W., and Sarah Jackson of Great Bustead, Essex, W.; by L. C.

7 Richard Holmes of St James, Westminster, Midx., W., and Sarah Malin of the same, S.; by L. C.

7 James Crosbie of St Paul, Shadwell, Midx., B., and Jane Spence of the same, S.; by L. C.

7 Richard Prideaux of St Magnus the Martyr, Lond., B., and Ann Goodchild of Wandsworth, Surry, S.; by L. C.

7 Thomas Leaper of St Dunstan in the West, Lond., B., and Elisabeth Phipps of Windsor, Berks, S.; by L. C.

8 Robert Chandler of St Andrew, Holborn, Midx., B., and Ann Stainbach of St Sepulchres, Lond., W.; by L. C.

8 William Cutleff of St George, Hanover Square, Midx., B., and Hannah Butler of Allhallows Barking, Lond., S.; by L. C.

1731

Oct. 9 Garston Harcourt of S[t] John, Hackney, Midx., B., and Susanna Chapman of Chuckfield, Sussex, W.; by L. C.

9 John Young of S[t] Mary, Aldermanbury, Lond., B., and Ann Gale of Dunstable, Bedfordshire, S.; by L. C.

10 Thomas Bevan of S[t] George, Hanover Square, Midx., B., and Sarah Ransteed of the same, S.; by L. C.

11 Thomas Hapeworth of Christ Church, Surry, B., and Catherine Goss of the same, S.; by L. C.

11 Edward Adams of Waltham upon Thames, Surry, B., and Letitia Waller of the same, S.; by L. C.

12 Francis Woodland of Barking, Essex, B., and Elisabeth Young of the same Parish, S.; by L. C.

12 Robert Chevin of Scopwick, Lincolnshire, B., and Ann Town of Chelsea, Midx., S.; by L. C.

13 Richard Cooper of Shipperton, Midx., B., and Mary Sedgwick of the same, S.; by L. C.

14 Joshua Brown of S[t] Dunstan in the West, Lond., B., and Rebecca Lucas of S[t] Martin in the Fields, Midx., S.; by L. C.

16 Samuel Paul of S[t] Gyles's in the Fields, Midx., B., and Mary Edwards of the same, S.; by L. C.

19 Peregrine Jones of S[t] Martin in the Fields, Midx., B., and Hester Loyd of the same, S.; by L. C.

19 Thomas Smith of Battersea, Surry, B., and Catherine Berry of the same, W.; by L. C.

20 Burges Clark of New Brentford in the Parish of Hanwell, Midx., B., and Sarah Franclin of the same, S.; by L. C.

20 William Elliott of Bromley, Kent, B., and Mary Axe of the same, S.; by L. C.

20 Thomas Shirley of S[t] Olave, Southwark, Surry, B., and Elisabeth Hall of S[t] John, Wappin, Midx., S.; by L. C.

21 James Worger of S[t] James, Westminster, Midx., B., and Jane Bickerton of S[t] Andrew, Holborn, Midx., S.; by L. C.

23 Daniel Bellamy of Cudham, Kent, B., and Eleanor Ockley of Oxstead, Surry, S.; by L. C.

23 William Cort of S[t] Paul, Deptford, Kent, B., and Jane Richardson of Islington, Midx., S.; by L. C.

23 William Jones of S[t] George the Martyr, Midx., B., and Mary Gatten of S[t] Andrew, Holborn, Midx., S.; by L. C.

24 William Burrough of S[t] Clement Danes, Midx., B., and Catherine Spring of S[t] George, Bloomsbury, Midx., S.; by L. C.

25 John Humfery of Linkfield, Surry, B., and Cloe Crease of East Greenstead, Sussex, S.; by L. C.

26 Henry Howard of Uxbridge, Midx., B., and Grace Maud of the same, S.; by M[r] Turner

26 Edward Hinton of S[t] Ann, Westminster, Midx., B., and Frances Blackshaw of the same Parish, W.; by M[r] Turner

26 Samuel Bayford of Bishop Storford, Hertford, W., and Mary Rowley of Saffron Walden, Essex, S.; by M[r] Turner

26 William Rolfe of West Tilbury, Essex, B., and Ann Dennis of East Tilbury, Essex, S.; by L. C.

27 Thomas Wickens of S[t] Sepulchre's, Midx., W., and Sarah Pick of the same, S.; by L. C.

28 Ezekiel Wharter of S[t] Mary, Whitechappell, Midx., B., and Sarah Percey of the same, W.; by L. C.

29 Thomas Jemson of S[t] Mary Woolnoth, Lond., W., and Sarah Holman of S[t] Gyles's in the Fields, Midx., W.; by L. C.

1731

Oct. 29 Thomas Chard of St Ann's in the East, Midx., W., and Eleanor Ward of the same, W.; by L. C.

30 William Pearson of Raysborough, Bucks, B., and Sarah Stanley of Twittenham, Midx., S.; by L. C.

30 Joseph Salway of Allhallows Barking, Lond., W., and Ruth Hedges of Deptford, Kent, W.; by L. C.

30 John Sheppard, Esq., of Cempsy Ash, Suffolk, W., and Mrs Hannah Wilmott, late of Mincing Lane, but now of Bridewell Precinct, Lond., S.; by L. C.

31 Thomas French of St Olave, Southwark, Surry, B., and Sarah Mason of the same, S.; by L. C.

Nov. 1 William Boffey of St Martin in the Fields, Midx., W., and Elisabeth Parker of St James, Westminster, Midx., W.; by L. C.

1 Edward Owers of St Paul, Covent Garden, Midx., B., and Martha Maybank of the same, S.; by L. C.

2 John Bowes of Battersea, Surry, B., and Mary Peck of Lambeth, Surry, W.; by Dr Watkinson

3 George Hagger of St Andrew, Holborn, Midx., B., and Sarah Wright of the same, S.; by L. C.

4 John Hart of St George the Martyr, Midx., B., and Elisabeth Keith of St Margaret, Westminster, Midx., S.; by L. C.

6 James Grant of St Olave, Southwark, Surry, B., and Elisabeth Young of the same, S.; by L. C.

7 Gilbert Grievell of St Saviour's, Southwark, Surry, B., and Elisabeth Andrews of Christchurch, Surry, S.; by L. C.

8 Thomas Dennis of St Gyles, Cripplegate, Lond., B., and Ann Smith of St Alphage, Lond., S.; by Dr Watkinson

11 John Naylor of St Gyles's in the Fields, Midx., W., and Ann Bullevant of the same, S.; by L. C.

11 Stephen Petty of St James, Westminster, Midx., B., and Elisabeth Haysom of the same, S.; by L. C.

11 Elijah Clark of St Leonard, Shoreditch, Midx., W., and Leah Agace of the same, W.; by L. C.

11 Joseph Gosdin of St Dunstan, Stepny, Midx., W., and Lydia Pratt of Poplar, Midx., W.; by L. C.

11 Griffith Pain of Old Radnor, Radnorshire, B., and Mary Green of New Radnor in the same County, S.; by L. C.

14 John Coles of Weybridge, Surry, B., and Frances Arnold of the same, S.; by L. C.

14 John Smite of Braesteed, Kent, W., and Ann Goad of St Clement Danes, S.; by Mr Wood

15 William Simpson of St Ann, Westminster, Midx., B., and Mary Smallbones of Christ Church, Lond., S.; by L. C.

15 George Russell of St Dunstan's in the West, Lond., W., and Sarah Rock of the same, S.; by L. C.

16 Thomas Fletcher of St Botolph, Aldgate, Lond., W., and Mary Jelly of the same, W.; by L. C.

16 John Russell of Epsom, Surry, B., and Martha Shepherd of the same, S.; by L. C.

17 Stephen Youl of St Mary Woolnoth, Lond., B., and Elisabeth Stone of St Mary, Newington, Surry, W.; by L. C.

18 John Hide of St Andrew, Holborn, Midx., B., and Abigael Munns of Charter House Square, Midx., S.; by L. C.

18 William Biddelcom of St George the Martyr, Midx., B., and Elisabeth Simpson of St Martin in the Fields, Midx., S.; by L. C.

19 William Jemmett of St Mildred, Bread Street, Lond., B., and Jane Sheldon of the same Parish, S.; by L. C.

1731

Nov. 20 John Hart of Egham, Surry, B., and Ann Glascock of Alhallows Barking, Lond., S.; by L. C.

21 Richard Baynes of St Andrew, Holborn, Midx., B., and Lucy Andrews of the same, S.; by L. C.

21 John King of St Gyles in the Fields, Midx., B., and Elisabeth Dontoun of St Andrew, Holborn, Midx., S.; by L. C.

24 Richard Rose of Croydon, Surry, B., and Mary Merrit of the same, S.; by L. C.

25 James Tudor Morgan of St Dunstan in the West., Lond., B., and Martha Bromhall of St Andrew, Holborn, Lond., S.; by Dr Watkinson

25 James Figgins of St Mary Woolnoth, Lond., B., and Susanna Smith of Battersea, Surry, S.; by L. C.

26 William Homes of Westham, Essex, B., and Sarah Graves of the same, S.; by Dr Watkinson

26 Clement Barker of Penham, Essex, B., and Mary Wright of Ugley, Essex, S.; by Dr Watkinson

28 Charles Howell of St George, Bloomsbury, Midx., W., and Sarah Judgson of St Andrew, Holborn, Midx., S.; by L. C.

29 William Boorer of St Ann, Limehouse, Midx., B., and Mary Pilkington of St Andrew, Holborn, Midx., S.; by L. C.

30 Robert Blagrove, B., and Elisabeth Wright, S., both of this Parish, by banns; by L. C.

Dec. 1 John Johnstone of St George, Hanover Square, Midx., B., and Charlott Vanlo of St James, Westminster, Midx., W.; by L. C.

1 Robert Rose of Tandridge, Surry, B., and Martha Woolf of the same place, S.; by L. C.

2 Roger Hendly of St James, Westminster, Midx., B., and Lucretia Palm of St George, Hanover Square, Midx., W.; by L. C.

2 John Vesenbeck of St Gyles, Cripplegate, Midx., B., and Ann Barlow of Kensington, Midx., S.; by L. C.

3 William Martain of East Mawlin, Kent, B., and Mary Gransden of the same, S.; by Dr Watkinson

3 Benjamin Wensley of Great St Hellens, Lond., B., and Elisabeth Beales of the same, S.; by Dr Watkinson

5 Thomas Feltwell of the Town of Cambridge, B., and Mary Thrussell of the same, S.; by L. C.

7 John Greener of St Ann's, Westminster, Midx., B., and Sarah Midwinter of St Martin in the Fields, Midx., S.; by L. C.

7 Gervas Neale, B., and Alice Jenkins, S., both of this Parish, by Banns; by Dr Watkinson

7 Lewis Douglass of Stow in Norfolk, B., and Mary Robinson of St James, Westminster, Midx., S.; by Dr Watkinson

7 Joseph Haines of St Gyles, Cripplegate, Midx., B., and Mercy Lucy of St Antholin's, Lond., S.; by Dr Watkinson

9 Thomas Goodson, Clerk of this Parish, W., and Mary Wilson of the same Parish, S.; by L. C.

9 William Bramfeild of St Andrew, Holborn, Midx., W., and Mary Stafford of the same, S.; by L. C.

11 William Phillips of St Martin in the Fields, Midx., W., and Bridget Radbourn of the same, W.; by L. C.

11 Jeffery Griffith of St John Zachary, Lond., B., and Elisabeth Cotton of St Dionis Backchurch, Lond., S.; by L. C.

11 Jeremiah Slow of Walthamstow, Essex, W., and Frances Cannon of Cheshunt, Hertf., S.; by L. C.

13 William Varty of Endfield, Midx., B., and Rebecca Cowdrey of the same, S.; by L. C.

1731

Dec. 13 Thomas King of S[t] John, Hackney, Midx., B., and Sarah Ogdon of S[t] Botolph, Bishopsgate, Lond., S.; by M[r] Horton of Highgate

14 Edward Sharp of S[t] James, Westminster, Midx., B., and Jane King of the same, S.; by L. C.

16 James Purcell of S[t] Ann's, Midx., B., and Catherine John of the same, W.; by L. C.

16 Josias Simmons of Westham, Essex, B., and Elisabeth Mayne of the same, S.; by M[r] Tho. Hillman

19 Josias Bainton of S[t] Dunstan in the West, Lond., B., and Elisabeth Paine of the same, S.; by L. C.

20 Thomas Smithen of S[t] Botolph, Aldgate, Lond., W., and Hannah King of the same, W.; by L. C.

21 Edward Yeamans of Stratford le Bow, Essex, B., and Eleanor Morley of the same, S.; by L. C.

22 Thomas Allison of East Greenwich, Kent, B., and Grace Davis of the same, S.; by L. C.

22 Thomas Alin of Bromly, Kent, B., and Mary Haynes of the same, W.; by L. C.

23 George Bambridge of Putney, Surry, W., and Elisabeth Clarke of the same, S.; by L. C.

23 Richard Owens of Christ Church, Surry, B., and Sarah Sparrow of the same, S.; by L. C.

23 Bartholomew Baker of S[t] George, Bloomsbury, Midx., B., and Elisabeth Lloyd of the same Parish, S.; by L. C.

23 Isaac Kent of Deptford, Kent, W., and Sarah Jones of S[t] Botolph without Aldersgate, Lond., W.; by L. C.

25 William Whitmash of S[t] Antholin's, Lond., B., and Sarah Jennings of the same, S.; by L. C.

25 Francis Giles of S[t] Pancras, Midx., W., and Margaret Cooke of S[t] Gyles's in the Fields, Midx., W.; by L. C.

26 John Jiggon, W., and Martha Bowen, W., both of this Parish, by Banns; by L. C.

27 Edward Burton of S[t] Michael, Crooked Lane, Lond., B., and Ruthe Lambeth of S[t] Paul, Covent Garden, Midx., S.; by L. C.

27 George Surridge of S[t] Sepulchre's, Lond., B., and Elisabeth Salt of S[t] Bride's, Lond., S.; by L. C.

27 Martin Champlin of Woolwich, Kent, B., and Matilda Townsend of Charlton, Kent, S.; by L. C.

27 Joseph Bull of S[t] John the Evangelist, Midx., B., and Sarah Wisdom of the same, S.; by L. C.

27 James Horne of Mitcham, Surry, W., and Elisabeth Cockram of Wimbledon, Surry, S.; by L. C.

29 Thomas Mills of S[t] James, Clerkenwell, Midx., W., and Ann Cullingworth of the same, S.; by L. C.

29 John Thompkins of Newton Longvile, Bucks, B., and Mary Mercer of Edmonton, Midx., S.; by L. C.

31 William Gerrard of S[t] Andrew, Holborn, Lond., B., and Oliva Arthur of the same, W.; by L. C.

Jan. 1 John Wicksteed of S[t] Gyles in the Fields, Midx., B., and Mary Lavington of S[t] Andrew, Holborn, Midx., S.; by L. C.

1 John Wall of S[t] Martin in the Fields, Midx., B., and Ann Colbatch of Kensington, Midx., S.; by L. C.

2 Robert Lloyd of Fulham, Midx., B., and Margaret Rookes of Richmond, Yorkshire, S.; by L. C.

4 John Rippon of S[t] Dunstan in the East, Lond., B., and Sarah Buncker of the same, S.; by L. C.

1731

Jan. 5 William Burton, W., and Rachael King, S., both of this Parish, by Banns; by L. C.

6 Richard Hanchett of S[t] Paul, Covent Garden, Midx., W., and Ann Lynd of the same, S.; by L. C.

6 Thomas Noble of Gravesend, Kent, B., and Mary Hodgson of the same, W.; by L. C.

6 George Creed of S[t] Mary, Whitechappel, Midx., W., and Mary Burrell of the same, S.; by L. C.

6 William Oder of Battersea, Surry, B., and Mary Juer of the same, S.; by L. C.

7 Edward Worsfold of Epsom, Surry, B., and Elisabeth Rogers of the same, S.; by L. C.

8 Thomas York of S[t] Michael's, Cornhill, Lond., B., and Ann Pawley of S[t] Clement Danes, Midx., S.; by L. C.

11 Thomas Lloyd of S[t] Andrew, Holborn, Lond., B., and Mary Bennett of S[t] James, Clerkenwell, Midx., S.; by D[r] Watkinson

12 Peter Nepueic of S[t] Botolph, Aldgate, Lond., W., and Mary Jackling of the same, W.; by L. C.

12 Thomas Low of Endfield, Midx., W., and Hannah Wakelin of the same, W.; by L. C.

12 George Hawkswell of S[t] James, Westminster, Midx., W., and Elisabeth Lloyd of the same, W.; by L. C.

13 Robert Burton of Hammersmith, Midx., B., and Elisabeth Carter of Fulham, Midx., S.; by L. C.

14 John Woole of S[t] Peters at the Chain in the Tower of London, B., and Mary State of the same, W.; by L. C.

15 Thomas Gray of Chelsea, Midx., W., and Elisabeth Holt of the same, S.; by L. C.

15 Robert Willis of S[t] Ann, Blackfryars, Lond., B., and Jane Hoddle of Bridewell Precinct, Lond., S.; by L. C.

17 Mark Marshall of S[t] George in the East, Midx., B., and Margaret Spencer of S[t] Martin's in the Fields, Midx., S.; by L. C.

18 Francis Flight of S[t] Olave, Silver Street, Lond., B., and Margaret Biston of S[t] Mary Woolchurch, Lond., S.; by L. C.

20 William Whitaker of S[t] Brides, Lond., B., and Lydia Buckle of the same, S.; by L. C.

20 Thomas Rollo of Christ Church, Midx., B., and Rachel Hamman of the same, S.; by L. C.

20 Abraham Cross of Wandsworth, Surry, W., and Ann Watts of the same, S.; by L. C.

21 Richard Downs of S[t] George, Bloomsbury, Midx., B., and Mary Watson of S[t] Martin, Ludgate, Lond., S.; by L. C.

25 William Harper of S[t] Dunstan in the West, Lond., B., and Ann Smart of the same, S.; by L. C.

26 William Jones of S[t] Sepulchre's, Lond., W., and Elisabeth Whiting of S[t] Brides, Lond., W.; by L. C.

27 Thomas Draper of Kensington, Midx., W., and Mary Lock of the same, W.; by L. C.

27 William Dawgs of S[t] Clement Danes, Midx., B., and Francis Cotton of the same, S.; by L. C.

27 John Piggott of Oxted, Surry, W., and Ann Burley of the same, S.; by L. C.

28 David Jones of S[t] Margaret, Westminster, Midx., B., and Jane Woodhouse of the same, W.; by L. C.

31 John Hoye of Woodford, Essex, B., and Jenny Matthews of the same, S.; by L. C.

1731

Feb. 1 John Fairland of Ware, Hertfordshire, W., and Alice Wright of the same, W.; by L. C.

1 Thomas Jones of S[t] Clement, Eastcheap, Lond., B., and Ann Spender of Wandford, Hertf., S.; by L. C.

2 Robert Bunyen of Hillinden, Midx., W., and Mary Mills of Brentford, Midx., S.; by L. C.

3 Rowland Reynolds of S[t] James, Westminster, Midx., Esq., B., and Mary Ann Duncombe of the same, S.; by L. C.

3 Samuel Bennett of S[t] John, Hackney, Midx., W., and Ann Bax of Low Layton, Essex, S.; by L. C.

3 Patrick Gibson of Tottenham, Midx., B., and Susanna Buckmaster of the same, S.; by L. C.

3 John Osborn of Sunbury, Midx., B., and Mary Bertrand of the same, S.; by L. C.

4 James Hume of S[t] Andrew, Holborn, Lond., B., and Elisabeth Rokeby of the same, S.; by L. C.

4 Jonas Powell of S[t] Gyles's in the Fields, Midx., W., and Mary Swan of S[t] Ann, Westminster, Midx., W.; by L. C.

5 Charles March of Denton, Bucks, B., and Mary Ealing of Little Norwood, Bucks, W.; by L. C.

6 George Bowen of Dulwich in the Parish of Camberwell, Surry, B., and Rose Cranwell of the same, S.; by L. C.

6 Henry Bate of S[t] Dunstan in the West, Lond., B., and Elisabeth Hinton of S[t] Andrew, Holborn, Lond., S.; by L. C.

6 Benjamin Godfrey of S[t] James, Westminster, Midx., B., and Elisabeth Bettew of the same, W.; by L. C.

7 John Hunt of S[t] James, Westminster, Midx., W., and Mary Dunnam of S[t] Mary le Bone, Midx., S.; by L. C.

8 John Patnall of Cheam, Surry, W., and Sarah Humphrey of the same, S.; by L. C.

9 William Went of S[t] George, Bloomsbury, Midx., B., and Esther Neale of East Greenwich, Kent, S.; by L. C.

9 William Barbour of S[t] James, Westminster, Midx., B., and Martha De Roach of the same, W.; by L. C.

9 Paul Lofpital of S[t] Martin in the Fields, Midx., B., and Mary Lacoste of the same, S.; by L. C.

10 Harrold Healey of S[t] Margaret, Westminster, Midx., B., and Margaret Tottenham of S[t] George the Martyr, Midx., S.; by L. C.

10 Thomas Lewington of S[t] Botolph, Bishopsgate, Lond., B., and Sarah Follett of S[t] Dunstan, Stepny, Midx., S.; by L. C.

12 David Steelle of S[t] George in the East, Midx., W., and Sarah Smith of the same, S.; by M[r] Turner

12 John Robinson of S[t] Mary's at Reading, Berks, B., and Mary Cooper of S[t] Gyles's in the Fields, Midx., S.; by M[r] Turner

13 Thomas Singer of S[t] Clement Danes, Midx., B., and Hannah Fear of the same, S.; by L. C.

13 Thomas Dixon of S[t] Mary Magdalene, Bermondsey, Surry, W., and Ann Rutter of the same, S.; by M[r] Price

14 Richard Upton of Deptford, Kent, B., and Mary Blackwell of Dartford, Kent, S.; by L. C.

14 Jasper Vangilder of S[t] John the Evangelist, Westminster, Midx., W., and Elisabeth Crawley of S[t] Saviour's, Southwark, Surry, W.; by L. C.

14 William Barling of S[t] Sepulchre's, Midx., W., and Ann Litchfield of the same, S.; by L. C.

14 Thomas Game of S[t] Mary le Strand, Midx., W., and Elisabeth Graves of S[t] Andrew, Holborn, Lond., S.; by L. C.

1731

Feb. 15 Edward Hemmings of Low Layton, Essex, W., and Elisabeth Blackbourn of Stratford le Bow, Midx., W.; by L. C.

15 Robert Aldridge of Cookham, Berks, B., and Elisabeth Newman of S[t] James, Westminster, Midx., S.; by L. C.

15 Thomas Haynes of Wandsworth, Surry, B., and Eleanor Walley of the same, S.; by L. C.

16 Joseph Whitaker of S[t] James, Westminster, Midx., B., and Elisabeth Blandy of the same, S.; by L. C.

16 George Petre of Clements Inn, Midx., B., and Anna Maria Fortescue of Droitwich, Worcestershire, S.; by L. C.

17 George Brooke of Halstead, Essex, B., and Ann Catherine Godfrey of the same, W.; by L. C.

17 Samuel Barker of S[t] Saviour's, Southwark, Surry, B., and Elisabeth Moore of the same, S.; by L. C.

17 Isaac Harman of S[t] Olave, Southwark, Surry, B., and Elisabeth Carter of the same, S.; by L. C.

17 James Spier of Ealing, Midx., B., and Hannah Woofendale of S[t] George, Hanover Square, Midx., S.; by M[r] Phipps

18 Ambrose Moore of S[t] Dunstan in the West, Lond., W., and Mary Winter of S[t] Saviour, Southwark, Surry, W.; by L. C.

18 George Wilkinson of S[t] James, Clerkenwell, Midx., W., and Sarah Bart of S[t] Olave, Southwark, Surry, W.; by L. C.

18 Thomas Smith of Mitcham, Surry, W., and Joanna Watson of the same, S.; by L. C.

19 Joseph Edmondson of S[t] Andrew, Holborn, Midx., W., and Elisabeth Boult of Waltham Holy Cross, Essex, S.; by L. C.

20 John Walmsley of S[t] Olave, Southwark, Surry, B., and Mary Rhodes of the same, S.; by L. C.

20 John Stow of S[t] Saviour's, Southwark, Surry, B., and Elisabeth Hopkin of S[t] Clement Danes, Midx., S.; by L. C.

20 Edward Wilcox of S[t] Saviour's, Southwark, Surry, B., and Margaret Birbeck of the same, S.; by L. C.

21 Richard Ayers of Poplar, Midx., B., and Elisabeth Vere of the same, S.; by L. C.

22 John Cock of Battersey, Surry, B., and Mary Ingram of Lambeth, Surry, S.; by L. C.

22 Richard Nethaway of S[t] Paul, Covent Garden, Midx., B., and Elisabeth Nuttal of the same, W.; by L. C.

22 Richard Stone of S[t] Martin, Ludgate, Lond., W., and Ann Powell of the same, S.; by L. C.

25 George Holroid of S[t] Sepulchre's, Lond., B., and Mary Grout of the same, W.; by L. C.

27 Abraham Cassal of S[t] George, Hanover Square, Midx., B., and Eleanor Hord of S[t] Paul, Covent Garden, Midx., S.; by L. C.

29 John Frathague [? Trathague] of S[t] Mary, Whitechappell, Midx., W., and Elisabeth Crump of the same, W.; by L. C.

Mar. 2 Edward Longshaw of Shipton, Oxfordshire, B., and Ann Randall of S[t] Bartholomew, near the Royal Exchange, Lond., S.; by L. C.

4 Richard Frewin of S[t] Michael's in the City of Oxford, W., M.D., and Elen Graves of Alhallows Barkin, Lond., W.; by Edward Cranke, Rector of Hatford, Berks

8 William Palmer of S[t] George's, Bloomsbury, Midx., B., and Ann Cramp of Milton, Bucks, S.; by L. C.

9 Isaac Friend of S[t] Mary Magdalene, Bermondsey, Surry, B., and Hannah Revett of Shoreham, Sussex, S.; by L. C.

9 Henry Tentwell of S[t] Martin in the Fields, Midx., W., and Margaret Carroll of the same, W.; by L. C.

1731

Mar. 16 Henry Williams of Alhallows the Great, Lond., W., and Catherine Blease of Christ Church, Lond., S.; by L. C.

16 John Reeves of Twittenham, Midx., B., and Ann Norris of St Gregory's, Lond., S.; by L. C.

22 Philip Hall of St Mary Magdalene, Bermondsey, Surry, B., and Rachael Lish of Wandsworth, Surry, S.; by L. C.

[*Change of writing begins here.*—Ed.]

1732.

Mar. 25 David Tom of St Martin's in the Fields, Midx., B., and Ann Lamdall* of the same, S.; by J. Wills

26 Samuel Starling of St Faith's, Lond., W., and Mary Jordan of St Bottolph's, Bishopsgate, Lond., S.

31 Charles Wells of St Mary Magdalen, Milk Street, Lond., B., and Mary Travers of St Dunstan's, Stepney, Midx., S.

April 8 Abraham Plaskett of St Andrews Undershaft, Lond., B., and Elisabeth Colhown of St James, Westminster, Midx., S.

9 William Nixon of St Clement Danes, Midx., B., and Mary Wilmot of the same parish, S.

9 Robert Plume of St Gregory's, Lond., B., and Mary Gillingwater of the same parish, S.

9 Edward Tottingham of St Botolph's, Aldersgate, Lond., W., and Elisabeth Thorpe of the same parish, W.

9 John Osmond of St Giles, Dorsetshire, W., and Lewis Elissold of St George's, Hanover Square, Midx., W.

10 Charles Vaughan of St George's in the East, Midx., B., and Sarah Pike of St Mary, Rotherhithe, Surry, S.

10 John Thomas of St Andrew's, Holborn, Lond., B., and Elizabeth Hewit of ye Inner Temple, Lond., S.

11 Duke Norton of Chatham, Kent, B., and Effery Hickes of the same, S.

11 Thomas Hasell of St James, Westminster, Midx., B., and Elizabeth Moody of the same, S.

12 William Ingersull of St Botolph, Aldersgate, W., and Mary Biggs of the same, W.

12 James Raymond of All-Hallows Barking, Lond., B., and Sarah Pettit of the same, S.

13 John Nisbett of St Brides, Lond., B., and Lucy Lillewhite of the same, S.

13 Richard Andrews of Merton, Surry, B., and Barbara Baker of St George's, Bloomsbury, Midx., S.

13 Henry Hallett of Fulham, Midx., W., and Mary Soper of the same, W.

13 John Crichlowe of St Nicholas Acons, Lond., B., and Christian Thompson of the same, S.

13 Thomas Brydges of St Michael's, Cornhill, Lond., B., and Susanna Wright of St Mary, Islington, Midx., W.

14 Joseph Cox of St Andrew's, Holborn, Midx., B., and Jane Kelley of the same, W.

15 George Arnold of Chiswick, Midx., W., and Ruth Denton of St James, Westminster, Midx., S.

16 Henry Weedon of Rickmonsworth in Hertfordshire and Susanna Weedon of Watford in same county, S.

17 James Corderoy of St Saviour's, Southwark, Surry, B., and Elizabeth Fuller of Abingdon, Berkshire, S.

17 Joseph Harris of St George's, Hanover Square, Midx., B., and Sarah Garskin of St James, Westminster, Midx., S.

* "Landal" in the margin.—Ed.

1732

April 17 John Mills of S[t] James, Westminster, Midx., B., and Elizabeth Mullineux of the same parish, S.

18 Richard Harris of S[t] James, Westminster, Midx., B., and Mary Moor of the same, S.

20 John Phillips of Deptford, Kent, B., and Sarah Boys of Lewisham in the same county, S.

20 John Satchell of S[t] Gyles, Cripplegate, Midx., B., and Elizabeth Hall of the same, S.

20 Francis Lett of Battersea, Surry, B., and Sarah Jelly of the same, S.

20 Thomas Lawrence of Christchurch, Lond., B., and Judith Willdon of Foster Lane, Lond., S.

20 Edward Gill of S[t] George, Midx., W., and Catherine Le Gall of the same, W.

22 Richard Benson of S[t] Mary, Rotherhith, Surry, B., and Mary Sheldon of the same, S.

22 Thomas Angell of S[t] George, Hanover Square, Midx., W., and Mary Hixon of the same, W.

23 William Shearsmith of S[t] Mary le Strand, Midx., B., and Ann Browne of the same, S.

25 William Body of S[t] Margaret's, Westminster, Midx., B., and Martha Chumley of the same, S.

25 William Gould of S[t] Mary, Lambeth, Surry, W., and Mary Willis of the same, W.

25 Thomas Cutler of S[t] Giles's, Cripplegate, Lond., W., and Jane Bradford of the same, S.

25 John Cotton of S[t] Mary athill, Lond., B., and Mary Hill of the same parish, S.

26 John Hoar of S[t] Nicholas, Deptford, Kent, B., and Ann Dudenee of Bromley in the same county, S.

27 John Gardner of S[t] Giles's, Cripplegate, Midx., W., and Sarah Woodhouse of S[t] James, Clerkenwell, Midx., W.

28 David Parry of Rotherhithe, Surry, W., and Elisabeth Ordway of ye Precinct of White Fryers, Lond., W.

28 John Wimbush of S[t] George's, Hanover Square, Midx., B., and Elisabeth Sweeting of Dunstable, Bedfordshire, S.

30 John Whitehead of S[t] James, Westminster, Midx., B., and Margaret Evans of S[t] Sepulchre's, Lond., S.

30 Robert Bailey of Heston, Midx., B., and Elizabeth Vergoe of the same, S.

May 1 *Thomas Stiddolph of Farningham, Kent, B., and Ann Harvey of Ainsford in the same county, S.

2 Peter Clowes of S[t] George the Martyr, Surry, B., and Hannah Leigh of S[t] Stephen, Coleman Street, Lond., S.

2 Hugh Boughton of S[t] Mary, Newington, Surry, W., and Mary Kinerly of the same, S.

3 Thomas Holland of S[t] Dunstan's, Stepny, Midx., B., and Sarah Smith of the same, S.

4 William Cornock of S[t] Stephen, Coleman Street, Lond., B., and Elizabeth Lane of the same, S.

4 Edward Foster of Mitcham in Surry, B., and Sarah Holyday of the same, S.

6 William Charsley of S[t] Andrews, Holborn, Midx., B., and Ann Newham of the same, W.

7 William Franklin of S[t] James, Westminster, Midx., B., and Mary Fillpot of S[t] George the Martyr, Midx., S.

* "Thomas" written over "Edward."—Ed.

1732

May 8 Robert Diggs of St Giles's in the Fields, Midx., B., and Elizabeth Strangwidge of St George the Martyr, Midx., S.

8 Jonathan Lewis of Hemelhempsted in Herfordshire, B., and Elizabeth Smith of Great Gaddesdon in same county, S.

8 James Graham of Kikeanders, Cumberland, B., and Elizabeth Dean of St Mary, Reading, Berks, S.

10 Richard Stradling of Barking, Essex, W., and Elizabeth Stockdill of the same, S.

11 Thomas Oakes of St George's, Queen Square, Midx., B., and Lucy Evans of the same, W.

12 Joseph Beete of St Martin's in the Fields, W., and Jane Colhown of the same, S.

13 James Reynolds of St James, Clerkenwell, Midx., W., and Ann Godfrey of St Mary, Islington, Midx., W.

13 Robert Wright of St John the Evangelist, Westminster, W., and Mary Leake of the same parish, Midx., S.

14 Peter Griffith of St Martin's in the Fields, Midx., B., and Anne Morris of the same, S.

16 Paul Meyer of St Leonard's, Shoreditch, Midx., B., and Sarah Mountfort of the same, W.

16 John Smith of St Mary Cray in Kent, B., and Mary Costen of the same, W.

18 Edward Butterfield of Hemmel-Hemsted in Hertfordshire, B., and Mary Lewis of the same, S.

18 Austin Tooly of Rickmondsworth in Hertfordsh., B., and Mary Skidmore of the same, S.

18 Philip Henry Bell of St Andrew's, Holborn, Lond., W., and Margaret Fletcher of the same, W.

19 Henry Wise, Esqr, of the Inner Temple, Lond., B., and Mary Tilson of St Margaret's, Westminster, Midx., S.

19 Joseph Alleen of St Giles's in the Fields, Midx., B., and Ann Garett of St Catherine Coleman, Lond., S.

21 Thomas Sheppard, B., and Mary Fildie, both of this Parish; by Banns

22 William Low of St Martin's in the Fields, Midx., B., and Mary Peat of the same, S.

22 Thomas Morris of St Martin's, Ludgate, Lond., W., and Ann Clare of St Andrew's, Holborn, Midx., W.

26 Phillip Lewis of St James's, Westminster, Midx., B., and Rebecca Morris of St Swithin's, Lond., S.

27 John Goodenough of Langford, Berkshire, B., and Catherine Bagwell of St Saviour's, Southwark, S.

27 Francis Winkworth of St Mary, Newington, Surry, W., and Mary Hughs of the same, W.

28 Paul Stirridge of St Clement Danes, Midx., B., and Mary Wharfe of the same, S.

28 Daniel Wright of Lewisham, Kent, B., and Esther Mainstone of the same, S.

29 John Woolley of St George the Martyr, Midx., B., and Jane Parker of the same, S.

29 William Stevens of St John, Hackney, Middx., B., and Elizabeth Underwood of the same, S.

30 Thomas Potts of St George, Bloomsbury, Midx., B., and Alice Dobney of St George, Hanover Square, Midx., S.

June 2 Timothy Edmunds of St Martin Orgars, Lond., B., and Elizabeth Tuttle of St Martin's in the Fields, Midx., S.

5 Thomas Hooker of St Margaret, Lothbury, Lond., B., and Anne Waggett of the same, S.

1732

June 5 John Eddowes of St Clement Danes, Midx., B., and Lucy Short of St George the Martyr, Midx., S.

7 Robert Palmer of Harmondsworth, Midx., B., and Mary Youle of the same, S.

7 John Edkins of Birmingham, Warwick, W., and Jane Ball of St Mary Aldermary, Lond., S.

8 Thomas Clark of St Mary, Rotherhith, Surry, B., and Elizabeth Pattaway of the same, S.

9 Thomas Martin of St Giles's in the Fields, Midx., B., and Mary Linnett of Hounslow in the said county, S.

10 Richard Fitzgerald of St George, Hanover Square, Midx., B., and Mary Stephens of the same, S.

12 Joseph Slade of St George, Bloomsbury, Midx., B., and Mary Stevens of Clapham in Surry, S.

13 William Burcomb of Charlton in Kent, B., and Elisabeth Gingell of St George, Hanover Square, Midx., S.

13 John Ravenfirth of St George, Bloomsbury, Midx., B., and Jane Manslow of the same, W.

14 William Wright of St Dunstan's, Stepny, Midx., W., and Ann Chapman of Old in Northamptonshire, S.

14 William Soan of Westram, Kent, B., and Barbara Wibern of Poles Cray in the same county, S.

14 John Gibson of Chelsea, Midx., B., and Louisa Hughes of the same, S.

14 Robert Mallick of St Giles's in the Fields, Midx., W., and Susannah Jones of the same, S.

18 Thomas Kidman of Stoke Newington, Midx., B., and Frances Perry of St Mildred, Poultry, Lond., S.

18 Philip Prosser of St James, Westminster, Midx. [*blank*], and Mary Barrell of St Clement Danes, Midx., S.

18 John Baker of St James, Clerkenwell, Midx., B., and Mary Box of St Andrew's, Holborn, Midx., S.

18 Francis Thomas of St George, Southwark, W., and Ann Redborn of St Andrew's, Holborn, Midx., W.

20 John Parfet of St Saviour's, Southwark, B., and Mary Higgins of St Giles's in the Fields [*blank*].

21 Thomas Beckett of St Foster, Lond., B., and Mary Garlant of the same, S.

22 George Wroth of St Leonard, Shoreditch, Midx., B., and Margaret Chandler of St Catherine, Coleman St., Lond., S.

22 John Gerring of St Margaret's, Westminster, Midx., W., and Jane King of the same, S.

23 Richard Heather of Horley in Surry, B., and Sarah Jordan of St Saviour, Southwark, S.

24 John Starrock of St Martin's in the Fields, Midx., B., and Catherine Dundas of the same, W.

24 Thomas Williams of St George, Hanover Square, Midx., B., and Lucy Trimnell of the same, S.

26 Thomas Hunt of St Giles's in the Fields, Midx., B., and Eleanor Jefferys of the same, S.

27 Cornelius Galvan of St Margaret, New-fish Street, Lond., B., and Elisabeth Winter of the same, S.

July 1 John Tunel of St Martin's in the Fields, Midx., B., and Susannah Lickeldike of Evisham, Surry, S.

3 Timothy Greeves of St Giles's in the Fields, Midx., B., and Sarah Richardson of St George's, Bloomsbury, Midx., S.

3 William Tyler of St Mary, Lambeth, Surry, B., and Grace Bethwin of the same, S.

1732

July 6 Mark Gregory of St Giles's in the Fields, Midx., W., and Theodosia Bullock of St Clement Danes, Midx., S.

6 Richard Fisher of St Brides, Lond., B., and Mary Copper of St Andrew Undershaft, Lond., W.

6 John Vaughan of St Mary, Newington, Surry, B., and Martha Smith of Christ Church, Surry, S.

7 John Hawkins of St Mary Athill, Lond., B., and Sarah Waxam of St Olave's, Southwark, Surry, S.

7 Alexander Flint of St Leonard's, Shoreditch, Midx., B., and Lucretia Eales of the same, S.

8 Thomas Cowell of St Martin's in the Fields, Midx., B., and Elisabeth Downing of the same, S.

8 Robert Beverly of St Anne near Limehouse, Midx., W., and Ann Lyell of the same, W.

10 John Westwood of Christ Church, Spittlefields, Midx., W., and Mary Russell of the same, S.

10 Thomas Pattney of St Giles's, Cripplegate, Midx., B., and Mary Murphy of St Michael's Bassishaw, Lond., S.

10 William Sawyer of Swanscomb, Kent, B., and Jane Badger of the same, S.

11 Richard Jackson of St Martin's in the Fields, Midx., B., and Mary Winspeare of St Clement Danes, Midx., S.

12 James Bland of St George's, Queen Square, Midx., B., and Anne Rolfe of the same, W.

12 Francis Stepens of Tottenham High Cross, Midx., B., and Martha James of the same, S.

12 John Ball of St Botolph's, Aldgate, Lond., B., and Anne Green of the same, S.

12 John Southern of St Martin's in the fields, Midx., B., and Hannah Primrose of St Martin's, Ludgate, Lond., W.

13 Robert Ewer of Braintree, Essex, B., and Prudence Nurse of St Catherine Coleman, Lond., S.

15 Walter King of St Clement Danes, Midx., B., and Frances Bush of the same, S.

16 Thomas Jenkins of St Martin's in the Fields, Midx., B., and Mary Purvis of St John the Evangelist, Westminster, S.

16 John Wall of St Stephen's, Coleman Street, Lond., B., and Ann Worrall of the same, S.

18 Elias de Gruchy Fassett of St John Evangelist, Lond., B., and Jane Maidstone of St Leonard, Eastcheap, Lond., S.

19 Thomas Milton of St Andrew's, Holborn, Midx., W., and Mary Ward of the same, W.

20 Thomas Ridlington of Great Ilford, Essex, B., and Rachael Shelley of the same, S.

20 Richard Manning of St Lawrence, old Jewry, Lond., W., and Elisabeth Burchett of St John, Hackney, Midx., W.

20 William Flecknall of St Giles in the Fields, Midx., W., and Mary Collinson of St Mary, Newington, Surry, W.

20 John Moores of St Andrew's Undershaft, Lond., B., and Elizabeth Webb of the same, S.

22 John Blower of St Mary, Islington, Midx., W., and Sarah Beamont of the same, S.

23 John Dungitt, W., and Jane Richford, S., both of this Parish; by Banns

26 Thomas Coleman of Long Buckby in Northtonsh., W., and Hannah Tanner of St Ann, Limehouse, Midx., W.

26 Hatton Green of St James, Westminster, Midx., B., and Anne Owen of the same, S.

1732

July 26 Hills Perry of S[t] Dunstan's, Stepny, Midx., B., and Ann Morgan of S[t] Ann, Limehouse, Midx., S.

27 Robert French of Northfleet, Kent, W., and Mary Bell of the same, S.

28 Fort Planta of S[t] George's, Midx., B., and Elisabeth Adams of the same, S.

29 Thomas Fisher of Greenford, Midx., W., and Ann Bladen of S[t] James, Westminster, Midx., W.

29 Benjamin Hawkins of S[t] Michael's, Queenhith, Lond., B., and Jane Greenwood of S[t] George's, Midx., W.

30 Thomas Worthington of Thavies Inn, Lond., W., and Mary Warden of S[t] Sepulchre's, Midx., W.

30 Peter Mourguett of S[t] Margaret, Lothbury, Lond., B., and Mary Ann Michellett of the same, W.

Aug. 2 Stephen Johnson of Woolwich, Kent, B., and Dorothy Bell of S[t] Giles's, Cripplegate, Lond., S.

2 Daniel West of Chiswick, Midx., W., and Emma Pike of S[t] Martin's in the Fields, Midx., W.

2 John Robinson of S[t] Giles's, Cripplegate, Lond., B., and Martha Danfield of S[t] James, Clerkenwell, Midx., S.

3 William Jewster of S[t] Leonard, Shoreditch, Midx., B., and Theodosia Phillips of S[t] Mary, Newington Butts, Surry, W.

3 James Cheney of S[t] George the Martyr, Surry, W., and Jane Betty of the same, S.

6 John Newcomb of Westham, Midx., B., and Usle Lettimore of the same [*blank*].

7 Edward Bentley of S[t] Mary Magdalen, Bermondsey, Surry, B., and Mary Hall of the same, S.

8 George Gill of Sunderland in the Bishoprick of Durham, B., and Abigail Hoalmes of the same, S.

8 Francis Carr of S[t] James, Westminster, Midx., B., and Christian Waters of S[t] Dunstan's, Stepny, Midx., S.

8 Edward Slade of S[t] George, Midx., B., and Mary Glandaning of S[t] Botolph's without Aldgate, Midx., S.

8 Thomas Westcott of S[t] Mary, Lambeth, Surry, B., and Penelope Gillom of the same, W.

8 David Ronin of S[t] Dunstan's, Stepny, Midx., B., and Elianor Barnes of the same, W.

10 Sarah Knight of S[t] George the Martyr, Midx., S., and George Shaw of S[t] Andrew's, Holborn, Lond., B. [*sic*]

10 Joseph Garrett of S[t] Giles's in the Fields, Midx., W.,* and Mary Ker of S[t] George, Hanover Square, Midx., W.

10 Thomas Watmore of S[t] Mary Magdalen, Bermondsey, Surry, W., and Rebecca Rowlstone of the same, S.

14 Thomas Bisenden of Croydon, Surry, B., and Jane Skelton of the same, S.

14 John Proudman of S[t] Saviour's, Southwark, B., and Sarah Wooders of the same, W.

14 Jasper Fitter of S[t] Margaret's, Westminster, Midx., B., and Henrietta Crumpton of the same, S.

15 John Fleming of Highgate, Midx., B., and Mary Webb of S[t] Giles's in the Fields, Midx., W.

16 Francis Grayling of New Haven in Sussex, B., and Elizabeth Cheesman of the same, S.

17 Robert Mackaris of Endfield, Midx., B., and Priscilla Slaughter of the same, W.

19 Thomas King of Mitcham, Surry, W., and Jane Dean of S[t] George's, Southwark, W.

* "W." written over "B."—Ed.

1732

Aug. 20 William Hall of St Paul's, Covent Garden, Midx., B., and Elisabeth Hicks of St Margaret, Westminster, S.

20 William Heycock of St Giles's, Cripplegate, Midx., B., and Elisabeth Johnson of the same, S.

22 Francis Booth of St George's, Hanover Square, Midx., B., and Elisabeth Dickson of St Martin in the Fields, Midx., S.

22 John Hills of Reygate, Surry, B., and Anne Shooe of the same, S.

23 John Stevens of St Olave, Southwark, B., and Arabella Bearcroft of St Giles's, Cripplegate, Midx., S.

23 John Bacon of St Andrew's, Holborn, Lond., B., and Catherine Lowther of St Ann's, Westminster, Midx., S.

24 Richard Strong of St Botolph's, Aldergate, Lond., W., and Hannah Leach of the same, W.

26 Antony Maccullock of St Ann's, Westminster, Midx., B., and Mary Towell of St Mary le Bone, Midx., S.

27 Joseph Peck of St Bennet-Finck, Lond., B., and Damaris Lewis of All Saints ye Greater, Lond., S.

28 Robert Noyce of St Margaret's, Westminster, Midx., B., and Sarah Clare of the same, S.

29 Thomas Bermingham of St Mary, White Chappel, Midx., B., and Mary Herbert of St Dunstan's, Stepny, W.

30 John Helmcke of St Martin's in the Fields, Midx., B., and Bridget Smith of the same, S.

29 William Nichols of Battersea, Surry, B., and Elisabeth Cox of the same, S.

30 Robert Coulson of St Olave, Southwark, B., and Mary Batmanson of St Catherine by the Tower, Lond., S.

31 David Strachan of St George's in the East, Midx., B., and Jane Clarke of the same, S.

31 Sebastian Vander Eyken of St George's, Hanover Square, Midx., W., and Temperance Young of the same, W.*

Sept. 1 Joseph Shurley of St Mildred, Bread Street, Lond., B., and Mary Pool of the same, S.

1 James Kirk of St Paul's, Shadwell, Midx., W., and Jane Bowlin of the same, W.

1 Stephen Bradstock of St Sepulchre's, Lond., B., and Dorothy Norris of the same, W.

1 William Godman of Tring, Herford, B., and Mary Sawell of Hunton bridge in the parish of Abbot's Langley in the said county, W.

3 Thomas Pillion of Lewisham, Kent, B., and Ann Allen of the same, S.

4 George Sparks of St Leonard, Shoreditch, Midx., B., and Jane Culpeper of the same, S.

4 William Lockwood of St John's, Wapping, Midx., B., and Elisabeth Sadler of the same, S.

5 Antony Appleford of St Lawrence, Reading, Berks, B., and Constance Honyborne of the same, S.

7 William Maudvitt of St Ann's, Westminster, Midx., B., and Elisabeth Tyers of All Hallows Barkin, Lond., S.

8 William Parsons of St John's, Wapping, Midx., W., and Sarah Darnell of St Catherine Creed Church, Lond., S.

9 Andrew Bow of Hatfield, Hertford, B., and Martha Davis of the same, S.

9 William Winkin of St John the Evangelist, Midx., W., and Joanna Pigott of the same, S.

9 Richard Cockett of Oxted, Surry, B., and Elisabeth Francis of Limpsfield in the said county, S.

* "S." has been altered into "W."—Ed.

1732

Sept. 10 William Smith of Christ Church, Lond., W., and Margaret Wright of S[t] Brides, Lond., S.

11 John Johnson of S[t] Olave, Southwark, B., and Ann Brown of S[t] John's, Wapping, Midx., W.

11 James Stafford of S[t] Stephen, Coleman Street, Lond., B., and Elisabeth Smith of the same, S.

13 Samuel Salter of S[t] Andrew's, Holborn, Lond., B., and Mary Baker of the same, W.

13 William Whitehouse of S[t] Dunstan in the West, Lond., B., and Susannah Bland of S[t] Botolph, Bishopsgate, Lond., S.

14 Thomas Monery of Kensington, Midx., B., and Agnes Stith of the same, S.

14 John Shireson of S[t] Sepulchre's, Lond., B., and Catherine Daniell of the same, S.

14 William Peem of Gravesend, Kent, B., and Sarah Latter of the same, S.

14 William Scott of S[t] Giles's, Cripplegate, Lond., B., and Margaret Harrison of S[t] Andrew's, Holborn, Midx., S.

16 Adam Van Diest of S[t] Martin's in the Fields, W., and Ann Turner of the same, W.

16 John Roubel of S[t] Ann's, Westminster, Midx., B., and Catherine Marchogay of S[t] Giles's in the Fields, Midx., S.

17 John Atterbury of S[t] Margarets, Westminster, Midx., B., and Ann Smith of the same, W.

17 Richard Meere of S[t] Bride's, Lond., B., and Catherine Leigh of S[t] James's, Westminster, Midx., S.

18 Richard Emes of S[t] James's, Westminster, Midx., B., and Martha Banes of the same, S.

19 Samuel Harris of S[t] Mary, Islington, Midx., B., and Susannah Carpenter of S[t] Gregory's, Lond., S.

19 John Kinaston of S[t] Leonard's, Shoreditch, Midx., B., and Ann Wright of the same, S.

19 Joseph Seymour of Thames Ditton, Surry, B., and Jane Hooke of the same [*blank*].

20 Joseph Betts of S[t] Mary, Rotherhithe, Surry, W., and Sarah Edmonds of the same, W.

20 William Littleton of S[t] Catherine near Tower, Lond., B., and Elisabeth Douglass of the same, W.

21 Thomas Robertson of S[t] George's, Midx., W., and Grace Grant of S[t] Olave, Southwark, W.

21 Jeremiah Hobson of S[t] Ann's, Midx., B., and Sarah Clarke of the same, W.

21 Nicholas Townsend of Wrotham, Kent, B., and Elisabeth Harman of Stone near Dartford in the said county, S.

22 John Logg of S[t] Mary, Rotherhith, Surry, B., and Elisabeth Keech of the same, S.

23 Richard Davis of S[t] George's, Hanover Square, Midx., W., and Ann West of the same, W.

25 Daniel Hornby of Kew in Surry, B., and Elisabeth Hillier of the same, S.

26 William Cox of S[t] Sepulchre's, Lond., B., and Ann Burchall of S[t] Botolph, Aldersgate, Lond. [*blank*].

27 Walter Higley of S[t] James's, Westminster, Midx., B., and Mary Barnes of Lambeth, Surry, S.

27 Thomas Goodson of Clapham, Surry, B., and Elisabeth Borer of the same, S.

27 Henry Bunn of S[t] Michael's le Quern, Lond., W., and Mary Barker of S[t] Magnus the Martyr, Lond., W.

29 Daniel Punter of Laiston, Hertford, B., and Mary Beedells of the same, W.

1732

Sept. 29 Thomas Marshall of Hempstead in Herfordsh., B., and Mary Watford of the same, S.

29 John Watts of Tottenham, Midx., W., and Ann Pratt of Hardingford Bury in Hertfordshire, W.

30 James Mercer of St John's, Stepny, Midx., W., and Sarah Phillips of the same, S.

30 Lewis Sermoise of St James's, Westminster, Midx., W., and Francis Keyets of the same, W.

30 John Slemaker of Dagenham, Essex, B., and Elisabeth Johnson of the same, S.

Oct. 1 Abraham Lecade lately of St Saviour's, Southwark, B., and Mary Price of the same, S.; by Mr. Worlich

2 Robert Bayuton of St George's, Hanover Square, Midx., B., and Francis Criche of St Sepulchre's, Lond., S.

7 Thomas Thumwood of Hartley Wingley in the county of Southampton, B., and Ann Whistone of the same, S.

8 Nicholas Nugent of St Mary, White Chappel, Midx., W., and Grace Gilmore of St John the Evangelist, Midx., W.

9 John Melven of St Paul's, Shadwell, Midx., B., and Dinah Bennett of the same, W.

9 Humphrey Frost of St Margaret's, Rochester, B., and Elisabeth Pusey of the same, S.

12 Richard Greenwood of Camberwell in Surrey, B., and Dorothy Allen of St Mary, Lambeth, Surry, S.

12 George Taylor of Chertsey, Surrey, B., and Hannah Bush of Laleham, Midx., S.

12 Thomas Major of St Buttolph's, Aldersgate, Lond., B., and Ellin Ilive of the same, S.

12 John Rogers of Preston Cape in Northamptonshire, B., and Catherine Finch of the same, S.

13 John Holden of St Ann's, Limehouse, Midx., W., and Eleanor Morren of Poplar in the parish of Stepny, W.

14 Joseph Stevenson of St James's, Westminster, Midx., W., and Elisabeth Marshall of Chigwell, Essex, W.

19 Philip Michell of St Andrew's, Holborn, Lond., B., and Mary Henley of the same, S.

19 John Knell of Tonbridge, Kent, B., and Sarah Lashley of the same, W.

19 Joseph Lea of St Giles's in the Fields, Midx., B., and Alice Ashe of St Mary Woolnoth, Lond., S.

20 William Morris of St Swithin, Lond., B., and Mary Webb of St Giles's, Cripplegate, Midx., S.

22 George Paynter of Yately in Southampton, B., and Mary Mapleton of Odiham in the said county, S.

23 Richard Merrin of St George's, Southwark, B., and Judith Gimber of St George's, Surry, W.

24 John Richards of St Giles's in the fields, Midx., B., and Jane Maggott of the same, S.

26 Thomas Belch of Coulsdon, Surry, B., and Amy Wood of Beddington in the said county, S.

26 John Halls of St Martin's in the fields, Midx., W., and Elisabeth Clayton of St Andrew's, Holborn, Lond., W.

28 Richard Metcalf of Greenwich, Kent, W., and Diana Brough of Whitehall in the parish of St Martin's in the fields, Midx., W.

29 John Farras of Dartford, Kent, W., and Mary Steene of the same, W.

29 Henry Langworthy of St Mary Magdalen, Bermondsey, Surry, W., and Elisabeth Pritham of the same, W.

1732

Oct. 29 Henry Bell of S[t] Andrew's, Holborn, Midx., B., and Mary Ashburner of the same, W.

31 Joseph Darcy of S[t] Paul, Covent Garden, Midx., W., and Ann Ginder of S[t] Giles's in the Fields, Midx., W.; by Dr. Watkinson

31 John Daniel of Bradwell, Bucks, B., and Rebecca Olney of Tilsworth, Bedfordshire, S.; by Dr. Watkinson

31 John Carter of S[t] Giles's in the Fields, Midx., B., and Rebecca Wood of the same, W.; by D[r] Watkinson

Nov. 1 John Sisum of Putney, Surry, B., and Rebecca Chittington of Wandsworth, Surry, S.; by D[r] Watkinson

1 Joshua Lumm of S[t] Botolph's without Aldgate, Midx., B., and Alice Lace of the same, W.; by D[r] Watkinson

2 George Marshall of S[t] Botolph, Aldgate, Lond., B., and Jane Howsell of the same, W.; by D[r] Watkinson

2 Mark Hamill of S[t] Ann's, Limehouse, Midx., B., and Lucy Griffin of the same, S.; by D[r] Watkinson

2 Benjamin Courtney of S[t] Saviour's, Southwark, B., and Sarah Wyan of the same, S.; by D[r] Watkinson

3 Peter Thompson of S[t] John's, Wapping, Midx., B., and Margaret Gourley of the same, S.; by D[r] Watkinson

4 William Watts of Bramley in Hampshire, B., and Mary Winter of S[t] Clement Danes, Midx., S.; by D[r] Watkinson

4 Richard Griffith of S[t] Dunstan's, Stepny, B., and Catherine Bramson of the same, W.; by D[r] Watkinson

7 Samuel Cawthorne of S[t] Andrew's, Holborn, Lond., B., and Ann Teboe of S[t] Martin's in the Fields, Midx., S.; by D[r] Watkinson

7 Francis Millson of S[t] Botolph, Aldgate, Lond., B., and Mary Tyson of S[t] Bartholomew by the Exchange, Lond., S.; by D[r] Watkinson

7 John Aubrey of S[t] John the Evangelist, Westminster, Midx., B., and Elisabeth Lloyd of the same, W.; by M[r] Rice Williams, Rect[r] of Stapleford Abbot, Essex

8 John Walker of Kensington, Midx., B., and Esther Skinner of Hampstead, Midx., S.

9 John Davis of West Horsley, Surry, B., and Elisabeth Falkner of the same, S.

9 William Pearis of S[t] Sepulchre's, Midx., B., and Elisabeth Rawlinson of S[t] Mary, White Chapell, Midx., S.

9 Joseph Richardson of S[t] Andrew, Holborn, Midx., B., and Diana Wright of the same, W.

9 John Sims of S[t] Leonard, Shoreditch, Midx., W., and Rebecca Higgins of S[t] Mary Axe, Lond., S.

9 John Cooper of S[t] Mary Cray, Kent, B., and Hannah Dadd of S[t] Paul's Cray, Kent, S.

11 Joseph Cooper of S[t] George's, Bloomsbury, Midx., W., and Mary Joseph of S[t] Margaret's, Westminster, Midx., S.

12 John Gates of Bow, Midx., B., and Sarah Bruce of Loughton, Essex, S.

12 John Robert Hartshorn of S[t] Andrew, Holborn, Midx., B., and Elisabeth Hebert of the same, S.

13 William Wise of S[t] Margaret Pattons, Lond., B., and Margaret Brayham of All Saints Staining, Lond., S.

13 John Golding of S[t] Martin's in the Fields, Midx., B., and Sarah Wilson of S[t] Paul's, Covent Garden, S.

16 George Gerrard of S[t] Catherine Creed Church, Lond., W., and Ann Ware of S[t] Botolph, Bishopsgate, Lond., W.

19 Solomon Harrison of S[t] Giles's, Cripplegate, Lond., B., and Alice Allen of S[t] Paul's, Covent Garden, Midx., S.

1732

Nov. 20 William Cockayne of Greenwich in Kent, B., and Mary Cole of the same parish, S.

20 Robert Hawkins of Chalfont St Peter, Bucks, B., and Sarah Copland of the same, S.

21 Thomas Stevens of Kingston upon Thames, Surry, W., and Elisabeth Bird of the same, S.

23 Joshua Sands of St Giles's in the Fields, Midx., B., and Elisabeth Crossman of St Andrew's, Holborn, S.

23 Samuel Barnsley of St Margaret's, Westminster, Midx., W., and Hannah Weeks of Camberwell, Surry, S.

24 Jonathan Gibson of St Mary, White Chapel, Midx., W., and Judith Gibson of the same, S.

24 John Cowdrey of Crowhurst, Surry, B., and Jane Green of the same, S.

25 James Maddox of St Sepulchre's, Lond., B., and Mary Rowlstone of St Mary Magdalen, Old Fish Street, Lond., S.

25 James Glan of St George's in the East, Midx., B., and Margaret Childs of the same, S.

26 Jonas Pearson of St Saviour's, Southwark, B., and Dorothy Turtin of the same, W.

27 Richard Browne of St Giles's, Cripplgate, Midx., B., and Sarah Maxfield of the same, S.

30 Edward Jones of St Martin's in the Fields, Midx., B., and Ann Noble of the same, S.

30 John Hall of St Stephen's Coleman, Lond., B., and Mary Fating of St Bartholomew the less, Lond., S.

Dec. 2 Nathanael Polhill of Newington Butts, Surry, W., and Sarah Furner of the same, S.

3 Philip Gadd of St Mary le Strand, Midx., B., and Ann Hewland of the same, W.

3 William Osborn of Bromley, Midx., B., and Elisabeth Jones of Christ Church, Midx., S.

3 William Dockwray of Christ Church, Spittlefields, Midx., W., and Ann Dennison of the same, S.

5 Joseph Love of Harrow on the Hill, Midx., B., and Rachel Rudd of Hendon in the said county, S.

6 Holland Wolley of St Clement Danes, Midx., B., and Sarah Wilkinson of the same, S.

7 Gabriel Lambeth of Reigate, Surry, B., and Elisabeth Burges of the same, S.

9 William Wakeland of St George's, Hanover Square, Midx., B., and Sarah Minchell of the same, S.

17 John Sharman of St James, Westminster, Midx., B., and Mary Brooks of the same, S.

18 Woodhouse Wood of St Leonard's, Shoreditch, Midx., W., and Elisabeth Gazey of St Peter's, Cornhill, Lond., W.

19 Henry Wetherhead of St George's, Hanover Square, Midx., B., and Mary Honyman of St James's, Westminster, Midx., W.

19 Copley Wilde of St Sepulchre's, Lond., B., and Elisabeth Style of St Andrew's, Holborn, Midx., S.

21 James Nicholson, Esq., of St Martin's in the Fields, Midx., B., and Elisabeth Fitzgerald of St Margaret's, Westminster, Midx., S.

23 Josiah Jones of Bermondsey, Surry, W., and Sarah Dell of the same, S.

26 John Towler of Barking, Essex, B., and Mary Chambers of White Chapple, Midx., W.

27 Thomas Poundlefieks of Bromley, Kent, B., and Joanna Coleson of the same, S.

1732-3

Jan. 1 Thomas Jackson of S[t] Sepulchre's, Lond., B., and Martha Bradbury of S[t] Giles's in the Fields, Midx., S.

2 William Stock of S[t] Margaret's, Westminster, Midx., B., and Elisabeth Hemes of the same, S.

3 Richard Harvey of Endfield, Midx., B., and Elisabeth Ellsom of the same, S.

4 John Hakewill of S[t] James's, Westminster, Midx., W., and Catherine Fisher of the same, W.

6 Thomas Smallwood of S[t] Giles's, Cripplegate, Lond., B., and Martha Simson of the same, S.

7 Richard Seagood of S[t] Leonard, Shoreditch, Midx., B., and Sarah Bucler of S[t] Giles's, Cripplegate, W.

8 Thomas Sibley of Eaton Suken, Bedfordsh., B., and Winifred Gray of the same, S.

9 James Dyer of Layer De la Hay, Essex, B., and Sarah Brydges of All Hallows Barking, W.

10 John Smith of Bovington, Hertford, B., and Elisabeth Smart of Norchurch, Hertford, S.

11 John Rederup of S[t] James, Westminster, Midx., W., and Elisabeth Smith of the same, W.

12 William Huggett of Rygate, Surry, B., and Rachael Hill of the same, S.

14 Michael M[c]Nemara of S[t] James's, Westminster, Midx., B., and Mary Wainwright of S[t] Bride's, Lond. [*blank*].

15 John Robinson of S[t] John the Evangelist, Midx., B., and Elisabeth Howson of the same, S,

16 Benjamin Underhill of S[t] Pancras, Soper Lane, Lond., B., and Elisabeth Hiller of the same, S.

16 John Furnett of the Isle of Jersey, B., and Elisabeth Simmonds of the same, S.

16 John Greeve of S[t] Paul's, Shadwell, Midx., B., and Jane Weymouth of the same, S.

19 George Fowke, Esq., of S[t] James, Westminster, Midx., B., and Mary Roath of S[t] Paul's, Covent Garden, Midx. [*blank*].

19 Nathaniel Gill of S[t] Paul's, Shadwell, Midx., B., and Elisabeth Dallby of the same, S.

20 William Glover of Teddington, Midx., B., and Ann Watts of the same, W.

23 James Dryhurst of S[t] Mary le Bone, Midx., W., and Ann Sidwey of S[t] George's, Hanover Square, Midx., S.

23 Phinees Deane of S[t] Bride's, Lond., B., and Ann Shute of the same, W.

24 John Baxter, B., and Ann March, W., both of S[t] Andrew's, Holborn, Lond.

24 John White of Westham, Essex, W., and Mary Ball of the same, W.

25 Edward Ellis of Breadist, Kent, W., and Susannah Hasting of the same, W.

25 John Thorn of Allhallows the Great, Lond., B., and Hannah Lewis of the same, W.

26 Thomas French of S[t] Andrew's, Holborn, Midx., B., and Avis Dobbs of S[t] Giles's in the Fields, Midx., S.

27 William Shirres of Rotherhith, Surry, B., and Ann Kenedy of the same, S.

27 Edward Holland of S[t] Giles's, Cripplegate, Midx., B., and Elisabeth Griffith of S[t] Leonard, Shoreditch, Midx., W.

27 John Hobbs of S[t] Margaret, Westminster, Midx., B., and Ann Bastian of the same, S.

1732-3

Jan. 28 John Towndrow of St Clement Danes, Midx., B., and Susanna Burnston of the same, S.

29 William Smoathman, B., and Alice Redhead, S., both of St Andrew's, Holborn, Midx.

29 Edward Burton, B., and Ann Glaisher, S., both of St Bride's, Lond.

30 John Pitcher, B., and Elisabeth Wild, S., both of St Swithin's, Lond.

30 John Sink, B., and Ann Smith, S., both of St Clement Danes, Midx.

Feb. 1 Thomas Streatch of South Mimms, Midx., W., and Sarah Eaton of the same, S.

1 Andrews Pankeman of St Giles's, Cripplegate, Lond., W., and Sarah Hargrave of St Peter's near Pauls Wharf, Lond., S.; by Dr Thomas

2 William Esling of St Ann's, Westminster, Midx., W., and Elisabeth Dyas of Cashalton, Surrey, W.

2 John Bunce of St Michael's, Queenhith, Lond., B., and Elisabeth Andrews of the same, W.

2 William Warren of St Leonard's, Shoreditch, Midx., B., and Elisabeth Raymond of the same, S.

3 Joseph Smith of St Mary, Rotherhith, Surry, B., and Susanna Norriss of the same, S.

3 John Squire of Tenn Deeton, Cambridge, B., and Alice Siant of St George's, Bloomsbury, Midx., S.

3 Richard France of Linsfield, Surry, B., and Elisabeth Debble of the same, S.

4 John Wright of St George's, Bloomsbury, Midx., W., and Mary Constable of the same, S.

4 John Price of Greenwich, Kent, B., and Elisabeth Pitts of Digswell, Hertford, S.

4 James King of St Ann's, Westminster, Midx., B., and Esther Ansell of St James's, Westminster, Midx., W.

5 John Grimsdell of St Mary, White Chappel, Midx., W., and Elisabeth Young of St George's, Bloomsbury, Midx., S.

5 John Smith of Mortlake, Surry, W., and Jane Bourne of the same, W.

6 Samuel Peirce of St Andrew's, Holborn, Midx., B., and Mary Cooke of the same, S.

6 John Munro of St Dunstan's, Stepny, Midx., B., and Margaret Richardson of the same, W.

6 William Matthews of St Clement Danes, Midx., B., and Bathsheba Wood of the same, S.

6 Lewis Johnson of St Giles's in the Fields, Midx., W., and Bridgett Daye of St George the Martyr, Midx., S.

6 Thomas Fielder of St Mary Woolnoth, Lond., B., and Rebecca Chumm of St Clement Danes, Midx., S.

6 John Barton of St Lawrence, Jewry, Lond., B., and Ann Freshwater of St James's, Clerkenwell, Midx., S.

6 Henry Beevor of St Margaret's, Westminster, Midx., B., and Catherine Preston of St James's, Westminster, Midx., S.

8 Christopher Watkins of St Dunstan's in the West, Lond., B., and Eleanor Harland of St Andrew's, Holborn, Midx., S.

8 John Griffin of St Ann's, Limehouse, Midx., B., and Sarah Stoakes of St Paul's, Covent Garden, Midx., S.

13 Thomas Harrison of St Mary, Whitechapple, Midx., B., and Mary Mitchell of the same, S.; by Dr Watkinson

13 John Ayres of Drs Commons, Lond., B., and Ann Overi of St Bennet, Paul's Wharf, Lond., S.; by Mr Piddington, Lecturer of St Bartholomew's the Great

15 John Church of St George the Martyr, Surry, W., and Margaret Burkitt of St Mary, White Chappel, Midx., W.; by Mr Piddington

1732-3

Feb. 21 Edward Tetstell of S[t] Olave's, Southwark, B., and Mary Bright of the same, S.; by D[r] Thomas

22 Thomas Wakeman of S[t] Mary, Islington, Midx. [*blank*], and Mary Hayesman of the same, S.; by M[r] Piddington

24 John Williams of S[t] George's, Hanover Square, Midx., B., and Elisabeth Hyde of S[t] James's, Westminster, Midx., S.; by the same

24 Humphrey Adams of Ware, Hertford, B., and Ann Cass of the same, W.; by the same

24 George Eyles of S[t] Mary, Rotherhithe, Surry, B., and Catherine Tye of the same, W.; by the same

Mar. 1 Charles Freeman of Isleworth, Midx., B., and Mary Stratford of the same, W.; by the same

2 John Hingston of S[t] Paul's, Shadwell, Midx., B., and Christian Morris of the same, S.; by D[r] Watkinson

3 Joseph Lawrence of S[t] Martin's in the Fields, Midx., B., and Ann Green of S[t] James's, Westminster, S.; by the same

4 Stephen Clench of S[t] James's, Westminster, Midx., B., and Hannah Thorndike of the same, S.; by M[r] Piddington

5 Jonathan Read of S[t] Andrew's, Holborn, Midx., B., and Ann Goulding of S[t] George's, Bloomsbury, Midx., S.; by M[r] Jackson, Curate of S[t] Austin's

5 Thomas Gill of Reading, Berks, B., and Elisabeth Haycock of the same, S.; by M[r] Jackson

6 William Howard of Fulham, Midx., B., and Elisabeth Fox of the same, S.; by M[r] Worlich, Lecturer of S[t] Nicholas Cole Abby

7 William Robinson of S[t] Thomas, Southwark, W., and Sarah Webb of S[t] Stephen, Coleman Street, Lond., W.; by D[r] Watkinson

8 Francis Lake of S[t] John's, Wapping, Midx., W., and Mary Buckley of All Hallows Barking, Lond., W.; by M[r] Thoresby, Rect[r] of Stoke Newington

8 William Marson of S[t] George's, Hanover Square, Midx., B., and Ann Hamerton of Cookham, Berks, S.; by M[r] Jackson

10 *Richard Norley of S[t] Ann's, Westminster, Midx., B., and Elisabeth Taylor of the same, S.; by the same

15 Thomas Candy of S[t] Dunstan's in the West, Lond., B., and Susannah Jones of the same, S.; by the same

18 Henry Lee of S[t] Swithin's, Lond., B., and Mary Leche of S[t] Mary Magdalen, Old Fish Street, Lond., S.

24 Charles Brent of S[t] Martin's in the Fields, Midx., W., and Sarah Lawes of S[t] James's, Westminster, Midx., W.

1733.

Mar. 25 James Baxter of S[t] John the Evangelist, Lond., B., and Sarah Rowlings of the same, S.

26 William Armstrong of Brackley, Northamptonshire, B., and Hannah Rose of S[t] Bride's, Lond., W.

26 Henry Lea of S[t] Martin's in the Fields, Midx., B., and Catherine Perrin of S[t] James's, Westminster, Midx., S.

26 John Huff of Stratford, Bow, Midx., B., and Elisabeth Crane of the same, S.

26 Thomas Collins of S[t] George's, Hanover Square, Midx., W., and Margaret Freeman of S[t] Ann's, Westminster, Midx., W.

26 John Buckle of S[t] Faith, Lond., B., and Catherine Hall of the same, S.

26 John Clason, junr., of Whitechapple, Midx., B., and Mary Alstrom of the same, S.

* "Richard" written over "William."—Ed.

1733

Mar. 27 Henry How of Beeley, Kent, B., and Elisabeth Allen of Chislehurst in the said county, S.

27 Matthew Robinson of St Dunstan's in the East, Lond., B., and Catherine Tomlinson of St John's, Wapping, Midx., S.

27 Robert Ingram of Battersea, Surry, W., and Mary Staples of the same, W.

29 John Palmer of Standon, Hertford, B., and Sarah Weedon of the same, S.

April 2 William Earlom of St Sepulchre's, Lond., B., and Mary Sculthorp of the same, S.

2 William Blondell of Northall, Midx., B., and Ann Nash of the same, S.

3 Thomas Fothergill of St George's, Bloomsbury, Midx., B., and Martha Fenn of St George's in the said county, W.

3 William Gardner of St Sepulchre's, Lond., W., and Eleanor Strange of St Andrew's, Holborn, Midx., S.

3 Benjamin Carter of St Saviour's, Southwark, W., and Jane Burnell of the same, S.

3 Hans Hinrick Steger of St John, Wapping, Midx., B., and Tralucia Ginn of St John Zachary, Lond., S.

3 Ebenezer Powell, B., and Sarah Hutcheson, W., both of this parish; by Banns

4 William Norris of Northampton, W., and Mary Crouch of High Barnett, Midx., S.

5 Thomas Allman of St Faith, Lond., W., and Judith West of Canterbury, S.

5 William Fernely of St Peter's, Cornhill, Lond., W., and Ann Chitley of the same, W.

5 Mark Thompson of Kensington, Midx., B., and Dorothy Morey of the same, S.

7 Thomas Moore of Whitechapel, Midx., B., and Mary Euzor of the same, W.

7 John Bayley of St Mary le Bone, Midx., B., and Jane Sadler of the same, S.

8 John Sarle of Colebrook in the parish of Langley, Berks, B., and Elisabeth Sayer of Ashbury, Wilts, S.

8 John Gildon of Hampton, Midx., B., and Elisabeth Fitzwater of the same, W.

9 John Mullins of Cullarn or Colhorne, Wilts, W., and Edith Cheltenham of Mortlake, Surry, S.

9 John Wadbrook of Kingston upon Thames, Surry, B., and Winifred Lloyd of the same, S.

11 John Drew of Wandsworth, Surry, B., and Ann Taylor of the same, S.

11 Richard Tallis of Myvord, Montgomery, B., and Sarah Needham of Wandsworth, Surry, S.

11 Peter Dupont of St Leonard, Foster Lane, Lond., B., and Sarah Spriggins of St Ann's, Aldersgate, Lond., W.

12 Daniel Reed of Rickmondsworth, Hertford, B., and Mary Copland of Denham, Bucks, S.

12 Oliver Silverthorne of St George's, Hanover Square, Midx., B., and Wilkins of the same, S.

13 John Sheffield of St James's, Westminster, Midx., B., and Mary Freeman of St George's, Hanover Square, S.

14 Thomas Churcher of St Olave, Southwark, W., and Elisabeth Carr of St Bartholomew the Great, Lond., W.

14 Mark Bawcutt of St Mary le Bone, Midx., W., and Susanna Whiskin of the same, S.

1733

April 14 William Rogers of St Peter's, Cornhill, Lond., W., and Jane Cullen of the same, S.; by Dr Jones, Rectr of Chipping Ongar, Essex

16 William Clements of Chislehurst, Kent, B., and Repentance Comport of the same, S.

17 Phinehas Smith of All Hallows Barking, Lond., B., and Sarah Low of St Dunstan's, Stepny, Midx., W.

17 William Stone of Uxbridge, Midx., B., and Mary Ravis of the same, S.

17 Edward Davis of Walton upon Thames, Surry, B., and Elisabeth Leader of St Margaret's, Westminster, Midx., S.

18 Jeffery Cooke of St Clement Danes, Midx., B., and Mary May of St Thomas's, Southwark, Surry, W.

18 William Wilson of Deptford, Kent, W., and Rose Turner of Old Brentford, Midx., W.

19 Daniel Brodbelt, Esqr, of the Inner Temple, Lond., B., and Charlotte Cardonnell of Chelsea, Midx., S.

19 George Carter of St Paul's, Covent Garden, Midx., B., and Mary Devereux of St Martin's in the Fields, Midx., S.

20 John Olive of Leaves in Sussex, W., and Katherine Pauncefort of Dorking, Surry, W.

20 William Surton of Bagington, Warwick, B., and Jane Baker of St George's, Hanover Square, Midx., S.

21 John May of St Margaret's, Westminster, Midx., B., and Martha Coster of St Andrew's, Holborn, Midx., S.

22 Edward Wellinton, B., and Elizabeth Iviory, W., both of St Peter's, Paul's Wharf; by Banns

23 Thomas Parker of St Clement's Danes, Midx., B., and Mary Bromley of St Martin's in the Fields, Midx., S.

23 John Gay of Endfield, Midx., B., and Mary Darlington of the same, S.

23 Richard Gunner of St James's, Westminster, Midx., B., and Ann Wright of the same, S.

24 William Gay of St Martin's in the Fields, Midx., B., and Elizabeth Gilder of St Paul's, Covent Garden, Midx., S.

24 John Thompson of St Botolph's, Bishopsgate, Lond., B., and Mary Morris of St Margaret's, Westminster, Midx., S.

24 John Allisson of St Paul's, Shadwell, Midx., B., and Mary Kendall of the same, S.

24 John Phillips of St George's, Southwark, B., and Hannah Lyford of St Giles in the Fields, Midx., S.

25 Edward Lamsdown of All Hallows the Great, Lond., B., and Ann Warren of the same, S.

26 James Hammond of St Dunstan's, Stepny, Midx., W., and Elizabeth Willoughby of Maidstone, Kent, S.

26 William Lagg of Walton upon Thames, Surry, B., and Catherine Cooper of the same, S.

26 Edmund James of St Saviour's, Southwark, Surry, W., and Ann Price of the same, W.

26 John Campart of Christ Church, Spittlefields, Midx., B., and Anne Vitall of St Leonard's, Shoreditch, Midx., S.

26 William Thompson of Peterson, Surry, W., and Ann Rich of the same, S.

27 Thomas Skilton of Harding, Hertford, B., and Elizabeth Hobbs of Redbourne in Hertford, S.

27 William Pix of Northiam, Sussex, B., and Ann Birch of the same, S.

28 Morgan Keene of New Sarum, Wilts, B., and Grace Camfield of St Martin's in the Fields, Midx., S.; by Mr Brotherton, Fellow of All Souls, Oxford

1733

April 28 Edmund Camper of St Paul's, Shadwell, Middx., W., and Ann Sutton of St John's, Wapping, Midx., W.

29 John Dunn of Bromley, Kent, B., and Easter Batchelder of St Peter le Poor, Lond., W.

30 George How of Walthamstow, Essex, B., and Martha Luckcraft of St Botolph, Aldgate, Lond., S.

30 John Buntin of Sandy, Bedford, B., and Hannah Haydon of the same, W.

May 1 Edward Chapman of Kingsdowne, Kent, B., and Jane Chapman of the same, S.; by Mr Hillman of St Paul's

2 Joseph Sweetting of St Mary Axe, Lond., B., and Ann James of the same, S.

3 William Towbe of St Clement's, Eastcheap, Lond., B., and Elizabeth Clifford of St Giles's, Cripplegate, Midx., S.

4 Edward Loveland of Lipsfield, Surry, B., and Elizabeth Burton of Westerham, Kent, S.

4 James Knight of Mortlake, Surry, W., and Mary Sergeant of the same, W.

7 Edward Whitehead of St Paul's, Covent Garden, Midx., B., and Mary Blanchard of the same, S.

7 John Grundy of St Mary Magdalen, Milk Street, Lond., B., and Elizabeth Fathers of St Lawrence, Jewry, Lond., S.

8 Richard Wabelin of Horndon on the Hill, Essex, B., and Anne Newport of Milton next Gravesend, Kent, S.

8 Thomas Sherley of St Clement Danes, Midx., B., and Arabella Watson of the same, S.

10 Andrew Solinus of St George, Hanover Square, Midx., B., and Susanna Mayhew of the same, S.

10 Stephen Philpot of Romney, Kent, W., and Elizabeth Bateman of Edmonton, Midx., S.

10 John Harlin of Crayford, Kent, W., and Eleanor Wiggin of the same, S.

10 James Serces of St Martin's in the Fields, Midx., Clerk, B., and Elizabeth Leige of the same, S.

14 Edmund Kinch of Hampton, Midx., B., and Elizabeth Langar of Kingston upon Thames, Surry, S.

14 Daniel Round of St James's, Westminster, Midx., W., and Elizabeth Richardson of St Botolph, Bishopsgate, Lond., S.

15 William Baker of Sevenoaks, Kent, B., and Elizabeth Lawrence of the same, S.

16 William Ockford of St Saviour's, Southwark, B., and Mary Clarke of the same, W.

19 John Hutchins of St Magnus the Martyr, Lond., B., and Philippa Hatch of the same, S.

19 Henry South of St Martin's in the Fields, Midx., B., and Jane Wilson of St Margaret, Westminster, Midx., S.

20 William Turner of St Martins in the Fields, Midx., W., and Eleanor Ask of the same, W.

22 Samuel Elly of New Windsor, Berks, B., and Catherine Winchcombe of Thames Ditton, Surry, S.

25 William Chancler of St Michael Bassishaw, Lond., B., and Jane Claverlay of the same, S.

25 Martin Preist of St Botolph, Aldgate, Lond., B., and Catherine Rolston of St Mary Magdalen, Old Fish Street, Lond., S.

25 Mark Donaldson of St John, Wapping, Midx., W., and Frances Read of St Hellen's, Lond., S.

25 Charles Bickerton of St Leonard, Foster Lane, Lond., B., and Sarah Edwards of St Ann's, Blackfyar's, Lond., S.

1733

May 26 Francis Best of Kingston on Thames, Surry, B., and Sarah Horsley of the same, S.

26 Thomas Ting of Roydon, Essex, B., and Mary Harris of Endfield, Midx., S.

26 Samuel France of St Ann's, Westminster, Midx., W., and Mary Elliot of St Martin's in the Fields, Midx., W.

28 Thomas Ingrams of Orpington, Kent, B., and Dorothy Everest of the same, S.

28 Fawnt Eyre of the Middle Temple, Lond., B., and Elizabeth Burleigh of St Martin's in the Fields, Midx., S.

29 Daniel Scott of St Mary, Rotherhith, Surry, B., and Hannah Nicholls of St Giles, Cripplegate, Midx., S.

29 George Rickards of St George's, Bloomsbury, Midx., B., and Ann Stevens of St Clement Danes, Midx., S.

29 John Starkey of Wrenbury, Cheshire, Esq., B., and Martha Gray of St James, Westminster, Midx., S.

30 George Maine of Piddleton, Northampton, B., and Elizabeth Heddige of St Margaret's, Westminster [*blank*].

31 John Robson of St James's, Westminster, Midx., B., and Deborah Bishop of the same, S.

31 William Parrat of St Martin's in the Fields, Midx., B., and Mary Leveridge of St Paul's, Covent Garden, Midx., S.

June 1 Anthony Briant of Beckenham, Kent, B., and Susannah Lodge of the same, W.

2 James Frazer of St James's, Westminster, Midx., Esq., B., and Rebecca Milne of St Mary le Strand, Midx., S.

2 John Hawksworth of St Andrew's, Holborn, Midx., B., and Mary Smith of the same, W.

3 Samuel Siddall of St Lawrence, Jewry, Lond., W., and Mary Grigry of St Christopher's, Lond., S.

6 Roger Prowse of Darlington, Devon, B., and Ann Clarke of St George's, Hanover Square, Midx., S.

6 Jeremiah Parmenter of Latten, Essex, B., and Sarah Boarum of the same, S.

7 George Gross of St John, Wapping, Midx., W., and Mary Tinmouth of St Peter's, Cornhill, Lond., S.

7 Thomas Cooch of St Michael, Queenhith, Lond., B., and Sarah Vaughan of St Faith the Virgin, Lond., W.

9 John Bullock, junr, of St Clement Danes, Midx., B., and Mary Bullock of St Mary, Whitechappell, Midx., S.

9 Thomas Egleton of St Mary, Bermondsey, Surry, W., and Elizabeth Allison of the same, S.

9 David Gwynn of Deptford, Kent, B., and Mary Hall of the same, S.

10 William Ghiselin of St Giles, Cripplegate, Midx., W., and Elianor Griffin of St Faith the Virgin, Lond., W.

11 Peter Renaux of Stepny, Midx., B., and Ann Cadon of St Margaret, Westminster, Midx., W.

12 William Watts of St Giles's in the Fields, Midx., W., and Sarah Sheppard of the same, S.

12 Samuel Farrington of St Ann's, Limehouse, Midx., B., and Elisabeth Harry of the same, S.

13 William Tharp of Borden, Kent, B., and Elisabeth Steward of St Andrew's, Holborn, Midx., W.

13 John Stow of St Mary, Rotherhith, Surry, B., and Martha Wade of the same, W.

14 William Folder of Lambeth, Surry, W., and Ann Couley of Hunsdon, Hertford, W.

1733

June 14 Thomas Ferriman of St George's, Botolph Lane, Lond., B., and Elisabeth Bamford of St Magnus the Martyr, Lond., S.

15 James Smorthwaite of St Albans, Hertford, B., and Elisabeth Pattison of the same, S.

15 John Allen of St James's, Westminster, Midx., W., and Hannah Jones of St Andrew's, Holborn, Midx., S.

17 William Irwing of ye Precinct of Norton Folgate, Midx., W., and Anna Maria Morgan of Slapton, Northampton, S.

23 William Wall of St Dunstan's in the West, Lond., B., and Mary Gold of the same, S.

23 John Proctor of St John the Evangelist, Westminster, Midx., B., and Ann Jackson of St James, Westminster, Midx., S.

23 William Stockham of St Paul's, Shadwell, Midx., B., and Mary Maxley of the same, S.

23 Thomas Stackhouse of St Vedast als. Foster, Lond., W., and Mary Chance of St Sepulchre's, Lond., W.

23 Henry Johnston, Clerk, LL.D., of Stow Market, Suffolk, B., and Hannah Harris of St Martin's in the Fields, Midx., S.

26 John Savery of Hammersmith, Midx., B., and Ann Binney of St James, Westminster, Midx., S.

27 Richard Holmes of St Clement Danes, Midx., B., and Alice Sleath of St Paul's, Covent Garden, Midx., S.

27 William Ivers, B., and Ann Newman, S., both of this Parish; by Banns

July 1 Henry Shakshaft of St Mary, Aldermanbury, Lond., B., and Mary Taylor of the same, S.

3 Abraham French of Wandsworth, Surry, B., and Jane Sturdy of Battersea, Surry, S.

3 Peter Odin of St Andrew's, Holborn, Lond., B., and Mary Hatch of St Brides, Lond., S.

3 James Read of St Giles's, Cripplegate, Midx., B., and Sarah Cuthbertson of the same, S.

4 John Martin of the Middle Temple, Lond., B., and Elizabeth Whitney of the same, S.

5 John Westifer of St Paul's, Covent Garden, W., and Sarah Palmer of St Martins in the Fields, Midx., W.

5 Peregrine Doyly of St Mildred, Bread Street, Lond., B., and Prudence Fenn of St Gabriel, Fenchurch, Lond., S.

7 Stephen Ogle of St Mary, Rotherhith, Surry, B., and Sarah Norriss of the same, S.

7 William Kendrick of St Dunstan's, Stepny, Midx., W., and Esther Christopher of the same, W.

8 Samuel Faulkner of St Leonard, Eastcheap, Lond., B., and Elisabeth Fellows of St Mary Athill, Lond., W.

8 George Palin, gent., of St Dionis Backchurch, Lond., B., and Mary Wade of the same, S.

9 Thomas Bourne of St Mildred, Poultry, Lond., B., and Mary Smith of Hampton, Midx., S.

10 Matthew Still of Stepny, Midx., B., and Abigael Fardin of the same, W.

10 Thomas Fetherston Leigh of Packwood, Warwickshire, W., and Mary Lane of Wolverhampton, Staffordshire, S.

11 Roger Bridges of Chatham, Kent, B., and Elizabeth Wood of the same, S.

12 Henry Hawes of Hammersmith, Midx., B., and Sarah Shepard of the same, W.

15 William Whiting of Teddington, Midx., B., and Elizabeth Gardner of the same, S.

1733

July 15 Robert Griffin of St Giles's, Cripplegate, Midx., B., and Mary Attwood of the same, S.

15 John Thompson of St James's, Westminster, Midx., B., and Mary Thresher of the same, W.

15 William Washington of St Giles's, Cripplegate, Lond., B., and Martha Woffendale of St Ann's, Westminster, Midx., S.

16 David Cole of Mortlake, Surry, B., and Martha Hebberly of the same, S.

16 Francis Pleasants of Deptford, Kent, B., and Diana Brooker of the same, S.

16 Jeremiah Pearson of St Clement Danes, Midx., B., and Martha Bennet of ye precinct of White Friars, Lond., S.

17 John Gibson of St Giles's, Cripplegate, Lond., W., and Hepzibeth Threllkeld of St Botolph without Aldersgate, Lond., S.

17 Thomas Browne of St Margaret's, Westminster, Midx., W., and Catherine Wishdish of the same, W.

17 Henry Kitchin of St Martin's in the Fields, Midx., W., and Sarah Sparrow of St Botolph, Aldersgate, Lond., W.

18 Arthur Kight, Clerk, Vicar of Orton upon Hill, Leicestershire, and Anna Austin of Chidingstone, Kent, S.

18 William Eastland of St Bartholomew the Less, Lond., B., and Hannah Walbank of Christ Church, Midx., S.

19 George Winterbottom of St Mary le Bone, Midx., B., and Rachael Hart of the same, S.

22 Henry Staines of St Botolph, Bishopsgate, Lond., B., and Margery Burwoss of the same, S.

22 Henry Martin of St Thomas the Apostle, Lond., W., and Abigael How of St Dionis Backchurch, Lond., S.

25 John Outerram of Chelsom, Surry, B., and Sarah Piggott of the same, S.

26 Thomas Richman of St John, Hackney, Midx., B., and Elizabeth Banbury of Trinity Parish in the Minories, Lond., S.

26 Thomas Hancock of Croydon, Surry, B., and Elizabeth Cooper of St James's, Clerkenwell, Midx., S.

27 John Harvey of Chiswick, Midx., B., and Sarah Wiggins of the same, S.

28 John Mason of St Sepulchre's, Lond., B., and Margaret Francis of the same, S.

29 John Fillon of St Dunstan's, Stepny, Midx., B., and Mary Lewington of the same, S.

29 Richard Jones of St Sepulchre's, Lond., B., and Mary Lardge of the same, S.

30 John Parkins of Mortlake, Surry, B., and Ann Lyford of the same, S.

31 Adam Sale of Deptford, Kent, B., and Sarah Simmons of the same, S.

31 John Moore of St Peter's, Cornhill, Lond., B., and Anne Blundell of the same, W.

Aug. 1 Thomas Martin of St George's, Hanover Square, Midx., B., and Mary Little of the same, S.

1 William Paul of St Dunstan's in the West, Midx., B., and Margaret Shirt of the same, S.

2 Caleb Jackson of St Mary, Newington, Surry, W., and Mary Beck of Catherum in Surry, S.

3 Josiah Woolley of St Lawrence, Jewry, Lond., B., and Frances Roak of the same, S.

3 Edmund Webb of St Clement Danes, Midx., B., and Elizabeth Odell of the same, S.

4 Henry Crowther of Lambeth, Surry, B., and Mary Loflis of the same, S.

1733

Aug. 5 Andrew Burton of Deddinghurst, Essex, B., and Alice White of the same, S.

5 Parker Allatt of S[t] Sepulchre's, Lond., B., and Mary Spencer of S[t] Dunstan's in the West, Lond., S.

5 William Bignell of S[t] George's, Bloomsbury, Midx., W., and Margaret Rivetts of S[t] Giles in the Fields, W.

8 Jonathan Bush of S[t] Giles in the Fields, Midx., B., and Mary Waring of S[t] Clement Danes, Midx., S.

9 John Hulse of S[t] Andrew Undershaft, Lond., B., and Ann Baxter of the same, S.

12 George Loo of Chinkford, Essex, B., and Ann Besgrove of the same, S.

12 William Simmons of Hadlow, Kent, B., and Ann Turley of the same, S.

12 Thomas Traver of Kensington, Midx., B., and Sarah Fry of S[t] Ann's, Westminster, Midx., S.

13 Henry Manley of S[t] Margaret's, Westminster, Midx., B., and Sarah Brawne of the same, S.

14 John Hill of S[t] Andrew's, Holborn, Lond., B., and Susanna Dalloway of the same, S.

14 Edward Garratt of Woolwich, Kent, B., and Mary Loyd of the same, S.

16 John Turnor, Esq., of Bury S[t] Edmonds, Suffolk, B., and Bridget Gery of S[t] Giles's in the Fields, Midx., S.; by M[r] Smith, Vicar of Hetchworth, Cambridgeshire

16 John Harris of S[t] Dunstan's, Stepny, Midx., B., and Elizabeth Fox of the same, S.

19 John Mynatt of S[t] George's, Hanover Square, Midx., B., and Elizabeth Davis of the same, W.

20 Michael Hill of S[t] Paul, Covent Garden, Midx., B., and Elizabeth Maddox of S[t] Andrew's, Holborn, Lond., S.

21 Paul Berland of St Martin in the Fields, Midx., B., and Anne Hardell of the same, S.

21 William Miller of St Botolph, Bishopsgate, Lond., B., and Hephzibah Prime of the same, S.

21 Richard Jackson of St Andrew's, Holborn, Midx., B., and Hester Holmes of the same, S.

21 Francis Jockim Gram Kañ of St Martin in the Fields, Midx., W., and Mary Williamson of the same, S.

22 John Barrot of St Giles in the Fields, Midx., B., and Esther Turner of St George the Martyr, Midx., S.

22 George Browne of St John's, Wapping, Midx., B., and Mary Potts of St Catherine's near the Tower, Lond., W.

23 Owen Porter of Stains, Midx., B., and Martha Mugglestone of the same, W.

23 Henry Bowland of S[t] Dunstan's, Stepny, Midx., W., and Elisabeth Collins of S[t] Paul, Shadwell, S.

24 Richard Heather of Deptford, Kent, B., and Martha Fossett of Allhallows Barkin, Lond., W.

25 William Mudge of S[t] Ann's, Limehouse, Midx., B., and Sarah Horton of S[t] Dunstan's, Stepny, Midx., S.

27 Richard Rylance of S[t] Giles's in the Fields, Midx., W., and Susannah Wood of S[t] James's, Clerkenwell, Midx., S.

28 William Russell of S[t] George's in the East, Midx., B., and Margaret Carter of the same, S.

28 Robert I:o:ny [*sic*], jun[r], of S[t] Michael's, Wood Street, Lond., B., and Sarah Goodchild of Kimbol, Bucks, S.

1733

Aug. 29 Daniel Wright of S[t] Faith's, Lond., B., and Mary Wright of Shenley, Hertford, S.

29 James Hughes of S[t] Ann's, Blackfryers, Lond., B., and Isabella Robinson of S[t] Andrew's, Holborn, Midx., S.

30 Francis Finton of Wivenhoe, Essex, B., and Dorothy Martin of S[t] Olave, Hart Street, Lond., W.

30 William Ford of S[t] Sepulchre's, Lond., B., and Mary Hall of Rumford, Essex, S.

30 Richard Edge of S[t] Mary at Litchfield, B., and Rebecca Swaine of S[t] Martin's le Grand, Lond., S.

31 Robert Robinson of S[t] Mary le Bow, Lond., B., and Esther Pearce of S[t] Andrew's, Holborn, Lond., S.

23* John Weaver of S[t] Peter's, Cornhill, Lond., B., and Mary Hargrave of S[t] Peter at Paul's Wharf, S.; by D[r] Watkinson

Sept. 1 John Petterson of Rochester, Kent, B., and Elisabeth Dirixon of Deptford, Kent, W.

2 Samuel Rogerson of S[t] Saviour's, Southwark, Surry, B., and Mary Armstrong of the same, S.

2 William Browne of S[t] Giles's, Cripplegate, Lond., B., and Henrietta Maria Duston of S[t] Leonard's, Shoreditch, Midx., S.

4 Charles Clay of S[t] James's, Westminster, Midx., B., and Mary Bromley of the Poultry, Lond., S.

5 William Shafford of Lambeth, Surry, W., and Mary Manly of S[t] Mary Magdalen, Bermondsey, Surry, W.

5 Emanuel Francis Silvey of S[t] Mary, Aldermanbury, Lond., B., and Ann Knight of the same, S.

6 James Allen of S[t] Georges, Midx., B., and Jane Evans of S[t] James's, Westminster, Midx. [*blank*].

6 Thomas Bean of S[t] Clement Danes, Midx., W., and Margaret Biggs of S[t] Bennet Finck, Lond., S.

7 Thomas Turnage of Wansted, Essex, B., and Elizabeth Dodd of S[t] Margaret's, Westminster, Midx., S.; by D[r] Thomas

8 John Beach of S[t] Clement Danes, Midx., B., and Mary Malcher of the same, S.

9 Thomas Chapman of S[t] Martin in the Fields, Midx., B., and Christian Chivers of S[t] Mary Abchurch, Lond., S.

9 Edward Cook of S[t] Saviour's, Southwark, Surry, B., and Ann Moor of S[t] James's, Westminster, Midx., S.

9 Solomon Rogers, B., and Miriam Moore, S., both of this Parish; by Banns

10 Thomas Elms of Mitcham, Surry, W., and Jane Jackson of the same, W.

10 Roger Whalley of S[t] James's, Westminster, Midx., B., and Elizabeth Webb of the same, S.

11 John Nash of Lambeth, Surry, B., and Elizabeth Wyatt of the same, S.

12 William Allison of Swanscombe, Kent, B., and Elizabeth Branch of the same, S.

13 Edward Cleaveland of S[t] James's, Westminster, Midx., B., and Elizabeth Smith of the same, S.

13 Thomas Clarke of Fulham, Midx., W., and Ann Holder of the same, W.

14 John Templeman of Esingdon, Hertford, B., and Isabella Rumney of the same, W.

16 John Woodin of S[t] Paul's, Covent Garden, Midx., B., and Mary Cole of the same, S.

16 Thomas Whitehead of S[t] Dunstan's in the East, Lond., B., and Elizabeth Lister of the same, S.

* Misplaced in original.—ED.

1733

Sept. 18 Thomas Oliver of St George's, Midx., W., and Mary Dixon of the same, S.

18 Benjamin Payne of St Giles's in the Fields, Midx., B., and Elizabeth Ives of the same, S.

18 Richard Whytaker of Basinghall Street, Lond., B., and Sarah Deeping of St Mildred, Bread Street, Lond., S.

18 Arnold Finchett of St Mary Aldermary, Lond., B., and Mary Mitchell of St Leonard's, Shoreditch, Midx., S.

20 Peter Marsh of St Bride's, Lond., B., and Catherine Crump of the same, S.

23 Thomas Reynolds of St Mary le Savoy, Midx., W., and Elizabeth Morris of Thaydon, Essex, S.

24 Nicholas Leech of Stepny, Midx., W., and Ann Robinson of All Hallows the Less, Lond., S.

25 Thomas Eve of Croydon, Surry, B., and Elizabeth Smallpeice of Guildford, Surry, S.

25 John Collyer of St Martin's in the Fields, Midx., W., and Patience Parker of Christchurch, Lond., S.

26 James Pennyall of Croydon, Surry, B., and Catherine Town of the same, S.

27 Richard Garbett of St Bartholomew's the Great, Lond., W., and Mary Brompton of the same, S.

29 James Beacham of Newington, Surry, W., and Mary Claridge of Stepney, Midx., S.

29 Edward Hodson of St James's, Westminster, Midx., W., and Joan Pety of St Giles's, Midx., W.

29 William Remington of St Botolph, Aldgate, Lond., B., and Hester Atterbrough of St Dunstan's, Stepny, Midx., W.

Oct. 3 John Manle of St James's, Westminster, Midx., B., and Ann Henderson of the same, W.

3 John Petor of Wandsworth, Surry, B., and Ruth Lucey of the same, W.

3 John Barefoot of Lalam, Midx., B., and Elizabeth Burges of the same, S.

4 James Corderoy of St Saviour's, Southwark, W., and Mary Hawkins of St Thomas, Southwark, Surry, S.; by the Revd Mr Casberd

4 John Hammond of Ruslipp, Midx., B., and Ann Ewer of the same, S.

5 Samuel Richardson of Stanway, B., and Susannah Lee of Colchester, Essex, S.

5 Peter Adams of St James's, Westminster, Midx., B., and Mary Edes of the same, S.

6 Robert Groney of St Mary Magdalen, Bermondsey, Surry, B., and Christian Baten of the same, S.

6 Henry Shade of Chigwell, Essex, B., and Ann Webb of the same, S.

6 David Tom of St Martin in the Fields, Midx., W., and Catherine Owens of All hallows Staining, Lond., S.

7 Francis Brooks of Christ Church, Lond., B., and Mary Cooper of St George's, Bloomsbury, S.

7 John Stephenson of St Saviour's, Southwark, Surry, B., and Christian Gaston of the same, S.

9 Thomas Hobbs of St Peter's, Canterbury, B., and Elizabeth Magson of St John, Wapping, Midx., S.

11 Richard Sumpner of Aveley, Essex, W., and Elizabeth Serle of Stableford Abbott, Essex, S.

11 John Dykes of Woburn, Bucks, B., and Sarah Price of the same, S.

1733
Oct. 13 George Gordon of St Paul's, Covent Garden, Midx., B., and Anne Baldwyn of Kensington, Midx., W.
13 Samuel Smith of St Giles's, Cripplegate, Lond., W., and Hannah Webb of All Hallows Staining, Lond., W.
18 William Truelove of Ruisslip, Midx., W., and Ann Lucas of Hayes, Midx., S.
18 William Saunders of Lambeth, Surry, B., and Mary Ludlow of St Michael Royal, Lond., S.
20 John Smallwood of Lewisham, Kent, B., and Mary Berry of the same, S.
20 Ralph Parkinson of Lewisham, Kent, B., and Mary Byers of the same, S.
22 Francis Merrit of St Stephen, Coleman Street, Lond., B., and Sarah Leigh of the same, S.
22 Richard Howard of Hickenham, Midx., W., and Elizabeth Day of Hillington, Midx., W.
24 Richard Carter of Wimbledon, Surry, W., and Elizabeth Harris of the same, W.
25 William Bromley of St Anne's, Westminster, Midx., B., and Ann Webb of the same, S.
25 Richard Corrall of North Mims, Hertford, B., and Bridget Bennet of the same, S.
27 Richard Winter of Lambeth, Surry, B., and Mary Holderness of the same, W.
27 John Jones of the Precinct of the Tower of London, B., and Elizabeth Roberts of St Antholin's, Lond., W.
28 John Lanchet of Chipsted, Surry, B., and Elizabeth Brooke of Nutfield, Surry, S.
29 Thomas Cowley of Christ Church, Surry, B., and Margaret Read of St Paul's, Covent Garden, Midx., S.; by Mr Worlich of St Nicholas, Cole Abbey
29 John Lamb of Battersea, Surry, B., and Mary Stables of the same, S.; by Mr *Jackson*, Curate of St Austins
29 John Bateman of St Giles's, Cripplegate, Midx., B., and Mary Hawkins of St Mary Staining, Lond., S.; by Mr Jackson aforesaid
30 Thomas Dunn of St Botolph, Bishopsgate, Lond., B., and Susan Bluett of St Mary Axe, Lond., S.; by Mr Jackson
30 William Constable of St Mary Magdalen, Bermondsey, Surry, W., and Elizabeth Neazar of St Giles's in the Fields, Midx., S.; by Mr Jackson
Nov. 1 John Dewes of St Clement Danes, Midx., B., and Sarah Chamberlayn of the same, S.; by Dr Thomas
1 Samuel Hallin of Bristol, B., and Ann Day of St Margaret, New Fish Street, Lond., S.; by Dr Thomas
2 Robert Leech of Dagenham, Essex, B., and Elizabeth Hudson of the same, W.; by Dr Thomas
2 Joseph Lee of St Mary, Rotherhith, Surry, W., and Sarah Hall of the same, S.; by Dr Thomas
2 John Spalding of Royston, Hertford, W., and Mary How of St Martin's in the Fields, Midx., S.; by Dr Thomas
4 Abraham Rogers of St Botolph, Aldgate, Midx., B., and Sarah Shillecorne of the same, S.; by Mr Jackson
5 John Harrison of St James's, Westminster, Midx., B., and Margaret Walter of St Giles's in the Fields, Midx. [*blank*]; by Dr Best of St Lawrence, Jewry
7 Henry Richard of Horton, Kent, B., and Mary Child of Sutton, Kent, S.; by Dr Thomas

1733

Nov. 7 Robert Bostock of Chevening, Kent, B., and Mary Rogers of Meopham, Kent, S.; by D[r] Watkinson

10 Samuel Belchier of Kingston upon Thames, B., and Elizabeth Smith of Windsor, Berks, S.; by D[r] Watkinson

10 Joseph Mill of S[t] Mary Magdalen, Bermondsey, Surry, B., and Mary Sallway of the same, W.; by D[r] Watkinson

12 John Chapman of S[t] Mary, Stratford le Bow, Midx., W., and Mary Jordan of Westham, Essex, W.

13 James Tough of S[t] Mary, Rotherhith, Surry, B., and Jane Allen of the same, S.; by M[r] Jackson

15 Thomas Millson of Esher, Surry, W., and Elizabeth Chitty of the same, S.

17 George Langdale of S[t] Clement Danes, Midx., B., and Elizabeth Bradwell of the same, S.

16 John Seymour of S[t] Mary Magdalen, Bermondsey, Surry, W., and Elizabeth Goulder of the same, S.

19 Anthony Langley of Kingston upon Thames, Surry, B., and Elizabeth Moore of the same, S.

22 Thomas Bonfflett of Christ Church, Spittlefields, Midx., B., and Mary Bouge of S[t] Leonard, Shoreditch, Midx., S.

22 Jacob Tallowgreen of Greenwich, Kent, B., and Ann Banham of the same, S.

26 Robert Pemberton of S[t] Martin in the Fields, Midx., W., and Mary Silvertop of S[t] Gregory, Lond., S.; by M[r] Piddington

26 John Grant of S[t] George, Midx., W., and Apollonia Graves of the same, S.; by D[r] Watkinson

27 Edward Watson of Low Layton, Essex, B., and Anne Page of the same, S.

27 Alexander Wood of Oxford, B., and Sarah Harvey of S[t] Martin's in the Fields, Midx., S.; by the Rev[d] M[r] Kenwrick

28 Joseph Clackston of Chiswick, Midx., B., and Phœbe Haynes of S[t] Ann and Agnes, Aldersgate, Lond., S.

29 William Vickers of S[t] George's, Bloomsbury, Midx., B., and Jane Reamy of the same, W.

29 Henry Crooks of Eltham, Kent, B., and Hannah Maria Le Vie of S[t] Andrew, Holborn, Midx., S.; by M[r] Jackson

30 John Willson of Deptford, Kent, W., and Mary Leonard of the same, W.

30 Edward Eveleigh of S[t] Mildred, Poultry, Lond., B., and Martha Moseley of the same, S.

Dec. 4 James Hawley of Paulers-pury, Northamptonshire, B., and Mary Pidgeon of S[t] Ann's, Westminster, Midx., S.

4 William Weston of Westham, Essex, B., and Catherine Huxley of Bow, Midx., S.

5 Joseph Wootton of Islington, Midx., W., and Dorothy Peck of the same, S.

5 Richard Addams of Stepny, Midx., W., and Dorothy Woollams of the same, S.

8 Thomas Sutton of the Inner Temple, Lond., B., and Katherine Schimmet Penninch* of S[t] Stephen, Walbrooke, Lond., W.

8 Henry Mitchell of S[t] James's, Westminster, Midx., B., and Elizabeth Ludby of the same, S.

8 John Bowen of S[t] Mary Magdalen, Bermondsey, Surry, B., and Mary Doset of Rotherhith, Surry, S.

10 Jeremiah Price of S[t] George's, Bloomsbury, Midx., B., and Esther Elson of the same, W.

* "Pennink" in the margin.—Ed.

1733

Dec. 15 William Gilbert of S[t] Antholin's, Lond., B., and Catherine Berkeley of the same, W.

18 William Beckett of Barming, Kent, B., and Anne Edwards of the same, S.; by D[r] Watkinson

18 Joseph Taylor of S[t] George's, Southwark, Surry, B., and Elizabeth Bray of S[t] Dunstan's in the West, Lond., S.; by D[r] Watkinson

18 John Ives of S[t] Olave, Southwark, Surry, B., and Margaret Johnson of the same, S.; by M[r] Jackson, Curate of S[t] Austin's

18 Francis Preist of Streatham, Surry, W., and Ann Smith of S[t] Saviour's, Southwark, Surry, W.; by M[r] Jackson aforesaid

20 Peter Neale of the Liberty of the Tower, Lond., W., and Rachael Verry of Christ Church, Midx., W.

22 Thomas Turner of All Hallows, Bread Street, Lond., B., and Barbara Kinier of S[t] Mary, Bermondsey, Surry, S.; by M[r] Worlich

22 Benjamin Louch of All Hallows the Great, Lond., W., and Ann Lilly of S[t] George the Martyr, Midx., S.

22 Walter Hay of S[t] Martin in the Fields, Midx., B., and Althea Bowden of S[t] Sepulchre, Lond., S.

25 Charles Day of S[t] Bride's, Lond., B., and Sarah Briggs of the same, S.

29 Thomas Sturges of S[t] Sepulchre's, Lond., B., and Frances Sculthorp of the same, S.

31 Henry Hillier of Nash, Bucks, B., and Elizabeth Cox of S[t] Ann's, Westminster, Midx., S.

Jan. 1 George Cooper of S[t] Andrew's, Holborn, Midx., W., and Ann Southen of S[t] Sepulchre's, Lond., S.; by M[r] Jackson

1 Thomas Morris of S[t] Clement Danes, Midx., B., and Elizabeth Jones of the same, W.

3 Henry Smith of S[t] Michael's Royal, Lond., B., and Lydia Redfern of S[t] Mary, Aldermanbury, Lond., S.

5 Joel Alderton of S[t] George's, Hanover Square, Midx., B., and Ann Vanderhelme of the same, W.

6 John Draper of S[t] Giles's in the Fields, Midx., B., and Mary Elton of the same, W.

6 Edward King of S[t] James's, Westminster, Midx., B., and Elizabeth Deacon of the same, W.

6 Zaccheus Willmot of the Precinct of S[t] Catherine by the Tower, Lond., B., and Elizabeth Davis of the same, S.

12 Richard Lucas of Wallingham, Surry, B., and Elizabeth Phillips of Chelsham, Surry, S.

13 John Rannison of S[t] Austin's, Lond., B., and Catherine Brealy of S[t] Mary Aldermary, Lond., S.

13 George Humphrey of S[t] George's, Midx., B., and Elizabeth Marshall of the same, S.

14 Richard Gray of S[t] James's, Westminster, Midx., B., and Susannah Brown of Eltham, Kent, S.

16 Richard Walker of S[t] James's, Westminster, Midx., B., and Elizabeth Owen of the same, S.

17 George Luckus of Twittenham, Midx., B., and Sarah Mobsworth of S[t] James's, Westminster, Midx., S.

24 Richard Newcome of Hursley in Southampton, Clerk, B., and Lydia French of S[t] James's, Westminster, Midx., S.

24 Edmund Drake of Redgrave, Suffolk, B., and Mary Ralph of S[t] Andrew's, Holborn, Lond., S.

25 Joseph Richards of S[t] Andrew's, Holborn, B., and Elizabeth Hill of Christ Church, Lond., S.

26 Nathaniel Mannister of S[t] John in Surry, B., and Elizabeth Stanley of the same, S.

1733-4

Jan. 28 Peter Crossleey of Sutton, Kent, B., and Hannah Symson of the same, S.
28 Samuel Pennick of Chelsea, Midx., B., and Jane Carter of the same, S.
29 John Yerbury of St Dunstan's in the West, Lond., B., and Mary Keeling of St George the Martyr, Midx., W.
31 John Loure of St Martin in the Fields, Midx., W., and Eleanor Thompson of the Liberty of the Rolls, Midx., S.
31 William Harris of St George's, Hanover Square, Midx., B., and Dorothy Jackson of the same, S.

Feb. 2 William Clarke of St Botolph, Aldersgate, Lond., B., and Ann Griffin of St George's, Bloomsbury, Midx., S.
4 Robert Rogers of St Andrew's, Holborn, Lond., B., and Elizabeth Hilliar of the same, S.
5 William Smith of St James, Westminster, Midx., B., and Mary Dee of Kensington, Midx., S.
5 Joseph Flood of Guildford, Surry, W., and Sarah Stout of the same, S.
6 Samuel Cobb of St James, Westminster, Midx., S., and Mary Rose of the same, S.
7 Henry Oram of St Mary, Whitechapple, Midx., W., and Judith Hall of St Botolph, Aldersgate, Lond., S.
9 Charles Nuthall of Redgrave, Suffolk, B., and Mary Gayford of Rendlessham, Suffolk, S.
9 Thomas Newcomb of St Margaret Moses, Lond., B., and Elizabeth Buck of St Lawrence, King Street, Lond., S.; by Dr Watkinson
11 Lewis James of St Clement Danes, Midx., B., and Sarah Justice of St Martin in the Fields, Midx., W.
13 John Robinson of St John, Wapping, Midx., B., and Josian Havard of St Mary, Whitechapple, Midx., W.
13 Samuel Rolt of St Luke the Evangelist, Midx., B., and Elizabeth Rideout of St George the Martyr, Midx., W.
14 Henry Winch of Warble, Berks, B., and Sarah Cobb of this parish, S.
14 Thomas Hambly of Deptford, Kent, B., and Lydia Kingston of the same, S.
14 John Cooke of St Dunstan's in the West, Lond., B., and Elizabeth Jarvis of St Brides, Lond., S.
14 Edward Chandler of St Bride's, Lond., W., and Jane Kentish of Knightsbridge, Midx., W.
15 Thomas Griffiths of Greenwich, Kent, W., and Araminta Steers of the same, S.
16 Peter Hunt of Becknam, Kent, B., and Jane Ayers of Kingston upon Thames, Surry, S.
18 Richard Russell of St Martin's in the Fields, Midx., B., and Elizabeth Phelps of St George's, Hanover Square, Midx., S.
18 William Gregory of St Peter, Cheap, Lond., B., and Martha Graves of the same, S.
21* Robert Burton of Barling, Essex, B., and Ann Wells of St Mary Hill, Midx., S.
18 Edward Owen of Clapham, Surry, B., and Ann Nelson of the same, S.
21 Charles Lee of St Martin's in the Fields, Midx., B., and Ann Halford of Uxbridge, Midx., S.
21 Richard Payne of St Olave, Southwark, Surry, B., and Ann Chinn of the same, S.
21 Orlando Arboll of St Leonard, Foster Lane, Lond., B., and Ann Ballard of the same, S.
21 Nathaniel Mathaier of St Margaret, Westminster, Midx., B., and Mary Short of the same, W.

* The date has been altered to 21st.—ED.

1733-4

Feb. 23 John Gage of St Paul's, Covent Garden, Midx., B., and Theodosia White of the same, S.

25 Robert Middlebrook of St James, Westminster, Midx., W., and Mary Ellis of St Martin in the Fields, Midx., S.

25 Mathew Cradock of St George's, Bloomsbury, Midx., B., and Mary Greenway of the same, S.

25 William Mohun, Esqr, of St Margaret's, Westminster, Midx., B., and Sibella Trefusis of the same, S.

26 John Wells of St Ann's, Westminster, Midx., B., and Elizabeth Riddall of St Andrew's, Holborn, Midx., S.

26 John Bradeley of Christ Church, Surrey, B., and Ann Shirt of the same, S.

26 Thomas Shelton of St Giles, Cripplegate, Lond., W., and Ann Cross of the same, S.

28 Edward Ingleton of St Ann's, Westminster, Midx., B., and Elizabeth Hatch of Bray, Berks, S.

28 Benjamin Baly of St George the Martyr, Surrey, B., and Mary Osborne of the same, S.

Mar. 1 Samuel Digweed of Wandsworth, Surrey, B., and Joanna Leott of the same, S.

6 George Phillips of St Clement Danes, Midx., W., and Hannah Lidget of the same, S.; by Mr Launce

7 James Bradshaw of St Mary Abchurch, Lond., B., and Elizabeth Harris of St Clement, Eastcheap, Lond., S.; by the same

10 Isaac Shepherd of St Andrew's Hubbard, Lond., B., and Catherine Shepherd of St Dunstan's in the East, Lond., S.; by the same

11 William Ward of St James, Clerkenwell, Midx., B., and Sarah Skingly of St Giles in the Fields, Midx., S.; by Mr Launce

14 John Ellits of Christ Church, Southwark, B., and Elizabeth Bulford of the same, S.; by Mr Jackson

21 Benjamin Ridgate of St James, Garlickhithe, Lond., B., and Mary Cornock of St Olave, Hart Street, Lond., S.; by Mr Launce

23 Samuel Hill of St George, Hanover Square, W., and Judith Faulkner of the same, S.; by Mr Launce

1734.

Mar. 28 John Gledhill of St Sepulchres, Lond., B., and Hannah Child of St Mildred's, Bread Street, Lond., S.; by Mr Launce

April 2 James Agnew of Blackheath, Kent, B., and Catharine Harrison of St Ann's, Blackfryars, Lond., S.; by Mr Launce

10 Edward Spencer of St James, Clerkenwell, Midx., B., and Mary Brown of the same, S.

14 George Tottingham of St Botolph, Aldersgate, Lond., B., and Anne Lloyd of St James, Westminster, Midx., S.

15 John Morris of Fulham, Midx., B., and Mary Martin of Chelsea, Midx., W.

16 Timothy Norrington of Milton near Gravesend, Kent, B., and Martha Parker of the same, S.

16 George Danock of St James's, Westminster, Midx., B., and Ann Tithmire of St George's, Hanover Square, S.

16 Joseph Holmes of Maidstone, Kent, W., and Rebecca Baly of St Saviour's, Southwark, W.

16 Charles Hammond of Hampton, Midx., B., and Warwick Stroud of the same, W.

17 George Rugely of Potton, Bedford, B., and Mary Auston of the same, S.

1734

April 17 John Penn of St Giles's in the Fields, Midx., B., and Constance Pye of the same, S.

17 Mark Hall of St George's, Bloomsbury, Midx., B., and Mary Wheeler of the same, W.

17 Archibald Murray of St James, Westminster, Midx., B., and Margaret Martin of St Martin's in the Fields, Midx., W.

18 James King of St Botolph, Aldersgate, Lond., B., and Ann Markey of St Botolph, Bishopsgate, Lond., S.

18 Lewis Griffithis of Chiswick, Midx., B., and Frances Triplett of the same, S.

18 Gabriel Alders of St Gregory's, Lond., B., and Dorothy Jones of the same, S.

18 William Freind of Newbury, Berks, B., and Sarah Stiff of Christ Church, Midx., S.

20 James Smallridge of Lambeth, Surrey, B., and Mary Gale of the same, W.

20 Christian Fleming of St George, Hanover Square, B., and Susanna Leach of Paddington, Midx., S.

22 Jonathan Hall of Tiverton, Devon, B., and Mary Adams of Hulls Bishop's, Somerset, W.

24 John Franklin of Much Hollingbury, Essex, W., and Sarah Small of Faydon Mount, Essex, S.

24 William Cole of St Saviour's, Southwark, B., and Elizabeth Katterns of the same, S.

25 Thomas Dennis of St Sepulchre's, Lond., B., and Martha King of the same, S.

25 William Bingley of Christ Church, Surrey, B., and Elizabeth Alloway of the same, S.

27 John Richmond of St George the Martyr, Midx., B., and Mary Ash of the same, S.

28 Forbes Wilson of St Andrew's Undershaft, Lond., B., and Sarah Radburne of All Hallow's Barking, Lond., S.

28 James Brandling of St Mildred, Poultry, Lond., B., and *Hannah Shipley of the same, S.

29 Richard Mitton of St George, Hanover Square, Midx., B., and Mary Parry of the same, S.

30 Daniel Whitehead of St George, Hanover Square, B., and Sarah Warren of the same, S.

30 James Francklyn of St Clement Danes, Midx., B., and Mary Jones of the same, S.

30 Thomas Clifford of Weybridge, Surrey, B., and Mary Jones of the same, W.

May 1 William Dobinson of St George, Hanover Square, Midx., B., and Ann Winbush of St James, Westminster, Midx., S.

1 Edmund Saggers of Endfield, Midx., W., and Mary Budworth of the same, S.

2 Thomas Furnell of Chiswick, Midx., W., and Mary Bourn of Isleworth, Midx., W.

2 Richard Jolland of St Leonard, Shoreditch, Midx., W., and Ann Hitchcock of the same, W.

2 William Gibson of St John the Evangelist, Westminster, Midx., B., and Isabell Wharton of the same, S.

4 Peter Antander of St Andrew's, Holborn, Lond., B., and Elizabeth Smith of St Martin's in the Fields, Midx., S.

4 John Wright of St Michael, Queenhith, Lond., W., and Margery Lynes of the same, W.

7 Richard Crook of Fulham, Midx., B., and Eutrisha Morriss of St Martin in the Fields, Midx., S.

* "Hannah" written over "Susanna."—Ed.

1734

May 7 John Hewke of St Dunstan's, Stepney, Midx., B., and Elizabeth Clinkard of St Margaret's, Westminster, Midx., S.

8 Michael Rone of St Ann, Blackfryars, Lond., B., and Sarah Hall of Deptford, Kent, S.

14 John Thomas of St Andrew's, Holborn, Lond., B., and Margaret Pain of St Clement Danes, Midx., S.

14 James Parrott of St James, Clerkenwell, Midx., B., and Elizabeth Blencow of St Mary, Islington, Midx., S.

16 James Smith of St James's, Westminster, Midx., B., and Sarah Avison of St Paul's, Covent Garden, Midx., S.

18 John Figg of Farnham, Hants, B., and Elizabeth Lingust of the same, S.

18 John Smith of St Christopher, Threadneedle St, Lond., B., and Sophia Daniel of St Magnus, Lond., S.

19 William Cantrell of St Peter, Paul's Wharf, Lond., B., and Mary Trevitt of St Thomas the Apostle, Lond., W.; by Dr Watkinson

19 John Abbott of St Mary Backchurch, Lond., B., and Hannah Dyer of St Catherine Coleman, Lond., W.

19 Edward Jones of Christ Church, Lond., B., and Catherine Tompson of St Ann's, Soho, Midx. [*blank*]

19 Richard Britton of Ware, Hertford, B., and Ann Dye of Ware in the parish of Great Amwell in said county, S.

19 Jenkin Griffith of St Margaret's, Westminster, Midx., W., and Elizabeth Phillips of St Clement Danes, Midx., S.

19 John Milbourne of St Sepulchre's, Lond., B., and Elizabeth Lewis of the same, S.

21 Thomas Arnold of St Saviour's, Southwark, B., and Catherine Lawrence of the same, W.

21 John Mulcaster of St Catherine's by the Tower, Lond., B., and Elizabeth Hester Cooter of St Clement Danes, Midx., S.

21 Edward Heathcote of St Martin's, Ludgate, Lond., B., and Mary Monk of St George, Hanover Square, Midx., S.

21 John Budding of Stonehouse, Gloucestershire, B., and Ann Humphrys of the same, S.

23 Walter Smith of St Mary, White Chapple, Midx., W., and Hannah Kingstone of the same, S.; by Edward Mores, Rector of Tunstall in Kent

26 Edward Hancock of St Ann's, Blackfryars, Lond., W., and Sarah Turfoot of All Hallows the Great, Lond., W.

26 John Neuenburchg of St Martins in the Fields, Midx., B., and Ann X'tophory of the same, S.

30 William Kingsley of St Bride's, Lond., W., and Ann Gibson of St James, Clerkenwell, Midx., S.; by Mr Beachcroft

June 1 Peter Bouvot, junr, of St Luke's, Midx., W., and Elizabeth Hearn of St James, Clerkenwell, Midx., W.; by Mr Jackson

3 Thomas Cooke of St John, Wapping, Midx., B., and Elizabeth Hill of the same, S.

4 Llewellin Davis of St Dunstan's, Stepney, Midx., W., and Ann Watkins of the same, S.

4 William Martin of Henley upon Thames, co. Oxford, B., and Mary Martin of St Olave, Silver Street, Lond., S.

4 Abraham Green of Godlyman, Surrey, B., and Mary Scott of St George, Hanover Square, Midx., S.

6 William Cæsar Strong of St James, Westmr, W., and Elizabeth Haslewood of the same, S.

6 Thomas Hanbury of All Hallows Barkin, Lond., B., and Mary Cæsar of Bromfield, Essex, S.

1734

June 6 John Creed of St Hellen's, Lond., B., and Elizabeth Myers of St Antholin's, Lond., W.

7 Edmund Relph of St Clement Danes, Midx., B., and Catherine Batty of St James, Westmr, Midx., S.

10 John Picket of Stepney, Midx., B., and Barbara Michilson of the same, S.

11 Jacob Harris of St Mary Staining, Lond., B., and Martha Haynes of the same, W.

13 William Lee of St Swithin, Lond., W., and Susannah Middleton of St Saviour's, Southwark, W.

17 Philip Reginald Ryley of Hockam, Norfolk, B., and Mary Keinsey of Epping, Essex, S.

18 Richard Bale of Horndon, Essex, B., and Ann Joyce of the same, W.

20 Nevill Prothero of St Luke, Midx., W., and Sarah Cook of St George, Hanover Square, Midx., S.

20 Isaac Simes of St Margaret's, Westmr, Midx., B., and Mary Everet of St Giles in the Fields, Midx., S.

21 Thomas Grice of Liverpool, Lancashire, B., and Sarah Gammage of St Ann's, Limehouse, Midx., S.

22 Samuel Dane of Eltham, Kent, B., and Susannah Week of the same, S.

22 John Torney of St James, Westmr, Midx., B., and Ann Fowle of the same, S.

23 Joseph Jackson of St Clement Danes, Midx., B., and Elizabeth Oliver of the same, S.

24 Thomas Wilson of St George, Hanover Square, Midx., B., and Peace Jenner of the same, S.

25 Francis Mason of St Mildred, Poultry, Lond., B., and Ann Whetnaw of the same, S.

25 Thomas Fisher of Putney, Surrey, B., and Hannah Bradley of the same, S.

26 William Dove of Christ Church, Surrey, B., and Margaret Price of St Martin in the Fields, Midx., S.

27 James Gower of St James, Westmr, Midx., B., and Jennett Thomas of the same, S.

28 John Clarke of Hanwell, Midx., B., and Dorothy Headly of the same, S.

29 Thomas Sheffield of St John, Wapping, Midx., B., and Ann Hammond of St George, Midx., S.

29 Thomas Pane of Northall, Hertford, B., and Elizabeth Eadds of St Leonard, Shoreditch, Midx., S.; by Mr Piddington

29 Samuel Harris of White Chapell, Midx., B., and Elizabeth Smith of St George in the East, Midx., S.; by Mr Piddington

29 John Wollaston of Christ Church, Lond., B., and Eleanor Hill of the same, S.; by Samuel Clarke, A.M.

July 1 John Widmore of Kingclere, Hampshire, W., and Ann Waldron of the same, S.

1 Charles Downing of St Margaret's, Westminster, Midx., W., and Henrietta Sara Margaretta Vandereyken of the same, S.

2 William Kay of St Giles, Cripplegate, Lond., B., and Sarah Perry of St Paul's, Covent Garden, Midx., S.; by Dr Best of St Lawrence, Jewry

2 John Henry Hier of St James, Westmr, Midx., B., and Christian Shilling of the same, S.; by Dr Best

2 Adam Willsone of St George, Southwark, B., and Rebecca Peacock of St Mary Magdalen, Bermondsey, Surrey, S.

2 Jeremiah Sanders of Woodfordbridge, Essex, B., and Ann Rix of the same, S.

1734
July 3 Thomas Hammond of Putney, Surrey, W., and Sarah Evans of the same, S.
4 William Hartley of S[t] Botolph, Aldersgate, Lond., B., and Mary Sherrock of the same, S.
6 Bartholomew Temple of Whitby, Yorkshire, B., and Esther Brewer of S[t] Paul's, Shadwell, Midx., S.
7 Charles Duran of S[t] Clement Danes, Midx., B., and Mary Manning of the same, S.
7 Thomas Jessup of S[t] Dunstan's in the East, Lond., B., and Elizabeth Cornwall of the same, S.
8 Thomas Hudson of S[t] Mary, Rotherhith, Surrey, B., and Joannah Hutt of S[t] Saviour's, Southwark, Surrey, W.; by M[r] Piddington
11 Thomas Gregory of East Greenwich, Kent, B., and Frances Smith of the same, S.
12 James Crawford of Milton, Kent, B., and Elizabeth Stephenson of the same, S.
12 Thomas Lander of S[t] Andrew's, Holborn, Lond., B., and Ann Smith of S[t] James, Dukes Place, Lond., S.
14 Joseph Askew of East Greenwich, Kent, B., and Elizabeth Richards of the same, S.
14 Thomas Wells of S[t] Mary Athill, Lond., B., and Sarah Woodhouse of the same, S.
17 Richard Noble of Poplar, Midx., B., and Margaret Bond of Limehouse, Midx., S.
18 Robert Webb of S[t] Clement Danes, Midx., B., and Ann Watson of the same, S.
21 Thomas Jackson of Croydon, Surrey, W., and Elizabeth Piper of the same, S.
21 Henry Thornton of All Hallows on the Wall, Lond., B., and Elizabeth Jones of the same, W.
23 John Green of S[t] Catherine Coleman, Lond., W., and Ann Russell of the same, S.
25 Thomas Burnell of Richmond, Surrey, W., and Sarah Fry of the same, S.
27 Henry Tiller of Belfound, Midx., B., and Dorothy Knevett of Ealing, Midx., S.
27 Thomas Rogers of Deptford, Kent, W., and Elizabeth Studley of S[t] Dunstan's in the West, Lond. [*blank*]
28 William Heacock of Christ Church, Spittlefields, Midx., W., and Mary Sheppard of the same, W.
28 William Ryall of S[t] Mary, White Chappell, Midx., W., and Ann Downes of S[t] Mildred, Poultry, Lond., S.
30 John Ward of Finchley, Midx., B., and Sarah Thomas of Hornsey, Midx., W.
Aug. 1 John Wilson of S[t] George, Midx., W., and Catherine Woods of the same, S.
1 John Beswicke of Fulham, Midx., B., and Silence Vigor of the same, S.
3 George Thatcher of S[t] George the Martyr, Midx., B., and Ann Richter of S[t] James, Westm[r], Midx., S.
3 Richard Antrobus Frith of S[t] Edmund the King, B., and Catherine Doughty of S[t] Magnus the Martyr, Lond., S.
4 John Mould of S[t] John Zachary, Lond., B., and Grace Wait of S[t] Mary Wolnoth, Lond., S.
4 William Mosdell of S[t] Giles in the Fields, Midx., B., and Elizabeth Walker of S[t] Andrew's, Holborn, S.
4 George Eaglesfield of S[t] John, Wapping, Midx., B., and Ann Ramsey of the same, S.

1734

Aug. 5 John Birks of St Clement Danes, Midx., B., and Ann Bright of the same, S.

5 Berry Anthony of Deptford, Kent, B., and Elizabeth Bradley of the same, S.

9 James Norris of St Dionis Backchurch, Lond., B., and Letitia Adams of the same, S.; by Mr Jackson

10 John Davis of Chatham, Kent, B., and Alice Lamb of the same, W.

15 Joseph Piner of St Margaret's, Westm^r, Midx., B., and Sarah Lucas of St Paul's, Covent Garden, Midx., S.

18 John Hill of St Sepulchre's, Lond., B., and Sarah Blackbourne of the same, S.

20 Thomas Young of St Olave, Southwark, Surrey, B., and Ann Nelson of the same, W.

21 Edward Drake of Oakham, Rutland, B., and Elizabeth Dowthat of St George, Hanover Square, Midx., S.

22 John Ayrs of Dawnay, Bucks, B., and Susan Banister of the same, S.; by Mr Worlich

25 Richard Wood of St Olave, Southwark, B., and Catharine Phillips of the same, S.

25 Thomas Carlton of St Dunstan's in the West, Lond., B., and Elizabeth Suff of St Martin's in the Fields, Midx., S.

27 John Pither of St John, Southwarke, B., and Elizabeth Eaton of St Lawrence in Berkshire, S.

29 John Fowlar of St Andrew's, Holborn, Midx., B., and Mary Duckett of St Giles, Cripplegate, Lond., S.; by Mr Jackson

30 William Gee of Bawtrey, Yorkshire, B., and Beatrix Loxley of Farningham, Kent, S.

Sept. 1 Roger Grant of St John, Southwark, Surrey, B., and Frances Peterson of the same, S.

3 Joel Robbins of St Saviour's, Southwark, B., and Catherine Starkey of the same, W.

3 John Ring of Westmeon, Hampshire, B., and Mary Prior of the same, S.

4 John Balding of St James, Dukes Place, Lond., W., and Ann Parvine of Walthamstow, Essex, W.

4 George Carrew of Rumford, Essex, B., and Martha Bartinton of St Andrew's, Holborn, S.

5 Thomas Booth of St Botolph, Bishopsgate, Lond., B., and Ann Colnett of St Catharine's by the Tower, W.

7 Paul Barrington of St James, Westminster, Midx., B., and Mary Watkins of the same, W.

7 John Atkins of St James, Clerkenwell, Midx., W., and Sarah Davenport of the same, W.

7 Thomas Gatchell of Bray, Berkshire, W., and Mary Snowden of New Windsor, Berkshire, S.

8 Herbert Snowsell of Lambeth, Surrey, W., and Elizabeth Purchaze of St Martin's in the Fields, Midx., W.

8 William Roberts of St Mary le Bow, Midx., B., and Mary Fenby of St George, Hanover Square, Midx., S.

9 Daniel Emerson of Ripley, Surrey, B., and Ann Inglesburt of the same, S.

12 James Turner of St Saviour's, Southwarke, B., and Elizabeth Edwards of St George, Southwark, Surrey, S.

12 Richard Acton, Esqr, of Gloverstone, Cheshire, B., and Sarah Ravenscroft of Pickhilt, Denbighshire, S.

15 Samuel Stevenson of St Clement Danes, Midx., B., and Mary Tolson of the same, S.

1734
Sept. 17 Benjamin Annable of White Chapple, Midx., W., and Elizabeth Hodgson of S[t] Andrew Undershaft, Lond., W.
17 John Homwood of S[t] Ann's, Westm[r], Midx., B., and Martha Bray of the same, S.
17 Mark Duckitt of S[t] George in the East, Midx., B., and Ann Bennett of the same, S.
19 John Jennings of S[t] Giles in the Fields, Midx., B., and Mary Harris of the same, S.
20 Edward Pollsue of S[t] Margaret's, Westm[r], Midx., W., and Joannah Wyatt of S[t] Paul's, Shadwell, Midx., W.
21 Samuel Salt of S[t] Dunstan's in the West, Midx., B., and Jane Norton of S[t] Andrew's, Holborn, Midx., S.
23 John Barfild of S[t] James, Westm[r], Midx., B., and Jane Hand of the same, S.
24 John Anthony Loubier of S[t] Michael Bassishaw, Lond., B., and Henrietta Charlotta Loubier of S[t] Andrew Undershaft, Lond., S.
26 James Pavey of Twickenham, Midx., B., and Margaret Bradfold of Epsom, Surrey, S.
26 Thomas Heald of S[t] James, Westminster, Midx., B., and Margarett Bolton of the same, S.
26 John Plummer of Chelsea, Midx., B., and Aney Raworth of Greenwich, Kent, S.
26 William Killock of Westham, Essex, B., and Ann Stockdell of the same, S.
26 John Lugg of S[t] Botolph, Aldgate, Midx., B., and Sara Wilkinson of the same, S.
29 Samuel Harford of S[t] Lawrence, Jewry, Lond., B., and Ann Dobson of S[t] Margarett Patten, Lond., S.
Oct. 1 William Gellett of S[t] John's, Southwark, W., and Catharine Drewry of S[t] Dionis Backchurch, Lond., W.
1 Rowland Rugely of S[t] Luke, Midx., B., and Hannah Evatt of the same, W.
3 Ralph Hodgson of S[t] Margaret, Westm[r], B., and Barbara Green of S[t] Ann's, Westmin[r], Midx., S.
3 Charles Hodskins of Twickenham, Midx., B., and Mary Hollis of the same, S.
3 Gregory Craster, W., and Jane Brown, W., both of this parish; by Banns
4 Frederick Miller of S[t] James, Westmin[r], Midx., B., and Hannah Roebuck of S[t] Martin in the Fields, Midx., S.
6 Nathaniel Gregory of S[t] Saviour's, Southwark, B., and Ursula Brice of S[t] James, Westm[r], Midx., S.*
6 Burdyn Anderson of S[t] Mary, White Chaple, Midx., W., and Alice Carroll of the same, S.
8 Thomas Grifas of Clapham, Surrey, B., and Eleanor Byers of S[t] Martin in the Fields, Midx., S.
8 Edward Hockaday of S[t] George the Martyr, Surrey, B., and Ann Matthews of the same, S.
10 Bainbridge Matthews of S[t] Pauls, Shadwell, Midx., W.,† and Elizabeth Child of the same, W.
10 Element [*sic*] Jones of S[t] Christopher le Stocks, Lond., B., and Elizabeth Jacobson of S[t] Giles, Cripplegate, Lond., S.
12 William Bishop of S[t] John, Southwarke, W., and Amy Knight of S[t] Mary Magdalene, Bermondsey, Surrey, W.
13 Francis Cremer of S[t] Giles in the Fields, Midx., B., and Mary Batrick of the same, S.
13 William Makins of Wells, Norfolk, B., and Ann Wilkinson of S[t] Antholin's, Lond., S.; by D[r] Watkinson

* "S." written over an erasure.—ED. † "W." written over an erasure.—ED.

1734

Oct. 14 Thomas Phillips of St Giles in the Fields, Midx., B., and Joan Davis of the same, S.

15 Phillip Green of Chiswick, Midx., B., and Elizabeth Brain of the same, W.

15 Edward Brasey of St Leonard, Shoreditch, W., and Mary Ward of St Luke, Midx., S.

15 Augistine Carloss of St Mary, White Chapel, Midx., B., and Elizabeth Burras of the same, S.

16 William Smith of St Mildred, Poultry, Lond., B., and Susannah Taylor of the same, S.

16 Thomas Carpenter of St Olave, Hart Street, Lond., W., and Elianor Turner of St Martin le Grand, Lond., W.

17 Henry Hall of St Mary Aldermary, Lond., B., and Elizabeth Fann of St Stephen, Coleman Street, S.

17 John Irwin of St Giles in the Fields, Midx., B., and Margaret Barnett of St James, Westmr, Midx., S.

19 Thomas Newton of St George the Martyr, Midx., W., and Elizabeth Heley of the same, S.

19 George Wetherhead of Barking, Essex, B., and Sarah Talbot of Wansted, Essex, S.

19 William Gebheart of Lambeth, Surrey, B., and Catharine Naylor of the same, S.

20 Thomas Bateman of St Sepulchre's, Lond., B., and Jane Gyles of the same, S.

22 Arthur Perkins of Lyons Inn, Midx., B., and Jane Graham of St Margaret, Westminster, Midx., W.

22 John Robinson of St Giles, Cripplegate, Midx., B., and Mary Anderson of the same, S.

24 Robert Heathcote of St James, Clerkenwell, Midx., B., and Mary Rich of Christ Church, Lond., S.

25 William Hunt of Chiswick, Midx., B., and Hannah Ottway of Chelsea, Midx., S.

26 James Seamour of Rislip, Midx., B., and Elizabeth Bugbey of the same, S.

27 John Fendall of St George, Southwark, Surrey, B., and Betty Casemore of the same, S.

28 John Goulding of East Ham, Essex, B., and Temperance Bowen of St Lawrence, Jewry, Lond., S.

28 William Heaps of St Andrew's, Holborn, Lond., B., and Elizabeth Everet of St Dunstan's in the East, Lond., S.

29 Simon Stratford of St Martins in the Fields, Midx., B., and Agatha Harbin of the same, S.; by Mr Bisse

30 Henry Clarke of St James, Westmr, Midx., W., and Frances Foster of the same, S.; by Mr Bisse

31 Samuel Drake of St Paul's, Covent Garden, Midx., B., and Elizabeth Dalton of St Mary le Strand, Midx., S.; by Mr Jackson

Nov. 2 John Howard of Harrow on the Hill, Midx., W., and Elizabeth Rumney of Greenford, Midx., W.; by Mr Worlich

3 Francis Strong of St Giles, Cripplegate, Lond., B., and Elizabeth Millward of the same, S.; by Mr Jackson

4 William Cowdrey of Deptford, Kent, W., and Margaret Wood of the same, S.; by Mr Bisse

7 William Dunbar of St Margaret's, Westmr, Midx., B., and Jane Mellone of the same, W.; by Mr Worlich

8 Thomas Sadler of Berkhampstead St Peter, Hertfordshire, B., and Frances Fenn of North Church, Herts, S.; by Mr Bisse

10 Henry Wells of Speen, Berks, B., and Elizabeth Wright of St Bartholomew the Less, Lond., W.

1734
Nov. 10 Thomas Sleeth of S[t] Giles in the Fields, Midx., B., and Elizabeth Webber of the same, W.
11 William Dockin of S[t] Mary, Whitechaple, Midx., B., and Susanna Skinsley of S[t] Saviour's, Southwark, Surrey, S.
13 John Fish of Farnham, Surrey, B., and Susannah Bernard of Chichester, Sussex, S.
12 Joseph Carlyle of S[t] George, Midx., B., and Sarah Alesbery of the same, S.
14 Thomas Church of S[t] Dunstan's, Stepney, Midx., B., and Mary Webb of the same, S.
14 Robert Gillett of Chertsey, Surrey, B., and Lucy Ravenell of S[t] Giles in the Fields, Midx., S.
14 Richard Meek of S[t] Clement Danes, Midx., B., and Ann Hall of the same, S.
17 Robert Foot of Twickenham, Midx., B., and Ann Leivers of the same, S.
19 John Martin of S[t] James, Westm[r], Midx., B., and Bridget Batts of S[t] Catherine near the Tower, Lond., S.
20 William Sharwood of Islington, Midx., B., and Mary Whitehead of the same, S.
21 Abraham Tovey of S[t] Paul's, Shadwell, Midx., W., and Sarah Cooke of the same, W.
23 Joseph Ford of S[t] James, Westm[r], Midx., B., and Rachel Gray of the same, S.
24 Joshua Jones of S[t] Giles in the Fields, Midx., B., and Elizabeth Alford of the same, S.
25 Nathaniel Shuttlewood of S[t] John, Wapping, Midx., B., and Ann Gascoigne of S[t] Stephen, Coleman Street, Lond., S.
26 William Seager of S[t] Dunstan's, Stepney, Midx., B., and Hester Maulendine of Christ Church, Spittlefields, Midx., S.
26 John Baddley of S[t] Andrew Undershaft, Lond., B., and Mary Clarke of the same, S.
26 Jacob Silver of New Romney, Kent, B., and Jane Reynolds of the same, S.
27 Edward Wood of Westerham, Kent, B., and Ann Rabb of the same, S.
29 John Aldridge of Woodford, Essex, B., and Anna Maria Rook of the same, S.
Dec. 3 Thomas Broadwater of S[t] Ann, Limehouse, Midx., W., and Sarah Hawkes of the same, W.
3 John Barton of S[t] George, Midx., B., and Ann Livingston of the same, S.
4 James Gray of S[t] Giles in the Fields, Midx., W., and Mary Frost of S[t] George, Bloomsbury, Midx., W.
5 Robert Ayliffe of S[t] Botolph, Aldgate, Midx., B., and Elizabeth Preist of the same, S.
9 John Brooks of Barking, Essex, B., and Elizabeth Thorndon of the same, W.
10 Joseph Turner of S[t] Mary Magdalen, Bermondsey, Surrey, B., and Mary Cobbet of the same, S.
10 Sharman Saving of S[t] James, Westm[r], Midx., W., and Mary Freeman of S[t] Andrew's, Holborn, Lond., S.
11 Edward Wetherly of Iver, Bucks, B., and Ann Cutler of the same, W.
11 John Waymark of Mitcham, Surrey, B., and Elizabeth Tomlyns of the same, S.
12 Thomas Harvey of Harwich, Essex, W., and Elizabeth Gardiner of S[t] Magnus the Martyr, Lond., W.

1734

Dec. 12 Thomas Britton of S[t] Margaret's, Westm[r], Midx., W., and Edith Mills of the same, S.

13 Joseph Shenton of Clapham, Surrey, B., and Elianor Hutchin of the same, S.

14 Edward Jones of Northall, Hertford, B., and Jane Spindler of the same, S.

17 Richard Crozer of S[t] Ann and Agnes, Aldersgate, Lond., B., and Ann White of S[t] Giles in the Fields, Midx., S.

19 William Cogdell of S[t] Alban, Wood Street, Lond., W., and Abigal Hene of S[t] Giles, Cripplegate, Midx., S.

19 Thomas Doughty of Hertford, W., and Elizabeth Feilding of the same, S.

19 Augustin Howland of S[t] Giles in the Fields, Midx., B., and Ann Maltas of the same, S.

22 John Randall of S[t] Mary, Rotherhith, Surrey, B., and Anna Maria Fenn of S[t] Mary Cole, Lond., S.

22 John Westbrook of Beckenham, Kent, B., and Dorothy Clemson of the same, S.

23 Jonathan Cotton, jun[r], of S[t] Olave, Southwark, B., and Sarah Maidstone of Clapham, Surrey, S.

24 John Halfhide of S[t] Botolph, Aldgate, Lond., W., and Elizabeth Hefford of the same, S.

25 George Gillett of Feversham, Kent, B., and Sarah Hooper of the same, S.

25 Samuel Parsons of S[t] James, Clerkenwell, Midx., W., and Anne Ashby of Albury, Hertford, S.

25 George Gibbs of S[t] John in Surrey, B., and Sarah Madham of the same, S.

26 Nathaniel Style of S[t] Olave, Silver Street, Lond., W., and Elizabeth Lewis of S[t] John, Southwark, Surrey, S.

26 Martin Woodham of Bromley, Kent, B., and Mary Gossage of Woolwich, Kent, S.

26 Joseph Flexman of Woodlands, Dorset, B., and Elizabeth Llewellin of S[t] Giles in the Fields, Midx., S.

27 William Vincaish of Barking, Essex, B., and Ann Eaton of the same, S.

30 William Smith of Hampton, Midx., B., and Mary Stacey of the same, S.

31 Adam Webb of S[t] Botolph, Bishopsgate, Lond., B., and Alice Crosfield of the same, S.

31 William Weeks als Cannon of S[t] Giles, Cripplegate, Lond., B., and Susanna Law of S[t] James, Clerkenwell, Midx., S.

31 Walter Mullaly of Tottenham High Cross, Midx., B., and Elizabeth Boldrow of Edmonton, Midx., S.

Jan. 1 Richard Collier of S[t] Botolph, Aldgate, Lond., B., and Anne Bishop of Walthamstow, Essex, S.; by M[r] Jackson

1 Louis Seleries of S[t] Martin in the Fields, Midx., B., and Elizabeth Brown* of S[t] Paul's, Covent Garden, Midx., W.

2 John Francklyn of Gravesend, Kent, B., and Ann Mason of Milton, Kent, S.

2 William Trotter of S[t] Paul's, Covent Garden, Midx., B., and Elizabeth Nickolls of the same, W.

2 Philip Jones of S[t] George, Hanover Square, Midx., B., and Susannah Crow of Chelmsford, Essex, S.

4 Robert Birks of S[t] George, Southwark, Surrey, B., and Mary Forster of the same, W.

5 John Thomas of S[t] Mary le Bone, Midx., W., and Elizabeth Roules of Croydon, Surrey, S.

* A final "e" has been added in different writing to Brown.—ED.

1734-5

Jan. 6 Joseph Smith of Parshore, Worcestershire, B., and Elizabeth Frith of All Hallows, London Wall, S.

7 Thomas Fidgett of St Michael, Cornhill, Lond., B., and Alice Peck of St George, Southwark, Surrey, W.

12 James Trime of St Mary Overies, Surrey, B., and Rebecca Clarke of the same, W.

12 Richard Harvey of St Giles in the Fields, Midx., B., and Eleanor Grundy of the same, S.; by Dr Watkinson

13 Andrew Lindberg of St John, Wapping, Midx., B., and Mary Hagg of the same, S.

14 Thomas Chandler of St James, Westmr, Midx., B., and Elizabeth Evans of the same, S.

16 William Kemp of St Stephen, Hertfordshire, B., and Ann King of the same, W.

16 Richard Nelson of St George, Bloomsbury, Midx., B., and Mary Leppington of St James, Westmr, Midx., S.

19 Richard Brady of St George, Midx., B., and Alice Gibbs of the same, S.

20 George Westron of St Paul's, Covent Garden, Midx., B., and Elizabeth Brock of St George the Martyr, Midx., S.

20 John Matthews of St John the Evangelist, Westmr, Midx., B., and Martha Rice of the same, S.

21 Anthony Jewet of Tottenham High Cross, Midx., W., and Elizabeth Russell of the same, W.

23 Edward Warren of Kingston, Surrey, B., and Ann Hedges of Isleworth, Midx., S.

23 David Odell of St Clement Danes, Midx., B., and Frances Gaywood of St Alphage, Lond., S.

29 Daniel Smith of South Mims, Midx., B., and Ruth Shackleton of St Ann's, Aldersgate, Lond., W.

Feb. 2 James Ellis of South Mims, Midx., B., and Dinah Barbour of St Gregory, Lond., S.

3 Philip Gosling of St James, Westmr, Midx., W., and Mary Wright of the same, S.

3 Thomas Richardson of St Margaret's, Westmr, Midx., W., and Hester Alexander of the same, S.

4 Henry Chipp of Henley upon Thames, Oxon, B., and Elizabeth Simmons of the same, S.

5 Benjamin Clapshew of St Andrew's, Holborn, Midx., B., and Catherine Warren of St Dunstan's in the West, Lond., S.

10 Allan Brett of Christ Church, Lond., B., and Esther Mills of St Nicholas Acons, Lond., S.

11 Richard Workman of North Nibley, co. Glocester, B., and Mary Wing of St John the Evangelist, Westmr, Midx., S.

12 John Garnar of S. Bartholomew by the Exchange, Lond., B., and Elizabeth Linch of the same, S.

12 David Rice of St Giles in the Fields, Midx., B., and Elizabeth Vaughan of St Martin in the Fields, Midx., S.

15 Henry Hallett of Hammersmith, Midx., W., and Sarah Lewis of Purfleet, Essex, W.

16 William Riley of Woolverhampton, co. Stafford, B., and Margaret Russell of the same, S.

16 Joshua Charlesworth of St George, Surrey, B., and Elizabeth Winson of the same, S.

16 Paul Whitmill of Cudsdon, Oxfordshire, B., and Ann Adams of the same, S.

16 Humphrey Gilbey of St John, Southwarke, Surrey, B., and Elianor Barton of the same, S.

1734-5

Feb. 17 John Boyce of St George, Hanover Square, Midx., B., and Elizabeth Stevenson of Fulham, Midx., S.

17 Charles Symonds of St Andrews, Holborn, Lond., B., and Mary Brooks of Godleman, Surrey, S.

17 Osmun Rogers of St Margaret Pattens, Lond., B., and Margaret Chidley of the same, S.

17 Samuel Hall of St Botolph, Aldgate, Lond., B., and Rachael Legg of St Saviours, Southwarke, Surrey, S.

17 James Charmasson of St George, Hanover Square, Midx., B., and Elizabeth Horbutt of the same, S.

17 John Joyce of St Lawrence Jewry, Lond., B., and Ann Peate of St Mary Magdalen, Milk Street, Lond., S.

17 Thomas Baldock of Gravesend, Kent, B., and Ann Stansfield of the same, W.

17 Ralph Howson of St Clement Danes, Midx., B., and Ann Massey of St Ann, Westmr, Midx., S.

18 William Wright of St Botolph, Bishopsgate, Lond., B., and Mary Gosford of the same, S.

18 William Hall of St Margaret, Westmr, Midx., B., and Mary Streat of the same, S.

18 Thomas Seacoal of St Andrew's, Holborn, Midx., W., and Mary Brant of St Dunstan's in the West, Lond., S.

18 James Dunton of Rislip, Midx., B., and Mary Bonnett of the same, S.

26 John Jarden of St George, Southwark, Surrey, B., and Christiana Simmons of St Andrew, Holborn, Midx., S.

Mar. 1 Evan Thomas of St Clement Dane, Midx., B., and Anne Watkins of St Ann's, Westmr, Midx., S.

3 Thomas Barrett of St Margaret, Westmr, Midx., B., and Rebecca Vernon of the same, W.

5 William Horner of St Margaret, Westmr, Midx., B., and Anne Ewens of the same, S.

8 Edward Fitzgerald of St Clement Danes, Midx., W., and Hannah Raven of St Martin in the Fields, Midx., W.

8 James Knight of Isleworth, Midx., W., and Philadelphia Carter of Twickenham, Midx., W.

9 Edward Beyellin of Christ Church, Surrey, W., and Mary Forster of St Saviours, Southwark, Surrey, S.

9 Patrick Burk of St Botolph, Aldersgate, Lond., B., and Martha Camden of the same, W.

10 William Rewse, Esqr, of St George the Martyr, Midx., W., and Martha Davis of the same, S.

11 Gabriel Fleming of St Michael, Cornhill, Lond., W., and Mary King of Edmonton, Midx., S.

13 Cornelius Willson of All Saints, Hertford, W., and Susannah Holham of St Andrew's, Holborn, Midx., S.

14 James Cameron of St James, Westmr, Midx., B., and Elizabeth Davis of St George, Bloomsbury, Midx., S.

16 Paul Baudrant of St Martin in the Fields, Midx., B., and Mary Danby of the same, S.

20 Weeton Whitfield of St Paul's, Shadwell, Midx., B., and Mary Dorkin of the same, W.

21 Thomas Barnard of Northall, co. Hertford, B., and Elizabeth Sills of the same, W.

22 James Hester of St George, Southwark, Surrey, B., and Sarah Teed of St Mary, Rotherhith, Surrey, S.

23 Edward Noone of St Martin in the Fields, Midx., B., and Hannah Stevens of St Margarett, Lothbury, Lond. [*blank*]

1735.

Mar. 30 Edward Spink of St Sepulchre's, Lond., B., and Ann Hilton of St Bartholomew the Great, Lond., S.

April 3 Matthew King of St James, Westm^r, Midx., B., and Mary Hooper of St George, Hanover Square, Midx., S.

3 John Stevens of Wathamstow, Essex, B., and Alice Collis of the same, W.

4 John Ware of Chesham, Esqr, Bucks, W., and Jane Burch of Hempstead, co. Hertford, W.

7 James Bennett of St Thomas, Salisbury, Wilts, B., and Mary Lewin of St Anne, Westm^r, Midx., W.

8 John Smith of Denham, Bucks, B., and Ann Pink of the same, S.

9 Henry Appleton of St Clement Danes, Midx., B., and Jane Gilburt of the same, S.

10 William Groom of St Botolph, Bishopsgate, Lond., W., and Sarah Henton of St Lawrence Jewry, Lond., S.

10 Richard Allen of St James, Westm^r, Midx., B., and Elizabeth Gibbs of the same, W.

13 William Spence of Greenwich, Kent, B., and Mary Sheldon of the same, S.

14 John Coowper of St Thomas, Southwark, Surrey, W., and Agnes Jennings of St Luke's, Midx., S.

14 Thomas Wilson of St James, Westminster, Midx., W., and Mary Miller of the same, S.

15 Robert Champion of St James, Westm^r, Midx., W., and Mary Grant of St Mary le Bone, Midx., S.

15 William Williams of St George, Bloomsbury, Midx., B., and Mary Cannell of St Giles, Cripplegate, Midx., S.

15 Abel Aldridge of Hillingdon, Midx., B., and Sarah Clater of St George, Bloomsbury, Midx., S.

17 Daniel Chapman of St Paul, Deptford, Kent, W., and Ann Greatrix of Lewisham, Kent, S.

17 John Bryant of Old Brentford in the parish of Ealing, Midx., B., and Elizabeth Page of Harrow on the Hill, Midx., S.

19 Robert Randall of Edmonton, Midx., B., and Mary Briggs of the same, S.

20 Owen Griffiths of St John, Hackney, Midx., B., and Mary Fowler of the same, S.

22 Clement Corderoy of St Mary, White Chappel, Midx., B., and Mary Fisher of the same, S.; by Mr Bisse

24 Thomas Bullevant of St Ann, Westmin^r, Midx., B., and Anne Athey of St George, Hanover Square, Midx., S.; by Mr Beachcroft

24 Thomas Ball of St George, Hanover Square, Midx., B., and Elizabeth Trottman of the same, S.; by Mr Beachcroft

25 Peter Umanden of Hawkhurst in Kent, B., and Hannah Miller of Gowdhurst, Kent, S.; by Mr Bisse

25 John Walgrave of St George, Hanover Square, Midx., B., and Barbara Carelton of St Margaret, Westm^r, Midx., W.; by Mr Bisse

25 Francis Hildyard of St James, Westm^r, Midx., B., and Sarah Bird of St Martin in the Fields, Midx., W.; by Mr Jackson

27 Edward Bowman of St Andrews, Holborne, Lond., B., and Elizabeth Ashurst of Hampstead, Midx., S.

28 Robert Lowndes of the Inner Temple, Lond., B., and Mary Shales of St James, Westm^r, Midx., S.

30 Robert Pollixfen of St John, Southwarke, Surry, W., and Jane Smith of St Olave's, Southwarke, in the said county

1735

April 30 Abraham Burley of St Giles in the Fields, Midx., W., and Catherine Biby of the same, W.

May 1 Edward Bright of St James, Westminster, Midx., B., and Elizabeth Hunt of Greenwich, Kent, S.

1 John Bray of St Botolph, Aldgate, Lond., B., and Martha Binder of St Andrew's, Holborne, S.

1 Arthur West of St Margarets, Westmr, Midx., B., and Elizabeth Webb of the same, S.; by Mr Beachcroft

1 John Pratt of St Paul, Deptford, Kent, B., and Mary Biggs of St Mary Cray, Kent, S.; by the same

1 Robert Whitfield of New Windsor, Berks, B., and Avis Hatch of the same; by ditto

1 John Turner of Hayes, Midx., B., and Martha Tyler of Denham, Bucks, S.; by Mr Beachcroft

4 Robert Brown of St Dunstan's, Stepney, Midx., W., and Anne Lewington of the same, S.

6 Thomas Peacopp of St Botolph, Bishopsgate, Lond., B., and Agnes Robinson of the same, S.

7 Benjamin Rice of St Stephen, Walbrook, Lond., B., and Mary Mayor of Winchmore Hill, Midx., S.

7 Shadrach Hammond of St John, Wapping, Midx., B., and Mary Smith of St Mary, White Chappell, Midx., S.

10 Henry Harry of St Margaret's, Westmr, Midx., B., and Penelope Newton of the same, S.

10 John Newton of this Parish, B., and Mary Jolloffe of All Hallows the Great, Lond. [*blank*]

11 Richard Prance of St Martin in the Fields, Midx., B., and Ann Tappentea of the same, S.

13 Thomas Boatswain of St Olave, Southwarke, Surry, B., and Elizabeth Jury of the same, S.

14 Thomas Peppering of St Martin in the Fields, Midx., B., and Susannah Morton of St Margaret, Westmr, Midx. [*blank*]

18 Thomas Turnham of St Brides, Lond., W., and Elizabeth Taylor of the same, S.

18 Nicholas Jourdain of Christchurch, Midx., B., and Mary Mollet of the same, S.

21 Charles Christian of St Andrew's, Holborn, Midx., B., and Jane Jennings of the same, S.

22 Waddis Pyke of Gold Hanger, Essex, B., and Mary Chamberlain of Malden, Essex, S.

22 Thomas Rice of Flixon, Suffolk, B., and Sarah Woods of Obbiston, Suffolk, S.

22 Edmund Boteler of St Dunstan's in the East, Lond., B., and Elizabeth Lucas of St John, Westmr, Midx., W.

22 Joseph Woollams of St Botolph, Bishopsgate, Lond., B., and Sarah Street of the same, W.

23 George Myhill of Portsmouth, Southton, W., and Elizabeth Austin of St Mary, Rotherhith, Surrey, W.

23 John Parker of Allhallows Barking, Lond., B., and Blandina Ward of the same, S.

23 Felix Perkins of St Mary, Rotherhith, Surry, B., and Elizabeth Parns of the same, W.

25 Samuel Newman of St Mary, Rotherhith, Surry, B., and Ann Gatward of St Olave's, Southwark, in the said county, S.

25 Isaac Rutson of St Saviour's, Southwarke, Surry, B., and Elizabeth Ann Woolston Craft of St Botolph, Bishopsgate, Lond., S.

27 William French of Kingston upon Thames, Surry, B., and Alice Burchett of the same, S.

1735

May 28 John Meloy of S[t] Olave, Southwarke, Surry, W., and Elizabeth Price of the same, W.

29 Cornelius Davis of S[t] Leonard, Shoreditch, Midx., B., and Ann Watkins of S[t] Botolph, Aldgate, Lond., S.

June 1 Francis Coster, W., and Mary Booz, S., both of this Parish

2 Thomas Hone of S[t] George the Martyr, Midx., B., and Frances Timms of the same, S.

4 Charles King of S[t] Stephen, Coleman Street, Lond., W., and Mary Cranfield of S[t] James, Clerkenwell, Midx., W.

5 Richard Salter of Christ Church, Midx., W., and Grace Edger of the same, W.

5 William Hicks of S[t] Martin in the Fields, Midx., W., and Sarah Marcy of the same, S.

6 Daniel Dunn of Richmond, Surrey, B., and Sarah Gray of Fulham, Midx., S.

7 Leonard Newman of Upton, Bucks, B., and Diana Sixe of the same, S.

7 Anthony Meymac of S[t] Martin in the Fields, Midx., B., and Ann Rouby Mareclein of S[t] Ann, Westm[r], Midx., S.

8 Morgan Cooke of S[t] George, Hanover Square, Midx., B., and Ann Templer of the same, S.

8 William Leach of S[t] James, Westm[r], Midx., W., and Hester Ashby of S[t] Martin in the Fields, Midx., S.

12 Newman Cartwright of S[t] Edmund the King, Lond., B., and Martha Unwin of West Meon, Southton, S.

12 John Roe of Streatham, Surry, W., and Diana Merrit of the same, S.

13 George Wheatley of Weybridge, Surry, B., and Sarah Barker of S[t] Martin Vintry, Lond., W.

14 James Razer of All Hallows the Less, Lond., W., and Mary Sheen of S[t] Martin in the Fields, Midx., S.

19 John Osborne of Bromley S[t] Leonards, Midx., W., and Magdalen Oliver of S[t] Dunstan's, Stepney, Midx., W.

22 Thomas Langford of S[t] Mary Magdalen, Bermondsey, Surry, B., and Mary Kemp of S[t] John, Southwarke, Surrey, S.

22 Robert Millard of Esher, Surry, W., and Elizabeth White of S[t] James, Westm[r], Midx., S.

22 James Mitchell of S[t] Mary le Bow, Lond., B., and Mary Hipson of S[t] Ann, Limehouse, Midx., W.

26 James Beale of S[t] Andrews, Holborn, B., and Joanna Hicks of S[t] James, Clerkenwell, Midx., W.

26 Thomas Warren of S[t] Bartholomew near the Exchange, Lond. [*blank*], and Elizabeth Gunter of the same, S.

26 Thomas Procter of Luton, co. Bedford, B., and Mary Jennings of the same, W.

26 Thomas Townsend of Stepney, Midx., W., and Ann Abbott of S[t] Peter the Poor, Lond., W.

26 Thomas Card of S[t] Paul's, Shadwell, Midx., B., and Susanna Minett of the same, S.

29 Thomas Baynes of Christ Church, Spittlefields, Midx., B., and Alice Baynes of the same, S.

29 Thomas Chitty of Westerham, Kent, B., and Frances Morer of Cudham, Kent, S.

30 John Ford of Lambeth, Surrey, W., and Sarah Miller of the same, W.

30 John Smith of Hornchurch, Essex, W., and Elizabeth Hadley of the same, S.

July 3 Corbett Neeves of S[t] Leonard, Shoreditch, Midx., B., and Ann Still of S[t] Botolph without Aldersgate, Lond., S.

1735

July 5 William Winn of Battersea, Surry, B., and Dorothy Wilson of the same, S.

6 William Heacock of Christ Church, Spittlefields, Midx., W., and Eleanor Foarth of White Chappel, Midx., S.

6 Thomas Colley of St Mary Somerset, Lond., W., and Elizabeth Owen of St Margaret, Westmr, Midx., S.

6 John Jenkins of St Mary Magdalen, Bermondsey, Surry, B., and Elizabeth Mayne of the same, S.

7 John Areskine of St Dunstan's, Stepney, Midx., W., and Dorothy Downham of the same, W.

7 Charles Gresham of Limesfield, Surry, B., and Sarah Reynolds of Bletchingly, Surry, S.

8 William Skinner of Chatham, Kent, B., and Sarah Brooke of Rochester, Kent, S.

9 Henry Owtram of St George, Hanover Square, Midx., B., and Mary Thomas of St James, Westminster, Midx., S.

9 James Price of Woodford, Essex, B., and Elizabeth Evans of St Stephen, Walbrook, Lond., S.

10 Thomas Dudfield of St George, Midx., W., and Mary Morgan of the same, S.

10 Robert Hawkins of St George, Southwarke, Surry, W., and Catharine Patten of the same, W.

10 Thomas Palmer of St John the Baptist, co. Hereford, B., and Sarah Gardiner of St Andrew's, Holborn, Midx., S.

10 Nicholas Pethor of Battersea, Surry, B., and Mary Evans of the same, S.

10 John Andrews of St Margaret, Westminster, Midx, W., and Elizabeth Vaughan of Camberwell, Surry, S.

14 Thomas Hannam of St Margaret, Westmr, Midx., W., and Bridget Green of the same, S.

15 John Werry of St John, Southwarke, Surry, B., and Jane Werry of the same, S.

15 John Rhodes of St Lawrence, Jewry, Lond., B., and Margaret Andra of St Hellen, Lond., S.

16 George Barr of St Mary le Bow, Midx., B., and Judith Rycroft of St John, Wapping, Midx., W.; by the Rev. Mr Lind

16 Josias Cottin of Walthamstow, Essex, B., and Jane Cunningham of the same, S.; by Mr Lind

17 James Hall of St Giles in the Fields, Midx., W., and Ellen Worthington of the same, W.; by the Rev. Mr Jackson

17 James Harrison of St Edmund the King, Lond., B., and Sarah Kell of St James, Clerkenwell, Midx., S.; by Mr Jackson

20 Stephen Gimber of St Botolph, Aldgate, Lond., B., and Mary Vaine of Charlton, Kent, S.

20 Robert Turbutt of St Dunstan's in the West, Lond., B., and Mary Worth of St Faith's, Lond., S.

21 John Dennison of Christ Church, Spittlefields, Midx., W., and Frances Sargeant of St Dunstan's, Stepney, Midx., S.

22 John Ayres, W., and Elizabeth Goodacker, S., both of this Parish

22 James Nicholls of Allhallows Barking, Lond., B., and Mary Parke of the same, W.

22 Edmund Waple of St Saviour, Southwarke, Surry, W., and Ann Mills of St Dunstan's in the West, Lond., S.

22 Vere Munn of St Clement Danes, Midx., B., and Margaret Grigg of the same, S.

22 William Paine of St Dunstan's in the West, Lond., B., and Mary Meek of the same, S.

1735
July 27 Thomas Booth of St Andrew's, Holborn, Midx., W., and Catharine Turner of the same, S.
29 John Baynard of Crayford, Kent, B., and Mary Mumford of the same, S.
30 Richard Bartrup of St John, Hackney, Midx., W., and Alice Swarbrook of the same, W.
31 Samuel Hamon of St Paul's, Shadwell, Midx., W., and Jane Cooke of the same, W.
31 Philip Walker of Clapham, Surry, B., and Elizabeth Poplett of the same, W.
31 Vincent Jones of St Mary Magdalen, Bermondsey, Surry, W., and Jane Sheppard of Stepney, Midx., W.
Aug. 2 Thomas Bell of St James, Westminster, Midx., B., and Catharine Swanland of St Giles in the Fields, Midx., S.
3 Robert Hill of Queenhithe, Lond., B., and Ann Breach of Christ Church, Spittlefields, Midx., S.
3 Richard Spearing of St Giles, Cripplegate, Lond., B., and Mary Rose of the town of Hertford, W.
4 Peter L'hommedieu of St Martin in the Fields, Midx., B., and Jane Martin ye Younger of St James, Midx., S.
5 John Prior, B., and Sarah Bringhurst, S., both of this parish
5 Hugh Child of St Peter Cheap, Lond., W., and Hannah Walker of Christ Church, Lond., S.
9 James Kettle of St Mary, White Chappel, Midx., W., and Elizabeth Corsellis of Whivenhoe, Essex, S.
10 Michael Bland of Love Lane, East Cheap, Lond., B., and Patience Jeffrey of St James, Clerkenwell, Midx., S.
10 Thomas Williams of St Antholin's, Lond., B., and Eleanor Watson of St Gregory's, Lond., S.
11 Thomas Fuller of Kingston, Surry, B., and Mary Gregory of the same, S.
11 Joseph Wright of St John, Wapping, Midx., B., and Mary Baley of the same, S.
11 Robert Browne of Woolwich, Kent, B., and Judith Sutton of St Martin in the Fields, Midx., W.
11 James Jay of St Martin in the Fields, Midx., B., and Mary King of the same, S.
12 John Barbar of St Mary, White Chapel, Midx., B., and Anne Newton of the same, S.
14 John Blinston of St Leonard, Shoreditch, Midx., B., and Elizabeth Bacon of Christ Church, Spittlefields, Midx., S.; by Mr Bailey, Curate of Queenhithe
15 Solomon Tovey of West Chester, B., and Mary Jones of the same, S.; by Mr Baily
19 Henry Hoadly of St Peters ad Vincula within the Liberty of the Tower, Lond., B., and Bridgett Blake of the same, S.
20 Robert Wilson of St Dunstan's, Stepney, Midx., B., and Ruth Huddle of Limehouse, Midx., S.
25 Charles Christian of St Andrew's, Holborne, Midx., W., and Martha Biddle of St Botolph, Aldersgate, Lond., S.
26 Henry Elmore of St Dunstan's, Stepney, Middx., B., and Elizabeth Young of the same, S.
28 Benjamin Domine of St John's, Southwarke, Surry, B., and Anne Brown of St Ann, Limehouse, Midx., S.; by Mr Bailey
31 Henry Torney of St James, Westm^r^, Midx., W., and Ann James of the same, W.
31 Robert Turner of Christ Church, Midx., B., and Catharine Slater of the same, S.

1735

Aug. 31 Edward Spur of St John, Southwarke, Surrey, W., and Deborah Day of St Mary Aldermary, Lond., S.; by Dr Watkinson

Sept. 4 John Bigg of St George, Hanover Square, Midx., B., and Anne Wragg of the same, W.

5 Thomas Porter of Putney, Surry, B., and Mary Body of Staines, Midx., S.

6 Arthur Brown of Christ Church, Midx., B., and Rebecca Seymour of this parish, S.

7 Oliver Tridwell of St Margaret's, Westminster, Midx., B., and Mary Paitfield of the same, S.

7 Joseph Scott of St Saviour's, Southwarke, Surry, B., and Elizabeth Carey of the same, S.

7 Thomas White of St Andrew's, Holborn, Lond., W., and Mary Ward of St James, Westmr, S.

11 Richard Skikelthorp of St Giles, Cripplegate, Lond., B., and Martha Lowe of St Dunstan's in the West, Lond., S.; by Mr Bailey of Queenhithe

11 Joseph Fish of Woodford, Essex, B., and Rose Griffin of Walthamstow, Essex, W.; by Mr Baily

11 Daniel Richards of Coopersale, Essex, W., and Ann Smith of the same, S.; by Mr Baily

11 Thomas Greffes of St George the Martyr, Midx., B., and Ann Wain of the same, W.; by Mr Jackson of St Austin's

13 James Peltro of St Ann's, Westmr, Midx., B., and Susan L'hommedieu of the same, S.

13 George Spencer of St George, Bloomsbury, Midx., B., and Jane Brown of St Martin in the Fields, Midx., S.

15 John Wilcox of St Clement Danes, Midx., B., and Anne Wright of St Mary, White Chappel, Midx., S.

15 William Taggart of St Helen's, Lond., B., and Elizabeth Holly of the same, S.

16 Thomas Meads of St Andrew, Holborn, Midx., W., and Mary Wilks of the same, S.

16 Samuel Snow of St Saviour's, Southwarke, B., and Mary Lewens of the same, S.

18 Peter Bennett of St George in the East, Midx., B., and Priscilla Bradford of St Botolph, Aldgate, Lond., S.

19 Thomas Merryfield of Rayleigh, Essex, W., and Jane Seggers of Runwell, Essex, S.

21 Samuel Willson of Rickmondsworth, co. Hertford, B., and Elizabeth Clement of Broadoak, Essex, S.

21 John Robuck of All Hallows Staining, Lond., B., and Hannah Shaw of Lambeth, Surry, W.

23 Robert Walling of St Gregory's, Lond., W., and Catharine Nicolson of the same, S.; by Mr Reyner of St Gregorys

24 Richard Chappell of St George in the East, Midx., W., and Susannah Ingram of the same, W.

25 John George Smith of St Martin in the Fields, Midx., B., and Jane Cheesborough of the same, S.

26 Samuel Perkins of Ware, co. Hertford, B., and Elizabeth Munns of Witford, co. Hertford, S.

27 John Reynier of St James, Westminster, Midx., W., and Jane Munk of St Martin in the Fields, Midx., S.

29 John Taylor of St Margaret's, Westmr, Midx., B., and Mary Tibbet of the same, S.

29 Allen Smith of Balcomb, Sussex, B., and Ann Wynn of the same, S.

Oct. 2 Thomas Porter of Hammersmith, Midx., W., and Mary Roberts of Chiswick, Midx., S.

1735

Oct. 5 Daniel Martinet of S[t] James, Westmin[r], Midx., B., and Rachael Le Self of the same, S.

6 Anthony Pickett of Southwell, Midx., B., and Sarah Thomas of S[t] Martin in the Fields, Midx., S.

6 Alexander Gordon of S[t] Giles in the Fields, Midx., W., and Mary Duke of S[t] Luke, Midx., S.

7 Paul Ferru of S[t] Ann's, Westm[r], Midx., B., and Elizabeth Altieri of S[t] Giles in the Fields, Midx., S.

8 Richard Holmden of Canterbury, B., and Elizabeth Horn of the same, S.

8 James Reeves of S[t] Matthew, Friday Street, Lond., B., and Elizabeth Bubb of the same, S.

8 Edward Coles of Husband Crawley, co. Bedford, B., and Elizabeth Sinfield of the same, S.

10 William West of Woolwich, Kent, B., and Hannah Bearkley of the same, W.

11 Nicholas Parades of Duke Street in the Royalty of the Tower, W., and Judith Hignon of Christ Church, Midx., W.

11 John Shakel of Aylesbury, Bucks, B., and Elizabeth Taylor of S[t] George, Hanover Square, Midx., S.

13 Henry Dickinson of Aldenham, co. Hertford, B., and Martha Tuly of the same, S.

14 Henry Walrond of S[t] Clement Danes, Midx., B., and Betty Glasse of the same, S.

14 Michael Hill of S[t] Mary le Bone, Midx., W., and Joyce Sinfield of S[t] Clement Danes, Midx., S.

16 Whitfield Murray of S[t] Paul, Shadwell, Midx., B., and Elizabeth Spalding of the same, W.

18 John English of S[t] Dunstan, Stepney, Midx., W., and Elizabeth Tiler of S[t] Gregory's by S[t] Paul, Lond., S.

18 John Meadows of Edgware, Midx., B., and Elizabeth Clarke of Stratford, Essex, S.

19 John Clarke of S[t] Saviour's, Southwarke, Surry, B., and Mary Warner of the same, S.

19 John Brady of S[t] Leonards, Foster Lane, Lond., W., and Elizabeth Morris of the same, S.

19 James Attfield of Farnham, Surrey, B., and Frances Wright of the same, S.

19 John Davis of S[t] Martin Vintrey, Lond., B., and Mary Freeman of the same, S.

21 William Jones of S[t] Paul, Covent Garden, Midx., B., and Sarah Bancks of the same, W.

21 Samuel Bowling of S[t] James, Westmin[r], Midx., B., and Susanna Lemmeray of the same, S.

27 James Mitchell of Marlborough, Wiltshire, W., and Catharine Carter of S[t] Mary le Strand, Midx., W.; by M[r] Beachcroft

28 Benjamin Brooks of S[t] Paul, Shadwell, Midx., B., and Ann Prudence of S[t] Mary, White Chappel, Midx., S.; by D[r] Thomas

29 Thomas Glegg of S[t] Martin in the Fields, Midx., B., and Ann Hollis of the same, S.; by M[r] Bailey

30 William Tichborne of S[t] Olave, Southwarke, Surry, W., and Martha Cort of Market Harborough, co. Leicester, W.; by M[r] Bailey

Nov. 4 Samuel Answorth of Hemel Hempstead, co. Hertford, B., and Ann Searles of Foots Cray, Kent, S.; by M[r] Beachcroft

4 Daniel Draper of S[t] Giles, Cripplegate, Lond., B., and Susannah Turner of the same, W.; by M[r] Beachcroft

4 George Cornelius of S[t] Clement Danes, Midx., B., and Mary Arnell of S[t] James, Westm[r], Midx., S.; by M[r] Beachcroft

5 John Exley of S[t] Clement Danes, Midx., B., and Easter Firmin of the same, S.; by M[r] Worlich

1735

Nov. 6 John Shipman of Rumford, Essex, B., and Elizabeth Smith of the same, W.; by Mr Beachcroft

6 James Kelse of St Peter le Poor, Lond., B., and Mary Purchase of the same, S.; by Mr Beachcroft

8 John Hutton of St George the Martyr, Midx., B., and Mary Rushberry* of Staverton, Shropshire, S.; by Mr Bailey

9 Joseph Wright of St Giles, Cripplegate, Lond., B., and Mary Cripple of the same, S.

9 William Milbourn of St Saviour's, Southwarke, Surry, B., and Margaret Dixon of the same, S.

11 Thomas Anderson of St George, Midx., B., and Margaret Berry of the same, W.

13 Ralph Huson of St Clement Danes, Midx., W., and Margaret Blenkinsopp of the same, S.

13 John Batten of the Artillery Ground, Midx., B., and Sarah Batchelour of the same, S.

15 Charles Townesend of Lincoln's Inn, Midx., Esqr, B., and Ann Snabling of Hamstead, Midx., S.

15 Robert Fairweather of St Buttolph without Aldgate, Midx., B., and Mary Cuthbert of the same, S.

15 Abraham Havers of Chipping Ongar, Essex, B., and Ann Mayne of Loughton, Essex, S.

16 John Cutting of St Sepulchres, Lond., B., and Anne Warden of the same, S.

17 Hubert Bonnot of St Giles in the Fields, Midx., B., and Lucy Evans of St James, Westmr, Midx., W.

25 Francis Fox of St George, Hanover Square, Midx., W., and Martha Keene of the same, W.

25 Richard Woodruff of St Dionis Backchurch, Lond., B., and Elizabeth Noble of the same, S.

25 James Hitchcock of St George the Martyr, Surry, B., and Sarah Newton Green of St Anne, Aldersgate, S.

26 Edmund Quay of St James, Westmr, Midx., B., and Elizabeth Cordis of the same, S.

26 Nathaniel Thomas of St Martin in the Fields, Midx., W., and Margaret Lovegrove of St Margaret, Westmr, Midx., W.

27 John Arnott of St Ann, Limehouse, Midx., B., and Mary Marshall of the same, W.

27 William Phillips of Wandsworth, Surry, B., and Mary Freeman of St Dunstan in the East, Lond., S.

29 John Overton of St Andrew, Holborn, Lond., B., and Hannah Baber of the same, S.

29 John Bell of St Paul, Shadwell, Midx., B., and Elizabeth Jackson of the same, W.

30 William Latton of the Middle Temple, B., and Sarah Chamberlain of St Clement Danes, Midx., S.

30 William Houldsworth of St Botolph without Bishopsgate, Lond., W., and Grace King of the same, S.

Dec. 2 Joseph Poynter of St Andrew's, Holborn, Lond., B., and Christian Clarkson of the same, S.

2 Nicholas Kempe of St Sepulchre's, Lond., B., and Sarah Gibson of Deptford, Kent, S.

4 Francis Ramond of St Martin in the Fields, Midx., B., and Elizabeth Caripell of the same, S.

5 Robert White of St Margaret's, Westmr, Midx., B., and Mary Dixon of the same, W.

* In the margin the surname is given as "Staverton." There is a parish of Rushbury in Shropshire.—Ed.

1735

Dec. 5 Arthur Culling of Sunbury, Midx., B., and Susannah Grumbald of the same, S.

7 James Knight of Clapham, Surrey, B., and Anne Stevens of the same, S.

10 William Osman of St Ann, Limehouse, Midx., B., and Jane Lee of the same, S.

11 John Kewell of Christ Church, Midx., B., and Mary Atkins of St Ann, Limehouse, Midx., S.

13 John Harvey of St Faith's, Lond., W., and Catharine Holmes of the same, S.

14 Josiah Swindell of St Mary at Hill, Lond., B., and Mary Davis of St Magnus the Martyr, Lond., S.

15 James Capstack of St Botolph, Aldersgate, Lond., W., and Sarah Worth of the same, W.

17 John Parker of St John, Wapping, Midx., B., and Mary Treadway of St Mary, Rotherhith, Surry, S.; by the Rev. Mr Wm Wilson

18 Robert Ball of St James, Clerkenwell, Midx., W., and Martha Longly of St Dunstan's in the West, Lond., S.

18 Edward Orpin of Christ-Church, Lond., B., and Lydia Sudlow of St Bride's, Lond., S.

21 George Harvest of St Bride's, Lond., W., and Ann Fenn of St Margaret's, Westm^r, Midx., W.; by Dr Thomas

24 William Robinson of Rotherhith, Kent, W., and Ann Ware of the same, S.

26 John King of Beckingham, Kent, W., and Mary Burton of the same, S.

27 Thomas Woodroffe of Loughborough, co. Leicester, B., and Ann Wild of St Martin in the Fields, Midx., W.

31 Edward Bonnick of St James, Clerkenwell, Midx., B., and Sarah Prompy of Hammersmith, Midx., W.

27 Henry Godsuff of St Nicholas Cole Abbey, Lond., W., and Martha Smith of the same, S.; by Mr Worlich

Jan. 1 William Puckridge of St Sepulchre's, Lond., B., and Mary Hall of St Andrew's, Holborn, Lond., S.

1 William Weeks alias Cannon of St Giles, Cripplegate, Lond., W., and Susannah Dixon of St James, Westm^r, Midx., S.

1 Henry Swetingham of St Giles in the Fields, Midx., B., and Sarah Bye of the same, S.

1 Peter Honore of the Tower Hamlett, Lond., B., and Elizabeth Towers of Dartford, Kent, W.

1 Philip Norris of St Mary Woolnoth, Lond., B., and Elizabeth Hobdell of St Andrew, Holborn, Midx., S.

4 Richard Goddard of St Peter Poor, Lond., B., and Alice Middleton of the same, S.

6 Edward Willett of St Mary le Bone, Midx., W., and Anne Mitchell of the same, S.

7 John Glue of Barking, Essex, W., and Elizabeth Hunt of the same, S.

7 Daniel Parry of Norton, co. Northampton, B., and Hannah Bedford of this Parish, S.

8 Thomas Tomlinson of White Chappel, Midx., B., and Hannah Sell of St Catherine Creed Church, Lond., S.

11 William Gamble of St Andrew, Holborn, Midx., B., and Catherine Duce of the same, S.

12 Thomas Golding of St Mary Magdalen, Old Fish Street, Lond., W., and Mary Lamb of the same, S.

15 Richard Bride of St Paul, Shadwell, Midx., B., and Ann Brooks of the same, S.

15 William Exton of Woolwich, Kent, B., and Martha Sherwood of St Olave, Surry, W.

1735-6

Jan. 16 Justinian Houchett of Chipping Ongar, Essex, W., and Mary Holdchain of the same, S.

17 Benjamin Vaughan of S[t] Dunstan's in the East, Lond., B., and Hannah Halfhide of S[t] Botolph, Aldgate, Lond., S.

20 Samuel Choell of Harrow on the Hill, Midx., B., and Mary Boncey of the same, S.

22 John Wright of S[t] Lawrence, Jewry, Lond., W., and Frances Palmer of S[t] Mary, Aldermanbury, Lond., S.

22 Joseph Hutt of Orsett, co. Essex, W., and Jane Davis of Chadwell, Essex, W.

22 Isaac Paulden of S[t] Martin in the Fields, Midx., W., and Jane Stephenson of S[t] Thomas, Southwarke, S.

24 Benjamin Rous of S[t] Osith, Essex, B., and Margarett Ellis of S[t] Andrew, Holborn, Midx., S.

24 John Dibley of Fulmore, co. Bucks, W., and Mary Davis of the same, W.

26 Simon Watson of Christ Church, Surry, W., and Hannah Marshall of the same, W.

26 John Chapman of S[t] Stephen, Coleman Street, Lond., B., and Anne Waldo of the Precinct of Bridewell, Lond., S.

27 William Green of Widford, co. Hertford, W., and Mary Barwick of Ware, co. Hertford, S.

29 Francis Broadhead of S[t] Giles in the Fields, Midx., B., and Mary Shippin of the same, W.

Feb. 2 Hugh Probort of S[t] Matthew, Friday Street, Lond., B., and Mary Lumbley of S[t] Martin in the Fields, Midx., S.

3 John Wills of S[t] Andrew's, Holborn, Lond., W., and Jane Young of S[t] James, Clerkenwell, Midx., S.

3 William Crampan of S[t] Botolph without Bishopsgate, Lond., B., and Mary Derry of the same, S.

7 Thomas Bird of S[t] Luke, Midx., W., and Elizabeth Bell of the same, W.

7 Thomas Hassell of S[t] Botolph without Aldgate, Lond., B., and Ann Delany of S[t] Faith, Lond., S.

8 Richard Whittaker of Oxted, Surry, B., and Elizabeth Phillips of the same, S.

10 Read Westbrook of S[t] Paul's, Deptford, Kent, B., and Martha Wilson of the same, S.

10 Edward Jones of S[t] Mary le Strand, Midx., W., and Elianor Gardiner of S[t] Sepulchre, Lond., W.

12 Henry Stephens of S[t] Thomas in Winchester, clerk, B., and Sarah Newton of Epsom, Surry, S.

12 David Cunningham of S[t] George, Midx., B., and Mary Lamb of the same, W.

13 John Tanswell of S[t] Saviour's, Southwarke, B., and Eleanor Burbero of the same, S.

17 John Hakewill of S[t] James, Westm[r], Midx., B., and Elizabeth Caillou of the same, W.

18 William Browning of S[t] George, Midx., B., and Martha Ruler of the same, S.

19 Robert Smith of S[t] George, Bloomsbury, Midx., B., and Mary Burges of the same, S.

19 Hugh Cathrall of S[t] George, Hanover Square, Midx., W., and Ann King of S[t] Martin in the Fields, Midx., W.

24 William Emes of S[t] James, Westm[r], Midx., B., and Elizabeth Jordan of S[t] Sepulchre, Lond., W.

26 Thomas King of Colchester, Essex, W., and Mary Gittings of S[t] Andrew, Holborn, Midx., W.

1735-6

Feb. 26 William Tate of S[t] Leonard, Shoreditch, Midx., W., and Martha Ryland of S[t] Botolph, Bishopsgate, Lond., W.

26 William Buck of S[t] Mary Somerset, Lond., B., and Mary Field of the same, S.

27 George Gale of Trowbridge, Wilts, B., and Mary Palmer of the same, S.

28 John Bromwell Jones of S[t] Dunstan, Stepney, Midx., Esq., B., and Mary Holden of the same, S.; by the Rev. M[r] J[n] Wright

29 John Claudius Bitton of S[t] Botolph, Aldgate, Lond., B., and Marianne Penus of Christ Church, Spittlefields, Midx., S.

Mar. 1 Thomas Kerr of Chislehurst, Kent, B., and Elizabeth Pearson of S[t] George, Southwarke, Surry, S.

1 James Andrews of Battersea, Surrey, W., and Mary Field of S[t] Peter y[e] Poor, Lond., S.

2 Thomas Thorp of S[t] James, Westm[r], Midx., B., and Mary Bedwell of S[t] Clement Danes, Midx., S.

4 Richard Morris of S[t] Mary, Newington, Surrey, B., and Sarah Salusbury of S[t] Mary Overy's, Surry, W.

4 Joseph Draper of Edmonton, Midx., B., and Hannah Chillingworth of the same, S.

4 John Squire of S[t] Buttolph, Aldersgate, Lond., B., and Catharine Hyatt of S[t] Stephen, Coleman Street, Lond., S.

5 Bernard Saunders of S[t] Martin, Ludgate, Lond., B., and Catherine Pigot of Croydon, Surry, S.

5 Charles Faugoin of Linton, co. Cambridge, B., and Mary Gager of S[t] Andrew's, Holborn, Midx., S.

6 Francis Brown of S[t] Ann and Agnes, Aldersgate, Lond., B., and Margaret Pasmore of Beckenham, Kent, S.

6 Edward Birchmore of S[t] Mary, Islington, Midx., W., and Hannah Greeves of the same, S.

7 William Casbard of S[t] Margaret Moses, Lond., B., and Sarah Richbell of the same, S.

7 William Howlett of Camberwell, Surry, B., and Elizabeth Jeanes of S[t] George, Southwarke, Surry, S.

8 Henry Geree of S[t] Olave, Southwarke, W., and Ann Salway of S[t] George, Southwarke, Surry, W.

8 John Jason of S[t] James, Westm[r], Midx., B., and Anne Fitzor of S[t] George, Hanover Square, Midx., S.

8 Morgan Morgan of S[t] Clement Danes, Midx., B., and Margaret Morgan of S[t] Andrew, Holborn, Lond., S.

11 Stephen Teissier of S[t] Margaret, Lothbury, Lond., B., and Elizabeth Loubier of S[t] Christopher's, Lond., S.

12 Thomas Whitehead of the Middle Temple, Lond., B., and Margaret White of S[t] Dunstan's in the West, W.

13 John Turner of S[t] John Baptist, Lond., B., and Mary Roussoa of the same, W.

20 John Lawson of the Inner Temple, Lond., Esq., B., and Ann Hurnall of S[t] Paul's, Covent Garden, Midx., S.

23 Jacob Hodgson of S[t] Paul's, Covent Garden, Midx., B., and Mary Larking of S[t] Ann's, Soho, Midx., S.

23 Robert Hill of Cranfield, co. Bedford, W., and Mary Cripps of Dunstable, co. Bedford, S.

1736.

Mar. 25 Joseph Luccock of S[t] Luke, Midx., W., and Phillis Gains of the same, S.

28 William Ponnard of S[t] James, Westm[r], Midx., B., and Susan Whittring of S[t] Margaret, Westm[r], Midx., S.

1736

Mar. 28 John Watson of S[t] Bottolph, Bishopsgate, Lond., B., and Jane Robinson of the same, S.

30 Charles Yardley of S[t] James, Westm[r], Midx., B., and Mary Yardley of the same, S.

30 William Hovell of S[t] Edmundsbury, Suffolk, B., and Elizabeth Burrell of Adstock, Bucks, S.

April 2 Edward Prosser of Great Shelsly, co. Worcester, B., and Mary Rawlins of Lower Handley, co. Worcester, S.

6 Josiah Baker of S[t] Dunstans, Stepney, Midx., B., and Susannah Palmer of the same, S.

6 Thomas Wollfryes of Wynterbourn Kingston, Dorset, B., and Penelope Malin of S[t] Martin in the Fields, Midx., S.

7 John Reeves of S[t] Mary Hill, Lond., B., and Sarah Lowth of S[t] Clement, East Cheap, Lond., S.

8 Joseph Potter of S[t] Dunstan, Stepney, Midx., B., and Ruth Trusham of the same, S.

9 Thomas Flower of Newington Butts, Surry, B., and Jane Fuller of S[t] Botolph, Aldersgate, Lond., S.

14 George Haines of S[t] Dunstan in the East, Lond., W., and Shibella Pomfrett of Lambeth, Surry, W.

15 John Whitfield of S[t] James, Westm[r], Midx., B., and Mary Clayton of the same, S.

16 Robert Cremer of S[t] Margaret's in Lyn, Norfolk, B., and Elizabeth Murden of Deal, Kent, S.

17 John Hawkins of S[t] Mary, White Chappel, Midx., B., and Ann Charington of S[t] John, Wapping, Midx., S.

21 Walwyn Morgan of Madley, co. Hereford, clerk, B., and Ann Wishaw of S[t] Lawrence, Jewry, Lond., S.

22 John Argent of Feversham, Kent, B., and Anne Bargrave of the same, S.

25 Jonathan Steward of S[t] Clement Danes, Midx., W., and Mary Judery of S[t] Pauls, Covent Garden, Midx., S.

26 Edward Edgson of Lewisham, Kent, B., and Sarah Peak of Bromley, Kent, S.

27 William Hubbard of S[t] Ann, Westm[r], B., and Elizabeth Green of the same, S.

27 William Watkins of S[t] George, Bloomsbury, Midx., B., and Ann Parsons of Allhallows, Lombard S[t], Lond., S.

28 Richard Frizer, W., and Elizabeth Ratchliff, S., both of this Parish; by Banns

29 William Smith of Rumford, Essex, B., and Sarah Denham of Sevenoaks, Kent, S.

29 Cornelius Cordiner of S[t] Martin in the Fields, Midx., B., and Ann Bell of S[t] Mary, White Chapell, Midx., S.

29 Alexander Dundas of S[t] Bartholomew the Less, Lond., B., and Mary Grimes of Stepney, Midx., S.; by the Rev. M[r] Swallow of Writtle, Essex

29 Robert Doughtey of S[t] Clement Danes, Midx., B., and Hannah Woodward of the same, S.

May 1 William Tuff of S[t] James, Westm[r], Midx., B., and Jane Legg of Allhallows Staining, Lond., S.; M[r] Worlich

3 John Chambers of Lambeth, Surrey, W., and Lydia Howit of the same, W.

4 Richard Squire of S[t] James, Garlick Hithe, Lond., B., and Jane Lawrence of the same, S.

8 Samuel Draper of Hampstead, Midx., B., and Mary Rodgers of the same, S.

1736

May 8 Cornelius Sarjant of St Catherine's near the Tower, Lond., B., and Elisabeth West of the same, S.

8 Francis Brown of St James, Westm^r^, Midx., B., and Hannah Jordan of the same, S.

11 Samuel Jaumard of St Ann, Westm^r^, Midx., W., and Mary Fraigneau of St James, Westm^r^, Midx., S.

11 Patrick Cannan of St Martin in the Fields, Midx., B., and Susannah Pomier of the same, S.

11 Antide Jennet of St James, Westm^r^, Midx., B., and Elizabeth Swain of St Giles in the Fields, Midx., S.

12 William Witheat of St Buttolph, Aldgate, Lond., B., and Mary Allen of the same, S.

13 Thomas Paine of St George, Bloomsbury, Midx., B., and Sarah West of the same, S.

13 John Rice of Midhurst, Sussex, B., and Anne Wooding of St Antholin's, Lond., S.

15 Thomas Winpenny of St Giles in the Fields, Midx., B., and Rolana Judd of the same, S.

16 Henry Norman of St James, Westm^r^, Midx., B., and Susannah Wilkinson of the same, S.

16 Abraham King of St Sepulchre, Lond., B., and Elizabeth Benson of St Bride's, Lond., S.

17 Richard Ward of Woolwich, Kent, B., and Elisabeth Smith of the same, S.

18 John Nicholas of Heese, Midx., B., and Ann Russell of the same, S.

18 Thomas Parncutt of Lambeth, Surry, W., and Mary Tanner of Stretham, Surry, S.

20 Stephen Thomas of St James, Westm^r^, Midx., W., and Mary Ashton of St Giles in the Fields, Midx., S.

20 John Morris of St Giles in the Fields, Midx., B., and Margaret Broome of the same, S.

22 Henry Biggs of St Sepulchre, Lond., B., and Susannah Lipscomb of the same, W.

25 George Gillett of St Margaret, Lothbury, Lond., B., and Ann Hammond of the same, S.

26 James Steere of St George, Bloomsbury, Midx., B., and Mary Smith of the same, S.

28 Edward Urling of Chiswick, Midx., W., and Alice Davidge of the same, W.

29 John Prissick of St John the Baptist, Lond., B., and Mary North of St Michael Royal, Lond., S.

29 John Papworth of Allhallows Barking, Lond., B., and Lydia Watton of the same, S.

30* Richard Swainston of the Inner Temple, Lond., B., and Judith Martin of St Martin in the Fields, Midx., S.

30 Joseph Woodward of St Clement Danes, Midx., B., and Hannah Chapman of the same, S.

June 3 John Fensham of Wormley, co. Hertford, B., and Hannah Lamb of Endfield, Midx., S.; by Mr Worlich

3 John Turner of Christ Church, Surry, B., and Sarah Hook of St Saviour's, Southwarke, Surry, S.; by the same

4 William Morris of St Swithin, Lond., W., and Mary Williamson of St Martin in the Fields, Midx., S.; by the same

4 John Edwards of Lambourne, Essex, W., and Mary Brown of Chigwell, Essex, S.; by Dr Thomas

5 Richard Gray of St Mary, White Chapell, Midx., B., and Penelope Knight of the same, S.; by the same

* Date altered from 29th to 30th.—Ed.

1736

June 10 John Boutflower of St Mary, Rotherhyth, Surry, B., and Sarah Cottam of the same, S.; by Mr Bayley

10 Willson Buxton of Clerkenwell, Midx., B., and Ann Simmonds of Lothbury, Lond., S.; by the same

15 William Martin of St James, Westmr, Midx., B., and Hannah Munday of the same, S.; by Dr Best

15 John Barnes of St George, Hanover Square, Midx., B., and Sarah Cross of Richmond, Surry, S.; by the same

16 William Pattinson of St Saviour's, Southwarke, Surry, B., and Jane Juck of the same, S.; by Dr Thomas

16 Robert Gibson of St Dunstan, Stepney, Midx., B., and Elizabeth Matthewson of the same, W.; by the same

17 Ralph Hall of St Andrew, Holborn, Midx., B., and Mary Baldwyn of the same, S.; by Dr Watkinson

18 Charles Halker of Stepney, Midx., B., and Hannah Dudley of the same, S.; by Mr Jones, Curate of St Gregory's

19 John Wheatland of St Andrew Undershaft, Lond., B., and Catharine Thompson of St Nicholas Cole Abbey, Lond., S.; by Dr Watkinson

24 Benjamin Bealing of St Paul, Shadwell, Midx., B., and Elizabeth Eves of the same, S.

27 Charles King of St Luke, Midx., W., and Mary Pearson of the same, S.

28 Edward White of St Sepulchre, Lond., W., and Mary Porter of the same, S.

28 Joseph Crutchley of St Catherine Creed Church, Lond., B., and Elizabeth Butler of St Catherine Coleman, Lond., S.

28 Spring Wyncoll of St Giles in the Fields, Midx., B., and Mary Broughton of the same, S.

29 James Swintoune of St Martin in the Fields, Midx., W., and Elizabeth Needham of St James, Westmr, Midx., S.

29 Thomas Norris of Lambeth, Surry, W., and Mary Waite of St Mary Woolchurch, Lond., W.

29 James Mallandain of Christ Church, Midx., B., and Susanna Rachel Motteux of the same, S.

29 John Ellitts of St Andrew, Holborne, Midx., W., and Elizabeth Beckwith of St Ann and Agnes, Aldersgate, Lond., S.

30 Robert Brownson of St Martin in the Fields, Midx., B., and Mary Page of Lambeth, Surry, S.

July 1 John Cromwell of Feltham, Midx., W., and Ann Foot of the same, S.; by Mr Hillman of St Paul's

5 Peter Dutens of St Martin in the Fields, Midx., B., and Elizabeth Charlotte of the same, S.

5 Samuel Buckland of St Clement Danes, Midx., B., and Ann Kennady of the same, S.

7 Henry Gawton of St Sepulchres, Lond., B., and Diana Williams of St James, Westmr, Middx., S.

8 Richard Nicholson of St James, Westmr, Midx., W., and Hannah Howson of St Mary le Savoy, Midx., W.

8 James Dodd of St Botolph, Bishopsgate, Lond., B., and Jane Greening of the same, S.

10 John Beaman of St Martin in the Fields, Midx., W., and Bridget Jolly of St Leonard, Shoreditch, Midx., W.

11 Thomas Greene, W., and Mary Fisher, S., both of this Parish; by Banns

11 John Seakins of St Botolph, Bishopsgate, Lond., W., and Margaret Clarke of Edmonton, Midx., S.

13 Henry Chester, Esq., of Stepney, Midx., W., and Mary Thomas of St Peter le Poor, Lond., S.; by Mr Audley, Lecturer of Rotherhithe

1736

July 14 Robert Scruton of St Clement Danes, Midx., B., and Ann Burfoot of St Stephen, Walbrook, Lond., S.

15 William Cox of St George, Midx., W., and Phœbe Nicholls of Stanford Le Hope, Essex, W.

16 John Jennings of Allhallows, Bread Street, Lond., B., and Mary Pearcy of the same, S.

17 John Waple of St James, Clerkenwell, Middx., W., and Jane Ellis of the same, S.

20 Joseph Kettle of St George, Hanover Square, Midx., B., and Ann Keeling of the same, W.

20 Charles Turner of St Catherine's near the Tower, Lond., W., and Elizabeth Edwards of St Bride's, Lond., W.

20 Thomas Reynolds of Bletchingly, Surry, B., and Mary Snelling of Godstone, Surry, S.

21 John Macklane of Stepney, Midx., B., and Elizabeth Davis of the same, S.

24 William Lee of St James, Clerkenwell, Midx., B., and Ann Day of the same, S.; by Mr Worlich

27 Roger Saunders of St Mary le Strand, Midx., W., and Elizabeth Southall of St Martin in the Fields, Midx., S.; by Mr Bayley

31 Robert Carr of Isleworth, Midx., Clerk, B., and Elizabeth Saville of the same, W.; by Mr Coliere of Richmond

Aug. 1 Robert Emery of St George, Bloomsbury, Midx., B., and Ann Allen of St Paul, Covent Garden, Midx., S.

1 Thomas Bullock of St Andrew, Holborn, Midx., B., and Judith Shergold of the same, S.

2 Henry Burton of Kennington, Midx., W., and Anna Doury of Chelsea, Midx., W.

2 Joseph Benson of St Saviour, Southwark, B., and Elizabeth Ireland of St Olave's, Southwark, Surry, W.

4 John Sugg of St John the Evangelist, Westmr, B., and Ann Allen of the same, S.

4 Samuel Dodd of Barnes, Surry, B., and Sarah Bates of the same, S.

5 Henry Worth of St Sepulchre's, Lond., B., and Martha Hoare of St Martin, Ludgate, Lond., S.

7 Robert Eldridge of Sevenoaks, Kent, B., and Mary Bond of Mitcham, Surry, S.

7 Edward Hornsbee of St Saviour's, Southwark, W., and Ann Long of St Paul, Shadwell, Midx., W.

8 Peter Coby of Allhallows, Thames Street, Lond., W., and Mary Shotton of the same, W.

10 William Platt of St Andrew's, Holborn, Lond., W., and Mary Lewis of the same, S.

13 Charles Stiff of St Saviour's, Southwark, B., and Elizabeth Hughes of the same, S.

15 John Benson of St Mary Aldermary, Lond., B., and Mary Halsaid of St Bartholomew near the Exchange, Lond., S.

17 Edward Young of St John the Evangelist, Westmr, Midx., W., and Jane Seadding of the same, S.

18 John Maillard of Christ Church, Spittlefields, Midx., B., and Martha Thompson of Stepney, Midx., S.

18 Thomas Sunn of Stepney, Midx., B., and Elizabeth Rawlings of the same, W.

19 William Hunt of Hammersmith, Midx., W., and Sarah Belcher of the same, S.

21 John Gilks of Langley, Bucks, B., and Jane Miller of the same, S.

1736

Aug. 21 William Goleborn of St Andrew's, Holborn, Midx., W., and Mary Axtell of Hampsted, Midx., W.

22 John Homeward of St Mary Magdalen, Bermondsey, Southwark, B., and Grace Horne of the same, S.

24 Anthony Johnson of Bromley, Kent, W., and Susan Bloume of the same, S.

24 Thomas Corless of St George the Martyr, Midx., B., and Eleanor Clowes of the same, W.

25 Hugh Gibb of St Martin in the Fields, Midx., B., and Elizabeth Williams of Clapham, Surry, S.

26 John Miller of St George, Hanover Square, Midx., B., and Mary Jennings of the same, S.

26 Thomas Lewin of St Peter's, Cornhill, Lond., B., and Jane Johnson of Berwick upon Tweed, S.

26 Matthew Boyer of St George, Botolph Lane, Lond., W., and Abigael Spackman of Lambeth, Surry, W.

26 Thomas Winter of Queenborough, Kent, B., and Ruth Brown of Barking, Essex, S.

26 John White of Waldorsher, Kent, B., and Ann Picket of St Andrew, Holborn, Lond., S.

27 Michael Robinson of Deptford, Kent, W., and Mary Cole of East Greenwich, Kent, S.

27 George Wright of Allhallows the Great, Lond., W., and Ann Gamble of St Clement Danes, Midx., W.

29 Thomas Nash of St Ann, Limehouse, Midx., B., and Mary Darby of the same, S.

29 John Hurst of St Mary le Bow, Lond., W., and Mary Dunkin of St Mildred, Bread Street, Lond., S.

29 John Halfhead of Gillingham, Kent, B., and Mary Eales of St Olave, Southwark, S.

31 John Battams of St Andrew, Holborn, Lond., W., and Mary Bull of the same, W.

Sept. 1 John Jackson of St Ann, Westmr, W., and Elizabeth Story of St James, Westmr, Midx., W.

2 Peter Pearson of Deptford, Kent, B., and Mary Faris of East Greenwich, Kent, S.; by Mr Badger

3 James Gordon of Alloa in North Britain, W., and Hannah Grindall of St James, Westmr, Midx., W.

6 Thomas Fowler of St Paul, Covent Garden, Midx., B., and Mary Plant of the same, S.

8 Thomas Sparkes of St Mary Magdalen, Bermondsey, Surrey, W., and Esther Horskins of the same, W.; by Mr Worlich

8 Benjamin Sherman of St Sepulchre's, Midx., B., and Elizabeth French of the same, W.; by Mr Bayley

9 William Huthwaite of Allhallows, Lombard Street, Lond., B., and Hannah Moore of the same, S.

11 John Jordane of St Saviour's, Southwarke, B., and Anne Spreakley of the same, S.

13 James Cope of Bushey, co. Hertford, B., and Eleanor Hickman of Harrow on the Hill, Midx., S.

13 Henry Wheatley of Deptford, Kent, B., and Mary Hartrup of the same, S.

13 Thomas Waller of St Anne, Blackfryars, Lond., B., and Ruth Jump of the same, S.

14 John Etheridge of St Mary, White Chapel, Midx., B., and Finis Vincent of the same, S.

14 Henry Sewell of Felstead, Essex, B., and Sarah Fuller of Horn Church, Essex, S.

1736

Sept. 14 Joseph Howard of S[t] Saviour's, Southwark, W., and Ann Taylor of Wickham, Kent, W.

16 Thomas Hooke of Pancras, Midx., B.,* and Ann Atkis of the same, W.

17 Robert Adams, Esq[r], Pancras, Midx., W., and Diana Thompson of S[t] Ann's, Westm[r], Midx., W.

17 William Carter of S[t] Peter Poor, Bread Street, Lond., B., and Martha Hinton of the same, S.

19 Thomas Grimward of Chelsea, Midx., B., and Margery Nevin of the same, S.

21 Gabriel Shonorey of S[t] Martin in the Fields, Midx., B., and Henrietta Ruffe of Wandsworth, Surry, S.

21 Isaac Pocock of S[t] Mary Magdalen, Bermondsey, Surry, B., and Susannah Barns of the same, S.

22 Samuel Roome of S[t] George, Bloomsbury, Midx., B., and Martha Dean of the same, S.

23 John Frank of Allhallows, Lombard Street, Lond., B., and Elizabeth Hicks of the same, S.

25 William Barker of S[t] Ann's, Westm[r], B., and Sarah Wyatt of S[t] Martin in the Fields, Midx., S.

28 Thomas Hutchins of S[t] Giles, Cripplegate, Lond., W., and Jane Cooper of the same, W.

28 John French of Bromley, Kent, B., and Catharine Hunter of the same, S.

28 John Jackson of Edmonton, Midx., B., and Ann Lewis of the same, S.

29 Gilbert Burnet of S[t] Paul, Covent Garden, Midx., B., and Mary Gately of S[t] Andrew's, Holborn, Midx., S.

30 William Bell, B., and Susannah Bland, S., both of this Parish; by Banns

30 Robert Green of Bermondsey, B., and Anne Blowen of S[t] Olave, Southwarke, Surrey, S.

30 William Needler of Mortlake, Surry, B., and Elizabeth Tacher of the same, S.

Oct. 1 Thomas Willis of Peckham, Surry, B., and Ann Burges of the same, S.

1 John Hooper of Harmondsworth, Midx., B., and Frances Rickards of S[t] George, Bloomsbury, Midx., S.

1 Andrew Houdten als Houdetn of Bermondsey, Surry, B., and Elizabeth Nixson of the same, S.

1 Joseph Keen of Twittenham, Midx., B., and Elizabeth Hartley of the same, S.

2 Thomas Jones of Chidingstone, Kent, B., and Susannah Long of Heaver, Kent, S.

2 Arthur Hebburne of S[t] Brides, Lond., B., and Elizabeth Howard of the same, W.

3 Henry Day of S[t] Saviour's, Southwark, B., and Ann Hughes of S[t] George the Martyr, Surry, S.

3 Edmund Peddell of S[t] Mary le Bone, Midx., B., and Ann Lowings of the same, W.

4 Joshua Atkins of this parish, B., and Ann Byng of S[t] Paul, Shadwell, Midx., W.

7 John Leaser of S[t] Martin in the Fields, Midx., W., and Mary Cleavland of the same, S.

7 George Cowrer of Mitcham, Surry, B., and Jane Henshaw of S[t] Georges, Southwark, S.

7 Thomas Turner of S[t] Botolph, Bishopsgate, Lond., B., and Elizabeth Nodes of the same, S.

10 Samuel Carter of S[t] Dunstan in the East, Lond., B., and Margaret Pates of the same, S.

* "B," has been written over "W."—Ed.

1736

Oct. 17 William Vincent of St Martin's, Ludgate, Lond., B., and Elizabeth Pridgeon of the same, S.

17 Edward Hales of Bermondsey, Surrey, B., and Edith Singer of St Giles in the Fields, Midx., S.

18 John Chigwell of Colchester, Essex, B., and Mary Perry of Little Baddowin, Essex, S.; by Mr Parry of St James, Westm^r

21 Richard Barber of St George, Hanover Square, Midx., B., and Ann Glover of St Martin in the Fields, Midx., S.

21 Samuel Barnett of St George, Bloomsbury, Middx., B., and Jane Pew of the same, S.

21 Richard Morris of St Michael, Cornhill, London, B., and Mary Badcock of St Ann, Blackfryars, London, S.

21 Charles Hodson of St Clement Danes, Middx., B., and Elizabeth Wallis of St Andrew, Holborn, Middx., W.

21 William Holmes of St James, Westminster, Middx., B., and Frances Ann Hart of St John the Evangelist, Westminster, Middx., S.

24 Robert Rampshire of St Thomas the Apostle, London, W., and Mary Smith of St Martin, Ironmonger lane, London, W.; by Dr Watkinson

27 Thomas Small of Darenth, Kent, B., and Judith Beale of Ash in Kent, S.

28 Thomas Jeffery of East Greenwich, Kent, B., and Tomlinson Mead of the same, W.

28 David Kidney of Market Harborough, co. Leic., B., and X^tian Kite of St Thomas, Southwark, Surry, S.

28 Hugh Cottrell of St George, Southwark, B., and Esther Osborne of St Botolph, Aldgate, London, S.

29 Benjamin Tomkins of St Saviour, Southwark, W., and Mary Lepidge of St John, Southwark, W.; by Mr Beachcroft

29 John Bennett of Bermondsey, Surry, W., and Elizabeth Backwell of St James, Clerkenwell, Middx., W.; by Mr Beachcroft

31 Joseph Harris of the Tower of London, B., and Anne Jones of Talgarth, co. Brecknock, S.; by Mr Bayley

Nov. 1 John Blanks of Southfleet in Kent, B., and Mary King of Chislehurst, Kent, S.; by Mr Beachcroft

3 Edward Fisher of St Lawrence Poutney, London, W., and Emm Bennet of St Martin Vintry, London, W.; by Mr Beachcroft

3 Charles Johnson of Bromley, Kent, B., and Elizabeth Greenwood of Orpenton, Kent, S.; by Mr Beachcroft

7 John Egleton of Lambeth, Surry, B., and Mary Pottinger of the same, S.

8 George Horner of Reading, co. Berks, B., and Isabella Wilson of St Martin in the Fields, Middx., S.

9 Isaac Percivall of St Dunstan in the West, London, B., and Elizabeth Nash of Chelsea, Middx., W.

11 James Linney of St Michael, Cornhill, London, B., and Rachael Moore of St Edmund the King, London, S.

11 Samuel Tomkiss of Wandsworth, Surry, W., and Rachael Palmer of St Mary Magdalen, Bermondsey, in the said County, S.

11 Thomas Edgerton of Bermondsey, Southwark, B., and Mary Burr of the same, S.

16 James Wignell of St Olave, Southwarke, B., and Mary Warray of the same, W.

12 Francis Bennett of St Martin in the Fields, Middx., B., and Ann Moor of Darwent in Kent, S.

12 William Sadgrove of Richmond, Surry, B., and Martha Cook of the same, S.

1736

Nov. 18 Christopher Hargreave of S[t] Clement Danes, Middx., B., and Amy Stephenson of the same, S.

20 Giles Aleyn of All Hallows Barking, London, B., and Mary Fisher of S[t] Margaret, Westminster, Middx., S.

24 Richard Easton of S[t] Martin, Ludgate, London, B., and Sarah Dicas of S[t] Andrew, Holborn, London, S.

24 Isaac Haines of S[t] Andrew, Holborn, Middx., B., and Mary Wilson of the same, S.

24 John Fisher of S[t] Giles in the Fields, Middx., B., and Catharine Jones of S[t] Andrew Undershaft, London, W.

25 John Bristo of S[t] James, Westminster, Middx., B., and Dorothy Hicks of the same, S.

25 William Harcott of Brentford, Middx., B., and Elizabeth Tillier of S[t] Margaret, Westminster, Middx., S.

26 Richard Broughton of S[t] George, Hanover Square, Middx., B., and Elizabeth Watson of the same, S.

27 Barrington Taverner of Colchester, Essex, B., and Frances Howland of the same, S.

27 James Bradshaw of S[t] Anne, Westminster, Middx., B., and Margaret Holt of S[t] Lawrence, Jewry, London, S.

30 Benjamin Fielder of Mortlake, Surry, W., and Mary Marshall of the same, S.

Dec. 1 Charles Corbet of S[t] Gregory, London, B., and Mabella Cox of the same, S.

1 Anthony Sharpe of Kings Cliffe, co. Northampton, W., and Elizabeth Newbourne of S[t] Gregory, London, S.

1 Francis Gaudin of S[t] Ann, Westminster, Middx., B., and Sarah Fountain of the same, S.

4 George Keepe of Wilmonton, Surry, B., and Mary Tanner of Wandsworth in the said county, S.

4 Lewis Evans of S[t] James, Westminster, Middx., W., and Dorothy Davies of S[t] Clement Danes, Middx., W.

9 William Ford of S[t] Michael Bassishaw, London, B., and Ann Chivers of the same, S.

9 Robert Wright of Great Burstead, Essex, B., and Catharine Biddle of the same, W.

9 John Morris of S[t] Saviour, Southwark, Surry, W., and Mary Ellett of the same, S.

12 Robert Aunger of S[t] James, Westminster, Middx., W., and Kezia Cates of S[t] Ann, Westminster, Middx., W.

12 Thomas Wright of S[t] Mary, White Chapple, Middx., B., and Mary Saunders of the same, W.

14 William Abercrombie of S[t] James, Westminster, Middx., B., and Sarah Youick of the same, S.

15 William Biddle of S[t] Andrew, Holborn, London, B., and Ann Graves of S[t] Clement Danes, Middx., S.

15 Matthew Ray of S[t] James, Westminster, Middx., W., and Elizabeth White of S[t] Giles in the Fields, Middx., W.

16 Alexander Ready of the Middle Temple, London, W., and Sophia Edwards of S[t] Paul, Covent Garden, Middx., S.

16 John Pero of S[t] Martin in the Fields, Middx., W., and Isabella Yarnton of the same [*blank*]; by M[r] Jones, Curate of S[t] Gregory's

21 Nathaniel Reeve of Finchley, Middx., B., and Mary Samm of Barnet, co. Herts, S.

21 John Baker of S[t] George, Southwark, Surry, W., and Ann Cross of the same, W.

21 Arthur Jones of Croyden, Surry, W., and Ann Wyatt of the same, W.

1736

Dec. 23 Peregrine Bertie of St Clement Danes, Middx., B., and Elizabeth Payne of St Andrew, Holborn, London, S.

23 George Putland of St Clement Danes, Middx., B., and Ann Bishop of St Margaret, Westminster, Middx., S.

25 Henry Glover of St Dunstan in the East, London, B., and Mary Sawyer of St Mary Somerset, London, S.

28 William Norwood of St Stephen, Coleman Street, London, B., and Rachael Sangar of the same, S.

30 Robert Williams of St James, Westminster, Middx., B., and Phœbe Robinson of the Precinct of White Fryers, London, W.

30 Robert Armorer of St Margaret, Westminster, Middx., B., and Mary Cornwall of Greenwich, Kent, S.

31 William Rowley of Bromsgrove, co. Worcester, W., and Sarah Poole of St Michael, Queenhithe, London, S.

31 John Tompson of Wormley, co. Herts, B., and Sarah Parish of the same, S.

Jan. 1 David Davies of St Martin in the Fields, Middx., B., and Mary Dickenson of St James, Westminster, Middx., S.

2 William Pyrke of St Giles, Cripplegate, London, B., and Mary Crooke of the same, S.

2 George Burch of St Andrew, Holborn, Middx., B., and Maria Bishop of the same, S.

3 Francis Brissart of St Andrew Undershaft, London, B., and Mary Hensketh of St Mary, Aldermanbury, London, W.

3 Thomas Andrews of Deptford, Kent, B., and Elizabeth Crouch of St John's in Surry, W.

6 James Thompson of All Hallows Barking, London, B., and Elizabeth Harling of St Andrew, Holborn, Middx., W.

6 Henry Wentworth of St Margaret Moses, London, B., and Honour Rusden of St Botolph, Aldgate, Middx., S.; by Mr Gibson of St Michael, Cornhill

7 William Cox of St Andrew, Holborn, Middx., W., and Hannah King of St Clement Danes, Middx., S.

10 Thomas Hall of St Mary, Aldermanbury, London, W., and Elizabeth Thorpe of St Martin in the Fields, Middx., S.

10 Daniel Philips of Brocksbon, co. Herts, W., and Sarah Benton of Endfield, Middx., S.

11 John Holt of Down in Kent, B., and Sarah Round of Shoreham, Kent, W.

12 Thomas Binon of Waltham Abby, Essex, B., and Hannah Hills of the same, S.

12 Patrick Quin of St James, Westminster, Middx., W., and Mary Topham of the same, S.

12 Joseph Ratcliffe of St Botolph, Bishopsgate, London, B., and Sibilla Roebuck of St George, Hanover Square, Middx., S.

13 Thomas Tod of Trinity parish, London, B., and Elizabeth Clarke of St Mary Aldermary, London, S.; by Dr Watkinson

13 Samuel Gray, B., and Sarah Jenkins, S., both of this parish. Banns

13 Daniel MacLean of St James, Westminster, Middx., B., and Elizabeth Dadicha of the same, W.

13 Thomas Thompson of St Dunstan in the West, London, B., and Elizabeth Wildman of St Swithin's, London, S.

17 Bradford Jefferies of Somerford Calnes, Wilts, B., and Mary Glover of St Martin in the Fields, Middx., S.

18 James Sidney of St Mary Magdalen, Bermondsey, Surry, W., and Hannah Bayley of St Olave, Southwarke, in the said County, S.

1736-7

Jan. 19 Thomas Bolas of St Nicholas Olave's, London, B., and Catherine Irish of the same, S.

19 Joseph Goodwin of St Giles, Cripplegate, Middx., B., and Amey Dowse of St Mary, Rotherhith, Surry, S.

20 Tristram Collins of Bishop's Aukland, co. Durham, B., and Agnes Jackson of the same, S.

20 William Cound of Hayes, Kent, B., and Rebecca Redhead of Adington, Surry, S.

20 John Morley of St George by Queen's Square, Middx., W., and Ann Wright of the same, S.

20 John Hunt of St Andrew, Holborn, Middx., B., and Elizabeth Horn of St Bride's, London, W.

21 John Andrews of Nosely, co. Leic., B., and Susanna Sturges of St Saviour, Southwarke, S.

24 John Giles of St George, Hanover Square, Middx., B., and Mary Leinthall of St Martin in the Fields, Middx., S.

24 Samuel Drury of Bromley, Kent, B., and Michall Jones of the same, W.

30 John Hiorn of St James, Clarkenwell, Middx., B., and Hesther Little of this parish, S.

30 William Praed of St Christopher le Stocks, London, B., and Frances Morgan of the same, S.

31 John Smith of St John, Southwark, Surry, W., and Elizabeth Blinston of the same, W.

Feb. 1 Andrew Cornwall of St Margaret, Westminster, Middx., B., and Mary Sugg of the same, S.

4 Richard Beale of St Saviour, Southwarke, B., and Sarah Plimpton of St Paul, Shadwell, Middx., S.; by Mr Cooke of Edmonton

6 Henry George of St Botolph, Aldgate, Middx., B., and Mary Stedman of St Luke's, Middx., S.

7 Thomas Farrand of St George, Hanover Square, Middx., B., and Elizabeth Lydall of the same, S.

8 Benjamin Jordan of Fulham, Middx., W., and Catherine Anderson of St Catherine by the Tower, London [*blank*]

9 George Wragg of St Giles, Cripplegate, Middx., B., and Alice Plummer of St Swithin, London Stone, S.

12 Thomas Dean of Boxley, Kent, B., and Elizabeth Porter of Maidstone, Kent, S.

13 Henry Feltman of St George, Hanover Square, Middx., B., and Anna Dutton of St Ann, Westminster, Middx., S.; by Mr Church

14 Robert Kitching of St Paul, Shadwell, Middx., B., and Elizabeth Perrett of St Saviour, Southwarke, S.

15 Henry Cook of St James in the Liberty of Westminster, Middx., W., and Mary Pell of St Ann, Aldersgate, London, W.

16 John Early of St Clement Danes, Middx., B., and Elizabeth Perry of the same, S.

17 John Barker of St Clement Danes, Middx., B., and Martha Pickett of the same, S.

17 Thomas Haslehurst of St Bride's, London, W., and Mary Belldom of St Dunstan in the West, London, S.

17 John Buxton of St James, Clarkenwell, Middx., B., and Catharine Waller of the same, S.

17 Michael Stacey of Sutton, Surry, B., and Mary Taylor of Clapham, Surry, S.

18 Samuel Freeman of St Dionis Backchurch, London, B., and Margaret Healey of the same, S.

18 William Heath of Wandsworth, Surry, B., and Frances Maynard of the same, W.

1736-7

Feb. 19 Francis Parnham of St Andrew, Holborn, Middx., B., and Mary Thompson of the same, S.

19 Richard Owen of St Martin in the Fields, Middx., B., and Elizabeth Robins of the same, W.

20 Edward Clarke of St Dunstan in the West, London, W., and Elizabeth Prince of St George, Southwark, Surry, S.

20 Joseph Liptrapp of St Margaret Pattens, London, B., and Elizabeth Smith of All Hallows, Lombard Street, London, S.

21 William Rimill of St Botolph, Aldergate, London, B., and Mary Russell of the same, S.

21 Thomas Wilmer of Cobham, Surry, W., and Mary Brown of Tetcham [*sic*] in the said county [*blank*]

21 Joseph Rollo of Xst Church, Middx., B., and Frances Collier of the same, S.

21 John Street of Erith, Kent, B., and Elizabeth Wheeler of St Martin in the Fields, Middx., W.

21 Isaac Sandford of Old Brentford, Middx., B., and Anne Walter of the same, S.

22 William Smith of Twickenham, Middx., W., and Sarah Davis of the same, W.

22 James Hessey of Walthamstow, Essex, B., and Hesther Cambell of the same, S.

22 Isaac Newbery of St Andrew, Holborn, Middx., B., and Elizabeth Gorthen of the same, S.

22 John Long of St Martin in the Fields, Middx., B., and Anne Cromwell of St George, Hanover Square, Middx., S.

22 William Chaddock of St Botolph, Aldersgate, London, W., and Jane Thompson of Tottenham, Middx., W.

27 Roger Rustat of St James, Westminster, Middx., B., and Sarah Lutman of St Luke's, Middx., S.

Mar. 3 Michael Tayleure of St Margaret Pattons, London, B., and Mary Mason of High Ongar, Essex, S.

5 John Worthington of St George in the East, Middx., B., and Mary Miller of the same, S.

5 William Davey of St Gyles in the Fields, Middx., W., and Joyce Houseman of St Clement Danes, Middx., S.

8 William Poole of Warmington, Wilts, B., and Elianor Jellett of St Olave, Southwarke, Surry, S.

8 Thomas Slade of St Saviour, Southwarke, Surry, B., and Jane Carter of the same, W.; by Mr Seagrave

13 Thomas Fearon of St John the Evangelist, Middx., B., and Joanna Wilkey of the same, W.

14 Young *Birdaway* Atkins of St John, Westminster, Middx., B., and Elizabeth Grace of Lambeth, Surry, S.

19 Thomas Hubbard of St Mary, White Chappell, Middx., B., and Elizabeth Saunders of St Catherine Coleman, London, S.

19 George Shelston of St Botolph without Aldgate, Middx., B., and Ann Gentleman of the same, S.

24 Nicholas Miller, B., and Mary Church, S., both of this parish

1737.

Mar. 25 Thomas Fear of St Clement Danes, Middx., B., and Mary Piper of Croydon, Surry, S.

26 Robert Sanders of St James, Westminster, Middx., B., and Mary Brown of the same, W.

1737
Mar. 27 David Hindson of St Martin in the Fields, Middx., B., and Hannah Thomas of the same, S.
30 James Dennis of Richmond, Surry, W., and Sarah Rose of this parish, W.; by Mr Hillman
30 James Beswell of Mitcham, Surry, B., and Elizabeth Smith of Wimbledon, Surry, S.; by Mr Hillman
31 Rice Morgan of Deptford, Kent, B., and Anne Farre of the same, W.; by Mr Hillman
31 James Dowding of St Saviour, Southwarke, Surry, W., and Anne Woodger of St Olave, Southwarke, Surry, S.; by Mr Beachcroft
31 Edward Spurling of Erith, Kent, W., and Isabella Carden of Grays, Essex, W.; by Mr Beachcroft
April 1 James Dennis of Fant [*sic*], Sussex, B., and Sarah Latter of the same, S.; by Mr Bayley
2 Thomas Stock of St George, Hanover Square, Middx., B., and Hannah Baker of Kensington, Middx., S.
3 John Mattocks of St Martin in the Fields, Middx., B., and Elizabeth Douglass of the same, W.
9 Richard Roberts of St Andrew, Holborn, Middx., W., and Mary Labby of the same, S.
10 Robert Littlewood of St Paul, Covent Garden, Middx., B., and Elizabeth Twisk of St James, Westminster, Middx., W.
11 John Kitchin of St Sepulchre, London, B., and Grace Burbridge of the same, S.
11 James Warner of St Mary le Bow, London, B., and Elizabeth Bowler of St Mary, Whitechapel, Midx., W.
11 Thomas Peplow of St Brides, London, B., and Rebecca Smeethes of St Giles in the Fields, Middx., S.
11 William Parsons of St Brides, London, B., and Hannah Bird of Kensington, Middx., S.
11 John Coleman of Strowd, Kent, W., and Susannah Paine of St Giles, Cripplegate, London, W.
12 Edward Boxall of East Wickham, Kent, B., and Ann Staples of the same, S.
12 William Pikes of St Andrew, Holborn, Middx., B., and Margaret Todd of the same, S.
13 William Hyte, B., and Prudence Ireson, S., both of this parish. Banns
14 Thomas Bell of St James, Westminster, Middx., B., and Mary Benson of Kensington, Middx., W.
16 William Bursey of St Saviour, Southwarke, Surry, W., and Sarah Norbury of Christchurch, Surry, W.
17 Kingston Cook of St Saviour, Southwark, Surry, B., and Elizabeth Lunn of the same, S.
18 John Peel of St Margaret, Lincoln, co. Lincoln, and Margaret Athis of St Brides, London, W.
21 Thomas Rice of X^st church, Surry, W., and Elizabeth White of St George the Martyr, Middx., S.
21 Robert Evans of St James, Westminster, Middx., W., and Elizabeth Houghton of the same, S.
22 Joseph Weston of Hagley, co. Worcester, B., and Anne Jennett of the same, S.
23 Phillip Reader of St Andrew, Holborn, Middx., W., and Mary Yeates of the same, S.
24 Thomas Wright of Stoke Newington, Middx., B., and Martha Swain of the same, S.
24 John Davies of All Hallows, Bread Street, London, B., and Elizabeth Saunders of the same, S.

1737

April 27 Charles Stokes of S[t] Vedast als. Foster Lane, London, B., and Jane Healy of S[t] Sepulchre, London, W.

29 Robert Polakely of S[t] Margaret, Westminster, Middx., B., and Ann Carter of the same, S.

29 Charles Lawrence of S[t] Dunstan in the West, London, B., and Mary Maria Daniel of the same, W.

30 Francis Asty of Northaw, co. Herts, B., and Elizabeth Asty of the same, S.

30 Christopher Potticary of Graies, Essex, W., and Elizabeth Honey of S[t] Mary, White Chapel, Middx., W.

May 1 Daniel Brock of S[t] James, Westminster, Middx., W., and Elizabeth Morton of the same, S.

2 Thomas Franklen of Branford, Middx., B., and Johanna Sharper of Stratford, Essex, S.; by M[r] Goodinge

3 Samuel Royle, B., and Gertrude Searle, S., both of this parish. Banns

5 Jacob Gosset of S[t] James, Westminster, Middx., W., and Constance Farr of S[t] Paul, Covent Garden, Middx., S.

5 John Law of Rotherham, co. York, W., and Abigael Moreton of S[t] Michael, Cornhill, London, S.

5 Mathew Lightfoot of S[t] John, Wapping, Middx., B., and Olivea Johnson of the same, S.

6 Frederick Lewis Leightheuser of Richmond, Surry, B., and Elizabeth Salt of S[t] Paul, Covent Garden, Middx., W.

7 Robert Pearce of S[t] Paul, Covent Garden, Middx., W., and Margaret Jacob of Fulham, Middx., W.

8 Michael Free of S[t] Olave, Southwarke, Surry, W., and Mary Lightfoot of the same, S.

9 Richard Simons of Blechingley, Surry, W., and Margaret Feake of S[t] George, Bloomsbury, Middx., S.

10 Robert Glascock of Clavering, Essex, B., and Anne Goose of Trumpington, co. Cambridge, S.

10 Thomas Woolven of S[t] Nicholas, Deptford, Kent, W., and Sarah Meacham of the same, W.

10 Lewen Mellichamp of S[t] James, Westminster, Middx., B., and Kezzia Allen of S[t] Margaret, Westminster, Middx., W.

11 David Griffith of S[t] Andrew, Holborn, Middx., W., and Mary Drury of S[t] Sepulchre, London, W.

11 Richard Peele of Chalgrave, co. Bedford, B., and Ann Embley of the same, S.

12 Thomas Nicholls of S[t] Anne, Westminster, Middx., W., and Catherine Hayworth of S[t] Giles in the Fields, Middx., W.

12 William Lewis of Winchester, Hants, B., and Mary Tovery of the same, S.

14 James Hurst of S[t] Dunstan in the East, London, W., and Anne Saxby of Lingfield, Surry, S.

14 John Blondel of S[t] Mildred, Poultry, London, B., and Susannah Arnaud of S[t] Bennett Fink, London, S.

16 Daniel Winn of S[t] Giles in the Fields, Middx., B., and Margaret Jones of the same, S.

16 George Everard of S[t] George, Hanover Square, Middx., B., and Ann Banks of Andover, Hants, S.

16 Thomas Townshend of S[t] James, Westminster, Middx., B., and Mary Reading of S[t] Mary Somerset, London, S.

18 John Mackie of S[t] Andrew, Holborn, Middx., B., and Sarah Roberts of S[t] Austin, London, S.

19 Joseph Bakewell of Albury, co. Herts, B., and Martha Barcock of S[t] Andrew, Holborn, London, S.

1737
May 19 James Fortune of S[t] Catherine Creed Church, London, B., and Mary Wish of S[t] James, Duke's Place, London, S.
19 Robert Cooke of Navestock, Essex, B., and Elizabeth Martin of Stapleford Abbott, Essex, S.
20 Jeffery Edwards of S[t] Margaret, Lothbury, London, B., and Ann Rigby of the same, S.
22 John Williams of Stratford Le Bow, Middx., B., and Mary Williams of S[t] George, Middx., W.
24 Thomas Paice of Ross, co. Hereford, B., and Margaret Machen of the same, W.
27 Joseph Clarke of S[t] Botolph without Aldgate, London, B., and Penelope Lamb of the same, S.
29 John Wright of S[t] Gregory, London, B., and Ann Martin of the same, S.
29 Alexander Gardner of S[t] Paul, Shadwell, Middx., W., and Mary Fallows of the same, W.
29 Joseph Purt of S[t] Botolph, Bishopsgate, London, B., and Sarah Taylor of the same, S.
30 Stephen Gilly of S[t] Botolph, Bishopsgate, London, W., and Mary Leask of S[t] Andrew, Holborn, Middx., S.
30 Thomas Maskew of S[t] Dionis Backchurch, London, B., and Phillis Bassett of S[t] Clement, East Cheap, London, S.
30 Peter Lenge of S[t] Martin in the Fields, Middx., B., and Martha Tyers of the same, S.
30 William Stephen Skey of S[t] Martin in the Fields, Middx., B., and Margaret Gregory of S[t] Paul, Covent Garden, Middx., S.
31 Edward Minton of S[t] James, Westminster, Middx., B., and Elizabeth Faulkner of the same, S.
June 4 William Elliot of S[t] James, Westminster, Middx., Esq., B., and the Right Hon. Lady Frances Nassau of S[t] George, Hanover Square, Middx., S.
4 William Baker of S[t] Clement Danes, Middx., B., and Horatia Harding of X[st] Church, London, S.
4 Jonathan Rayner of S[t] George, Hanover Square, Middx., B., and Anne Cowley of S[t] James, Westminster, Middx., S.
6 Edward Pollen of S[t] Clement Danes, Middx., B., and Elizabeth Welch of S[t] James, Westminster, Middx., S.; by M[r] Peters
7 William Smith, B., and Sarah Goldsmith, S., both of S[t] Peter, Paul's Wharfe. Banns
8 William Brookes of S[t] Mary le Bone, Middx., W., and Ann Atmar of S[t] James, Westminster, Middx., W.
9 Ralph Parker of All Hallows, London Wall, B., and Mary Clay of S[t] Ethelburgh, London, S.
9 William Lang of Fulham, Middx., B., and Elizabeth Linn of Hamersmith, Middx., S.
9 Potter Cackett of All Hallows, Lombard Street, London, B., and Mary Togwell of the same, S.
11 Daniel Rogers of Richmond, Surry, B., and Elizabeth Baugh of the same, S.
12 George Coulton of S[t] Martin in the Fields, Middx., B., and Ann Walker of S[t] Andrew, Holborn, Middx., S.
13 Thomas Roberts of Ryegate, Surry, B., and Sarah Baker of the same, W.
14 Christoffell le Roy of S[t] Ann, Westminster, Middx., B., and Mary Bullevant of S[t] Giles in the Fields, Middx., S.
16 John Crosier of S[t] Dunstan in the East, London, B., and Mary Flood of S[t] Andrew, Holborn, Middx., S.

1737

June 16 John Farmer of St John, Southwark, Surrey, W., and Mary Matthews of St Dionis Backchurch, London, S.

16 William Bingham of St Anne, Limehouse, Middx., B., and Eleanor Bubb of St Ann without Aldersgate, London, W.

17 Rice Lawrence of St Margaret, Westminster, Middx., B., and Elizabeth Gill of the same, S.

18 Thomas Ives of St James, Clarkenwell, Middx., W., and Ann Lee of the same, W.

18 John Croudson of St Saviour, Southwark, Surrey, B., and Mary Williamson of X^st Church, Surrey, S.

19 Edward Bunce of Sulham, co. Berks, B., and Ann Store of St Mary, Queenhyth, London, S.

21 John Penny of St Andrew Undershaft, London, B., and Mary Arnold of the same, S.

22 John Sley of St Bride's, London, B., and Mary Foster of Hornsey, Middx., S.

23 William Buttery of St Paul, Shadwell, Middx., W., and Mary Lewman of the same, W.

24 George Shearer of St James, Westminster, Middx., B., and Letitia Blackham of the same, W.

26 Sir Richard Anderson of St George the Martyr, Southwarke, Surry, Bart., B., and Mary Hutson of the same, W.

26 Richard Ellis of St James, Westminster, Middx., B., and Alice Forster of the same, S.

29 John Chapman of Rotherhith, Surry, W., and Jane Tow of Eltham, Kent, W.

30 George Talmadge of Staples Inn, London, B., and Mary Weaver of St Sepulchre, Middx., S.

30 Jonathan Daniells of St Andrew, Holborn, London, W., and Mary Lawrence of St George, Bloomsbury, Middx., W.

July 2 Jonathan Bradley of St George, Hanover Square, Middx., B., and Mary Nickols of the same, S.

5 Edgar Edlyne of St Alphage, London, W., and Ann Barradell of St Dunstan in the West, London, W.

6 William Lucas of Croydon, Surry, W., and Mary Clear of the same, W.

7 George Wentworth of St Andrew, Holborn, London, B., and Sarah Tothaker of the same, S.

8 Samuel Banner of St Thomas, Southwark, Surry [*blank*], and Mary Bazson of the same, S.

8 Paul Gosset of X^st Church, London, B., and Mary Chandler of St John's, Clarkenwell, Middx., S.

10 John Box of St Sepulchre, Middx., B., and Mary Lazenby of the same, S.

12 Moses Williams of X^st Church, Surry, W., and Sarah Elgar of the same, W.; by Mr Nickoll

14 Thomas Cowlard of Deptford, Kent, B., and Sarah Christopher of Seal, Kent, S.; by Mr Bayley

14 Edward Hammers of St Martin in the Fields, Middx., B., and Joyce Green of the same, W.; by Mr Bayley

14 James Dawson of Aldermanbury, London, B., and Elizabeth Hardman of Stoke Newington, Middx., S.; by Mr Bayley

17 Thomas Storer of St George, Bloomsbury, Middx., W., and Ann Gulliver of St Botolph, Bishopsgate, London, W.; by Mr Worlich

18 Sampson Barber of St George, Hanover Square, Middx., B., and Sarah Peirson of the same, S.; by Mr Worlich

22 Thomas Barrett of St James, Westminster, Middx., B., and Elizabeth Blissett of the same, S.; by Mr Bayley

1737
July 23 Charles Marsh of Winslow, co. Bucks, W., and Jane Herbert of St Clement Danes, Middx., S.; by Mr Bayley
24 Martin Clarke of St Giles in the Fields, Middx., B., and Margaret Stanbury of the same, S.
24 Francis Cranwell of East Greenwich, Kent, B., and Margaret Reeves of the same, S.
26 Daniel Cownden of St Saviours, Southwark, Surry, B., and Hannah Whitpaine of the same, W.
26 George Wright of Ilford, Essex, W., and Martha Davis of Low Layton, Essex, S.
27 Joshua Pearson of St Mary, White Chapel, Middx., B., and Jane Corter of St Martin in the Fields, Middx., S.
27 John Shaw of St Martin in the Fields, Middx., W., and Beatrix Gardiner of St Paul, Covent Garden, Middx., S.
30 Charles Lamy of Egham, Surry, B., and Mary Bissell of Putney, Surry, S.
31 James Sufflee of St Dunstan, Stepney, Middx., B., and Abigael Briggs of the same, S.
Aug. 1 George Charrington of Windsor, co. Berks, B., and Mary Phillips of St Dunstan in the West, London, S.
1 Henry Loat of Wandsworth, Surry, B., and Mary Peircy of Clapham, Surry, S.
2 Quested Simmons of St Stephen, Coleman Street, London, B., and Mary Fosters of St Leonard, Shoreditch, Middx., S.
4 James King of St Mary Magdalen, Bermondsey, Surry, B., and Hannah Minett of the same, W.
4 William Vincent of St Mary, White Chapel, Middx., W., and Jane Furney of the same, W.
5 John Matthews of St George, Southwark, Surry, B., and Elizabeth Hiller of the same, S.
7 John Winchester of St Margaret Moses, London, B., and Elizabeth Derry of All Hallows, Thames Street, London, S.
9 Richard Hudson of St Olave, Southwarke, Surry, B., and Jane Mills of the same, W.
9 Gervas Smith of St Paul's, Covent Garden, Middx., B., and Mary Foull of Ewell, Surry, S.
12 Thomas Rumbold of St Catherine Cree Church, London, B., and Sarah Stevens of St Clement Danes, Middx., S.
13 Edward Baxter of St Martin in the Fields, Middx., W., and Anne Edwards of the same, W.
16 Philip Mannooch of St Saviour, Southwark, Surry, B., and Elizabeth Nelson of the same, S.
17 Henry Agas of Low Layton, Essex, B., and Elizabeth Jackson of the same, S.
18 Samuel Crunden of St Margaret, Westminster, Middx., B., and Jane Walker of St John the Evangelist, Middx., S.
19 William Calvert of the Middle Temple, London, B., and Catherine York of St Martin in the Fields, Middx., S.
20 John Macleod of St Dunstan, Stepney, Middx., B., and Jane Mackenzie of St Catherine by the Tower of London, S.
21 Edward Vaughan of Xst Church, Surry, B., and Elizabeth Newman of St Mary, White Chapel, Middx., S.
21 Thomas Cam of St George, Hanover Square, Middx., B., and Emma Barton of St Botolph, Aldersgate, London, S.
21 Detlef Miller of St Stephen, Walbrooke, London, B., and Dorothy Spooner of the same, S.
23 Benjamin Odling of St Mary, Rotherhith, Surry, B., and Ursula Pettyt of the same, S.

1737

Aug. 24 William Barlow of Trinity in the Minories, London, B., and Mary Cater of the same, S.

31 John Castolow of Low Layton, Essex, B., and Susanna Flower of the same, W.

31 Arthur Eaves of Coleshill, co. Warwick, B., and Anne Tysell of St James, Westminster, Middx., S.

Sept. 1 Thomas Challo of St Ann, Limehouse, Middx., B., and Mary Powell of the same, S.

2 William Holton of Aylesbury, co. Bucks, W., and Mary Wheeler of Rotherhith, Surry, W.

3 Christopher Yates of St Paul, Covent Garden, Middx., B., and Frances Horwell of St Clement Danes, Middx., S.

4 James Promfritt of Richmond, Surry, B., and Mary English of St James, Westminster, Middx., S.

5 William Arthur of St Thomas the Apostle, London, B., and Mary Lovick of St Catherine, Coleman Street, London, S.

6 David Davis of St Dunstan in the East, London, B., and Elizabeth Hely of the same, S.

8 Peter Fontanan of St Dunstan, Stepney, Middx., B., and Lucy Elizabeth Roullet of Xst Church, Middx., W.

8 John Francis of St John, Surry, B., and Elizabeth Dungate of Rygate, Surry, S.

13 Thomas Town of St George, Bloomsbury, Middx., B., and Margaret Hinchliff of the same, W.

14 Moses Allnutt of St Martin Vintry, London, B., and Abigail Shaw of the same, W.

15 Daniel Monk of St Paul, Deptford, Kent, W., and Barbara Christopher of Seal, Kent, S.

15 Thomas Veal of St Martin in the Fields, Middx., B., and Mary Barrett of the same, S.

15 John Wilkinson of St Martin in the Fields, Middx., B., and Elizabeth Hopegood of the same, S.

16 Thomas Davis of St George, Hanover Square, Middx., B., and Elizabeth Perks of the same, W.

19 Thomas Short of St Dunstan, Stepney, Middx., B., and Ann Christian of the same, S.

19 Edward Muns of East Ham, Essex, W., and Eleanor Partridge of St Bride's, London, W.

23 James Lowther of Xst Church, London, B., and Martha Penavayre of Maxfield, Cheshire, S.

23 Robert Gladdish of Ash, Kent [*blank*], and Elizabeth Dunstan of the same, S.

24 John Schultz of St Clement Danes, Middx., W., and Hannah Harris of Islington, Middx., S.

24 Jonas Rowlandson of St Dunstan, Stepney, Middx., B., and Elizabeth Hewitt of the same, S.

25 John Pecknell of Arundell, Sussex, W., and Anne Heath of the same, W.

26 Edward Sawyer of Cookham, co. Berks, B., and Mary Coleman of St Swithin, London, S.

26 Thomas Stratton of All Hallows, co. Herts, W., and Elizabeth Faint of Cheshunt, co. Herts, W.

26 Lewis Jenkins of Dunwick, co. Glamorgan, B., and Frances Wharram of Wharram Pacy [*sic*], co. York, S.

26 Daniel Prosser of Lambeth, Surry, B., and Jane Sutton of the same, S.

26 Henry Lucas of St George, Hanover Square, Middx., B., and Catherine James of the same, S.

1737

Sept. 27 John Gardner of S[t] Margaret, Westminster, Middx., B., and Mary Debatt of the same, S.; by M[r] Bailey

29 John Davis of S[t] Anne, Westminster, Middx., B., and Esther Hammond of the same, S.

Oct. 1 Thomas White of S[t] James, Westminster, Middx., B., and Elizabeth Williams of the same, W.

3 George Roffey of Sevenoake, Kent, B., and Sarah Norton of the same, S.

4 Thomas Cole of X[st] Church, Surry, B., and Harriot Howard of S[t] Margaret, Westminster, Middx., S.

4 John James of S[t] Andrew, Holborn, Middx., B., and Ann King of the same, S.

6 John Fell of S[t] Dunstan in the East, London, B., and Dorothy Smith of S[t] Mary Abchurch, London, S.

6 Thomas Brown of S[t] Mary le Strand, Midx., B., and Ann Beven of S[t] James, Westminster, Middx., S.

9 Septimus Loveday of Chelsea, Middx., B., and Ann Duke of the same, S.

11 William Woodard of S[t] Olave, Southwark, Surry, B., and Rachael Stephens of the same, S.

11 Philip Durnford of S[t] Mary le Strand, Middx., B., and Mary Drew of S[t] Ann, Westminster, Middx., S.

12 Francis Reece of S[t] Giles in the Fields, Middx., B., and Elizabeth Davis of the same, W.

13 Thomas Bourne of S[t] Luke, Middx., W., and Catharine Collier of S[t] Botolph, Aldgate, London, S.

13 John Sedgwick of S[t] Margaret, Westminster, Midx., W., and Grace Berry of the same, S.

13 David Humphreys of Hackney, Middx., B., and Anne Pearce of the same, S.

13 John Hart of Romford, Essex, B., and Mary Davies of the same, W.

16 Joseph Burton of S[t] Saviour, Southwarke, Surry, B., and Elizabeth Lambert of S[t] Margaret, Westminster, Middx., S.

16 John Lee of All Hallows, Lombard Street, London, B., and Sarah Gurnell of S[t] Leonard, Shoreditch, Middx., S.

17 William Kyte of S[t] Mildred, Bread Street, London, B., and Mary Beaucheamp of Wandsworth, Surry, S.

18 James Stedman of S[t] George, Bloomsbury, Middx., B., and Catherine Triggs of the same, S.

18 Richard Martin of Sunbury, Middx., B., and Anne King of the same, S.

19 John Randall of Woolwich, Kent, W., and Mary Dilkes of S[t] Sepulchre, London, S.

21 Philip Aubin of S[t] Catherine by the Tower of London, B., and Jane Brock of the same, W.

22 David Davies of S[t] Martin in the Fields, Middx., W., and Elizabeth Perry of S[t] James, Westminster, Middx., S.

25 Samuel Simmons of Bosham, Sussex, B., and Mary Birch of the same, S.

29 Robert Brough of S[t] Paul, Shadwell, Middx., B., and Mary Cannaway of the same, S.

31 James Townsend of Chelsea, Middx., B., and Sarah Jones of the same, W.

Nov. 1 John Buteux of S[t] Botolph, Bishopsgate, London, B., and Mary Moore of S[t] Dunstan, Stepney, Middx., W.

1 Robert Paradine of S[t] Botolph, Aldgate, Middx., W., and Elizabeth Savage of S[t] Mary, White Chapell, Middx., S.

2 Thomas Norris of Lambeth, Surry, B., and Anne Wright of the same, S.

1737

Nov. 3 Thomas Sedgwick of S[t] George, Southwark, Surry, W., and Sarah Sanders of the Little Minories, London, S.

3 John Axe of All Hallows Barking, London, B., and Mary Wilson of the same, S.

5 Edward Bryant of S[t] James, Westminster, Middx., B., and Mary Alchorne of the same, S.

6 Thomas Schacklady of S[t] Luke, Middx., B., and Mary Harrison of the same, S.

7 John Royston of S[t] Leonard, Shoreditch, Middx., W., and Elizabeth Harraby* of X[st] Church, Middx., S.

8 Adam Wheeler of S[t] Mary, White Chapel, Middx., B., and Sarah Crosley of S[t] Leonard, Shoreditch, Middx., S.

8 John Treadway of S[t] Ann, Westminster, Middx., B., and Armin Bower of S[t] Paul, Covent Garden, Middx., W.

8 John Skinner of Sundrich, Kent, B., and Mary Overy of the same, S.

9 Robert Paine of S[t] Margaret, Westminster, Middx., W., and Mary Gray of S[t] Giles in the Fields, Middx., W.

10 John Boulton of S[t] Mary, White Chapel, Middx., W., and Jane Gilkes of Fulham, Middx., W.

10 Thomas Inwood of Church Cobham, Surry, B., and Susannah Withread of the same, S.

10 William Kerr of this parish, B., and Elizabeth Day of the same, W.

13 Stephen Inwood of Sherness, Kent, B., and Elizabeth Farley of the same, S.

14 William Johnson of S[t] Mary, White Chapel, Middx., B., and Anne Hall of the same, S.

17 David Duncomb of S[t] Dunstan, Stepney, Middx., B., and Margaret Clemens of the same, S.

17 John Chantry of S[t] Saviour, Southwark, Surry, W., and Hannah Shepherd of the same, W.

17 John Martin of S[t] Giles, Cripplegate, London, B., and Elizabeth Jones of S[t] James, Clarkenwell, Middx., W.

18 Thomas Chilton of S[t] Giles in the Fields, Middx., B., and Martha Raper of S[t] Mary le Bone, Middx., S.

23 Thomas Hodgson of S[t] Anne, Limehouse, Middx., W., and Mary Chaplin of the same, S.

24 William Sheappard of S[t] Martin in the Fields, Middx., B., and Anne Smith of S[t] Paul, Covent Garden, Middx., S.

24 Samuel Phelps of Fulham, Middx., B., and Mary Morris of the same, W.

24 Stephen Chilman of Wrotham, Kent, B., and Ann Baldwyn of the same, W.

24 Michael Evans of S[t] Mary le Savoy, Middx., B., and Elizabeth Ainsworth of S[t] Giles in the Fields, Middx., S.

24 John Hume of S[t] Botolph, Aldgate, London, B., and Elizabeth Buckett of S[t] Mary Magdalen, Bermondsey, Surry, S.

26 John Summers of S[t] Mary le Bow, London, B., and Elizabeth Bakewell of the same, S.

26 John Maskall of Lambeth, Surrey, B., and Ann Purvis of the same, S.

27 John Pittom of S[t] George, Hanover Square, Middx., W., and Hannah Gale of S[t] Anne, Soho, Middx., S.

27 Richard Whytaker of S[t] Mary, White Chapel, Middx., W., and Elizabeth Lewis of the same, W.

27 Benjamin Delahay of S[t] Bennet Fink, London, B., and Mary Pashley of S[t] John the Evangelist, Westminster, Middx., S.

28 Richard Harrington of Endfield, Middx., B., and Elizabeth Bagshaw of the same, S.

* "Harrowby" in margin.—Ed.

1737

Nov. 29 Thomas Button of Finchley, Middx., B., and Ursula Elmore of the same, S.
29 Edward Scarlett, jun^r, of St Anne, Westminster, Middx., B., and Ann Wright of the same, S.; by Dr Thomas

Dec. 1 Thomas Bray of St Dunstan in the West, London, W., and Elianor Stokes of the same, S.
3 Henry Maynard of Mortlake, Surry, B., and Sarah Westwood of the same, S.
5 Thomas Bennett of St George, Hanover Square, Middx., W., and Cary Dear of the same, W.
6 John Lermont of Kingston upon Thames, Surry, B., and Sarah Hambleton of Hackney, Middx., S.
6 Ezra Jackson of St George, Southwarke, Surry, W., and Martha Wynn Pembroke of the same, S.
6 Tibal Bell of St Andrew, Holborn, London, B., and Martha Smith of St Botolph, Aldgate, London, S.
8 William McDonald of St Edmund the King, London, B., and Elizabeth Lowther of the same, S.
9 James Lewin of St George, Hanover Square, Middx., B., and Catherine Clann of the same, S.
9 James Lawson of St Clement Danes, Middx., B., and Frances Frederick of St Margaret, Westminster, Middx., S.
9 St John Hawkings of St Leonard, Shoreditch, Middx., W., and Frances Clark of the same, W.
11 John Snelling of All Hallows, Bread Street, London, W., and Elizabeth How of the same, S.
12 Richard Vincent of St James, Westminster, Middx., W., and Elizabeth Binks of St Paul, Covent Garden, Middx., S.
15 Thomas Warland of Fulham, Middx., B., and Lydia Dwight of the same, S.
16 William Roberts of Poplar in Stepny, Middx., B., and Sarah Long of the same, W.
20 John Hawes of St Giles in the Fields, Middx., B., and Elizabeth Potts of St James, Westminster, Midx., S.
20 William Davis of All Hallows the Great, London, B., and Mary Angell of Totness, Devon, S.
21 John James of St James, Clarkenwell, Middx., B., and Susan Wright of St Andrew, Holborn, London, S.
24 William Churchill of Greenford, Middx., B., and Mary Early of the same, W.
24 Thomas Head of St Luke, Middx., B., and Sarah Loomes of St Mary, Islington, Middx., S.
25 James Arthur of St John, Southwark, Surry, B., and Constance Furminger of St Mary, Newington, Middx., S.
25 Thomas Eyre of St Dunstan in the West, London, B., and Sarah Wigmore of St Andrew, Holborn, London, S.
28 John Poulter of Hampton, Middx., B., and Ann Ray of the same, S.; by Mr Worlich
29 Samuel Johnstone of St Paul, Covent Garden, Middx., B., and Anne Bourk of St Martin in the Fields, Middx., S.
29 Joseph Handley of St Albans, co. Herts, W., and Sarah Hartrup of Deptford, Kent, S.
29 Samuel Trowell of the Inner Temple, London, B., and Mary Goodwyn of St Sepulchre, London, S.
30 John Ewer Finch of Wilsdon, Middx., B., and Elizabeth White of the same, S.
30 John Edwards of Hayes in Kent, B., and Margaret Walker of Greenwich, Kent, S.

1737-8

Jan. 2 Richard Cutler of S[t] George, Bloomsbury, Middx., W., and Ann Francis of the same, S.

3 William Purvis of S[t] John, Southwark, Surry, B., and Joanna Langley of the same, S.; by M[r] Worlich

4 Isaac Birdwhissell of S[t] Sepulchre, London, B., and Sophia Sargeant of S[t] Bride's, London, S.

4 Samuel Ore of East Greenwich, Kent, B., and Elizabeth Williams of S[t] James, Westminster, Middx., S.

5 Richard Parker of S[t] Mary Magdalen, Bermondsey, Surry, W., and Anna Lidyeard of S[t] John, Wapping, Middx., W.

5 Robert Newton of S[t] Martin in the Fields, Middx., B., and Mary Warren of the same, S.

5 Cornelius Ford of S[t] Andrew, Holborn, London, W., and Mary Kyte of S[t] Sepulchre, London, S.

5 John Cabread of S[t] Dunstan in the West, London, W., and Sarah Baker of the same, S.

5 Richard Burchard of S[t] George, Hanover Square, Middx., W., and Mary Thomas of the same, S.

7 William Cosser of S[t] Ann, Limehouse, Middx., B., and Ann Young of S[t] Paul, Shadwell, Middx., S.

7 Adam Steward of S[t] Mary, Rotherhyth, Surry, B., and Mary Harding of S[t] Botolph, Aldgate, London, W.

7 Richard Pool of S[t] Paul, Covent Garden, Middx., B., and Elizabeth Halstead of the same, W.

7 Benjamin Vines of X[st] Church, Surry, B., and Ann Sparrow of the same, S.

7 Samuel Hearne of S[t] Michael, Crooked lane, London, B., and Diana Rown of S[t] Catherine Coleman, London, S.

8 John Morton of S[t] Ann, Westminster, Middx., B., and Mary White of the same, W.; by D[r] Thomas

9 Henry Leigh of S[t] Bennet, Grace Church, London, B., and Sarah Crow of the same, S.

11 Philip Vinsley of S[t] Andrew, Holborn, London, B., and Agatha Norris of the same, S.

11 Charles La Fortune of S[t] Martin in the Fields, Middx., B., and Sarah Kendall of S[t] Faith's, London, S.

12 James Hawley of Paulus Perry, co. Northampton, W., and Elinor Turner of S[t] John, Wapping, Middx., S.

14 Samuel Ouldknow of S[t] Giles in the Fields, Middx., B., and Elizabeth Hopkins of the same, S.

17 John Townsend of S[t] Martin in the Fields, Middx., B., and Ann Williams of S[t] Andrew, Holborn, Middx., S.

17 Benjamin Picart de la Forte of X[st] Church, Middx., B., and Mary Elliott of S[t] Saviour's, Southwark, Surry, S.

18 Robert Carter of S[t] Ann, Westminster, Middx., B., and Anne Battey of S[t] George, Hanover Square, Middx., S.

19 John Turner of Ealing, Middx., B., and Elizabeth Hallford of S[t] Margaret, Westminster, Middx. [*blank*]

20 Edward Horne of Eversham, co. Worcester, B., and Anne Jew of the same, S.

26 George Dobbins of S[t] George, Bloomsbury, Middx., B., and Frances Coggin of S[t] Thomas the Apostle, London, S.

26 George Townsend of S[t] James, Westminster, Middx., W., and Alice Wright of Bedford Row, Middx., S.

30 Peter Charles Leviez of S[t] Giles in the Fields, Middx., B., and Elizabeth Boney of S[t] Paul, Covent Garden, Middx., S.

31 John Frederick Lampe of S[t] George, Hanover Square, Middx., B., and Isabella Young of the same, S.

1737-8

Feb. 2 Jeremiah Bowne of Hackney, Middx., B., and Martha Coose of the same, W.

2 Andrew William Bourne of the Liberty of the Rolls, London, B., and Sarah Templer of S[t] Clement Danes, Middx., S.

2 Henry Gellibrand of S[t] Martin in the Fields, Middx., B., and Elizabeth Hayes of the same, W.

4 William Callcott of Kensington, Middx., B., and Sarah Long of the same, S.

4 John Watts of S[t] Leonard, Shoreditch, Middx., W., and Elizabeth Claudius of the same, W.

5 John Mathews of S[t] Swithin, London, B., and Mary Greenham of the same, W.

7 Thomas Hunt of S[t] Martin, Ironmonger lane, London, B., and Sarah Rainsford of the same, W.

7 Thomas Ingree of Stanford Rivers, Essex, B., and Mary Curtis of S[t] Giles in the Fields, Middx., S.

7 Thomas Reynolds of S[t] Lawrence Pountney, London, B., and Margaret Luntley of the same, S.

8 John Peploe of S[t] Magnus by London Bridge, B., and Ann Chandler of the same, S.

9 William Hollier of S[t] Pancras, Soper lane, London, B., and Marguerritta Wynne of Deptford, Kent, S.

9 John Trymmer of S[t] Vedast, Foster Lane, London, B., and Elizabeth Seyliard of S[t] Saviour, Southwark, S.

9 Benjamin Foulgeir* of this parish, B., and Sarah Sell of Fulham, Middx., S.

12 Andrew Young of S[t] George in the East, Middx., B., and Hannah Matthews of Whitny, co. Oxford, S.

13 Francis Pearce of S[t] Botolph, Aldersgate, London, B., and Judith Willmott of the same, W.

13 William Driver of Bostow, Surry, B., and Ann Dodd of Blechingly, Surry, S.

13 William Holt of S[t] John the Evangelist, Middx., W., and Frances Parke of the same, S.

13 Thomas Mathews of S[t] Sepulchre, Middx., B., and Ann Higgins of S[t] Andrew, Holborn, London, S.

14 Solomon Goldsmith of S[t] Sepulchre, London, B., and Elizabeth Arnold of S[t] Saviour, Southwarke, S.

14 Nicholas Smith of S[t] James, Duke's Place, London, B., and Mary Eaves of S[t] Michael, Queenhythe, London, S.; by M[r] Beachcroft

14 John Killock of Hampstead, Middx., B., and Elizabeth Hack of Edmonton, Middx., S.; by M[r] Beachcroft

14 Moses Griffith of the Precinct of White Fryers, London, B., and Mary Williams of S[t] Saviour, Southwark, W.; by M[r] Beachcroft

14 Michael Oddy of Grimstead, Essex, B., and Hannah Crabe of Shalley, Essex, S.; by do.

14 John Hudson of S[t] John, Wapping, Middx., W., and Catharine Paxton of S[t] George in the East, Middx., S.; by do.

14 Jacob Morgan of S[t] George, Hanover Square, Middx., B., and Sarah Smith of S[t] James, Westminster, Middx., S.; by do.

28 John Blake of Isleworth, Middx., B., and Elizabeth Nicholson of this parish, S.

Mar. 5 William Lacey of S[t] Stephen, Colman Street, London, B., and Elizabeth Harrison of Hackney, Middx., S.

* "Foulgier" in the margin.—ED.

1737-8

Mar. 9 John Bovell of St George, Middx., W.,* and Mary Needham of St Catherine by the Tower of London, S.

16 Thomas Piner of Clewer, co. Berks, W., and Elizabeth Parish of Easher, Surry, W.; by Mr Dolben, Vicar of Stoke Poges, co. Bucks

23 Robert Erskine of Chatham, Kent, B., and Mary Anderson of the same, S.; by Mr Hillman of St Paul's

23 Richard Kinnersley of St Dunstan in the West, London, B., and Sarah Peck of the same, S.; by Mr Hillman of St Paul's

1738.

Mar. 28 John Jones of St Olave, Southwarke, W., and Eleanor Jennings of Clapham, Surry, S.

28 Isaac Hardy of Ham, Essex, B., and Elizabeth Manchester of the same, W.

30 Joseph Hurt of St Gregory, London, B., and Frances Fuller of St Botolph, Aldersgate, London, S.

April 1 Francis Wynantz of St Mary Bothaw, London, B., and Margaretta Morgan of Norton Folgate, Middx., W.

2 William Burgess of St John, Wapping, Middx., W., and Elizabeth Bainbridge of St Mary le Bow, London, S.

3 Lewis Bowen of this parish, B., and Joanna Smith of the same, S.

3 Thomas Hale of Dartford, Kent, W., and Mary Beest of Crayford, Kent, S.

3 Richard Hedger of X^st^ Church, Middx., B., and Ann Matthews of Taplow, co. Bucks, S.

3 William Wingrove of St Andrew, Holborn, Middx., B., and Jane Rayndolls of the same, S.

3 Nathaniel Roberts of St Stephen, Coleman Street, London, B., and Mary Crittall of Crutched Friars, London, S.

4 Samuel Savage of the Liberty of the Tower of London, B., and Martha Fann of St Stephen, Coleman Street, London, S.

4 Edmund Borman of Tottenham High Cross, Middx., B., and Sarah Lacey of Hackney, Middx., S.

6 Thomas Parker of Goldhanger, Essex, B., and Sarah Swain of the same, W.

6 Thomas Sanderson of Chelsea, Middx., B., and Martha Maddock of the same, S.

10 James Coleman of Luton, co. Bedford, B., and Ann Burt of the same, S.

10 Faustin Puddefort of Redburn, co. Herts, B., and Mary Ashby of Luton, co. Bedford, S.

11 John Ferguson of St Botolph, Aldgate, London, B., and Catherine Turner of the same, W.

13 Charles Auterac of St Ann, Westminster, Middx., W., and Sarah Martin of St Sepulchre, London, W.

13 Riches Girling of Shipdhan, Norfolk, B., and Rose Frances of St Danes, Westminster, Middx., S.

13 Cleave Greenhill of Abbots Langley, co. Herts, clerk, W., and Mary Smith of Crutched Friars, London, S.; by the Rev. Mr Ramsey

13 William Cook of St John, Wapping, Middx., W., and Mary Clegg of the same, W.

14 John Blake of X^st^ Church, London, B., and Sarah Bedingfield of Hornsey, Middx., S.

16 Benjamin Jones of St George, Middx., W., and Mary Hughes of St George the Martyr, Surry, W.

* "W." written over an erasure.—ED.

1738

April 16 James Perry of S[t] James, Westminster, Middx., B., and Elizabeth Robinson of S[t] Olave, Hart Street, London, S.; by D[r] Thomas

19 George Hewson of Fulham, Middx., W., and Mary Harrison of Chiswick, Middx. [*blank*]; by D[r] Thomas

19 Joseph Jackson of New Town, Cumberland, W., and Margaret Benn of Well, Norfolk, S.

20 Nicholas Yearley of Ockham, Surry, W., and Rachael Hallett of Chiswick, Middx., W.

20 John Partridge of S[t] George, Middx., W., and Anne Stace of S[t] Sepulchre, London, S.

20 Alexander Murray of Thames Ditton, Surry, B., and Elizabeth Heath of Farnham, Surry, S.

20 Robert Speaks of Fetcham, Surry, B., and Elizabeth Hale of the same, S.

21 Richard Sewell of S[t] Mary Staining, London, B., and Sarah Mitchell of the same, S.

24 Patrick Barry of S[t] Sepulchre's, London, B., and Catherine Lane of S[t] George, Middx., W.

25 Edward Burford of S[t] George, Southwarke, Surry, W., and Elizabeth Copper of S[t] Andrew Undershaft, London, S.

27 Robert Morgan of S[t] Michael le Querne, London, B., and Mary Chapman of the same, S.

28 Archibald Campbell of S[t] Olave, Southwarke, B., and Elizabeth Hollis of S[t] Thomas, Southwarke, Surry, S.

28 William Carson of Ewell, Surrey, W., and Mary Mason of Epsom, Surry, S.

May 4 John Quiney of S[t] Leonard, Shoreditch, Middx., B., and Eleanor Greenhalgh of the same, W.

8 William Badcock of Tetcott, Devon, B., and Mary Shingle of S[t] Mary le Bone, Middx., S.

9 Henry Chapman of Eastling, Kent, B., and Milbrow Weaver of Otterden, Kent, S.

9 John Pancutt of S[t] Mary, Newington, Surry, B., and Catherine Fuller of Headington, co. Oxford, S.

9 Robert Cumber of S[t] George, Hanover Square, Middx., B., and Martha Mantle of Charlton, Kent, S.

11 John Hoffman of S[t] Olave, Old Jewry, London, B., and Mary Orme of S[t] Andrew, Holborn, London, S.

11 Edward Brown Atherton of S[t] James, Westminster, Middx., B., and Jane Williams of S[t] Mary le Bone, Middx., W.

13 John Batcheler of Stepney, Middx., B., and Mary Magdalen Gourgas of the Artillery Ground, London, S.

14 James Morgan of S[t] Andrew, Holborn, Middx., B., and Frances Collyn of the same, S.

14 John Poole of S[t] Dunstan in the West, London, B., and Mary Langley of the same, W.

16 John Andrews of West Ham, Essex, B., and Mary Lowe of the same, S.; by M[r] Worlich

16 Richard Allen of S[t] James, Westminster, Middx., B., and Jane Bird of S[t] Mary le Bone, Middx., S.; by M[r] Worlich

18 John Smith of Iver, co. Bucks, W., and Esther Watkins of S[t] Mary, Aldermanbury, London, W.

20 Robert Skinner of X[st] Church, London, B., and Sophia Browning of Offley, co. Herts, S.

20 Jasper Spencer of S[t] Andrew, Holborn, London, W., and Mary Oseland of S[t] Sepulchre, London, W.

20 John George Elliott of S[t] Margaret, Westminster, Middx., W., and Lucy Clements of S[t] John the Evangelist, Westminster, Middx., S.

1738

May 21 Richard Jesson of St Martin in the Fields, Middx., B., and Sarah Cope of the same, S.

22 Thomas Howell of St Mary Magdalen, Bermondsey, Surry, B., and Mary Line of St John the Evangelist, Middx., S.

23 John Saunders of St Stephen, Coleman Street, London, B., and Hannah Groves of Hertford, co. Hertford, S.

23 Joseph Jarvis of St George, Hanover Square, Middx., B., and Anne Belles of Xst Church, London, S.

24 Thomas Cotes of St Martin in the Fields, Middx., B., and Mary Ayres of the same, S.

25 Henry Moseley of Crayford, Kent, B., and Elizabeth Gilbert of the same, S.

25 Elias Venassell of St James, Westminster, Middx., W., and Ann Pickering of the same, W.

25 Thomas Hammond of St Martin in the Fields, Middx., W., and Margaret Stone of the same, S.

25 Charles Young of St George the Martyr, Middx., W., and Mary Bettesworth of the same, W.

25 John Bird of St Saviour, Southwarke, Surry, B., and Elizabeth Bellow of St George the Martyr, Surrey, W.

26 Gerard Bromley of Charleton, Kent, B., and Hannah Dawson of the same, W.

27 Richard Langford of St James, Westminster, Middx., B., and Elizabeth Threlkald of the same, S.

29 Richard Goring of Sunbury, Middx., B., and Hannah Heather of Chiswick, Middx., S.

30 Thomas Ravis of Uxbridge, Middx., B., and Sarah Baldwyn of the same, W.

June 1 John Vaughan of St James, Westminster, Middx., W., and Jane Bullen of the same, W.

1 John Halaway of St Saviour, Southwarke, Surry, B., and Mary Masterman of the same, W.

1 Robert Lewin of St Mary Aldermary, London, W., and Sarah Kirke of St Helen, London, S.

6 Richard Eccleston of Liverpool, Lancashire, B., and Rebecca Summers of the same, S.

8 James Sherwood of Xst Church, London, W., and Alice Watts of St Dunstan, Stepney, Middx., S.

9 William Shirley of Chertsey, Surry, W., and Sarah Yoeill of Lambeth, Surry, S.

11 William Symmonds of St Mary Somerset, London, B., and Catharine Cornish of the same, S.

11 Richard William Thompson of St Anne, Blackfryars, London, B., and Alice Parker of St Giles, Cripplegate, London, S.

12 John Harmar of Hadley, Kent, B., and Elizabeth Miles of the same, S.

13 John Cartlitch of St Giles in the Fields, Middx., B., and Elizabeth Rogers of St Ann, Soho, Middx., S.

15 William Rufus Chetwood of St Paul, Covent Garden, Middx., W., and Anne Brett of the same, S.

15 John Bennett of St Andrew, Holborn, London, B., and Elizabeth Ray of St Olave, Southwarke, S.

20 William Smith of Greenwich, Kent, B., and Mary Elmes of St Giles, Cripplegate, Middx., S.

21 Christopher Dent of St Bartholomew the Less, London, B., and Elizabeth Fuller of St James, Clerkenwell, Middx., S.

21 Richard Beard of St Ann, Westminster, Middx., W., and Elizabeth Bishop of St Giles in the Fields, Middx., S.

1738
June 21 John Daves of S[t] Martin in the Fields, Middx., W., and Martha Moore of S[t] Bartholomew the Less, London, W.
22 John Forman of S[t] James, Westminster, Middx., B., and Ann Coleby of S[t] George the Martyr, Surrey, S.
23 William Edmonds of S[t] Ann, Blackfriers, London, W., and Anne Brockbank of S[t] Andrew, Holborn, Middx., W.
25 William York of S[t] Martin in the Fields, Middx., B., and Martha Bishop of S[t] Paul, Covent Garden, Middx., S.
25 Joshua Pearson of S[t] Michael, Wood Street, London, W., and Amey Clarke of S[t] Botolph, Aldgate, London, W.
26 William Bell of S[t] Mary Bothaw, London, B., and Mary Field of the same, S.
28 John Coulty of S[t] Clement Danes, Middx., B., and Mary Westmorland of S[t] George the Martyr, Middx., S.
July 2 Richard Whitfield of Grays Inn, Middx., B., and Sarah Mansell of S[t] Luke's, Middx., S.
3 Francis Davies of S[t] Bride's, London, B., and Sarah Gough of Hampstead, Middx., S.
3 Julian Onfuy of S[t] Giles in the Fields, Middx., W., and Mary Ann Brewer of the same, W.
4 Thomas White of Scarborough, co. York, B., and Sarah Lane of S[t] Catherine by the Tower of London, S.
6 Robert Nobs of Wareham, Norfolk, B., and Sarah Ranby of S[t] James, Westminster, Middx., S.; by M[r] Worlich
6 William May of Eshire, Surry, B., and Letitia Thomas of the same, S.; by M[r] Worlich
6 John Reeves of S[t] James, Westminster, Middx., W., and Elizabeth Steemson of the same, W.; by M[r] Evans
6 Phillip Apps of S[t] James, Clerkenwell, Middx., W., and Mary Rhodes of S[t] Pancras, Middx., S.; by the same
9 Thomas Stanly Browne of S[t] Mary Abchurch, London, B., and Elizabeth Oustin of S[t] Mary, Aldermanbury, London, W.
10 Joacim Oaker of S[t] Andrew Undershaft, London, B., and Mary Lord of Hampstead, Middx., S.
13 William Lowen of S[t] Mary, White Chappel, Middx., W., and Elizabeth Newbould of the same, W.
13 Joseph Farrah of S[t] Botolph, Billingsgate, London, B., and Elizabeth Scowen of the same, W.
15 Charles Buchanan of All Hallows, Bread Street, London, W., and Elizabeth Brearley of S[t] Mildred, Bread Street, London, W.; by M[r] Worlich
21 William Merrick of S[t] Margaret, Westminster, Middx., B., and Elizabeth Granger of S[t] John the Evangelist, Westminster, Middx., S.
24 Richard Webb of Shepton Mallet, Somerset, W., and Elizabeth Caten of S[t] Margaret, Westminster, Middx., S.
27 John Nash of S[t] Nicholas, Coventry, B., and Sarah Humphrys of S[t] Clement Danes, Middx., S.
29 William Craven of S[t] Andrew, Holborn, Middx., B., and Anne Hadley of the same, S.
29 Thomas Bimson of S[t] Martin in the Fields, Middx., B., and Elizabeth Says of the same, S.
30 John Corrock of S[t] Botolph, Aldgate, London, B., and Mary Stanley of the same, W.
30 Richard White of Eling, Middx., W., and Mary Oakley of Kensington, Middx., W.
Aug. 1 Benjamin Tudor of S[t] Mary, White Chapel, Middx., W., and Elizabeth Nunns of S[t] Catherine Cree Church, London, S.

1738

Aug. 2 Benjamin Cousins of St Andrew, Holborn, Middx., B., and Elizabeth Hayton of St Martin in the Fields, Middx., S.

3 John Mills of St Bartholomew, near the Royal Exchange, London, B., and Elizabeth Ewers of Earith, Kent, S.

3 Robert Nelson of All Hallows on the Wall, London, B., and Henrietta Maria Pitches of St Mary le Bow, London, S.; by Mr Sandford

4 Henry Everall of Deptford, Kent, W., and Arabella Streek of the same, S.

5 Thomas Groom of St Ann's, Westminster, Middx., W., and Esther Asten of the same, W.

5 Thomas Murry of Deptford, Kent, B., and Elizabeth Barham of Rotherhith, Surry, S.; by Mr Audley

5 George Churchey of St Mary Somerset, London, W., and Mary Lawson of St Mary Aldermary, London, S.

6 William Hayes of St Mary Magdalen, Old Fish Street, London, B., and Elizabeth Ride of St Nicholas Cole Abbey, London, S.

6 Nathaniel Stephens of St George, Hanover Square, Middx., B., and Elizabeth Calah of St James, Westminster, Middx., S.

6 Charles Chillingworth of All Hallows Barking, London, B., and Jane Bliss of the same, S.

7 William Glazier of Chelsea, Middx., B., and Hannah Dormer of the same, S.

8 Quince Blackburn of St Giles in the Fields, Middx., W., and Anne Eppley of St Mary le Bone, Middx., S.; by Mr Worlich

8 Thomas Bates of Camberwell, Surrey, W., and Alice Weeden of the same, S.; by Mr Worlich

9 William Raynes of Uxbridge, Middx., W., and Martha Woods of the same, S.

9 John Godfrey of Salisbury, B., and Anne Copland of the same city, W.

11 Francis Dorrell of St Giles, Cripplegate, London, W., and Elizabeth Lee of Loughborough, co. Leic., W.

13 Henry Addis of St Bride's, London, W., and Susannah Earl of St Andrew, Holborn, Middx., W.

20 Richard Matthews of St John the Evangelist, Westminster, Middx., B., and Tryphosa Laws of the same, S.

24 Edward Welton of St George, Bloomsbury, Middx., W., and Jean Holt of St Martin in the Fields, Middx., S.; by Dr Best

24 John Wilkinson of St Paul, Covent Garden, Middx., B., and Mary Balley of St Bartholomew the Great, London, S.; by Mr Worlich

27 Charles Browell of St Dunstan in the West, London, B., and Letitia Fernell of St James, Clarkenwell, Middx., S.

28 Richard Streatly of Fulham, Middx., W., and Mary Penny of St Dunstan in the West, London, S.

28 John Connoway of St Alban, Wood Street, London, B., and Elizabeth Boote of St Clement Danes, Middx., S.

31 John Hillyard of St Botolph, Bishopsgate, London, B., and Mary Phillips of St Michael Royal, London, S.

31 Richard Wood of St Giles in the Fields, Middx., B., and Mary Panton of the same, S.

Sept. 2 William Snow of Plaistow, Essex, B., and Jane Brazier of St Botolph, Bishopsgate, London, S.; by Mr Keighley

3 William Beilles of St George the Martyr, Middx., B., and Mary Cally of the same, S.

3 John Craner of St Clement, East Cheap, London, B., and Ann Richardson of the same, S.

5 Raby Griggs of St Botolph, Aldersgate, London, W., and Hannah Wheatly of the same, S.

1738
Sept. 6 Matthew Wilson of S[t] Giles, Cripplegate, London, W., and Elizabeth Burgesse of the same, S.
6 Thomas Brayley of Mitcham, Surry, B., and Catharine Parry of the same, S.
7 Job Cole of S[t] Margaret, Westminster, Middx., B., and Elizabeth Wilson of the same, S.
7 Richard Wainwright of S[t] Mary le Strand, Middx., W., and Ann Bridges of the same, S.
9 William Hales of S[t] Martin in the Fields, Middx., W., and Ann Wood of S[t] Paul, Covent Garden, Middx., W.
9 John Burye of S[t] Leonard, Shoreditch, Middx., B., and Sarah Phillipps of the same, S.
12 John Tildsley of S[t] Andrew, Holborn, Middx., B., and Ann Sprigg of S[t] George, Hanover Square, Middx., W.
14 Henry Henshaw of S[t] George the Martyr, Surrey, B., and Sarah Nicholson of All Hallows, Lombard Street, London, W.
14 James Catterns of S[t] Saviour, Southwarke, Surry, B., and Susannah Kerwell of S[t] Olave, Southwarke, W.
14 John Huddy of S[t] Ann, Lymehouse, Middx., B., and Jane Watkinson of the same, S.
17 William Turnbull of S[t] James, Garlickhyth, London, B., and Jane Hindmarsh of the same, S.
19 George Stevens of All Hallows, Lombard Street, London, B., and Anne Reynolds of S[t] Leonard, Shoreditch, Middx., S.
19 John Pruce of Paddington, Middx., B., and Mary West of the same, W.
19 John Moor of Weybridge, Surrey, B., and Catherine Gould of the same, W.
20 John Satchell of S[t] Dunstan, Stepney, Middx., W., and Sarah Payne of the same, S.
22 Joseph Jones Lloyd of X[st] Church, London, B., and Anne Salisbury of S[t] Mary le Strand, Middx., S.
23 William Brasfield of Hammersmith hamlet in Fulham, Middx., W., and Alice Avery of S[t] Martin in the Fields, Middx., W.
25 Martin Search of Chiswick, Middx., W., and Elizabeth Blacklock of Edmonton, Middx., W.
25 James Nicholson of S[t] Mary, Rotherhith, Surry, B., and Elizabeth Simms of S[t] Margaret, Westminster, Middx., S.
25 John Pigeon of S[t] Margaret, Westminster, Middx., W., and Jane Wilks of S[t] George the Martyr, Middx., S.
25 Simon King of S[t] George, Middx., W., and Elizabeth Loving of the same, W.
25 Alexander Spurling of Hackney, Middx., W., and Mary Reynolds of S[t] Leonard, Shoreditch, Middx., W.
27 Isaac le Doux of Bednall Green Hamlett in S[t] Dunstan, Stepney, Middx., B., and Elizabeth Rouge of X[st] Church, Middx., W.; by D[r] Thomas
29 Matthew Mills of S[t] Olave, Southwarke, Surry, B., and Margaret Davis of S[t] James, Westminster, Middx., S.
30 William Huddelson of S[t] Mary le Bone, Middx., W., and Anne Church of the same, S.
Oct. 2 Thomas Dewick of Broxburn, co. Herts, B., and Anne Bentley of the same, S.; by M[r] Keighly
5 Robert Cottrell of All Hallows, Lombard Street, London, W., and Jane Sussex Butcher of SS. Ann and Agnes, Aldersgate, London, W.
8 William Bouch of S[t] Clement Danes, Middx., W., and Elizabeth Oliver of Isleworth, Middx., W.
8 Noah Green of S[t] Botolph, Aldgate, London, W., and Elizabeth Screen of S[t] Mary le Bow, London, S.

1738

Oct. 8 Richard Shepherd of Helsham, Surry, B., and Elizabeth Leigh of the same, S.

9 James Kent of S[t] Michael in Winchester, Hants, B., and Elizabeth Freeman of S[t] Andrew, Holborn, Middx., S.

10 John Hosey of Fulham, Middx., B., and Sarah Fisher of Eaton, co. Bucks, S.

10 Charles Mallory of S[t] Clement Danes, Middx., B., and Elizabeth Hardy of S[t] Mary le Strand, Middx., S.

11 Philip Gard of Penryn, Cornwall, W., and Mary Atkins of S[t] Mary, Aldermanbury, London, S.

11 Ralph Twyford of S[t] Faith's, London, B., and Mary Staples of the same, S.

12 Samuel Broadbent of X[st] Church, London, B., and Mary Sheppard of Barham, Kent, S.

12 John Solie of S[t] Martin in the Fields, Middx., B., and Rebecca Davis of the same, S.

14 Henry Young of West Ham, Essex, B., and Elizabeth Hook Jacob of the same, S.

15 Thomas Mudghett of Twickenham, Middx., B., and Elizabeth Toten of the same, S.

15 Littleton Pryce of S[t] John, Wapping, Middx., B., and Mary Luxford of the same, S.

16 John James of S[t] John the Evangelist, Westminster, Middx., B., and Mary Warren of S[t] George, Hanover Square, Middx., S.

17 Thomas Maclery of S[t] Giles in the Fields, Middx., B., and Sarah Bly of S[t] James, Westminster, Middx., S.

17 Thomas Burnett of S[t] Mary, White Chapel, Middx., B., and Mary Renalds of the same, S.

19 Robert Gordon of SS. Ann and Agnes, Aldersgate, London, B., and Ann Wharrie of S[t] Michael, Wood Street, London, W.

24 Thomas Butler, Esq., of S[t] George, Hanover Square, Middx., W., and Margaret Davis of the same, S.

24 William Henderson of S[t] James, Westminster, Middx., B., and Jane Ellwood of the same, S.

28 Thomas Haywood of Thavies Inn, London, B., and Sarah Patfull of Isleworth, Middx., S.

29 John Gawthearn of S[t] Andrew, Holborn, Middx., B., and Mary Maverley of the same, S.

30 Charles Harrison of S[t] George, Middx., W., and Sarah Collett of the same, W.; by M[r] Hillman

30 Richard Haines of Lambeth, Surry, W., and Susan Seaker of the same, S.; by M[r] Hillman

30 Philip Chapman of Sutton, Kent, B., and Mary Northall of the same, S.; by M[r] Hillman

30 John Angell of Cobham, Kent, B., and Ann Chapman of Swainscam, Kent, S.; by the same

31 Richard Fell of S[t] Michael Basishaw, London, B., and Elizabeth Langdale of S[t] Matthew, Friday Street, London, S.; by M[r] Keighly, curate at the Poultry

31 John Thatcher of Paddington, Middx., B., and Ann Meyrick of the same, S.; by M[r] Keighly

31 Edward Low of S[t] Michael, Cornhill, London, B., and Rhoda Merser of the same, S.; by ditto

*Nov. 2 John Collis of S[t] Andrew, Holborn, Middx., B., and Mary Green of the same, W.; by ditto

* A vacant space for an entry between 31 Oct. and 2 Nov.—Ed.

1738

Nov. 5 John Hollis of St Olave, Southwark, Surry, B., and Elizabeth Robinson of the same, W.; by Mr Hillman

5 Thomas Wilson of St Andrew, Holborn, London, W., and Barbara Sheldon of St Gyles, Cripplegate, London, W.; by Mr Hillman

5 Vincent Hotchkiss of St Clement Danes, Middx., Clerk, B., and Anna Christiana Honywood of St Mary le Strand, Middx., S.; by Mr Hillman

6 Nathaniel Sykes of St George, Hanover Square, Middx., B., and Elizabeth Crump of Coopersale, Essex, S.; by Mr Worlich

7 John Biford of Barking, Essex, B., and Elizabeth Quantrill of the same, W.; by Mr Hillman

7 John Search of St James, Westminster, Middx., B., and Margaret West of St George, Middx., S.; by the same

7 John Bryan of St George the Martyr, Surrey, W., and Mary Bunpas of the same, W.; by Mr Worlich

13 Edmund Larken of St Dunstan, Stepney, Middx., B., and Jane Campion of the same, S.

14 John Copeland of St Paul, Shadwell, Middx., B., and Mary Owen of the same, S.

14 Robert Taylor of Wandsworth, Surry, B., and Sarah Simmons of the same, S.

15 William Langford of Endfield, Middx., B., and Mary Shirley of the same, S.

16 Richard Griffith of St John, Wapping, Middx., W., and Ann Benson of St John, Southwarke, Surry, S.

18 John Norcott of Friarn Barnett, Middx., B., and Mary Wood of Sunbury, Middx., W.

21 William Perrin of St John the Evangelist, Middx., B., and Honor Williams of the same, S.

23 William Saunders of St Ann, Westminster, Middx., B., and Elizabeth Lester of St Saviour, Southwark, Surry, S.

24 William Stafford of St Martin in the Fields, Middx., B., and Martha Smith of St Leonard, Shoreditch, Middx., S.

25 John Anthony D'Esgens of Stoke Pogeis, co. Bucks, B., and Ann Jackson of St Margaret, Westminster, Middx., S.

26 Martin Watson of St Olave, Southwarke, Surry, B., and Martha Browne of St Saviour, Southwarke, Surry, S.

Dec. 1 Richard Grandee of Carshalton, Surry, W., and Martha Jackman of Plaistow, Essex, S.

4 John Dunkarton of St Martin in the Fields, Middx., W., and Elizabeth Foxly of the same, W.

4 John Fennell of the Hamlett of Hammersmith in Fulham, Middx., W., and Anne Evans of the same, S.

4 John Mayer of St James, Westminster, Middx., B., and Amey Shrimpton of the same, S.

10 Thomas Cartwright of St Giles, Cripplegate, London, B., and Mary Wright of the same, W.

14 Robert Swain of Chiswick, Middx., B., and Elizabeth Batson of the same, S.

18 James Baynes of St Mary Bothaw, London, W., and Rachael Warner of the same, S.

18 Joshua Cooper of Ulcomb, Kent, B., and Susanna Waterman of East Sutton, Kent, S.

20 Theophilus Cross of St Sepulchre, London, B., and Catharine White of St Luke, Middx., S.

20 Philip Stoddart of St Clement Danes, Middx., B., and Mary Spriggs of St George, Hanover Square, Middx., S.

1738

Dec. 21 Charles Hassell of Acton, Middx., B., and Susanna Johnson of Hormead, co. Herts, S.; by Mr L. Jones

23 John Rogers of St Dunstan in the East, London, B., and Mary Walker of the same, S.

23 Rice James of St Paul, Covent Garden, Middx., B., and Margaret Jones of the same, S.

23 Daniel Trim of St Martin in the Fields, Middx., B., and Sarah Whitlock of the same, S.

23 Richard Towell of Kensington, Middx., B., and Elizabeth Street of Petworth, Sussex, S.

24 James Cutler of St Stephen, Coleman Street, London, B., and Ann Evans of St Leonard, Shoreditch, Middx., S.

25 James Waller of St James, Clerkenwell, Midx., B., and Elizabeth Beswick of Hornsey, Midx., W.

26 William Hill of Battersea, Surry, W., and Elizabeth Shayler of St Andrew, Holborn, Lond., S.

26 Samuel Diaper of Mile End in Stepny, Midx., W., and Mary Bowles of St Bottolph, Bishopgate, Lond., S.

28 Humphrey Davis of Edmonton, Midx., B., and Elizabeth Everden of the same, S.

30 William Beach of Hammersmith, Midx., B., and Jane Soper of the same, S.

30 Thomas Towett, B., and Mary Cooper, S., both of this parish. Banns

Jan. 1 Owen Hughes of St Martin in the Fields, Midx., B., and Martha Rogers of St Andrew, Holborn, Midx., S.

1 Richard Moore of Christ Church, Lond., W., and Prudence Howard of St Faith's, Lond., S.

1 Robert Simpson of the Inner Temple, Lond., B., and Elizabeth Bolton of St Andrew, Holborn, Midx., S.

2 Thomas Cotham of St Mary Magdalen, Bermondsey, Surry, B., and Elizabeth Keene of St Saviour's, Southwark, Surry, S.

3 Edward Horne of St Vedast als. Foster, Lond., B., and Parnell Gray of this parish, S.

3 Robert Russell of Horton Kirby, Kent, B., and Mary Wood of the same, S.

5 David Oxley of St Paul, Shadwell, Midx., B., and Deborah Matthews of St Mary, Rotherhith, Surry, W.

6 Henry Ealy of St Andrew, Holborn, Lond., W., and Sarah Weaver of the same, S.

7 Thomas Minchin of St Augustine, Lond., B., and Elizabeth Chandler of the same, W.

9 Thomas Maxfield of St Martin in the Fields, Midx., B., and Hannah Murray of St Clement Danes, Midx., S.; by Mr Keighly

9 Thomas Green of St Dunstan in the West, Lond., B., and Elizabeth Crane of St Mary le Strand, Midx., S.; by the same

10 Henry Speke of Portsmouth, Hants, B., and Elizabeth Meade of St Andrew's, Holborn, Midx., W.; by the same

14 Ellis Thomas of St Clement Danes, Midx., B., and Jane Edwards of the same, W.

16 William Smith of St Clement Danes, Midx., B., and Margaret Humphreys of St George, Hanover Square, Midx., S.

17 James Higgens of St John, Westmr, Midx., B., and Anne Hanford of the same, S.

18 Thomas Cherry of Newington, Surry, W., and Jane Cheney of St George, Southwark, Surry, W.

22 Samuel Chapman of St James, Clerkenwell, Midx., B., and Mary Bradley of the same, W.

1738-9
Jan. 23 George Watkins of Allhallows the Great, Lond., B., and Anne Hedley of the same, S.
26 Richard Chester of Egham, Surry, B., and Mary Lane of the same, W.
27 William Sopp of St Saviour's, Southwarke, Surry, B., and Sarah Nicholls of the same, W.
31 Richard Mascall of St Andrew Undershaft, Lond., B., and Anna Walshaw of the same, S.
Feb. 2 William Taylor of St Botolph, Aldgate, Midx., W., and Elizabeth Middleditch of St Michael Bassishaw, Lond., S.
3 William Barber of Hornchurch, Essex, B., and Jane Smith of Upminster, Essex, S.
4 Armado Limbrey of Woolwich, Kent, W., and Elizabeth Cambell of St Margaret, Westmr, Midx., W.
6 Samuel Shatford of St Ann, Westmr, Midx., B., and Elizabeth Vernon of the same, S.
6 Hills Thomson of St Mary, White Chapel, Midx., W., and Mary Stone of the same, S.
7 John Gibson of St Ann's, Westmr, Midx., B., and Ann Sykes of the same, W.
8 Thomas Molesworth of St George, Bloomsbury, Midx., B., and Elizabeth Porter of the same, S.
10 William Brown of St Ann, Westmr, Midx., W., and Phillis Caridus of the same, S.
10 Isaac Kimber of St Olave, Southwarke, Surry, B., and Alice Banks of the same, S.
13 Jacob Bannister of St Dunstan in the West, Lond., B., and Hannah George of the same, W.
14 Edward Edwards of St Dunstan in the West, Lond., B., and Letitia Smart of St Martin's Lane in Thames Street, Lond., S.
16 John Mason of St Ann, Aldersgate, Lond., B., and Susannah Prosser of the same, S.
22 John Richardson of St Mary Magdalen, Bermondsey, Surry, B., and Mary Allison of the same, S.
24 William Pigeon of St James, Westmr, Midx., B., and Jane Coales of the same, S.
25 Richard Holford of Avebury, Wilts, Esq., W., and Aurea Otway of Bocton Malherbe, Kent, S.; by Mr Otway
25 William Goodall of St Mary, White Chapel, Midx., B., and Sarah Ingham of St George, Midx., S.
27 Thomas Jones of St Clement Danes, Midx., B., and Mary Fitz Gerald of St Andrew, Holborn, Midx., S.
27 Thomas Newbee of St Saviour's, Southwarke, Surry, B., and Ann Wright of the same, S.
Mar. 1 Edmund Boddington of St Martin in the Fields, Midx., W., and Elizabeth Thompson of the same, W.
2 John Raoult als. Row of Christ Church, Midx., B., and Catharine Gardiner of St Dionis Back Church, Lond., S.; by Mr Batho
3 Daniel Gallier of St Mary, White Chapel, Midx., B., and Mary Rudduck of St Sepulchre, Lond., S.
4 James Alvey of St James, Westmr, Midx., W., and Dorothy Bedder of the same, S.
4 John Fretts of St Botolph, Aldersgate, Lond., B., and Ann Hickman of St Giles, Cripplegate, Lond., S.
5 Thomas Wilson of St Sepulchre, Lond., B., and Martha Carter of the same, S.
6 George Groome of St James, Clerkenwell, Midx., B., and Agnes Burt of the same, S.

1738-9

Mar. 6 James Hayter of St Luke, Midx., W., and Margaret Harding of Lambeth, Surry, S.

6 Thomas Orton of St Sepulchre, Lond., W., and Sarah Cranwell of Hoxton, Midx., S.

6 John Holbeche of St Botolph, Aldgate, Midx., B., and Jane Pearson of the same, S.

19 Richard Stone of St George, Hanover Square, Midx., B., and Ann Richley of the same, S.

21 Thomas Letherbarrow of St James, Westm^r, Midx., B., and Phebee Booth of the same, S.

1739.

April 1 George Freeman of St James, Westm^r, Midx., W., and Catharine Roberts of Bath, Somerset, W.

6 John Norris of Glimpton, co. Oxford, B., and Elizabeth Low of the same, S.

8 Edward Bradley of Lambeth, Surry, W., and Elizabeth Burton of St George, Hanover Square, Midx., S.

10 Edward Manby of St Clement Danes, Midx., B., and Anne Whitehead of Woodford, Essex, S.

10 Richard Sutton of Kensington, Midx., B., and Alice Babb of St Dunstan in the West, Lond., S.

10 Archibald Pitcairn of St Botolph, Aldgate, Midx., B., and Jane Gaer of the same, S.

17 Richard Brittain of St Andrew, Holborn, Lond., B., and Susannah Bumsted of the same, W.

22 Benjamin Bleathman of St George, Hanover Square, Midx., B., and Mary Turner of St James, Westm^r, Midx., S.

23 John Cox of St Martin in the Fields, Midx., W., and Mary Owen of the same, W.

23 Joseph Bolland of St Martin in the Fields, Midx., W., and Ann Nay of St George, Bloomsbury, Midx., W.

25 George Liddell of Ramsey, co. Southampton, B., and Diana James of St Andrew, Holborn, Midx., S.

28 Thomas Harris of Putney, Surry, B., and Jane Baxter of the same, S.

29 William Austin of SS. Ann and Agnes, Aldersgate, Lond., B., and Elizabeth Otter of St Peter le Poor, Lond., S.

29 Allan Ramsay ye Younger, Esqr, of St Paul, Covent Garden, Midx., B., and Anne Bayne of St Martin in the Fields, Midx., S.

May 1 Robert Dade of Diss, co. Norfolk, W., and Mary Peck of the same, W.

3 George Spencer of St Dunstan in the West, Midx., B., and Elizabeth Sanders of St Andrew, Holborn, Midx., W.; by Mr Keighly

3 Christopher Balmout of Lambeth, Surry, B., and Sarah Abbut of Clapham, Surry, S.; by the same

5 Lawrence John Ossibrooke of St Saviour's, Southwarke, Surry, W., and Catharine Robins of the same, W.

5 Thomas Millward of St George, Midx., W., and Margaret Smith of St John, Wapping, W.

7 Richard Pearson of Evesham, Surry, B., and Priscilla Coussins of St Andrew, Holborn, Lond., S.

8 John Emmell of Fulham, Midx., B., and Elizabeth Brasell of the same, S.

10 John Adams of St James, Westm^r, Midx., B., and Susannah Rushworth of St Martin in the Fields, Midx., S.

15 William Phillips of Isleworth, Midx., B., and Ann Roach of New Brentford, Midx., S.

1739

May 16 John Lewis Favre of S[t] Catherine near the Tower [*blank*], and Susannah Delzanne of S[t] Giles in the Fields, Midx., S.

17 Edward Sutton of Town Sutton, Kent, W., and Amy Earl of East Sutton, Kent, S.

17 John Dorsett of S[t] Clement Danes, Midx., B., and Mary White of S[t] Edmund the King, Lond., W.

18 George Curtis of Mortlake, Surry, B., and Jane Bourne of the same, S.

18 John Wright of S[t] Paul, Covent Garden, Midx., B., and Mary Dickenson of S[t] Martin in the Fields, Midx., S.

21 Thomas Fleetwood of Hendon, Midx., B., and Carr Gray of the same, S.

21 Thomas Eling of Twickenham, Midx., B., and Sarah Bocksell of Kingston upon Thames, Surrey, S.

26 Thomas Willes of S[t] Mary, White Chapell, Midx., B., and Elizabeth Martin of the same, S.

26 Francis Goodinge of Fawley, Bucks, B., and Mary Toovey of Henly upon Thames, co. Oxford, W.

27 Andrew Johannot of Eynsford, Kent, B., and Jane Jones of Sevenoaks, Kent, S.

28 Joseph Storey of Cheshunt, co. Herts, W., and Mary Cowell of the same, W.

28 James Taylor of S[t] John the Evangelist, Westminster, Middx., B., and Catherine Denson of the same, S.

30 George Webb of Kingston upon Thame, Surry, B., and Mary Weston of S[t] Paul's, Covent Garden, Middx., S.

31 Charles Laycock of S[t] Ann, Westminster, Middx., B., and Mary Boon of S[t] George, Bloomsbury, Middx., W.

31 Abraham Addams of S[t] Dionis Back Church, London, B., and Sarah Smith of X[st] Church, Middx., S.

June 3 William Gibson of S[t] Saviour, Southwark, Surry, B., and Mary Bent of S[t] Paul, Covent Garden, Middx., S.

3 Matthew White of S[t] Leonard, Shoreditch, Middx., W., and Elizabeth Staines of S[t] Botolph, Bishopsgate, London, W.

3 Thomas Spyers of Isleworth, Middx., B., and Lowdey Batchelor of S[t] Dunstan in the East, London, S.

3 Thomas Sanders of S[t] Peter le Poor, London, B., and Sarah Taylor of the same, S.

4 Daniel Jones of Kensington, Middx., B., and Mary Taylor of S[t] James, Westminster, Middx., S.

5 Daniel Tonge of S[t] Andrew, Holborn, Middx., W., and Elizabeth Neilson of Richmond, Surry, W.

8 John Salmon of S[t] Saviour, Southwarke, Surry, B., and Mary Catterns of the same, S.

10 James Walker of X[st] Church, Surry, B., and Ruth Cox of S[t] Saviour, Southwarke, S.

10 William Robinson of S[t] Clement Danes, Middx., B., and Sarah Colton of S[t] Mary, White Chapel, Middx., S.

11 William Binford of Bridgewater, Somerset, Esq., B., and Elizabeth Newland of S[t] Peter le Poor, London, S.

12 James Achison of S[t] Andrew, Holborn, London, B., and Mary Davies of the same, S.

12 Joshua Dinsdale of S[t] Andrew Undershaft, London, B., and Mary Jackson of the same, S.

13 William Slow of Hitchin, co. Herts, B., and Mary Lepine of S[t] Bennet, Grace Church, London, S.

14 Bainbridge Mathew of S[t] George in the East, Middx., W., and Elizabeth Graham of S[t] Mary, White Chapel, Middx., W.

1739

June 15 Humphry Roby of S[t] Olave, Old Jewry, London, W., and Elizabeth Percival of the same, S.

15 William Gomery of S[t] Dunstan, Stepny, Middx., B., and Ann Wright of the same, S.

15 William Crow of S[t] James, Westminster, Middx., B., and Bridget Bold of the same, S.

19 Thomas Leather of S[t] Margaret, Westminster, Middx., B., and Margaret Jenkins of S[t] Martin in the Fields, Middx., S.

21 James Brown of S[t] Andrew, Holborn, Middx., B., and Elizabeth Barton of S[t] Michael, Wood Street, London, S.

21 Richard Waddington of S[t] Clement Danes, Middx., B., and Elizabeth Kerby of S[t] Paul, Covent Garden, Middx., W.

22 Thomas Swift of Hernhill, Kent, B., and Diana Dawes of Boughton under the Blen, Kent, S.

22 John Bell of S[t] Mary Stratford, Bow, Middx., B., and Sarah Fletcher of Welling, co. Herts, S.

23 Arthur Maynwaring, Esq., of S[t] Paul, Covent Garden, Middx., B., and Catharine Pyne of S[t] Ann, Westm[r], Middx., S.

24 John Colliber of Trinity Parish, London, W., and Hannah Waley of Dartmouth, Devon, W.

26 Thomas Robinson of S[t] James, Westminster, Middx., B., and Joannah Cooke of the same, S.

26 William Beakley of S[t] Saviour, Southwarke, Surry, W., and Margaret Tillie of the same, W.

30 Roger Offty of the Precinct of White Friars, London, W., and Mary Holloway of the same, W.

July 1 Robert Wynn of S[t] Clement Danes, Middx., B., and Mary Williams of the same, S.

2 John Risoliere of X[st] Church, Middx., W., and Ann Mollet of the same, S.

2 Thomas Cadrwry of Hammersmith, Middx., B., and Martha Cardman of All Hallows Barking, London, S.

3 William Tegny of S[t] John, Wapping, Middx., W., and Elizabeth Sackett of the same, S.

5 John Head of Chelsea, Middx., B., and Cornelia Lynn of the same, W.; by M[r] Keighly

6 John Hussey of S[t] Margaret, Westminster, Middx., B., and Susannah Hannam of the same, S.

7 Matthew Wild of S[t] James, Westminster, Middx., W., and Sarah Richardson of the same, S.

8 Robert Wallis of S[t] John the Evangelist, Westm[r], Middx., W., and Anne Waters of the same, W.

8 William Pickering of S[t] Gyles in the Fields, Middx., B., and Ursula Doe of the same, W.

9 John Bosworth of S[t] Gyles in the Fields, Middx., B., and Mary Clark of the same, S.

9 Moses Cates of S[t] Andrew, Holborn, London, B., and Grace Milborn of the same, S.

9 John Prignan of S[t] Martin in the Fields, Middx., W., and Mary Wilkes of the same, S.

10 John Francklin of S[t] Martin in the Fields, Middx., W., and Polehampton Hemet of S[t] Ann, Westminster, Middx., W.

11 Stephen Grosvenor of S[t] George, Hanover Square, Middx., B., and Elizabeth Totty of the same, S.; by M[r] Bailey

12 Thomas Bourne of Great Bookham, Surry, W., and Elizabeth Gerrard of S[t] Magnes the Martyr, London, S.

13 Thomas Dinsdale of All Saints in the Town of Hertford, B., and Mary Brassey of Hartingfordbury, co. Herts, S.

1739

July 15 John Dell of St Andrew Hubbard, London, B., and Susannah Adye of the same, S.

16 Walter Chittick of St James, Westmr, Middx., B., and Ann Shank of St Saviour, Southwarke, Surry, S.; by Mr Bailey

16 George Long of St Ann, Westmr, Middx., B., and Elizabeth Daniel of the same, W.; by Mr Bailey

18 William Stocker of St Ann, Westmr, Middx., B., and Elizabeth Liney of St George, Hanover Square, Middx., S.; by Mr Worlich

20 John Knell of St Mary's in Kent, B., and Ruth Chapman of Pembury, Kent, S.

20 Lachlin Leslie of St Gyles in the Fields, Middx., B., and Alice Pettiver of the same, S.

23 Richard Pamphilon of Croydon, Surry, B., and Mary Touching of the same, S.

24 John Smith of Kings Walden, co. Herts, B., and Mary Larner of the same, S.

26 Thomas Tatnall of Cowsden, Surry, B., and Elizabeth Killick of Chipsted, Surry, S.

27 David Jones of New Cross in Deptford, Surry, B., and Jane Rickwood of the same, W.

27 Francis Johnston of St George, Hanover Square, Middx., B., and Jane Wray of the same, S.

29 Thomas Farr of St George, Middx., B., and Mary Norton of Bath, Somerset, S.

29 Richard Poole of St Botolph, Aldgate, London, B., and Mary Smith of the same, W.

29 Richard Lancake of Wandsworth, Surry, B., and Dorothy Fitzer of St Dunstan in the West, London, S.

29 Samuel Hawkins of Hadleigh, Middx., W., and Hannah Williams of the same, S.

29 John Kent of St Dunstan in the West, London, B., and Margaret Reay of St Martin in the Fields, Middx., S.

29 John Jefferson of St George, Botolph lane, London, B., and Jane Astley of St Bartholomew the Less, London, S.

29 Joseph Chapman of Northfleet, Kent, W., and Magdalen Callagham of St Xstopher, London, W.; by Mr Godbold

30 Peter Ardouin of St Ann, Westmr, Middx., W., and Elizabeth Hooper of the same, S.

Aug. 1 William Malcher of St John the Evangelist, London, B., and Elizabeth Fellows of Xst Church, Surry, S.

3 Thomas Gillman of All Saints, co. Hertford, B., and Mary Clarke of the same, S.

4 Richard Ashford of St Clement Danes, Middx., W., and Elizabeth Cockayne of St Michael, Queenhith, London, W.

5 John Forrest of St Olave, Hart Street, London, B., and Ellinor Scarsee of the same, S.

6 Thomas Neale of Chiswick, Middx., W., and Mary Wells of the same, S.

7 Samuel Salt of St Andrew, Holborn, Middx., W., and Elizabeth Huntingford of the same, S.; by Mr Noble

7 William Baker of Kentish Town, Middx., B., and Mary Maris of the same, S.

9 William Colbron of Brackley (2), co. Northampton, W., and Ann Wrangham of St Paul, Covent Garden, Middx., W.*

8 James Affleck of St Margaret (1), Westmr, Middx., B., and Anne Ceely of the same, S.*

* These two entries have figures in brackets placed over the name in the original which they follow here.—Ed.

1739

Aug. 12 John Reeve of Ewell, co. Oxford, B., and Rachel Hogan of Uxbridge, co. Middx., S.

16 Henry Perkins of St Margaret, Westm^r^, Middx., W., and Hannah Marshall of St Paul, Covent Garden, Middx., W.

21 William Wiggins of St Ann, Blackfryars, London, W., and Elizabeth Osmond of X^st^ Church, London, W.

31 Robert Parrott of St Saviour, Southwarke, Surry, B., and Mary Wollon of the same, S.

31 Peter Hull of the city of Rochester, B., and Avis Hartwell of the Liberty of the Tower of London, W.

Sept. 1 George West of St Luke, Middx., W., and Hannah Wells of the same, W.

4 Charles Keightley of St James, Westm^r^, Middx., B., and Elizabeth Portman of the same, S.

4 Hugh Roberts of Chiswick, Middx., W., and Elizabeth Miller of the same, W.

6 William Hebort of Hanwell, Middx., B., and Mary Wolle of Fulham, Middx., S.

7 George Haughton of St Paul, Covent Garden, Middx., B., and Mary Cobus of Deptford, Kent, S.

8 John Carter of St Botolph, Aldersgate, London, W., and Mary Bran of St George the Martyr, Middx., S.

9 Benjamin Brown of All Hallows, Bread Street, London, B., and Sarah Smith of the same, S.

10 William Orrock of St Martin in the Fields, Middx., B., and Ann Hatley of St George, Hanover Square, Middx., S.

11 William Smith of St Anne, Limehouse, Middx., B., and Margaret Innis of Stepney, Middx., S.

13 Richard Stevens of St James, Garlickhyth, London, B., and Margaret Broadbridge of the city of Canterbury, S.

13 John Daniell of St Dunstan, Stepney, Middx., W., and Ann Brown of the same, W.

13 Timothy Dewell of Wootton Bassett, Wilts, B., and Mary Goddard of the same, S.

17 Stephen Turner of St George the Martyr, Southwarke, W., and Rebecca Pritchard of the same, W.

17 William Whittaker of St Sepulchre, London, B., and Katherine Taylor of St Lawrence, Jewry, London, S.

18 James Rokes of St Clement Danes, Middx., B., and Esther Blastock of Hornsey, Middx., S.

18 John Oakey of St Andrew, Holborn, London, B., and Elianor Arnold of the Liberty of the Tower of London, W.

19 John Yates of St Olave, Southwarke, B., and Elizabeth Twyford of St Margaret Pattons, London, S.

20 George Moore of St George, Hanover Square, Middx., B., and Elizabeth Larrett of the same, S.

21 William Eldridge of St Martin in the Fields, Middx., B., and Sarah Jolly of St James, Westminster, Middx., S.

22 Thomas Burton of the Middle Temple, London, B., and Bridgett Brereton of St Martin in the Fields, Middx., S.

23 John Stuartup, W., and Ann Staples, S., both of this parish. Banns

25 Gilbert Gordon of St Martin in the Fields, Middx., B., and Mary Bates of St Mary Magdalen, Bermondsea, Surry, S.

27 James Macey of St Mary, Newington Butts, Surrey, B., and Mary Giles of the same, W.; by Mr Worlich

27 William Weatherhead of St Botolph, Aldgate, London, W., and Mary Record of the Precinct of St Catherine by the Tower of London, S.; by Mr Keighly

1739

Sept. 28 Richard Sharp of St Dunstan in the East, London, B., and Mary Butcher of the same, W.; by Mr Keighly

28 George Palmer of St George, Bloomsbury, Middx., B., and Anne Browne of the same, S.; by Mr Worlich

Oct. 3 John Pratt of Deptford, Kent, W., and Amy Wood of Shoreham, Kent, S.

4 William Barber of St Matthew, Friday Street, London, B., and Margaret Bailey of St Andrew, Holborne, London, S.

4 John Stead of Putney, Surrey, W., and Elizabeth Lobbs of St Martin in the Fields, Middx., S.; by Mr Worlich

7 William Gibbs of St Clement Danes, Middx., W., and Mary Cason of St Olave, Hart Street, London, S.

9 Robert Kellaway of St Nicholas Accorn, London, B., and Susannah Farrow of Edmonton, Midx., S.

10 Edward Cramp of St George, Southwarke, B., and Elizabeth Browne of the same, S.

11 Charles Bathurst of the Middle Temple, London, B., and Mary Brian of Harrow on the Hill, Middx., S.

13 Peter Harris of Lambeth, Surrey, B., and Mary Asten of the same, S.

14 William May of St Leonard, Foster lane, London, W., and Catharine Bull of St Botolph, Aldersgate, London, S.

14 John Lillie of St Olave, Southwarke, B., and Millicent Greenhill of St Andrew, Holborn, London, S.

18 Henry Chapman of St James, Middx., B., and Catherine Whitfield of St Anne, Westminster, Middx., S.

21 John Vere of St James, Westminster, Middx., W., and Mary Sankey of the same, W.

22 Samuel Wood of Twickenham, Middx., B., and Mary Davis of the same, S.

25 Richard Spencer of St Clement Danes, Middx., W., and Elizabeth Wood of Hays, Middx., S.

25 Richard Strong of All Hallows the Great, London, B., and Lettice Drury of St Paul, Covent Garden, Middx., S.

27 John Collyer of St Paul, Covent Garden, Middx., W., and Dorothy Carr of St Michael, Garlickhith, London, S.

28 Francis Johnson of St Leonard, Shoreditch, Middx., B., and Esther Prisly of the same, S.

28 William Hill of St Dionis Back Church, London, W., and Mary Oxendon of Richmond, Surry, W.

29 John Holman of North Ochington, Essex, B., and Mary Rogers of the same, S.

30 Morris Bailey of Mitcham, Surry, B., and Ann Smith of the same, S.; by Dr Thomas

30 John Cross of St Mary Magdalen, Bermondsey, Surry, B., and Elizabeth Fendall of the same, S.; by Mr Baily

31 James Burges of St Anne, Limehouse, Middx., W., and Elizabeth Bishop of St Dunstan, Stepney, Middx., W.; by Mr Keighly

Nov. 1 George White of Quorndon, co. Leic., B., and Mary Turvylle of the borough of Leicester, W.; by Mr Worlich

2 John Rawlins of St Mary Magdalen, Bermondsey, Surry, W., and Elizabeth Collins of St Buttolph, Aldgate, London, S.; by the same

2 Berry Manly of Windsor, co. Berks, W., and Mary French of the same, S.; by Mr Keighly

7 George Churchey of St Mary Somerset, London, W., and Anne Ougelsby of Ealing, Middx., W.; by Dr Thomas

7 Thomas Norris of Chiswick, Middx., B., and Susan Kitchen of the same, S.; by Mr Worlich

1739

Nov. 8 John Hill of St George the Martyr, Middx., B., and Mary Charlton of St Margaret, Westmr, Middx., S.; by Mr Sandford

11 Richard Wood of St Leonard, Shoreditch, Middx., B., and Mary Goswell of Norton Folgate, Middx., W.

11 Joseph Briggs of Langwith Bassett, co. Derby, B., and Frances Flint of the same, S.

14 John Searle of Barking, Essex, B., and Catharine Davies of Epping, Essex, S.

15 John Hough of Stockport, Cheshire, B., and Susannah Harris of Hammersmith, Middx., W.

15 John Tindell of St Andrew, Holborn, Middx., B., and Phebe Sicker of the same, S.

16 William Child of Farnham Royal, co. Bucks, W., and Dorcas Dorrell of the same, S.

19 Robert Wilson of Uxbridge, Middx., B., and Frances Egerton of St George, Hanover Square, Middx., S.

21 Thomas Hiller of St Dunstan in the West, London, B., and Mary Ann Memberry of the same, S.

24 John Bailey of St Saviour, Southwarke, B., and Anne Hanch of Dartford, Kent, W.

26 Edward Bingham of St Michael, Crooked lane, London, B., and Elizabeth Hart of the same, S.

29 Joseph Pricar of Norton Folgate, Middx., B., and Elizabeth Burssey of St Dunstan, Stepney, Middx., S.

Dec. 1 Ebenezer Coker of St James, Clarkenwell, Middx., W., and Elizabeth Ramsey of the same, S.

1 John Briggs of Dorking, Surry, B., and Ann Matthew of Epsom in the said county, S.

2 Daniel Cooksey of St Gyles, Cripplegate, Middx., B., and Lucy Warwick of St Botolph, Billingsgate, London, S.

6 John Burscoe of St Mary, White Chappel, Middx. [*blank*], and Henretta Gaston of St Edmund the King, London, S.; by Mr Hillman

7 Thomas Godman of St Luke, Middx., W., and Sarah Ganderton of Xst Church, London, W.

11 William Henton of Great Dalby, co. Leic., B., and Margaret Lumley of Hampstead, Middx., S.

13 Edmund Robottom of Hampstead, Middx., B., and Susanna Lomas of the same, S.

13 John Phillips of Dinder, Somerset, W., and Grace White of Battersea, Surry, S.

13 Richard Poppellwell of Putney, Surry, B., and Mary Perkehus of St George, Hanover Square, Middx., S.

15 Anthony Nicholls of St Dunstan in the West, London, W., and Elizabeth Buckland of St Andrew, Holborne, London, W.

15 William Ray of Willsdon, Middx., B., and Frances Downing of St Mary at Hill, London, S.

15 Christopher Mayor of Chatham, Kent, B., and Hannah Sanders of the same, S.

20 Richard Evans of St Clement Danes, Middx., B., and Alice Holmes of St Vedast, Foster lane, London, S.

22 Xstopher Roe of St Stephen, Walbrook, London, B., and Susanna Price of St Mary at Hill, London, S.

27 Richard Cook of St Ann, Westmr, Middx., B., and Sarah Howard of the same, W.

Jan. 1 Robert Woodifield of St Martin in the Fields, Middx., B., and Margaret Hyde of St Paul, Covent Garden, Middx., S.

1 Thomas Day of St Saviour, Southwarke, B., and Mary Day of the same, S.

1739-40

Jan. 1 Carlile Hathaway of St Luke, Middx., B., and Anne Cole of the same, S.

4 John Trussell of King's Newton, co. Derby, B., and Dorothy Cowlisher of the same, W.

5 Richard Hargrave of Grays Inn, Middx., B., and Henrietta Cox of Kensington, Middx., S.

5 Thomas Howson of Hackney, Middx., W., and Mary Cunningham of the same, W.

8 John McClye of St Nicholas, Deptford, Kent, B., and Mary Moor of the same, S.

10 James Severn of St Andrew Undershaft, London, W., and Ann Green of St Andrew, Holborn, Middx., S.

15 Benjamin Payne of St Dunstan in the West, London, W., and Priscilla Burt of St Margaret, Westm^r, Middx., S.

17 George Woolmor of Weald, Essex, B., and Mary Terry of the same, S.

19 Matthew Purdue of St John the Evangelist, Westm^r, Middx., B., and Elizabeth Thomas of the same, S.

21 William Holbroke of Manchester in Lancashire, B., and Elizabeth Credocke of St Lawrence, Jewry, London, S.

27 Robert Johnson of St Leonard, Shoreditch, Middx., B., and Catherine Wright of St Dunstan, Stepney, Middx., S.

27 John Peters of St Mary Magdalen, Bermondsey, Southwarke, B., and Hannah Nixon of the same, S.

29 Abraham King of St James, Westm^r, Middx., B., and Sarah Vass of Edmonton, Middx., S.

29 Robert Curn of St Alban, Wood Street, London, B., and Mary Hobbs of Stratford, Middx., S.

29 Edmund Elgar of St Botolph, Aldgate, London, W., and Priscilla Horrocks of St Dunstan, Stepney, Middx., W.

31 John Dawson of St Saviour, Southwark, B., and Anne Dongworth of St Mary, White Chapel, Middx., W.

31 John French of Hounslow, Middx., B., and Anne Shelton of the same, S.

31 Thomas Smith of St George the Martyr, Middx., B., and Margaret Brookes of St Ann, Westm^r, Middx., S.

Feb. 2 Thomas Richardson of St James, Clarkenwell, Middx., B., and Margaretta Champion of the same, W.

5 John Brett of St Paul, Covent Garden, Middx., B., and Anne Metcalfe of the same, S.

6 John Swallow of St Martin in the Fields, Middx., B., and Sarah Frith of St Margaret, Westm^r, Middx., W.

7 Jacob Saunders of St Dunstan in the East, Middx., B., and Esther Burroughs of the same, S.

7 Joseph Hall of Esher, Surry, B., and Hannah Cockram of the same, S.

7 John Goodchild of Hoxton, Middx., B., and Sarah Spire of the same, W.

7 Ludford Palmer of St Giles, Cripplegate, London, B., and Diana Yardstanley of St Alban, Wood Street, London, W.; by Mr Yates, curate of St Dionis Back Church

7 Matthew Bailey of Hampsted, Middx., W., and Ann Purbeck of St James, Clarkenwell, Middx., W.

10 John Arden of this parish, B., and Ann Clemson of St Andrew, Holborn, London, S.; by Mr Pearce of St Paul's

10 Richard Ward of Ammersden, co. Oxford, B., and Ann Millians of the same, S.; by the same

10 Thomas Sawyer of St Martin in the Fields, Middx., B., and Sarah Harvey of the same, S.; by the same

1739-40

Feb. 11 Thomas Tew of S[t] George, Hanover Square, Middx., B., and Jane Hoskinson of the same, S.

14 Anthony Marle of S[t] Dunstan in the West, London, B., and Margaret Poole of the same, S.

14 John Staines of Walthamstow, Essex, B., and Jane Plaisted of the same, S.

14 Peter Smalt of S[t] Brides, London, B., and Pheby Evans of S[t] James, Clarkenwell, Middx., W.

18 Thomas Graham of Buckland, Surry, W., and Alice Pride of S[t] James, Westminster, Middx., S.

18 John Rumball of Edmonton, Middx., B., and Susannah Blizzard of S[t] Leonard, Shoreditch, Middx., W.

19 Richard Ball of S[t] Gyles, Cripplegate, London, B., and Sarah Reviss of S[t] Luke, Middx., S.

19 Samuel Bowyer of Hays, Middx., B., and Ann Bradford of the same, S.

19 John Ewer of Pinnor, Middx., B., and Phœbe Hill of the same, S.

25 Samuel Lillie of S[t] Dunstan, Stepney, Middx., B., and Elizabeth Elmore of the same, S.

26 William Coyd of S[t] George the Martyr, Middx., W., and Sarah Srayton of the same, S.

28 Elias Waymark of S[t] Saviour, Southwarke, W., and Susannah Leydger of the same, W.; by M[r] Worlich

28 Robert Brealey of S[t] Pancras, Middx., B., and Elizabeth Wilkinson of S[t] Clement Danes, Middx., W.; by M[r] Pearce of S[t] Paul

Mar. 1 John Sugar of S[t] Dunstan, Stepney, Middx., B., and Mary Easter Delajaille of S[t] Mary, White Chapell, Middx., S.; by M[r] Worlich

5 Thomas Leigh of S[t] Dunstan in the West, London, B., and Alice Smith of S[t] Giles, Cripplegate, London, W.

8 Francis Haskins Eyles Styles of Rumford, Essex, B., and Sybilla Egerton of S[t] Ann, Westm[r], Middx., S.; by M[r] Fletcher of Rumford

11 Jasper Wrangle of S[t] Ethelburgh, London, B., and Barbara Moreley of the same, S.

19 John Singleton of Richmond, Surry, B., and Anne Freind of S[t] Mary, Islington, Middx., S.

20 William Arvin of S[t] Saviour, Southwarke, W., and Jane Chase of the same, W.; by M[r] Worlich

1740.

Mar. 26 William Sims of S[t] John, Wapping, Middx., W., and Mary Ann Williams of the same, S.

27 James Grimault of Stepney, Middx., B., and Ann Raine of Christ Church, Middx., S.; by M[r] Keighly

28 William Baker of S[t] Clement Danes, Middx., B., and Catherine Duffield of Chelsea, Middx., S.

29 George Pottinger of Lambeth, Surry, W., and Ann Bradley of S[t] Dionis Back Church, London, S.

30 William Stephens of S[t] Clement Danes, Middx., B., and Mary Clark of the same, S.

April 1 Simon Sell of S[t] Mary Axe, London, B., and Elizabeth Taylor of the same, W.; by M[r] Chambers

6 Thomas Giles of S[t] Martin in the Fields, Middx., B., and Mary Rowlls of the same, S.

6 James Harnsworth of S[t] Bride's, London, B., and Winefrid Skeff of Christ Church, Surry, S.

7 Robert Aiton of S[t] Martin in the Fields, Middx., B., and Mary Evans of S[t] Clement Danes, Middx., S.

7 John Hallsted of S[t] Margaret, Westm[r], Middx., B., and Mary Smith of the same, S.

1740

April 8 Thomas Barnett of S[t] Dunstan in the East, London, B., and Rachael Sherwin of S[t] Leonard, Shoreditch, Middx., S.

9 James Barker of Stepney, Middx., B., and Anne Mackett of S[t] Paul, Shadwell, Middx., W.

10 John Marshall of S[t] Giles in the Fields, Middx., B., and Anne Upton of the same, S.

12 Richard Ryder of S[t] Nicholas Cole Abby, London, B., and Sarah Browning of S[t] Mildred, Bread Street, London, S.

13 Thomas Hutchings of S[t] Gyles in the Fields, Middx., W., and Sarah Green of S[t] Michael Bassishaw, London, S.

13 John Wall of S[t] Clement Danes, Middx., W., and Mary Darnbroff of the same, W.

15 John Cole of S[t] Margaret, Westm[r], Middx., B., and Elizabeth Evans of X[st] Church, Spittalfields, Middx., S.

15 William Bird of S[t] George, Middx., B., and Frances Warrener of the same, W.

17 Alexander Storey of Sunderland, co. Durham, B., and Mary Bowman of S[t] Andrew, Holborn, London, S.

17 Joseph Cooke of S[t] George, Hanover Square, Middx., W., and Sarah Vero of S[t] Andrew, Holborn, Middx., S.

19 Robert Barrington of S[t] Mary, Rotherhith, Surry, B., and Mary Gibson of the same, W.

19 Richard Pain of Willsdon, Middx., B., and Anne Paine of Watford, co. Herts, S.

20 Christopher Imber of S[t] George the Martyr, Surry, W., and Ann Williams of the same, W.

22 Barton Miles of Yarmouth in the Isle of Wight, W., and Martha Miles of S[t] John, Southwark, Surry, S.

24 George Hickleton of S[t] Clement Danes, Middx., B., and Mary Brown of S[t] Andrew, Holborn, Middx., W.

27 Henry Marr of S[t] Paul, Covent Garden, Middx., B., and Martha Brown of S[t] Giles in the Fields, Middx., S.; by M[r] Lloyd

27 Abraham Jones of S[t] Luke, Middx., W., and Mary Moor of S[t] George, Bloomsbury, Middx., S.

27 William Ogborne of Wandsworth, Surry, B., and Sarah English of the same, S.

29 Joseph Smith of S[t] Botolph, Aldersgate, London, B., and Sarah Scott of the same, S.

May 5 Isaac Webb of S[t] Martin in the Fields, Middx., W., and Anne Sellman of S[t] Andrew, Holborn, Middx., S.

6 John Wilson of X[st] Church, Middx., B., and Rebecca Wood of S[t] Mary, White Chapel, Middx., S.

7 Richard Carter of S[t] Giles in the Fields, Middx., B., and Anne Harrison of S[t] Mary Magdalen, Bermondsey, Surry, S.; by M[r] Keighly

8 James Allix of S[t] Giles in the Fields, Middx., B., and Adriane Girod of the same, W.

8 Joseph Lockwood of Hanworth, Middx., B., and Rebecca Barlow of S[t] George, Hanover Square, Middx., S.

8 John Hutchinson of Osmaston, co. Derby, B., and Lucy Monk of S[t] James, Westminster, Middx., S.

10 Benjamin Tovey of S[t] Olave, Southwark, Surry, B., and Ely Hope of S[t] Mary Magdalen, Bermondsey, Surry, S.

10 Theodosius Reed of S[t] George, Bloomsbury, Middx., B., and Anne Dobson of S[t] Thomas the Apostle, London, S.

11 Gaspar Deliot of S[t] James, Westm[r], Middx., B., and Elizabeth Maingett of S[t] Giles in the Fields, Middx., S.

12 Samuel Challinge of Deptford, Kent, W., and Sarah Bishop of the same, S.

1740

May 13 Henry Howson of St Luke, Middx., W., and Ellenor Devenport of All Hallows, London, S.

13 Thomas Cock of St Dionis Backchurch, London, W., and Rachael Reed of Hampstead, Middx., S.

14 John Kemp of St George, Hanover Square, Middx., B., and Anne Butt of the same, S.

14 John Partington of St Magnus, London, B., and Elizabeth Rowlands of St George, Botolph Lane, London, W.

14 Joseph Carr of St James, Clerkenwell, Middx., B., and Dorothy Spencer of the same, S.

14 John Keet of St Mary Monthaw, London, W., and Sarah Allen of St Giles in the Fields, Middx., S.

14 Moses Gentleman of St Botolph, Aldgate, London, B., and Mary Sell of the same, S.; by the Rev. Dr Thomas

14 Thomas Coghell of Bushey, co. Herts, B., and Martha Weedon of St Michael, Cornhill, London, S.; by the same

14 John Wills of this parish, clerk, B., and Margaret Busby of St Martin, Ludgate, London, S.; by the Rev. Dr Thomas

15 Luke Pope of Hillingdon, Middx., W., and Sarah Hampton of Hayes, Middx., S.

15 John Godsalve of Much Baddow, Essex, B., and Catherine Mathew of the same, W.

21 William Quintin of St Sepulchre, London, B., and Mary Griffith of St James, Clerkenwell, Middx., S.; by the Rev. Mr Worlich

22 Samuel Frankling of St George, Hanover Square, Middx., W., and Joane Brice of the same, W.

22 Robert Doughty of the Middle Temple, London, B., and Margarett Lee of St Clement Danes, Middx., S.

22 Lewis John of St Martin in the Fields, Middx., B., and Elinor Holdsworth of St George, Hanover Square, Middx., S.

22 John Banfield of Ealing, Middx., B., and Mary Willis of St George, Hanover Square, Middx., S.

23 John Gray of East Greenwich, Kent, B., and Ann Thayer of St James, Westminster, Middx., W.

24 Robert Ewin of St Botolph, Aldgate, London, B., and Mary Newell of the same, W.

24 John Atkinson of Hackney, Middx., B., and Sarah Morell of the same, S.

25 William Adams of St Martin in the Fields, Middx., B., and Ann Cole of St Clement Danes, Middx., S.

26 Richard Puttenam of St James, Westminster, Middx., B., and Mary Abraham of the same, S.

26 Richard Harper of Wellington, Salop, B., and Elizabeth Ladds of the same, S.

27 Thomas Millbank of Woodford, Essex, B., and Anne Tanner of Raynham, Essex, S.

28 John Page, clerk, vicar of Penn, co. Bucks, W., and Dorothy Cotton of St George, Hanover Square, Middx., S.

29 William Essex of St Clement Danes, Middx., W., and Jane Crosby of the same, W.

31 Roger Beck of Camberwell, Surry, B., and Sarah White of the same, S.

June 2 The Hon. Heneage Legge, Esq., of the Inner Temple, London, B., and Catherine Fogg of East Sheen, Surry, S.; by the Rev. Mr Upton

2 Thomas Newton of St George in the East, Middx., B., and Anna Maria Smith of Newington, Surry, W.

4 John White of St Thomas the Apostle, London, B., and Elizabeth Clark of Xst Church, Surry, S.; by Rev. Dr Watkinson

1740

June 6 Richard Owens of Maidstone, Kent, B., and Sarah Slendon of the same, W.

7 John Moore of St Clement Danes, Middx., W., and Dorrington Dowbiggin of St Bride's, London, W.

7 John Gibbs of St James, Westmr, Middx., B., and Catherine Dignell of St Martin in the Fields, Middx., S.

8 Thomas Waller of St Andrew, Holborn, London, B., and Amme [*sic*] Creed of the same, W.

8 William Ellwood of St Brides, London, B., and Mary Graham of St Martin in the Fields, Middx., S.

15 Richard Cox of St Saviour, Southwark, Surry, B., and Mary Stevens of the same, W.

16 John Greensmith of St James, Westmr, Middx., B., and Dorothy Stevens of the same, W.

17 Bartholomew Hodgson of Hackney, Middx., B., and Rachael Grey of St Paul, Covent Garden, Middx., S.

17 Thomas Hill of Islington, Middx., B., and Sarah Pritchard of the same, S.

18 Ralph Wilkinson of Broughton, co. York, B., and Anne Shute of St Catherine by the Tower of London, S.

18 Devereux Cooke of St George, Bloomsbury, Middx., B., and Sabrina Smith of the same, S.

19 Francis Lewis Robert of St Ann, Westmr, Middx., B., and Charlotta Louisa Homot of St Mary Le Bone, Middx., S.

19 John Chick of Twickenham, Middx., B., and Elizabeth Shuttleworth of Richmond, Surry, S.

22 Daniel Nell of St John, Wapping, Middx., B., and Beneria Gibson of the same, S.

22 William Rubidge of St George the Martyr, Surry, W., and Mary Cotsal of St Saviour, Southwarke, S.

24 John Gaspard Ringmacher of St Bartholomew the Less, London, B., and Ann Aiskell of St Sepulchre, London, S.

25 William Nash of SS. Ann and Agnes, Aldersgate, London, B., and Ruth Ven of St James, Clerkenwell, Middx., S.

26 John Davis of St Gregory, London, B., and Mary Lonsdale of the same, S.

27 Henry Egleton of St Margaret, Westmr, Middx., W., and Mary Curtis of the same, W.

28 Edward Jones of St Clement Danes, Middx., W., and Mary Buckley of St James, Westminster, Middx., W.

29 John Booley of Leostoff near Yarmouth, Suffolk, B., and Sarah Coleman of the same, S.; by the Rev. Mr Worlich

29 John Eastop of St John, Southwarke, Surry, B., and Mary Rooding of St Luke, Middx., S.

30 William Trotter of St Giles in the Fields, Middx., B., and Joyce Horne of St George in the East, Middx., S.

30 Francis Delaballe of St Ann, Westmr, Middx., B., and Mary Bayeux Cauvin of the same, S.

July 1 Thomas Kent of St Giles in the Fields, Middx., W., and Elizabeth Ebrall of Bletchingly, Surry, S.

1 James Hill of St Martin in the Fields, Middx., B., and Anne Adams of the same, W.

3 John Ranking of Mortlack, Surry, B., and Ann Harrod of Barnes in the said county, S.

5 Daniel Hull of St Martin, Ludgate, London, B., and Dorothy Atwell of St Martin in the Fields, Middx., S.

5 William Cross of St Botolph, Aldgate, London, B., and Anne Chalkey of St Mary, White Chapel, Middx., S.

1740

July 5 Nicholas Cooth of St Saviour, Southwarke, W., and Rachael Robins of the same, S.

10 William Godwin of St Margaret, Lothbury, London [*blank*], and Ann Harding of the same, S.

13 Thomas Turford of St Dunstan, Stepney, Middx., B., and Anne Wyburd of St Mary, White Chapel, Middx., S.*

15 John Rogers of Camberwell, Surry, W., and Ann Bayly of the same, S.; by the Rev. Mr Sandford

15 George Mace of Orpington, Kent, B., and Alice Eades of Beddington, Surry, S.; by Mr Sandford

17 Ambrose Evans of St Martin in the Fields, Middx., W., and Margaret Pert of St Andrew, Holborn, Middx., S.; by Rev. Mr Keighly

18 John Lockwood of St Saviour, Southwarke, B., and Mary Drucce of St Bride's, London, S.; by Rev. Dr Thomas

22 William Hill of Whitby, co. York, B., and Mary Goddard of North Sheilds in Northumberland, S.

24 Marker Head of Battersea, Surry, B., and Mary Stevens of St James, Westminster, Middx., S.

26 Jeremiah Collins of Richmond, Surry, B., and Margaret Pritchard of the same, S.

27 Charles Spendelow of St Giles in the Fields, Middx., B., and Hannah Pattison of the same, S.

27 James Showell of St George, Hanover Square, Middx., B., and Anne Charity of the same, S.

28 Charles Edwards of Lambeth, Surry, B., and Charity Pilbury of the same, S.

28 George Thomas of St James, Westm^r, Middx., B., and Mary Browning of the same, S.

28 John Manoury of Stepney, Middx., W., and Esther Grimault of the same, S.

29 William Crouch of St Giles in the Fields, Middx., B., and Elizabeth Hutchinson of St Margaret, Westm^r, Middx., S.

30 Richard Thurlow of Cambridge, B., and Jemima Bourne of the same, S.

30 Michael Jones of St Ann, Westminster, Middx., W., and Elizabeth Harper of the same, S.

31 John Pope of Acton, co. Middx., B., and Margaret Hawdon of St George, Bloomsbury, Middx., S.

Aug. 2 John Machin of St Ann, Westm^r, Middx., W., and Ann Hodson of the same, S.; by the Rev. Dr Thomas

4 Robert Cook of Stepney, Middx., W., and Joanna Linn of St Mary, Rotherhith, Surry, W.

5 Robert Syrett of St George, Middx., B., and Margaret Clayton of St Mary, Aldermanbury, London, W.

7 William Barton of St Mary Magdalen, Bermondsey, Surry, B., and Mary Parker of the same, S.

8 Thomas Neverson of St Margaret, Westm^r, Middx., B., and Ann Metcalfe of Richmond, Surry, S.

9 John Rotherford of X^st Church, Surry, B., and Mary Willoughby of the same, W.

10 Samuel Pett of Eye, Suffolk, B., and Anne Kerry of the same, S.

11 George Woillenge of St Martin in the Fields, Middx., B., and Susannah Ridor of the same, W.

12 Thomas Walker of Stepney, Middx., B., and Mariana Tonstill of X^st Church, Middx., S.

* This entry is at the end of July in the original, with a note that it is misplaced.—Ed.

1740
Aug. 12 Thomas Reid of St Mary, White Chapple, Middx., B., and Elizabeth Read of the same, S.
14 Edward Agar of St Bartholomew the Great, London, B., and Elizabeth Briggs of the same, S.
14 Robert Wray of St Dunstan in the West, London, B., and Mary Smith of this parish, W.
14 William Pye of St James, Clerkenwell, Middx., W., and Sarah Edwards of the same, W.
16 Richard Grant of St Margaret, Westmr, Middx., B., and Deborah Bolton of the same, W.; by the Rev. Mr Worlich
17 Thomas Martin of St Clement Danes, Middx., B., and Mary West of the same, W.
18 Xstopher Bond of St Mary Woolnoth, London, B., and Ann Palhthorp of St Swithin, London, S.; by Mr Worlich
19 Edward Bowman of St Clement Danes, Middx., W., and Anna Maria Jackson of the same, S.
22 James Thomas of Mortlake, Surry, B., and Millicent Taylor of the same, S.
25 Blackburn Poulton of Barking, Essex, B., and Mary Smith of St Clement Danes, Middx., S.
27 William Jefferies of West Ham, Essex, B., and Hannah Hobson of the same, S.
29 John Haines of St Paul, Covent Garden, Middx., B., and Martha Ewer of the same, S.
30 John Poole of St Leonard, Shoreditch, Middx., B., and Elizabeth Rose of the same, S.; by the Rev. Mr Keighly
Sept. 1 Chiverton Cooper of St Anne, Middx., B., and Mary Donne of the same, S.
1 Thomas Rickword of St Martin in the Fields, Middx., B., and Jane Hutcheson of the same, S.
2 Andrew Chapman of Deptford, Kent, W., and Frances Attwood of St Edmund the King, London, S.
2 John Scott of St Botolph, Aldgate, London, B., and Anne Reynolds of the same, S.
3 Henry Gibson of St Sepulchre, London, W., and Elizabeth Jones of the same, W.
4 Richard Funstone of Wandsworth, Surry, W., and Grace Dowle of St Andrew, Holborn, London, S.
4 Thomas Gray of St Dunstan, Stepney, Middx., B., and Margaret Cooper of St Magnus, London, S.
5 John Hodgson of Ham, Essex, B., and Mary Corbett of the same, S.
8 Andrew Crackan of Chelsea, Middx., B., and Pasky Bagwell of Hammersmith, Middx., S.
9 Clem Davis of Stepney, Middx., B., and Elizabeth Stephens of the same, S.
13 John Guy of Speldhurst, Kent, B., and Ann Beezon of Bromley, Kent, S.
13 James Thornton of St Martin in the Fields, Middx., B., and Sarah Royall of St George, Hanover Square, Middx., S.
15 Joshua Hallows of St Luke, Middx., B., and Martha Manwaring of the same, S.
16 James Cooper of St John the Evangelist, Westmr, Middx., W., and Jane Paul of the same, W.
18 Thomas Gibbs of Chipping Norton, co. Oxford, B., and Sarah Norgrove of the same, W.
18 James Knight of Eaton, co. Bucks, B., and Margaret Ware of St James, Westminster, Middx., S.

1740

Sept. 20 James Hind of West Ham, Essex, W., and Ann Woodbridge of the same, W.
24 George Wills of S[t] Martin in the Fields, Middx., W., and Ann Tappley of the same, S.
25 Thomas Ranson of S[t] Anne, Westminster, Middx., B., and Mary Hill of S[t] George, Hanover Square, Middx., S.
25 Thomas Brent of Plymouth, co. Devon, B., and Elizabeth Dodemead of S[t] Paul, Covent Garden, Middx., S.
25 Xstopher Anderson of S[t] James, Westm[r], Middx., B., and Margaret Hill of the same, S.
27 Andrew Duncan of S[t] Botolph, Aldgate, London, W., and Elizabeth Nicholson of S[t] John, Wapping, Middx., S.
28 John Hitchin of Stevenage, co. Herts, B., and Mary Bradnam of the same, S.
29 John Tuckwell of S[t] Martin in the Fields, Middx., W., and Martha Tiffin of the same, W.
30 William Standfast of S[t] Mary Magdalen, Old Fish Street, London, W., and Jane Haskins of the same, S.

Oct. 2 John Chapman of S[t] Lawrence Pountney, London, W., and Susannah Warren, W.
2 Jonas Rhodes of Reading, co. Berks, B., and Elizabeth May of S[t] George the Martyr, Middx., S.
6 Berrisford Bacon of S[t] John, Wapping, Middx., W., and Elizabeth Fearne of S[t] Mary, Rotherhith, Surry, S.
8 John Goodwin of Bermondsey, Southwarke, B., and Elizabeth Standley of the same, S.
8 Edward Ling of Barkin, Essex, B., and Ann Davis of the same, S.
9 Thomas Drury of Foremarke, co. Derby, B., and Elizabeth Lamken of Whorwell, Hants, S.
9 Joseph Freeman of Battersea, Surry, B., and Sarah Margetts of the same, S.
10 John Thompson of Shadwell, Middx., B., and Wealthany Lamb of the same, W.
12 Richard Holbeche of Queenhythe, London, W., and Elizabeth Goodfreind of S[t] George, Bloomsbury, Middx., W.
13 Joseph Downs of All Hallows the Great, London, B., and Sarah Curryer of Battersea, Surry, S.; by the Rev. M[r] Church
14 William Jackson of Bushey, co. Herts, B., and Anne Humphreys of the same, W.; by the Rev. M[r] Worlich
16 John Rounsivell of S[t] Bartholomew behind the Exchange, London, B., and Elizabeth Wood of S[t] Catherine by the Tower, London, S.
16 John Willson of S[t] Michael, Cornhill, London, B., and Elizabeth Perlour of the same, S.
17 John Ewen of S[t] Margaret Pattons, London, B., and Susannah Brookhouse of S[t] Mary Le Bow, London, W.
18 John Richardson of S[t] Andrew, Holborn, London, B., and Isabella Dilley of S[t] Giles in the Fields, Middx., W.
19 Joshua Hardye, B., and Mary Trantham, S., both of this parish
21 James Crown of S[t] John, Wapping, Middx., W., and Phillis Johnson of S[t] George in the East, Middx., S.
21 Humphrey Rand of S[t] Botolph, Aldgate, Middx., W., and Margaret Honeywell of S[t] Helen's, London, S.
26 Robert Paine of S[t] Margaret, Westm[r], Middx., W., and Margaret Eaton of the same, W.
26 John Eaton of S[t] Margaret, Westm[r], Middx., B., and Jane Howard of the same, S.
28 Thomas Bolland of Uxbridge, Middx., B., and Elizabeth Mason of the same, W.

1740
Oct. 28 John Harvey of X^st Church, London, W., and Susanna Williams of St Faith, London, S.; by the Rev Mr Worlich

29 William Bunch of St Mildred in the Poultrey, London, W., and Mary Read of St Miles, Crooked Lane, London, W.

31 Matthew Sainsbury of East Greenwich, Kent, B., and Jane Hubley of the same, S.

Nov. 1 Thomas Conway of Wanstead, Essex, B., and Catharine Rebend of St Gyles in the Fields, Middx., S.

2 Thomas Simkins of St Sepulchre's, London, W., and Elizabeth Hopkins of the same, S.

2 Caspar Claussen, B., and Sarah Hewkin, S., both of this parish. Banns

4 William Beckett of St George, Hanover Square, Middx., B., and Elizabeth Cranedge of the same, S.

5 George Elliott of Wapping Wall, Middx., B., and Anne Johnson of St Paul, Covent Garden, Middx., S.

6 Richard Pavey of St Margaret, Westm^r, Middx., W., and Susanna Rathbone of the same, S.

6 William Dormer of St James, Westm^r, Middx., W., and Catharine Venables of St Anne, Westm^r, Middx., W.

8 John Mayhew of St Botolph, Aldgate, London, B., and Hester Cheney of the same, S.

8 Thomas Fox of St Martin in the Fields, Middx., B., and Elizabeth Harris of the same, W.

8 John Arthur of St Anne, Westminster, Middx., W., and Ann Bayeux of the same, S.

9 Charles Forster of St Gyles in the Fields, Middx., B., and Mary Griszel of St Anne, Westminster, Middx., S.

9 Even Evens of St Paul, Covent Garden, Middx., B., and Ann Housman of the same, S.

9 Francis Hussey of St George, Bloomsbury, Middx., B., and Susannah Hurst of the same, S.

10 Thomas Prichard of St George the Martyr, Middx., W., and Ann Wallton of St James, Clerkenwell, Middx., W.

11 Adam Eve of Poplar in Stepney, Middx., B., and Elizabeth Linsley of St Anne, Limehouse, Middx., S.

12 James Hawkins of St Mary, White Chapple, Middx., B., and Anne Hawkins of the same, S.

12 John Dumas of St James, Westm^r, Middx., B., and Mary Youll of the same, S.

13 Joseph Whittaker of St Clement Danes, Middx., B., and Ann Long of the same, S.

13 John Tomson of St Leonard, Shoreditch, Middx., B., and Mary Holmes of St Mary, Newington, Middx., S.

15 William Kinleside of St Magnus, London, W., and Mary Galton of St Thomas, Southwarke, W.

16 Stephen Jenkins of St Dunstan, Stepney, Middx., B., and Phebe Fulford of St John, Wapping, Middx., S.

18 Joseph Merry of Gayton, co. Northampton, W., and Elizabeth Wood of Windsor, co. Berks, W.

20 John Goodinge of Richmond, Surry, B., and Ann Piggott of Isleworth, Middx., S.

25 George Stocks of St George, Middx., B., and Barbara Robinson of the same, S.

27 Lawrence Eakman of St Paul, Shadwell, Middx., B., and Mary Lilly of the same, S.

27 Thomas Lewis of St Margaret Pattons, London, B., and Ann Miller of the same, S.

1740

Nov. 27 John Wakerell of Beckenham, Kent, W., and Amey Muggeridge of the same, S.

27 William Musgrove of Maidstone, Kent, B., and Martha Newton of the same, S.

30 Samuel Rogers of Lay in Grashford, co. Denbigh, Esq., W., and Sarah Enstone of Newbury, co. Berks, W.

Dec. 1 James Littlejohn of S[t] Michael, Cornhill, London, B., and Eleanor Winder of Peter Le Poor, London, S.; by the Rev. M[r] Charles

2 John Crooke of S[t] James, Westminster, Middx., B., and Mary Jones of S[t] Peter, Paul's Wharfe, S.

4 Henry Edmund Herbert of S[t] James, Westm[r], Middx., W., and Mary Allen of the same, S.

4 Thomas Woodford of S[t] George, Hanover Square, Middx., B., and Sarah Adams of the same, S.

7 Thomas Tooner of S[t] Dunstan, Stepney, Middx., B., and Elizabeth Burnell of the same, S.

7 Thomas Barton of Chertsey, Surry, B., and Martha Ellis of the same place, S.

9 William Allchin of Wallingham, Surry, B., and Sarah Gilbert of the same, S.

9 George Paine of S[t] George in the East, Middx., W., and Jane Emmett of S[t] Olave, Hart Street, London, S.

10 Richard Saxby of Itham, Kent, B., and Sarah Rawlinson of Chevening, Kent, S.

11 John Pellon of S[t] Paul, Covent Garden, Middx., B., and Elizabeth Tyson of S[t] Michael, Wood Street, London, S.

11 Edward Harland of S[t] George, Hanover Square, Middx., B., and Anne Coates of the same, S.

11 Thomas Jones of S[t] Clement Danes, Middx., W., and Lettice Edwards of S[t] Dunstan in the West, London, W.

12 James Page of S[t] Martin in the Fields, Middx., W., and Elizabeth Wescott of Deptford, Kent, S.

13 William Wragg of the Middle Temple, London, Esq., B., and Mary Wood of S[t] Clement Danes, Middx., S.

13 William Davies of S[t] Martin, Ludgate, London, B., and Margaret Matthews of the same, W.

14 Elisha Whitchurst of S[t] George, Middx., W., and Elizabeth Johnson of S[t] Stephen, Coleman Street, London, W.

14 Francis Cremer of S[t] Gyles in the Fields, Middx., W., and Anne Bridges of S[t] Bennet Sherehog, London, S.

14 Thomas Chapman of S[t] James, Westm[r], Middx., B., and Rose Barnes of the same, S.

14 William Lewis of All Hallows the Great, London, B., and Rachael Frances of S[t] Thomas the Apostle, London, S.

16 Thomas Squire of Thrapston, co. Northampton, B., and Elizabeth Bletso of Wringstead, co. Northampton, S.

18 Michael Kistell of S[t] Paul, Covent Garden, Middx., B., and Mary Cradock of S[t] Andrew, Holborn, Middx., S.

20 John Walker of Leigh, Kent, B., and Sarah Powis of Greenwich, Kent, S.

25 Duncan Wright of S[t] Margaret, Westminster, Middx., B., and Isabell Hunter of S[t] George, Hanover Square, Middx., S.

27 James Osmond of Shenley, co. Herts, B., and Elizabeth Baker of the same, S.

27 Edward Shipley of S[t] Mary Overy's, Surry, B., and Elizabeth Gee of the same, S.

30 Benjamin Sidey of S[t] Sepulchre's, Middx., B., and Elizabeth Bayes of Low Leighton, Essex, S.

1740

Dec. 30 John Prentice of the Island of Foulness in Essex, B., and Hannah Preston of the same Island, S.

31 Henry Carpenter of S[t] Saviour, Southwark, B., and Elizabeth Partridge of the same, S.

Jan. 1 John Walker of S[t] Paul, Covent Garden, Middx., W., and Ann Elledge of the same, S.

1 Stephen Kingston of Hampstead, Middx., B., and Louisa Fletcher of S[t] Paul, Covent Garden, Middx., S.

5 Humphrey Winder of Wilsden, Middx., B., and Rebecca Mills of S[t] James, Westminster, Middx., S.

5 Richard Baxter of S[t] Mary at Hill, London, B., and Martha Cookson of the same, S.

7 James Magrath of S[t] John, Wapping, Middx., B., and Frances Donaldson of the same, W.

8 Louis Baud of S[t] Ann, Westminster, Middx., B., and Ann Ellis of S[t] Stephen, Coleman Street, London, S.

12 John Sore of Amberstone, co. Derby, B., and Mary Gibson of S[t] James, Westm[r], Middx., S.; by M[r] Keighly

12 Daniel Williams of S[t] Luke, Middx., B., and Jane Stalker of S[t] Sepulchre, London, S.; by M[r] Pearce of S[t] Paul's

13 John Lewis of S[t] Sepulchre's, London, W., and Selena Turner of the same, W.; by ditto

15 Robert Martin of S[t] Catherine Creed Church, London, W., and Anne Johnson of S[t] Peter, Cornhill, London, S.; by M[r] Keighly

16 Peter Pemell of Westerham, Kent, B., and Mary Richbell of S[t] Martin in the Fields, Middx., S.; by the same

16 Robert Barnard of S[t] Olave, Southwarke, Surry, B., and Isabella Bell of the same, S.; by M[r] Worlich

19 Richard Lee of Ingarstone, Essex, B., and Mary Hasildon of S[t] Martin in the Fields, Middx., S.

20 Benjamin Holloway of Coventry, co. Warwick, B., and Sarah Smith of Uxbridge, Middx., S.

21 William Drew of Mitcham, Surry, B., and Elizabeth Harman of Lambeth, Surry, W.

22 Martin Bird of Richmond, Surry, B., and Mary Jesson of Mortlake, Surry, S.

24 Robert Cayer of S[t] Andrew, Holbourn, London, B., and Anne Mannering of S[t] Mary Woolnoth, London, S.

26 John Chipsis of S[t] Andrew, Holbourn, London, B., and Mary Bowden of the same, S.

27 John Gregory of All Hallows Barking, London, W., and Mary Gates of S[t] Dunstan in the East, London, W.

27 John Allen of Hemelhampsted, co. Herts, B., and Sarah Paine of Bovingdon, co. Herts, S.

27 John Christopher Gohl of All Hallows, Lombard Street, London, B., and Catherine Thompson of the same, S.

28 William Borlase of S[t] Martin in the Fields, Middx., B., and Mary Merrick of the same, W.

28 William Wheeler of S[t] James, Clerkenwell, Middx., B., and Elizabeth Martin of the same, W.

28 Thomas Lovejoy of X[st] Church, London, B., and Elizabeth Phillips of S[t] Mary Somerset, London, S.

30 Thomas Goostrey of S[t] Clement Danes, Middx., B., and Mary Ansell of S[t] George the Martyr, Middx., S.

Feb. 2 John Maples of S[t] Dunstan, Stepney, Middx., B., and Hannah Archer of S[t] Botolph, Bishopsgate, London, S.

2 John Oxley of S[t] Michael, Cornhill, London, B., and Ann Becket of S[t] Michael, Wood Street, London, S.

1740-41

Feb. 5 James Goodes of S[t] Giles, Cripplegate, London, B., and Mary Crampton of S[t] Brides, London, S.

5 James Simpson of S[t] Lawrence, Jewry, London, B., and Hannah South of the same, S.

7 Samuel Trowell of Hammersmith, Middx., W., and Rebecca Dare of the same, S.

8 John Thompson of S[t] Andrew, Holbourn, Middx., B., and Jane Pears of the same, S.

8 Thomas Gibbs of Hendon, Middx., B., and Elizabeth Laws of the same, S.

8 Richard Burges of Thames Ditton, Surry, B., and Elizabeth Lee of S[t] Saviour, Southwarke, Surry, S.

8 John Nash, B., and Anne Atwell, S., both of this parish. Banns

9 Thomas Dawes of S[t] John, Wapping, Middx., B., and Anne Grant of S[t] Peter, Paul's Wharfe, London, S.

9 Joshua Roberts of Clapham, Surry, B., and Alice Pinfold of the same, S.

10 George Hartley of S[t] George, Hanover Square, Middx., B., and Mary Mason of the same, S.

10 Joseph Compton of S[t] James, Westm[r], Middx., B., and Elizabeth Bethell of S[t] George, Hanover Square, Middx., S.

10 Richard Watkis of S[t] Giles in the Fields, Middx., B., and Mary Hughes of the same, S.

10 William Robinson of S[t] Andrew, Holborn, London, W., and Elizabeth Taylor of S[t] Botolph, Aldersgate, London, S.

10 John Griffiths of Swansey, co. Glamorgan, B., and Ann Romaine of S[t] Mary, Rotherhith, Surry, S.

10 James Harres of Ewell, W., and Alice Oulsan of Epsom, Surry, S.

10 Francis Allum of S[t] Saviour, Southwarke, B., and Hannah Norris of Lambeth, Surry, S.

10 Thomas Burgoyne of S[t] Margaret, Westm[r], Middx., W., and Jane Millward of the same, S.; by M[r] Keighly

12 Francis Stone of S[t] Mary le Bone, Middx., B., and Anne Blandy of S[t] Nicholas Olave, London, S.

14 Richard Sharpe of S[t] Leonard, Shoreditch, Middx., B., and Sarah Waller of Waltham Abbey, Essex, S.

19 Richard Grundy of S[t] Botolph, Aldgate, Middx., B., and Bridgett Newman of the same, W.

19 William Prisley of S[t] Paul, Covent Garden, Middx., B., and Jane Dunster of the same, W.

21 Hope Hazard of S[t] Ann, Blackfryers, London, B., and Mary Leech of S[t] Bride's, London, S.

23 Jeffery French of the Middle Temple, London, Esq., B., and Catharine LLoyd of S[t] George, Hanover Square, Middx., S.

26 Robert Shaw of S[t] Dunstan, Stepney, Middx., B., and Elizabeth Leadstone of the same, S.

Mar. 3 Mark MacCarty of S[t] Andrew, Holbourn, Middx., W., and Catherine MacCarty of S[t] Dionis Backchurch, London, W.

3 Thomas Place of S[t] Andrew, Holborn, London, B., and Mary Frye of the same, S.

3 Robert Powney of S[t] Mary Le Strand, Middx., W., and Susanna Matthews of S[t] Pancras, Middx., W.

4 George Paris of S[t] Mary Magdalen, Bermondsey, Surry, B., and Mary Jennings of the same, S.

5 William Methuen of S[t] Clement Danes, Middx., B., and Mary Videll of S[t] John the Evangelist, Westminster, W.

7 Thomas Parry of S[t] Saviour, Southwark, Surry, W., and Elizabeth Sidy of S[t] Dunstan, Stepney, Middx., S.

1740-41

Mar. 9 Stavely Parker of Cambridge, B., and Elenor Postlethwaite of Portsmouth, Hants, S.

10 William Masters of S[t] Mary Magdalen, Bermondsey, Surry, W., and Hannah Cole of Wandsworth, Surry, W.

12 William Hubbard of Edmonton, Middx., B., and Rachael Surredge of the same, S.

14 John Garret of Chelsea, Middx. [*blank*], and Elizabeth Hutchins of the same, S.

17 Samuel Smith of S[t] Saviour, Southwark, Surry, B., and Elizabeth Brown of the same, S.; by Mr. Hillman

1741.

Mar. 28 George Sarling of Low Layton, Essex, B., and Susannah Hunt of Wanstead, Essex, W.

28 Xstopher Humphreys of S[t] Brides, London, B., and Mary Fox of S[t] Sepulchre, London, S.

28 Joseph Copes of S[t] Paul, Shadwell, Middx., B., and Margaret Hart of X[st] Church, Middx., S.

29 James Chipperfield of S[t] Leonard, Shoreditch, Middx., B., and Debora Darby of the same, S.

30 John Kensett of Putney, Surrey, B., and Elizabeth Hart of the same, S.

31 Caleb Jope of S[t] Luke, Middx., B., and Elizabeth Blackwell of Lambeth, Surry, S.

31 Joseph Patrick of Petersfield, Hants, B., and Elizabeth Pissey of All Hallows Staining, London, S.

April 2 Edward Gilby of Ryslip, Middx., B., and Rachael Page of the same, S.

2 Charles Kenyon of S[t] Edmundsbury, Suffolk, B., and Mary Kenyon of the same, W.

4 William Hipwell of S[t] Martin in the Fields, Middx., W., and Elizabeth Carter of this parish, S.

5 John Campbell of S[t] Mary Somerset, London, B., and Ann Bryan of S[t] Dunstan, Stepney, Middx., S.

6 John Allen of Halstead, Essex, B., and Mary Crowhurst of Greenwich, Kent, S.

8 Edward Meades of Putney, Surry, W., and Mary Woodroffe of the same, S.

9 John Ashley of S[t] James, Clerkenwell, Middx., W., and Hannah Allen of the same, S.

10 Francis Perrin of S[t] Botolph, Aldgate, Middx., W., and Elizabeth Foster of the same, S.

11 Daniel Willson of S[t] Andrew, Holbourne, London, B., and Anne Stringer of S[t] Bride's, London, W.; by M[r] Keighly

12 William Middleton of S[t] George, Southwark, Surry, B., and Sarah Nixon of S[t] Dionis Backchurch, London, S.

12 Joseph Robins of East Greenwich, Kent, B., and Ann Dibbil of S[t] Swithin, London, S.

12 Jeremiah Colman of Whymondham, Norfolk, B., and Elizabeth Causton of S[t] Botolph, Aldersgate, London, W.

19 John Holloway of S[t] Gregory, London, W., and Elianor Brown of the same, S.

21 John Steele of S[t] Sepulchre's, Middx., W., and Catherine Stubbs of S[t] Mary, Newington Butts, Surrey, W.

23 James May of West Wickham, Kent, B., and Ann Uridge of the same, S.

25 Thomas Hunter of Abbots Langley, co. Herts, W., and Mary Ballard of S[t] Stephen near S[t] Albans, co. Herts, S.

26 Vincent Hinton of S[t] Paul, Shadwell, Middx., B., and Elizabeth Stevens of the same, S.

1741

April 26 William Dolman of S[t] Andrew, Holborn, Middx., W., and Elizabeth Constable of S[t] Giles, Cripplegate, London, S.

26 William Elderton of S[t] Gyles, Cripplegate, London, B., and Elizabeth Farrin of the same, S.

27 Theophilus Newstead of S[t] Andrew, Holborn, Middx., B., and Elizabetha Sophia Venden of the same, S.

28 William Manning of S[t] Martin in the Fields, Middx., B., and Ellinor Greenfield of the same, S.

28 James Smith of S[t] Sepulchre, London, B., and Sarah Smartfoot of the same, W.

30 Michael Kirby of S[t] James, Clerkenwell, Middx., B., and Elizabeth Adams of the same, W.

30 John Vincent of S[t] Martin in the Fields, Middx., B., and Anne Poynton of S[t] George, Hanover Square, Middx., S.

30 Abraham Ravenell of X[st] Church, Spittlefields, Middx., W., and Mary De Caux of the same, S.

May 4 Abraham Ogier of S[t] Michael, Cornhill, London, B., and Martha Turquand of X[st] Church, Middx., S.

6 Caleb Chips of S[t] Martin in the Fields, Middx., B., and Mary Mortimor of the same, S.

7 Robert Gooding of S[t] James, Westminster, Middx., B., and Margaret Cox of S[t] Ann, Westminster, Middx., W.

8 Josiah Mickelfield of West Ham, Essex, B., and Elizabeth Williams of the same, W.

8 Joseph Thompson of Woolwich, Kent, W., and Johannah Sparks of the same, S.

10 Edward White of S[t] George in the East, Middx., B., and Mary Hack of the same, W.

10 Simon Williams of S[t] Margaret, Westminster, Middx., B., and Joanna Cobden of the same, S.

12 Stephen Langford of S[t] Luke, Middx. [*blank*], and Elizabeth Low of the same, W.

12 Abraham Skegg of Hitchin, co. Herts, B., and Hannah Shilford of Stevenage, co. Herts, S.; by D[r] Thomas

15 Nathaniel Jeffreys of X[st] Church, Surry, W., and Sarah Smith of S[t] Andrew, Holborn, London, S.; by M[r] Bailey

15 Joseph Bell Simmors of Chatham, Kent, B., and Anna Ince of Sheerness, Kent, W.; by M[r] Worlich

15 Thomas Fitzherbert of Beckenham, Kent, B., and Sarah Belchcoben of the same, W.; by M[r] Worlich

17 Zachary Gisborne of S[t] Andrew, Holborn, Middx., B., and Ann White of the same, S.

18 William West of S[t] Paul, Deptford, Kent, B., and Mary Attwood of S[t] Luke, Middx., S.

19 Thomas Hunt, W., and Mary Whiskins, W., both of this parish. Banns*

20 William Barker of Stroud, Kent, W., and Anne Cox of the same, S.

21 Richard Hinton of S[t] Margaret, Westm[r], Middx., W., and Anne Stevens of the same, S.

21 Thomas Paddey of Tottenham High Cross, Middx., B., and Catharine Byworth of S[t] Dunstan in the West, London, S.

21 Edward Snowdin of Leeds, co. York, W., and Elizabeth Pitt of Thaden, Essex, W.

23 Joseph Joyce of S[t] Clement Danes, Middx., W., and Eleanor Morley of Hampstead, Middx., W.

* Entered by error at the end of May on next page of the Register.—Ed.

1741

May 24 John Alderman of St Peter in the Town of Bedford, W., and Beatrice Tubman of Barnwell, co. Northampton, S.

25 Gabriel Payne of Stifford, Essex, B., and Susannah Milton of St George, Hanover Square, Middx., S.

26 William Evans of Hendon, Middx., B., and Mary Machan of the same, S.

26 John Grace of St Saviour, Southwark, Surry, B., and Elizabeth Harrison of the same, W.

26 Nicholas Child of Clapham, Surry, W., and Ann Glanvill of Milton, Kent, S.; by Mr Bailey

28 Philip Wynell of Lincoln's Inn, Middx., B., and Betty Salt of Betley, co. Stafford, S.

28 William Clark of St Paul's, Canterbury, B., and Elizabeth Carter of the same, S.

28 Henry Walter of Woking, Surry, B., and Margaret LLoyd of St Alban, Wood Street, London, W.; by Mr Saunders

29 Joseph Hurdle of St John, Hackney, Middx., B., and Elizabeth Hutson of the same, S.

31 Timothy Truman of St Magnus the Martyr, London, B., and Elizabeth Whitchouse of the same, S.

June 4 Edward Hewett of St Dunstan in the West, London, B., and Mary Hopkins of White Cleve, Wilts, S.

5 William Kitchingman of St John, Wapping, Middx., B., and Elizabeth Mewburne of Northshields, Northumberland, W.

5 William Sanders of Pancras, Middx., B., and Mary Elkins of the same, W.

6 Peter Clerke of St James, Westminster, Middx., B., and Esther George of Fulham, Middx., S.

6 John Simpson of St Martin in the Fields, Middx., W., and Elizabeth Higgins of the same, S.

10 Joseph Heighington of Kingston upon Thames, Surry, B., and Elizabeth Palmer of the same, S.

10 William Charlesworth of St Mary le Strand, Middx., B., and Martha Robinson of St Peter Cheape, London, S.

11 Lancelot Burton of St Clement Danes, Middx., B., and Hannah Sedgwick of St Ann, Limehouse, Middx., S.; by Mr Bayley

11 Thomas Arnold of St Saviour, Southwarke, Surry, W., and Martha Collins of Endfield, Middx., S.; by Dr Best

13 Robert Dunbar of St Giles in the Fields, Middx., B., and Mary Alcock of St James, Westminster, Middx., S.

15 William Jourdain, the elder, of Edmonton, Middx., W., and Elizabeth Tirau of St Dunstan, Stepney, Middx., S.

17 Henry Howard of Isleworth, Middx., B., and Elizabeth Hethwell of the same, S.

18 Moses Carter of St Dionis Back Church, London, B., and Sarah Woodley of the same, S.

22 John Marsh of Wandsworth in Surrey, B., and Edith Taylor of the same, S.

23 Thomas Wolfall of St Paul, Covent Garden, Middx., W., and Hester Dove of St George, Bloomsbury, Middx., W.

23 John Fowler of Blechingly, Surry, B., and Susannah Rowed of Caterham, Surry, S.

23 William Jordan of Richmond, Surry, W., and Emery Fairclue of the same, S.

28 William Loveland of St Gregory, London, B., and Elianor Bilson of the same, S.

28 John Hurst of Ware, co. Herts, W., and Dorothy Bateman of St Clement Danes, Middx., S.

1741

June 29 Thomas Drury of S[t] Paul, Shadwell, Middx., W., and Susannah Vaughan of S[t] Peter le Poor, London, S.

30 Lionel Longdon of S[t] George, Hanover Square, Middx., B., and Dorothy Larmer of the same, S.

July 2 Richard Miles of Lambeth, Surry, W., and Elizabeth Hill of Battersea, Surry, S.

2 Richard Monk of S[t] Margaret, Westm[r], Middx., B., and Mary Davies of the same, S.

3 Thomas Whare of S[t] Botolph, Aldersgate, London, B., and Margaret Wagstaffe of the same, S.

5 Charles Hare of S[t] Clement Danes, Middx., B., and Hester Mashborne of the same, S.

8 Robert Bell of Bocking in Essex, B., and Priscilla Prime of S[t] Buttolph without Aldgate, London, W.

9 Robert Taylor of S[t] John, Southwarke, Surry, B., and Elizabeth Martin of the same, S.

12 Jonathan Crook of S[t] Mary le Bone, Middx., B., and Elizabeth Pearsehouse of the same, S.

12 Charles Fynmore of S[t] James, Clerkenwell, Middx., B., and Beata Pollard of the same, S.

12 Daniel Pearson of S[t] Mary, Rotherhith, Surry, B., and Jane Constable of the same, S.

12 Thomas Berridge, B., and Lydia Flawn, S., both of this parish. Banns

13 John Payes of Bishop Starford, co. Herts, B., and Margaret Brasier of the same, W.

16 John Cobham of S[t] Andrew, Holborn, London, B., and Mary Eysham of S[t] Luke, Middx., S.; by M[r] Bailey

17 James Bourdien of S[t] Leonard, Bromley, near Bow, Middx., B., and Hannah Gill of the same, W.; by M[r] Sparkes

21 Ralph Jackson of Harrow on the Hill, Middx., B., and Elizabeth Goodwin of Shepperton, Middx., S.

22 Henry Griffith of S[t] Dunstan in the West, London, B., and Mary Hobbs of the same, S.

28 Henry Canham of Layston, Suffolk, B., and Mary Pingstone of West Ham, Essex, W.

30 Robert Cook of Woodford, Essex, B., and Margaret Dench of the same, S.

30 Richard Stradling of Barking, Essex, W., and Anne Shepard of the same, W.

30 Thomas Godbor of S[t] Martin in the Fields, Middx., B., and Elizabeth Fenton of the same, S.

31 Robert Sopp of Forneux Pelham, co. Herts, B., and Elizabeth Clarke of the same, S.

31 Xstopher Braithwaite of Isleworth, Middx., B., and Dorothy Place of the same, S.

Aug. 2 Benjamin Stables of Battersea, Surry, B., and Mary Ingram of the same, S.

3 Jonathan Andrews of Tottenham High Cross, Middx., W., and Elizabeth Skegg of Edmonton, Middx., S.

4 Henry Brougham of S[t] Andrew, Holborn, Middx., B., and Mary Freeman of the same, S.

5 William Parr of Wandsworth, Surry, B., and Alice Ledger of Croydon, Surry, S.

5 William Smyth of S[t] Gyles in the Fields, Middx., W., and Ann Hood of the same, S.

7 William Rowles of S[t] James, Westminster, Middx., B., and Elizabeth Yates of the same, W.

1741

Aug. 9 Robert Palmer of S[t] Sepulchre, London, B., and Mary Phillis of the same, S.

9 George Butcher of S[t] Martin in the Fields, Middx., B., and Elizabeth Upp of Twittenham, Middx., S.

10 William Maitland of S[t] Martin in the Fields, Middx., B., and Ann Ferguson of the same, S.

11 William Ross of S[t] John, Wapping, Middx., B., and Ann Leek of the same, W.; by M[r] Mead

12 Amos Brown of S[t] Paul, Shadwell, Middx., B., and Elizabeth Amy of S[t] Anne, Westm[r], Middx., S.; by M[r] Pearce

13 John Bickerton of S[t] Giles, Cripplegate, London, B., and Mary Stevens of S[t] Leonard, Shoreditch, Middx., S.; by M[r] Pearce

13 James Hayes of S[t] Margaret, Rochester, Kent, W., and Mary Butler of Chatham, Kent., W.; by M[r] Mead

16 William Wilks of Eling, Middx., B., and Mary Sarmer of the same, S.

22 Richard Drinkwater of S[t] Clement Danes, Middx., B., and Elizabeth Drinkwater of the same, S.

23 Richard Pendrill of S[t] Clement Danes, Middx., B., and Ann Hopkins of the same, S.

23 Ralph Jennings of S[t] Mary, Rotherhith, Surry, B., and Elizabeth Clemens of the same, S.

27 William Scafe of S[t] Margaret, Westm[r], Middx., B., and Mary Gronlow of the same, S.

30 John Riley of S[t] Dionis Back Church, London, B., and Sarah Green of S[t] Dunstan in the East, London, S.

31 John Hughes of S[t] Paul, Covent Garden, Middx., B., and Mary Smith of the same, W.

31 Job Gibbons of S[t] George, Hanover Square, Middx., W., and Mary Truesdale of the same, W.

31 Thomas Davison of S[t] George, Hanover Square, Middx., B., and Blanch Williams of S[t] Giles in the Fields, Middx., S.

Sept. 3 Charles Vandallum of S[t] Mary, White Chappel, Middx., B., and Elizabeth Haynes of the same, S.

3 William Grove of S[t] Mary Le Strand, Middx., W., and Anne Mitchell of Uxbridge, Middx., W.

3 Benjamin Longworth of S[t] Saviour, Southwarke, W., and Sarah Hill of the same, S.

3 Richard Stevens of S[t] Leonard, Shoreditch, Middx., B., and Sarah Street of S[t] Giles, Cripplegate, London, W.

6 John Pricquett of Norwood Barningham, Norfolk, Esq., W., and Winnifred Hoare of S[t] James, Westm[r], Middx., S.

7 Thomas Bush of S[t] Giles in the Fields, Middx., B., and Anne Bell of S[t] Andrew, Holbourn, Middx., W.

8 Bartholomew Bernard of S[t] Dunstan, Stepney, Middx., W., and Elizabeth De La Haie of the same, S.; by M[r] Worlich

10 James Trenhaile of Windsor, co. Berks, W., and Mary Yrndal of the same, W.; by M[r] Worlich

10 William Bowen of S[t] Lawrence, Jewry, London, W., and Mary Paget of the same, W.; by the same

14 John Fryer of Hampstead, Middx., B., and Mary Colishaw of the same, S.

17 William Parrett, jun[r], of S[t] Martin in the Fields, Middx., B., and Joanna Pulley of Isleworth, Middx., S.

17 John Edmeads of Ightham, Kent, B., and Anne Taylor of the same, S.

21 Peter Lamborn of S[t] Giles in the Fields, Middx., W., and Sarah Blinkarne of S[t] Leonard, Foster lane, London, S.

1741

Sept. 21 William Norman of Tolsberry, Essex, W., and Mary Manson of St Catherine near the Tower of London, S.

21 Robert Deane of Chiswick, Middx., B., and Anne Webb of New Brentford, Middx., S.

21 Richard Wells of Grays, Essex, B., and Jane Clark of St Andrew, Holborn, Middx., W.

22 John Gasse of Battersea, Surry, B., and Elizabeth White of St Saviour, Southwark, Surry, S.

22 Edward Pratt, B., and Margery Johnson, S., both of this parish. Banns

24 Richard Maundrell of Mile End New Town, Middx., W., and Joanna Wiltshire of the same, S.

24 John Price of St Mary le Bow, London, B., and Anne Wilson of St Mildred, Bread Street, London, S.

24 Richard Wood of Coulsdon, Surry, W., and Elizabeth Haswell of the same, S.

24 John Robinson of St Mary Magdalen, Bermondsey, Surry, B., and Mary Searles of West Ham, Essex, S.

25 Nicholas Ritter of St George, Hanover Square, Middx., B., and Jane Roberts of the same, S.

25 William Roberts of St Clement Danes, Middx., B., and Mary Brewer of the same, S.

28 David Jones of St Mary Magdalen, Bermondsey, Surry, B., and Susannah Betton of St Saviour, Southwark, Surry, W.

29 Robert Hilton of St Edmund the King, London, B., and Jane Berkeley of this parish, S.; by Dr Thomas

29 William Palmer of St George in the East, Middx., B., and Isabella Reull of St John, Wapping, Middx., S.

29 John Long of St James, Westmr, Middx., W., and Elizabeth Hillton of Oakingham, co. Berks, S.

30 John Whitpaine of St Mary Magdalen, Bermondsey, Surry, B., and Hannah Sears of the same, S.

Oct. 1 Richard Sutor of St Giles in the Fields, Middx., B., and Mary Spaldin of St Paul, Shadwell, Middx., S.

4 John Hardy of St Bride's, London, W., and Sarah Owen of the same, S.

5 Daniel Lambie of St Matthew, Friday Street, London, B., and Ann Brodhurst of the same, S.

7 Thomas Coleman of St John, Southwark, Surry, W., and Ann Wayman of the same, S.

8 Thomas Woolley of All Hallows the Great, London, W., and Ann Maylard of St John Baptist, London, W.

8 William Limmer of St George the Martyr, Midx., W., and Elizabeth Murrell of St Clement Danes, Midx., S.

8 Richard Guest of Mortlake, Surry, W., and Jane Alexander of the same, S.

11 David Thomas of St John, Wapping, Midx., W., and Hannah Fitzgerald of St Martin in the Fields, Midx., W.

12 Joseph Parlebien of All Hallows Barking, Lond., W., and Mary Roberts of the same, S.

12 Robert Palmer of St Dunstan, Stepney, Midx., B., and Elizabeth Gregory of St Giles, Cripplegate, Lond., W.

14 Gilbert Lloyd of St George, Hanover Square, Midx., B., and Susannah Dellow of Hornsey, Midx., S.

14 Andrew Trench of the Liberty of Brickinton within the town of Hertford, B., and Anne Mallard of All Saints, co. Hertford, S.

15 William Baddiley of St Lawrence, Jewry, Lond., B., and Maria Susannah Morrice of Kingsland, Midx., S.

1741

Oct. 15 John Beardshaw of Stanmore Magna, Midx., B., and Mary Berry of the same, S.

15 John Popham of S[t] Clement Danes, Midx., B., and Susannah Walker of the same, W.

16 Francis Barrs of S[t] Nicholas Cole Abbey, Lond., W., and Elizabeth Peckwell of S[t] Martin, Ludgate, Lond., S.; by D[r] Thomas

17 Richard Domvile of S[t] Andrew Wardrobe, Lond., B., and Mary Lawton of the same, S.

18 Richard Wright of S[t] Anne, Westminster, Midx., B., and Jane Gorsuch of the same, S.

18 William Pottit of S[t] George, Hanover Square, Lond., W., and Martha Fowles of S[t] Dionis Backchurch, Lond., W.

19 Edward Harwood of Lambeth, Surry, B., and Jane Downing of the same, S.

21 Henry Cole of S[t] Mary Magdalen, Bermondsey, Surry, B., and Susannah Stubbs of the same, S.

23 Samuel Longbothom of S[t] Nicholas Acons, Lond., B., and Mary Parr of the same, S.

25 George Smith of S[t] George, Hanover Square, Midx., B., and Susan Start of the same, S.

29 John Cartwright of S[t] Leonard, Shoreditch, Midx., B., and Mary Leech of the same, S.

31 William Montgomery of S[t] Botolph, Aldgate, Lond., B., and Sarah Complen of the same, W.

Nov. 1 Lewis Jones of S[t] John, Wapping, Midx., B., and Mary Wall of the same, S.

6 James Ellis of S[t] Paul, Shadwell, Midx., B., and Honor Rawlinson of S[t] Mary, White Chapel, Midx., S.

7 Arthur Best of Hayes, Midx., B., and Mary Talbott of the same, S.

7 John Hulce of the Middle Temple, Lond., B., and Jane Platt of S[t] Mary le Strand, Midx., S.

8 Henry Nell of S[t] John, Wapping, Midx., B., and Ursula Dawson of the same, S.

8 John Nortrop of S[t] Mary, White Chapel, Midx., B., and Ann Cope of S[t] Mildred, Poultry, Lond., S.

12 John Farnall of S[t] Martin in the Fields, Midx., B., and Anne Lawes of the same, S.

12 Nathaniel Pilgrim of S[t] Clement Danes, Midx., W., and Jemimah Collins of Laindon Fields, Essex, S.

12 Thomas Wilkinson of S[t] George, Midx., W., and Agnes Wood of S[t] Buttolph, Bishopsgate, Lond., W.

13 John Sowerby of S[t] Michael, Wood S[t], Lond., B., and Arabella Goodred of S[t] Margaret, Westm[r], Midx., S.

14 George Harvey of S[t] George, Hanover Square, Midx., B., and Martha Wilmott of the same, S.

14 Henry Norman of S[t] Botolph, Aldgate, Midx., B., and Grissell Sprat of the same, S.

14 Robert Griffith of S[t] James, Westm[r], Midx., B., and Sarah Gray of the same, S.

16 John Phillip of Hampstead, Midx., B., and Elizabeth Page of the same, S.

19 John Bynon of S[t] John, Hackney, Midx., B., and Mary Estwick of the same, W.

19 John Loyns of S[t] Leonard, Shoreditch, Midx., W., and Elizabeth Sawyer of S[t] Mary Magdalen, Bermondsey, Surry, S.

21 Isaac Goodwin of Shepperton, Midx., B., and Eleanor Till of the same, S.

1741

Nov. 22 Jacob Hodgson of St Olave, Southwarke, W., and Theodosia Chester of St Hellens, Lond., S.

25 John Wells of Whitstable, Kent, W., and Anne Robinson of East Greenwich, Kent, S.

27 Thomas Bright of Deptford, Kent, W., and Mary Selsby of St Mary, White Chapel, Midx., S.

Dec. 1 John Smith of St John, Wapping, Midx., B., and Margaret Prophet of St Martin in the Fields, Midx., W.

3 Henry Smith of Richmond, Surrey, B., and Catherine Young of the same, S.

3 John Capps of St James, Westmr, Midx., B., and Elizabeth Sifford of St George, Hanover Square, Midx., S.

3 Thomas Adcock of St Martin in the Fields, Midx., B., and Mary Elliott of the same, S.; by Mr Pearce

4 Robert Ellis of St Mary, White Chapel, Midx., B., and Elizabeth Murcutt of the same, W.

8 Peter Gazey, B., and Mary Attwell, S., both of this parish. Banns

8 Edward Westley of Margam, co. Glamorgan, B., and Anne Cressell of Playestead, Essex, S.

8 Alexander Eynard of St Botolph, Bishopsgate, Lond., W., and Elizabeth Labrum of the same, S.

9 Michael Wilson of St Mary le Bow, Lond., B., and Margaret Walker of St Paul, Covent Garden, Midx., S.; by Mr Hillman

9 Solomon Jeddere of St Giles in the Fields, Midx., B., and Esther Bryan of St George, Hanover Square, Midx., W.; by Mr Hillman

10 Abraham Goodwin of St James, Clerkenwell, Midx., B., and Margery Divett of the same, S.

10 Edmund Trott of St James, Westmr, Midx., B., and Mary Marsh of Dorchester, co. Oxford, S.

11 Thomas Sparrow of Hockley, co. Bedford, B., and Elizabeth Jones of Great Oakley, co. Northampton, S.

12 George Mortimore of Fulham, Midx., W., and Mary Bullock of the same, S.

15 Shaw Price of St Margaret, Lothbury, Lond., B., and Esther Starkey of Lambeth, Surrey, S.

17 Richard Seagood of St Leonard, Shoreditch, Midx., W., and Mary Elliston of St James, Clerkenwell, Midx., S.

17 John Hall of St James, Clerkenwell, Midx., B., and Sarah Padder of the same, S.

19 John Udall of St John, Wapping, Midx., B., and Sarah Moore of St George, Midx., S.

20 Stephen Brice of St Paul, Covent Garden, Midx., B., and Margaret Morley of Lambeth, Surrey, S.

20 Jarvis Smith of St Leonard, Shoreditch, Midx., W., and Mary Desbrough of the same, W.

24 William Potts of St Giles in the Fields, Midx., B., and Elizabeth Hall of the same, S.

24 William Lane of St Brides, Lond., B., and Elizabeth Sanderson of St Ann, Blackfryers, Lond., S.

26 John Keep of Barking, Essex, B., and Isabell Waller of the same, S.; by Mr Bayley

27 Allen Sharrett of West Malling, Kent, W., and Mary Richards of St Vedast als Foster, Lond., W.

29 Joseph Hyde, junior, of St Saviour's, Southwarke, B., and Mary Holland of the same, S.

30 Alexander Mason of Edmonton, Midx., B., and Margaret Gomery of St Mary, White Chapel, Midx., S.

1741-2
Jan. 1 *George Rossiter of S[t] Andrew, Holborn, Lond., B., and Mary Bradshaw of the same, W.
2 Peter Bath of Chelsea, Midx., B., and Arabella Susanna Stubley of the same, S.
2 Daniel Johuston of S[t] Sepulchre, Lond., B., and Elizabeth Lowe of the same, S.
5 Thomas Vaughan of S[t] Andrew, Holborn, Midx., B., and Alexandrina Anna Macleod of the same, S.
5 James Nayler of S[t] Catharine's near the Tower, Lond, B., and Catherine James of S[t] Botolph, Aldgate, Midx., W.
6 James Spratly of the Precinct of White Fryars, Lond., B., and Martha Worthy of the same, S.
6 James Tong of S[t] Paul, Shadwell, Midx., B., and Alice Perry of Poplar, Stepney, Midx., W.
6 John Chitty of Staines, Midx., W., and Avice Capper of S[t] Margaret, Westm[r], Midx., W.
7 Grundey Hooper of S[t] Ann, Westm[r], Midx., B., and Mary Laval of the same, S.
10 Robert Smith of S[t] Dunstan in the West, Lond., W., and Mary Bartrem of S[t] Giles in the Fields, Midx., S.
12 John Palmer of S[t] Peter's, Cornhill, Lond., B., and Elizabeth Meadows of the same, W.
12 James Gresham of S[t] Alban, Wood Street, Lond., W., and Elizabeth Mabby of S[t] Giles, Cripplegate, Lond., W.
14 Thomas Aspelee of Mortlake, Surry, W., and Sarah Woddall of the same, S.; by M[r] Worlich
14 William Earl of Spalding, co. Lincoln, B., and Anne Taylor of S[t] Margaret, New Fish S[t], Lond., S.
19 Richard Litton of S[t] Margaret, Westm[r], Midx., W., and Esther Beckett of the same, S.†
19 Thomas Young of S[t] Saviour's, W., and Anne Wimpey of S[t] Thomas, Southwarke, S.
20 Nathaniel Smith of S[t] George the Martyr, Surry, B., and Mary Slapp of S[t] Mary, Newington Butts, Surry, W.
22 Robert Garwood of S[t] George in the East, Midx., W., and Mary Ansell of the same, W.
25 Gideon Barbaud of Wandsworth, Surry, B., and Mary Milton of the same, S.
26 John Hoyland of S[t] Alphage, Lond., W., and Elizabeth Bedford of the same, S.
27 Dennis Doyle of Cork, Ireland, B., and Isabella Boyd of Sheerness, Kent, W.
27 John Inward of Wimbledon, Surrey, B., and Lettice Street of the same, S.
30 Christopher Horsnaile of S[t] Andrew, Holborn, Lond., B., and Mary Jones of S[t] George, Bloomsbury, Midx., W.; by M[r] Worlich
31 William Stacey of Maidstone, Kent, W., and Mary Flint of the same, S.
Feb. 1 George Higgs of Ealing, Midx., B., and Elizabeth Lynn of Lambeth, Surry, S.
1 John Miles of New Brentford, Midx., B., and Marcy Martin of Oaking, Surry, S.
2 James George of S[t] George, Hanover Square, Midx., B., and Elizabeth Ratford of S[t] Martin in the Fields, Midx., S.
3 John Powell of S[t] James, Westm[r], Midx., B., and Mary Kingham of Gadsden, co. Hertford, S.

* Entry misplaced in Register.—Ed.

† "S." written over "W." erased.—Ed.

1741-2

Feb. 4 Bartholomew Field of S[t] John, Hackney, Midx., B., and Sarah Lake of the same, S.

4 William Connop of S[t] John, Wapping, Midx., B., and Susannah Waller of S[t] George, Midx., S.

4 Joshua Burton of Wandsworth, Surry, B., and Mary Barbaud of the same, W.

4 Joseph Smith of Stanmore, Midx., clerk, B., and Mary Martin of the same, S.

6 John Dawson of S[t] George, Bloomsbury, Middx., B., and Catharine Miles of the same, S.

7 Isaac Ogdin of S[t] Peter's, London, B., and Ann Barnard of S[t] Gabriel, Fenchurch Street, London, S.

10 William Alldridge of S[t] Mary, Newington, Surry, B., and Sarah Ogdon of the same, W.

11 Thomas French of S[t] Clement Danes, Middx., B., and Mary Smith of S[t] Margaret, Westminster, Middx., S.

11 James Welch of Barnett, co. Herts, B., and Sarah Williams of Totteridge, co. Herts, S.

13 John Durham of S[t] Andrew, Holborn, Middx., B., and Elizabeth Totter of the same, S.

15 John Jones of S[t] Botolph, Aldgate, Middx., W., and Mary Enewen of the same, W.

16 Samuel Penford of S[t] Mary Magdalen, Bermondsey, Surry, W., and Phillis Romaine of the same, S.

16 Samuel Glover of Sutton at Hone, Kent, B., and Martha Nethercoat of the same, S.

18 John Roman of S[t] Martin in the Fields, Middx., B., and Priscilla Webb of the same, S.

18 Thomas Turner of S[t] George, Hanover Square, Middx., B., and Elizabeth Bowers of the same, S.

18 James Phillips of S[t] Botolph, Aldersgate, London, B., and Mary Blasstock of Hornsey, Middx., S.

20 William Beamish of S[t] John, Wapping, Middx., B., and Susannah Stock of the same, S.

21 William Westmore of Greenwich, Kent, B., and Margaret Watkins of S[t] Thomas, Southwark, W.

22 John Patten of Lambeth, Surry, B., and Mary Lynn of the same, S.

22 John Ogdon of Camberwell, Surry, W., and Mary Tisdale of the same, W.

23 William Simmons of Edmonton, Middx., B., and Mary Luckings of the same, S.

26 Thomas Chapman of S[t] Peter Cheap, London, B., and Louisa Fullom of S[t] Lawrence, Jewry, London, S.

26 John Drinkwater of S[t] George, Hanover Square, Middx., B., and Elizabeth Napper of S[t] James, Westm[r], Middx., S.

27 John Arney of Lambeth, Surry, B., and Elizabeth Hall of the same, S.

28 James Wainewright of S[t] Giles, Cripplegate, London, W., and Elizabeth Stennett of S[t] Austin's, London, S.

28 Joseph Butcher of S[t] Peter, Cornhill, London, B., and Mary Mackee of S[t] Luke's, Middx., S.; by D[r] Thomas

Mar. 1 William Pearce of Farnham, co. Bucks, B., and Mary Deen of Beckonsfield, co. Bucks, W.

1 Richard Gabbitas of S[t] George, Hanover Square, Middx., B., and Martha Mathewman of same, W.

2 Michael Clocner of S[t] Clement Danes, Middx., B., and Martha Clarke of the same, S.

1741-2

Mar. 2 John Slark of Mortlake, Surrey, B., and Susannah Raynes of S[t] Botolph, Bishopsgate, London, S.

2 Thomas Slape of S[t] Bartholomew the Less, London, W., and Anne Margetts of Battersea, Surry, W.

6 William Pullen of S[t] Dunstan in the East, London, B., and Elizabeth Veal of the same, S.

10 John Fall of S[t] John, Wapping, Middx., B., and Elizabeth Hancock of the same, S.

10 Richard Winckley of S[t] Martin in the Fields, Middx., W., and Myrtilla Mayhew of S[t] Giles in the Fields, Middx., S.

11 Charles Devenport of S[t] Mary Axe, London, B., and Phillis Littlefield of S[t] George, Botolph lane, London, S.

18 Richard Beale, jun[r], of Biddenden, Kent, B., and Anne Cooke of Cranbrook, Kent, S.

19 John Wheeler of Bridport, Dorset, B., and Leonora Bingham of Sergeant Inn, Fleet Street, London, S.

20 Michael Combrune of S[t] Giles in the Fields, Middx., B., and Mary Bayeux of S[t] Ann, Westminster, Middx., S.

1742.

Mar. 27 William Coleston of S[t] James, Westm[r], Middx., B., and Catharine Monk of the same, S.

30 Samuel Hutson of Kensington, Middx., B., and Ann Francks of the same, S.

31 Thomas Milnes of the town of Derby, W., and Frances Prime of the same, S.

April 4 William Rance of S[t] Margaret, Westm[r], Middx., W., and Margaret Willis of the same, S.

4 Joseph Gootheridge of S[t] James, Westm[r], Middx., B., and Lydia Oney of Hamton, co. Herts, S.

8 James Grinwell of S[t] Ann, Blackfryers, London, W., and Esther Iron of this parish, W.

11 Robert Crosbie of S[t] Bartholomew the Great, London, W., and Anne Simnell of the same, W.

14 Richard Woofe of Clifford's Inn, London, B., and Mary Higgins of S[t] Giles in the Fields, Middx., S.

14 John Pain of S[t] Andrew, Holborn, London, W., and Elizabeth Monk of the same, W.

19 John Hooker of Brasted, Kent, B., and Elizabeth Hunt of the same, S.

19 Thomas Allen of High Wickham, co. Bucks, B., and Sarah Waterson of S[t] Luke, Middx., S.

20 John Maxey of Islington, Middx., B., and Mary Chapman of Ongar, Essex, S.

21 James Knight of Great Gatesden, co. Herts, B., and Susannah Johnson of S[t] George, Hanover Square, Middx., S.

21 Thomas Butcher of Penshurst, Kent, W., and Elizabeth Strutfield of the same, W.

22 John Curtiss of S[t] Dunstan in the West, London, W., and Frances Blackburne of S[t] Andrew, Holborne, London, S.

22 George Woolley of Wootton Bassett, Wilts, B., and Hannah Holderness of Colnbrook, Middx., W.

22 Andrew Paterson of S[t] James, Westm[r], Middx., B., and Sarah Tuff of the same, S.

24 Benjamin Johnson of Waltham Abby, Essex, B., and Mary Player of the same, S.

1742

April 25 Robert Cannaway of North Shields in Tinmouth, Northumberland, and Alice Brough of the same, S.

25 Richard Merriott of St Botolph, Aldgate, Middx., B., and Mary Peterson of the same, S.

30 Thomas Perkins of St Ann, Westm^r, Middx., B., and Mary Sheldon of St Martin in the Fields, Middx., S.

30 Richard Thompson of Carshalton, Surry, W., and Alice Saunders of the same, W.

May 1 Hugh Searchwell of Plymouth, Devon, B., and Mary Marshall of St Andrew, Holborn, London, S.

6 Daniel Cooper of St Andrew, Holborn, Middx., B., and Elizabeth Green of St John the Evangelist, Middx., S.

6 John Kent of Crayford, Kent, B., and Anna Maria Walker of the same, S.

9 Thomas Beech of X^st Church, London, B., and Elizabeth Ransden of Addington, Kent, S.

10 James Wall of East Greenwich, Kent, B., and Ann Jeffs of Waltham in Essex, S.

11 Robert Foster of St George in the East, Middx., B., and Elizabeth Stafford of St George, Southwarke, S.

12 George Dartnall of Stretham, Surry, B., and Hannah Taylor of the same, S.

13 Henry Harding of St George, Middx., W., and Mary Moyes of the same, W.

13 Timothy Hutchinson of St James, Westm^r, Middx., B., and Anne Roach of the same, S.

13 John Browne of St George, Hanover Square, Middx., B., and Mary Brookhouse of the same, S.

14 William Clark of Chatham, Kent, W., and Sarah Nash of the same, W.

15 William Burrough of All Hallows on the Wall, London, B., and Mary Marr of the same, S.

17 Richard Holmes of St James, Westm^r, Middx., W., and Elizabeth James of the same, W.

17 Richard Broughton of St George, Hanover Square, Middx., B., and Isabella Colling of the same, W.

18 William Stansall of Reading, co. Berks, B., and Susannah Paris of the same, S.

19 John West of New Windsor, co. Berks, B., and Anne Allen of St George, Hanover Square, Middx., S.

19 Xstopher Martin of St Bride's, London, B., and Teresa Tevenan of St James, Clarkenwell, Middx., S.

20 Peter Devallee of St James, Westm^r, Middx., W., and Magdeleine Osmont of the same, W.

24 Thomas Forbes of St Gyles in the Fields, Middx., B., and Martha Udny of St Bartholomew by the Royal Exchange, London, S.

24 Peter Ogier of X^st Church, Spittlefields, Middx., B., and Elizabeth Cadet of the same, S.

24 William Lestar of Hanmeorth, Middx., B., and Frances Lad of the same, S.

25 John Glover of St Giles, Cripplegate, Middx., B., and Alice Street of the same, W.

25 Joseph Hill of St James, Westm^r, Middx., B., and Frances Lane of the same, S.

26 James Makemault of St Margaret, Westm^r, Middx., B., and Martha Westmore of the same, S.

27 Thomas Smith of St Thomas à Beckett in Sussex, W., and Mary Richards of St John's parish, Sussex, W.

1742

May 27 John Woolley of St Ann, Westmr, Middx., B., and Ann Easton of St Martin in the Fields, Middx., S.

29 Evan Cadlan of St Martin in the Fields, Middx., B., and Sarah Cottrell of the same, S.; by Mr Worlich, curate of St Nicholas Cole Abbey

29 Joseph Monk of St Andrew, Holborn, London, B., and Mary Cox of the same, S.; by Mr Worlich

June 2 Thomas Stables of Battersea, Surry, B., and Martha Ingram of the same, S.

3 John Coys of Chatham, Kent, W., and Mary Kam of the same, S.

5 John Tomlyn of Wrutham, Kent, W., and Sarah Wingate of the same, S.

6 Thomas Todd of St Magnus the Martyr, London, B., and Sarah Joyce of the same, S.

8 Richard Wyatt of St James, Westmr, Middx., B., and Ruth Simmons of St Paul, Covent Garden, Middx., S.

10 William Thompson of St Catherine near the Tower, London, W., and Martha Harvey of the same Precinct, S.

10 Charles Leadbetter of St Leonard, Shoreditch, Middx., W., and Sarah Hall of St Giles in the Fields, Middx., S.

10 Joseph Ince of St Dunstan in the East, London, B., and Sarah Taverner of All Hallows the Great, London, S.

11 William Baxter of Feversham, Kent, W., and Judith Luckett of the city of Canterbury, S.

11 Francis Johnston of Wingfield, co. Berks, B., and Anne Knife of the same, W.; by Mr Worlich

12 Walter Ray of St Martin, Ludgate, London, B., and Rachael Nynn of Dartford, Kent, S.

15 Thomas Jones of Hornchurch, Essex, W., and Anne Welett of the same, S.

15 William Evans of Epsom, Surry, W., and Sarah Stacey of the same, S.

17 George Edwards of St Mary Aldermary, London, B., and Mary Uirvine of the same, S.; by Dr Watkinson

17 Robert Clarke, Esq., of St Botolph without Aldgate, Middx., B., and Anne Mitchell of St Anne, Middx., S.

17 James Bocock of Woodford, Essex, B., and Elizabeth Lawson of the same, S.

17 William Smith of St James, Westmr, Middx., B., and Mary Nicholls of the same, S.

19 Thomas Tyler of Fobing, Essex, W., and Elizabeth Walker* of St Bride's, London, S.

20 Ellis Jones of St James, Clerkenwell, Middx., W., and Mary King of the same, S.

20 John Stotesbury of St Mary, White Chapel, Middx., W., and Mary Hare of Edmonton, Middx., S.

20 Charles Warner of St Nicholas Cole Abby, London, B., and Elizabeth Troute of the same, S.

20 Thomas Padmore of St George, Bloomsbury, Middx., B., and Mary Edgley of St Mary Wolnoth, London, W.†

24 Robert Elve of St Paul, Shadwell, Middx., B., and Elizabeth Earle of St George the Martyr, Middx., S.

24 William Burr of Farningham, Kent, B., and Mary Penury of Horton Kerby, Kent, S.

27 Luke Mitchilson of St Dunstan, Stepney, Middx., B., and Elizabeth Colly of the same, S.

27 Richard Wood of St James, Clerkenwell, Middx., W., and Ann Scrivener of St Dunstan in the West, London, S.

* This name is given as "Fobing" in the margin of the Register.—Ed.

† "W." written apparently over "S."—Ed.

1742

June 27 John Morris of St John, Hackney, Middx., W., and Mary Puppin of the same, S.

28 William Grant of Clownish, co. Monaghan, Ireland, B., and Eleanor Gregg of St John, Bedwardine, co. Worcester, W.

28 Thomas Taylor of Eaton Bridge, Kent, B., and Mary Turley of Braseted, Kent, S.

29 Thomas King of St John, Hackney, Middx., W., and Anna Rowley of Stepney, Middx., S.

July 1 Richard Low, B., and Mary Kent, S., both of this parish. Banns

7 Edward Bird of St Andrew, Holbourn, London, B., and Anne Cave of Endfield, Middx., S.; by Mr Campbell

8 Henry Powell of St James, Westm^r, Middx., B., and Mary Lucas of X^st Church, London, S.; by ditto

9 John Merigeot of X^st Church, Spittlefields, Middx., W., and Elizabeth Campart of the same, W.; by ditto

10 John Best of St James, Westm^r, Middx., B., and Mary Parsons of the same, W.; by ditto

11 Thomas Lewen of Barking, Essex, B., and Mary Sterrop of St Mary le Bow, London, S.; by Mr Lushington

15 Thomas Hose of Islington, Middx., B., and Elizabeth Jackson of St Dunstan in the West, London, W.; by Mr Lewis

19 Matthew Hale of Westhamlet, Sussex, B., and Susan Paternoster of Hitching, co. Herts, S.; by Mr Campbell

19 Thomas White of St Margaret, Westm^r, Middx., B., and Mary Hunter of St Martin in the Fields, Middx., S.; by ditto

20 William Barradell of St Clement Danes, Middx., W., and Mary Atkins of Chelsea, Middx., W.; by ditto

21 Thomas Hutchcroft of Eastington, co. York, B., and Frances Henley of St Margaret, Westm^r, Middx., S.; by ditto

21 Joseph Rawlinson of St Saviour, Southwarke, W., and Elizabeth Smith of St Ann, Soho, Middx., S.; by ditto

25 Thomas Bosvile of St Mary Magdaline, Milk Street, London, B., and Bridget Bosvile of Elkington, co. Linc., S.; by ditto

25 John Shaw of St Clement Danes, Middx., W., and Anne Jones of the same, W.; by ditto

27 John Bowler of St Paul, Shadwell, Middx., W., and Anne LLoyd of the same, W.; by ditto

28 James Beech of Boxley, Kent, B., and Margaret Hooker of the same, S.; by ditto

29 William Skillton of Edmonton, Middx., W., and Hannah Hill of Endfield, Middx., W.; by ditto

30 Edward Stevens of Putney, Surrey, B., and Sarah West of St Paul, Shadwell, Middx., S.; by ditto

Aug. 1 Thomas Arthur of St Margaret, Lothbury, London, B., and Elizabeth Hoar of St Martin Outwich, London, S.

1 John Croxen of St Catherine near the Tower of London, B., and Susannah Smith of the said Precinct, S.

2 William Day of St James, Westm^r, W., and Elizabeth Mary Darsy of the same, S.

4 Joseph Kettle of St George, Hanover Square, Middx., W., and Grace Pease of the same, S.

5 John Lincoln of St Andrew, Holbourn, Middx., W., and Margaret Brooks of the same, W.

8 William Van Wych of St Mary Woolnoth, London, W., and Anne Morris of the same, S.

11 Stanhope Dickson of St John, Hackney, Middx., B., and Mary Rufford of the same, S.

1742
Aug. 12 Francis Eld of Sighford, co. Stafford, B., and Ann Arblaster of the city of Litchfield, S.
14 Joshua Noble of Wandsworth, Surry, B., and Mary Cumlyn of the same, S.
14 Richard Sadler of this parish, W., and Deborah Brown of St Martin, Ludgate, London, S.
15 Richard Milward of St Olave, Old Jewry, London, B., and Ann Robinson of St Brides, London, S.
16 William Sage of Woolwich, Kent, W., and Jane Butcher of St Gabriel, Fenchurch, London, S.
21 Hutton Perkins of Barnard's Castle, co. Durham, B., and Sarah Smith of St Buttolph, Aldgate, London, S.
22 Michael Erskine of St Catherine Coleman, London, B., and Ann Matthews of St Martin in the Fields, Middx., S.; by Mr Worlich
24 Charles Birkett of St Saviour, Southwarke, B., and Elizabeth Johnson of St Antholin, London, W.
28 John Bowyer of Deptford, Kent, W., and Susanna Lemon of St George, Southwarke, Surrey, W.
28 Thomas Sutton of St Martin in the Fields, Middx., W., and Sarah Harding of the same, S.
28 Thomas Goodchild of St James, Westmr, Middx., B., and Elizabeth Morehead of St George, Hanover Square, Middx., S.
30 Joshua Ambler of St Giles, Middx., W., and Ann Redhead of St Andrew, Holbourn, London, S.
Sept. 2 Samuel Backman of St John, Southwarke, B., and Elizabeth Whitford of the same, W.
5 Humphrey Giles of Chiddingstone, Kent, B., and Philippa Longhurst of Hadlow, Kent, S.
9 Samuel Rance of Staines, Middx., W., and Elizabeth North of St Dunstan, Stepney, Middx., W.
10 William Hare of St George, Hanover Square, Middx., B., and Mary Hixson of St James, Westmr, Middx., S.
12 Richard Pritchard of St Dionis Backchurch, London [*blank*], and Anne Goodyer of All Hallows Barking, London, S.
14 Thomas Bickham of Clapham, Surrey, W., and Sarah Palmer of the same, W.
16 James Letchford of Lewisham, Kent, B., and Sarah Fist of Croydon, Surry, S.
18 John Earle of St George, Middx., W., and Elizabeth Gates of Gravesend, Kent, W.
23 John Clarke of Enfield, Middx., B., and Ann Donde of the same, W.
24 John Meadwell of St Mary le Bow, London, B., and Catherine Perrin of St Paul, Covent Garden, Middx., S.
24 Samuel Shephard of Yealing, Middx., B., and Anne Turner of the same, S.
26 James Backhouse of St Mary, White Chapel, Middx., B., and Elizabeth Wright of St Saviour, Southwarke, S.
30 Richard Williams of St Andrew, Holbourn, Middx., W., and Ann Saill of the same, W.
30 William Collins of Staines, Middx., W., and Mary Randall of St Margaret, Westmr, Middx., S.
Oct. 2 Daniel Statter of St Clement Danes, Middx., B., and Elizabeth Groves of the same, W.
2 Alexander L'huillier of St Ann, Westmr, Middx., B., and Susanna Mauret of the same, S.
3 John Killick of St Giles, Cripplegate, London, W., and Anne Daniel of St Mary, Aldermanbury, London, S.

1742

Oct. 5 John Howell of S[t] Peter, Paul's Wharfe, B., and Alice Swayls of S[t] Mary, White Chappel, Middx., S. Banns

5 Michael Foster of S[t] Botolph, Bishopsgate, London, B., and Ann Horsfield of S[t] John, Stepney, Middx., S.

5 Humphrey Tarry of Hamstead, Middx., B., and Olive Minion of the same, S.

6 Richard Rennells of S[t] Mary, White Chappel, Middx., W., and Mary Cadogan of S[t] Bride's, London, S.

7 Isaac Sperin of All Hallows, Bread Street, London, B., and Ann Guest of the same, S.

7 John Game of S[t] Mary, White Chappel, Middx., B., and Elizabeth Perry of the same, W.

7 William Whetstone of S[t] Ann, Limehouse, Middx., W., and Mary Penhallow of the same, W.

9 John Strachan of S[t] James, Westm[r], Middx., Esq., B., and Jane Puxty of the same, S.

10 Joseph Drury of S[t] Stephen, Coleman Street, London, W., and Mary Lovitt of the same, S.

12 John Hislop of S[t] George in the East, Middx., B., and Margaret Donaldson of S[t] John, Wapping, Middx., W.

14 William Weed of S[t] Sepulchre, London, B., and Elizabeth Coatham of S[t] Giles in the Fields, Middx., S.

14 Samuel Wells of S[t] Sepulchre, London, W., and Sarah Spring of Beckamsfield, co. Bucks, S.

15 John Fillby of Richmond, Surry, B., and Hannah Kendrick of the same, W.

16 Penyston Powney of Bray, co. Berks, Esq., B., and Elizabeth Portlock of S[t] Martin in the Fields, Middx., S.

19 John Haslam of S[t] Luke, Middx., W., and Frances Wise of the same, S.

20 Charles Riley of the Inner Temple, London, B., and Jane Boothby of S[t] Margaret, New Fish Street, London, S.

24 James Porter of S[t] Margaret, Westm[r], Middx., W., and Adeiena Shield of the same, W.

28 John Rogers, Esq., of Westhoe, Devon, B., and Hannah Trefusis of S[t] Botolph without Aldgate, London, S.

30 James Thompson of S[t] Michael Bassishaw, London, B., and Ann Easthem of S[t] Edmund the King, London, S.

31 George Griffin of S[t] Bride's, London, B., and Mary Edlyne of S[t] Dunstan in the West, London, S.

31 Hugh Russell of All Hallows, Bread Street, London, B., and Elizabeth Jones of S[t] George, Southwarke, W.

Nov. 2 John Waite of Greenwich, Kent, B., and Sarah Housson of the same, S.

2 Edward Jones of S[t] Bennet, Grace Church, London, W., and Sarah Sampson of S[t] Luke, Middx., S.

2 John Jones of S[t] Mary, Rotherhith, Surry, W., and Mary Randall of S[t] Dunstan in the East, London, W.

4 Benjamin Tucker of S[t] Gregory, London, B., and Sarah Wells of S[t] Magnus the Martyr, London, S.

6 William Stevens of X[st] Church, Spittlefields, Middx., W., and Mary Youell of the same, W.

9 William Cushnie of South Mimms, Middx., B., and Elizabeth Legg of the same, W.

10 John Niblett of S[t] George, Southwarke, W., and Susannah Hanson of the same, S.; by M[r] Reyner

14 Charles Jones of S[t] Saviour, Southwarke, W., and Jane Marsh of S[t] Bride's, London, S.

1742

Nov. 16 Henry Whittnoll, B., and Elizabeth Sible, S., both of this parish. Banns

18 James Gastine of St Paul, Covent Garden, Middx., B., and Rebecca Heaton of St Andrew, Holbourn, London, S.

18 William Lockstone of All Hallows, Bread Street, London, B., and Sarah Stevens of the same, S.

18 Thomas Spriggs of All Hallows, London Wall, W., and Mildred Stevenson Blundell of St Peter's, Cornhill, London, S.

18 Isaiah Lucas of St Dunstan, Stepney, Middx., W., and Ann Peart of Xst Church, Middx., W.

19 Richard Hardy of St Mary, Aldermanbury, London, B., and Jane Tate of the same, S.

20 Thomas Brooks of St Paul, Deptford, Kent, B., and Margaret Isaacs of the same, S.

22 John Browne of Stepney, Middx., W., and Mary Gunn of the same, W.

22 John Cole of St Luke, Middx., W., and Elizabeth Clarke of the same, S.

22 Thomas Vaughan of St Martin in the Fields, Middx., B., and Mary Mills of Speldhurst, Kent, S.

25 Stephen Parker of St Andrew, Holbourn, London, W., and Catherine Clark of St Sepulchre, London, W.; by Mr Bayley

Dec. 1 Richard Evans of St George, Bloomsbury, Middx., B., and Mary Bird of St Andrew, Holborn, London, S.; by Dr Thomas

2 Loyd Middleton of St Catherine Cree Church, London, B., and Sarah Drake of Kensington, Middx., S.

3 George Wise of Cranbrook, Kent, W., and Elizabeth Winterflood of St James, Westmr, Middx., W.

4 Garvess Reeve of St Dunstan in the West, London, W., and Margaret Ferry of St Mary le Strand, Middx., S.

5 George Hall of St Mary le Strand, Middx., W., and Mary Lowder of St Margaret, Lothbury, London, W.

8 George Ayres of All Hallows Barking, London, W., and Sarah Burch of the same, W.

9 John Cottingham of St John the Evangelist, Westmr, Middx., B., and Elizabeth Wood of St Margaret, Westmr, Middx., S.

14 Thomas Collett of St Paul, Shadwell, Middx., B., and Mary Gregory of Camberwell, Surrey, W.; by Mr Aylmer

16 Robert Carless of St Giles in the Fields, Middx., W., and Fridayesweed Tidmarsh of the same, W.; by Mr Bayley

16 Patrick Doolin of Deptford, Kent, B., and Elizabeth Hooper of St Mary, Rotherhith, Surrey, S.; by Mr Bayley

17 Daniel Banton of Edmonton, Middx., B., and Mary Johnson of the same, S.

18 Amos Angles of St Mary Magdalen, Bermondsey, B., and Homer Smith of the same, W.; by Mr Maldus

19 Joseph Fleetwood of St Peter's Cheap, London, B., and Hannah Brown of St Leonard, Shoreditch, Middx., S.

21 John Atkinson of Xst Church, Middx., B., and Mary Chandler of St Botolph, Bishopsgate, London, S.

21 Henry Wood of St Botolph, Bishopsgate, London, B., and Anne Mounce of the same, S.

22 John Dilley of St Stephen, Coleman Street, London, B., and Anne Blizard of the same, S.

23 John Baker of St Alban, Wood Street, London, B., and Elizabeth Pocock of the same, S.

25 Edward Maurice of St George, Hanover Square, Middx., B., and Sarah Saunders of Hampstead, Middx., S.

1742

Dec. 26 Collingwood Garratt of St Mary le Bow, London, B., and Elizabeth Fleming of the same, S.

27 John Summers of St George the Martyr, Middx., B., and Mary Brickwood of St Peter le Poor, London, S.

29 George Oliver of St Ann, Limehouse, Middx., B., and Elizabeth Exall of Poplar, Middx., S.

29 John Miller of Ockingham, co. Berks, B., and Elizabeth Taylor of the same, S.

End.

On the inside of the cover of this volume is written "James Burdieu," also "Commencem^t of the year changed in Jany 1732/3, the year having previously commenced March 25th," and in pencil, "See Register of Marriages for March 30, 1725, from which period it appears the new Epoch commenced."

[End of Volume E.]

BOOK F.

St. Bene't & St. Peter.

MARRIAGES FROM 1ST JAN^Y 1742-3 TO 24 MARCH 1754.

A Register of Marriages in the Parish of St Benedict, Paul's Wharfe, in the City of London, Beginning on the first day of January 1742-3.

MARRIAGES.

1742-3.

Jan. 1 John Holloway of St James, Westminster, Midx., B. & Elizabeth Dixon of St Mary Magd., Bermondsey, Surrey, S.

1 Elias Ivy of St Botolph, Bishopsgate, London, B., & Mary Kirke of St Helen's, London, S.

2 John Clegg of X^t Church, Spittlefields, Midx., W., & Ellen Powell of St George, Bloomsbury, Middx., W.; by Mr Hillman of St Paul's

4 Giles Stevens of St James, Middx., B., & Mary Crisp of St Martin in the Fields, Middx., S.

8 Charles Dodd of St John, Southwarke, B., & Elizabeth Guppey of St Thomas, Southwarke, S.

11 Benjamin Kendall of St Bride's, London, B., & Mary Shutter of St Clement Danes, Middx., S.

13 John Spradbery of Barking in Essex, B., & Margaret Flewster of ye same place, S.

13 John Jenivar of St Andrew, Holbourn, London, B., & Margaret Crafts of ye same par., S.

16 Charles Nourse of St Andrew, Holborn, London, B., & Margaret Hedington of ye same par., S.

17 Thomas LLoyd of St George, Southwarke, B., & Elizabeth King of ye same parish, S.

20 Stephen Bell of St Botolph, Aldersgate, London, B., & Agnes Noble of ye same par., S.

1742-3

Jan. 20 Henry Barker of S[t] Pancras, Middx., B., & Sarah Heddinton of y[e] same par., S.

20 Adam Rayner of S[t] Andrew Hubbard, London, B., and Mary Johnson of S[t] Peter's, Cornhill, London, S.

20 Anthony Weltden, Esq., of S[t] Clement Danes, Middx., B., & Mary Holt of y[e] same par., S.

22 Edward Jackson of S[t] Olave, Southwarke, B., & Jane Foots of y[e] same par., S.

22 Edward Russell of S[t] Mary Magd., Bermondsey, Surry, W., & Elizabeth Wakeling of Bromley in Kent, S.

23 William Middelditch of S[t] James, Westminster, Middx., B., & Rebeccah Kerton of S[t] Martin, Ludgate, London, S.

24 John Hinton of S[t] James, Westm[r], Middx., B., & Catharine Phithion of S[t] Anne, Westm[r], Middx., S.; by D[r] Thomas.

27 Andrew Strode of S[t] James, Westm[r], Middx., W., & Susanna Mayo of y[e] same parish, S.

29 Thomas Bridgen of S[t] Andrew, Holborn, Middx., B., and Anna Maria Dalton of y[e] same par., S.

Feb. 1 John Furlonger of S[t] Paul's Crane [*sic*] in Kent, B., and Ann Day of S[t] Mary Crane [*sic*] in Kent, S.

2 William Edwards, B., & Catherine Parrance, S., both of this parish. Banns.

2 Ephraim Hopwood of Edmonton, Midx., W., & Mary Pickman of S[t] George, Bloomsbury, Middx., S.

3 Samuel Grant of X[st] Church, London, B., and Dorothy Green of S[t] Giles in y[e] Fields, Middx., S.

5 Henry Vaughan of S[t] John, Hackney, Middx., W., & Elizabeth Beckworth of S[t] Andrew, Holborn, Middx., W.

5 George Fletcher of y[e] Town & county of Newcastle, B., & Sarah Moore of S[t] George, Middx., W.

6 Thomas Kippax of S[t] Sepulchre's, London, W., & Sarah Gale of Clapham, Surrey, S.

7 Robert Bell of S[t] James, Westminster, Middx., B., & Ann Denton of the same, S.; by M[r] Clare.

10 John Butler of Woodford, Essex, W., & Elizabeth Hubberd of y[e] same parish, S.

10 William Abson of S[t] George in y[e] East, Middx., W., & Sarah Naylor of y[e] same parish, W.

11 Thomas Gulliver of S[t] Margaret, Westm[r], Middx., B., & Elizabeth Lynch of y[e] same parish, S.

11 John Dalton of Deptford, Kent, B., & Anne Cole of S[t] George, Hanover Square, Middx., S.

12 Henry Barton of S[t] Dunstan in y[e] East, Middx., B., & Catharine Lambeth of y[e] same, S.

13 John Sopp of S[t] Saviour, Southwark, W., & Sarah Keen of y[e] same, W.

14 Richard Archer of S[t] Botolph without Bishopsgate, London, W., & Mary Collins of X[st] Church, Spittlefields, Middx., W.

14 George Bickley of S[t] Giles, Cripplegate, London, B., & Jane Woolford of X[st] Church, Surry, S.

14 Richard Dobson of Clapham, Surrey, W., & Mary Slade of y[e] same place, W.

15 John Goulds of Redbourn, co. Herts, B., & Dorothy Bowles of Gadesden, co. Herts, S.

17 Edward Hulitt of Rotherhith, Surry, W., & Phebe Winter of y[e] same, W.; by D[r] Watkinson.

25 Richard Bright of Barnes, Surrey, B., & Elizabeth Pagett of Mortlake in Surrey, S.

1742-3

Feb. 26 Jacob Hall of St Anne, Limehouse, Middx., B., & Hannah Smith of ye same, S.

Mar. 1 Richard Smith of Coney Hatts, Middx., B., & Susanna Warner of Hampstead, Midx., S.

3 William Meridith of St James, Westmr, Middx., B., & Elizabeth Pepper of Richmond, Surry, S.; by Mr Bayley.

7 Musgrave Brisco of St James, Westmr, Middx., B., & Mary Fletcher-Dyne of ye same, S.

17 Matthew Bingley of St Olave, Southwarke, B., & Sarah Stokes of ye same, S.

21 John Shellito of St Andrew, Holborn, Middx., B., & Mary Sharwood of St John, Hackney, Middx., S.

1743.

Mar. 26 Thomas Howell of St George, Middx., B., & Mary Hoxley of St John, Wapping, Middx., S.

30 William Fuller of Mayfield in Sussex, B., & Elizabeth Langham of Wadhurst in Sussex, S.; by Mr Johnson.

April 1 Joseph Rogers of St Dunstan in the West, London, B., & Elizabeth Earl of St Clement Danes, Middx., S.

2 John Davis of St Saviour, Southwarke, B., & Rachael Brown of ye same, S.

4 Thomas Watson of St George, Middx., B., & Sarah Nitten of ye same, S.

4 Abraham Witley of Colchester in Essex, B., and Ann Delemar of St Dunstan, Stepney, Middx., S.

4 James Woodroffe of St Dionis Backchurch, London, B., & Mary Zealy of Chelsea, Middx., S.

5 Andrew Heude of St Mary le Bone, Middx., B., & Mary Greaton of ye same, S.

6 Timothy Miles of Stanstead, co. Herts, W., & Hannah Hall of St Anne, Limehouse, Middx., W.

6 William Fearon of St George ye Martyr, Middx., W., & Elizabeth Eyres of St Margaret, New Fish Street, London, S.

6 Robert Beachamp, B., & Elizabeth Stretton, S., both of St Peter's near Paul's Wharfe. Banns.

7 Thomas Mailes, B., & Elizabeth Adams, S., both of St Peter's near Paul's Wharfe. Banns.

7 Rice Jones of St Nicholas Cole Abbey, London, B., & Elizabeth Holder of ye same, S.

7 Richard Strong of St Mary, Whitechappel, Midx., B., & Elizabeth Maples of St George, Middx., S.

9 Charles Banson of St Saviour, Southwarke, B., & Elizabeth Perry of St Andrew, Holbourn, Midx., S.

14 John Bosley of St Bride's, London, W., & Elizabeth Kent of ye same, S.

14 Edward Tucker of St Olave, Hart Street, London, B., & Sarah Smale of the same, S.

15 James Thompson of St Anne, Middx., B., & Mary Thompson of the same, S.

15 John Phelps of Chiswick, Middx., W., & Ann Hooke of Fulham, Middx., S.

15 Anthony Fothergill of Gravesend in Kent, B., & Mary Barker of the same, S.

19 John Merryweather of St Martin in ye Fields, Middx., W., & Martha Rogers of ye same, S.

21 Charles Woodroffe of Sherfield, Hants, B., & Eleanor Nicholls of St Botolph, Aldgate, London, S.

25 Daniel Maingett of St James, Westmr, Middx., W., & Jane Bouche of the same, S.

1743

April 26 Robert Davis of S[t] James, Westm[r], Middx., B., & Ann Goodge of S[t] Giles in the Fields, Middx., S.

26 Henry Elsegood of S[t] Ann, Westm[r], Middx., W., & Catherine Williams of y[e] same, W.

27 Deni Rene Gastecloux of S[t] Ann, Westm[r], B., & Mary Magdalen Griblin of S[t] Martin in the Fields, Middx., S.

May 2 William Wapels of S[t] James, Westm[r], Middx., B., & Elizabeth Hillam of y[e] same, W.

2 Robert Thornton of Stanton, co. Worcester, clerk, B., & Elizabeth Hardwell of S[t] Ann, Westm[r], Middx., S.

3 Isaac Stiedenroth of S[t] James, Westm[r], Middx., B., & Hannah Harlow of Fulham, Middx., W.

3 Robert Cross of y[e] Precinct of S[t] Catherine near the Tower of London and Mary Delabertauche of S[t] Martin in the Fields, Middx., S.

7 James Bodicoat of S[t] Luke's, Middx., B., & Mary Yarwood of Y[e] Town of Leicester, W.

10 Tayler Bates of S[t] Catherine, Coleman Street, London, W., & Ann Holt of y[e] same, S.

11 John Hughes of Bloxham, co. Oxford, B., & Hannah Partridge of S[t] Mary le Strand, London, Middx., S.

12 Lancelot Ride of Twickenham, Middx., B., & Betty Adams of Westbury, co. Bucks, S.

12 Thomas Harris of S[t] Andrew, Holbourn, London, B., & Patience Jenkins of y[e] same, S.

14 Joseph Deboust of S[t] Dunstan, Stepney, Middx., W., & Mary Mackenzey of y[e] same, W.

14 Robert Colley of S[t] Saviour, Southwarke, B., & Mary Hawkins of y[e] same, S.

16 Robert Liddell of Dover, Kent, B., & Ann Lucas of y[e] same, W.

17 Richard Dowell of S[t] Brides, London, B., & Ann Callis of y[e] same, S.

19 Thomas Waker of Lambeth, Surrey, B., & Judith Hope of S[t] Mary Magd., Bermondsey in Southwarke, S.

19 Thomas Dean of Chiswick, Midx., W., & Grace Morgan of y[e] same, S.

23 Tobias Payne of S[t] John y[e] Evangelist, Westm[r], Middx., B., & Anne Unthank of y[e] same, S.

23 William Harman of S[t] Mary, Whitechapple, Middx., W., & Elizabeth Pittman of y[e] same, W.

23 James Kellock of S[t] Ann, Middx., W., & Mary Walton of S[t] Dunstan, Stepney, Middx., S.

24 Henry Baker of S[t] Martin in y[e] Fields, Middx., W., & Mary Greenwood of y[e] same, W.

26 William Snook of Deptford, Kent, W., & Susannah Davis of y[e] same, W.

26 Samuel Wake of S[t] Saviour, Southwarke, B., & Elizabeth Jones of S[t] Catherine by y[e] Tower of London, S.

26 William Eglese of S[t] Mary, Whitechapple, Middx., B., & Ann Mott of y[e] same, S.

27 William Groom of Stoke Pogis, co. Bucks, B., & Martha Farmer of X[st] Church, London, S.; by D[r] Watkinson.

30 John Le Sueur of S[t] Mary Magd[n], Bermondsey, Surry, B., & Mary Broadway of y[e] same, S.

31 James Camper of Rochford, Essex, W., & Sarah Davison of S[t] Thomas, Southwarke, W.

June 7 William Reynolds of S[t] Botolph without Aldgate, London, B., & Sarah Harrold of Endfield, Middx., S.

1743

June 7 David Mackcullach of St James, Westmr, Middx., B., & Margaret Brown of ye same, W.

13 Jonas Bull of St Dunstan, Stepney, Midx., B., & Elizabeth Storer of St George ye Martyr, Middx., W.

13 Jennings Wood of St George, Hanover Square, Middx., B., & Bridget Rugeiro of ye same, S.

16 Shute Adams of St Bride's, London, B., & Kerenhappuch Forrest of Battersea, Surry, S.

16 Stephen Tripp of St Olave, Southwarke, W., & Bridgett Savory of St James, Westmr, Middx., S.; by Mr Worlich.

18 John Gunn of St Paul's, Shadwell, Middx., B., & Mary Dawson of ye same, W.

18 Charles Rhodes of Isleworth, Middx., W., & Anne Hill of Windsor, co. Berks, S.

18 John Belfour of St Botolph, Aldgate, Midx., W., & Carolina Sneath of ye same, S.

18 William Saxby, Esq., of Penshurst, Kent, B., & Margaret Wyatt of Oxted, Surrey, S.

20 Thomas Okes of St James, Westmr, Middx., B., & Mary Freeman of St George, Hanover Square, Middx., S.

21 Alexander Alexander of St Martin in the Fields, Middx., B., & Isabella Wilson of St Clement Danes, Middx., S.

23 George Lockhart of St Saviour, Southwarke, B., and Elizabeth Clarke of the same, S.

23 Hancox Whitehouse of St Saviour, Southwarke, B., and Elizabeth Parrott of the same, W.

23 Richard Doody of Chelsea, Middx., W., and Elizabeth Russell of Edgware, Middx., W.

24 John Poch of St Andrew, Holborn, Middx., B., and Ann Shaw of St Paul, Shadwell, Middx., S.; by Mr Pinckney.

25 Isaac Pevey of St Luke's, Middx., W., and Mary Nicholls of St Botolph without Aldgate, W.

26 Mark Bryant of St Olave, Southwarke, W., and Elizabeth Long of St Saviour, Southwarke, W.

26 John Wynne of Christchurch, London, B., and Sarah Pointon of this parish, S.

26 Isaac Peach of St Magnus the Martyr, London, W., and Elizabeth Phipps of St John's in the city of Gloucester, S.

27 John Sampson of Isleworth, Middx., B., and Elizabeth Taylor of Richmond, Surry, S.

29 John Edge of St George, Hanover Square, Midx., W., and Ann Williamson of the same, S.

29 Samuel Spencer of St Paul, Covent Garden, Middx., W., and Ann Wainwright of St Martin in the Fields, Midx., W.

30 Jenkin Lewis of St George's, Bloomsbury, Middx., W., and Sarah Piper of the same, S.

30 Alexander Norcott of Fryern Barnett, Middx., W., and Elizabeth King of St Andrew Wardrobe, London, W.

July 1 Henry Peirce of Amwell Parva, co. Herts, B., and Elizabeth Booth of the same, S.

1 Stephen Towne of St Mary le Bone, Middx., B., and Elizabeth Edmones of Mortlake, Surry, S.

3 John Moore of St Lukes, Middx., B., and Anne Harrett of All Hallows Barking, London, S.

6 Thomas Moore of Bishop's Hatfield, co. Herts, W., and Eleanor Dobson of Hornchurch, Essex, W.; by Mr Campbell.

7 Thomas Reddish of St George, Hanover Square, Middx., B., and Margaret Heathitt of Westerham, Essex, W.; by the same.

1743

July 13 Pierre Le Saumery of St Ann, Westminster, Middx., B., and Margueritte Brunyer of the same, S.; by Mr Pearce of St Paul's.

14 Joseph Wesley of St Saviour, Southwarke, B., and Grace Beal of the same, S.; by the same.

17 John Robin of Gosport, co. Hants, B., and Jane Martin of St Martin in the Fields, Midx., S.; by Mr Foxley of St Edmund ye King.

17 Samuel Leigh of St Lawrence, Jury, London, B., and Mary Crow of Richmond, Surry, S.

17 Harry Dashwood of St Clement Danes, Midx., B., and Jane Hickson of Christchurch, London, S.

19 William Markinfield of East Greenwich, Kent, W., and Elizabeth Conway of St Olave, Southwarke, S.

19 Joshua Nash of Clapham, Surry, W., and Lydia Taylor of the same, S.

20 Thomas Payne of St Michael, Cornhill, London, B., and Elizabeth Grumball of St Dunstan, Stepney, Middx., S.

20 Xstopher Creed of St James, Westminster, Middx., W., and Mary Lee of the same, W.

21 James Haines of Woolwich in Kent, B., and Hannah Ifoell of the same, S.

23 Richard Jones of St Mary Ax, London, B., and Ann Moore of St Catherine Creed church, London, S.

25 William Barker of Camberwell, Surry, B., and Elizabeth Waite of the same, S.; by Mr Worlich.

26 Robert Cleaver of St Saviour, Southwarke, W., and Jane Eustace of St Mary, Whitechapel, Middx., S.

26 Thomas Reynal, Esq., of Bexfields in Essex, B., and Elizabeth Boughton of St Andrew, Holborn, Middx., S.

29 John Cordery of Deptford, Kent, W., and Sarah Beaumont of St John, Southwark, S.

31 Humphry Jackson of St Margaret, Westminster, B., and Elizabeth Savory of St James, Westminster, Middx., S.

31 Richard Garratt of St John, Southwark, B., and Ann Wallis of the same, W.; by Mr Worlich.

Aug. 1 Isaac Mills, Serjeant in 2nd Regt of Foot Guards, B., and Dorothy Thompson of Kensington, W.

3 William Bugbee of Maldon, Essex, B., and Ancee Batsford of Ilford, Essex, S.

9 Joseph Whitamore of St Sepulcre, London, B., and Elizabeth Spencer of St Bartholomew the Great, London, S.; by Mr Pinckney of St Paul's.

10 Charles Mackintosh of St Olave, Jewry, London, B., and Mary Bolton of the same, S.; by the same.

12 Charles Jerdein of St John, Wapping, Middx., B., and Phillis Crown of the same, W.; by the same.

13 Francis Gotobed of St Botolph, Aldgate, Midx., B., and Rebecca Wood of St James, Clarkenwell, Middx., S.; by Mr Worlich.

18 Isaac Lugnes of St Martin in the Fields, Middx., W., and Mary Pignet of St Anne, Westminster, Middx., S.; by Mr Mead.

20 Joseph Brown of St Lukes, Middx., B., and Mary Bonnett of the same, S.; by Mr Swynfen.

21 Edward Roberts of St Alphage, London, B., and Elizabeth Acland of St Giles, Cripplegate, London, S.

21 Joseph Upton of St John, Hackney, Middx., B., and Mary Goodge of St Magnus near London Bridge, S.

21 John Stewart of All Hallows Steyning, London, W., and Anne Mitchell of the same, S.

1743

Aug. 21 John Simmons of St Botolph, Aldersgate, London, B., and Frances Coleman of the same, W.

24 Thomas Page of Hornsey, Middx., B., and Martha Bayes of the same, S.

27 Thomas Arnold of St Saviour, Southwarke, W., and Anne Mylett of St Botolph, Bishopsgate, London, S.

28 George Temple of St Dunstan in the West, London, B., and Elizabeth Smith of St Margaret, Lothbury, London, S.

Sept. 3 William Harris of Hadlow, Kent, W., and Elizabeth Meriton of St Mary le Strand, Middx., S.

3 John King of Chiswick, Middx., W., and Rebecca Bagnall of St Margaret, Westminster, Middx., S.

4 Robert Sadler of St Saviour, Southwark, B., and Grace Price of the same, S.

5 Thomas Bailey of St George, Southwark, B., and Elizabeth Holmden of the same, S.

7 Peter le Moine of Holy Cross, Westgate, Canterbury, B., and Jane Bomble of St Anne, Westminster, Middx., S.

8 John Cogger of Lambeth, Surry, B., and Hannah Hutchins of the same, S.

8 William Wharton of St Martin in the Fields, Midx., W., and Esther Singleton of St George, Hanover Square, Middx., W.

8 Roger Sampson of St Dunstan in the East, Lond., B., and Sarah Free [? Tree] of the same, W.

10 Henry Long of St James, Westminster, Middx., B., and Elizabeth Price of the same, S.

10 Robert Pennett of St Martin in the Fields, Middx., W., and Jane Harris of the same, W.

11 John Sealy of St John the Evangelist, Westminster, Middx., B., and Elizabeth Smith of the same, S.

11 Peter Aylway of St Margaret, Westminster, Middx., W., and Mary Curtis of the same, S.

12 Thomas Stacy of St John, Hackney, Middx., W., and Elizabeth Johnson of St Olave, Hart Street, London, W.

13 Robert Phillipshill of St Andrew, Holborn, London, B., and Elizabeth Boots of Christ church, London, S.

13 Henry Kelly of St Mary le Strand, Middx., B., and Affabilia Morphet of the same, S.

14 William Metcalf of St Andrew, Holborn, Middx., W., and Margaret Brabant of the same, S.

14 Gerrard Atmar of Sunderland in the Bishoprick of Durham, B., and Ann Perkins of St Margaret, Westminster, Middx., S.

15 Frederick Pingeon of St Ann, Westminster, Middx., B., and Hellena Wilson of the same, S.

16 Francis Loder of Holy Trinity parish, London, B., and Mary Green of All Hallows Staining, London, S.

18 Alexander Bell of St Peter, Cornhill, London, B., and Sarah Cater of St Botolph, Bishopsgate, Middx., S.

19 John Bateman of Guilsborough, co. Northampton, B., and Mary Buckby of the same, S.

22 Isaac Dobson of St Anne, Aldersgate, London, B., and Elizabeth Shilbick of the same, S.

22 Daniel Kirton of Little Greenford, Middx., B., and Elizabeth Woodbridge of the same, S.

24 John Butterfield of St Andrew, Holborn, Middx., B., and Dorothy Lambert of St Dunstan in the West, London, W.

24 John Mottier of St Bartholow behind ye R. Exchange, London, B., and Jane Jourquet of St Anne, Westminster, Middx., S.

1743

Sept. 25 John Dobbins of S[t] George, Bloomsbury, Middx., B., and Elizabeth West of the same, S.

26 John Shaw of S[t] Botolph, Aldgate, Middx., B., and Deborah Roxby of S[t] Margaret, Westminster, Middx., S.

28 Anthony Shepherd of S[t] Mary Magdalen, Bermondsey in Southwarke, B., and Sarah Shepherd of Wandsworth, Surry, S.

29 William Blakes of S[t] Catherine Coleman, London, B., and Rebecca Bancroft of the same, S.; by M[r] Pinckney of S[t] Pauls.

29 Thomas Luton of S[t] Saviour, Southwarke, W., and Dorothy Green of the same, W.

29 John Hanslapp of Loughton, co. Bucks, B., and Elizabeth Jones of the same, S.

30 Walter Wyatt of S[t] Sepulchre, London, W., and Sarah West of the same, S.

Oct. 2 Benjamin Johnson of Walton upon Thames, Surrey, W., and Elizabeth Coward of S[t] Saviour, Southwarke, S.

6 Richard Leland of S[t] John, Hackney, Middx., B., and Mary Trussel of S[t] Clement Danes, Middx., S.

8 George Whitfield of S[t] Dunstan, Stepney, Middx., B., and Elizabeth Wright of the same, S.

9 Samuel Robinson of S[t] John the Evangelist, Westminster, Middx., B., and Susannah Church of the same, S.

10 Thomas Curtis of Newberry, co. Berks, B., and Ann Casebroock of New Windsor, co. Berks, W.

12 Martin Watson of S[t] Olave, Southwarke, W., and Elizabeth Hyde of S[t] Saviour, Southwarke, S.; by M[r] Knapp.

13 John Butcher of S[t] James, Clerkenwell, Middx., W., and Rachael Robinson of S[t] Peter, Cornhill, London, S.

17 James Stanley of S[t] Mary le Bone, Middx., B., and Frances Hoe of the same, S.

21 Edward Hopkins of Leatherhead, Surry, W., and Mary Twine of Thames Ditton, Surry, W.

24 Thomas Cooke of S[t] Helen's, London, B., and Mary Scarlett of Wodnesborrough, Kent, S.

25 Daniel Booth, Esq., of S[t] Botolph, Bishopsgate, London, W., and Martha Bodicoate of Stretham, Surry, W.

25 Henry Leetham of S[t] Clement, East Cheap, London, W., and Jane Kamp of S[t] Anne, Limehouse, Middx., W.

27 John Davis of S[t] Andrew, Holborn, Middx., B., and Mary Wilson of S[t] Luke, Chelsea, Middx., S.

27 John Wilkes of S[t] Mary, Newington, Surry, W., and Anne Peake of the same, W.

29 Benjamin Clark of S[t] George, Hanover Square, Middx., B., and Mary Gent of the same, S.

Nov. 3 William Noyes of Devizes, co. Wilts, W., and Catherine Nutt of the same, S.

3 Thomas Smith of Christchurch, Surry, B., and Ann Randolph of S[t] Olave, Southwarke, S.

3 Thomas Tub of S[t] James, Clerkenwell, Middx., W., and Sarah Shore of the same, W.

4 Samuel Banks of S[t] Saviour, Southwarke, B., and Sarah Smith of the same, S.

6 Archibald Scott of S[t] James, Westminster, Middx., Esq., B., and Christian Moncrieff of S[t] Margaret, Westminster, Middx., S.

12 William Evans of S[t] Leonard, Foster Lane, London, B., and Elianor Bull of the same, S.

24 Peter Hull of S[t] Peter ad Vincula, Middx., W., and Mary Alder of S[t] James, Clerkenwell, Middx., W.

1743

Nov. 27 Henry Bovill of St Dunstan in the West, London, B., and Mary Green of the same, S.

Dec. 4 George Baker of Christ church, Surry, B., and Sarah Smith of the same, S.

6 John Edgson of Lewisham, Kent, B., and Margaret Woodhouse of the same, W.

7 John Swindil of St George, Hanover Square, Middx., B., and Ann Sheppard of the same, S.

8 Alexander Vanderdussen of St Martin in the Fields, Middx., Esq., W., and Elizabeth Maggott of St James, Westminster, Middx., S.

8 John Ditton of St Mary, Islington, Middx., B., and Elizabeth Lowe of the same, S.

10 Benjamin Hughes of All Hallows, London Wall, B., and Margaret Blacknell of the same, S.

15 Matthew Bates of St Giles in the Fields, Middx., B., and Mary Nevill of the same, S.

20 Thomas Buckle of St Andrew, Holborn, Middx., B., and Martha Maynard of Taunton, Somerset, S.

20 Henry Button of St John, Southwarke, W., and Flower Johnson of St Bride's, London, W.

21 Edward Gough of St Peter Poor, London, B., and Joanna Jordine of St Peter near Paul's Wharfe, London, S.; by ye Rev. Dr Thomas.

22 Richard Eyre of Bright Walton, co. Berks, B., and Alice Willis of Whaddon, co. Bucks, S.; by ye Rev. Dr Thomas.

22 Isaac Du-Hamel of St Martin in the Fields, Middx., W., and Ann Markham of St Dunstan in the West, London, W.

27 William Coleman of St Botolph, Aldersgate, London, B., and Ann Coleman of the same, S.

27 Frederick Horner of St Luke's, Middx., B., and Mary Fisher of Christ church, London, S.

27 Thomas Eales of Morden, Surry, B., and Lucy Bordeaux of West Ham, Essex, S.

31 Samuel Payce of St Andrew, Holborn, London, B., and Elizabeth Lofthouse of the same, S.

31 William Lovell of Chatham, Kent, B., and Mary Ward of St John, Hackney, Middx., S.

Jan. 1 Thomas Stocks of Christchurch, Surry, B., and Mary Cooke of St Andrew, Holborn, London, S.

2 Gilbert Scott of St Andrew, Holborn, London, B., and Elizabeth Bowler of Woodcott Clump, co. Oxford, S.

5 Thomas Walker of St Mary Cole, London, W., and Elizabeth Bealey of St Giles, Cripplegate, London, S.

5 Hugh Vincent of Sherman Bury in Sussex, B., and Mary Hayward of Tatsfield in Surry, S.

5 Benjamin Pewtress of St Ethelburgh's, London, W., and Mary Spurrier of St John in Surrey, W.

6 Abraham Mendez of St Botolph, Aldgate, B., and Margaret Turner of St John, Wapping, Middx., S.

8 Kimble Nixon of St John, Wapping, Middx., B., and Susannah Falcon of St Leonard, Foster Lane, London, S.

9 Thomas Charlton of Sutton, Surrey, W., and Martha Kingett of Netley, Hants, S.

11 John Lambert of St Martin in the Fields, Middx., B., and Ann Gertrude Stam of St George, Hanover Square, Middx., S.

11 Richard Morris of St George, Hanover Square, Middx., B., and Mary Young of the same, S.

1743-4

Jan. 12 Benjamin Pearce of S[t] James, Westminster, Middx., B., and Elizabeth Treece of S[t] Andrew, Holborn, Middx., S.

12 William Brightwell of Wandsworth, Surry, B., and Elizabeth Burr of the same, S.

12 Howell Lewis of S[t] James, Westminster, Middx., B., and Elizabeth Jones of the same, S.

12 Richard Nevill of S[t] Giles in the Fields, Middx., B., and Mary Hakewill of the same, S.

17 Thomas Hodgkin of S[t] Botolph, Aldersgate, London, B., and Mary Coleman of the same, S.

17 Peter Triggs of S[t] James, Westminster, Middx., W., and Fanny Ball of the same, W.

19 Garvas Spencer of S[t] James, Westminster, Middx., B., and Margaret Carrig of the same, S.

19 John Harley of S[t] James, Westminster, Middx., B., and Elizabeth Nell of S[t] George, Hanover Square, Middx., S.

19 Joseph Woolley of S[t] Margaret Pattons, London, W., and Johannah Holloway of S[t] Peter, Cornhill, London, S.

21 Thomas Stafford of S[t] Mary le Bone, Middx., B., and Mary Mortimer of S[t] Ann, Westminster, Middx., S.

22 William Clark of S[t] Clement Danes, Middx., B., and Amy Smith of the same, W.

23 William Herritage of S[t] James, Westminster, Middx., W., and Hannah Parsons of the same, S.

25 William Sharp of Farningham, Kent, B., and Mary How of the same, S.

26 John Barnett of S[t] George, Hanover Square, Middx., W., and Elizabeth Graham of the same, W.

30 John Wallis of Eastbead, Surry, B., and Magdalen Hollier of Lambeth, Surry, S.; by M[r] Pearce of S[t] Paul's.

Feb. 2 Daniel Mills of S[t] Nicholas Acons, London, B., and Anne Dorsett of S[t] Clement Danes, Middx., S.

3 James Barker of Lambeth, Surry, B., and Jane Ward of the same, S.

3 Edward Willson of S[t] Botolph, Aldgate, London, W., and Elizabeth Vokens of S[t] Bennet, Grace church, London, W.

4 Robert Roffey of Sutton, Surry, W., and Margaret Allen of S[t] Saviour, Southwarke, W.

5 William Cosins of Whitney, co. Oxford, W., and Ann Kent of the same, W.

7 John Hembrough of St Martin in the Fields, Middx., W., and Ann Briggs of the same, S.

7 John Price of Low Layton, Essex, B., and Elizabeth Jordan of the same, S.

8 Thomas Wright of Dorking, Surry, B., and Elizabeth Giles of St Martin in the Fields, Middx., S.

8 Peter De Béta of Christ church, Middx., B., and Mary Godard of St Leonard, East Cheap, London, S.

11 Silvester Devonish of St James, Westminster, Middx., B., and Elizabeth Plunkett of the same, S.

11 Charles Newport of Lambeth, Surry, W., and Frances Bradley of the same, S.; by Mr Mead of Foster Lane.

13 Robert Bateman of Ipswich, Suffolk, B., and Mary Greenwood of Winchester, Hants, S.

17 Alexander Fall of S[t] Martin in the Fields, Middx., B., and Jannet Old of the same, S.

21 Robert Thompson of S[t] Mary, Rotherhith, Surry, B., and Kaziah Whetstone of the same, W.

1743-4

Feb. 22 John Paine of St Dunstan, Stepney, Middx., B., and Sarah Gilman of the same, W.

22 John Leigh of St Mary, Newington, Surry, B., and Susannah Fawcett of St Thomas, Southwarke, W.

23 Joseph Jones of St George, Bloomsbury, Middx., B., and Mary Willoughby of the same, S.

23 William Everard of St Mary, White chapel, Middx., W., and Dorothy Pickard of St James, Westminster, Middx., S.

Mar. 1 Henry Hotchen of St George, Bloomsbury, Middx., B., and Anne Sison of the same, S.

1 Thomas Harman of Rumford, Essex, W., and Dorothy Sandford of the same, S.; by ye Rev. Mr Fletcher.

8 John Burnett of Reading, co. Berks, Clerk, B., and Catharine Stanton of Berwick on Tweed, S.

8 Samuel Franks of St Andrew, Holborn, Middx., B., and Mary Gardner of the same, S.

1744.

Mar. 26 Richard Higham of Christ Church, Surry, W., and Sarah Ward of St Peter Le Poor, London, S.

27 Thomas Barlow of St Andrew, Holborn, London, W., and Rebecca Say of Deptford, Kent, S.

28 John Atkinson of Farningham in Kent, B., and Mary May of Horton in Kent, S.

29 Richard Smith of Hampstead, Middx., W., and Mary Holford of Edmonton, Middx., S.

29 Peter Whitehead of St George, Hanover Square, Middx., B., and Elizabeth LLoyd of the same, S.

29 Joseph Sowter of St John, Hackney, Middx., W., and Elizabeth Claxon of the same, W.

29 Jonas Magnus Edberg of St John, Wapping, Middx., B., and Christiana Westfall of the same, S.

30 Nathaniel Wedd of ye old Artillery ground in ye Liberty of ye Tower of London, B., and Mercy Sunter of St Martin Vintry, London, S.

31 Henry Kidney of Harrow on the Hill, Middx., B., and Mary Westmore of the same, S.

April 2 John Cossens of St Ann, Westminster, Middx., B., and Mary Woodcock of the same, S.

4 John Jenkins of St Luke's, Middx., W., and Susannah Gill of St Bartholomew the Less, London, W.

6 John Bayly of St Andrew, Holborn, Middx., B., and Mary Cumberlidge of St Paul, Covent Garden, Middx., S.

8 Samuel Burgess of St Clement Danes, Middx., B., and Ann Jones of the same, S.

8 John Franklin of St Martin in the Fields, Middx., B., and Margaret Wildman of St Michael, Cornhill, London, S.

10 John Giles of Lambeth, Surrey, W., and Elizabeth Selby of St Paul, Covent Garden, Middx., W.; by Mr Pearce of St Paul's

13 Henry Harris of St Peter Le Poor, London, B., and Ann Stevens of the same, S.

17 John Stiles of Wandsworth, Surry, B., and Elizabeth Anne Van Bargen of the same, W.

17 Edward Hide of St Brides, London, B., and Margaret Meakin of St Mary le Savoy, Middx., S.

19 Richard Browne of St Leonards, Shoreditch, Middx., W., and Joan Curtis of St Luke, Middx., W.; by Mr Worlich.

1744

April 22 Robert Richardson of S[t] Andrew, Holborn, London, B., and Elizabeth Kight of the same, S.

25 John Cantrill of Windsor, co. Berks, B., and Jane Swain of Stanwell, Middx., S.

25 Robert Hooper of Deptford, Kent, B., and Elizabeth Haynes of the same, W.

25 Jenkin Jones of S[t] Mary at Hill, London, B., and Ellinor Winterburn of the same, S.

26 Samuel Ryley of S[t] Dunstan in the West, London, B., and Elizabeth Coulston of the same, S.

26 Charles Courteen of S[t] Paul, Covent Garden, Middx., B., and Jane Price of S[t] Andrew, Holborn, Middx., S.

27 John Jackson of Borton Mallard, Kent, B., and Margaret Bradley of the same, S.

May 1 George Watts of East Barnett, co. Herts, B., and Elizabeth Quarry of the same, S.

2 John Woodward of S[t] Mary at Hill, London, B., and Esther Varley of the same, S.

3 Robert Ritchie of S[t] Butolph, Aldgate, London, B., and Ann Pimperton of the same, S.

4 Edward Powell of S[t] Andrew, Holborn, London, B., and Mary Haslehurst of S[t] Bride's, London, S.

5 Thomas Griffith of S[t] Giles in the Fields, Middx., W., and Mary Bost of S[t] Andrew, Holborn, Middx., W.

6 George Wheeler of y[e] Precinct of y[e] Savoy, Middx., W., and Anne Abbot of S[t] Gregory, London, S.

7 James Wright of S[t] Pancras, Middx., B., and Jane Hurlock of S[t] John, Hackney, Middx., S.

10 William Henry Haucks of S[t] Mary le Strand, Middx., W., and Hannah Tabourn of S[t] Giles in the Fields, Middx., W.

12 John Cock of S[t] Botolph without Aldgate, Middx., B., and Abia Gordon of the same, S.

13 Jude Kitt of S[t] John, Wapping, Middx., B., and Sarah Leagoe of S[t] Leonard, Shoreditch, Middx., S.

13 Thomas Noots of Maidstone, Kent, B., and Susannah Missing of the same, S.

14 Thomas Farnes of Croydon, Surry, B., and Sarah Appleby of the same, S.

14 James Johnson of S[t] Mary Magdalen, Bermondsey, Surry, W., and Prudence Whitell of the same, W.

14 William Green of S[t] Dunstan in the East, London, B., and Susannah Bound of All Hallows Barking, London, S.

15 William Woolley of S[t] Andrew, Holborn, Middx., B., and Ellin Slaughter of the same, W.; by M[r] Bradley.

17 Laurence Rudyerd of Winchfield, Hants, B., and Jane Hodson of S[t] Anne, Westminster, Middx., S.

17 John Bynon of S[t] John, Hackney, Middx., W., and Alicia Rayson of the same, S.

17 Christian Godfriet Wiseman of S[t] George, Hanover Square, Middx., B., and Anne Mason of the same, W.

19 George Field of S[t] Paul, Covent Garden, Middx., B., and Emma Fickus of S[t] John, Westminster, Middx., S.

21 William Wrenford of S[t] James, Westminster, Middx., W., and Dorothy Rowth of S[t] Olave, Southwarke, S.

21 John Gardner of Isleworth, Middx., B., and Elizabeth Green of S[t] Olave, Hart Street, London, S.

21 Samuel Quay of S[t] Paul, Covent Garden, Middx., W., and Elizabeth Rivers of the same, W.

1744

May 22 John Hall of Ealing, Middx., W., and Elizabeth Wilkins of Fulham, Middx., S.

25 William Jewell of Seven Oak, Kent, B., and Hester Mortimer of Seal in Kent, S.

26 Henry Vaughan of S[t] Giles in the Fields, Middx., B., and Mary Norman of S[t] Martin in the Fields, Middx., S.

26 Robert Meldrum of S[t] Botolph, Aldgate, Middx., W., and Elizabeth Wallgrave of the same, S.

28 William Phelps of Endfield, Middx., B., and Ann Cooling of the same, S.

30 John Eatt of the Town of Cambridge, W., and Mary Hume of Deptford, Kent, S.

31 William Snook of Deptford (S[t] Paul's), Surry [*sic*], W., and Mary Potter of S[t] Nicholas, Deptford, Kent, W.

31 Thomas Sisum of S[t] Giles in the Fields, Middx., B., and Rebecca Edwards of Stepney, Middx., S.

31 Xstopher Appleby of S[t] Sepulchre, London, B., and Ann Tinson of the same, S.

June 3 John Dobson of S[t] John, Southwarke, W., and Ann Jones of S[t] Michael, Queenhith, London, S.

5 William Porter of S[t] Clement Danes, Midx., W., and Ann Bry of the same, S.

7 John Paul of Hornchurch, Essex, W., and Sarah Webster of the same, W.

9 Reuben Borer of S[t] Martin in the Fields, Middx., B., and Esther Cox of S[t] Giles in the Fields, Middx., S.

10 John Callis of S[t] Botolph, Aldersgate, London, W., and Rebecca Pugh of the same, W.

13 William Dick of S[t] Martin in the Fields, Middx., B., and Mary Ward of the same, S.

14 Francis Moulcer of S[t] John, Hackney, Middx., W., and Martha Greenaway of S[t] Lawrence, Jewry, London, S.

14 Robert Dawson of S[t] James, Westminster, Middx., B., and Elizabeth Howard of S[t] Martin in the Fields, Middx., S.

14 Ambrose William Bartlett of S[t] Peter's, Paul's Wharfe, London, B., and Mary Wass of S[t] Lawrence, Jewry, London, S.; by M[r] Pinckney of S[t] Pauls.

15 John Hugens of S[t] Paul, Covent Garden, Middx., B., and Ann Rahn of the same, W.

17 John Bowler of S[t] Paul, Shadwell, Middx., W., and Mary Gandae of the same, W.; by M[r] Pinckney.

19 Alexander Cushnie of S[t] Saviour, Southwarke, W., and Bethiah Ray of the same, W.

24 Michael Worth of S[t] Botolph, Bishopsgate, London, W., and Mary Swaine of the same, S.

29 Thomas Parker of Godstone, Surry, B., and Ann Francis of the same, S.

July 5 Joshua Beck of Amersham, co. Bucks, W., and Elizabeth Chalkley of Watford, co. Herts, S.; by M[r] Ellison.

11 Charles Newman of S[t] James, Clerkenwell, Middx., [*blank*], and Joannah Slatham of the same; by M[r] Pearce of S[t] Paul's, [*blank*].

11 Samuel Smith of Sabridgeworth, co. Herts, W., and Mary Corney of Gileston, co. Herts, S.; by M[r] Pearce.

15 Richard Howe of S[t] Catherine near the Tower of London, B., and Barbara Matthew of the same Precinct, W.

15 Robert Gaskill of S[t] Paul's, Deptford, Kent, B., and Hannah Martin of S[t] John, Wapping, Middx., S.

25 Richard Harford of Trowbridge, co. Wilts, W., and Mary Hawkins of S[t] Clement Danes, Middx., S.

1744

July 25 Thomas Barnett of S[t] Margaret, Westminster, Middx., B., and Frances Green of S[t] Ives, co. Huntingdon, S.

25 John Skaines of Deptford, Kent, B., and Sarah Eaton of the same, W.

27 Maurice Ireland of Rudgwick in Sussex, B., and Leah Mitchell of the same, S.

27 Henry Trower of Wisborough Green in Sussex, B., and Mary Mitchell of Rudgewick in Sussex, S.

30 William Burgeyne of Islington, Middx., B., and Elizabeth Bird of the same, W.

Aug. 2 Robert Jamesson of S[t] George, Middx., W., and Margaret Clark of the same, W.

5 William Leake of S[t] Michael, Cornhill, London, B., and Elizabeth White of Christ church, Middx., W.

9 Samuel Hoy of S[t] Botolph, Aldgate, Middx., W., and Mary Perkins of S[t] Mary Magdalen, Old Fish Street, London, W.; by M[r] Tillotson.

9 Richard LLoyd of S[t] Mary, Islington, Middx., B., and Judith Matthews of Lambeth, Surry, W.; by M[r] Tillotson.

9 John Holloway of S[t] Brides, London, W., and Mary Betts of the same, W.; by M[r] Tillotson.

9 Francis Nisbitt of Tinmouth, Northumberland, B., and Mary Clark of Gravesend, Kent, W.; by M[r] Tillotson.

13 Joseph Grigg of S[t] Nicholas, Deptford, Kent, B., and Susannah Challenger of the same, S.; by M[r] Worlich.

14 Thomas Williams of S[t] John, Hackney, Middx., B., and Jane Forster of the same, S.; by M[r] Pearce.

14 William Ford of S[t] Martin in the Fields, Middx., W., and Anne Hurst of the same, W.

15 Thomas Randel of S[t] Anne, Limehouse, Middx., B., and Elizabeth Dixon of the same, S.; by M[r] Hillman.

16 Benedict Pysing of East Chinick, Somerset, B., and Jane Moor of West Coker in Somerset, S.; by M[r] Grainger.

16 George Pawley of Lullingstone, Kent, B., and Mary Hampton of the same, S.; by M[r] Pearce.

21 Charles Gwilt of S[t] Saviour's, Southwark, W., and Mary Le Bass of S[t] Martin in the Fields, Middx., W.

25 James Elcock of Barking in Essex, B., and Betty Arthur of the same, S.

26 Thomas Norwood Ashfield, B., and Mary Wass, S., both of S[t] Peter's, Paul's Wharf. Banns.

27 David Peirson of S[t] Stephen, Coleman Street, London, W., and Elizabeth Berley of the same, W.

27 William Wood of S[t] Botolph, Aldgate, London, B., and Anne Wood of the same, W.

28 George Marshall of St Andrew's, Holborn, London, B., and Anne Jones of the same, S.

Sept. 1 William Boston of Mitcham, Surrey, B., and Hannah Davis of the same, W.

1 William Johnson of St Saviour, Southwarke, W., and Susannah Gillings of St Paul, Shadwell, Middx., W.

2 Edward Büshop of Chipping Barnett, co. Herts, W., and Mary Downer of the same, S.

3 John Chittenden of St Mary Magdalen, Bermondsey, Southwarke, W., and Anne Maynard King of Camberwell, Surry, S.

3 Henry Jacob Gynander of St James, Westminster, Middx., B., and Anne Catherine Ernst of the same, W.

4 William Smith of Kensington, Middx., W., and Mary Bass of the same, W.

1744

Sept. 5 Robert Wrench of Epsom, Surry, W., and Elizabeth Latter of the same, S.

5 Jeremiah Milner of St Mary, White Chapel, Middx., B., and Anne Bradley of St Giles in the Fields, Middx., S.

6 William Patrick of St Clement Danes, Middx., W., and Mary Davis of St Andrew, Holborn, Middx., S.

6 Edward Simson of St Clement Danes, Middx., B., and Elizabeth Hayward of the same, S.

9 Joseph Sturt of St Catherine Cree, London, B., and Mary North of St James, Westminster, Middx., S.

15 Matthew Shaw of St George, Hanover Square, Middx., B., and Dorothy Choice of the same, S.

17 Lawrence Stanroyd of St Mildred, Poultry, London, B., and Mary Curle of St Alban, Wood Street, London, W.

26 Thomas Croft of St John Zachary, London, B., and Ann Francis of St George, Middx., S.

Oct. 2 Robert Gundry of St George, Hanover Square, Middx., W., and Mary Miles of the same, S.

2 Samuel Ogier of Christ church, Middx., B., and Mary Marsillat of the same, S.

3 George Allison of Edmonton, Middx., B., and Penelope Edmunds of the same, S.

7 Richard Post of St Lawrence, Poultney, London, B., and Ann Webb of St Lukes, Middx., S.

8 Alexander Grigg of Woolwick, Kent, B., and Elizabeth Challenger of Deptford, Kent, S.

8 James Pearsey of Old Brentford, Middx., B., and Alice Parr of the same, S.

10 Ambrose Filber of St Paul, Shadwell, Middx., B., and Ann Witherden of St Peter, Isle of Thanet, Kent, W.

11 Robert Osbaldeston of St Luke, Middx., B., and Sarah Wittingham of St Lawrence Jury, London, W.

12 Roger Brewster of Cheshunt, co. Herts, W., and Jane Milson of Windsor, co. Berks, S.

13 Thomas Bayliss of St John, Southwarke, W., and Ellenor Cherry of the same, W.

14 Jenkin Coward of St Clement Danes, Middx., B., and Anna Maria Barker of the same, W.

16 James Parroissien of Christ church, Middx., B., and Anne Pouchet of Bethnel Green, Middx., S.

16 Peter Bargeau of St Mary, White Chapel, Middx., W., and Mary How of All Hallows, Thames Street, London, S.

20 John Walker of Cheshunt, co. Herts, B., and Mary Keys of the same, S.

22 John Collyer of St Paul, Covent Garden, Middx., W., and Frances Merrick of St Martin in the Fields, Middx., W.

25 John Wake of St Catherine by the Tower of London, B., and Sarah Peene of Gravesend, Kent, W.

29 John Ross of St Andrew, Holborn, Middx., B., and Anne Hunter of Wandsworth, Surry, S.

30 John Barry of St Bartholomew the Great, London, W., and Frances LLoyd of St Mary, Islington, Middx., S.

30 Thomas Fryer of Isleworth, Middx., B., and Jane Goffe of the same, S.

Nov. 1 John Chandler of St Andrew, Holborne, Middx., [*blank*], and Rhoda Heardson of the same, [*blank*].

3 Henry Kitchen of St John the Evangelist, Westminster, B., and Elizabeth Knight of the same, S.

1744

Nov. 3 William Sheappard of S[t] Martin in the Fields, Middx., B., and Elizabeth Langworthy of the same, W.

4 Charles Appley of S[t] James, Westminster, B., and Elizabeth Jenkins of the same, S.

5 Henry West of Old Brentford, Middx., B., and Elizabeth Louch of Richmond, Surry, S.

6 William Taylor of Frant in Sussex, W., and Philadelphia Luck of the same, S.

7 John Gray of S[t] James, Clerkenwell, Middx., B., and Mary Henson of the same, S.

11 Joseph Clegg of S[t] Thomas, Southwarke, B., and Mary Carlton of the same, S.

13 John Blackford of S[t] James, Westminster, B., and Mary Greasham of the same, S.

20 William Fearon of Tinmouth, Northumberland, B., and Christina Lance of S[t] John, Wapping, Middx., S.

23 Thomas Fielder of Kensington, Middx., B., and Elizabeth Singler of the same, W.

25 Ralph Lawson of S[t] Peter's, Cornhill, London, B., and Elizabeth Newton of the same, S.

25 Henry Wadham of S[t] Mary Magdalen, Bermondsea, Southwarke, B., and Sarah Beazley of S[t] Faith under S[t] Paul, London, W.

Dec. 1 Henry Hurley of S[t] Mary, Islington, Middx., W., and Elizabeth Field of S[t] Andrew, Holborn, Middx., S.

2 Ambrose Jagg of S[t] Thomas, Southwarke, B., and Margaret Westmore of the same, S.

6 John Lefevre of S[t] Olave, Hart Street, London, B., and Judith Spencer of the same, W.

6 William Parker of Bray, co. Berks, B., and Hester Slade of S[t] James, Westminster, Middx., S.

12 Michael Laybank of Chinkford, Essex, B., and Elizabeth Groves of the same, S.

13 Richard Mitchell of S[t] Paul's, Shadwell, Middx., B., and Mary Gillings of the same, W.

16 John Cock of S[t] James, Westminster, Middx., W., and Mary Michie of Aberdeen, North Britain, S.

19 Thomas Fawknor of SS. Ann and Agnes within Aldersgate, London, W., and Elizabeth Burges of S[t] Sepulchre, London, S.

20 Thomas Patfull of S[t] Giles, Cripplegate, London, B., and Elizabeth Saunders of S[t] Mary, Rotherhith, Surry, S.

24 Henry Child of Rislip, Middx., B., and Sarah Beake of Harrow, Middx., S.

25 John Parker of All Hallows Staining, London, B., and Ann Stoker of the same, W.

27 John Horton of S[t] Nicholas Olave, London, B., and Alice Shadwell of Wolverhampton, co. Stafford, S.

30 William Humphry of S[t] Mary, White Chapel, Middx., B., and Sarah Thomas of S[t] Botolph, Aldgate, London, S.

30 Nathaniel Oldham of S[t] George, Hanover Square, Middx., W., and Sarah Buxton of S[t] Pancras, Middx., S.

31 David Bataille of Christ church, Middx., W., and Anne Louisa Grellier of Norton Folgate Precinct, Middx., S.

Jan. 4 Hans Erick of S[t] George, Middx., B., and Dorothy Smart of the same, W.

5 Benjamin Hart of Cookham, co. Berks, B., and Mary Worster of the same, S.

8 John Masterman of Northfleet, Kent, B., and Sarah Crowcher of Chatham in Kent, S.

1744-5

Jan. 9 Robert Machan of Wandsworth, Surry, B., and Anne Moseley of St Stephen, Coleman Street, London, S.

10 John Smith of St John's, Southwarke, W., and Elizabeth Ewell of the same, S.

10 Richard Mayle of St Andrew, Holborn, Middx., B., and Mary Williams of the same, S.

12 Edward Lovibond, Esq., of Kingston in Surry, B., and Catherine Hamilton of Hampton, Middx., S.; by Mr Fisher, curate of Hampton.

15 John Dell of St Luke's, Middx., B., and Elizabeth Beck of the same, [*blank*].

16 Henry Lusancy of Bethnall Green, Middx., B., and Eleanor Gandy of the same, S.

17 Thomas Moses of St Dunstan, Stepney, Middx., B., and Mary Bacon of the same, S.

17 Thomas Felton of Towcester, co. Northampton, B., and Mary Muskett of St Sepulchre, Middx., W.

19 John Griffiths of Old Windsor, co. Berks, B., and Hannah Clark of St Martin in the Fields, Middx., S.

22 William Gardiner of St Margaret, Westminster, B., and Mary Tomlyn of the same, S.

24 Richard Malkin of St Catherine, Coleman Street, London, B., and Elizabeth Vallett of the same, S.

26 Thomas Akers of Streatham, Surry, B., and Mary Phillips of the same, S.

28 William Bennett of New Windsor, co. Berks, B., and Ann Hill of Clapham, Surry, S.

30 Joseph Smallman of Lugwardine, co. Hereford, B., and Grace Baldwin of Upton, co. Berks, S.

31 Thomas Whitaker of St John, Wapping, Middx., B., and Elizabeth Tayler of the same, S.

Feb. 3 George Yeatts of St Mary, Aldermanbury, London, B., and Sarah Walton of St Martin in the Fields, Middx., S.

9 John Colchin of Hams in Sussex, B., and Mary English of Bromley in Kent, S.

9 William Toll of Kensington in Middx., W., and Elizabeth Delarene of the same, S.

13 Cowdery Milson of New Windsor, co. Berks, B., and Eleanor Gilman of the same, S.

13 Joseph Cox of Edmonton, Middx., W., and Jane Bonam of the same, S.

14 William Wright of Froome, Somerset, B., and Rebecca Wright of Islington, Middx., S.

14 John Quincy of St Martin in the Fields, Middx., B., and Margaret Detton of St Olave, Silver Street, London, S.

15 Samuel Horsman, D^r^ of Physick, of St Andrew, Holborn, Middx., W., and Mary Reynolds of Tottenham High Cross, Middx., S.; by Mr Berrow, Lecturer of this parish.

15 Samuel Cornish of St George, Southwarke, B., and Lydia Killick of the same, S.

16 James Kennedy of St Martin in the Fields, Middx., B., and Rebecca Piers of St Margaret, Westminster, Middx., S.

17 Francis Starks of St Nicholas in Rochester, B., and Elizabeth Pilcher of the same, S.

18 John Gregory of St Mary, Rotherhith, Surry, B., and Henrietta Meirvin of St Mary Magdalen, Bermondsey, Surry, S.

19 William Bettsworth of St Saviour, Southwarke, W., and Elizabeth Quinton of the same, W.

1744-5

Feb. 19 Rowland Berkeley of St Lawrence, Jewry, London, B., and Ann Eccles of Macklesfield, Cheshire, S.

21 Edward Arnott of St Giles in the Fields, Middx., B., and Elizabeth Chamberlain of St Andrew, Holborn, London, W.

21 Charles Carter of St Sepulchre's, Middx., W., and Sarah Bolsford of the same, W.

21 William Poole of Lambeth, Surry, B., and Mary Cannon of the same, S.

21 Henry Dawson of St Dunstan, Stepney, Middx., W., and Hannah Ralfe of the same, S.

24 George Brewer of St Mary, co. Southampton, B., and Mary Backhouse of St Michael's, co. Herts, S.

25 Hugh Charnock of Christ church, London, B., and Ann Smith of the same, S.

25 Mark Jordan of Elmstead, Kent, B., and Elizabeth Valyer of the same, S.

26 Samuel Collchen of Bromley, Kent, B., and Elizabeth Best of St Nicholas Acons, London, S.

26 John Truman of St Anne, Limehouse, Middx., B., and Alice Graves of the same, S.

Mar. 1 John Warick of Barking, Essex, B., and Mary Eaton of Wanstead, Essex, S.

3 Peter Woodnoth of St Clement, East Cheap, London, B., and Margaret Lofting of St George the Martyr, Middx., S.

6 John Hutchison of St Dunstan, Stepney, Middx., W., and Mary LLoyd of St Luke's, Middx., S.

10 John Murton of Kennington, Kent, B., and Sarah Brice of St Andrew, Holborn, Middx., S.

13 Thomas Laming of East Greenwich, B., and Catherine Hattinborow of St Dunstan, Stepney, Middx., W.

14 Abraham Debart of St Peter's in Colchester, Essex, W., and Elizabeth Cundall of this parish, S.

16 William Adams of Wanstead, Essex, B., and Mary Webster of the same, S.

21 Thomas Hearn of Chiswick, Middx., W., and Rachael Lawrence of the same, S.

1745.

Mar. 28 Edward Eagleton of Town Malling, Kent, B., and Martha Johnson of St Margaret, Westminster, Middx., S.; by Mr Welles.

28 Benjamin Dillingham of Epsom, Surry, W., and Susan Anderson of the same, W.; by Mr Welles.

April 1 Robert Gideon of St Martin in the Fields, Middx., B., and Ann Agnes Hambleton of St Margaret, Westminster, Middx., S.

2 Henry Byng of the City of Rochester, Kent, B., and Elizabeth Nixon of St George the Martyr, Middx., S.

2 Charles Chapman of St Michael, Cornhill, London, B., and Mary Nowers of Westerham, Kent, S.

6 Thomas Stevenson of St Margaret Pattens, London, B., and Elizabeth Speller of the same, S.

9 Robert Yeates of All Hallows the Great, London, B., and Ann Kingdon of the same, S.

14 Henry Lettington of St Mary, Newington, Surry, B., and Joanna Hunt of St Olave, Southwarke, S.

15 Robert Bingham of St Margaret, Westminster, Middx., B., and Sarah Hawtyn of St Clement Danes, Middx., S.; by Mr Tillotson.

1745

April 15 Richard Sale of St Dunstan in the West, London, B., and Mary Ralfe of the same, S.

16 William Pitfield of St James, Clerkenwell, Middx., W., and Mary Wallis of St Dunstan in the East, London, W.

17 George Meebourne of St George, Bloomsbury, Middx., B., and Sarah Welbrough the Younger of St Margaret, Westminster, Middx., S.

20 George Welch of St Mary le Strand, Middx., W., and Philadelphia Surger of St Clement Danes, Middx., S.

21 Peter Ives of St Andrew Hubbard, London, B., and Elizabeth Hughes of the same, S.

25 William Judge of St James, Westminster, Middx., B., and Frances Gillman of the same, S.

25 John Williams of St Catherine near the Tower of London, B., and Susannah Underwood of the same, S.

27 Jerehjah Finch of Christ church, London, B., and Anna Maria Fisher of Hackney, Middx., S.

27 William Taylor of St Mary le Bow, London, B., and Charlotte Fisher of Hackney, Middx., S.

28 John Mitchener of St Martin in the Fields, Midx., B., and Elizabeth Taylor of the same, S.

28 Robert Kimin of St Mary, Newington Butts, Surrey, W., and Lucy Messenger of Chepstead, Kent, W.

May 2 John Lewis of St Margaret, Westminster, Middx., B., and Mary Boon of the same, S.

2 William Probert, B., and Jane Smith, S., both of this parish. Banns.

2 William Thacker of Poplar Hamlett in Stepney, Middx., W., and Mary King of the same, W.

3 Henry Hennings of St Mary le Strand, Middx., B., and Esther Newsham of the same, S.

4 Jacob Jamet of the Liberty of Norton Falgate, Middx., B., and Ann Du Bec of St Andrew Undershaft, London, S.

4 Benjamin Golden of St Olave, Southwarke, W., and Lucy Boan of the same, S.

5 John Cowdery of St Margaret, Westminster, Middx., B., and Elizabeth Thomas of the same, S.

7 James Weston of St Mary Magdalen, Milk Street, London, B., and Susanna Delarne of Christ church, London, S.

14 Hugh Pattrickson of All Hallows, Bread Street, London, B., and Jane Dalton of St James, Westminster, Middx., S.; by Mr Pearce.

16 James Boulter of Wimbledon, Surrey, B., and Sarah Bayley of St George, Hanover Square, Middx., S.

16 Richard Edwards of St George, Hanover Square, Middx., B., and Mary Minnitt of the same, S.

16 William Arvin of St John, Southwarke, Surry, W., and Mary Clevell of St Paul, Deptford, Kent, S.

21 John Hawley of St George, Hanover Square, Middx., B., and Mary Talbot of the same, S.

21 Thacker Nightingale of Roxwell, Essex, B., and Mary Tyler of Hornchurch, Essex, S.

22 John Veck of St Andrew, Holborn, London, B., and Elizabeth Woolmer of St Paul, Shadwell, Middx., S.

22 William Havard of St Paul, Covent Garden, Middx., B., and Elizabeth Kilby of St Martin in the Fields, Middx., W.

26 John Rogers of St Clement Danes, Middx., B., and Mary Tomson of St Mary le Strand, Middx., S.

27 Thomas Sterling of Mortlake, Surry, B., and Mary Stretton of the same, S.

1745

May 27 John May of S[t] John, Southwarke, W., and Sarah Hanson of the same, W.

28 John Leach of Deptford, Kent, B., and Elizabeth Wayman of the same, S.; by M[r] Worlich.

28 Robert Gusthart of S[t] Martin, Ludgate, London, B., and Adiliza Goner of S[t] Andrew, Holborne, London, S.; by M[r] Pinckney.

28 Henry Groom of S[t] Paul, Covent Garden, Middx., B., and Jemima Metcalfe of S[t] Mary le Bone, Middx., W.; by the same.

29 George Porter of S[t] Stephen, Coleman Street, London, B., and Sarah Frencham of S[t] George, Hanover Square, Middx., S.; by M[r] LLoyd.

30 George Ashdowne of S[t] George the Martyr, Middx., B., and Sarah Ashdowne of the same, S.; by M[r] Worlich.

30 Peter Poupard of y[e] old Artillery Ground in the Tower Hamlett, Middx., B., and Sarah Combers of Brentwood, Essex, S.; by M[r] Worlich.

30 James Currant of S[t] Andrew, Holbourn, London, B., and Jane Olaphant of the same, W.

30 William Steel of Long Ditton, Surrey, B., and Elizabeth Martins of the same, S.

June 3 Henry Secrett of S[t] Alban, Wood Street, London, W., and Ann Hawkins of Dunstable, co. Beds, S.

3 Richard Brandon of Dartford, Kent, B., and Ann Shott of the same, S.

3 James Wheeler of Hornsey, Middx., B., and Dorothy Shilton of the same, S.

4 James Moulton of S[t] Botolph, Aldgate, London, B., and Elizabeth Parr of S[t] Martin, Ludgate, London, S.

5 David Witchell, B., and Elizabeth Richards, S., both of this parish. Banns.

7 Richard Turner of Wandsworth, Surry, B., and Elizabeth Thorndell of Battersea, Surry, W.

7 William Hall of S[t] Paul, Shadwell, Middx., B., and Mary Cain of the same, S.

10 William Black of Disert, Fifeshire, W., and Isabella Smith of Vidressa in Nairnshire, North Britain, S.

11 Joseph Essex of Christchurch, Southwarke, W., and Mary Cary of S[t] Anne, Westminster, Middx., W.; by M[r] Swinfen.

13 Henry Leetham of S[t] Clement, East Cheap, London, W., and Deborah West of the same, W.

13 James Matthews of S[t] Peter, Cornhill, London, W., and Rebecca Bowden of S[t] Anne, Soho, Middx., S.

19 William Tanner of S[t] James, Westminster, Middx., B., and Mary Owen of S[t] George, Hanover Square, Middx., S.

22 Thomas Hewitt of S[t] George, Hanover Square, Middx., W., and Catherine Read of the same, W.

22 Peter Brookes of Newington Butts, Surry, B., and Jemima Parsons of the same, S.

24 John Stace of Epping, Essex, B., and Martha Craswell of S[t] Mary, White Chapel, Middx., S.; by M[r] Steward.

24 Samuel Buckland of Deptford in Kent, W., and Ann Lamborn of Lewisham, Kent, S.; by M[r] Steward.

26 William Haynes of S[t] Thomas, Southwarke, B., and Susanna Flemming of the same, W.

27 Peter Didier of S[t] Leonard, Shoreditch, Middx., W., and Jane Jeudine of Christchurch, Middx., S.

27 Alexander Mackay, Esq., of S[t] Margaret, Westminster, Middx., B., and Elizabeth Kipps of the same, W.

1745

June 27 William Tonge of S[t] Gregory's, London, W., and Sarah Farly of S[t] Andrew, Holborn, London, W.

28 William Dinton of the Hamlett of Bethnell Green, Stepney, Middx., B., and Penelope Lawson of the same, W.

July 1 William Mortimer of S[t] James, Westminster, Middx., B., and Mary Kane of the same, S.

2 John Barkley of S[t] James, Clerkenwell, Middx., B., and Elizabeth Mol or Maul [*sic*] of the same, W.; by M[r] Pemberton.

11 Joseph Westfield of Chipping Wycomb, co. Bucks, B., and Mary Peirson of the same, S.

13 Robert Rogers of S[t] Botolph, Aldgate, Middx., W., and Frances Brightlidge of the same, S.

13 Edward Acton of S[t] Clement Danes, Middx., B., and Ann Acton of the same, S.; by M[r] Pinckney.

14 John Fidler of Battersea, Surry, W., and Johannah Wyatt of S[t] Clement Danes, Middx., S.

18 John Maxfield of S[t] Catherine near the Tower of London, B., and Mary Dunkun of S[t] John, Wapping, Middx., W.

20 John Peel of Kensington, Middx., B., and Theodosia Milburn of the same, S.

21 Thomas Page of S[t] Margaret, Westminster, Middx., B., and Elizabeth Cock of the same, W.

22 James Jones of S[t] Martin in the Fields, Middx., B., and Susannah Hill of S[t] Mary, White Chappel, Middx., S.

23 John Conder of Hackney, Middx., gent., B., and Rebeckah Wightman, W.

23 Henry Russell of Tottenham, Middx., B., and Ann Howard of the same, S.

25 William Chesher of Waltham Abbey, Essex, W., and Edeth Bradshaw of the same, S.; by M[r] Pearce.

25 William Eastham of S[t] Martin in the Fields, Middx., W., and Mary Browne of S[t] George, Middx., W.

25 William Daniel of S[t] George in the East, Middx., W., and Mary Bevens of S[t] Paul, Shadwell, Middx., S.

25 Charles Blagrave of S[t] James, Clerkenwell, Middx., W., and Hannah Cornwell of the same, W.

27 Richard Biddell of S[t] George, Hanover Square, Middx., W., and Sarah Dryer of the same, W.

27 James Eagle of Walthamstow, Essex, B., and Mary Welby of the same, S.

Aug. 1 Robert Young of S[t] Dunstan, Stepney, Middx., B., and Elizabeth Jones of the same, S.

2 John Haycraft of S[t] Mary, Rotherhith, Surrey, B., and Mary Tomkis of the same, S.

3 Joshua Mollineaux of S[t] Luke, Middx., W., and Ann Deane of the same, W.

6 Thomas Squier of S[t] Ann, Blackfryars, London, B., and Jane Keele of the same, S.

8 Daniel Burford of Sheerness, Kent, B., and Sarah Day of the same, S.

8 Solomon Sammon of S[t] Clement Danes, Middx., B., and Anne Pembrooke of Christchurch, London, S.

14 Henry Loup of Rippon, co. York, [*blank*], and Elizabeth Calvert of S[t] Gabriel, Fenchurch Street, London, S.

15 Roger Bilby of S[t] Andrew, Holborn, B., and Sarah Nash of the same, S.; by M[r] Williams.

15 Richard Green of S[t] Andrew, Holbourn, Middx., B., and Ann Gallberth of Clapham, Surry, S.

1745
Aug. 15 Richard Slatter of St Saviour, Southwarke, B., and Ann Carter of St Mary, Newington, Surry, S.
15 James Dixon of Woolwich, Kent, B., and Mary Cottam of Chatham, Kent, S.
16 John Taylor of Walthamstow, Essex, B., and Ann Renshaw of St Botolph, Bishopsgate, London, S.
17 Edmund Jones of St Margaret, Lothbury, London, W., and Mary Quelch of St Magnus, London, W.
18 James Bennett of St Martin in the Fields, Middx., W., and Elizabeth Dodwell of St Ebb's in the City of Oxford; by Mr Steward.
18 John Unwin of St Mary Woolnoth, London, B., and Ann Collier of St Vedast alias Foster Lane, London, S.
18 William Costellow of Lambeth, Surry, W., and Mary Fletcher of the same, W.
22 William Masters of St Martin in the Fields, Middx., W., and Ann Legat of St Margaret, Westminster, Middx., S.; by Mr McGilchrist.
25 Mark Shergold of St George, Botolph Lane, London, W., and Ann Lawrence of the same, W.
25 Thomas Warfield of Wandsworth, Surrey, B., and Dennis Browne of the Town of Southampton, S.
26 Joseph Blackwell of St James, Clerkenwell, Middx., W., and Ann Paxton of St James, Westminster, Middx., S.
28 John Farrell of St James, Westminster, Middx., B., and Martha Gibson of St Martin in the Fields, Middx., S.
29 John Perham of St John, Wapping, Middx., B., and Rebecca Frith of St Dionis Backchurch, London, S.
29 William Symonds of St Peter in the city of Hereford, B., and Amor Bayes of St James in the city of Bath, S.
29 Benjamin Foulger of Fulham, Middx., W., and Sarah Debank of the same, S.
30 Norman Mills of Upminster in Essex, B., and Sarah Sewell of Raynham, Essex, S.
31 James Le Sueur of St Leonard, Shoreditch, Middx., B., and Susan Patenotre of the same, S.
Sept. 1 Thomas Griffith of St Giles in the Fields, Middx., W., and Frances Wilson of St Martin in the Fields, Middx., S.
1 John Kirke of All Hallows, Lombard Street, London, W., and Mary Bowley of St Sepulchre's, London, S.
2 James Black of Christ church, Middx., B., and Abigail Langley of St Giles in the Fields, Middx., W.
3 William Overitt of Epping, Essex, B., and Elizabeth Nunn of the same, S.; by Mr McGilchrist.
7 Thomas Sherwin of St Martin in the Fields, Middx., B., and Catherine Hanscombe of Shillington, co. Bedford, S.
7 Benjamin Jones of St George, Bloomsbury, Middx., B., and Susanna Stevenson of the same, S.
7 Thomas Calvert of St Botolph, Billingsgate, London, B., and Alice Parker of the same, S.; by Mr Williams.
8 Thomas Granger of St Martin in the Fields, Middx., B., and Hannah Johnson of St Bride's, London, S.; by the same.
10 James Valentine of Christ church, London, B., and Elizabeth Wilson of the same, W.; by Mr McGilchrist.
13 Thomas Milburne of St Mary, White Chapel, Middx., W., and Elizabeth Lodge of the same, W.; by Mr Pinckney.
15 John Johns of Camberwell, Surrey, B., and Sarah Chapman of the same, S.; by Mr Williams.
15 Samuel Brookland of St Martin in the Fields, Middx., B., and Anne Leeson of the same, S.; by Mr McGilchrist.

1745

Sept. 17 Richard Hansard Barry of St Bride's, London, W., and Leonora Hansard of St Martin in the Fields, Middx., S.; by the same.

19 Richard Colley of St James, Westminster, Middx., B., and Ann Smelt of St Clement Danes, Middx., S.

22 Enos Dexter of St Margaret, Westminster, Middx., B., and Frances Jackson of the same, W.

24 Thomas Baker of St Mary Magdalen, Bermondsey, Surrey, B., and Anne Chargeley of the same, S.; by Mr Worlich.

24 William Hart of St George, Middx., B., and Penelope Yeates of St Martin in the Fields, Middx., S.; by the same.

24 William Weaver of St Giles, Cripplegate, London, B., and Barbara Baughan of the same, W.; by the same.

24 George Jackson of All Hallows Barking, London, B., and Mary Ward of St Dunstan in the West, London, S.; by the same.

26 Maurice Hiller of Great St Hellen's, London, W., and Ann Kelk of Wallbrook, London, W.; by Mr Wilmot.

29 Jonas Pearson of St Saviour, Southwarke, W., and Elizabeth Harris of the same, S.

29 Richard Burrows of St Peter, Cornhill, London, B., and Rachael Geldert of the same, S.

Oct. 3 William Massam of Lambeth, Surrey, B., and Hannah Sutton of the same, W.

4 John Budder of Camberwell, Surrey, B., and Mary Budder of the same, S.

9 William Bull of St Martin in the Fields, Middx., B., and Elizabeth Woodhouse of the same, S.; by Mr Pinckney.

10 Peter Van Bleeck of St Paul, Covent Garden, Middx., B., and Alice Cony of St George the Martyr, Queen Square, Middx., S.

11 John Harrison of St Giles in the Fields, Middx., W., and Martha Webb of the same, W.

11 James Pampelloune of Chelsea, Middx., W., and Mary Boiton of the same, S.

11 William Pettifer of St Peter, Cornhill, London, W., and Anne Phipps of the same, S.

13 Edward Robinson of St George, Hanover Square, Middx., B., and Anne Huxley of St James, Westminster, Middx., S.

14 John Beal of Gosport, Hants, B., and Elizabeth Wake of St John, Wapping, Middx., S.

16 Edward Okey of St George, Hanover Square, Middx., W., and Hannah Robinson of the same, S.

17 William Shearer of St John, Wapping, Middx., B., and Sally Freeman of the same, S.

17 Edward Scovell of Christ church, Surrey, W., and Frances Steen of St Mary Magdalen, Bermondsey, Surrey, W.

19 Samuel Clarke of Northaw, co. Herts, B., and Mary Matthews of the same, S.

21 Richard Reed of St Mary Magdalen, Old Fish Street, London, B., and Ann Reed of the same parish, S.

25 John Marshall of St Leonard, Shoreditch, Middx., B., and Deborah Catherine Mackdonell of the same, S.

25 John Dilley of St Stephen Coleman, London, W., and Mary Darling of St Giles, Cripplegate, London, W.

26 Christopher Buckle of Chelsea, Middx., B., and Anne Bird of the same, S.

26 James Vallett of Plymouth, Devon, B., and Mary Whitebread of St George, Bloomsbury, Middx., S.

27 Randle Norris of Greenwich, Kent, B., and Sarah Whiteid of St Dunstan in the West, London, S.

1745

Oct. 29 John Swan of S[t] Saviour's, Southwarke, W., and Mary Allom of the same, W.

29 William Orpin of Wateringbury, Kent, B., and Jane Tomlin of Eltham, Kent, S.

31 Jabez Tuckey of S[t] John the Evangelist, Westminster, Middx., B., and Amy Toll of the same, W.

Nov. 1 Daniel Rock of S[t] Margaret, Westminster, Middx., W., and Sarah Lamb of S[t] Clement Danes, Middx., S.

3 Richard Keene of S[t] Botolph, Bishopsgate, London, B., and Mary Payne of the same, S.

10 Isaac Beal of S[t] Andrew Hubbard, London, B., and Eleanor Baxter of the same, S.

11 Henry Chaloner of S[t] Giles, Cripplegate, London, W., and Sarah Scarborough of S[t] Sepulchre's, London, W.

12 Edward Taillsfor of the Town of S[t] Hilary in Jersey Island, B., and Perine Grillier of Christ church, Middx., S.

14 Thomas Mortimer of S[t] George, Bloomsbury, Middx., B., and Jane Knell of S[t] Pancras, Middx., W.

14 William Martin of Thirsk in the North Riding of York, Esq., B., and Catherine Elizabeth Lewis of Windsor, co. Berks, S.

16 John Lambert of S[t] Dunstan in the West, London, B., and Sarah Capon of Shoreham, Kent, S.

18 John Jenkins of S[t] Andrew, Holborn, London, B., and Margaret Norman of the same, S.

22 Hugh Hodgson of S[t] James, Westminster, Middx., B., and Mary Baldwin of the same, S.

23 John Windell of S[t] Olave, Southwarke, W., and Susannah Coleman of the same, W.

23 Isaac Palmer of S[t] Mary Magdalen, Bermondsey in Southwarke, B., and Elizabeth Lissney of the same, W.

24 James Reneuf of S[t] George, Middx., B., and Christian Thomas of the same, S.

26 Edward Murdock of Chertsey, Surry, W., and Catherine Soane of the same, W.; by M[r] Oakeley, Vicar of Chertsey.

30 John Sibthorpe of S[t] George, Bloomsbury, Middx., W., and Elizabeth Westerman of the same, W.; by M[r] LLoyd.

Dec. 1 Caleb Paris, [*blank*], and Ann Undrey, [*blank*], both of S[t] Peter, Paul's Wharfe. Banns. By D[r] Thomas.

2 Samuel Biss of Kensington, Middx., B., and Mary Fry of the same, W.; by M[r] LLoyd.

8 Richard Rugg of S[t] Gregory, London, B., and Mary Brockel of S[t] Martin le Grand, London, W.

10 John Grolmen of S[t] Paul, Covent Garden, Middx., B., and Elizabeth Haynes of the same, S.

12 Joseph Fisher of S[t] Antholine, London, B., and Mary Magdalen Parades of S[t] Andrew, Holborn, London, S.

12 John Forth of East Greenwich, Kent, B., and Martha Jobson of S[t] Margaret Patten, London, S.

14 James Ventris of S[t] Luke, Middx., B., and Elisha [*sic*] Hussey of S[t] Andrew Wardrobe, London, S.

17 George West of S[t] Mary le Bow, London, W., and Hannah Rugeley of S[t] Luke, Middx., W.; by Rev. M[r] Sawrey.

24 John Stordy of S[t] Dunstan in the East, London, B., and Jane Baker of the same, S.

24 John Reynolds of Chelmsford, Essex, B., and Mary Wright of Stoke in Essex, W.

25 Vere Warner of S[t] Michael, Cornhill, London, B., and Mary Hutchins of Chelsea, Middx., W.

1745

Dec. 26 John Taylor of Chislehurst, Kent, B., and Mary Willcox of St Mary le Strand, Middx., S.

27 William Pittkin of Finchley, Middx., B., and Mary Nettleship of the same, S.; by Dr Thomas.

28 Thomas Wingrove of Harefield, Middx., B., and Hannah Goodchild of the same, S.

Jan. 1 John Knight of St George, Hanover Square, Middx., B., and Elizabeth Furburrow of the same, S.

2 Francis Stevens of St James, Westminster, Middx., W., and Elizabeth Adcock of St Ann, Westminster, Middx., S.

5 Joseph Starkey of St Vedast alias Foster lane, London, B., and Jane Howell of the same, S.

5 William Gouldhawk of Martin, Surry, B., and Priscilla Pockinhorn of St Georges, Southwarke, S.

7 Charles Colman of St George the Martyr, Middx., W., and Sarah Landrey of St Clement Danes, Middx., W.

9 George Wright of St George, Hanover Square, Middx., B., and Elizabeth Johnston of Clapham, Surrey, W.

10 Alexander Henderson of St Mary Magdalen, Bermondsey, Surry, B., and Mary Brett of the same, W.

11 Thomas Roch of Islington, Middx., B., and Eleanor Strode of the same, W.

11 Henry Carter of West Ham, Essex, B., and Sarah Whitfield of St John, Clerkenwell, Middx., S.

16 Edward Sumner of St John, Southwarke, B., and Hannah Stow of the same, S.

23 Edward Holding of Great St Hellen's, London, B., and Jane Carr of St Giles, Cripplegate, London, W.

24 William Bland of St Andrew, Holborn, Middx., B., and Elizabeth Chandler of the same, S.

24 Henry Smith of Wingfield, co. Berks, B., and Priscilla Gayson of Kensington, Middx., W.

24 Augustin Carloss of St Mary, White Chapel, Middx., W., and Elizabeth Wallis of the same, W.

26 John Cook of St Botolph without Bishopsgate, London, B., and Elizabeth Cox of the same, S.

Feb. 2 Silvester Oliver of St Neots, co. Huntingdon, B., and Mary Lansdell of St Ann, Westminster, Middx., S.

5 Francis Dawes of St Magnus the Martyr, London, B., and Judith Hall of Trinity parish, co. Cambridge, S.

6 Thomas Edwards of East Greenwich, Kent, B., and Margaret Roby of Richmond, Surrey, S.

8 John Harbert of Low Layton, Essex, B., and Ann Mason of Chigwell, Essex, S.

8 William Adnett of Ealing, Middx., B., and Ann Stane of the same, S.

9 George Friswell of St Margaret, Westminster, Middx., B., and Elizabeth Dudman of St John the Evangelist, Westminster, Middx., S.

10 Thomas Plester of Mile End in St Dunstan, Stepney, Middx., W., and Jane Herring of the same, W.

10 William Edwards of Chelsea, Middx., B., and Mary Lacy of the same, S.

11 John Fustnidge, [*blank*], and Ann Bond, [*blank*], both of this parish. Banns.

13 John Hopwood of Bromley near Bow, Middx., B., and Sarah Rementon of the same, S.

Mar. 1 John Vanneil of St Martin in the Fields, Middx., B., and Fanny Nice of the same, S.

1745-6

Mar. 6 Thomas Bolney of Tilbury Fort, Essex, W., and Mary Blamyre of S[t] Dunstan, Stepney, Middx., S.

6 Wallwyn Shepheard of Donnington, co. Hereford, Esq., B., and Mary Collins of Richmond, Surrey, S.

11 John Crookshanks of All Hallows Barking, London, B., and Jane Seldon of the same, S.

11 John Brine of S[t] Luke, Middx., W., and Mary Parker of S[t] Andrew Undershaft, London, W.

20 Robert Smith of Greenwich, Kent, B., and Martha Andrews of the same, S.; by M[r] Hunt.

1746.

Mar. 25 Martin Pemell of Deptford, Kent, B., and Elizabeth Kirton of same, S.; by M[r] Pearce.

30 Thomas Price of S[t] Pancras, Soper lane, London, B., and Anne Falconer of the same, S.

31 Bartholomew Shercliff of S[t] Giles in the Fields, Middx., B., and Hannah Jones of the same, S.

April 1 James Edwards of S[t] John, Westminster, Middx., B., and Sarah Walker of the same, S.

3 Isaac Garratt of S[t] John, Hackney, Middx., B., and Mary Field of the same, S.

3 John Kent of S[t] Mary, Stratford, Bow, Middx., B., and Martha Webb of the same, S.

3 David Duncombe of S[t] Botolph, Aldgate, Middx., B., and Elizabeth Hutchinson of the same, S.

5 Robert Bevis of S[t] Giles, Cripplegate, London, B., and Hannah Ashton of the same, S.

5 Samuel Parry of S[t] Peter, Cornhill, London, B., and Nanny Freeman of S[t] Mary Staining, London, S.

5 Robert Baylis of Tewkesbury, co. Gloucester, W., and Elianor Knox of Putney, Surry, W.

6 Robert Townley of Tunbridge, Kent, B., and Ann Coleman of S[t] George, Hanover Square, Middx., S.

7 Edward Penner of Kingston upon Thames, Surry, B., and Elizabeth Vincin of the same, S.

8 James Webb of S[t] Dunstan in the West, London, B., and Sarah Blair of S[t] Martin Orgars, London, W.

8 John Harding of S[t] Austin, London, W., and Sarah Smith of Camberwell, Surrey, W.

8 Edward Elliot of S[t] Sepulchre's, London, W., and Ann Groom of the same, S.

9 John Halfhide of S[t] Olave, Southwarke, W., and Susannah Lee of S[t] George, Southwarke, W.

9 Paul Turquand of S[t] Mary, White Chapel, Middx., W., and Ann Blondell of the same, S.

9 Joseph Fuller of S[t] Luke's, Middx., B., and Elizabeth Ruslen of the same, S.

9 Xstopher Hawkins of S[t] Mary, Rotherhith, Surry, W., and Harryard Oglethorpe of the same, S.

10 Jacob Phillips of Rotherhith, Surrey, B., and Sophia Norris of the same, S.

10 Richard Lawman of Bexley, Kent, B., and Mary Smith of Mottingham, Kent, S.

13 Philip Petrie of Woolwich, Kent, B., and Elizabeth Prichard of the same, S.

1746

April 14 William Pitt of Harvely in Essex, B., and Sarah Collins of the same, S.

14 John Wood of Woolwich, Kent, B., and Elizabeth White of the same, W.

14 George Hudson of St Bartholomew the Less, London, B., and Mary Holmes of St Bartholomew the Great, London, S.

17 John Salthouse of Battersea, Surry, B., and Sarah Hargrave of the same, S.

19 Harris Sharp of St Michael, Queenhithe, London, B., and Sarah Tichbourn of St John, Southwarke, S.

21 Hector Heathe of St Anne, Westminster, Middx., W., and Elizabeth Franklin of the same, S.

22 George Pratt of St Martin in the Fields, Middx., B., and Mary Howard of St Andrew, Holborn, Middx., S.

24 Edward Callis of St Bride's, London, B., and Margaret Ratcliffe of St Andrew, Holborn, London, W.

27 Robert Abbiss of Deptford, Kent, B., and Sarah Street of the same, S.

29 Robert Adams of St John, Southwarke, W., and Mary Hull of St Katherine near the Tower of London, S.

May 1 George Wells of Stratham, Surry, W., and Elizabeth Jackson of Addington, Surry, W.

3 John Sydebothom of St Edmund the King, London, B., and Mary Hall of St Bride's, London, S.

5 John Wyle of Tycehurst, Sussex, B., and Elizabeth Winch of the same, S.

9 Joel Peircy of Croydon, Surry, B., and Mary Pamphylion of the same, W.

10 Robert Hinton of St James, Westminster, Middx., B., and Anne Collett of the same, S.

12 Anthony Langley of Kingston upon Thames, Surry, W., and Sarah Reeves of the same, S.

14 Philip Sherer of St Sepulchre's, Middx., W., and Mary Farnell of St Brides, London, W.

14 Michael Page of Chatham, Kent, W., and Mary Smith of the same, W.

15 William Hill of St Andrew, Holborn, Middx., B., and Elizabeth Pearce of the same, S.; by M^r McGilchrist.

15 John Quested of St Catherine Coleman, London, B., and Ann Cope of St Giles in the Fields, Middx., S.; by M^r McGilchrist.

16 David Jones of St Helen, London, B., and Elizabeth Hansher of St Peter-le-Poor, London, W.; by the same.

17 John Preswick of St George, Middx., B., and Sarah Bennet of St John, Wapping, Middx., S.; by the same.

17 Joseph Dewbery of St Paul, Covent Garden, Middx., B., and Mary Baldwin of the same, W.; by the same.

19 James Bull of Christ church, Surry, B., and Mary Still of the same, S.; by Mr Berrow.

19 John Hargrave of St James, Westminster, Middx., W., and Elizabeth Chandler of Lambeth, Surry, W.; by M^r McGilchrist.

20 Richard Jones of St George the Martyr, Southwarke, W., and Abia Thomas of Camberwell, Surry, W.; by the same.

20 Edward Hales of St Peter, Cornhill, London, W., and Mary Deniord of St Dunstan, Stepney, Middx., S.; by the same.

20 Richard Jackson of St Martin in the Fields, Middx., B., and Elinor Hadwin of St Clement Danes, Middx., S.; by Mr Berrow.

20 Samuel Hopperton of Fulham, Middx., B., and Elizabeth Scott of the same, S.; by the same.

22 James Crook of St Faith's, London, B., and Mary Vincent of the same, S.; by M^r McGilchrist.

1746

May 24 Haddon Hopkins of S[t] Mary Magdalen, Bermondsey, Surry, B., and Ann Arnold of S[t] Saviour, Southwarke, Surry, S.; by the same.

25 Frederick Finck, B., and Jane Bentley, S., both of this parish. Banns. By the same.

27 William Edsell of Chiswick, Middx., W., and Elizabeth Winter of S[t] Olave, Silver Street, London, W.

27 Benjamin Tolley of S[t] Martin in the Fields, Middx., B., and Hannah Everingham of the same, S.

29 Body Spearman of S[t] Mary Magdalen, Bermondsey, Surry, B., and Ann Browne of Tottenham, Middx., S.; by M[r] Audley.

29 George Elkins of S[t] Margaret, Westminster, Middx., W., and Jane Stubbs of S[t] George, Hanover Square, Middx., W.; by M[r] Williams.

29 John Dawkes of S[t] James, Clerkenwell, Middx., B., and Hannah Richardson of the same, S.

29 Alexander Glasse of S[t] Dunstan in the West, London, B., and Frances Jernegan of S[t] Paul, Covent Garden, Middx., W.

June 1 John Shower of S[t] Paul, Covent Garden, Middx., W., and Frances Fancourt of the same, S.

4 Roger Hines of Harwich, Essex, B., and Elizabeth Whiting of S[t] Dionis Backchurch, London, W.

4 John Craven of S[t] George, Southwarke, B., and Mary Hooker of the same, S.

10 Anthony Vere of S[t] George, Bloomsbury, Middx., B., and Elizabeth Williams of the same, S.

11 Joseph Stockdill of Finchley, Middx., B., and Elizabeth Howland of S[t] Faith's, London, S.

12 John Chivers of S[t] Lawrence, Jewry, London, B., and Hannah Turner of the same, S.

13 John Hobson of S[t] Clement Danes, Middx., B., and Mary Stevens of Hitchin, co. Herts, S.

15 Thomas Russell, B., and Martha Crabb, S., both of S[t] Peters, Paul's Wharfe. Banns.

16 George Osborne of Richmond, Surry, B., and Penelope Mann of S[t] George the Martyr, Middx., S.

19 Edward Bailey of Stock in Essex, B., and Edith Hare of the same, W.

22 William Shemelt of All Hallows the Less, London, W., and Martha Ditchfield of S[t] George the Martyr, Surrey, S.

23 Walter Copestake of S[t] Mary le Strand, Middx., B., and Mary Gordon of S[t] Luke's, Middx., W.

24 Thomas Johnson of Rochester, Kent, B., and Mary Curtis of the same, S.

28 Blaise Willioc of S[t] Ann, Westminster, Middx., B., and Mary Durand of the same, W.

July 7 Jeffery Findall of Deptford, Kent, W., and Amelia Ariskin of the same, W.

8 James Chatine de Roche of S[t] Martin in the Fields, Middx., W., and Susannah Bosquam of the same, S.; by M[r] M[c]Gilchrist.

8 Edward Bromley of S[t] Thomas, London, W., and Ann Moore of S[t] Sepulchre, London, W.; by the same.

8 John Chamberlain, Esq., of Sheffield, co. York, B., and Mary Methwold of S[t] Andrews, Holborn, Middx., S.; by M[r] LLoyd.

10 Christopher Gray of Fulham, Middx., B., and Ann Loader of Chelsea, Middx., S.

10 Cæsar Saunders of Hertford, co. Herts, W., and Mary Nash of the same, S.; by Mr Williamson.

1746

July 15 John Cowgill, B., and Eleanor Dickers, S., both of this parish. Banns. By Mr McGilchrist.

17 Humphrey Henchman, clerk, Rector of Littleton, Midx., B., and Ann Keywood of Woodstock, co. Oxford, S.; by Mr Harris.

19 Peter Heron of St Martin in the Fields, Middx., B., and Elizabeth Harding of White Hall in the same parish, S.; by Mr McGilchrist.

21 Thomas Lisle of Bradford, Surrey, B., and Ann Phelps of West Chester, W.; by the same.

22 Thomas Green of Chiswick, Middx., W., and Mary Neale of the same, W.; by the same.

26 Edmund Ferrers of the Middle Temple, London, B., and Hannah Broomfield of St George the Martyr, Middx., S.; by the same.

27 Thomas Stoble of Harding, co. Oxford, B., and Ann Brown of St Stephen, Coleman Street, London, S.; by the same.

28 Matthew Jones of St Giles in the Fields, Middx., W., and Susannah Manton of St Andrew, Holborn, Middx., W.; by the same.

Aug. 2 Edward Robinson of St Dionis Backchurch, London, B., and Sarah Bryne of the same, S.

8 John Thatcher of St Olave, Southwarke, W., and Mary Waters of the same, W.

10 John Wicks of this parish, B., and Elizabeth Bolton of St Peter's, Paul's Wharfe, S. Banns.

13 William Ashton of St George, Hanover Square, Middx., W., and Sarah Smith of the same, W.; by Mr McGilchrist.

14 Gabriel Hurry of Great Yarmouth, Norfolk, B., and Ann Scoffin of the same, S.; by the same.

19 Samuel Smart of St Luke, Middx., B., and Elizabeth Grove of the same, W.; by the same.

19 Titus Nevill of Twickenham, Middx., B., and Jane Cook of the same, S.; by the same.

24 Joseph Cox of Edmonton, Middx., W., and Elizabeth Godfrey of the same, S.; by the same.

26 William Hudson, W., and Elizabeth Curtis, W., both of this parish. Banns. By the same.

Sept. 4 John Roberts of St Andrew, Holborn, Middx., B., and Mary Parran of the same, S.; by the same.

4 William Wisdom of Streatham, Surry, B., and Mary Cole of the same, S.; by the same.

4 Anthony Cook of Deptford, Kent, W., and Elizabeth Berry of Christ church, Surry, W.; by the same.

7 William Rushton of St Saviour, Southwarke, B., and Elizabeth Rawlings of Dartford, Kent, S.; by the same.

9 Joseph West of Edmonton, Middx., B., and Elizabeth Peters of the same, S.; by the same.

11 Gabriel Leeky [? Lecky] of St Dunstan, Stepney, Middx., B., and Ann Blamyre of the same, S.; by the same.

13 William Richards of St James, Clerkenwell, Middx., W., and Jane Walker of the same, S.; by the same.

14 John Richardson of the Precinct of Norton Falgate, Middx., B., and Elizabeth Bampton of the same, S.; by Mr McGilchrist.

18 Giles Powell of St George, Hanover Square, Middx., B., and Anne Keynton of Chelsea, Middx., S.; by the same.

21 John Long of St Bride's, London, B., and Mary Johnson of the same, S.

21 Abraham Rasor of St James, Westminster, Middx., B., and Jane Bankworth of the same, S.

22 William Cumlyn of Wandsworth, Surrey, B., and Mary Parker of the same, S.

1746

Sept. 25 William Vigers of S[t] George the Martyr, Middx., B., and Margaret Williams of S[t] Giles, Cripplegate, London, S.

25 Willoughby Stevens of Multon, Surry, B., and Margaret Cockin of the same, S.

25 William Dean of S[t] George, Hanover Square, Middx., W., and Mary Moor of the same, S.

26 William Lea of S[t] George the Martyr, Hanover Square, Middx., B., and Rebecca Bengerfield of S[t] Paul, Shadwell, Middx., S.

27 Richard Hoare of S[t] Andrew, Holborn, London, B., and Eleanor Wacket of the same, S.

29 John Grub of Tottenham High Cross, Middx., B., and Mary Hart of Hornsey, Middx., S.

29 John Perry of Cambridge, B., and Anne Claus of S[t] Paul, Covent Garden, Middx., W.

Oct. 1 John Woraker of Chelsea, Middx., B., and Elizabeth Slaughter of the same, S.

5 James Clapham of Streatham, Surry, B., and Sarah Herbert of Tooting, Surrey, S.

6 William Bartee of S[t] George, Hanover Square, Middx., B., and Elizabeth Sayer of S[t] Andrew, Holborn, London, S.

7 Richard Stewart of S[t] Gyles in the Fields, Middx., B., and Mary Lea of the same, S.; by M[r] Lally.

8 Henry Watts of New Windsor, co. Berks, B., and Barbara Hilbert of the same, S.; by M[r] Lally.

10 Waters Rolfe of North Pickenham in Norfolk, clerk, W., and Phœbe Bowman of the same, S.

13 William Porter of S[t] Botolph, Aldgate, London, B., and Mary Sellers of S[t] Gyles, Cripplegate, London, W.

15 John Beech of S[t] Ann's, Middx., B., and Mary Stagg of S[t] Pancras, Middx., S.

18 Stephen Smith of Shoreham, Kent, W., and Elizabeth Walker of the same, S.

19 Bartholomew Bigg of S[t] Saviour, Southwarke, Surry, B., and Elizabeth Vass of the same, S.

22 Squire Porter of S[t] George, Hanover Square, Middx., B., and Elizabeth Peirson of the same, S.

23 William Clunn of S[t] George, Southwarke, W., and Elizabeth Meller of the same, W.; by M[r] M[c]Gilchrist.

24 Samuel Stokes of Fulham, Middx., B., and Mary Tiller of the same, S.; by the same.

27 Peter Johnson Bomhoff of S[t] John, Wapping, Middx., B., and Catherine Williamson of the same, W.

30 Dymock Morris of Deptford, Kent, B., and Ann Briggs of S[t] James, Westminster, Middx., S.

31 John Weeden of Harrow on the Hill, Middx., B., and Rebecca Beek of the same, S.

Nov. 6 Richard Moore of S[t] James, Westminster, Middx., B., and Ann Raworth of the same, S.

6 John Todd of Frant alias Fant, Sussex, W., and Anne Powell of S[t] Margaret, Westminster, Middx., S.; by M[r] M[c]Gilchrist.

7 Samuel Smith of S[t] Saviour, Southwarke, W., and Hannah Farrall of S[t] Paul, Covent Garden, Middx., W.; by the same.

8 James Haythorn of Lambeth, Surry, B., and Elizabeth Harley of the same, W.

8 Robert Craig of S[t] Clement Danes, Middx., B., and Mary Anthony of Greenwich, Kent, S.

10 William Ashmore of S[t] George, Southwarke, W., and Elizabeth Smith of S[t] John, Southwarke, W.

1746

Nov. 12 Vertue Hughes of St Matthew, Bethnell Green, Middx., B., and Ann Harmon of Christ church, Middx., W.

14 Joseph Howlett of St Peter, Cornhill, London, B., and Mary Fenner of St Benet, Grace Church, London, S.

14 George Duncan of St Martin in the Fields, Middx., B., and Catherine Thorn of the same, W.

16 Robert Penn of St James, Garlickhith, London, W., and Jane Wilson of St Mary Somerset, London, W.

18 George Williams of Woolwich, Kent, B., and Mary Chalende of the same, S.

18 Richard Woolley of St Giles in the Fields, Middx., B., and Catherine Lawley of the same, S.

19 Henry Bowman of St George, Middx., B., and Elizabeth Dunn of the same, S.

19 Samuel Cope of St Martin Vintry, London, W., and Mary Carter of St Luke's, Middx., S.

19 John Tyther of St Stephen, Coleman Street, London, B., and Elizabeth Carter of St Luke's, Middx., S.

21 John Darton of Christ Church, London, B., and Sarah Hooker of Tottenham, Middx., W.

24 James Warren of the City of Chester, W., and Mary Johnson of St James, Westminster, Middx., S.

27 John West of St Paul's, Covent Garden, Middx., W., and Mary Harris of St Martin in the Fields, Middx., S.

*27 John Knight of Deptford, Kent, W., and Henrietta Maria Hume of the same, S.; by Mr Hinton.

29 Rene Grilliet of St Martin in the Fields, Middx., W., and Susannah Allington of Christ church, Middx., W.

Dec. 1 Baston Sorletta of St Mary, Rotherhith, Surrey, W., and Mary Randall of the same, S.

9 William Kent of St Luke's, Middx., W., and Mary Witton of St Andrew, Holborn, Middx., S.

9 John Richards of Christ church, Surry, W., and Ann Ayrton of St Dunstan in the West, London, S.

9 Redwood Bull of St Saviour, Southwarke, Surry, B., and Mary Woolford of the same, S.

11 Philip Jones of St Clement Danes, Middx., B., and Elizabeth Pedley of Endfield, Middx., W.

15 William Clapham of Rumford, Essex, B., and Jane Heron of the same, S.

15 Thomas Bruce of St Saviour, Southwarke, Surry, B., and Catherine Southerland of St James, Westminster, Middx., S.

16 Richard Burton of Wakefield, co. York, B., and Frances Ward of the City of Stockholm in Sweden, S.

17 Nicholas Dark of Woolwich, Kent, B., and Sarah Ashworth of St Catherine Creed church, London, S.

20 John Pippin of St Leonard, Shoreditch, Middx., B., and Jenny Jenks of St John, Hackney, Middx., S.

22 William Dawson of St Peter's, Wood Street, London, W., and Hannah Weston of St Faith's, London, W.

24 William Worthington of the Liberty of the Tower of London, B., and Sarah Whitworth of St George, Southwarke, S.; by Mr Williams.

27 John Latimer and Ann Whitfield, both of this parish. Banns.

31 Richard Short of St Clement Danes, Middx., B., and Hannah Tickner of St Gyles in the Fields, Middx., S.

Jan. 3 George Baker of St Lukes, Middx., B., and Mary Harrison of St Mary Magdalen, Old Fish Street, London, S.

* Entry misplaced in Register.—Ed.

1746-7
Jan. 3 John Pratt of Farningham in Kent, B., and Mary Sandwell of the same, W.
5 Bartholomew Haws of Lambeth, Surry, B., and Elizabeth Martin of the same, S.
6 Obadiah Chadd of East Greenwich, Kent, W., and Hannah Davies of the same, S.
10 James Goodchild of St Clement Danes, Middx., B., and Susanna Winn of the same, W.; by Mr Fearon.
12 Thomas Fowler of St Mary Magdalen, Bermondsey, Surrey, B., and Eleanor Parker of the same, S.
12 Joseph Lawrence of St Saviour, Southwarke, B., and Letitia Baker of the same, S.
13 James Gordon of St Paul, Covent Garden, Middx., W., and Mary Hitchcock of the same, W.
13 Joseph Farmer of Wansted, Essex, B., and Martha Stedman of the same, S.
17 George Wybourn of St Mary, Islington, Middx., W., and Mary Weston of the same, S.
18 Francis, Lord Olephant, of St Paul, Covent Garden, Middx., W., and Mary Linley of St Martin, Ludgate, London, S.
21 John Whiteaves of St Margaret, Westminster, Middx., B., and Mary Manly of the same, S.
22 William Bendall of St Mary Magdalen, Bermondsey, Surry, W., and Elizabeth Lock of the same, W.
22 William Mynton of St George, Bloomsbury, Middx., B., and Ann Parry of the same, S.
22 Miles Fox of St Andrew, Holborn, Middx., B., and Lydia Landry of St George the Martyr, Middx., S.
25 Joseph Host of St George the Martyr, Middx., W., and Elizabeth Traugh of the same, S.
Feb. 1 George Lawrence of St Mary le Strand, Middx., B., and Dorothy Griffith of St James, Westminster, Middx., W.
7 William Whittle of Lambeth, Surry, B., and Ann Buscarlett of the same, S.; by Mr Pemberton.
8 James Flather of St Olave, Southwarke, Surry, B., and Elizabeth Kember of St Thomas, Southwarke, S.
8 Thomas Chapman of St Ann, Limehouse, Middx., B., and Elizabeth Clements of St Mary at Hill, London, W.
9 John Wood of Nutfield,* Surry, B., and Sarah Hayward of Wallinghame, Surrey, S.
12 Michael Shewell of Christ church, Surry, B., and Mary Low of the same, S.
15 John Willoughby of St Mary Somerset, London, B., and Mary Hayes of the same, S.
17 Robert Swain of St James, Westminster, Middx., W., and Bridget Hadley of St George, Hanover Square, Middx., S.
19 John Franks of St John, Southwarke, W., and Mary Fish of St Catherine near the Tower of London, W.
19 James Middlehurst of Warrington, Lancashire, B., and Mary Cooper of St Mary Magdalen, Bermondsey, Surrey, S.
19 John Prosser of St Andrew, Holborn, Middx., B., and Martha Lawson of the same, S.
20 Cheesman Peircy of St John, Southwarke, B., and Sarah Fullicks of the same, S.
20 Alexander Smith of Orpinton, Kent, B., and Ann Dennis of the same, S.
22 George Needham of St Bride's, London, W., and Ann Lacey of St Ann, Westminster, Middx., S.; by Mr Pemberton.

* Blotted in Register.—Ed.

1746-7

Feb. 23 John Wood of St Ann, Blackfryars, London, B., and Ann Steed of St Magnus the Martyr, London, S.; by the same.

23 Benjamin Dossett of St Ann, Westminster, Middx., W., and Elizabeth Lowen of the same, S.; by Mr Williams.

24 James Cotsford of St Alban, Wood Street, London, B., and Hannah Jones of this parish, S.; by Mr Berrow.

26 Thomas Churchill of St James, Clerkenwell, Middx., B., and Eleanor Hunt of the same, S.; by Mr Pinckney.

28 Thomas Cobham of St Olave, Hart Street, London, B., and Jane Gurney of St Peter le Poor, London, S.

28 William Pyke of St Leonard, Shoreditch, Middx., B., and Sarah Day of the same, W.

28 William Booth of St John, Westminster, Middx., B., and Ann Page of Heston, Middx., S.

Mar. 1 Richard Fulbrook of St Sepulchre, London, B., and Sarah Wilder of the same, S.

1 William Barnard of St Ann, Soho, Middx., B., and Joan Tripp of the same, S.

2 Edward Hieatt of St Margaret, Westminster, Middx., B., and Frances Button of the same, S.

2 Charles Eyre of Ewelm, co. Oxford, B., and Ann Perks of Stockton, Salop, S.

3 Edward Bridges, Esq., of Wotton, Kent, B., and Jemima Egerton of Lullingstone, Kent, S.

3 Neal Maxwell of St Paul, Shadwell, Middx., B., and Ellis Innes of the same, S.

3 Arthur Stanley of St Botolph, Aldgate, London, B., and Elizabeth Barber of the same, S.

3 Henry Hunt of Bracested, Kent, B., and Ann Hooker of Cudham, Kent, S.

4 James Bunn of Lincoln's Inn, Middx., W., and Hannah Tomlyns of St Mary Calenders in the city of Winchester, S.

12 Gwin LLoyd, Esq., of St James, Westminster, Middx., B., and Sarah Hill of the same, S.

14 Henry Hawes of Leighton, co. Bedford, B., and Frances Emes of the same, S.

23 Mordecai Andrews of the Precinct of Old Artillery lane, near Spittlefields, Middx., Clerk, W., and Sarah Fann of St Stephen, Coleman Street, London, S.

24 John Townsend of St James, Westminster, Middx., W., and Elizabeth Beaver of the same, S.

1747.

April 1 Stephen Powell of St John in Devizes, Wilts, B., and Sarah Adlam of the same, S.; by Mr Hunt.

17 John Wood of Hillingdon, Middx., B., and Elizabeth Phillips of the same, S.

18 Litchfield Howes of St Botolph, Aldersgate, London, W., and Penelope Stirzacker of St Margaret, Westminster, Middx., W.

18 William Frimble of St Ann, Westminster, Middx., B., and Susannah Sutton of St Paul, Covent Garden, Middx., S.

19 John Lee of St Gyles in the Fields, Middx., B., and Elizabeth Lee of St Bartholomew the Great, London, S.

19 George Street of St Mildred, Poultry, London, B., and Sarah Bullin of St Mary Magdalen, Old Fish Street, London, S.

19 William Sleter, B., and Margaret Collins, S., both of this parish. Banns.

1747

April 20 William Bushnell of Ealing, Middx., W., and Elizabeth Holloway of the same, S.; by Mr Vaughan.

20 Littleton Hill of St Paul, Covent Garden, Middx., B., and Margaret Lilly of St James, Westminster, Middx., S.

21 John Hyder of All Hallows Barking, London, B., and Mary Burton of the same, S.

21 William Beamon of Hillingdon, Middx., B., and Elizabeth Kentish of the same, S.

22 James Branscombe of St Giles in the Fields, Middx., B., and Elizabeth Heard of the same, S.

22 Thomas Parker of St Saviour, Southwarke, W., and Mary Stevens of Newington, Surry, W.

29 David Pettre of St Ann, Westminster, Middx., W., and Jennet Greeves of the same, S.

29 William Stone of St Margaret, Westminster, Middx., B., and Mary Clarke of the same, S.

May 3 George Adams of St Sepulchre's, Middx., B., and Jane Oudart of Christ church, Spittlefields, Middx., W.

6 Thomas Topham of High Barnet, co. Herts, B., and Sarah Dean of the same, W.; by Mr Ellison.

7 Thomas Pittman of Richmond, Surrey, B., and Massey Marsh of St Martin in the Fields, Middx., S.; by Mr Pearce.

7 Philip Bourne of St Martin in the Fields, Middx., W., and Catherine Fitzgerald of St Lawrence Pountney, London, W.; by Mr Land.

14 Robert Mundy of Norwood, Middx., W., and Amy Mayan of the same, S.

21 William Baycock of Epping, Essex, B., and Ann Boreham of the same, S.

23 James Deliot of St James, Westminster, Middx., W., and Frances Letouzey of St Giles in the Fields, Middx., S.

24 Ferdinand Myon of Lee in Kent, B., and Mary Siddell of the same, S.

28 Thomas Bowlby of St Botolph, Bishopsgate, London, B., and Elizabeth Crawford of the same, S.

31 Jonathan Hornsby of St Martin in the Fields, Middx., B., and Anne Slater of Enfield, Middx., S.

June 4 Richard French of Deddington, co. Oxford, B., and Hannah Hanwell of St Olave, Southwarke, Surry, S.; by Mr Wight of St Paul's.

6 John Chantry of Lambeth, Surrey, B., and Hannah Hart of the same, S.; by the same.

8 Anthony Suttle of St Clement Danes, Middx., B., and Eleanor Morton of the same, W.

9 *Thomas Hays of Rotherhith, Surry, B., and Mary Hall of Deptford, Kent, S.

10 Benjamin Waterhouse of St Dunstan in the East, London, W., and Ann Massey of St Giles in the Fields, Middx., S.

11 Philo Hovord of Hornchurch, Essex, W., and Ann Spencer of the same, W.

15 Henry Trott of St Sepulchre's, London, B., and Mary Cress of the same, S.

29 Nathaniel Percival of Tooting, Surrey, B., and Elizabeth Simmonds of the same, S.; by Mr Pemberton.

July 2 John Puzey of All Hallows Staining, London, B., and Dorcas Aston of St Botolph, Aldgate, London, S.; by Mr Steward.

3 William Armstrong of St George, Southwarke, B., and Mary Hunt of Petworth, Sussex, S.

5 Edward LLoyd of St Michael, Crooked lane, London, W., and Elizabeth Whiton of St Magnus the Martyr, London, W.

* Part of this entry is written over an erasure.—Ed.

1747

July 5 John Snowden of St Botolph, Aldersgate, London, B., and Elizabeth Rutley of St Stephen, Walbroke, London, S.

9 Thomas Layton of St Botolph, Aldgate, Middx., W., and Sarah Shaw of the same, W.

9 John Knowles of Deptford, Kent, B., and Elizabeth Raggett of the same, S.

10 Bartholomew Shercliff of St Giles in the Fields, Middx., W., and Mary Bickford of St George the Martyr, Middx., S.

16 Edward Mount of St George the Martyr, Middx., W., and Sarah Spurgin of St Lawrence, Jewry, London, W.; by Mr Shackleford.

18 William Green of Godston, Surry, B., and Mary Arnold of the same, S.

18 Thomas Lovett of St Andrew, Holborn, Middx., W., and Elizabeth Hardey of the same, S.

20 Lyonel Lyde of the city of Bristol, B., and Rachael Lyde of St Andrew, Holborn, London, S.; by Mr Wight of St Pauls.

23 William Bull of St Andrew, Holborn, Middx., B., and Margaret Wood of St Botolph without Aldersgate, London, S.; by Mr Wight.

23 Moses Gentleman of St Botolph, Aldgate, London, W., and Mary Richardson of the same, S.; by Mr Sandiford.

25 Thomas Milward of St Giles, Cripplegate, London, W., and Sarah Suraties of the same, S.

25 John Jerratt of St Giles in the Fields, Middx., B., and Rachael Bouch of St Paul, Covent Garden, Middx., S.

25 John Passall of Islington, Middx., B., and Elizabeth Smith of the same, S.

27 Henry Elstow of Deptford, Kent, B., and Elizabeth Cambell of the same, W.

27 Nicholas Welsh of St Botolph, Bishopsgate, London, B., and Ann Greenvill of St Mary, Rotherhithe, Surry, W.

29 Joseph Liles of St Gabriel, Fenchurch, London, B., and Anne Sibley of Bishop Stortford, co. Herts, S.

29 John Meierhoff of St Martin Vintry, London, B., and Sarah Franklin of St Ethelburgh, London, S.

30 Richard Storrs of St Andrew, Holborn, Middx., W., and Mary Johnson of St Clement Danes, Middx., S.

Aug. 1 Francis Donnall of St Saviour, Southwarke, B., and Ann Huddleston of Lambeth, Surry, S.

6 James Moring of Clapham, Surrey, B., and Margaret Holyoak of the same, S.

9 Francis Gallant of St Andrew, Holborn, Middx., W., and Grace Mays of St Giles in the Fields, Middx., S.; by Mr Buckby.

9 John Hilldreth of St George the Martyr, Middx., B., and Elizabeth North of St Peter, Cornhill, London, S.; by the same.

9 Richard Sergent of St Martin Vintry, London, B., and Elizabeth Courtis of All Hallows the Great, London, S.; by the same.

11 Samuel Cobb of St Mary le Bone, Middx., B., and Grace Loggin of the same, W.; by the same.

15 Peter Wilkinson of St George, Hanover Square, Middx., B., and Jane Crowley of the same, S.; by the same.

17 James Robards of St Leonard, East Cheap, London, W., and Ann Summers of St George, Southwark, W.; by the same.

20 Isaac Toms of Hadleigh, Suffolk, B., and Sarah Say of St Margaret, Westminster, Middx., [*blank*]; by the same.

25 John Jones of St Lawrence, Jewry, London, B., and Mary Crosby of the same, S.; by Mr Buckby.

26 Giles White of St Clement Danes, Middx., W., and Mary Todd of the same, W.; by the same.

27 William Wild of St Paul, Shadwell, Middx., W., and Hannah Chatwin of St Saviour, Southwark, S.; by the same.

1747

Aug. 30 Daniel Mawley of S[t] Giles in the Fields, Middx., B., and Elizabeth Russell of the same, S.; by the same.

Sept. 1 Matthew Bromley of Putney, Surry, B., and Mary King of the same, S.; by the same.

1 John White of All Hallows the Less, London, W., and Mary Scurrier of S[t] Martin, Ludgate, London, S.; by the same.

2 Thomas White of S[t] Andrew, Holborn, Middx., B., and Rebecca Jones of the same, S.; by the same.

3 Matthew Biggs of Chertsey, Surry, B., and Elizabeth Sizemor of the same, S.; by the same.

8 Thomas Smith of Grantham, co. Lincoln, W., and Christian White of the same, W.; by the same.

8 William Vicaris of Endfield, Middx., B., and Rebecca Gin of the same, S.; by the same.

14 Robert Binfield of S[t] Andrew, Holborn, Middx., B., and Martha Johnson of the same, S.; by the same.

19 Thomas Holmes of Cheshunt, co. Herts, B., and Elizabeth Dixon of the same, W.; by the same.

19 Amos White of S[t] Brides, London, B., and Margaret Hide of S[t] Dunstan in the West, London, W.; by the same.

20 James A'Dean of West Ham, Essex, W., and Mary Forster* of S[t] Dunstan in the East, London, S.; by M[r] Buckby.

21 Francis Paine of S[t] Dunstan in the East, London, W., and Mary Holmden of the same, S.; by the same.

21 James Cromp of Dartford, Kent, B., and Mary Beadle of the same, S.; by the same.

22 Thomas Crookenden of S[t] George, Middx., W., and Jane Hallum of S[t] Botolph, Aldgate, Middx., W.; by the same.

23 Hugh Morgan of S[t] Mary, White Chapel, Middx., B., and Hannah Alexander of the same, S.; by the same.

24 George Newstead of S[t] Benet Finck, London, B., and Dorothy Elizabeth Jackson of the same, S.

24 Roger Billby of S[t] Nicholas, Deptford, Kent, W., and Margaret Beezly of S[t] Bartholomew the Great, London, W.

24 Warder Vanderiste of Croydon, Surry, B., and Elizabeth Keil of S[t] Saviour, Southwark, S.

29 James Harriott of All Hallows, Lombard Street, London, B., and Mary Dickenson of S[t] Mary, Aldermanbury, London, S.

30 Samuel Smith of Elton, co. Huntingdon, B., and Susanna Skemp of S[t] Mary, Newington, Surry, S.

Oct. 4 John Hallett, B., and Ann Scott, S., both of S[t] Peter, Paul's Wharfe. Banns.

4 Thomas Hiron of S[t] Saviour, Southwark, B., and Clare Vernon of the same, S.

7 Edward Benham of Houndslow, Middx., B., and Johanna Sorrell of the same, S.

8 George Barnicoat of Falmouth, Cornwall, W., and Anne Wood of All Hallows Barking, London, S.

8 John Crabb of Epping, Essex, B., and Mary Bridges of the same, S.

9 John Rumney of S[t] Mary, Newington, Middx., B., and Mary Fisher of S[t] James, Westminster, Middx., S.

12 Robert Lane, B., and Elizabeth Willby Flowers, S., both of S[t] Peter, Paul's Wharfe. Banns.

12 Isaac Leggett of Godstone, Surry, B., and Mary Mathews of Westram, Kent, S.

* "Forster" written over "Fowler" struck out.—Ed.

1747

Oct. 13 James Parrott of St James, Clerkenwell, Middx., W., and Elizabeth Bryers of the same, S.

16 Moses Jacobs of St John, Wapping, Middx., B., and Sarah Jacobs of the same, S.

19 Daniel Kemp of Barking, Essex, B., and Elizabeth Wood of the same, S.

22 John Askew of St Magnus the Martyr, London, B., and Mary Saver of the same, S.

22 Samuel Da Costa of St Botolph, Bishopsgate, London, B., and Rebecca Lopez of St Dunstan in the East, Lond., S.

22 John Jay of St Matthew, Friday Street, London, B., and Sarah Clarke of St John Zachary, London, S.

22 John Fling of St Dunstan, Stepney, Middx., B., and Elizabeth Walnite of the same, W.

25 John Payce of St Andrew, Holborn, London, B., and Elizabeth Worrell of St Giles in the Fields, Middx., S.

27 Ralph Wilkinson of St George, Middx., B., and Anne Brown of the same, W.

27 William Cheale of Camberwell, Surry, B., and Jane Pollett of Stretham, Surry, S.

Nov. 3 John Bennett of St Olave, Southwarke, B., and Sarah Owen of St Saviour, Southwarke, S.

5 John Branson of St Saviour, Southwark, B., and Mary Chatwin of the same, S.

6 William Adams of Ware, co. Herts, B., and Anne Robinson of Royston, co. Herts, S.

9 Gibbs Owen of St Ann, Aldersgate, London, B., and Hannah Whitbourne of St Andrew, Holbourn, Middx., S.

10 James Atkins, B., and Joyce Sell, S., both of St Peter, Paul's Wharfe. Banns.

10 William Randell of St Michael, Queenhith, London, W., and Eleanor Parker of St Luke, Middx., S.

12 Joseph Farr of St Sepulchre, London, B., and Anna Maria Price of St James, Clerkenwell, Middx., S.

12 Edmund Popplewell of St James, Clerkenwell, Middx., W., and Mary Gillett of St Bride's, London, W.; by Mr Campbell.

14 William Wells of Brightwell, co. Oxford, B., and Mary New of the same, S.; by Mr Pearce.

14 Thomas Stock of Standstead Mount Fitchet, Essex, B., and Mary Mayne of Kensington, Middx., S.

14 Jonathan Widmer of St Sepulchre's, London, B., and Ann Corbett of the same, W.

17 Solomon Spetigue of St John the Evangelist, Westminster, Middx., W., and Jane Whinyates of the same, W.

24 Xstopher Wood of Grays Thurrocks, Essex, B., and Mary Garrett of Orset, Essex, S.

24 Francis Godfrey of St James, Westminster, Middx., B., and Mary Vincent of the same, S.

26 Mark Robinson of St Michael, Cornhill, London, B., and Elizabeth Reade of Portsmouth, Hants, S.

26 Benjamin Palmer of St Andrew, Holborn, Middx., W., and Sarah Holliday of Rumford, Essex, S.

27 Henry Fielding of the Middle Temple, London, W., and Mary Daniel of St Clement Danes, Middx., S.

29 Samuel Freind of St John the Evangelist, Westminster, Middx., B., and Catherine Jones of St Clement Danes, Middx., S.

Dec. 10 John Simmons of Ospring, Kent, W., and Ann Chambers of Selling, Kent, S.

1747

Dec. 10 James Goodwin of S[t] James, Westminster, Middx., B., and Frances Greening of the same, S.

15 Charles Raworth of S[t] James, Westminster, Middx., B., and Mary Lawrence of S[t] Paul, Covent Garden, Middx., S.

21 William Bromfield of S[t] Clement Danes, Middx., B., and Susanna Margett of the same, S.; by M[r] LLoyd.

22 John Nelson of S[t] John, Wapping, Middx., W., and Hannah Stevens of Deal, Kent, S.

26 Thomas Stanton of Deptford, Kent, B., and Mary White of the same, W.

26 John Moor of Windsor, co. Berks, B., and Averilda Skipton of Woolwich, Kent, S.

31 Edward Pindar of S[t] Edmund the King, London, B., and Elizabeth Seamark of Greenwich, Kent, S.

Jan. 1 Joseph Appleton of All Hallows, Thames Street, B., and Mary Wilkinson of S[t] Martin Vintry London, S.

1 Thomas Lally of S[t] George the Martyr, Middx., B., Clerk, and Elizabeth Saunders of the same, S.

1 Robert Derby of Wimborne, Dorset, B., and Ann Harris of Lewisham, Kent, S.; by M[r] LLoyd.

3 William Webb, B., and Mary Newby, S., both of S[t] Peter, Paul's Wharfe, London. Banns.

7 John Prosser of Battersea, Surry, B., and Margaret Whitaker of the same, S.

9 Charles Coltson of S[t] Mary le Bone, Middx., B., and Ann Field of S[t] James, Westminster, Middx., S.

11 Edward Thurgood of Danbury, Essex, B., and Ann Cooper of the same, S.; by Mr Tillotson.

12 Elias Lecousteur of St Mary, White Chapel, Middx., B., and Elizabeth Watts of the same, S.; by Mr Pemberton.

12 Patrick Spencer of St Leonard, Shoreditch, Middx., B., and Susanna Green of the same, S.; by Mr Wight.

14 Thomas Williams of Wernddû, co. Carmarthen, B., and Anna Maria Miller of St Martin in the Fields, Middx., W.

14 Thomas Stevens of Hornsey, Middx., B., and Eleanor Devey of the same, S.

16 Paschen Kuse of St Margaret, Westminster, Middx., B., and Priscilla Guidot of the same, S.

19 William Rybe of St Botolph, Aldgate, Middx., B., and Elizabeth Galt of the same, S.

20 Thomas Woods of Godalming, Surry, B., and Anne Meale of Dartford, Kent, S.

21 Robert Buxton of S[t] Dunstan in the West, London, B., and Bliss Biddle of the same, S.

23 Charles Cooper of S[t] Paul, Deptford, Kent, B., and Elizabeth Chiballs of the same, S.

24 Giles Panchen of S[t] Gregory, London, B., and Mary Allcock of the same, S.

28 Benjamin Miller of S[t] Botolph without Bishopsgate, London, B., and Ann Bayley of the same, W.

28 Thomas Walthall of S[t] Peter le Poor, London, W., and Hester Haynes of S[t] Mary Aldermary, London, S.

28 John Clark of S[t] Sepulchre, London, B., and Elizabeth Toll of Kensington, Middx., W.

28 Thomas Ireland of S[t] George, Hanover Square, Middx., B., and Anne Gabriel Rocher of the same, S.

29 Thomas Mitford of S[t] George, Hanover Square, Middx., B., and Abigail Holride of S[t] Andrew, Holborne, Middx., S.; by M[r] Buckby.

1747-8

Jan. 31 William Lister of New Windsor, co. Berks, B., and Mary Kay of Kellum, co. Notts, S.

31 William Sprules of St Botolph, Bishopsgate, London, B., and Mary Hopper of the same, S.

31 John Eaton of St Margaret, Westminster, Middx., W., and Sarah Mumbee of St James, Westminster, Middx., S.

Feb. 2 Samuel Nicoll of Hillingdon, Middx., B., and Sarah Newdegate of the same, W.

3 Ralph Bradford of St Peter's in Leeds, co. York, B., and Hannah Horsley of Christ Church, Surrey, S.

5 Richard Simpson of St Andrew, Holborn, Middx., B., and Ann Haswell of the same, S.

8 John *Gilphilling* of St Martin in the Fields, Middx., B., and Sabrine Philpott of the same, S.

9 Charles Harman of St Peter, Paul's Wharfe, B., and Elizabeth Dakin of St Olave, Hart Street, S. Banns.

15 John Warren of St George, Hanover Square, Middx., B., and Mary Hill of St George, Bloomsbury, Middx., S.

15 James Spence of St John, Wapping, Middx., B., and Dorothy Ray of Newcastle upon Tyne, S.

17 Thomas Power of St Brides, London, B., and Mary Baxter of the same, W.

20 John Farrer of St Clement Danes, Middx., B., and Elizabeth Farrow of Great St Bartholomew, London, S.

21 John Bowler of St Saviour, Southwarke, B., and Mary Nash of Mortlake, Surrey, S.

21 Henry Copper of St Leonard, Foster lane, London, B., and Elizabeth Rands of SS. Ann and Agnes, London, S.

22 John Bristow of St Mary Magdalen, Bermondsey, Surrey, W., and Ann Roberts of St Mary, Rotherhith, Surrey, W.; by Mr Shakleford.

22 Edmond Mitten of Hadleigh, Middx., W., and Ann James of the same, W.

22 Thomas Arman of St George the Martyr, Middx., W., and Arabella Cuthbert of the same, S.

23 John Hammond of St Clement Danes, Middx., B., and Hannah Bradbury of St Giles in the Fields, Middx., S.

23 Richard Skinner of St Saviour, Southwarke, W., and Jane Cleaver of the same, W.; by Mr Evans.

23 Mark Davis of St Austin's, London, W., and Margaret Leadbetter of St Dunstan in the West, London, W.; by the same.

23 Martin Heinrick of St James, Westminster, Middx., B., and Sarah Terry of the same, W.

Mar. 1 Robert Howlett of St Sepulchre's, London, B., and Mary Briley of the same, S.

1 Emanuel Mendes da Costa of St Peter le Poor, London, B., and Lea de Prado of Ethelburga, London, S.

2 Richard Rowden Baynham of Kensington, Middx., W., and Sophia Hayes of St James, Westminster, Middx., W.

5 The Honble George Compton, Esqr, of St James, Westminster, Middx., B., and Frances Payne of St Margaret, Westminster, Middx., S.

6 Herbert Barbur of St Andrew, Holborn, Middx., W., and Mary Bourne of the same, S.

8 William Brown Lucey of St Mary, White Chapel, Middx., W., and Mary Sheilds of the same, S.; by Mr Shackleford.

10 Henry Adshead of this parish, B., and Hannah Hall of Rostbury in Cheshire, S.

1747-8

Mar. 10 William Spicer of S[t] John, Wapping, Middx., W., and Martha Browning of S[t] George, Middx., W.

13 Daniel Fenton of Antony in Cornwall, B., and Susanna Langman of S[t] Clement Danes, Middx., S.

16 Robert Towell of Kensington, Middx., W., and Rebecca Griffin of S[t] George, Hanover Square, Middx., S.; by M[r] LLoyd of S[t] Paul's.

16 Edward Lawrence of S[t] Nicholas, Deptford, Kent, B., and Sarah Smith of Rotherhith, Surrey, W.

24 William Smith of S[t] Saviour, Southwarke, B., and Susannah Cock of Christ church, Surrey, S.

24 Edward Giles of Alverstoke, Hants, B., and Elizabeth Stevens of S[t] Botolph, Aldgate, London, W.

24 Edward Kynaston, Esq[r], of Ellesmere, Salop, B., and Victoria LLoyd of S[t] James, Westminster, Middx., S.

1748.

Mar. 25 Francis Bryant of S[t] Nicholas, Deptford, Kent, B., and Elizabeth Hawes of the same, S.

April 10 John Wyatt of S[t] Clement Danes, Middx., B., and Mary Stevens of the same, S.

10 John Wright of S[t] Martin in the Fields, Middx., W., and Elizabeth Slater of the same, W.

12 Edmund Wickes of Kingston, Surry, B., and Ann Dudley of Darking, Surry, S.

14 Joseph Skelding of S[t] Andrew Undershaft, London, W., and Mary Webster of the same, W.

17 Edward Cowles of S[t] Stephen, Walbrook, London, B., and Elizabeth Woodhams of the same, S.

18 Thomas Spencer of East Barnet, co. Herts, B., and Mary Trumble of the same, S.

18 Thomas Clarke, W., of S[t] Bennets, Paul's Wharfe, and Mary Griffith of the same, S. Banns.

18 Henry Keen of S[t] Peter's parish, B., and Sarah Castel of the same, S. Banns.

21 Thomas Bolton of S[t] John the Evangelist, Westminster, W., and Mary Beck of S[t] Margaret, Westminster, W.; by M[r] Foulkes.

25 Thomas Eldridge of S[t] Ann, Westminster, Middx., W., and Catherine Fitzgerald of the same, S.

28 John Finch of Waltham Abbey, Middx., B., and Mary Juda of the same, S.

30 Thomas Jones of S[t] Ann, Westminster, Middx., B., and Charlotte Milward of the same, S.

May 3 John Millington of S[t] George the Martyr, Middx., B., and Elizabeth Campbell of the same, S.

6 Josiah Allen of S[t] Luke, Middx., B., and Elizabeth Vanhuffleing of S[t] Botolph, London, S.

7 William Reynolds of Cheltsham, Surry, B., and Mary Reeve of Tatsfield, Surry, W.

9 Daniel Maycock of Barnes, Surrey, B., and Anne Cook of the same, S.

9 Thomas Baldwin of S[t] Giles, Cripplegate, London, B., and Sarah Curtis of the same, S.

15 Benjamin Gandar of S[t] Paul, Shadwell, Middx., B., and Theophilee Walkley of the same, S.

15 John Hodgson of S[t] Mary Mounthaw, London, B., and Grace Triffin of the same, W.

1748

May 18 William Frost of Tottenham High Cross, Middx., B., and Mary Hall of the same, S.

19 John Hall of Maidenhead, co. Berks, B., and Elizabeth Freeland of Kingston upon Thames, S.

22 Charles Barnett of St Bartholomew the Great, London, B., and Alice Leverett of St Clement Danes, Midd., S.

23 James Morgan of St Anne, Limehouse, Middx., B., and Elizabeth West of the same, S.

24 Thomas Smith of Marlborough, Wilts, W., and Rebecca Swanston of St Michael, Queenhith, London, S.

24 Samuel Cox of the Liberty of the Tower of London, B., and Anne Trout of St Martin in the Fields, Middx., S.; by Mr Wills.

24 Isaac Clemens of St Botolph, Aldgate, London, B., and Sarah Long of St John's, Wapping, Middx., S.; by Mr Wills.

25 William Sowthwood of Christ church, Middx., B., and Sarah Cooke of St Bride's, London, S.

25 Robert Baxter of St Michael, Queenhith, London, B., and Susanna Hasse of the same, S.

28 Edward King of High Wicomb, co. Bucks, B., and Martha Sargent of the same, S.

28 Joseph Archer of Tottenham, Middx., W., and Ann Norcross of St Matthew, Bethnal Green, S.

28 John Lestie of Woolwich, Kent, B., and Ann Nurse of West Ham, Essex, S.

30 Godin Meekins of St James, Westminster, Middx., B., and Ann March of the same, S.

June 12 Richard Furnish of St George, Hanover Square, Middx., B., and Sarah Banks of St Clement Danes, Middx., S.

18 William Mitchell of Camberwell, Surrey, W., and Sarah Woodyer of the same, S.; by Mr Aylmer, Vicar of Camberwell.

20 James Gale of St George, Hanover Square, Middx., W., and Hannah Cooper of the same, S.

23 John King and Dinah Dicker, both of St Bennet, Paul's Wharfe, London. Banns.

24 Francis Searle of Stoke near Guilford, Surry, W., and Mary Bennett of Holy Trinity, Guilford, Surrey, S.

27 William Cooke of St Giles in the Fields, Middx., B., and Mary Cockin of St George, Hanover Square, Middx., S.

29 Francis Rodes of St John, Clerkenwell, Middx., B., and Mary Bagnall of the same, W.

29 Thomas Carter of St George, Hanover Square, Middx., W., and Mary Turner of the same, S.

30 John Rogers of St Sepulchre, Midx., B., and Amy Thorpe of the same, W.

July 2 John Sigismund Tanner of the Tower of London, W., and Margaret Langford of St Mary le Bon, Middx., W.

3 John Tilladams of St Michael, Crooked Lane, London, B., and a minor, and Honor Grove of the same, S.

6 John Harrison of Chilham, Kent, B., and Susannah Barker of Wandsworth, Surry, S.

7 James Wheatcroft of Tooting, Surry, B., and Mary Wheatley of the same, S.

8 Ralph Wright of St Margaret, Westminster, Middx., B., and Sarah Ripley of St George, Hanover Square, Middx., S.

12 John Unwin of Hornchurch, Essex, B., and Martha Lambert of the same, S.

12 John Sellman of Whitney, co. Oxford, B., and Ann Boulton of St Botolph, Aldersgate, London, S.

1748

July 16 William Alexander of Martin, Surry, B., and Grace Stiles of Wimbledon, Surry, W.

20 William Brooks of Litchfield, co. Stafford, W., and Elizabeth Sherrat of Bromley, Kent, S.

22 Joshua Brogden of St Paul, Covent Garden, Middx., W., and Sarah Pistor of the same, S.

22 George Miller of St James, Westminster, Middx., B., and Ann Quick of the same, S.

23 Robert Barber of All Hallows the Less, London, W., and Ann Wale of the same, W.

28 George Caffey of St Mary, Whitechapple, Middx., W., and Elizabeth Sheppard of the same, W.

28 Cuthburd Henson of Christ church, Surry, W., and Mary Bullock of New Brentford, Middx., S.

28 Robert Cowdrey of St Paul, Deptford, Kent, B., and Isabella Haynes of the same, S.

Aug. 1 Samuel Winder, Junr, of Putney, Surry, B., and Mary Bernard of the same, S.

1 Elisha Cook of St Mary, Lambeth, Surry, B., and Hester Batts of Chelsea, Middx., S.

2 William Pendridge of St Michael, Cornhill, London, B., and Mary Summers of the same, S.

2 Isaac Besly of All Hallows, London Wall, B., and Mary Waltor of the same, S.

4 Francis Boxhammer of St George, Hanover Square, Middx., B., and Sarah Wright of St Ann, Westminster, S.

4 Thomas Brown of St Botolph, Aldgate, London, B., and Mary Sutton of the same, S.

5 James Matthews of Hunsdon, co. Herts, B., and Martha Morton of the same, S.

7 William Littleton of St John, Wapping, Middx., W., and Theodosia Darby of St Botolph, Aldgate, London, S.

7 Thomas Smith of St Botolph, Aldersgate, London, B., and Elizabeth Barber of the same, W.

9 William Wood of St Mary, Lambeth, Surry, B., and Mary Season of St Saviour, Southwark, Surry, W.

12 William Povey of St Andrew, Holborn, London, B., and Ann Haydon of St Ann, Westminster, Middx., S.

16 Henry Taylor of Christ church, Surry, B., and Margaret Starkey of the same, S.

18 William Summersett of Christ church, London, B., and Ann Curthberthson of St Clement Danes, Middx., S.

19 Alexander Johnson of St Paul, Deptford, Kent, W., and Barbara Jubber of St Nicholas, Deptford, Kent, W.

20 Thomas Sneath of Christ church, Surry, W., and Elizabeth Farnsworth of the same, S.

21 Joseph Moorhouse of St Mary Woolnoth, London, B., and Anne Fynes of St Lawrence, Jewry, London, S.

21 Charles Eastwood of St Helen's, London, B., and Sarah Smith of St Martin in the Fields, Middx., S.

29 James Ogilvie of St John, Wapping, Middx., B., and Dorothy Wakefield of the same, W.

Sept. 1 William Smith of St Botolph without Bishopsgate, London, B., and Ann Wilson of St Dunstan, Stepney, Middx., S.

2 William Southwell of St James, Westminster, Middx., B., and Hannah Okey of St George, Hanover Square, Middx., W.

2 William Stitkin of Greenwich, Kent, B., and Sarah Beale of the same, S.

1748

Sept. 3 Thomas Baker of St Mary, Lambeth, Surrey, W., and Ann Wise of the same, W.

4 John Keen of St Leonard, Shoreditch, Middx., B., and Elizabeth Provey of Christ Church, Middx., S.

4 Benjamin Braffett of Wimborne, Dorset, B., and Hannah Newman of St Dunstan in the West, London, W.

8 Jeremiah Carroway of St Nicholas, Deptford, Kent, B., and Mary Husband of the same, S.

9 William Risbrook of Teddington, Middx., B., and Sarah Sashell of the same, S.

9 Humphry Matthews of St Giles in the Fields, Middx., B., and Jane Jones of Chelsea, Middx., S.

10 Thomas Harvey of St John, Westminster, Middx., W., and Mary Beauchamp of the same, W.

11 Thomas Varney of St Mary le Strand, Westminster, Middx., B., and Elizabeth Steemson of St James, Westminster, Middx., S.

11 James Smith of St John, Wapping, Middx., B., and Sarah Hales of the same, S.; by Mr Greet.

12 Allen Boutwell of the Hamlett of Poplar in St Dunstan, Stepney, Middx., B., and Mary Nobbs of the same, S.

13 Benjamin Scarlett of St Mary Magdalen, Bermondsey, Surry, B., and Ann Mathews of St Mary, Lambeth, Surrey, S.

14 William Duplessy of St James, Westminster, Middx., B., and Hannah Peckham of St Mary, Whitechapell, Middx., W.

15 John Mottley of St Mary, Lambeth, Surrey, B., and Mary Harris of the same, S.

22 Henry Whiffin of Farnborough, Kent, B., and Anne Redford of the same, S.

22 Thomas Harding of St Clement Danes, Middx., B., and Ann Bulline of St Giles in the Fields, Middx., S.

22 William Gregory of Portsmouth, Hants, W., and Mary Ward of St Margaret, Westminster, Middx., W.

27 John Dewes of St Clement Danes, Middx., W., and Mary Cooke of St George, Hanover Square, Middx., S.

30 John Galleher of Woolwich, Kent, B., and Jane Sage of the same, S.

Oct. 1 Adam Hill of St Catherine near the Tower of London, B., and Elizabeth Campbell of St Martin in the Fields, Middx., S.

1 Thomas Sweatman of St Dunstan in the East, London, B., and Jane Pindar of the same, S.

4 George Foggo of St Mary, Whitechappel, Middx., W., and Judith Guy of the same, W.; by Mr Wills.

6 Phillip Hewes of St Martin in the Fields, Middx., B., and Elizabeth French of St James, Westminster, Middx., S.

6 Richard Warwick of St George the Martyr, Middx., B., and Hannah Butterfield of the same, S.

8 John Knight of St Dunstan, Stepney, Middx., W., and Elizabeth Carr of St Martin in the Fields, Middx., W.

12 Thomas Stevenson of St Margaret Pattens, Lond., W., and Sarah Pinder of St George, Middx., W.

13 James Patterson of St Botolph, Aldgate, London, B., and Ellen Hughes of the same, S.

14 John Stillwell of Darking, Surry, Carman, and Margaret Letts of St Benedict, Paul's Wharfe, London, S.

22 Samuel Root of St Mary Magdalen, Bermondsey, Surry, W., and Elizabeth Wilkinson of St James, Clerkenwell, Middx., S.; by Mr F. Maltus.

23 Joseph Falkner of this parish, B., and Mary Ireland of the same, W.

1748
Oct. 24 Thomas Lake of S[t] Botolph, Bishopsgate, London, B., and Elizabeth Russel of Putney, Surry, S.
24 Thomas Dudley of S[t] Mary Magdalen, Bermondsey, Surrey, B., and Margaret Walker of the same, S.
28 John Dixon of All Hallows Barking, London, W., and Jane Bowen of the same, W.; by M[r] Shakleford.
28 Obadiah Jones of S[t] Andrew, Holborn, London, W., and Sarah Hare of S[t] Thomas, Southwarke, Surry, S.; by M[r] Wills.
31 Samuel Makepeace of Ware, co. Herts, B., and Jane Cobham of the same, [*blank*].
31 Samuel Sewell of All Hallows, Lombard Street, London, B., and Anne Shepherd of the Precinct of the Savoy, Middx., S.
Nov. 2 Robert Shallerass of Tandridge, Surry, B., and Sarah Terry of the same, S.
3 Richard Loyde of Bromley S[t] Leonard, Middx., W., and Ann Simpson of the same, S.
8 Godfrey Webster of S[t] James, Westminster, Middx., Esq[r], B., and Elizabeth Gilbert of S[t] Paul, Covent Garden, Middx., S.
10 William Hornblower of S[t] Luke, Middx., B., and Ann Sully of S[t] James, Westminster, Middx., S.
10 Mansel Pavey of S[t] Ann, Blackfryers, London, B., and Mary Bradbury of S[t] Giles in the Fields, Middx., S.
10 George Roch of Christ church, London, B., a blak, and Mary Timson of S[t] Andrew, Holborn, London, S.
15 Francis Marshall of Dagenham, Essex, B., and Anne Carr of S[t] Bride's, London, S.
16 Peter Stapel of S[t] Mary Abchurch, London, B., and Anne Emilie of Putney, Surry, S.
17 Richard Paynter of S[t] Sepulchre, Middx., W., and Martha Lambin of the same, W.
19 John Jones of the city of Oxford, B., and Mary Babb of Greenwich, Kent, S.
20 William Stephenson of S[t] Mary, White Chapel, Middx., W., and Mary Francis of S[t] Dunstan in the West, London, S.
22 Edward Hawkes of S[t] Nicholas, Deptford, Kent, B., and Elizabeth Johnson of the same, S.
24 John Grant of S[t] Magnus the Martyr, London, W., and Margaret Young of S[t] John, Westminster, Middx., S.
24 William Rees of S[t] Andrew, Holborn, Middx., W., and Mary Wordington of the same, S.
29 Martin Bird of Richmond, Surry, W., and Lydia Vigno of the same, S.
30 William Smith of S[t] George, Middx., B., and Ann Norton of S[t] Mary, Whitechapel, Middx., S.
30 John Young of S[t] Botolph, Aldersgate, London, B., and Hannah Bird of S[t] Luke, Middx., S.
Dec. 1 Richard Fitzpatrick of S[t] George, Hanover Square, Middx., Esq[r], B., and Susanna Young of S[t] James, Westminster, Middx., S.
2 Isaac Rimington of Armley in Leeds parish, co. York, B., and Sarah Denzer of Lambeth, Surry, S.
2 Daniel Webb of S[t] Dunstan, Stepney, Middx., W., and Frances Lister of S[t] James, Clerkenwell, Middx., S.
3 Henry Burt of Sheer, Surry, B., and Elinor Elston of the same, S.
4 Thomas Everitt of S[t] Leonard, Shoreditch, Middx., B., and Susannah Long of the same, W.
6 Robert Gilfillan of Portsmouth, Hants, B., and Elizabeth Stringer of the same, W.

1748

Dec. 7 George Sarmon of Milton near Gravesend, Kent, W., and Elizabeth Frost of the same, W.

8 Thomas Walker of St Mary, Rotherhith, Surry, W., and Rebecca Thomas of the same, W.

8 Stephen Amiot of St Martin in the Fields, Middx., W., and Magdalen Paon of St Mary, Whitechapel, Middx., S.

14 George Tregeare of Woolwich, Kent, B., and Ann Johnson of the same, S.

15 James Brayley of Mitcham, Surrey, W., and Sarah Franklin of the same, W.

15 John Barry of Land Rothall, co. Hereford, B., and Lucy Hodgson of Utexeter, co. Stafford, S.

18 William Chomley of Sheerness, Kent, B., and Mary Morris of Portsmouth, Hants, S.

18 George Phillips, Junr, of All Hallows the Less, London, B., and Susannah King of St Dunstan in the West, London, W.

20 The Revd Benjamin Gutteridge of St Nicholas Cole Abbey, clerk, B., and Ann Goole of the same, W.

22 Obert Lafeuilliade of St James, Westminster, Middx., B., and Jane Miller of the same, S.

25 John Baptist Elzabeth Morean of St James, Westminster, Middx., B., and Elizabeth Delabertanche of St Martin in the Fields, Middx., S.

27 John Butterfield of St George, Southwark, Surry, W., and Elizabeth Morris of the same, S.

29 Thomas Morgan of Kensington, Middx., W., and Susanna Pavey of the same, W.

29 William Roberts of St Catherine Creechurch, London, B., and Ann Taylor of St Martin Outwich, London, S.

29 Henry Griffin of St Leonard, Shoreditch, Middx., B., and Mary Collior of the same, S.

31 Joseph Oldham of St Martin in the Fields, Middx., B., and Jane Turnbull of St Bride's, London, S.

31 Thomas Pike of Woolwich, Kent, B., and Elizabeth Cavel of the same, S.

Jan. 4 Richard Connop of Presteign, co. Hereford, B., and Ann Newell of St Leonard, Shoreditch, Middx., S.

5 Charles Keyzer of St Gabriel, Fenchurch, London, B., and Mary Flexney of the same, S.; by Mr Wills.

5 Fredrick Bund of St Martin in the Fields, Middx., W., and Catherine Cuthbert of St George the Martyr, Middx., S.; by Mr Wills.

7 James Wilks of St Clement Danes, Middx., W., and Margaret Miller of the same, S.

8 John Butcher of Camberwell, Surry, B., and Eleanor Ducker of St Bennet Finck, London, S.

8 Thomas Jackson of Greenwich, Kent, B., and Elizabeth Clayton of the same, S.

10 Robert Walker of St Mary le Strand, Middx., B., and Bridget Feild of the same, S.

13 Thomas Quartermayn of St James, Westminster, Middx., W., and Sarah Twigg of the same, S.

13 James Danniell of St John, Southwark, Surry, B., and Alice Gray of St Catherine Coleman, London, S.

14 Edward Howle of Aylesford, Kent, B., and Jane Long of Chatham, Kent, S.

14 John Woodbridge of St Dunstan in the East, London, W., and Elizabeth Noyes of the same, W.; by Mr Aylsford, Vicar of Camberwell.

1748-9

Jan. 18 Andrew Smith of Battersea, Surry, B., and Cœlia Pedder of Clapham, Surrey, W.

19 James Walker of Christ Church, Spittlefields, Middx., B., and Elizabeth Edwards of the same, S.

19 John Bartin of St Ann, Limehouse, Middx., B., and Amy Stow of the same, S.

20 John Brewer of St Catherine, Coleman Street, London, B., and Margaret Franklin of St Mary Magdalen, Bermondsey, Surry, W.

22 Henry Rumsey of Wandsworth, Surry, B., and Margaret Powell of St Andrew, Holborn, Middx., S.

24 Thomas Veal of St Martin in the Fields, Middx., W., and Ann Johnson of Hampstead, Middx., S.

29 James Vincent, B., of St Bennets, and Sarah Humphreys of the same. Banns.

Feb. 2 John Hunt and Amy Runting, both of St Anne, Westminster, Middx., B. and S.

2 Nicholas South, B., and Mary Picherd, W., both of St Bennett's. Banns.

3 Charles Page of St Faith's, London, B., and Mary Edwards of the same, S.

4 John Cuthbert of St Peter, Paul's Wharfe, London, B., and Elizabeth Neale of the same, S. Banns.

4 Samuel Higgs of this parish, B., and Mary Newton of the same, S. Banns.

4 Samuel Hatton of St George, Hanover Square, Middx., B., and Mary Hall of St Mary Le Bone, Middx., W.

4 John Acors of Woolwich, Kent, B., and Hannah Harrison of Croydon, Surry, S.

5 Timothy Stransom of Barking, Essex, W., and Mary Plummer of the same, W.

5 William Whitaker of St Bride's, London, W., and Mary Billington of Bridewell Precinct, London, S.

5 John Hodges of St Dionis Backchurch, Lond., B., and Sarah Murgatroyd of the same, S.

6 John Whiteway of St Mary, Whitechapel, Middx., B., and Sarah Webb of the same, S.

7 Alexander Temple of St Martin in the Fields, Middx., B., and Ann Harris of the same, S.

7 Ralph Williams of Market Drayton, Salop, B., and Margaret Venables of Whitechurch, Salop, S.

9 Thomas Davis of St Clement Danes, Middx., W., and Elizabeth Seabrook of St Giles in the Fields, S.

14 William Lester of St Dunstan, Stepney, Middx., B., and Mary Minion of East Ham, Essex, S.

15 William Hayes of the parish of Aldates in the city of Oxford, B., and Sarah Rogers of East Greenwich, Kent, S.; by Mr Pinckney of St Paul's.

23 Robert Wright of St George, Middx., B., and Anne Bland of the same, S.

27 James Cowey of St Leonard, Shoreditch, Middx., B., and Mary Peircy of the same, W.

Mar. 2 Peter Brozet of St Martin in the Fields, Middx., B., and Sarah Righton of the same, S.

7 Robert Fretwell of Wakefield, co. York, B., and Elizabeth Steer of the same, S.

10 James Short of St James, Westminster, Middx., B., and Mary Hammond of Alverstoke, Hants, S.

1748-9

Mar. 14 William Chubb of All Hallows, London Wall, W., and Ann Watts of S[t] Botolph, Bishopsgate, London, W.

19 Charles Sheen of S[t] Leonard, Shoreditch, Middx., B., and Esther Jewkes of the same, W.

1749.

Mar. 25 Samuel Smith of Boston, co. Lincoln, B., and Catherine Gilson of S[t] George, Bloomsbury, Middx., S.

27 James Jagger of S[t] Mary le Bone, Middx., B., and Elizabeth Baker of Pancras, Middx., S.

28 John Hutchinson of S[t] James, Clarkenwell, Middx., B., and Esther Crowther of the same, S.

28 John Vivian of S[t] Paul, Covent Garden, Middx., B., and Jane Rybe of the same, S.

30 Thomas Henry John Toone of S[t] Saviour, Southwark, Surry, W., and Susanna Philips of the Liberty of the Tower, S.

April 1 Joseph Bayley of S[t] Alphage, London, B., and Martha Robinson of the same, W.

1 Robert Baker of All Hallows, Lombard Street, London, B., and Mary Russell of the same, W.

4 Robert Fauntleroy of S[t] Mary Magdelen, Bermondsey, Surry, W., and Mary Mason of S[t] Mary, Rotherhith, Surry, W.

4 John Winckles, Esq[r], of S[t] James, Westminster, Middx., B., and Ann Chambers of the same, [*blank*].

6 George Clempson of S[t] John the Evangelist, Westminster, Middx., W., and Sarah Collins of S[t] Nicholas, Deptford, Kent, S.

7 Matthew Jenkinson of Stoney Stratford, co. Bucks, W., and Elizabeth Fenton of Longlofthouse, co. York, S.

15 George Bucknot of Woolwich, Kent, B., and Elizabeth Smith of S[t] Mary Le Bone, Middx., S.

15 Bartholomew Hyatt of St Ann, Westminster, Middx., B., and Catherine Turner of the same, S.; by Mr Winstanley.

16 John Abbot of St George, Hanover Square, Middx., B., and Ann Clousinger of St Martin in the Fields, Middx., S., a minor.

16 Benjamin Sprong of St Botolph, Bishopsgate, London, B., and Elizâbeth Proview of the same, S.

22 Randle Norris of Greenwich, Kent, W., and Jane Whiteid of the same, S.

22 John Trow of Lambeth, Surry, B., and Ann Halsey of St Saviour, Southwark, Surrey, S.*

23 Thomas Humphryes of Harwich, Essex, W., and Elizabeth Garwood of the same, W.

24 William Russen of Deptford, Kent, B., and Hannah Roberts of the same, W.

25 Walter Stubbe of Mersworth, co. Bucks, B., and Elizabeth Wright of Berkhemstead, co. Herts, W.

28 Richard Finch of S[t] George the Martyr, Surry, B., and Elizabeth Jones of S[t] Saviour, Southwark, Surry, S.

May 1 Tanneguy Clark of Fulham, Middx., B., and Henrietta Brassett of the same, S.

6 George Marshall and Mary Fuller, both of this parish. Licence.

7 William Boydell of S[t] Clement Danes, Middx., B., and Mary Crossman of the same, W.

7 Samuel Mynnes of S[t] Saviour, Southwark, Surry, B., and Sarah Warren of the same, S.

* "Wid." is inserted, above the line, after Southwark in the original.—Ed.

1749

May 8 William Bignall of St Mary, Rotherhith, Surry, W., and Ann Freeman of the same, W.

11 Phillip Michell of Highgate, Middx., W., and Ann Brown of the same, S.

14 Richard Morley of St Margaret, Westminster, Midd., B., and Elizabeth Richardson of the same, S., a minor.

15 William Winter of Eaton, co. Bucks, B., and Elizabeth Wilkinson of St Michael's in St Alban's, co. Herts, S.

15 Thomas Stow of Farnborough, Kent, W., and Anne Cooper of Croydon, Surry, S.

16 John French of Meopham, Kent, B., and Margaret Kettle of Wrotham, Kent, S.

18 Thomas Siggins of Twickenham, Middx., W., and Elizabeth Best of Hampton, Middx., S.

18 Robert Nutkins of Edmonton, Middx., B., and Elizabeth Church of the same, S.

24 William Steward, W., and Margaret Goodridge, W., both of this parish. Banns.

25 James Mouser of Stifford, Essex, B., and Mary Radley of Orset, Essex, S.

25 John Bishop of St Ann, Soho, Middx., B., and Ann Jourdan of St James, Westminster, Middx., S.

27 Richard Howell of Langley Marsh, co. Bucks, W., and Martha Hatchett of Harlington, Middx., W.

29 John Turner of Hayes, Middx., B., and Mary Chandler of St Sepulchre's, London, W.

June 3 William Goldstone of St George, Hanover Square, Middx., B., and Sarah Legarde of Fulham, Middx., S.

3 John Davies of St Luke's, Middx., B., and Margaret Rosser of St Martin in the Fields, Middx., S.

4 Thomas Webber of St Mary, Whitechappel, Middx., B., and Elizabeth Matthews of St Luke's, Middx., W.

4 James Wheeler of St Catherine by the Tower of London, B., and Hannah Banister of the same, S.

5 Gabriel Rivalin of the Precinct of Norton Folgate, Middx., B., and Ann Nedel of St Matthew, Bethnall Green, S.

6 Thomas Coke, Esqr, of St Martin in the Fields, Middx., W., and Anne Paysant of St Margaret, Westminster, Middx., S.

7 John Muddin of St Ann, Limehouse, Middx., W., and Elizabeth Mason of the same, W.

7 The Rt Honable Charles, Lord Viscount Fane, Baron of Loughgur in Ireland, B., and Dame Susanna Juxon of Little Compton, co. Gloucester, W. "By a Special Licence at ye house of Mr Stevens ye Proctor."

8 John Hicks of St Margaret Pattens, London, B , and Sarah Barboure of Richmond, Surry, S.

8 Thomas Warburton of St Andrew, Holborn, Middx., B., and Elizabeth Hinsell of the same, S.

8 Thomas Holmes of St James, Westminster, Middx., B., and Elizabeth Simms of Oakingham, co. Berks, S.

8 William Keys of St Ann, Westminster, Middx., B., and Ann Haszell of St James, Westminster, Middx., S.

9 Thomas Bethell of St George, Hanover Square, Middx., B., and Mary Morris of the same, S.

13 Peter Sallaway of St Saviour, Southwark, Surry, B., and Mary Brown of St Mary Magdalen, Bermondsey, Surry, S.

17 Moses Dawson of St Botolph, Aldgate, London, B., and Frances Barrett of the same, S.

1749

June 18 William Smith, B., and Sarah Bowes, [*blank*], both of this parish. Banns.

20 John Wright of S[t] Luke's, Middx., B., and Martha Hirons of the same, S., a minor.

22 Thomas Warren of S[t] Stephen's, Walbrook, London, B., and Elianor Williams of S[t] George, Bloomsbury, Middx., S.

22 John Curtis of S[t] Mary Woolnorth, London, W., and Ann Feather of S[t] George, Hanover Square, Middx., W.

22 George Hoskins of Chiswick, Middx., W., and Sarah Isles of the same, S.

24 Thomas Bowman of S[t] George, Hanover Square, Middx., W., and Ann Newbey of S[t] James, Westminster, Middx., S.

24 George Ashby of Quenby Hall, co. Leicester, Esq., B., and Deborah Sparke of the town of Cambridge, S.

26 Henry White of S[t] Mary, Lambeth, Surry, B., and Mary Ann Marsh of S[t] Saviour, Southwark, S.

29 Henry Jenks of Brentford, Middx., W., and Deborah Honor of Isleworth, Middx., W.

29 James Ware of Deptford, Kent, W., and Elizabeth Blake of Deal in Kent, S.

July 1 Nicholas Statton of S[t] Ann, Middx., B., and Dorcas Packwood of the same, S.

2 Edward Pugh of S[t] George, Bloomsbury, Middx., B., and Margaret Midgley of the same, S.

3 John Mills of Stapleford Tawny, Essex, B., and Ann Keep of Stanford Rivers, Essex, S.

4 John Good of Folkstone, Kent, W., and Mary Hampton of the same, W.

4 Francis Weaver of S[t] Alban, Silver Street, London, B., and Ann Mills of S[t] Andrew, Holborn, Middx., S.

5 William Wallis of S[t] George in the East, Middx., B., and Ann Patling of S[t] Mary, White Chapel, Middx., S.

9 John Henkell of S[t] Paul, Shadwell, Middx., B., and Sarah Spakeman of the same, W.

10 John Mobbs of S[t] Sepulchre's, Middx., B., and Catherine Stubbs of the same, S.

11 Evan Edwards of S[t] George, Hanover Square, Middx., B., and Susannah Sansom of the same, W.

13 Thomas Scudder of Boxly, Kent, W., and Ann Clark of Dartford, S.

15 John Werge of Hitching, co. Herts, B., and Sarah Wigmore of the same, S.

15 William Hemans of S[t] Andrew, Middx., B., and Catherine Carr of the same, S.

15 John Petre Barbier of S[t] Mary le Bone, Middx., W., and Anne Chennebre of S[t] George, Hanover Square, Middx., W.

16 Thomas Hains of S[t] Olave, Jewry, London, B., and Elizabeth Dawson of Christ Church, Middx., S.

16 Timothy Veale of S[t] Andrew, Holborn, Middx., W., and Elizabeth Singer of S[t] Clement Danes, Middx., S.

19 James Hargreaves of S[t] Andrew, Holborn, Middx., B., and Ann Lamplugh of the city of Oxford, W.

19 Martin Fox of Fulham, Middx., B., and Elizabeth Beetham of the same, S.

22 Daniel Chardavoyn of Sunbury, Middx., W., and Elizabeth Susy of the same, S.; by the Rev. M[r] Cronkshaw, Curate of Chertsey in Surry.

24 Edward Kyffin of S[t] Martin in the Fields, B., and Frances Edgforth of the same, S.

1749

July 27 William Cutford of Wandsworth, Surry, B., and Phillis Northridge of the same, S.

27 Edward Parker of St George, Bloomsbury, Middx., W.,* and Elizabeth Tyson of St Saviour, Southwark, Surry, W.

30 William Jones of St Clement Danes, Middx., B., and Elizabeth Murthwaite of the same, S.

30 Thomas Buster of St Giles, Cripplegate, London, B., and Mary Clarke of the same, S.

Aug. 1 Thomas Gibson of Christ Church, Surry, B., and Margaret Wright of St Saviour, Southwark, Surry, W.

2 Anthony Brunn of St George, Hanover Square, Middx., B., and Mary Hinde of the same, S.

3 Thomas Gillman of the Inner Temple, London, B., and Catherine Proudman of St Saviour, Southwark, Surry, S.

5 Joseph Tomlin of Christ Church, Surry, B., and Elizabeth Meader of the same, S.

7 Joseph Hardin of South Mimms, Middx., W., and Sarah Scott of Enfield, Middx., W.

8 John Nicholson of St Sepulchre's, London, W., and Rebecca Lawrence of St Vedast, Foster lane, London, S.

10 Charles Vaughan of St Andrew, Holborn, B., and Sarah Taylor of the same, S.

10 John Evans of St Peter, Paul's Wharfe, London, W., and Elizabeth Wilson of St Giles, Cripplegate, London, W.

18 John Simpson of St George, Southwark, Surry, B., and Elizabeth Aeiry of the same, S.

20 Archibald Bower of St James, Westminster, Middx., B., and Dorothy Conner of the same, W.

21 William Feild of St Nicholas, Deptford, Kent, B., and Rebecca Webb of Wandsworth, Surry, S.

22 James Preston of Newport, Isle of Wight, B., and Mary Salkeld of St Dunstan in the West, London, S.

22 Henry Sexton of St Martin in the Fields, Middx., B., and Elizabeth Harris of the same, S.

23 William Mallett of Fryan Barnett, Middx., W., and Rebecca Spiller of the same, W.

25 John Goodall of Woodbridge, Suffolk, W., and Amey Ward of the same, W.

29 Henry Kitchin of St Martin in the Fields, Middx., W., and Mary Mudge of St Andrew, Holborn, London, W.; by Mr Pugh.

29 Daniel Shepley of St Andrew, Holborn, Middx., W., and Sarah Booth of the same, S.; by Mr Pugh.

31 Edward Thornbrough of Reading, Berks, W., and Mary White of Totford, Southampton, S.; by Mr Pugh.

Sept. 9 George Batholomew of All Hallows, London Wall, B., and Mary Denison of Wakefield, co. York, S.

11 John Grubb of Hornsey, Middx., W., and Martha Page of St James, Clarkenwell, Middx., S.

12 Richard May of St John Baptist, London, B., and Frances Winsmore of St Sepulchre's, London, S.

13 Henry Pearson of St Mary Magdalen, Milk Street, London, W., and Arabella Mawson of St Mary Aldermary, London, W.

18 Jacob Pearce of St George, Hanover Square, Middx., B., and Sarah Fry of the same, W.

19 Charles Wilkinson of St James, Westminster, Middx., B., and Mary Bire of the same, W.

* "W." is written over "B."—Ed.

1749

Sept. 20 Marmaduke Rawdon of St Andrew, Holborn, Middx., W., and Rebecca Seignoret of the same, W.

21 Benjamin Riggleswortli* of Layndon Hills, Essex, B., and Susannah Mabbs of Mountnessing, Essex, S.

23 William Marsden of St Giles in the Fields, Middx., B., and Susannah Cartwright of St Paul, Shadwell, Middx., S., a minor.

23 Robert Gore of St Mary, White Chapel, Middx., B., and Elizabeth Kelley of the same, W.

24 Richard Mason of SS. Ann and Agnes, London, B., and Anne Palser of Christ Church, London, S.

27 William Smith of Enfield, Middx., B., and Margaret Phillips of the same, S.

28 John Edwards of St James, Clerkenwell, Middx., B., and Elinor Davis of Barnet, co. Herts, S.

28 John Tealing of Wandsworth, Surry, B., and Magdalen Bernard of St Matthew, Bethnall Green, Middx., S.

30 Thomas Stringfield of Hendon, Middx., B., and Theodosia Milbourne of St James, Westminster, S.; by Mr Buckby.

Oct. 2 Joachim Johan Lodewick Warnich of the Cape of Good Hope in Africa but at present residing at the parish of Endfield, Middx., B., and Joanna Bullen of Enfield aforesaid, S. By Special Licence in the church about 7 o'clock at night in the presence of Mr Josias Farrer, Proctor, and several others.

4 Henry Gunner of Epping in Essex, W., and Dorothy Schooling of the same, W.

7 Edward Maybank of St George, Southwark, Surry, W., and Mary Duke of the same, S., a minor.

9 Thomas Field of St Mary, Lambeth, Surry, W., and Sarah Prince of St Leonard, Shoreditch, Middx., S.

15 Thomas Ashman, B., and Ruth Barns, S., both of St Peter, Paul's Wharfe, London. Banns.

16 Frederick Bernard of St Matthew, Bethnall Green, Middx., B., and Mary Anvache of St Botolph, Bishopsgate, London, S.

16 Joseph Howlatson of St Catherine near the Tower of London, B., and Mary Richardson of St Botolph, Aldgate, London, S.

18 Thomas French of Ludsdon, Kent, B., and Elizabeth Gray of Chelsea, Middx., S.

19 Joseph Mascall of St Bennett Finck, London, B., and Catherine Buckley of St Christopher's, London, W.

20 Thomas Sisum of Kensington, Middx., W., and Judith Palmer of the same, S.

21 John Wills of St Bennet Finck, London, W., and Anne Davis of St Martin in the Fields, Middx., S.

21 John Croasdell of St Paul, Covent Garden, Middx., B., and Katherine Milward of Battersea, Surry, S.; by Mr Pinckney of St Paul's.

26 William Alexander of St Andrew, Holborn, Middx., B., and Mary Parker of the same, S.

28 John Keeling of St James, Clerkenwell, Middx., W., and Ann Reynolds of the same, S., a minor.

Nov. 2 James Cadywould of St Bennet, Gracechurch, London, B., and Sarah Davies of St Dunstan in the West, London, S.

2 William Fillingham of St Mary, White Chapel, Middx., B., and Jane Taylor of the same, W.; by Mr Cronkshaw.

4 John Swaisland of St John, Southwark, Surry, B., and Mary Evlutton of the same, S.

4 William Ash of St Botolph, Aldersgate, Middx., W., and Margaret Cooke of St Luke's, Middx., W.; by Mr Cronkshaw.

* "Riglesworth" in margin.—Ed.

1749
Nov. 7 Richard Riley of Woodford, Essex, B., and Elizabeth Cannon of Walthamstow, Essex, W.
9 John Rose of St Ann, Middx., B., and Alice Gibbs of the same, S.; by Mr Cronkshaw.
20 Joseph Kingston Alloway of Christ Church, Surry, B., and Elizabeth Pearce of the same, S.
20 Robert Goslin of the Precinct of White Fryers, London, B., and Mary Reeves of Christ Church, Middx., S.
21 John Davis of St John, Southwark, Surry, B., and Martha Lester of the same, S.
23 John Gayler of Armsworth, Middx., B., and Sarah Atkins of the same, S.
26 Bartholomew Nutt of Battersea, Surry, W., and Susanna Turner of the same, S.
29 John Wood of St Luke, Middx., B., and Urania Harriott of the same, S.
Dec. 7 William Taylor of St Luke's, Middx., W., and Ann West of the same, W.
7 Samuel Tabor of Bocking, Essex, B., and Anne Crakenthorp of the same, S.
7 Richard Wyatt, W., and Amey Pennill, S., both of this parish. Banns.
8 Nathaniel Cawne of Woolwich, Kent, B., and Sarah Wilson of Greenwich, Kent, S.
9 William Shaw of St Martin in the Fields, Middx., B., and Elizabeth Godde of the same, S.
10 Timothy Collins, [*blank*], and Elizabeth Brooks, [*blank*], both of this parish. Banns.
10 Young Benn Allen of St Dunstan in the West, London, B., and Mary Dodd of St Andrew, Holborn, Middx., W.
13 William Rooke of Enfield, Middx., B., and Anne Simmonds of the same, S.
19 Edmund Crawley of Hampstead, co. Herts, B., and Martha Metilda Rundle of Stoke Damerell, Devon, S.
21 George Cook of St Martin in the Fields, Middx., B., and Sarah Gardner of St Paul, Covent Garden, Middx., S.
22 John Redding of Berkhampstead, co. Herts [*sic*], B., and Susannah Geary of the same, S.; by Mr Pugh.
22 William Ringsted of St Martin in the Fields, B., and Martha Temple of the same, S.; by Mr Pugh.
27 Hambury Gyles of St Paul, Covent Garden, Middx., B., and Mary Gattlyffe of St Dunstan in the West, London, S.
28 Thomas Johnson of Colchester, Essex, B., and Alice Spencer of St Clement Danes, Middx., S.
31 Walter Hall of St Saviour, Southwark, Surry, B., and Grace Gray of St Thomas, Southwark, Surry, S.
31 James Humphreys of St Paul, Shadwell, Middx., W., and Elizabeth Wright of St Mary, White Chapel, Middx., W.
Jan. 1 Samuel Finch of St Mary, Rotherhithe, Surry, B., and Elizabeth Machen of the same, S.
1 Thomas Okell of St Margaret's, Westminster, Middx., B., and Elizabeth Harwood of St Andrew, Holborn, Middx., S.
2 John Clarke of St Andrew, Holborn, Middx., B., and Ann Baroott of the same, [*blank*].
3 John Jones of St Martin in the Fields, Middx., B., and Mary Goodshaw of the same, W.
6 Burton Hudson of St Martin in the Feilds, Middx., B., and Amey West of St Mary le Bow, London, S.
7 Robert Gibson of St Andrew, Holborn, Middx., B., and Martha Perkins of the same, S.
7 John Lunn of St Botolph, Aldgate, London, B., and Sarah Benton of St George in the East, Middx., S.

1749-50

Jan. 9 James Hume of S[t] John, Wapping, Middx., B., and Anne Gowling of the same, W.

11 Samuel Walker of S[t] George, Southwark, Surry, B., and Judith Boodall of the same, W.

12 Thomas Jefferies of S[t] Andrew, Holborn, London, B., and Mary Woodcock of the same, S.

13 Henry Barber of S[t] Botolph, Aldgate, London, W., and Hannah Bowzer of Clapham, Surry, S.

13 John Powell of S[t] George, Bloomsbury, Middx., W., and Sarah Pullen of the same, S.

15 James East of Ware, co. Herts, B., and Elizabeth Tilbary of Woodford, Essex, S.

17 John Collin, B., and Hannah Grant, S., both of this parish. Banns.

18 Jonas Phipps of S[t] George, Middx., B., and Jane Wells of the same, W.

23 John Lisle of Bristol Causeway, Surry, B., and Margaret Newman of S[t] James, Westminster, S.

25 Thomas Whithead of Whitton in Twickenham, Middx., B., and Sarah Taylor of the same, S.

28 John Parrott of S[t] Saviour, Southwark, Surry, B., and Rebecca Jones of S[t] Martin, Ludgate, London, W.

28 Francis Plastow of Acton, Middx., B., and Rebecca Cornell of the same, S.

Feb. 1 James Miller of S[t] Michael, Crooked lane, London, B., and Dorothy Hammond of Battersea, Surry, S.

3 Thomas Reynolds of Croydon, Surry, B., and Ann Willimot of the same, S.

9 James Bennett of Totteridge, co. Herts, B., and Mary Reeve of Finchley, Middx., S.

10 George Allcock of S[t] Martin in the Fields, Middx., W., and Mary Salisbury of the same, S.

13 William Windham of Felbrigge in Norfolk, Esq., B., and Sarah Lukin of Braintree in Essex, W. By a Special Licence at the house of M[r] Henry Stevens, Proctor at Doctors' Commons, and in the presence of the said M[r] Stevens and M[r] William Field of Brick Court in the Temple.

14 Thomas Stevens of Sutton, Kent, B., and Jane Small of the same, S.

15 Samuel Gregory of S[t] John, Wapping, Middx., B., and Molly Wright of S[t] Magnus the Martyr, London, S.

17 Vincent Stokoe of S[t] Martin in the Fields, Middx., B., and Sarah Darlington of S[t] Ann, Westminster, Middx., S.

18 William Godfrey of S[t] Sepulchre, London, B., and Anne Pardon of S[t] Brides, London, S.

20 William Bowman of All Hallows Barking, London, B., and Susanna Sterey of S[t] Olave, Hart Street, London, S.

20 James Blake of Chipsted, Surry, B., and Jane Garland of S[t] Mary le Bone, Middx., S.

21 Lewis Nicholson of S[t] Peter le Poor, London, B., and Ann Yeatts of Mortlake, Surry, S.

21 Paul Meslier of S[t] Martin in the Fields, Middx., B., and Mari Ann Rouson of the same, S.

24 Henry Irving of S[t] Andrew Undershaft, London, B., and Frances Ferminger of the same, S.

24 William Cock of S[t] George, Southwark, Surry, W., and Prudence Stowards of Christ Church, London, S.

25 Humphrey Roberts of S[t] Brides, London, B., and Mary Pack of S[t] Martin in the Fields, Middx., S.

1749-50

Feb. 25 Richard Aston of St Andrew, Holborn, Middx., B., and Elizabeth Jackson of St George the Martyr, S.

27 John Pridham of St Giles in the Fields, Middx., W., and Frances Sex of the same, W.

27 Adam Fairchild Fowler of Stoke Newington, Middx., B., and Mary Derigo of the same, S.

28 Joseph Salway of Ashford, Middx., W., and Margaret Collier of Chertsey, Surry, W.

25 [*sic*] John Nelson of St Martin in the Fields, Middx., B., and Ann Driver of St Brides, London, S.; by Mr Wills.

Mar. 8 George Franklin of Eltham, Kent, B., and Margaret Coates of the same, S.

8 John Burrup of Kensington, Middx., B., and Mary Fitzwater of the same, S.

15 John Pilkington Morgan of St Clement Danes, Middx., B., and Esther Hilton of the same, S.

1750.

Mar. 29 Thomas Stephenson of St James, Westminster, Middx., W., and Mary Bickseall of St Sepulchre, Middx., W.

April 1 Richard Curtis of St Andrew, Holborn, London, B., and Elizabeth Holmes of the same, S.

5 Thomas Chettle of St Bridget, London, B., and Elizabeth Tugwell of the same, S.

16 William Baker of St Giles in the Fields, Middx., B., and Rebecca Samwell of the same, S.

17 John Jarvis of St Margaret, Westminster, Middx., B., and Amelia Lawrence of Isleworth, Middx., S.

18 Thomas Matson of St Botolph, Aldgate, London, B., and Elizabeth Redding of St Margaret Pattens, London, S.

20 John Brasier of St James, Westminster, Middx., B., and Diana Haley of the same, S.

21 Samuel Hunt of Rickenhall, Suffolk, B., and Margaret Laws of Clare in Suffolk, S.

22 John Clapham of St Giles in the Fields, Middx., B., and Henrietta Clarentia Watts of the same, W.

23 William Banson of Tottenham, Middx., B., and Mary Banson of the same, S.

23 William Royall of St Stephen, Coleman Street, London, B., and Ann Barton of the same, S.

24 John Harris of St Mary, White Chapel, Middx., B., and Alice Bampton of St Leonard, Shoreditch, S.

24 John Dalton of St Bartholomew behind the Royal Exchange, London, W., and Mary Sunter of St Botolph, Bishopsgate, London, W.; by Mr Cronkshaw.

24 Thomas King of Sunbury, Middx., B., and Elizabeth Smith of the same, S., a minor.

25 William Bradford of St Olave, Hart Street, London, B., and Sarah Obrian of St Martin Vintry, London, S.

25 Henry Wilson of Christ Church, Middx., W., and Margaret Farrar of the same, S.

26 Abraham Gill of Deptford, Kent, B., and Hannah Browning of the same, S.; by Mr Cronkshaw.

26 William Cullerne of St John the Evangelist, London, B., and Martha Baylie of the same, S.

27 Samuel Bonne of the Inner Temple, London, Esq., [*blank*], and Jane Brooke of the same, S.

1750

April 27 James Lyttler of St Martin in the Fields, Middx., B., and Elizabeth Welch of the same, S.

28 John Wilkinson of St Martin in the Fields, Middx., B., and Jane Allin of St Margaret, Westminster, S.

28 John Peacock of Clapham, Surry, B., and Elizabeth Barecroft of the same, S.

29 Henry Jones of St Michael Royal, London, B., and Mary Perry of St Andrew Hubbard, London, S.

May 8 Joseph Bilton of St Bartholomew the Great, London, B., and Elizabeth Bramley of St James, Clerkenwell, S.

14 Robert Copland of St Stephen, Coleman Street, London, B., and Ann Farmer of St Ann, Westminster, Middx., S.

16 William White of St Saviour, Southwark, Surry, W., and Sarah Stevens of St Mildred, Bread Street, London, S.

21 Abraham Holloway of Deptford, Kent, B., and Mary Spalding of the same, S.

29 Edward Dod of St Bartholomew the Great, London, B., and Elizabeth Cawood of the same, S.

30 James Smith of St Edmunds Bury, Suffolk, B., and Ann Smith of the same, S.

31 Robert Magson of St James, Westminster, Middx., B., and Frances Ann Deliott of the same, W.

31 Thomas Sequin of St Andrew, Holborn, Middx., B., and Esther Cumenge of the same, S.

June 2 Samuel Smith of St Saviour, Southwark, Surry, B., and Sarah Holford of the same, S.

4 Edward Benton of St George, Middx., B., and Mary Hill of the same, S.

4 Nicholas Andrews of Oxted, Surry, B., and Elizabeth Burges of Limpsfield, Surrey, S.

5 Thomas Coates of St Andrew, Holborn, Middx., W., and Ruth Mumford of St Clement Danes, W.

10 James Bernard of this parish, B., and Mary Whitehead of St Sepulchre, London, S.

13 William Dawes of Fen Stanton, co. Hunts, W., and Margaret Forster of the same, S.

17 Edward Prior of St Clement Danes, Middx., B., and Elizabeth Middleton of St Paul, Covent Garden, Middx., S.

17 Charles Arnott of St Margaret, Westminster, Middx., B., and Henrietta Ferguson of the same, S.

17 John Halbert, B., and Jane Dimock, S., both of St Peter's, Paul's Wharfe, London. Banns.

18 Robert Davis of St Clement Danes, Middx., B., and Mary Price of Richmond, Surry, S.

20 Anthony Murphy of St James, Westminster, Middx., B., and Mary Middlebrook of the same, W.

21 Jonathan Shillingford of St James, Westminster, Middx., B., and Elizabeth Thomson of the same, S.

21 Francis Fletchet of St Clement Danes, Middx., B., and Elizabeth Wallis of Chelsea, Middx., S.

29 Thomas Edwards of St George, Hanover Square, Middx., B., and Ruth Watkins of the same, S.

July 1 James Cowdon of St Clement Danes, Middx., B., and Martha Walker of the same, S.

3 George Hodgson of St George, Southwark, Surry, B., and Mary Millson of the same, S.

5 Titus Angus of St George, Hanover Square, Middx., B., and Rebecca Whitaker of St James, Clerkenwell, Middx., S.

1750

July 5 William Spong of S[t] Margaret near Rochester, Kent, B., and Mary Stark of S[t] Nicholas in Rochester, Kent, S.

7 William Wyatt of S[t] Sepulchre, London, W., and Ann Jones of the same, W.

8 Francis Watts of S[t] Olave, Silver Street, London, B., and Elizabeth Grimmit of S[t] Clement Danes, Middx., S.

11 Samuel Burch of S[t] Martin, Leicester, B., and Elizabeth Pritchard of the same, W.

11 Jonathan Smith of S[t] Sepulchre, Middx., W., and Ann Wyatt of the same, S.

13 Harry Goodyer of S[t] Dunstan in the West, London, B., and Mary Armstrong of Guildford, Surry, S.

17 Robert Hinton of Battersea, Surry, B., and Elizabeth Yates of the city of Oxford, S.

19 Edward Jones of Croydon, Surry, B., and Elizabeth Healey of Mitcham, Surry, S.

19 Joseph Salway of S[t] Paul, Deptford, Kent, B., and Rebecca Maynard of Christchurch, Surry, S., a minor.

27 Richard Cartwright of S[t] George, Hanover Square, Middx., B., and Lucy Collett of the same, S.

27 William Warren of S[t] Andrew, Holborn, Middx., W., and Jane Burdett of Whetstone in Fryan Barnett, Middx., W.

28 John Marham of S[t] Botolph, Aldgate, London, B., and Mary Clarkson of the same, W.

31 George Wood of S[t] Clement Danes, Middx., B., and Joyce Bagnell of S[t] Andrew, Holborn, London, S.

Aug. 1 William Paggett of S[t] Albans, co. Herts, W., and Mary Smith of Camberwell, Surry, S.

2 Thomas Stephens of S[t] Dunstan in the West, London, B., and Mary Bundock, a minor, of S[t] Botolph, Aldgate, Middx., S.

5 Thomas Thayen of Chelmsford, Essex, B., and Edith Bailey of Haverstock, Essex, W.

5 John Vibert of S[t] George, Bloomsbury, Middx., W., and Ann Ducar of S[t] George the Martyr, Middx., S.

5 James Rice of S[t] Faith's, London, B., and Mary Cossens of the same, S.

7 John Staines of Woodford, Essex, B., and Jane Ward of Lambourne, Essex, S.

8 Thomas Ringwood of New Windsor, co. Berks, W., and Jane Thomas of S[t] Martin in the Fields, Middx., S.

9 James Patterson of S[t] George, Middx., B., and Ann Farrow of All Hallows on the Wall, London, S.; by M[r] Wills.

11 William Stell of S[t] Mary Woolnoth, London, B., and Ruth Evererd of S[t] James, Garlickhith, London, S.; by M[r] Wills.

22 William Wells of Ewell, Surry, B., and Sarah Jubb of the same, W.

22 John Townsend of S[t] Luke, Middx., B., and Martha Broncker of S[t] John, Southwark, Surry, S.

23 Henry Rich of Battersea, Surry, B., and Ann Berry of the same, S.

25 James Clark of S[t] James, Westminster, Middx., B., and Mary Hellier of the same, W.; by M[r] Pugh.

26 John Kay of S[t] Mary Magdalen, Bermondsey, Surry, B., and Rose Hill of S[t] Olave, Southwark, Surry, S.; by M[r] Pugh.

27 Thomas Phillips of S[t] Mary Magdalen, Bermondsey, Surry, B., and Frances Gowith of the same, S.; by M[r] Pugh.

29 John Barrett of Dartford, Kent, B., and Elizabeth Webb of Chipstead, Kent, S.

29 John Pitman of S[t] George, Hanover Square, Middx., B., and Elizabeth Tatlow of S[t] Paul, Covent Garden, Middx., W.

1750

Sept. 1 Peter Denis, Esq., of S[t] Ann, Soho, Middx., B., and Elizabeth Pappett of S[t] James, Westminster, Middx., S.

1 Christopher Felton of S[t] Dunstan, Stepney, Middx., B., and Sarah Biddell of S[t] Paul, Shadwell, Middx., S.

3 Matthew Corbey, B., and Sarah Glover, S., both of this parish. Banns.

5 Thomas White of S[t] John, Southwark, Surry, B., and Maria Dallin of S[t] Saviour, Southwark, Surry, S.

5 San Hancock of S[t] Mary, White Chapel, Middx., W., and Jane Ogilby of S[t] Mary, Lambeth, Surry, W.

6 James Goodwin of All Hallows, Lombard Street, London, B., and Elizabeth White of S[t] Antholins, London, S.

9 William Dove of S[t] Clement Danes, Middx., B., and Elizabeth Hoar of the same, S.; by M[r] Pugh.

10 Robert Freeman of S[t] Mary, White Chapel, Middx., B., and Elizabeth Hall of the same, S.; by M[r] Benett.

10 Thomas Wright of S[t] Giles in the Fields, Middx., W., and Catharine Bell of S[t] Margaret, Westminster, Middx., W.; by M[r] Bennet.

12 Francis Chappell of S[t] Clement Danes, Middx., B., and Sarah Crouch of S[t] Dunstan in the West, London, S.; by M[r] Bennet.

12 John Perkins of S[t] George, Middx., B., and Sarah May of the same, S.; by M[r] Bennet.

15 Jarvis Langford of S[t] Olave, Southwark, Surry, B., and Alice Jones of the same, W.

15 John Petley of East Langdon, Kent, B., and Sarah Chambers of Sandwich, Kent, S.

15 James Palmer of S[t] George, Southwark, Surry, W., and Hester Sloper of the same, W.

16 John Fynney of All Hallows the Less, London, B., and Hannah Sims of the same, S.

17 Henry Harrison of S[t] George, Hanover Square, Middx., B., and Anne Price of the same, S.

20 John Peacock of Dagenham, Essex, B., and Susannah Seabrook of the same, S.; by M[r] Pugh.

23 John Honychurch of S[t] Dunstan in the West, London, B., and Mary Vigurs of Penzance, Cornwall, W.

27 Matthew Bedford of S[t] Mary, White Chapel, Middx., B., and Dianah Jones of the same, S., a minor.

27 John Costidell of Westerham, Kent, B., and Jane Browne of the same, S.

29 Thomas Hopkins of S[t] Margaret, Westminster, Middx., B., and Elizabeth Phillips of S[t] John the Evangelist, Westminster, Middx., W.

30 James Chapman of S[t] Martin in the Fields, Middx., W., and Rebecca James of the same, W.

Oct. 2 John Hood of S[t] Ann, Westminster, Middx., B., and Allison Neillson of S[t] James, Westminster, Middx., S.

3 John Eeles of Westlip, Middx., W., and Hannah Taylor of Aikenham, Middx., S.

4 Edward Adams of S[t] John, Hackney, Middx., B., and Mary Owen of S[t] Sepulchre, London, S.

6 Roger Pemberton of S[t] Bennet Finck, London, B., and Elizabeth Leyson of S[t] Clement Danes, Middx., S.

9 Edward Wellum of Bromley, Kent, B., and Ann May of the same, S.

10 Josias Whitely of S[t] George, Southwark, Surry, W., and Elizabeth Day of S[t] Martin, Ludgate, London, S.

15 Alexander Morhead of S[t] George, Middx., B., and Bridget Patterson, W.; by M[r] Bennet.

16 Stockley Cobham of S[t] Luke, Middx., B., and Sarah Clarke of S[t] Stephen, Walbroke, London, [*blank*]; by M[r] Bennet.

1750

Oct. 16 Joseph Clare of S[t] Luke, Middx., B., and Elizabeth Norris of S[t] Giles, Cripplegate, London, S.; by M[r] Bennet.

17 Charles Newton of S[t] Ann, Middx., B., and Sarah Wood of the same, S.; by M[r] Bennet.

23 Reuben Borer of S[t] Giles in the Fields, Middx., W., and Elianor Nicholls of S[t] Margaret, Westminster, Middx., W.

24 Andrew Bruce of S[t] James, Westminster, Middx., B., and Elizabeth Tellfer of the same, S.

27 Benjamin Allen of S[t] Paul, Shadwell, Middx., B., and Sarah Cush of the same, S.

30 Thomas Pindin of Farningham, Kent, B., and Mary Loynes of the same, S.

31 Henry Tom of S[t] Martin in the Fields, Middx., B., and Mary Scott of the same, W.

Nov. 1 George Keddey of S[t] James, Westminster, Middx., B., and Martha Barnes of the same, S.

1 George Colson Smith of the Hamlet of Poplar in Stepney, Middx., B., and Elizabeth Watlington of the same, S.

3 John Grant of S[t] Olave, Southwark, Surry, W., and Mary Willson of S[t] Botolph, Aldgate, London, S.

6 James Willson of S[t] Dunstan, Stepney, Middx., B., and Mary Arnold of S[t] Mary, Rotherhith, Surry, S.

14 Hanameel Rogers of Bromley, Middx., B., and Elizabeth Eaton of the same, S.

14 Thomas Garway Budgen of Hampstead, Middx., B., and Ann Ladyman of the same, S.

15 John Healey of S[t] Mary Magdalen, Bermondsey, Surry, W., and Hannah Fleming of S[t] Luke, Middx., W.

15 William Odber of S[t] Mary, Newington, Surry, B., and Ann Treadway of S[t] Saviour, Southwark, S.

19 George Wassell of Woolwich, Kent, B., and Elizabeth Smith of the same, S.

20 Nicholas Rich of Chatham, Kent, B., and Cordelia Alexander of the same, W.

21 Thomas Tapper of S[t] Clement Danes, Middx., B., and Elizabeth Venables of S[t] Ann, Black Fryars, London, S.

24 Samuel West of S[t] Mary Magdalen, Bermondsey, Surry, W., and Beater Kebal of the same, S.

10 [*sic*] James Reynolds of S[t] James, Clerkenwell, Middx., W., and Mary Berry of Finchley, Middx., W.; by M[r] Doughty.

Dec. 1 Ferdinando Clarke of S[t] Paul, Shadwell, Middx., W., and Elizabeth Turpin of the same, S.

1 Henry Wallis of Ducksford, co. Cambridge, W., and Alice Pettit of Great Shelford, co. Cambridge, W.

2 Prince Myles of S[t] Matthew, Bethnell Green, Middx., B., and Anne Parroissieu of the same, W.

3 Thomas Williams of All Hallows, London, B., and Jane Barnes of the same, W.

4 Thomas Stephens of S[t] Paul, Covent Garden, Middx., B., and Catherine Pye of S[t] Ann, Westminster, Middx., S.

6 William Hubbard of S[t] Saviour, Southwark, Surry, B., and Sarah Stubbs of the same, W.

6 James Currie of Barnes, Surry, B., and Hannah Burdit of the same, S.

7 Charles Cartwright of S[t] Andrew, Holborn, London, B., and Rebecca Logon of the same, W.

7 Thomas Jefferies of S[t] Mary Magdalen, Bermonsey, Surry, B., and Elizabeth Francis of S[t] John, Southwark, Surry, S.

1750

Dec. 10 Zachary Nelson of St John, Westminster, Middx., B., and Tobitha Kell of St Margaret, Westminster, Middx., S.

12 Nathaniel Lott of St Clement Danes, Middx., B., and Elizabeth White of Devizes, Wilts, S.

12 Nathaniel Eardley of Lambeth, Surry, B., and Susannah Sadler of the same, S.

15 Ferrers Nash of St Margaret, Westminster, Middx., W., and Charlotte Brice of the same, S.

18 The Rev. Stanhope Ellison of this parish, W., and Elizabeth Slemaker of Aldermanbury, London, S.; married by Dr Sanford, minister of Aldermanbury.

20 Joseph Holney of St Sepulchre, London, W., and Mary Ford of the same, W.

20 Henbury Freeman of St Giles, Cripplegate, London, B., and Elizabeth Stuck of the same, S.

25 John Steele of St Sepulchre, Middx., W., and Mary Sherer of the same, W.

29 George Griggs of Much Canvell, Essex, B., and Patience Hunnix of St Ann, Limehouse, Middx., W.

Jan. 1 John Twist of St Sepulchre, Middx., B., a minor, and Alice Edwards of St Luke, Middx., S.

5 John Salliar of St James, Westminster, Middx., Esq., and Martha Brame of St Paul, Covent Garden, Middx., S.

6 William Pain of St Andrew, Holborn, London, B., and Elizabeth Marshall of the same, S.

18 Richard Moore of St Michael Bassishaw, London, B., and Sarah Cotton of St Stephen, Coleman Street, London, S.

21 John Humpherys of St Saviour, Southwark, Surry, W., and Eleanor Ross of St Paul, Shadwell, W.

21 Thomas Griggs of St Lawrance Pountney, London, B., and Mary Budd of the same, W.

23 William Slade of St John near Winchester, Hants, B., and Hannah Pain of St Mary Calendar in the city of Winchester, S.

26 John Post of St John, Southwark, Surry, W., and Mary Cooke of St Mary, Lambeth, Surry, S.

29 Alexander Young of St Andrew, Holborn, Middx., W., and Sarah Bishop of the same, [*blank*].

30 Charles Bettenham of St James, Clerkenwell, Middx., B., and Elizabeth Parker of the same, S.

30 Charles Broadwater of Woolwich, Kent, B., and Ann Garner of the same, S.

31 Matthew Mitchell of St John, Southwark, Surry, W., and Mary Rawlings of St Peter le Poor, London, S.

Feb. 5 Morgan Rice of St Martin in the Fields, Middx., W., and Mary Perdue of the same, W.

6 Abraham Willis of St James, Westminster, Middx., B., and Mary Turner of St Botolph, Bishopsgate, London, S.

7 Edward Green of Walthamstow, Essex, B., and Emma Osborn of the same, S.

8 Michael Allanson of St Dunstan in the East, London, B., and Sarah Bland of the same, S.

9 John Crowder of St George, Bloomsbury, Middx., W., and Elizabeth Warden of the same, S.

11 James Waterman of Woodford, Essex, B., and Ann Bevan of the same, S.

12 Richard Spencer of Croydon, Surry, B., and Catherine John of the same, S.

1750-1

Feb. 13 John Jones of Ednum, co. Lincoln, B., and Mary Parker of the same, S.

14 Peter Cordwell of S[t] Leonard, Foster lane, London, B., and Elizabeth Cookson of S[t] Bartholomew the Less, London, S.

16 Richard Slaughter of S[t] James, Westminster, Middx., W., and Sarah Holloway of the same, S.

16 David Harris of S[t] Peter le Poor, London, B., and Ann Ford of Woodford, Essex, S.

17 Samuel Burch of S[t] James, Westminster, Middx., B., and Christian Germerod of S[t] Martin in the Fields, S.

17 James Clarkson of S[t] George, Hanover Square, Middx., B., and Sarah Singleton of S[t] Ann, Black Fryers, London, S.

18 John Townshend of Ockham, Surry, B., and Mary Mathews of Guildford, Surrey, S.

19 Joseph Stevens of S[t] Giles in Dorset, B., and Elianor Franklin of Gaisbrook in the City of York, S.

19 John Robson of Chelsea, Middx., B., and Elizabeth Percivall of the same, W.

19 John Laban of S[t] Magnus the Martyr, London, B., and Susannah Bradley of S[t] Olave, Southwark, Surry, W.

19 John White of S[t] Mary le Bone, Middx., B., and Anne Goodchild of the same, S.

19 Richard Graham of S[t] Giles in the Fields, Middx., W., and Susanna Westerman of S[t] Luke, Middx., S.

Mar. 1 John Leach of SS. Ann and Agnes, Aldersgate, London, [*blank*], and Mariah Pears of the same, S.

10 James Turner of S[t] Martin in the Fields, Middx., B., and Jane Campbell of the same, S.

10 George Walker of All Hallows Barking, London, B., and Elizabeth Armstrong of the same, S.

11 Thomas Sharpe of Chelsea, Middx., W., and Ann Firebrace of the same, S.

14 Adam Edgar of S[t] Margaret, Westminster, Middx., B., and Ann Kelleck of S[t] Andrew, Holborn, S.

14 Henry Marshall of Chelsea, Middx., W., and Grace Lowe of S[t] John Zachary, London, W.

18 John Hays of S[t] John, Southwark, Surry, B., and Elizabeth Judge of the same, S.

1751.

Mar. 28 William Newell of S[t] James, Clerkenwell, Middx., B., and Hephzibah Apletree of the same, S.; by M[r] Campbell.

31 John Wright of S[t] Lawrence, Jewry, London, W., and Sarah Brown of S[t] Martin in the Fields, W.

April 2 James Dickinson of S[t] Leonard, Shoreditch, Middx., B., and Susannah Crook of S[t] Giles, Cripplegate, London, S.

7 Joseph Cropley of S[t] Giles, Cripplegate, London, B., and Elizabeth Cole of the same, S.

8 Philip Crow of South Ockingdon, Essex, B., and Sarah Dennis of the same, W.

9 Jonathan Steward of S[t] Clement Danes, Middx., W., and Ann Chester of the same, W.

10 Thomas Harrison of S[t] Austins, London, B., and Ann Mitchell of the same, S.

13 Richard Pargeter of S[t] Olave, Silver Street, London, W., and Ann Barber of All Hallows the Less, London, W.

14 Theophilus Buckworth of Spalding, co. Lincoln, B., and Elizabeth Clay of Bourn, co. Lincoln, S.

1751

April 16 Edward Fothergill of S[t] Dunstan in the East, London, W., and Catherine Stibbs of the same, S.

17 Robert Haswell of Portsmouth, Hants, B., and Sibella Crossby of S[t] Clement Danes, Middx., S.

17 William Coates of S[t] John, Southwark, Surry, B., and Hannah Oram of the same, W.

18 Joseph Hawkins of S[t] Andrew, Holborn, London, B., and Mary Smith of the same, S.

20 John Baileys of Hampstead, Middx., B., and Mary Forrester of S[t] Andrew, Holborn, Middx., S.

22 John Smith of S[t] Mary Woolnorth, London, W., and Catherine Ayscough of S[t] Paul, Covent Garden, Middx., S.

29 Thomas Nightingale of S[t] Martin in the Fields, Middx., W., and Edith Jeffs of the same, S.

30 Edward Sullings of Barking, Essex, W., and Sarah Bayes of Low Layton, Essex, W.

30 William Daniels of Sawbridgeworth, co. Herts, W., and Mary Campin of the same, S.

May 1 William Wood of S[t] Dunstan, Stepney, Middx., B., and Jane Marriott of the same, S.

4 Ralph Harwell of S[t] Gregory, London, B., and Jemima Wyatt of the same, S.

5 Richard Williams of S[t] Olave, Southwark, Surry, B., and Ann Robinson of the same, S.

11 John Stone of S[t] Giles, Cripplegate, London, B., and Hannah Barnard of the same, S.

13 William Poulton of S[t] Andrew, Holborn, Middx., B., and Sarah Clayton of the same, S.

13 Thomas Bullock of S[t] James, Westminster, Middx., W., and Isabella Waving of S[t] Catherine Coleman, London, W.

18 John Hattersley of S[t] John, Hackney, Middx., B., and Sarah Garrington of the same, W.

18 Robert Cade of S[t] Clement Danes, Middx., B., and Ann Burrell of S[t] Andrew, Holborn, S.

18 William Vale of S[t] Paul, Covent Garden, Middx., B., and Elizabeth Wall of Preston, Lancashire, S.

19 John Browne of Saffron Walden, Essex, B., and Margaret Kelley of S[t] Swithin, London Stone, London, W.

20 John Setchwell, B., and Sarah Williams, both of this parish. Banns.

25 Martin Armstrong of S[t] Andrew, Holborn, London, B., and Ann Brown of the same, S.

25 John Rocque of S[t] Martin in the Fields, Middx., W., and Ann Bew of the same, W.

29 Daniel Pickance of S[t] Martin in the Fields, Middx., W., and Alice Nowell of the same, W.

30 Richard Richardson of New Brentford in Hanwell, Middx., B., and Elizabeth Percival of the same, W.

30 John Waite Wade of S[t] Dunstan, Stepney, Middx., W., and Elizabeth Rice of the same, S.

June 2 Cuthbert Softley of S[t] Giles in the Fields, Middx., W., and Carah Carter of the same, W.

2 Nathaniel Barrow of Christ Church, London, B., and Hannah Watson of the same, S.

5 James Bond of S[t] James, Westminster, Middx., B., and Jane Bullock of the same, W.

5 Lancelot Palmer of S[t] Mary, White Chappel, Middx., B., and Mary Martin of the same, S.

1751

June 6 Charles Friquet of Norton Folgate, Middx., B., and Mary Anne Merle of St Buttolph, Bishopsgate, London, S.

11 John Paradise of St Michael, Cornhill, London, B., and Maria Amory of St Mildred, Bread Street, London, S.

11 John Alsop of St Mary Magdalen, Milk Street, London, W., and Ann Randall of St Mary, Islington, Middx., W.

16 John Smith of St Giles in the Fields, Middx., B., and Mary Worrall of the same, S.

23 Thomas Love of Beckington, Somerset, B., and Frances Winwood of St Clement Danes, Middx., S.

25 Bernard Arnold of St George, Hanover Square, Middx., B., and Ann Hitchcock of Putney, Surry, S.

25 John Wilkins of St Mary, Islington, Middx., B., and Alice Dillo of Hornsey, Middx., S.

26 Robert French of St Paul, Covent Garden, Middx., B., and Elizabeth Hull of the same, S.

27 Benjamin Smith of Blechingley, Surry, B., and Sarah Clement of the same, W.

29 William Pickering, [*blank*], and Mary Smith, [*blank*], both of St Peter, Paul's Wharfe, London. Banns.

July 2 Samuel Harding of West Ham, Essex, B., and Ann Butts of the same, S.

5 Thomas Bookham of Chelsea, Middx., W., and Martha Basford of the same, S.

6 William Cubbidge of St Clement Danes, Middx., W., and Ann Lawson of the same, W.

14 Solomon Knaggs of St Paul, Shadwell, Middx., B., and Ann Hunt of St Saviour, Southwark, Surry, S.

20 William Blackwell of Cashalton, Surry, B., and Ann Griffiths of the same, S.

25 Adam Gladman of Studham, co. Herts, B., and Rebecca Niccoll of Studham, co. Bedford, S.

31 Robert Panling of Shaw, co. Berks, B., and Elizabeth Cooper of Newbury, co. Berks, S.

Aug. 1 Joseph Birch of Lavisham, Kent, W., and Susannah Cray of Greenwich, S.

4 Robert Edden, [*blank*], and Hannah Hawkins, [*blank*], both of this parish. Banns.

8 Stephen Underdown of St Peter in the Isle of Thanet, Kent, B., and Susannah Freeman of St John in the Isle of Thanet, Kent, S.

10 Thomas Winter of Battersea, Surry, B., and Mary Taaffe of the same, S.

15 William Gelpine of Stepney, Middx., B., and Sarah Goodwin of the same, S.

15 William Pearson of St Clement Danes, Middx., B., and Ann Walker of the same, W.

17 William Johnson of St Mary Somerset, London, B., and Susannah Tarver of the same, W.

18 James Sherwood of St Botolph, Lond., B., and Elizabeth Perry of the same, S.

22 George Wilkinson of St Swithin, London, B., and Anne Clark of St James, Westminster, Middx., S.

24 William Penlington of Kensington, Middx., B., and Jone Lowndes of the same, S.

24 Richard Walklin of Richmond, Surry, B., and Martha Herbert of the same, S.

25 John Todd of St Bartholomew the Great, London, B., and Ann Pollet of St Dunstan in the West, London, W.

1751

Aug. 25 Thomas Atkins of St Thomas, Southwark, Surry, B., and Phillis Hughes of the same, S.

26 Benjamin Munday of Clapham, Surry, B., and Elizabeth Davis of Tottenham, Middx., S.

26 Joseph Grigg of St Nicholas, Deptford, Kent, W., and Mary Simms of the same, S.

27 John Bishop of St Ann, Middx., B., and Joan Christopher of the same, S., a minor.

27 Henry Baratt of Kidlington, co. Oxford, W., and Frances Williams [of] Ivingo, co. Bucks, W.

28 William Hill of St Lawrence Poutney, London, B., and Mary Hillyear of St Andrew, Holborn, S.

29 John Glover of Sutten, Kent, B., and Elizabeth Cannum of the same, S.

31 Jeffry Dinsdale of Kensington, Middx., B., and Elizabeth Herly of the same, W.

Sept. 3 John Heardman of St Andrew, Holborn, London, B., and Rachael Swan of St Sepulchre, London, S.

10 William Saunders of Deptford, Kent, B., and Sarah Pretty of the same, W.

12 Thomas Stanley of St Margaret, Westminster, Middx., B., and Ruth Chalkley of the same, S.

12 William Godard of St Mary, Rotherhithe, Surry, W., and Hannah Belitha of the same, S.

17 Arthur Baynes of St Andrew, Holborn, Middx., B., and Judith Lambert of Chelsea, Middx., S.

19 Paul Townsend of St Mary Magdalen, Bermondsey, Surry, B., and Fortune Brown of St Clement Danes, Middx., W.

19 William Peckham of St Giles without Cripplegate, London, B., and Jane Penney of Reading, co. Berks, S.

22 Robert Mabb of Mountnessing, Essex, B., and Susannah Hawys of Great Buckstead, Essex, S.

22 William Wackett of St Thomas, Southwark, Surry, B., and Arabella Harvey of St Margaret, Lothbury, London, S.

*26 John Leapidge of St Margaret, Lothbury, London, B., and Sophia Christiana Maples of St George, Middx., S.; by Mr Audley.

*26 Robert Cornwell of South Okendon, Essex, B., and Ruth Clark of the same, S.

29 John Godard of Christ Church, Middx., B., and Susannah Lepine of St Matthew, Bethnall Green, Middx., S.

Oct. 5 Peter Michell of St Mary, White Chapel, Middx., B., and Elizabeth Bebb of the same, S.

5 Edmund Parker of St George, Hanover Square, Middx., W., and Jane Walker of the same, S.

7 Thomas Richards of All Saints, Hants, B., and Rachel Brawer of the same, S.

8 Edward Peate of Ealing, Middx., B., and Phillis Hickson of St George the Martyr, Middx., S.

10 Francis Musgrave of St Margaret, Westminster, Middx., B., and Ann Lunn of the same, S.

10 Edmund Critchett of West Ham, Essex, B., and Sarah Henriks of the same, S.

10 George Calbreath of St Dunstan, Stepney, Middx., B., and Martha Hurst of Lambeth, Surrey, S.

13 Thomas Preston of St James, Westminster, Middx., B., and Fanny Musgrove of St Paul, Covent Garden, Middx., S.

13 Francies Heath of St Paul, Covent Garden, Middx., B., and Ann Ward of St Andrew, Holborn, London, W.

* Date altered from 27th to 26th.—Ed.

1751
Oct. 13 James Dempey of S[t] Andrew, Holborn, Middx., W., and Elizabeth Harvey of Christ Church, London, S.
17 Joseph Buckett of S[t] Mary Magdalen, Bermondsey, Surry, B., and Elizabeth Alexander of the same, S.
19 William Wray of S[t] Paul, Covent Garden, Middx., B., and Susannah Nelson of the same, S.
19 John Knight, B., and Margret Saunders, S., both of S[t] Peter's parish, London. Banns.
19 Thomas Paulin of S[t] James in the city of Bath, Somerset, B., and Elizabeth Vere of S[t] Peter and Paul in the same city, S.
26 Thomas Bagshaw of Lambeth, Surry, W., and Mary Coleman of the same, S.
31 James Kingman of S[t] Faith, London, B., and Leah James of S[t] Olave, Hart Street, London, S.
Nov. 4 Samuel Medley of S[t] Andrew, Holbourn, Middx., B., and Sarah Pooler of the same, S.
5 William Page of S[t] Clement Danes, Middx., B., and Elizabeth Knott of S[t] Mary at Reading, co. Berks, S.
9 Peter Tabois of S[t] Giles in the Fields, Middx., B., and Mary Wooldridge of S[t] Lawrence, Jewry, London, S.
11 James Cannum of Sutton at Hare [*sic*], Kent, W., and Mary Bateman of Stone, Kent, W.
12 John Raines of Eaton, co. Bucks, B., and Jane Bradford of Hayes, Middx., S.
14 John Harrison of S[t] Ann, Blackfryers, London, W., and Mary Cutler of the same, W.
18 William Bell of S[t] John, Southwark, Surry, W., and Elizabeth Newell of the same, W.
20 James Sands of S[t] John, Southwark, Surry, B., and Anne Johnson of the same, S.
21 John Harrison of S[t] Bartholomew the Great, London, B., and Mary Roalfe of the same, S.
21 Samuel Willott of Rusden, co. Northampton, clerk, B., and Elizabeth Newbon of S[t] George, Hanover Square, Middx., S.
26 Edward Bradley of S[t] Hellen, London, B., and Mary Bryant of S[t] Lawrence, Jewry, London, S.
Dec. 2 John Dillingham of S[t] Andrew, Holborn, Middx., B., and Jane Watson of the same, S.
3 James Sisson of S[t] Andrew, Middx., B., and Elizabeth Bricheno of Papworth, co. Hunts, S.
5 Charles Hooton of S[t] Sepulchre, London, B., and Mary Stafford of S[t] Paul, Covent Garden, Middx., S.
7 Richard Millward of S[t] Clement Danes, Middx., B., and Elizabeth Woodin of S[t] James, Westminster, Middx., S.; by M[r] Pugh.
8 William Wood of S[t] Bride's, London, B., and Mary Greathead of the same, S.; by M[r] Pugh.
8 Peter Sufflee of S[t] Dunstan, Stepney, Middx., B., and Elizabeth Jourdain of S[t] Botolph, Bishopsgate, London, W.; by M[r] Pugh.
8 James Holt of S[t] Mary, Abchurch, London, B., and Hannah Coates of the same, S.
10 Martin Mocho of S[t] Giles in the Fields, Middx., B., and Elizabeth Chesterfield of S[t] Martin in the Fields, S.; by M[r] Allen.
20 Michael Bell of S[t] Nicholas, Deptford, Kent, B., and Elizabeth Porter of the same, S.; by M[r] Pugh.
22 John Gregory of S[t] Matthew, Bethnal Green, Middx., B., and Elizabeth Bibben of the same, S.; by M[r] Ely.
24 Joseph Taylor of Hammarsmith, Middx., B., and Elizabeth Bond of the same, S.; by M[r] Pugh.

1751

Dec. 26 James Hassell of Eynsford, Kent, B., and Mary Hayward of the same, S.; by M[r] Pugh.

26 John Grove of S[t] Andrew, Holborn, Middx., B., and Alice Mucklow of the same, W.; by M[r] Ely.

1752.

Jan. 1 Edward Bartles of S[t] Clement Danes, Middx., B., and Eleanor Humphreys of S[t] Saviour, Southwark, Surry, W.

1 John Sennitt of S[t] Bennett in Cambridge, B., and Susannah Nicholson of S[t] Botolph in that county, S.

2 Thomas Gibbon Boykett of Dover, Kent, B., and Jane Fletchar of S[t] Paul, Covent Garden, Middx., S.

4 John Burnett of Wandsworth, Surry, W., and Elizabeth Collier of Greenwich, Kent, S.

5 Martin Carr of S[t] Botolph, Aldersgate, London, B., and Elizabeth Costen of S[t] Antholin's, London, S.

6 James Nind of S[t] Ann, Westminster, Middx., B., and Elizabeth Lakin of S[t] George the Martyr, Middx., S.

9 John Hosier of S[t] Mary, Rotherhith, Surry, B., and Anne Gillam of the same, S.; by M[r] Negus.

15 James Button of Chuckfield, Sussex, B., and Elizabeth Guillman of the same, S.

16 Joseph Smith of S[t] Mary, Lambeth, Surry, B., and Elizabeth Wilson of Greenwich, Kent, S.

19 George Gibson of S[t] Mary Woolnoth, London, B., and Joyce Higgins of S[t] Bartholomew behind the Royal Exchange, London, S.

19 William Bithell of All Hallows the Great, London, B., and Mary Kirby of S[t] Mary Magdalen, Old Fish Street, London, S.

23 Joseph Butcher of S[t] Leonard, Shoreditch, Middx., W., and Jane Hayward of Deptford, Kent, S.

27 Samuel Door of S[t] Peter in Malden, Essex, B., and Sarah Goodman of S[t] Mary at Hill, London, S.

28 William Thomas of Woolwich, Kent, B., and Mary Woodman of Portsmouth, Hants, S.

29 Thomas Sheppard of S[t] Albans, co. Herts, B., and Sarah Nicholls of Hendon, Middx., S.

29 Luke Budworth of South Mimms, Middx., W., and Mary Knight of Edmonton, Middx., S.

Feb. 2 John Murgatroyd of S[t] Dionis Backchurch, London, B., and Anne Smith of All Hallows, Lombard Street, London, S.

2 Joseph Stephens of S[t] Clement Danes, Middx., B., and Mary James of the same, S.

2 Josiah Howard of S[t] Mary le Bow, London, B., and Mary Bone of All Hallows on the Wall, London, W.

4 Roger Beck of Camberwell, Surry, W., and Katharine Hudson of the same, S.

8 Thomas James of S[t] Mary, Lambeth, Surry, W., and Ann James of the same, W.

9 Mark Stafford of Kelvedon, Essex, B., and Rebecca Storr of S[t] John, Southwark, Surry, W.

9 George Reid of S[t] Dunstan in the West, London, W., and Sarah Frier of Chelsea, Middx., S.

9 Robert Wheeler of S[t] John, Westminster, Middx., B., and Mary Atkins of the same, W.

9 James Waggett of S[t] Martin Ongar, London, B., and Hester Skey of S[t] Bennet Shear Hog, London, S.

1752

Feb. 9 Richard Foster of St George, Southwark, Surry, B., and Ann Cox of the same, S.

11 John Hunter of Liverpoole, Lancashire, B., and Jane Hayes of St Ann, Middx., S.

15 Samuel Baxter of St Mary, White Chappell, Middx., W., and Hannah Moulton of the same, S.

17 Anthony Kitching of St Leonard, Shoreditch, Middx., W., and Alice Fairland of Ware, co. Herts, W.

25 John Rogers of St James, Westminster, Middx., B., and Mary Cox of St John, Hackney, Middx., S.

Mar. 1 William Hall of St Paul, Covent Garden, Middx., W., and Ann Colegrave of St George, Queen Square, S.

1 George Bowser of Greenwich, Kent, B., and Elizabeth Parkinson of St Luke, Middx., S.

5 Thomas Perkins of St Clement Danes, Middx., B., and Elizabeth Cropp of Old Ford, Middx., S.

10 John Millin of St Saviour, Southwark, Surry, W., and Mary Hollowell of the same, W.

15 James Holt of St Mary, Rotherhith, Surry, W., and Elizabeth Wheatley of the same, W.

17 Thomas Nicholson of St Mary, Rotherhith, Surry, W., and Joyce Floyd of the same, S.

30 William Mertins of Richmond, Surry, B., and Mary Barnes of the same, S.

31 John Bond of St Stephen, Coleman Street, London, W., and Alice Burnham of the same, W.

April 2 Abraham Bence of the Old Artillery Ground within the Liberty of the Tower of London, W., and Susannah Loste of All Hallows, Bread Street, London, S.

3 John Clark of Hounslow, Middx., B., and Ann Messiter of the same, S.

5 Joseph Palmer of Christ Church, Surry, B., and Ann Margett of Battersea, Surry, S.

7 Charles Blanch of St John, Southwark, Surry, W., and Elizabeth Hinket of the same, S.

10 William Henry Hamill of All Hallows, Bread Street, London, B., and Elizabeth Reynolds of the same, S.

16 John Barns of Tottenham High Cross, Middx., B., and Martha Wicksted of the same, S.

23 Thomas Skerrett of St Paul, Covent Garden, Middx., B., and Margaret Penlington of Kensington, Middx., S.

23 Christopher Buckle of Chelsea, Middx., W., and Barbara Maude of St Bride's, London, S.

26 Samuel Stephens of St Botolph, Algate, London, B., and Mary Hopkins of St Martin Vintry, London, S.

26 John Berry of St Lawrence, Old Jewry, London, B., and Elizabeth Collier of St Leonard, Shoreditch, Middx., S.

May 10 Nathaniel Thorley of St Mildred in the Poultrey, London, W., and Hannah Knowles of the same, S.

13 John Morgan of Wandsworth, Surry, B., and Elizabeth Ramsay of the same, [*blank*].

14 William Richardson of Staines, Middx., B., and Elizabeth Love of the same, W.

16 George Long of St Ann, Westminster, Middx., W., and Hester Prudom of the same, S.

19 John Norton of Hunton, Kent, B., and Elizabeth Tanner of the same, S.

23 John Barber of St Matthew, Bethnal Green, Middx., W., and Mary Foo of the same, S.

1752

May 29 John Sedding of St Gabriel, Fenchurch, London, B., and Ann Harmsworth of Alverstoke, Hants, S.

June 2 Andrew Viner of St Andrew, Holborn, London, B., and Ann Stacey of the same, S.

7 Morgan James, [*blank*], and Sarah Corke, [*blank*], both of this parish. Banns.

8 Henry Hall, B., and Sarah Hester, S., both of this parish. Banns.

9 Joseph Field of St Sepulchre, London, B., and Margaret Simkins of the same, S.

10 Edward Degrare of St Ann, Westminster, Middx., B., and Hannah Hawton of the same, S.

14 Cornelius Neep of St James, Westminster, Middx., B., and Sarah Ingham of the same, S.

16 Andrew Reed of St Martin in the Fields, Middx., B., and Mary Lithgow of St Bridget alias St Brides, London, S.

20 Richard Stanes of Rickmansworth, co. Herts, B., and Elizabeth Alden of the same, S.

21 Isaac Palmer of St Alphage, London, B., and Catherine Osborn of St Botolph, Aldersgate, London, S.

22 Edward Nicholas of Rowndway in Bishops Canning, Wilts, Esqre, B., and Jenny Neate of the Devizes in Wilts, S.

25 William Bettsworth of St Saviour, Southwark, Surry, W., and Mary Ball of the same, W.

29 William Meredith of St Mary le Strand, Middx., W., and Susannah Grenous of St Andrew, Holborn, Middx , S.

30 Thomas Deasley of West Ham, Essex, B., and Thomasin Cracknall of the same, S.

July 9 William Gordon of St Brides, London, W., and Elizabeth Robinson of St Andrew, Holborn, London, W.

13 Thomas Pagget of All Hallows the Less, London, B., and Ann Laylow of this parish, W.

18 Thomas Lumley of St George, Hanover Square, Middx., B., and Elizabeth Darlow of the same, S.

21 George Tickner of Kingston upon Thames, Surry, B., and Ann Jefferys of the same, W.

23 Jonathan Dunn of Christ Church, Middx., B., and Sarah Kerly of St Mary, Lambeth, Surry, S.

31 Thomas Bradshaw of All Hallows the Great, London, W., and Sarah Bassil of Hatfield, co. Herts, S.

Aug. 1 John Cullinfor of St James, Westminster, Middx., B., and Sarah Wood of the same, S.

2 Thomas Wartham of St Dunstan, Stepney, Middx., B., and Martha Stone of the same, S.

3 John Gregory, Junr, of St Andrew, Holborn, Middx., W., and Mary Walton of the same, S.

4 John Collen, B., and Ann Williams, S., both of this parish. Banns.

6 Samuel Hill of St Mary le Bone, Middx., W., and Ann Morton of St George, Bloomsbury, Middx., W.

7 Thomas Toone of St Olave, Southwark, Surry, B., and Mary Dyer of St Mary Magdalen, Bermondsey, Surry, S.

16 John Willis of St Clement Danes, Middx., B., and Mary Hoare of the same, S.

22 Haddon Hopkins of St Saviour, Southwark, Surry, W., and Mary Hoare of the same, S.

23 Robert Matthews of St James, Clerkenwell, Middx., B., and Catherine Gardner of the same, S.

1752

Aug. 25 Anthony Beech of Uffington, co. Lincoln, B., and Esther Wigmore of S[t] George the Martyr, Middx., S.

28 William Jelfe of S[t] Margaret, Westminster, Middx., B., and Mary Hodgkinson of S[t] Bridget alias S[t] Brides, London, S.

29 George Clempson of S[t] Nicholas, Deptford, Kent, W., and Frances Timberlake of S[t] Martin in the Fields, Middx., S.

30 John Steele of S[t] Sepulchre, Middx., W., and Susannah Jones of S[t] Andrew, Holborn, Middx., [*blank*].

30 John Dilley of S[t] Martin in the Fields, Middx., W., and Margaret Page of S[t] James, Westminster, Middx., W.

Sept. 14 George Smith of S[t] Margaret, Westminster, Middx., B., and Elizabeth Paul of S[t] John the Evangelist, Middx., S.

16 Charles Chambers of the Inner Temple, London, B., and Rachel Yeates of S[t] Martin in the Fields, Middx., S.

16 William Jackson of Lambeth, Surry, B., and Elizabeth Applebee of this parish, S.

17 Francis Williams of S[t] Mary, White Chappel, Middx., B., and Lydia Munday of S[t] Giles in the Fields, Middx., S.

21 John Lemaistre of the Liberty of the Artillery Ground, Middx., B., and Henrietta Ponterdant of Christ Church, Middx., S.

21 Joseph Ancott of S[t] Sepulchre, London, B., and Catherine Haynes of S[t] James, Clerkenwell, Middx., S., a minor.

21 Benjamin Andertan or Anderton of S[t] James, Clerkenwell, Middx., B., and Elizabeth Faithfull of S[t] Botolph, Aldgate, London, S.

23 Richard Clarke of South Ockenden, Essex, B., and Elizabeth Robinson of East Ham, Essex, S., a minor.

30 John Day of S[t] Giles in the Fields, Middx., W., and Johanna Longbotham of S[t] Andrew, Holborn, Middx., W.

Oct. 3 John Edwards of S[t] Luke, Middx., B., and Catherine Stowards of S[t] Thomas the Apostle, London, S.

3 Alexander Mackenzie of S[t] Leonard, Shoreditch, Middx., W., and Mary Morris of S[t] John, Hackney, Middx., W.

6 William Breach of S[t] Olave, Southwark, Surry, B., and Mary Edmeston of S[t] Margaret, Westminster, Middx., S., a minor.

9 Henry Whitefoot of Barking, Essex, W., and Elizabeth Wicks of S[t] Sepulchre, London, W.

12 Robert Ball of S[t] Mary, Rotherhith, Surry, W., and Mary Gillet of the same, W.

12 Redburn Tomkins of S[t] Mary, White Chappel, Middx., B., and Rebecca Humfreys of S[t] Mary, Newington, Surry, S.

16 William Norton of Sevenoakes, Kent, W., and Mary Loft of Farningham, Kent, S.

19 Charles Payn of Clapham, Surry, B., and Mary Shipley of the same, S.

24 John Stafford of Camberwell, Surry, B., and Susannah Clifford of Leigh, Essex, S.

26 Henry Hancock of S[t] Nicholas, Deptford, Kent, W., and Margaret Eisdon of S[t] Mary Magdalen, Bermondsey, in said County [*sic*], S.

26 Robert Long of S[t] Mary Magdalen, Bermondsey, Surry, B., and Ann Harwood of the same, S.

31 Thomas Heather of Great Marlow, co. Bucks, B., and Elizabeth Burton of Hammersmith, Middx., S., a minor.

Nov. 2 John Shaw of the city of Hereford, B., and Mary Bassel of Tillington, Sussex, S.

2 John Ward of S[t] Alban, Wood Street, London, B., and Elizabeth Kemp of S[t] Martin Vintry, London, S.

8 Richard Mayfield of Feny Stanton, co. Hunts, B., and Sarah Cooke of Hoddesdon, co. Herts, S.

1752

Nov. 8 Thomas Davies of Taunton, Somerset, B., and Mary Bryan of St Ann, Westminster, Middx., S.

11 David Whilton of St James, Westminster, Middx., B., and Elizabeth Hart of St George, Hanover Square, Middx., S.

12 Daniel Mason of St Ann, Westminster, Middx., W., and Sarah Taylor of Kensington, Middx., S.

13 Richard Martin of St Margaret, Westminster, Middx., B., and Sarah Sidney Evans of the same, S.

13 John Collison of Marden, Kent, B., and Sarah Norton of the same, S.

16 John Lewis of St Lawrence Jewry, London, B., and Rose Edwards of St Luke, Middx., S.

21 Richard Carr of St Gregory, London, W., and Susannah Jucks of St Botolph, Aldersgate, London, W.

23 Henry Street of St Catherine Cree church, London, B., and Martha Crudge of Barking, Essex, S.

25 James Green of St James, Clerkenwell, Middx., B., and Elizabeth Tyler of the same, S.

26 Thomas Parker of St Lawrence, Jewry, London, B., and Elizabeth Mould of St Sepulchre, Middx., S.

27 John Stone of St Mary, White Chappel, Middx., W., and Martha Crompton of All Hallows Barking, London, W.

28 Nathaniel Gray of St Botolph, Aldersgate, London, W., and Elizabeth Thornton of St Giles, Cripplegate, London, W.

30 Francis Baker of Blakemoor, Essex, B., and Sarah Ramsey of the same, S.

Dec. 3 Cuthbert Lowden of St Luke, Middx., B., and Ann Halloway of the same, W.

4 Daniel Gibbins of St Nicholas, Deptford, Kent, B., and Ann Cottrill of the same, S.

6 The Rev. Samuel Goodinge of Newdigate, Surry, W., and Elizabeth Boote of St Mary, White Chappel, Middx., S.

22 William Levett of North Fleet, Kent, B., and Mary Whiskin of the same, S.

23 Robert Stiell of St Martin in the Fields, Middx., B., and Elizabeth Middleton of the same, W.

24 Samuel Rutter of St James, Clerkenwell, Middx., B., and Anne Belson of the same, [*blank*].

27 John Emblen of St Botolph, Aldersgate, London, W., and Jane Randall of St Mary, *Aldermanbury*, *London*, W.

28 Joseph Hart of St Dunstan in the West, London, W., and Mary Lamb of the same, S.

28 Thomas Hawkins of St Martin, Ironmonger Lane, London, B., and Lener Lea of the same, S.

31 Samuel Collyer of St Bennet Fink, London, B., and Susanna Streames of the same, S.

31 Peter Cornud of St Peter Le Poor, London, B., and Sarah Oughton of St Botolph, Bishopsgate, London, S.

1753.

Jan. 1 Charles Gibbs of the Liberty of the Tower Royal, London, B., and Elizabeth Nevill of St Clement Danes, Middx., S.

8 George Gillie of Fryern Barnett, Middx., B., and Ann Skipper of the same, S.

12 Thomas Chown of Richmond, Surry, B., and Elizabeth Skiggs of the same, S.

1753

Jan. 13 Edward Cole of St Luke, Middx., B., and Sarah Lee of St James, Clerkenwell, Middx., S.

14 Thomas Rimmer of Christ Church, Southwark, Surry, W., and Lucy Porringer of St Mary, Lambeth, Surry, S.

17 James Gardner of Queenborough, Kent, B., and Ann Langrum of the same, S.

18 John Tapson of Barking, Essex, B., and Jane Cox of the same, S.

27 William Bennett of St Martin in the Fields, Middx., W., and Jane Prosser of Chelsea, Middx., S.

Feb. 1 Daniel Jones of St Giles, Cripplegate, London, B., and Rebecca Andrews of the same, S.

5 John Coke of St Bride's, London, B., and Edith Hodgson of St Bartholomew the Less, London, S.

12 Edward Gibbons of Uxbridge, Middx., B., and Bethiah Collier of the same, S.

12 Robert Bennett of St Botolph, Aldgate, London, B., and Catherine Purkess of the same, S.

18 Robert Adamson of St George, Middx., B., and Ann Pittullo of the same, W.

21 William Staines of St George, Middx., W., and Sarah Ash of the same, S.

22 John Passo of St Martin, Ludgate, London, B., and Jane Baker of St Clement Danes, Middx., S.

22 Matthew Byrne of St Mary Bow near Stratford, Middx., W., and Jane Kent of the same, W.

24 William Foster of St Botolph, Aldersgate, London, B., and Sarah Remington of the same, S., a minor.

25 Lewis Miraut of St Martin in the Fields, Middx., B., and Jane Martin of the same, W.

27 John Balthasar Knecht of St Ann, Westminster, Middx., B., and Isabella Jolly of St Mary, White Chapel, Middx., S.

27 John Martin of St Martin in the Fields, Middx., B., and Mary Moore of the same, S.

Mar. 3 Thomas Bunn of St Vedast als. Foster lane, London, B., and Mary Thurston of St Mary Mounthaw, London, S.

5 John Jee of St Peter Le Poor, London, B., and Elizabeth Stoddart of the same, S.

6 John Dupree of St Mary Le Bone, Middx., B., and Ann Reynolds of the same, W.

6 Richard Tull of St John, Westminster, Middx., W., and Joyce Swanton of the same, W.

7 Joseph Webb of Christ Church, Middx., B., and Ann Patrick of St Matthew, Bethnal Green, Middx., S.

14 Charles Burrows of St John the Evangelist, Westminster, Middx., B., and Abigale Cager of the same, W.

20 William Hughes of Chelmsford, Essex, W., and Jane Branch of All Hallows the Great, London, S.

April 19 Thomas Edwards of St Antholin, London, B., and Susannah Wheely of the same, S.

21 Timothy Brent of St James, Westminster, Middx., B., and Hannah Howard of St Dunstan in the West, London, S.

22 Tristram Vinton of St George, Bloomsbury, Middx., W., and Mary Tayler of the same, S.

26 Alexander Nelson of St Antholin, London, B., and Mary Dighton of the same, W.

26 Henry Cook of Battersea, Surry, B., and Sarah Fulker of Putney, Surry, S.

1753

April 26 John Howdell of Detling, Kent, clerk, B., and Patience Rugg of the same, S.

26 Henry Bedford of S[t] Martin in the Fields, Middx., B., and Mary Field of the same, S.

May 6 Nicholas Mackelcan of S[t] Martin Vintry, London, B., and Ann Vanderclusе of St Matthew, Bethnal Green, Middx., S.

6 Thomas Sparepoint of St Mary, White Chapel, Middx., B., and Deborah Rawlings of the same, W.

10 Thomas Powlter of Godalming, Surry, W., and Ann Harvey of St Andrew, Holborn, London, W.

10 John Morgan of Endfield, Middx., B., and Cælia Walters of the same, S.

11 Thomas Shipton of St James, Westminster, Middx., B., and Sarah Crump of St Giles in the Fields, Middx., S.

21 Samuel Watts of St James, Clerkenwell, Middx., B., and Ann Threlkield of St Michael, Wood Street, London, S.

25 David Russell of Richmond, Surry, B., and Mary Field of Weighbridge, Surrey, S.

29 John Biggs of Paddington, Middx., B., and Elizabeth Burt of Kensington, Middx., S.

30 John Weekes of S[t] Mary, Islington, Middx., W., and Margaret Eels of the same, S.

June 2 William Ride of S[t] Margaret, Westminster, Middx., B., and Catherine Blinckhorn of S[t] James, Westminster, Middx., S.

8 Thomas Naylor of Guildhall, London, B., and Margaret North of S[t] Martin Outwich, London, S.

9 Peter Foucault of Lambeth, Surry, W., and Mary Sabatier of S[t] Ann, Westminster, Middx., S.

12 Benjamin Franklin of S[t] Mary, Islington, Middx., B., and Margaret Figgins of the same, S.

12 James Coperthwaite of S[t] Martin in the Fields, Middx., W., and Hannah Spendelow of the same, W.

14 Richard Roffey of Coulsdon, Surry, B., and Patience Hassell of the same, S.

20 William Severy of Chatham, Kent, W., and Mary Dummer of the same, W.; by M[r] Hugill.

21 Samuel Cook of S[t] Sepulchre, Middx., W., and Mary Rudgley of Potton, co. Bedford, W.

26 Henry Webb of Fulham, Middx., B., and Amy Streatley of the same, S.

28 Robert Willard of Sutton, Surry, W., and Mary Preistley of Tootting, Surry, W.

July 1 John Taylor of S[t] Dunstan, Stepney, Middx., B., and Rachael Simes of S[t] Paul, Covent Garden, Middx., S.

4 John Austin of S[t] Mary, Lambeth, Surry, B., and Mary Wise of the same, S., a minor.

7 Abraham Hebert of the Tower Hamlet in S[t] Matthew, Bethnal Green, Middx., B., and Mary Delaferte of S[t] Matthew, Bethnal Green, Middx., S.

8 James Pugh of S[t] Nicholas, Deptford, Kent, B., and Hester Tryer of the same, S.

11 Matthias Neale of S[t] Austin, London, W., and Elizabeth Tranter of S[t] Andrew, Holborn, London, S.; by M[r] Keighly.

15 Thomas Richards of S[t] Paul, Covent Garden, Middx., B., and Ann Ellwood of the same, S.; by M[r] Buckby.

17 James Perkin of S[t] George, Hanover Square, Middx., B., and Elizabeth Rathburn of the same, S.

21 Robert Houlton of S[t] Mary, Rotherhith, Surry, B., and Mary Ann Barnard of the same, S.

1753

July 25 David Thomson of S[t] Martin in the Fields, Middx., B., and Henrietta Forman of S[t] Margaret, Westminster, Middx., S.

26 Thomas Boon of S[t] Dionis Backchurch, London, B., and Rebecca Baxter of the same, S.

30 John Hutchinson of S[t] George, Hanover Square, Middx., B., and Sarah Bradley of the same, S.

30 James White of S[t] Mary Magdalen, Bermondsey, Surry, B., and Elizabeth Nicholls of the same, S.

Aug. 1 Moses Wingrove of Christ Church, London, B., and Ann Sandell of the same, S.

2 Joseph Pallett of the Precinct of S[t] Catherine near the Tower of London, B., and Mary South of the same, W.

2 Henry Burrows of Speldhurst, Kent, B., and Judith Carden of Penshurst, Kent, W.

4 John Hay of S[t] Andrew, Holborn, Middx., W., and Mary Jackson of the same, S.

5 Joseph Thropp of S[t] Paul's, Deptford, Kent, B., and Mary Prockter of the same, S.

8 James Mann of S[t] Paul, Covent Garden, Middx., B., and Sarah Calvert of the same, S.

9 William Stokes of S[t] George, Bloomsbury, Middx., B., and Johanna Munden of the same, S.

10 Robert Francis of S[t] Martin in the Fields, Middx., B., and Anne Sherlock of S[t] Paul, Covent Garden, Middx., S.

14 Thomas Jemmitt of Chelsea, Middx., W., and Rebecca Carter of Eltham, Kent, S.; by M[r] Cronkshaw.

20 John Maryat of S[t] James, Westminster, Middx., W., and Joanna Ring of the same, S.

21 Thomas Duffield of S[t] George, Bloomsbury, Middx., B., and Ann Pember of the same, S.

21 Joseph Welch of Christ Church, Surry, B., and Elizabeth Lacey of the same, S.

23 Henry Atkins of Tooting Graveney, Surry, B., and Elizabeth Sheldon of Mitcham, Surry, S.; by M[r] Cronkshaw.

23 Hymners Taylor of S[t] James, Westminster, Middx., B., and Amelia Ludbey of the same, S.; by M[r] Cronkshaw.

26 John Burton of S[t] Matthew, Friday Street, London, B., and Elizabeth Jull of S[t] Mildred, Bread Street, London, S.

28 Joseph Willcockson of S[t] Luke, Middx., B., and Anne Gillebrand of S[t] Mary Abchurch, London, S.

30 Thomas Burroughs of S[t] Nicholas, Deptford, Middx., B., and Saince Webster of Eltham, Middx., S.

Sept. 2 John Callow of S[t] James, Westminster, Middx., B., and Elizabeth Evans of the same, S.

5 Gabriel Mathias of S[t] Paul, Covent Garden, Middx., B., and Elizabeth Griffin of S[t] Martin in the Fields, Middx., S.

16 Alexander Parker of S[t] Giles in the Fields, Middx., B., and Mary Pryar of Woodford, Essex, S.

16 Edward Abraham of this parish, B., and Martha Dearmor of S[t] Dionis Backchurch, London, S.

20 Seth Nelson of S[t] Paul, Covent Garden, Middx., B., and Anna Riding of Ramsden, Essex, W.; by M[r] Nelson.

22 John Dykes, W., and Mary Mathews, W., both of this parish. Banns.

23 John Fair of S[t] Mary Le Strand, Middx., B., and Mary Lilly of the same, S.

24 Samuel Days of S[t] George the Martyr, Middx., W., and Mary Ann Williams of the same, S.

1753

Sept. 25 Robert Morty of S[t] Sepulchre, London, W., and Ann Nicholas of Bow alias Stratford Bow, Middx., S.

Oct. 9 William Bell of Braintree, Essex, B., and Mary Prime of S[t] Botolph, Bishopsgate, London, S.

9 The Right Honourable George Bentinck, commonly called Lord George Bentinck, of the Parish of S[t] Ann, Westminster, Middlesex, Esquire, a Batchelor, and Mary Davies of the parish of Hanwell in the same County, Spinster.

11 Thomas Smith of S[t] Botolph, Bishopsgate, Middx., W., and Sarah Bird of the same, W.

18 William Mascall of S[t] Catherine Cree Church, London, B., and Mary Kilbye Anderson of S[t] Mary, White Chapel, Middx., S.

20 William Runting of S[t] Margaret, Westminster, Middx., B., and Mary Percivall of the same, S.

25 Robert Freeman of S[t] Botolph, Aldgate, London, B., and Mary Wright of the same, W.

31 John Winter of St John, Clerkenwell, Middx., B., and Ann Merriman of the same, S.

Nov. 4 William Smithson of St Botolph, Aldgate, London, B., and Mary Wells of the same, S.

9 Thomas Munns of Christ Church, Surry, B., and Elizabeth Norcutt of St George, Middx., S.

10 Cæsar Hughes of the Temple, London, W., and Elizabeth Houlton of Blockley, co. Worcester, S.

13 William Wells of Cobham, Kent, W., and Mary Pemble of the same, S.

18 Edward Green of All Hallows Barking, London, B., and Elizabeth Browning of the same, W.

18 Edward Mara of St Luke, Middx., B., and Hannah Bradish of S[t] Bride, London, S., a minor; by M[r] John Mara, A.B.

24 Samuel Hodges of S[t] George, Hanover Square, Middx., B., and Katherine Greene of the same, S.

26 James Alexander Doig of S[t] James, Westminster, Middx., B., and Joan Nell of S[t] John, Wapping, Middx., S.

27 John Bingley of S[t] Mary Magdalen, Bermondsey, Surry, B., and Dorothy Smith of S[t] Mary, Rotherhith, Surry, S., a minor.

27 William Griffies of S[t] Margaret, Westminster, Middx., W., and Sarah Delany of S[t] Ann, Westminster, Middx., S.

29 Joseph Staines of S[t] Catherine Cree Church, London, B., and Elizabeth Harker of the same, S.; by M[r] Nowell.

30 John Harrington of S[t] Andrew, Holborn, Middx., B., and Mary Gray of the same, S.

Dec. 1 William Hassall of S[t] Mary, White Chapel, Middx., W., and Elizabeth Franke of S[t] George, Middx., W.

3 Josias Pattenson of Ashford, Kent, B., and Elizabeth Dyne of the same, S.

5 Robert Sturt of S[t] George, Hanover Square, Middx., B., and Judith Witherell of S[t] Andrew, Holborn, Middx., S.

8 Thomas Peters of S[t] George the Martyr, Middx., W., and Catherine Poole of S[t] Bridget alias Brides, London, S.

8 Richard Holmes of S[t] Giles, Cripplegate, London, W., and Mary White of S[t] Gregory, London, S.; by M[r] Pinkney.

18 Francis Hayes of S[t] Giles, Cripplegate, London, B., and Mary Bullingham of S[t] Olave, Southwark, Surry, S.

18 Giles Bond of S[t] Mary, White Chappel, Middx., B., and Mary Hill of the same, S.

22 John Fuller of S[t] James, Westminster, Middx., B., and Ann Ludbey of the same, S.

1753-4
Dec. 25 John Letchworth of Christ Church, Middx., B., and Diana Webb of S[t] Botolph, Bishopsgate, London, S.
25 Daniel Manning of Stratford in West Ham, Essex, B., and Elizabeth Joslin of the same, S.
29 Edward Argles of S[t] Peter ad Vincula in the Tower of London, B., and Elizabeth Halsey of the same, W.
30 Thomas Sibthorpe of the Middle Temple, London, B., and Mary Jelly of Thursley, Surry, S.
30 Nathaniel Ricketts of S[t] Ann, Blackfryars, London, W., and Isabella Banbury of S[t] Dunstan in the West, London, S.
31 John Sperinck of S[t] Giles, Cripplegate, London, W., and Mary Browne of the same, W.

1754.

Jan. 2 William Clay of S[t] Mary Le Bone, Middx., B., and Sarah Stuckey of the same, W.
2 Thomas Lack of S[t] Botolph, Bishopsgate, London, W., and Mary Munt of S[t] Leonard, Shoreditch, Middx., S.
5 Abraham Mortier of Fulham, Middx., B., and Martha Naden of the same, W.
9 John Bracher of Hindon, Wilts, B., and Elizabeth Bowles of Hythe, Kent, S.
13 Simon Marcham, B., and Elizabeth Gooding, [*blank*], both of this parish. Banns.
19 George Bacon of Clapham, Surry, B., and Elizabeth Johnson of All Hallows Barking, London, S.
21 Nicholas Farmer of S[t] Mary Magdalen, Bermondsey, Surry, B., and Martha Grace of S[t] Mary, Rotherhith, Surry, S.
23 Henry Huish of S[t] George the Martyr, Southwark, Surry, Esq., B., and Mary Powell of S[t] James near the city of Bristol, S.
24 John Parker of S[t] Mary Le Strand, Middx., B., and Elizabeth Braithwaite of the same, S.
27 Henry Jenkins of All Hallows Barking, London, B., and Martha Watson of the same, S.
29 William Mountain of S[t] Martin in the Fields, Middx., B., and Rachel Williams of S[t] George, Bloomsbury, Middx., S.
Feb. 1 John Revell of S[t] Olave, Southwark, Surry, W., and Mary Whitaker of the same, W.
5 Thomas Windley of Deptford, Kent, B., and Rachel Brillet of the same, W.
6 Anthony Wright of S[t] Olave, Southwark, Surry, W., and Christain Pretty of the same, W.
7 John Boulton of Walthamstow, Essex, B., and Ann Perry of Tottenham, Middx., S.
12 Thomas Cureton of S[t] Mary, Lambeth, Surry, B., and Ann Holmes of the same, S.
12 Edward Haswell of S[t] James, Westminster, Middx., B., and Judith Tarrant of S[t] Peter Le Poor, London, S.
12 Charles Landsell of Chistlehurst, Kent, B., and Hannah Bushell of the same, S.
16 John Bennett of S[t] George the Martyr, Middx., B., and Sarah Ballett of the same, W.
17 James Scudamore of S[t] Luke, Middx., B., and Jane Fitchall alias Fitsall of S[t] Margaret, Westminster, Middx., S.
21 Stephen Brookman of S[t] Mary Woolnoth, London, B., and Jane Wheeler of the same, S.
21 John Culver of S[t] Mary, White Chappell, Middx., B., and Elizabeth Redman of the same, S.

1754

Feb. 25 Giles Powell of St George, Hanover Square, Middx., W., and Elizabeth Crane of the same, S.

26 Samuel Walter of Ickenham, Middx., B., and Jane Macklin of the same, S.

26 James Empson of St Luke, Chelsea, Middx., B., and Rebecca Brewer of Mortlake, Surry, S.

26 George Feild of St John, Hackney, Middx., B., and Grace Hulett of the same, S.

28 Matthew Hawks of Newport Pagnell, co. Bucks, B., and Anne Bunker of the same, S.

Mar. 5 William Page of St Mary, Aldermanbury, London, B., and Mary Hosley of St Mary Le Bow, London, S.

6 Ring Shepherd of Feversham, Kent, B., and Anne Argent of the same, W.

8 John Davie of St Alban, Wood Street, London, B., and Mary Dickenson of the same, S.

10 John Henry Dray of St Michael, Queenhith, London, W., and Elizabeth Griffith of the same, S.

14 Benjamin Seymour of St John, Southwark, Surry, B., and Joanna Judge of the same, S.

16 George Ellerton of St Saviour, Southwark, Surry, B., and Sarah Widdows of the same, W.

21 Thomas Skeggs of Dartford, Kent, B., and Ann Higgins of this parish, S.

21 Robert Steedman of St Martin in the Fields, Middx., W., and Eleanor Row of St Clement Danes, Middx., W.

22 Marvin Bowles of St Ann, Westminster, Middx., B., and Mary Hobbs of the same, S.

24 Thomas Millner of St Bridget alias Brides, London, B., and Ann Kellfull of the same, S., a minor.

24 John Douthwait of St Andrew, Holborn, Middx., B., and Elizabeth Cobb of St James, Westminster, Middx., S.

24 Richard Denyer of Staines, Middx., B., and Mary Gilbert of Egham, Surry, S.

[End of Book F.]

G.

St. Benet & St. Peter.

MARRIAGES FROM 25 JULY 1754 TO 22 JAN^Y 1778.

[On the Cover.]

*"The united parishes of St Benedict & St Peter Paul's Wharf."

MARRIAGE REGISTER 1754.

1754.

July 25 John Power of this parish, W., and Mary Hayward of the same, S.; by Stanhope Ellison, curate. Lic. Wit.: Richard Foddy, Elizabeth Foddy.

Sept. 9 William Shemelt of All Hallows the Less, London, W., and Sarah Woodward† of this parish, W.; by Matthew Smith, curate. Lic. Wit.: Francis Coster, Daniel King.

* There is a MS. note on the printed page immediately following the title page, to the effect that the marriages in this book were solemnized *in the Parish Church of St. Benedict, Paul's Wharf, London.*—ED.

† Signs by mark.—ED.

1754-6

Sept. 16 John Sculscup of this parish, W., and Winifread Verney of the same, S.; by Richard Hannot Bennett, Minister. Banns. Wit.: James Browne, Thomas Verney.

21 John Wagstaff of St Peter, Pauls Wharf, London, W., and Mary Newhouse* of the same, W.; by R. Hannot Bennett, Minister. Banns. Wit.: Will. Ford, Francis Coster.

Nov. 10 John Amies of St Giles in the Fields, B., and Susannah Hutchinson* of this parish, S.; by Stanhope Ellison, Curate. Banns. Wit.: Mary Chambers, Walter Maperley.

Dec. 29 Joshua Laughton of St Bennet's, Pauls Wharf, London, B., and Ann Collett of the same, [*blank*]; by Stanhope Ellison, curate. Banns. Wit.: Samuel Preston, Matha Preston.

1755.

Feb. 6 John Phelps of this parish, W., and Maria King of the same, W.; by Stanhope Ellison, curate. Lic. Wit.: B. Glandfield, Walter Maperley.

9 Abraham Purchas of this parish, W., and Mary Lawrance* of St Botolph, Billingsgate, London, S.; by S. Ellison, curate. Lic. Wit.: William Burton, Sarah Lawrance, her mark.

April 1 John Phillips of St Benedict, Pauls Wharf, London, B., and Elizabeth Stewart* of the same, W.; by S. Ellison, curate. Banns. Wit.: Simon Maid, Walter Maperley.

May 5 Richard Mackrell of St Benedict, Pauls Wharf, London, W., and Deborah Flower, W., of the same; by S. Ellison, curate. Banns. Wit.: James Spurrier, Walter Maperley.

11 John Moull of St Benedict, Pauls Wharf, London, B., and Lydia Sinfield of the same, S.; by S. Ellison, curate. Banns. Wit.: Thos Ault, Walter Maperley.

June 24 Benjamin Lewis* of St Peter, Pauls Wharf, London, B., and Sarah Carey of St Botolph, Bishopsgate, London, S.; by W. Morgan, curate. Lic. Wit.: Fran^s Coster, Daniel Hodges.

July 15 John Paterson of St Margaret, Lothbury, London, W., and Ann Harford of St Benedict, Pauls Wharf, London, W.; by W. Morgan. Lic. Wit.: Fran^s Coster, Daniel Hodges.

19 Robert Carter of St Bennet, Pauls Wharf, London, W., and Dorothy London of the same, W.; by W. Morgan, curate. Lic. Wit.: Walter Maperley, Ann Maperley.

Sept. 21 John Gisnir of St Bennet, Pauls Wharf, London, W., and Esther Courtien, S., of the same; by William Morgan, curate. Lic. Wit.: David M. Chelu [?], Walter Maperley.

Oct. 26 Nicholas Hall* of St Peter, Pauls Wharf, London, B., and Elizabeth Allen of the same, S.; by S. Ellison, curate. Lic. Wit.: Sarah Day, Deborah Thomas.

Nov. 4 Samuel Huntley of this parish, W., and Catherine Bradstreet, S., of the same; by Stanhope Ellison, curate. Banns. Wit.: Thos Ives, Samuel Mann.

Dec. 30 Thomas Atkinson of St Mary, Newington, Surrey, W., and Sarah Smith of St Peter, Pauls Wharf, London, [*blank*]; by S. Ellison, Curate. Lic. Wit.: Daniell Hodges, Fran^s Coster.

1756.

Feb. 5 Samuel Edwards of St Antholine, London, B., and Mary Biggs of this parish, S.; by Richard Elliot, Minister. Banns. Wit.: Joseph Brown, Mary Lewington.

* Signs by mark.—ED.

1756-7

Feb. 11 William Burchmore of this parish, W., and Jane Trevailer of the same, W.; by S. Ellison, curate. Lic. Wit.: Walter Maperley, Francis Coster.

24 Thomas Sims of S[t] Peter, Pauls Wharf, London, B., and Hannah Tubb of Allhallows the Great, London, W.; by Stanhope Ellison, Curate. Lic. Wit.: John Smith, Walter Maperley.

28 George Harris, Doctor of Laws of Doctors Commons in this parish, B.,* and Hannah Price of the same, S.; by S. Ellison, curate. Lic. Wit.: John Johnson, Walter Maperley.

29 Thomas Kennett of this parish, B., and Frances Price of the same, [*blank*]; by Stanhope Ellison, curate. Banns. Wit.: Walter Maperley, Fran[s] Coster.

April 6 Richard Bolt of this parish, B., and Elizabeth Price of All Hallows Barking, London, S.; by S. Ellison, curate. Lic. Wit.: William Lowden, Edward Abraham.

21 John Driver of this parish, B., and Ann Holland of the same, S.; by S. Ellison, curate. Lic. Wit.: James Sell, Walter Maperley.

24 Richard Attwood† of this parish, B., and Ann Buttler† of the same, S.; by S. Ellison, curate. Banns. Wit.: Edward Thorpe, Walter Maperley.

May 22 Joseph Corney† of this parish, B., and Ann Eudy‡ of the same, S.; by S. Ellison, curate. Lic. Wit.: Mary Saunderson, Walter Maperley.

June 21 Deark Peatar Koop of this parish, B., and Elizabeth Lane† of the Precinct of S[t] Katherine near the Tower of London, S.; by S. Ellison, curate. Lic. Wit.: Clements Wightman, John Turben.

July 14 Samuel Maynard of this parish, B., and Martha Shepherd§ of the United parishes of S[t] Margaret, New Fish Street, and S[t] Magnus the Martyr, S.; by S. Ellison, curate. Banns. Wit.: William Maynard, Walter Maperley.

Aug. 15 John Butler of S[t] Peter, Pauls Wharf, London, B., and Catherine Russell of the same, S.; by S. Ellison, curate. Lic. Wit.: Samuel Ellwood, Daniel Hodges.

Oct. 17 James Here Pemolber† of this parish and Bathsheba Watson of the same, S.; by S. Ellison, curate. Banns. Wit.: Charles Biggs, Sarah Ibberson.

24 Robert Wellwood of S[t] George, Middx., B., and Mary Reed of this parish, W.; by S. Ellison, Curate. Lic. Wit.: Anne Murrey, Walter Maperley.

24 John Linell† of S[t] Mary le Bone, Middx., B., and Eleanor Dean of this parish, S.; by S. Ellison, curate. Lic. Wit.: George Verney, Ann Starkis.

Nov. 9 David Morier of this parish, B., and Mary Carter of Christ church, Surrey, S.; by S. Ellison, curate. Lic. Wit.: B. Glandfield, Edward Atkinson.

Dec. 13 Charles Chick of S[t] Peter, Pauls Wharf, London, B., and Elizabeth Boffree† of the same, S.; by S. Ellison, curate. Banns. Wit.: William Chick, Mary Erry.

1757.

Feb. 6 John Phillips of this parish, B., and Hannah Alston of S[t] Gabriel, Fenchurch, London, S.; by S. Ellison, curate. Lic. Wit.: John Pickering, William Alston.

April 9 John Paty† of this parish, B., and Jane Pickett† of S[t] Mary Abchurch, London, W.; by S. Ellison, curate. Lic. Wit.: Jonathan Whebell, James Lyndes.

* "Batchelor" has been erased.—Ed. † Signs by mark.—Ed.
‡ Marginal note: "Ann Eudy not Nudey by mistake.—S. Ellison."—Ed.
§ Signs "Shephard."—Ed.

1757-8

April 14 Thomas Chapman of S[t] Peter, Pauls Wharf, London, B., and Hannah Higgins of the same, S.; by S. Ellison, curate. Lic. Wit.: Thomas Sibson, Ann Bonner.

25 John Smithers of this parish, B., and Elizabeth Moore of the same, S.; by S. Ellison, curate. Banns. Wit.: Mary Monds, Mary Collibor.

July 5 Thomas Worsley, Esq., of S[t] Martin in the Fields, Middx., B., and Elizabeth Lister of the same, S.; by Stanhope Ellison, Rector. Special Licence. Wit.: R. Knight, Josias Farrer.

Aug. 7 Thomas Robson of S[t] Peter, Pauls Wharf, London, B., and Ann Wallin of the same, S.; by Stanhope Ellison, Rector. Banns. Wit.: Thomas Mailes, Ann Turner.

Sept. 11 Samuel Spragg of S[t] Bennett's, Paul's Wharf, [*blank*], and Mary Jacob* of All Hallows, Lombard Street, London, [*blank*]; by David Price, minister. Lic. Wit.: Fran[s] Coster, Walter Maperley.

29 George Ann Burchett of S[t] Margaret, Westminster, Esq., W., and Elizabeth Bullythorpe of Chelmsford, Essex, W.; by Stanhope Ellison, Rector. Special Licence. Wit.: LLwyd E. [*sic*], Fran[s] Coster.

Oct. 6 Sir William Barnaby,† Knt., of Broughton Hall in the parish of Broughton, co. Oxford, and Grace Ottley of S[t] Andrew, Holbourne, London; by D. Price, minister. Special Licence. Wit.: James Southgate, Alice Crutchley.

16 John Litton of this parish, W., and Catherine Fox‡ of S[t] John, Wapping, Middx., W.; by S. Ellison, Rector. Lic. Wit.: Alice + Crowder, her mark, Fran[s] Coster.

27 John White of Woolwich, Kent, W., and Jane Forrest of the same, W.; by S. Ellison, Rector. Special Lic. Wit.: Lott [?] Smart, James Southgate.

28 John Bargrove of Southfleet, Kent, B., and Elizabeth Wickham‡ of this parish, S.; by S. Ellison, Rector. Lic. Wit.: Thomas Ives, Elizabeth Ives.

Nov. 17 Samuel Walter of S[t] George the Martyr, Middx., B., and Amy Whattam of the same, S.; by Stanhope Ellison, Rector. Special Lic. Wit.: James H. Maskelyne, Walter Maperley.

Dec. 5 William Rogers of Tooting, co. Surry, B., and Mary Bowman of this parish, S.; by S. Ellison, Rector. Lic. Wit.: John + Low, his mark, William Waine.

15 William Miller of S[t] Ann, Blackfryars, London, B., and Lucy Creswell of S[t] Peter, Pauls Wharf, S.; by S. Ellison, Rector. Lic. Wit.: Esther Walker, Daniel Hodges.

24 Joseph Ford‡ of this parish, B., and Lucy Nisbett of S[t] Bridgett als. Brides, London, S.; by S. Ellison, Rector. Lic. Wit.: John Nisbett, Eli. Sell.

1758.

Feb. 9 Felix Calvert of S[t] Giles, Cripplegate, London, Esq., and Rebecca Bayly of Allesby, co. Warwick; by George Lewis Jones, Minister. Special Licence. Wit.: John Shepherd, Peter Calvert.

Mar. 19 George Anne Cooke of S[t] James, Westminster, Middx., Esq., W., and Catherine Robins of the same, W.; by S. Ellison, Rector. Special Licence. Wit.: Elizabeth Chandler, Walter Maperley.

26 Walter Fishley of this parish, B., and Elizabeth Franklin of the same, S.; by S. Ellison, Rector. Banns. Wit.: George Tomkinson, Mary + Tomkinson, her mark.

28 Peter Leset of S[t] Matthew, Bethnal Green, Middx., B., and Ann Coles of this parish, S.; by S. Ellison, Rector. Lic. Wit.: William Cramp, Michael Coles.

* Signs "Jacobs."—Ed. † Signs "Burnaby."—Ed. ‡ Signs by mark.—Ed.

1758-9

May 17 William Prosser of this parish, B., and Mary Barns of St Luke, Chelsea, [*blank*]; by S. Ellison, Rector. Banns. Wit.: Abraham Crawley, Mary + Crawley, her mark.

24 William Milbourne of this parish, B., and Deborah Cookman of Christ Church, Surry, S.; by S. Ellison, Rector. Lic. Wit.: William Burchmore, John Scandrett.

July 16 Peter Davis of All Hallows the Great, London, B., and Sarah Bargery of this parish, S.; by James Adams, minister. Lic. Wit.: John Todd, William Korton.

Aug. 1 Edward Tanner of this parish, B., and Elizabeth Burrell* of the same, W.; by William Collins, pro vice minister. Lic. Wit.: Thos Castleman, Walter Maperley.

3 John Roobotham of this parish, W., and Elizabeth Padmore of St Giles in the Fields, Middx., W.; by Francis Humphreys, clerk pro vice. Lic. Wit.: John Woods and Fran^s Coster.

20 Alexander Clark, B., of St Peter, Paul's Wharf, and Elizabeth West, S., of the same; by James Adams, minister. Lic. Wit.: William Clark, Daniel Hodges.

Oct. 1 John Eason* of this parish, B., and Mary Guy of St Mary Somerset, London, S.; by James Adams, Minister. Lic. Wit.: John Smyth [?], Richard Higgins.

1 Samuel Green of St Peter's, Paul's Wharf, B., and Elizabeth Winslow of St Botolph, Aldersgate, London, S.; by James Adams, Minister. Lic. Wit.: Thos Robson, Ann Robson.

9 Thomas Nayler of St Bennets, Pauls Wharf, London, B., and Sarah Dunn of St John, Westminster, Middx., W.; by James Adams, Minister. Lic. Wit.: Will: Jones, Drs Commons, Walter Maperley.

13 Richard Danals* of St James, Westminster, Middx., B., and Elizabeth Cooper of this parish, S.; by S. Ellison, Rector. Banns. Wit.: Mary Brockett, Walter Maperley.

28 William Jackson of St Giles, Cripplegate, London, W., and Ann Wilkinson of this parish, S.; by S. Ellison, Rector. Lic. Wit.: Joseph Pomroy, Alex^r Anderson, James Gibbons.

Nov. 7 Trew Jegon of this parish, B., and Mary Atkins of the same, W.; by S. Ellison, Rector. Lic. Wit.: James Brynnan, Mary Shaw.

Dec. 3 John Cunningham of St Michael, Queenhith, B., and Elizabeth Miller of this parish, S.; by Richard Hannot Bennett, Minister. Lic. Wit.: William Fanjoux, Walter Maperley.

10 Richard LLoyd of St Sepulchre, Middx., B., and Alice Nutter* of St Peter, Pauls Wharf, London, S.; by S. Ellison, Rector. Lic. Wit.: John Smith, Walter Maperley.

1759.

Jan. 7 Joshua Bedford of Christ Church, Middx., W., and Martha Cole* of this parish, S.; by S. Ellison, Rector. Lic. Wit.: Tho: Harrington, Phillip Baker.

23 Thomas Burchett of this parish, B., and Elizabeth Armistead of St Margaret, Westminster, Middx., S.; by S. Ellison, Rector. Lic. Wit.: Walter Maperley, Fran^s Coster, Fran. Coster.

Feb. 5 Giles Trinder of St Peter, Pauls Wharf, London, W., and Elizabeth Dickson* of the same, S.; by S. Ellison, Rector. Banns. Wit.: Thos Tarver, Daniel Hodges.

April 28 James Maidment of St Peter, Pauls Wharf, London, B., and Martha Welch of the same, W.; by S. Ellison, Rector. Lic. Wit.: Clement North, Sam: Chatfield.

* Signs by mark.—ED.

1759-61
July 31 John Knight of this parish, B., and Sarah Boar* of the same, S.; by Arthur Dawes. Banns. Wit.: The mark of John Warr, Fran[s] Coster.

Aug. 19 William Oxley of S[t] John the Evangelist, West., W., and Johanna Roach* of S[t] Benedict, London, S.; by Francis Humphreys. Lic. Wit.: Thomas Wignall, Walter Maperley.

Sept. 16 Samuel Brinklett of this parish, B., and Martha Woodward the same, S.; by Francis Sherondell, minister. Banns. Wit.: Sarah Ibberson, Walter Maperley.

16 Humphrey Davis* of this parish, W., and Mary Dunn of the same, S.; by Francis Sherondell, minister. Banns. Wit.: Walter + Maperly, M[rs] Maynard, William Maynard.

Oct. 28 James Wallis of this parish, B., and Frances Draper of S[t] Mary Magdalen, Old Fish Street, London, S.; by S. Ellison, Rector. Lic. Wit.: Patrick Baxter, Tho[s] Lewis.

Dec. 2 John Carrell of this parish, B., and Ann Ball* of the same, S.; by S. Ellison, Rector. Banns. Wit.: John Fitzpatrick, Jemima + Dowd, her mark.

30 Robert Macey of S[t] Peter, Pauls Wharf, London, B., and Elizabeth Harding* of the same, S.; by S. Ellison, Rector. Banns. Wit.: Edward Winspear, Charity Hollis.

1760.

Jan. 12 Robert Stringer of Christ church, London, B., and Dorothy Vanderplank of S[t] Peter, Pauls Wharf, London, S.; by S. Ellison, Rector. Lic. Wit.: John Vanderplank, Sam[l] Green.

Feb. 2 Timothy Jee of this parish, W., and Rebecca Baker of the same, W.; by S. Ellison, Rector. Lic. Wit.: Tho[s] Slater, Elizabeth Slater.

Mar. 27 William Bartlett of this parish, W., and Mary Gebarson of the same, S.; by S. Ellison, Rector. Banns. Wit.: Judith + Robins, her mark, Ann + Armson, her mark.

April 6 William Bruce* of this parish, B., and Mary Goodill* of the same, S.; by S. Ellison, Rector. Banns. Wit.: James Bloor, Susanna + Bloor.

27 William Braswell,† B., and Elizabeth Armstrong, S., both of S[t] Peter's; by Richard Hannot Bennett, minister. Banns. Wit.: M[r] John Allen, Fran. Coster, Daniel Hodges.

June 28 Henry Payne of S[t] Faith's, B., and Mary Bentley of this parish, S.; by John Dobey. Lic. Wit.: J. [?] Payne, Elizabeth Payne.

29 John Austin of this parish, B., and Catherine Wall of the same, S.; by John Dobey, minister. Banns. Wit.: Humphry Seger, Mary Davis.

July 6 Edward Hopkins of this parish, B., and Ann Siddall of the same, S.; by John Dobey. Lic. Wit.: Edward Porter, Elizabeth Stoddart.

Sept. 29 Alexander Palmer of this parish, W., and Christian Whicket* of the same, W.; by John Dobey, minister. Banns. Wit.: John White, Edward Harman.

Oct. 3 William Burton of this parish, W., and Mary Warner* of the same, W.; by S. Ellison, Rector. Lic. Wit.: Richard Loughlin, Joan [? Ann] Loughlin.

Nov. 29 John Harvey of this parish, W., and Elizabeth Mitchell* of S[t] John, Wapping, Middx., S.; by S. Ellison, Rector. Lic. Wit.: Jane Brand, Fran. Coster.

1761.

Mar. 12 John Hutchinson of this parish, B., and Mary Harrison of S[t] Mary, Whitechapel, Middx., S.; by S. Ellison, Rector. Lic. Wit.: William Henry Hamill, Fran. Coster.

* Signs by mark.—ED.

† Signs "Brasewell."—ED.

1761-2

April 5 William Ball of S[t] Michael, Queenhith, London, W., and Margaret Stilwell* of S[t] Peter, Pauls Wharf, London, W.; by S. Ellison, Rector. Lic. Wit.: John Ball, John Farrell.

13 Edward Harman of this parish, B., and Sarah Ibberson of the same, S.; by James Challis. Banns. Wit.: George Brignall, John Bishop.

June 6 George Churchill* of S[t] Faith's, London, B., and Ann White* of this parish, S.; by S. Ellison, Rector. Banns. Wit.: Frances Cock, Michael Coles.

19 John Rieth of this parish, B., and Henrietta Day* of Christ Church, Surry, W.; by S. Ellison, Rector. Lic. Wit.: Dunton Littler, Elizabeth Goff.

July 21 Henry Harrow of S[t] Benedict, Pauls Wharf, London, B., and Sarah Hornsby* of S[t] George, Hanover Square, Middx., S.; by James Adams, minister. Lic. Wit.: James Thwaits, Elizabeth + Winter, her mark.

25 Edward Frame of S[t] Benedict, Paul's Wharf, London, W., and Susannah Debbit* of East Greenwich, Kent, W.; by Henry Hayman, minister. Lic. Wit.: Matthew Vine, Jane Brand.

Aug. 28 John Davies of this parish, B., and Mary Matthews of the same, S.; by S. Ellison, Rector. Banns. Wit.: John Griffith, Mary Pritchard.

Sept. 14 John Martin Leake, Esq., of this parish, B., and Mary Calvert of Lambourn in Essex, S.; by S. Ellison, Rector. Lic. Wit.: F. Sherriff, E. Winter.

Oct. 15 Francis Harris of S[t] Peter, Paul's Wharf, London, B., and Elizabeth Watkins* of S[t] Michael, Queenhith, S.; by S. Ellison, Rector. Lic. Wit.: Sam. Keyes, Daniel Hodges.

Nov. 23 William Spry of this parish, LL.D., B., and Amelia Pitt of S[t] Martin in the Fields, Middx., S.; by Stanhope Ellison, Rector. Lic. Wit.: John Blake, Michael Fountain.

Dec. 6 John Laybank of this parish, B., and Mary Davis of this parish, S.; by S. Ellison, Rector. Banns. Wit.: John Todd, Jun[r], Michael Coles.

21 Thomas Roberts of Paul, Deptford, Kent, B., and Mary Blake of this parish, S.; by S. Ellison, Rector. Lic. Wit.: William James, Michael Coles.

1762.

Jan. 6 Joseph Daves of Hampstead, Middx., B., and Anne Robinson of this parish, S.; by S. Ellison, Rector. Lic. Wit.: William Thompson, Ann Urmson [?].

10 Patrick Baxter of S[t] Peter, Pauls Wharf, London, B., and Sarah Wilcox of the same, S.; by S. Ellison, Rector. Lic. Wit.: Robert Black, Mary Burnell.

Feb. 11 John Vanhagan of this parish, B., and Elizabeth Pool of S[t] Faith's, S.; by S. Ellison, Rector. Banns. Wit.: Robert Burston, Ruth Harris.

16 George Fielder* of Chelsea, B., and Elizabeth Weatherhead of this parish, S.; by S. Ellison, Rector. Banns. Wit.: Mary Booke, Michael Coles.

20 Robert Gosling of S[t] Dionis Backchurch, London, B., and Rachael Booth of this parish, S.; by S. Ellison, Rector. Lic. Wit.: George Booth, J. Phillips.

April 11 William Dawson of this parish, B., and Ann Wisken of the same, S.; by S. Ellison, Rector. Banns. Wit.: William Barber, Olive Jacob.

11 Thomas Goddard of this parish, B., and Mary White of the same, S., a minor, with consent of her father; by S. Ellison, Rector. Lic. Wit.: Richard Jordan, Tho[s] Grove.

* Signs by mark.—ED.

1762-3

April 20 John Strong of this parish, B., and Sarah Wright* of the same, S.; by William Collins, minister. Banns. Wit.: Ann Mayor, Richard Allum.

May 16 John Suter of St Mary, Lambeth, Surry, B., and Jane Griffitt of this parish, S.; by S. Ellison, Rector. *Lic.* Wit.: James Aingworth, Sibbell Griffitt.

28 Alexander Cheek of this parish, B., and Mary Barnard of the same, S.; by Ab^m^ Hurley, curate for this time. Banns. [Signature as Mary Cheek, written after it "Late Mr Barnard."] Wit.: Ben. Worthy, Mary Empy.

July 10 Charles Bosher of St Dunstan, Stepny, Middx., B., and Mary Raymant† of St Peter, Pauls Wharf, S.; by W. Taswell, Minor Canon of St Paul's Cathedral. Lic. Wit.: Christian Raymen, Mary Easterby.

Aug. 10 Thomas Waterman of St George, Bloomsbury, Middx., B., and Jane Hallett of St Peter, Paul's Wharf, S.; by Stephen Roe, curate. Banns. Wit.: William Panckridge, Moley Gibbs.

Sept. 23 William Scott of St Benedict, Paul's Wharf, London, B., and Margaret Hunt* of the same, S.; by Stephen Roe, curate. Banns. Wit.: James Coles, Ann Mose, Fran^s^ Coster.

Oct. 10 Joachim Poohl of St George in the East, B., and Ann Symonds of St Peter's, Pauls Wharf, London, S.; by S. Ellison, Rector. Banns. Wit.: Abr^m^ Brooksbank, Godfry William Smith.

14 Christopher Kaslar* of this parish, B., and Ann Morton* of the same, S.; by S. Ellison, Rector. Lic. Wit.: George Deveral, Jane Brand.

17 James Lockhart of St Dunstan in the East, London, W., and Mary Harriot Gray of this parish, S.; by S. Ellison, Rector. Lic. Wit.: John Vernon, Fran. Coster.

29 John Bell, a soldier in H.M. 36th Reg^t^ of Foot (Lord Robert Manners, Commander), B., and Elizabeth Moule of this parish, S.; by S. Ellison, Rector. Lic. Wit.: Sarah Hurst, Michael Coles.

Nov. 6 George Chamberlain‡ of St Thomas the Apostle, London, [*blank*], and Elizabeth Swhartz of St Peter, Paul's Wharf, London, [*blank*]; by S. Ellison, Rector. Lic. Wit.: William Jones, Rebecca Jones.

7 John Barnsley* of St Peter, Pauls Wharf, London, B., and Elizabeth Tyler* of the same, W.; by S. Ellison, Rector. Banns. Wit.: Deborah Thomas, Daniel Hodges.

9 Charles Williams of St Martin in the Fields, Middx., B., and Rachael Jones of this parish, S.; by S. Ellison, Rector. Lic. Wit.: William Green, Matthew Whitehead.

21 Robert Knight of St Bennett, Paul's Wharf, London, W., and Elizabeth French* of St Augustine's, London, S.; by S. Ellison, Rector. Lic. Wit.: Benjamin Church, Mary Church.

23 John Bishop of this parish, B., and Mary Cooper* of the same, W.; by S. Ellison, Rector. Lic. Wit.: John + Hill, his mark, Michael Coles.

Dec. 21 Thomas Woodcock* of this parish, B., and Sarah Nunn* of the same, S.; by S. Ellison, Rector. Lic. Wit.: Edward Barnard, Mary Barnard.

25 John Moos of this parish, B., and Elizabeth Ball* of the same, S.; by S. Ellison, Rector. Banns. Wit.: John Stroke, Mary Priest.

1763.

Feb. 14 Thomas Stone of St Peter, Paul's Wharf, B., and Ann French* of the same, W.; by S. Ellison, Rector. Lic. Wit.: William Barham, Michael Coles.

* Signs by mark.—ED. † Signs "Mary Raymen."—ED.
‡ Signs "Chamberlin."—ED.

1763-4

Feb. 28 Josiah de Ponthieu of this parish, B., and Mary Spencer* of the same, W.; by S. Ellison, Rector. Banns. Wit.: Thos Boswell, Sarah + Conn, her mark.

April 7 Russell Penn of Newington, Surry, B., and Ann Stevens of this parish, S.; by S. Ellison, Rector. Lic. Wit.: James Buck, Elizabeth Penn.

May 8 James Robinson of this parish, B., and Mary Comfort of the same, S.; by S. Ellison, Rector. Banns. Wit.: John Comfort, Mary Anthoney.

20 Thomas Collass of St Andrew, Plymouth, Devon, B., and Mary Owen* of St Benedict, S.; by James Penn, for the Rector. Lic. Wit.: William Ford, Michael Coles.

June 14 William Calvert of St Benedict, B., and Catherine Langston of the same, S.; by James Penn, for the Rector. Banns. Wit.: Ann + Millonton, her mark, Francis Coster.

26 Edward Owen of St Peter's, B., and Sarah Blunt* of the same, S.; by James Penn. Banns. Wit.: Richard Webb, Sarah Smith.

July 7 Thomas Ives of St Benedict, B., and Susannah Cooart† of the same, S.; by James Penn. Banns. Wit.: Hendrick Nodrum, Elizabeth + Estaff, her mark.

31 John Comfort of St Benedict, B., and Ann Parden* of the same, S.; by James Penn. Banns. Wit.: John Stockall, Sarah Stockall.

Sept. 6 Joseph Windred of Harrow on the Hill, Middx., W., and Jane Darwell* [signature Darvell] of St Peter's, S.; by James Penn. Lic. Wit.: John Ryder, Michael Coles, Fran. Coster.

Oct. 1 John Wood of St Peter's, Paul's Wharf, London, W., and Mary Ball of St Dunstan in the West, London, W.; by S. Ellison, Rector. Lic. Wit.: John Paulin, Daniel Hodges.

5 Simeon Clifton of this parish, B., and Ann Goodwin* of the same, W.; by S. Ellison, Rector. Lic. Wit.: John + Urrey, his mark, Michael Coles.

24 William Webster of this parish, B., and Sarah Tucker* of the same, S.; by S. Ellison, Rector. Banns. Wit.: William Townsend, An Duning.

Nov. 15 Thomas Forster of this parish, B., and Elizabeth May,* S.; by S. Ellison, Rector. Banns. Wit.: Hannah Willson, Sarah Gibson.

Dec. 16 David Hinton* of this parish, B., and Mary Collins* of St Bartholomew the Great, London, W.; by S. Ellison, Rector. Lic. Wit.: John Brasier, Susannah Brasier.

1764.

Jan. 1 John Cotham of this parish, B., and Ann Stubbins of All Hallows Barking, S.; by S. Ellison, Rector. Lic. Wit.: Samuel Ford, Michael Coles.

3 Richard Lunn* of St Peter, Paul's Wharf, London, B., and Elizabeth Scarlett of the same, W.; by S. Ellison, Rector. Banns. Wit.: George Briggs, Elizabeth + Joselyn, her mark.

‡ James McLean of St Margaret, Westminster, Middx., W., and Elizabeth Westerbey of this parish, S.; by S. Ellison, Rector. Lic. Wit.: W. Richardson, David Richards.

Feb. 10 Harry Fabian of St Ann, Blackfryars, London, B., and Elizabeth Minton of St Peter, Paul's Wharf, London, S.; by S. Ellison, Rector. Lic. Wit.: Frans Coster, Michael Coles.

Mar. 14 George Pettit of this parish, B., and Elizabeth Evans* of St Andrew, Holborn, Middx., S.; by S. Ellison, Rector. Lic. Wit.: Andrew Rook, Catherine Clark.

* Signs by mark.—Ed. † Signs "Susannah Coore."—Ed.
‡ Date is omitted.—Ed.

1764-5

April 22 The Rev. Stanhope Ellison of St Benedict, Paul's Wharf, clerk and W., and Sarah Wilby of St Mary, Islington, Middx., S.; by Edward Wilby, curate. Lic. Wit.: Mary Brewster, Richard Allum.

June 13 Charles Egerton of St Benedict, Paul's Wharf, London, [*blank*], and Constantia Skynner of St Mildred, Poultry, London, [*blank*]; by Edward Wilby, curate. Lic. Wit.: Elizabeth Musgrave, Richard Allum.

16 William Rutland of Dartford, Kent, W., and Elizabeth Silkwood of St Benet, Paul's Wharf, London, W.; by Edw. Wilby, curate. Lic. Wit.: Tho: Hyde, Anne Fry.

18 Edward Keate of St Benet, Paul's Wharf, London, B., and Elizabeth Rhodes of the same, S.; by Edw. Wilby, Curate. Banns. Wit.: Richd Allum, Sarah Waguit [?].

28 William Braxton of St Peter's, B., and Elizabeth Veriner of the same, S.; by Edw. Wilby, curate. Banns. Wit.: Anthony Braxton, James Mottley.

July 1 Richard Wingfield of Christ church, London, B., and Susanna Webb of St Benets, Pauls Wharf, S.; by Edw. Wilby, curate. Lic. Wit.: John Green, Richd Allum.

19 William Drew of this parish, B., and Sarah Lawson of St Olave, Southwark, Surry, W.; by S. Ellison, Rector. Lic. Wit.: Thos Boswell, Richd Allum.

Aug. 4 Thomas Lyon of this parish, B., and Elizabeth Pyke of the same, S.; by Edw. Wilby, curate. Banns. Wit.: Richd Allum, Michael Coles.

Sept. 30 William Paine of this parish, B., and Elizabeth Fletcher of the same, S.; by S. Ellison, Rector. Lic. Wit.: Millicent Abdy, Richd Allum.

Nov. 29 Richard Underhill of this parish, B., and Mary Maynard of Christ Church, Surry, S.; by S. Ellison, Rector. Lic. Wit.: William Maynard, Martha Underhill.

Dec. 2 William Trinder of St Peter's, Pauls Wharf, London, B., and Sarah Church of St Sepulchre's, London, S.; by S. Ellison, Rector. Banns. Wit.: Binson Hawkins, Thomas Langfield, Ann Church, Elizabeth Church.

9 Nicholas Sweeting Richards of St Luke, Middx., W., and Mary Wilson* of this parish, S.; by S. Ellison, Rector. Lic. Wit.: Andrew + Jones, Mary Jones.

23 Christopher Ahlman of this parish, B., and Mary Tinkler of the same, S.; by S. Ellison, Rector. Banns. Wit.: Johann Lötter [?], Richd Allum.

30 Piggott Radburn of this parish, B., and Mary Chipp† of the same, S.; by S. Ellison, Rector. Banns. Wit.: Thomas Erllam, Elizabeth + Erllam, her mark.

31 James Shaw of this parish, B., and Mary Buckley† of St Bridget als. Bride, London, S.; by S. Ellison, Rector. Lic. Wit.: Michael Coles, Richd Allum.

1765.

Feb. 28 Thomas Hyde of this parish, B., and Anne Fry of Dartford, Kent, S.; by S. Ellison, Rector. Lic. Wit.: John Howlett, Susanna + Jones, her mark.

Mar. 19 Archer Blake of this parish, B., and Phillis Reece of the same, S.; by S. Ellison, Rector. Banns. Wit.: Elizabeth Leyton, Richd Allum.

April 6 Henry Kendall of St Bennett, Grace Church, London, W., and Elizabeth Pittway of St Peter, Pauls Wharf, London, S.; by S. Ellison, Rector. Lic. Wit.: John Pittway, Mary Rouse.

* Signs "Mary Willson."—Ed. † Signs by mark.—Ed.

1765-6

April 7 William Hancock of this parish, B., and Betty Dyment* of the same, S.; by S. Ellison, Rector. Banns. Wit.: Philip Main, Martha + Main, her mark.

16 Isaac Peat of St Giles, Cripplegate, London, W., and Elizabeth Fellows of this parish, S.; by S. Ellison, Rector. Lic. Wit.: Trew Jegon, Mary Jegon.

20 William Browne of this parish, B., and Sarah Williams of the same, W.; by S. Ellison, Rector. Banns. Wit.: Elizabeth Stone, Ann + Allen, her mark.

27 George Goulding of St Augustin als. Austin, London, B., and Sarah Norris of this parish, S.; by S. Ellison, Rector. Lic. Wit.: John Leach, James Montgomerie.

May 3 Thomas Webb of St Luke, Middx., W., and Mary Fletcher of this parish, S.; by S. Ellison, Rector. Lic. Wit.: George Cary, Mary Cary.

June 10 Samuel Banner of this parish, B., and Jane Gunn* of the same, S.; by S. Ellison, Rector. Banns.† Wit.: Ann + Williams, her mark, Elizabeth Brooks.

Sept. 9 Thomas Offield of St Saviour, Southwark, W., and Elizabeth Marshall of this parish, S.; by Edw. Wilby, Minister. Banns. Wit.: William Marshall, Sarah Marshall.

30 John Jones of this parish, B., and Jane Owen of the same, S.; by S. Ellison, Rector. Banns. Wit.: Samuel LLoyd, Evan Rowland.

Oct. 11 John Lawrance of this parish, W., and Elizabeth Minn of the same, W.; by S. Ellison, Rector. Lic. Wit.: William Carpenter, Richd Allum.

17 John Penny of this parish, B., and Hester Hume of St Gregory, London, W.; by S. Ellison, Rector. Lic. Wit.: Thos White, Sarah Roberts.

17 Thomas Rose of St George, Southwark, Surry, W., and Mary Mayfield* of this parish, W.; by S. Ellison, Rector. Lic. Wit.: John Gom, J. Ashford.

Nov. 10 David Wise of this parish, B., and Hannah Smith* of St Olave, Southwark, Surry, S.; by S. Ellison, Rector. Lic. Wit.: Thomas Wild, Jonathan Wise.

Dec. 4 Charles Cooper of Walton upon Thames, Surry, B., and Mary Woodhatch of this parish, S.; by S. Ellison, Rector. Lic. Wit.: Richard Middleton, Thomas Marsh.

1766.

Jan. 1 William Halliwell of St Peter, Pauls Wharf, London, B., and Elizabeth Knowles of the same, S.; by S. Ellison, Rector. Banns. Wit.: William Edwards, James Montgomerie.

Feb. 2 Edward Clark of this parish, B., and Hannah Aylward of the same, S.; by S. Ellison, Rector. Lic. Wit.: Thos Holloway, Grace + Clark, her mark.

25 Edward Cheney of St Botolph, Aldersgate, London, W., and Sarah Blower of this parish, S.; by S. Ellison, Rector. Lic. Wit.: John Hawkshaw, Sarah Hawkshaw.

25 John Webb of this parish, B., and Sarah Lemon of the same, S.; by S. Ellison, Rector. Lic. Wit.: Margaret + Wilkinson, her mark, Michael Coles.

Mar. 11 Daniel Hodges of St Peter, Pauls Wharf, London, B., and Ann Mayo of St Botolph, Aldgate, London, S.; by S. Ellison, Rector. Banns. Wit.: Joseph Mayo, Daniel Mayo.

May 29 James Wenham,* W., and Ann Bayly, S., both of this parish; by Chrisr Armstrong, curate. Banns. Wit.: Thos Archer, William Bertell.

* Signs by mark.—Ed. † "Banns" altered from "Licence."—Ed.

1766-7

July 20 George Surman of this parish, B., and Margaret Boaird of the same, S.; by Thomas Higgins, Minister. Banns. Wit.: Marg[t] Morgan, James Coles.

Aug. 10 Joseph Gaulock* of this parish, B., and Christian Glandfield of the same, S.; by William Rider, Minister. Banns. Wit.: John Truman Tredwell, Margeat Mackoy.

Sept. 14 John Ward of this parish, B., and Jane Ferrell* of the same, S.; by Thomas Higgins, Minister. Banns. Wit.: Robert Jones, James Montgomerie.

Oct. 26 Thomas Watson* of S[t] Martin in the Fields, Middx., B., and Jane Hanson of this parish, S.; by John More, curate pro hac vice. Lic. Wit.: James Montgomerie, Michael Coles.

Nov. 10 John Cadman* of S[t] Peter, Pauls Wharf, London, B., and Hannah Stiles of the same, S.; by S. Ellison, Rector. Banns. Wit.: Jane + Batt, her mark, Daniel Hodges.

1767.

Feb. 5 Joseph Akam of this parish, B., and Sarah Gray* of the same, S.; by Tho[s] Higgins, Minister. Banns. Wit.: Sarah + Core, her mark, James Montgomerie.

28 John French of S[t] Paul, Covent Garden, Middx., W., and Isabella Harrison of S[t] Peter, Pauls Wharf, S.; by S. Ellison, Rector. Lic. Wit.: John Law, Ann Shuttleworth.

Mar. 23 George Filley of this parish, B., and Margaret Clark of the same, S.; by S. Ellison, Rector. Banns. Wit.: F. Sawyer, Susannah Sawyer.

April 7 John Hobman of S[t] Andrew Undershaft, London, B., and Hannah Newcomb of this parish, S.; by S. Ellison, Rector. Lic. Wit.: John Browne, James Montgomerie.

20 Benjamin Lee of this parish, B., and Margaret Williams of the same, S.; by S. Ellison, Rector. Banns. Wit.: Bennett Davis, John Truman Tredwell.

May 10 Alexander Waters* of S[t] Peter's, W., and Ann Gresham of the same, W.; by Tho. Higgins, Minister. Banns. Wit.: John May, Daniel Hodges.

12 John Heskey* of this parish, B., and Elizabeth Reynolds* of the same, W.; by Tho. Higgins, minister. Banns. Wit.: John Singelton, Mary Singelton.

16 George Rattray of S[t] Peter's, B., and Mary Cooper of the same, S.; by Tho. Higgins, minister. Lic. Wit.: James Montgomerie, Michael Coles.

June 1 John Tyhurst of Eltham, Kent, B., and Sarah Willard of this parish, S.; by Tho. Higgins, Minister. Lic. Wit.: Mary Willard, James Montgomerie.

4 William Green of S[t] Ann, Blackfryars, London, B., and Elizabeth Walker of this parish, S.; by Tho. Higgins. Lic. Wit.: John Read, Sarah Miller.

22 Richard Sills of S[t] Peter, Pauls Wharf, W., and Mary Cooper* of the same, S.; by Tho. Higgins, minister. Banns. Wit.: Augustus Kennedy, Tho[s] Sculthorp.

[*One form not filled in.*]

July 2 Stephano Barow De Bissye of Kensington, Middx., B., and Catherine Thornhill of this parish, a minor, by consent of her father Joseph Thornhill; by T. Higgins, Minister. Lic. Wit.: Joseph Thornhill, Elizabeth Payne.

* Signs by mark.—ED.

1767-8

July 26 William Brown of St Dionis Backchurch, London, B., and Henrietta Rogers* of this parish, S.; by Tho. Higgins, Minister. Lic. Wit.: James Montgomerie, Michael Coles.

Sept. 15 George Saunders* of Fulham, Middx., B., and Elizabeth Wooley of this parish, S.; by Tho. Higgins, minister. Lic. Wit.: Thos Baker, Anne Coles.

23 John Wynn* of Chiddingly, Sussex, W., and Mary Willard of this parish, S.; by Tho. Higgins, Minister. Lic. Wit.: John Smith, James Montgomerie.

Oct. 17 John Mays of St Peters, W., and Elizabeth Haines* of St Faith's, London, W.; by Tho. Higgins, minister. Lic. Wit.: Susan Keyes, James Montgomerie.

[*A form not filled in.*]

1768.

Jan. 2 John Buxton of St Peter, Pauls Wharf, London, B., and Mary Money of St Mary Magdalen, Bermondsey, Surry, S.; by R. P. Finch. Lic. Wit.: Saml Enderby, Elizabeth Enderby, H. Enderby.

17 John Thompson of this parish, B., and Elizabeth Eastaff* of the same, S.; by S. Ellison, Rector. Banns. Wit.: Jane + Coar, her mark, Thos Ives.

Feb. 15 Christopher Warren of St Peter, Pauls Wharf, W., and Elizabeth Armstrong of the same, S.; by S. Ellison, Rector. Banns. Wit.: Mercy Aspley, Sophia Keyes.

May 15 William Pitt of this parish, B., and Mary Wilson of the same, S.; by Tho. Higgins, minister. Banns. Wit.: Tho. Garrett, Mary Pacose [?], Sarah Wilson.

June 6 William Bunten of St Peter's, B., and Ann Ebbutt† of the same, S.; by Tho. Higgins. Lic. Wit.: Edward Gwillim, James Montgomerie.

13 George Everett of St Peter's, B., and Elizabeth Saunders of Woburn, co. Bucks, S.; by Tho. Higgins, minister. Lic. Wit.: Robert Hewes, James Montgomerie.

14 Francis Page* of this parish, W., and Mary Perry of this parish, W.; by Tho. Higgins, minister. Banns. Wit.: William Dawson, Ann Dawson.

16 Richard Rawlins of this parish, B., and Ann Dobson* of St Peter's, S.; by Tho. Higgins, minister. Lic. Wit.: Thos Robinson, James Montgomerie.

20 James Maccarty of this parish, B., and Mary Hoare* of the same, S., a minor, with consent of her father; by Tho. Higgins, minister. Banns. Wit.: Walter Hoare, William + Welldon, his mark.

26 James Norrington of this parish, B., and Elizabeth Bandon of the same, W.; by F. G. Bennett, minister. Lic. Wit.: John Middleton, James Montgomerie.

July 4 John Banister of this parish, B., and Sarah Lee* of the same, S.; by F. G. Bennet, minister. Banns. Wit.: Henry Burgess, James Montgomerie.

5 Tudor Jones of this parish, B., and Elizabeth Sellers of the same, [*blank*]; by Tho. Higgins, minister. Banns. Wit.: Sarah Patman, James Montgomerie.

Aug. 7 Patrick Hanly of this parish, B., and Mary Eaton‡ of the same, S.; by Thomas Howes, A.B. Banns. Wit.: Michael + Heaton, his mark, Martin Hanly.

* Signs by mark.—Ed. † Signs "Ann R. Ebbutt."—Ed.

‡ In the entry the name is "Eaton," the bride's signature is "Heaton," and one witness is written "Heaton."—Ed.

1768-9

Sept 25 John Elvert* of this parish, B and Elizabeth Swallow† of the same, S ; by Tho Higgins Banns. Wit George Sapnell, James Montgomerie

Oct 28 John Douglas† of this parish, B , and Seabia Jones† of the same, S , by S Ellison, Rector Banns Wit Mary + Jones, her mark, Elizabeth + Jones, her mark

30 Joseph Lacey of this parish, B , and Sarah Pike of the same, S ; by S Ellison, Rector Banns Wit Jonathan Richard Brown, Peter Nadall

Nov. 14 John Woolled of this parish, B , and Sarah Chamberlain† of the same, S , by S. Ellison Banns Wit . Elizabeth + Green, her mark, James Montgomerie

1769

Jan 3 John Lewis of this parish, B , and Eleanor Wilks of the same, S , by S Ellison, Rector Banns Wit Jos Porter, William Fowkes

30 John How of this parish, B , and Ann Pecoret† of the same, S , by S Ellison, Rector Banns Wit. Tho Ives, James Montgomerie

Feb 5 Benjamin Moore of this parish, B , and Mary Davis of the same, S , by S Ellison, Rector Lic Wit James Montgomerie, James Coles

Mar 12 Benjamin Smith† of St John, Southwark, Surry, W , and Ann Stovell of this parish, S , by S Ellison, Rector Lic Wit William Cole, Mary + Cole, her mark

April 23 John Chatterton of this parish, B , and Grace Upton of the same, S., by Abm Hurley, curate for this time Banns Wit Elizabeth Outhwaite, Benjamin Geary

30 Robert Hammond of St Peter's, B , and Mary Woodford† of the same, S , by Abm Hurley, curate Banns. Wit Mary Jones, James Montgomerie

May 27 William Snow of this parish, B , and Sarah Dewell of the same, S , by H Foster, minister Banns Wit James Montgomerie, Michael Coles

June 18 Edward Phillipson of St John's, Wapping, Middx , B , and Sarah Wrigglesworth‡ of this parish, S , by Tho Higgins, Minister Lic Wit . Michael Coles, James Montgomerie

25 William Bate† of St Peter, Pauls Wharf, B , and Isabella Waller of the same, S , by Chrisr Armstrong, curate Banns Wit James Sarney, James Montgomerie, Daniel Hodges

July 9 Edward Hedges of this parish, B , and Sarah Austin† of the same, S , by Tho Higgins, minister Banns Wit William Worland, Elliss Taylor.

30 Thomas Lane of this parish, B , and Sarah Bachouse† of the same, S , by Tho Higgins, minister Banns Wit Ralph Narwell, Ann Watts

Aug 8 John Rider of this parish, B , and Catherine Gray of St Paul's, Deptford, Kent, S , by S Ellison, Rector Lic Wit Mary Gray, H Goodwyn, Junr

Oct 1 George Stoddart of St Gregory's, London, W , and Sussannah Smith† of St Benedict, Pauls Wharf, W , by Tho Higgins, minister Lic. Wit John Sardneer, James Montgomerie

1 John Tongue of this parish, W , and Mary Ann Truesdell† of the same, W , by Tho Higgins, minister Banns Wit Robert Ayres, William Hatt

5 William Matthews of St Bennets, Pauls Wharf, W , and Hannah Alsop of the same, S , by Christopher Armstrong, curate Lic Wit Adams Alsop, James Montgomerie

* Signs " Elfert "—Ed. † Signs by mark.—Ed ‡ Signs " Wigglesworth "—Ed.

1769-70

Oct. 9 James Sarney of St Peter's, B., and Mary Robyne of the same, S., a minor, by the consent of parents; by Tho. Higgins, curate. Banns. Wit.: George Rous, Joseph Humble.

11 Thomas Hill* of this parish, B., and Sarah Rigby* of Wandsworth, Surry, S.; by Richard Sugden, minister. Lic. Wit.: Saml Angier, James Montgomerie, James Aylward, Michael Coles.

18 Thomas Adams of this parish, B., and Nancy Smith of St George, Hanover Square, Middx., S.; by T. Richards, minister. Lic. Wit.: James Montgomerie, Michael Coles.

24 William Purnell of this parish, W., and Sarah Lacey of the same, W.; by Tho. Higgins, minister. Banns. Wit.: James Montgomerie, Michael Coles.

Dec. 14 Thomas Whitby of this parish, B., and Mary Hare of the same, W.; by S. Ellison, Rector. Lic. Wit.: Hugh Gibbes, Emelen Whitby.

24 Henry Butler of this parish, B., and Alice Cloak† of St Mary Magdalen, Bermondsey, Surry, S.; by S. Ellison, Rector. Lic. Wit.: James Montgomerie, Michael Coles.

1770.

Jan. 21 John Robinson of this parish, B., and Jane Nixon* of the same, S.; by S. Ellison, Rector. Banns. Wit.: Edward Hedges, Sarah + Ayeress, her mark.

25 Richard Varley* of St Peter's, B., and Jane Crawford* of the same, S.; by Chr Armstrong, curate. Banns. Wit.: James Montgomerie, Thomas Harvey.

28 John Hill of this parish, B., and Judith King of the same, S.; by Tho. Higgins, minister. Banns. Wit.: William Law, Stephen Simson.

Feb. 1 John Davies‡ of this parish, B., and Sarah Core of the same, S.; by Tho: Higgins, minister. Banns. Wit.: James Lee, James Montgomerie.

13 Charles Brown* of this parish, B., and Arabella Alvey§ of St Paul, Deptford, Kent, S.; by J. Jones, minister. Lic. Wit.: Maurice Dolley, Mary Jones, James Montgomerie, Michael Coles.

27 Thomas Turner of this parish, B., and Elizabeth Luckings of the same, S.; by Tho. Higgins, minister. Banns. Wit.: Mary Stacey, James Montgomerie.

Mar. 12 William Brown of St Peter's, W., and Elizabeth Francis of the same, S.; by Tho. Higgins, minister. Banns. Wit.: Thos Butterfield, Jane Butterfield.

12 William Webb of St John, Wapping, Middx., W., and Mary Powell of St Peter's, Paul's Wharf, S.; by Tho. Higgins, minister. Lic. Wit.: Joseph Burton, Sarah Walker.

June 24 James Dawson of St Peter's, Pauls Wharf, B., and Rebbecca Allen* of the same, S.; by Tho. Higgins, minister. Banns. Wit.: Wm Quinton, Thos Morgan.

July 5 William Quinton of this parish, B., and Mary Fidler of the same, S.; by J. Jones, minister. Banns. Wit.: John Barnes, Samuel Hollier.

15 Thomas Purrett* of this parish, W., and Ester Offield of the same, W.; by Tho. Higgins, minister. Banns. Wit.: Daniel Allen, Jane Barnes.

Aug. 6 William Marks of this parish, B., and Ann Smith of the same, S.; by Tho. Higgins, minister. Banns. Wit.: Richard Peither, Ann Smith.

Sept. 8 Peter Powell of this parish, B., and Elizabeth Conyers of the same, S.; by Christopher Armstrong, curate. Banns. Wit.: Patrick Gilchrist, Hannah + Shonsey, her mark.

* Signs by mark.—Ed.

† Signs "Alice Cloake."—Ed.

‡ Signs "John Davis."—Ed.

§ Signs "Arabella Allvey."—Ed.

1770-71

Oct 19 John Perbrite* of St Peter, Pauls Wharf, B, and Eleanor Bartlee of the same, S, by Christ^r Armstrong, curate Banns Wit John Hilton, James Montgomerie

25 George Gordon of St Peter, Paul's Wharf, B, and Ann Spencer of the same, W, by Christ^r Armstrong, curate Banns Wit William Drake, Iscalader Smith

Nov 25 Thomas Whebell of this parish, B, and Mary Drury of the same, S, by Tho Higgins, minister Banns Wit Joseph Beecham, Jane Wilson

Dec 3 William Rayner† of St Peter, Pauls Wharf, B, and Sarah Plailet† of the same, S, by J Jones, minister Banns Wit James Montgomerie, William Still Buckingham

12 Edward Catliff of this parish, B, and Mary Hammond† of the same, S, by J. Jones, minister. Banns Wit James Montgomerie, Michael Coles

26 Charles Beamish of this parish, B, and Mary Buckland† of the same, S, by Mark Holberry, minister Banns. Wit. James Montgomerie, Michael Coles.

1771

Jan. 6 William Webb of St Peter's, W, and Mary Luck of the same, W; by Tho Higgins, minister Banns. Wit Abraham Dennison, James Montgomerie

21 William Bowden‡ of this parish, B, and Mary Verity of the same, S, by Christ^r Armstrong, Curate Banns Wit. Josiah Langdon, W Graham.

27 Robert Stephenson of this parish, W, and Jane Taylor of the same, S; by Tho Higgins, minister Lic Wit Edmund Hodgson, Sarah Castlow

28 William Seller of this parish, W, and Mary Humble of the same, W; by J Jones, Minister Lic Wit John Whiter, James Sarney

Feb 9 John Scatliff of this parish, W, and Ann Whitton† of St George the Martyr, Middx, S, by J Jones, Minister Lic Wit William Whitton, Hannah Scatliff

12 George Marpole† of St Antholin, London, B, and Mary Gibbard of St Peter's, W, by J Jones, minister Lic Wit William March, Ann Marpole

April 1 William Taubman of this parish, B, and Elizabeth Collins† of the same, S, by Christ^r Armstrong, curate Banns Wit John + Smith his mark, Nathaniel Taubman

May 19 Nathan Veazey of this parish, B, and Elizabeth Speed† of the same, S, by Chr^r Armstrong, curate Banns Wit. George Drinkwater, Hannah Fryer

July 2 Orlando Pearse of St Mary le Strand, B, and Elizabeth Preston† of St Peter, Pauls Wharf, S, by Tho Higgins, Minister Banns Wit · James Freeman, James Montgomerie

21 John Houlton of St Peter, Paul's Wharf, W, and Isabella Helder† of the same, W, by Chr^r Armstrong, curate Banns Wit James Montgomerie, Daniel Hodges

Aug 11 Thomas Seker of this parish, W., and Sarah Murray† of the same, W, by Tho Higgins, minister Banns Wit James Montgomerie, Elizabeth Baines.

18 Thomas Peckett† of this parish, W, and Lydia Evans† of the same, W, by Chr^r Armstrong, curate. Banns. Wit Charles White, Tho Bosville

* Signs "Porbrite."—Ed † Signs by mark —Ed ‡ Signs "Bauden"—Ed

1771-2

Sept. 15 Francis Hammond* of St Peter's, W., and Ann Burchall* of the same, W.; by Edw. G. Foote. Banns. Wit.: George + Gover, his mark, James Montgomerie.

25 John Halsted Deere of St Martin in the city of Norwich, B., and Ann Huitson of this parish, S.; by Tho. Morden. Lic. Wit.: Danl Gillman, James Montgomerie.

Nov. 2 William Turner of this parish, B., and Hannah Harrison of the same, S.; by Chrr Armstrong, curate. Banns. Wit.: James McKaine, Sarah Jones.

12 William Bethell* of this parish, B., and Elizabeth Ibbertson* of the same, S.; by Chrisr Armstrong, curate. Banns. Wit.: Alexander Jones, John Lebenrood.

21 James Crisp of this parish, B., and Catherine Tanner of the same, S.; by Chrisr Armstrong, curate. Banns. Wit.: Peter Chasnie, Charlotta Hill.

1772.

Jan. 1 William Dredge of this parish, B., and Martha White of the same, S.; by Chrisr Armstrong, Curate. Banns. Wit.: Benjamin Worthy, Elizabeth Gradey.

19 Gabriel Long of St Pancras, Middx., B., and Elizabeth Bailey* of this parish, S.; by Chrisr Armstrong, curate. Lic. Wit.: William Bailey, Thomas Petley.

30 John Muffett of St Peter's, B., and Mary Letts of the same, S.; by Chrisr Armstrong, curate. Banns. Wit.: John Pain [? Price], Ann Hand.

Mar. 14 William Compton, LL.D., of this parish, B., and Caroline Glover of St James, Westminster, W.; by James Hallifax, minister. Lic. Wit.: S. Compton, Pen. Compton.

29 William Sherwin of St Ann, Blackfryers, B., and Mary Bourn of this parish, W.; by Chrisr Armstrong, curate. Lic. Wit.: Judith Bourn, Loader Bourn.

April 26 John Ingly* of this parish, B., and Elizabeth Harris of the same, S.; by Chrisr Armstrong, curate. Banns. Wit.: James Montgomerie, John Mears, James Dowling.

27 Edward Wells of this parish, B., and Ann Huffam Norgate of the same, S.; by Chrisr Armstrong, curate. Banns. Wit.: Edward Wells, senr, Christian Norgate.

May 17 James Headling* of this parish, B., and Sarah Every* of the same, S.; by Chrisr Armstrong, curate. Banns. Wit.: Sarah Terry, Elizabeth Ramsey.

June 14 George Inch of this parish, B., and Elizabeth Brown* of the same, S.; by Christr Armstrong, curate. Banns. Wit.: Charles Horne, Geo. Byworth.

23 James Waylett of this parish, B., and Ann Paxford of St Swithin, London, S.; by Tho. Richards. Lic. Wit.: James Montgomerie, John Mears.

July 5 Richard Proberts* of St Peter's, Paul's Wharf, B., and Mary Jones* of the same, S.; by Tho. Higgins, minister. Banns. Wit.: James Montgomerie, Daniel Hodges.

6 Richard Mansbridge* of this parish, B., and Ann Hands* of the same, W.; by Tho. Higgins, minister. Banns. Wit.: James Montgomerie, John Mears, James Bignell, Elizabeth Jerves.

Aug. 24 Thomas Lewis of this parish, B., and Ann Watts of the same, S.; by Chr. Armstrong, curate. Banns. Wit.: John Goodridge, Thomas Young.

* Signs by mark.—Ed.

1772-3

Sept. 1 Charles Poynter of S[t] Peter's, B., and Elizabeth Shaw of the same, S.; by Chr. Armstrong, curate. Lic. Wit.: Eliz. Almon, Mary Jackson.

13 Charles Iliffe of S[t] Peter's, B., and Rebecca Heylin of the same, S.; by Chr[r] Armstrong, curate. Lic. Wit.: Rachell Groves, John Heylin.

13 Joseph Sharp* of this parish, B., and Francis [*sic*] Tumber* of the same, S.; by Chr[r] Armstrong, curate. Banns. Wit.: James Montgomerie, James Dowling, Phillip Williams, John Mears.

20 William Austin* of this parish, B., and Mary Coulson* of the same, S.; by T. Richards, min[er]. Banns. Wit.: James Keynock, James Montgomerie, John Masters, John Mears.

27 Zachariah Gisborne of S[t] Margaret Pattens, London, B., and Esther Rogers of S[t] Peter, Paul's Wharf, London, S.; by Chr[r] Armstrong, curate. Lic. from the Archbishop of Canterbury. Wit.: John Rogers, Geo. Chapman.

Oct. 17 Robert Roberts of this parish, W., and Mary Humphries of S[t] Peter, Paul's Wharf, W.; by T. Richards, minister. Banns. Wit.: Charles Horne, John Mears.

Nov. 8 William Brett of this parish, B., and Isabella Perry of the same, S.; by Geo. Steers, minister. Banns. Wit.: Tho. Wilkinson, James Montgomerie.

11 Edward Edwards of this parish, B., and Elizabeth Ambler of the same, S.; by T. Richards, minister. Banns. Wit.: Thomas Dean, James Montgomerie.

Dec. 3 Thomas Turten of S[t] Bennett, Pauls Wharf, London, W., and Susannah Symons of Ealing, Middx., W.; by Thomas Pollen, Min[r]. Lic. Wit.: Joseph Wilkinson, James Montgomerie.

22 John Casey* of S[t] Peter's, B., and Anne Broadway of the same, [*blank*]; by John Naish, minister. Banns. Wit.: John Merritt, James Montgomerie.

29 James Jackson of this parish, B., and Mary Roper* of the same, S.; by Geo. Steers, minister. Banns. Wit.: Joseph Wilkinson, James Montgomerie.

1773.

Jan. 5 John Player of this parish, B., and Mary Biggs of West Ham, Essex, S.; by T. Richards, minister. Lic. Wit.: Thomas Beart, James Montgomerie.

Feb. 21 Samuel Wells of this parish, B., and Mary Sutton* of the same, S.; by G. Steers, Min[r]. Banns. Wit.: Edward Wells, Edward Wells, jun[r], James Montgomerie.

Mar. 7 Richard Harding of this parish, B., and Catherine Dallain of the same, S.; by Geo. Steers, min[r]. Banns. Wit.: Samuel Warren, Ann Warren, James Montgomerie.

11 Isaac Lewis of the city of Chichester, B., and Sally Ashford of this parish, S.; by Geo. Steers, Min[r]. Lic. Wit.: John Ashford, Easther Lewis, James Montgomerie.

27 Luke Sykes of S[t] Dunstan, Stepney, Middx., B., and Mary Rouse of this parish, S.; by Geo. Steers, min[r]. Lic. Wit.: John Pittway, Elizabeth Kendall.

May 14 Thomas Burton of this parish, W., and Mary Allen of the same, S.; by G. Steers, min[r]. Banns. Wit.: James Montgomerie, John Mears.

June 19 Robert Moser of S[t] Michael, Queenhithe, B., and Elizabeth Crawshay of S[t] Bennets, Paul's Wharf, S.; by Geo. Steers, Min[r]. Lic. Wit.: Richard Crawshay, James Montgomerie.

* Signs by mark.—ED.

1773-4

June 24 John Taylor of the parish Extra parochial of Norton Falgate, B., and Ann Smith of S[t] Peter, Pauls Wharf, S.; by William Rider, Lecturer of S[t] Vedast. Licence of the Archbishop of Canterbury. Wit.: Henry Smith, Jun[r], Charlotte Edgar.

Aug. 1 Francis Stennett of S[t] Peter, Paul's Wharf, W., and Ann Barker of S[t] Mildred, Bread Street, S.; by G. Steers, Min[r]. Lic. Wit.: Dorothy Lodge, James Montgomerie.

Sept. 6 Robert Clavering of this parish, B., and Eleanor Turner of the same, S.; by G. Steers, Min[r]. Banns. Wit.: Hannah Asser, Charles Horne.

7 Thomas Burrell of this parish, W., and Mary Fitzgerald of the same, W.; by Geo. Steers, Min[r]. Banns. Wit.: John Cawne, Richard Allum.

27 James Jeffery of this parish, W., and Rebecca Hands of the same, S.; by Geo. Steers, Min[r]. Banns. Wit.: James Montgomerie, William Purnell.

Nov. 7 Isaac Montague* of this parish, B., and Sarah Carbarcy of the same, W.; by M. M. Merrick. Banns. Wit.: Tho. Spedding, James Montgomerie, John Mears.

10 Nathaniel Wheatley of Greenwich, Kent, B., and Mary Enderby of S[t] Peter, Paul's Wharf, London, S.; by S. Ellison, Rector. Lic. Wit.: Jane Enderby, Elizabeth Enderby.

Dec. 16 William Hayes, Clerk of the Inner Temple, London, B., and Ann Thomas Soaper of this parish, S.; by John Gibbons, curate. Lic. Wit.: Philip Hayes, Samuel Johnson [?].

25 Samuel Stephens of this parish, B., and Jane Coar of the same, S.; by John Gibbons, curate. Banns. Wit.: John Davis, Ann + Stephens, her mark.

27 Samuel Walker of this parish, B., and Susannah Bates of the same, S.; by John Gibbons, curate. Banns. Wit.: Samuel Hodson, Susanna Bolt.

1774.

Jan. 8 Christopher Barber of this parish, W., and Elizabeth Pulford of the same, W.; by John Gibbons, curate. Banns. Wit.: James Montgomerie, John Mears.

30 John Orr of Christ Church, Surrey, W., and Mary Brentnall of S[t] Peter's, S.; by John Gibbons, curate. Banns. Wit.: J. Brentnall, Jane Lander.

Feb. 12 Daniel Allen of this parish, W., and Isabella Wright of S[t] Mary Magdalen, Old Fish Street, London, S.; by John Gibbons, curate. Lic. Wit.: Charles Horne, James + Suffolk, his mark.

Mar. 13 William Morgan of this parish, B., and Martha Humphreys of the same, S.; by John Gibbons, curate. Banns. Wit.: Charles Horne, John Mears.

17 Thomas Coare of this parish, B., and Ann Bettsworth of the same, S.; by John Gibbons, curate. Banns. Wit.: James Ayres, Ann Ayres.

20 Thomas Longbottom of this parish, W., and Mary Simmonds* of the same, S.; by John Gibbons, curate. Banns. Wit.: Rich[d] Allum, Charles Horne.

24 Thomas Blyth of this parish, B., and Mary Ellis of the same, W.; by John Gibbons, curate. Lic. Wit.: Tho. Wingfield, Sarah Partridge.

April 3 Nicholas Dove of S[t] Peter, Pauls Wharf, W., and Elizabeth James* of S[t] Saviour, Southwark, Surrey, W.; by John Gibbons, curate. Banns. Wit.: Charles Horne, John Mears.

5 John Dicker* of this parish, B., and Hannah Marsh* of the same, S.; by John Gibbons, curate. Banns. Wit.: John Tilbury Williams, Charles Horne.

* Signs by mark.—Ed.

1774-5

April 8 Thomas Thomas of this parish, B, and Elizabeth Moore of S[t] Catherine Cree church, London, S, by John Gibbons, curate Lic Wit Charles Horne, John Mears

May 6 Francis Lambert of S[t] Bennett, Paul's Wharf, London, B and Rebecca Moore* of Woolwich, Kent, S, by John Gibbons, curate Lic Wit Charles Moore, Charles Horne

June 29 Gervass Elliot of this parish, B, and Elizabeth Potter* of S[t] Leonard, Shoreditch, W, by John Gibbons, curate Lic. Wit James Avis, Charles Horne

July 10 John Henry Manly of this parish, B, and Johannah Morris of the same, W., by John Gibbons, curate. Banns Wit Mary Hubbard, Alice Barum

15 William Lang of this parish, B, and Elizabeth Marlow of S[t] Mary le bone, Middx, S., by John Gibbons, curate Lic Wit Tho Spedding, Charles Horne

Aug 7 Philip Tranter of this parish, B, and Elizabeth Morris* of the same, W, by John Gibbons, curate. Banns Wit. Charles Horne, John Mears

Oct 9 James Letchford* of this parish, B, and Elizabeth Onyon of the same, S., by John Gibbons, curate Banns Wit William Tort, Christopher Gardner

13 Edward Rust of this parish, B, and Alice Turner* of S[t] Leonard, Shoreditch, S; by John Gibbons, curate Lic. Wit Charles Porter, Mary Porter.

Nov 21 Robert Kitson of this parish, W, and Mary Jennaway of the same, S, by John Gibbons, curate Banns Wit. William Birkwood, Rebeckah Birkwood

1775.

Jan. 22 Lewis Braeutigam of this parish, B, and Ann Forces of the same, S, by John Gibbons, curate. Banns. Wit James Montgomerie, John Mears.

Feb. 19 Thomas Hilliard of this parish, W, and Mary Gay* of the same, S, by John Gibbons, curate Banns Wit Robert Westley, Mary Westley.

Mar 26 George Clapham of S[t] Bennett, Pauls Wharfe, London, B, and Sarah Metcalfe of S[t] George, Bloomsbury, Middx, S, by John Gibbons, curate Lic Wit Charles Horne, James Montgomerie

April 4 Samuel Hare of Trinity, Minories, London, B, and Mary Lashley of S[t] Peter, London, S, by John Gibbons, curate Lic Wit James Montgomerie, Stephen Ball

June 13 Thomas Harris* of S[t] Peter, London, B, and Catherine Hughes* of the same, S, by John Gibbons, curate Banns Wit James Montgomery, John Mears

19 John Lawrence of this parish, B, and Susanna Morris* of the same, S, by Tho Richards, Min[r] Banns Wit Charles Horne, James Montgomerie

24 Jacob Smith of this parish, B, and Mary Gale of the same, S, by John Gibbons, curate Banns. Wit. Joseph Blunt, M Morisson

July 16 Richard Worrall of this parish, B, and Mary Grindley of the same, S, by John Gibbons, curate. Banns Wit.: John Grindley, Mary Marcellus

23 Christopher Lewis Steip of S[t] Bennett, Paul's Wharfe, London, B and Jane Charlton of the same, S; by John Gibbons, curate Lic Wit · Jane Andrew, Charles Horne.

* Signs by mark.—Ed

1775-6

Aug. 6 John Jones* of this parish, B., and Sarah Davis* of the same, S.; by John Gibbons, curate. Banns. Wit.: Esther Foster, Charles Horne.

Nov. 9 Edward Higgs of this parish, B., and Sarah Horsey of the same, S.; by John Gibbons, curate. Banns. Wit.: Gilbert Edwards, Sarah Horsey.

12 John Cowderoy of St Benedict, Paul's Wharfe, London, B., and Ann Deverill of St Mary le Bone, Middx., S.; by John Gibbons, curate. Lic. Wit.: Luke Lyney, Charles Horne.

20 William Gooding* of this parish, B., and Elizabeth Amonent* of the same, S.; by John Gibbons, curate. Banns. Wit.: James Montgomerie, Lucy Clarke, John Mears.

Dec. 25 Samuel Butt* of this parish, B., and Grace Hawkshaw* of the same, W.; by John Gibbons, curate. Banns. Wit.: Allen Helsdon, James Montgomerie.

1776.

Jan. 18 William Puckridge of St Sepulchre, London, B., and Mary Boyles of St Benedict, Paul's Wharf, S.; by John Gibbons, curate. Lic. Wit.: William Puckridge, Charles Puckridge.

28 John Beveridge of St Mary, White Chappel, Middx., B., and Mary Booker of St Benedict, Pauls Wharfe, London, S.; by John Gibbons, curate. Lic. Wit.: Charles Horne, James Montgomerie.

Feb. 19 James Fross of St Peter's, B., and Mary Oliver* of the same, S.; by John Gibbons, curate. Banns. Wit.: James Montgomerie, John Mears, Rebecca Morris.

Mar. 16 Thomas Stephens of this parish, B., and Hannah Hoppey* of the same, W.;† by John Gibbons, curate. Banns. Wit.: Charles Horne, James Montgomerie.

April 10 Edward Chapman of this parish, B., and Mary Stanton of the same, S.; by John Gibbons, curate. Banns. Wit.: Charles Horne, James Montgomerie.

14 Robert Guy* of St Sepulchre, London, B., and Theodora Grange of St Bennett als. Benedict, Pauls Wharfe, London, S.; by John Gibbons, curate. Lic. Wit.: Henry Boston, Mary Love.

May 5 James Ford* of this parish, B., and Sarah Tyler* of Staines, Middx., S.; by John Gibbons, curate. Lic. Wit.: John Taylor, James Montgomerie.

9 John Rofe of this parish, B., and Ann Ward* of the same, S.; by John Gibbons, curate. Banns. Wit.: Elizabeth Butler, George Fowler.

12 John Tayler of this parish, B., and Elizabeth Harris of the same, S.; John Gibbons, curate. Banns. Wit.: Nancy Welch, Charles Horne.

20 Richard Sanders of this parish, B., and Sarah Felton* of the same, S.; by John Gibbons, curate. Banns. Wit.: Charles Horne, Jane Parson.

21 Charles Ackland of this parish, B., and Elizabeth Heather of the same, S.; by John Gibbons, curate. Banns. Wit.: W. Cruthwell, Charles Horne.

26 William Pyke* of this parish, B., and Esther Swaine* of the same, S.; by John Gibbons, curate. Banns. Wit.: Aaron Woods, William Harris.

June 30 Thomas Brentnall of St Peter, Pauls Wharf, London, W., and Sarah Moor of Holy Trinity, London, W.; by John Gibbons, curate. Lic. Wit.: John Redford, Catherine Redford.

July 21 William Clanfield of this parish, B., and Elizabeth Broadwater* of the same, S.; by William Hayes, Minister. Banns. Wit.: Charles Horne, James Harris.

* Signs by mark.—Ed. † "Widow" written over apparently "Spinster."—Ed.

1776-7

Aug. 12 Henry Gilder of this parish, B., and Avis Wallford of the same, S.; by William Hayes, minister. Banns. Wit.: Ed. Crabb, Charles Horne.

Sept. 1 John Shaw of this parish, B., and Ann Sanders of the same, S.; by John Gibbons, curate. Lic. Wit.: Richard Read, Mary Hastings.

8 Daniel Hodgkin of this parish, B., and Mary Towle of the same, W.; by Tho. Richards, Min[r]. Banns. Wit.: James Killer, William Attwood.

21 Joseph Camp* of this parish, B., and Elizabeth Hambleton of the same, S.; by John Gibbons, curate. Lic. Wit.: Balguy Hart, John Mears.

29 John Jackson* of this parish, B., and Mary Worthy* of the same, S.; by John Gibbons, curate. Banns. Wit.: James Pybell, Elizabeth Depear.

Oct. 7 Richard Lee* of S[t] Giles in the Fields, Middx., B., and Rebecca Payne* of S[t] Bennett, Pauls Wharfe, London, S.; by John Gibbons, curate. Lic. Wit.: Charles Horne, John Mears.

[*A form not filled in.*]

21 William Rowlatt of S[t] Ann, Blackfriers, London, B., and Ann Haley of S[t] Benedict, Pauls Wharfe, London, W.; by John Gibbons, curate. Lic. Wit.: William Pontyfie, Nathaniel Veazey.

29 William Isaac Hayden of this parish, B., and Jane Griffiths of the same, S.; by John Gibbons, curate. Banns. Wit.: Andrew Newland, John Clapp.

Nov. 3 Simeon Clifton of S[t] Bennet, Pauls Wharfe, London, W., and Elizabeth Gouldin of the same, W.; by John Gibbons, curate. Lic. Wit.: Charles Griffiths, John Mears.

21 William Cook of S[t] Bennetts, Pauls Wharf, London, W., and Mary Seears of Ryslip, Middx., S.; by John Gibbons, curate. Lic. Wit.: James Montgomerie, John Mears.

26 Samuel Weddell of this parish, B., and Sibella Clark of the same, S.; by John Gibbons, curate. Banns. Wit.: Anne Hodgson, Geo. Keyes.

Dec. 2 William Timms of this parish, W., and Jane Jeshope of the same, S.; by John Gibbons, curate. Banns. Wit.: James Jackson, Ann Davis.

1777.

Jan. 18 Henry Allum of S[t] Benedict, Pauls Wharfe, London, B., and Ann Burtenwood of S[t] Saviour, Southwark, Surry, S., a Minor; by John Gibbons, curate. Lic. Wit.: Mary Thompson, Thomas Burtenwood.

Mar. 6 Isaac Hemingway of this parish, B., and Elizabeth Leach of the same, S.; by John Gibbons, curate. Lic. Wit.: James Jackson, James Montgomerie.

8 John Jackson of S[t] Peter, Paul's Wharfe, B., and Catherine Yates of S[t] Gabriel, Fenchurch, W.; by John Gibbons, curate. Lic. Wit.: Elizabeth Whitthorn, James Montgomerie.

16 John Dix of this parish, B., and Mary Roberts of the same, S.; by John Gibbons, curate. Banns. Wit.: William Liddon, Mary Hutchings.

23 James Hayward of this parish, B., and Ann Kemp* of the same, S.; by John Gibbons, curate. Banns. Wit.: William Kemp, Mary Kemp.

May 10 Thomas Smith of this parish, B., and Ann Morris of S[t] Leonard, Shoreditch, Middx., S.; by John Gibbons, curate. Lic. Wit.: Mary Lewis, D. Morris.

June 2 William Clarke of this parish, B., and Ann Ayres of the same, S.; by John Gibbons, curate. Banns. Wit.: Edward Hedges, Mary Whitely.

* Signs by mark.—Ed.

1777-8

June 22 Daniel Eberhard of this parish, B., and Elizabeth Cox of St Margaret Pattens, London, S.; by John Gibbons, curate. Lic. Wit.: James Jackson, John Mears.

30 John Barrow of this parish, W., and Martha Fassett of the same, W.; by John Gibbons, curate. Banns. Wit.: Ann Webb, Richard Webb.

30 Walter Fishley of St Peter, Pauls Wharf, W., and Mary Glandfield of this parish, W.; by John Gibbons, curate. Banns. Wit.: Charles Horne, John Mears.

Aug. 10 James Wilson the younger of St Benedict, Pauls Wharfe, London, B., and Sarah Johnson of St Mildred, Bread Street, London, S.; by Tho. Evans, min^r. Lic. Wit.: Charles Horne, John Mears.

Nov. 9 John Archer of St Bennett, Paul's Wharfe, London, B., and Elizabeth Chantrey of the same, S.; by John Gibbons, curate. Lic. Wit.: William Barham, Charles Horne.

10 William Lake of this parish, B., and Ann Collins of the same, S.; by John Gibbons, curate. Banns.* Wit.: John Lake, Geo. Markham.

Dec. 1 John Willson of St Nicholas Cole Abbey, London, B., and Jane Sparkes of this parish, S.; by John Gibbons, curate. Lic. Wit.: John Mears, James Montgomerie.

1778.

Jan. 22 John Edge of this parish, W., and Mary English of St Sepulchre, London, W.; by John Gibbons, curate. Lic. Wit.: Charles Horne, John Mears.

NOTE.—An entry of "John Beedell of this parish, B., and Rosanna Willan of St Ann, Westminster. Licence. 24 Jan. 1778," has been left incomplete and marked out.

[*Two forms not filled in.*]

[End of this Volume.]

[On the Cover.]

†The united parishes of St Benedict & St Peter, Pauls Wharf. Marriage register.
EDMUND GIBSON, Rector 1777.

H.

St. Benet & St. Peter.

MARRIAGES FROM 12TH APRIL 1778 TO 15 DEC^R 1796.

1778.

April 12 Simon Allen of St George, Hanover Square, Middx., B., and Prudence Helliar of this parish, S.; by John Gibbons, curate. Lic. Wit.: Richard Wheadon, Charles Horne.

May 16 Joseph Allen Boggis of St Peter, Pauls Wharfe, London, B., and Elizabeth Gulliver of Walcot in Somerset, S.; by John Gibbons, curate. Lic. Wit.: Margaret Savage, Edm. Bick.

* "Banns" written over "Licence."—ED.

† There is a MS. note on the printed page immediately following the title page, to the effect that the marriages in this book were solemnized *in the Parish Church of St. Benedict, Paul's Wharf, London.*—ED.

1778-9

May 19 Thomas Clarke of St Luke, Middx, W, and Mary Jameson* of this parish, S, by John Gibbons, curate Lic Wit Stephen Wolfe, Elizabeth Clifton

July 26 Charles Moore of St Bennett, Pauls Wharfe, London, W, and Elizabeth Titterington of St George, Southwark, Surry, W, by John Lawson Lic Wit Charles Horne, Ann Titterington

Aug 29 John Tomlin† of this parish, B, and Susannah Walker† of the same parish, S, by Tho Richards, curate Banns Wit. David Porter, Charles Horne

Sept 28 George Lake of this parish, W, and Sarah Brand of the same, W, by John Gibbons, curate Banns Wit. Ann Lake, William Lake

29 Robert Barton of Cheshunt, co Herts, B, and Mary Hanscombe of St Peter, Pauls Wharfe, London, S., by George Baxter, A M Lic. Wit. Charles Horne, John Mears

Oct 1 John Seal of this parish, B, and Jane Stephens of the same, W, by John Gibbons, curate Banns. Wit William Sharp, Charles Horne

6 Richard Sears of St Bennett, Pauls Wharfe, London, W, and Ann Deely† of the same, W, by James Watkins Lic Wit. Charles Horne, John Mears

22 John Price of this parish, B, and Margaret Williams of the same, S; by John Gibbons Banns Wit Tho Williams, Margery Hoole.

23 Francis Walker of this parish, B, and Elizabeth Mathews of the same, S, by John Gibbons, curate. Banns Wit Charles Horne, John Mears

Nov 24 Thomas Fuller of this parish, B, and Frances Slade of the same, S, by John Gibbons, curate Banns Wit John Bushnell, Mary Bushnell

Dec 10 John Thorowgood† of this parish, B, and Mary Lake of the same, S, by John Gibbons, curate Banns Wit Charles Horne, John Mears

19 James Sheridan of this parish, W, and Joyce Carter† of the same, W, by John Gibbons, curate Banns Wit .. Thomas, John Mears

1779

Jan 3 Dennis Egan† of this parish, B, and Rebecca Peters‡ of the same, W, by John Gibbons, curate. Banns Wit. Barry Connolly, Sarah Connolly

4 John Pearce of this parish, B, and Mary Lane† of the same, S, by John Gibbons, Curate Banns Wit Sarah Owen, the mark of Thomas Pearce

16 John Raban of this parish, W, and Mary Smith of St Andrew, Holborn, S; by John Gibbons, Curate Licence Wit William Stephens & Hester Robinson

28 William Cook of this parish, W., and Mary Claro† of Heese, Midx., S, by John Gibbons, Curate Licence. Wit. Mary Nicholas & John May

Feb. 21 Henry Richards† of this parish, B, and Sarah Wallis of the same, S; by John Gibbons, Curate Banns Wit Charles Horne & John Mears

Mar. 8 Augustin King George of this parish, B, and Lucy Berner of Endfield, Midx, S, by John Gibbons, Curate. Licence. Wit Dutton Greenwood, Charles Horne

14 John Nelson of this parish, B, and Sarah Webb† of Bury Saint Edmunds, Suffolk, S, by John Gibbons, Curate. Licence Wit. Samuel Shepherd, Charles Horne

* Signs "Joneson."—ED. † Signs by mark—ED. ‡ Signs "Petters"—ED.

1779

April 4 William Loveday Lord of this parish, B., and Ann Goodwin of the same, S.; by Robert Dolling, Vicar of Aldenham. Banns. Wit.: Elizabeth Goodwin, Thomas James, Richard Ball.

21 William Crookshank of this parish, B., and Hannah Holloway* of the same, W.; by John Gibbons, Curate. Banns. Wit.: James Fell & Mary Fell.

24 William Avery of St John, Wapping, Midx., W., and Mary Patriarch of this parish, S.; by John Gibbons, Curate. Licence. Wit.: Charles Horne, John Mears.

May 3 William Chalklen of this parish, B., and Sarah Weller of Mitcham, Surrey, W.; by John Gibbons, curate. Licence. Wit.: Gideon Ernest Charpentier & Mary Reddish.

9 Joseph King of this parish, B., and Hester Adams* of the same, S.; by John Gibbons, Curate. Banns. Wit.: Edward Harrison & James Hills.

16 Edward Rocket of this parish, B., and Elizabeth Mosely of the same, S.; by John Gibbons, Curate. Banns. Wit.: Andrew Bilton & John Mears.

June 1 Thomas Richards of St Peter, B., and Mary Mears of the same, S.; by John Gibbons, Curate. Banns. Wit.: John Mears & Charles Horne.

2 William Boon of this parish, B., and Mary Barton* of the same, S.; by John Gibbons, Curate. Banns. Wit.: Charles Horne & John Mears.

6 William Hurst* of St Benedict, Paul's Wharf, Lond., B., and Elizabeth Barthrow* of the same, S.; by John Gibbons, Curate. Licence. Wit.: Charles Horne, John Mears.

8 Samuel Baldwin of this parish, W., and Ann Sutton of the same, S.; by John Gibbons, Curate. Banns. Wit.: Charles Horne & John Mears.

July 11 Charles Curtis of St Peter, Paul's Wharf, B., and Elizabeth Cole of the same, S.; by John Gibbons, Curate. Banns. Wit.: Sarah Bale, William Dolton.

11 William Wheadon of this parish, B., and Mary Wheadon of the same, S.; by John Gibbons, Curate. Licence. Wit.: Elizabeth Wheadon, Thomas Wheadon.

Sept. 6 John Thompson* of this parish, B., and Sarah Hitchcock* of the same, S.; by John Gibbons, Curate. Banns. Wit.: Thomas Taverner & Charles Horne.

16 Samuel Perry of St Luke, Midx., W., and Ann Bone* of St Peter near Paul's Wharf, Lond., S.; by David Matthias, Min^r. Licence. Wit.: William Gates, Charles Horne.

Nov. 9 William Wright of this parish, B., and Mary Pike* of the same, S.; by John Gibbons, Curate. Banns. Wit.: W. Purnell, Charles Horne.

21 William Glasscock of St Peter, B., and Margaret Loggan of the same, S.; by John Gibbons, Curate. Banns. Wit.: Andrew Billton & John Mears.

21 Henry Brickman of this parish, B., and Dorothy Horn* of the same, S.; by John Gibbons, Curate. Banns. Wit.: John Auhlmann, Jane Gibbs.

24 Michael Thomas* of St Michael, Queenhithe, B., and Mary Lawes* of St Peter, S.; by John Gibbons, Curate. Licence. Wit.: Robert Benham & Charles Horne.

Dec. 15 John Titcomb of St George, Midx., W., and Mary Clarke* of this parish, S.; by John Gibbons, Curate. Licence. Wit.: John Cruse & William Page.

* Signs by mark.—Ed.

1780

1780-81

Feb. 20 Samuel Murray of Tynemouth, co Northumberland, B, and Ann Fielding of S[t] Peter, Paul's Wharf, S, by John Gibbons, Curate. Licence Wit.. Ann Cooper & Charles Horne

Mar 18 William Hood of this parish, B, and Elizabeth Maria Lowes of the same, S, by John Gibbons, Curate Licence Wit George Davidson & Harriot Lowes

May 11 John Stevens of this parish, W, and Ann Bigg of the same, W., by John Gibbons, Curate. Banns. Wit Charles Horne & John Mears

June 6 William Manby of Downham, Norfolk, B, and Elizabeth Paine of S[t] Benedict near Paul's Wharf, S, by John Gibbons, Curate Licence Wit C Law, Charles Horne

25 Elisha Byrne of S[t] Mary, White Chapel, Midx, W, and Margaret Sinnett of S[t] Benet, Paul's Wharf, Lond, S, by John Gibbons, Curate Licence Wit Aaron Hale & Charles Horne

28 George Jennings of Greenwich, Kent, B, and Mary Dunn of S[t] Bennet, Paul's Wharf, Lond, S, by John Gibbons, Curate Licence Wit · Thomas Powis, Charles Horne

Oct 6 John Forrest of S[t] James, Westm[r], Midx, B, and Sarah Quincey of S[t] Benedict near Paul's Wharf, Lond, W, by John Horner, Minister Lic Wit Benjamin Smith, Charles Horne

17 Peter Smith of this parish, B, and Rebecca Berry* of the same, S, by John Gibbon, Curate Banns Wit Edward Edwards & Charles Horne

26 Isaac Ivory of S[t] Leonard, Shoreditch, Midx, a Minor & a B, and Charlotte Truckler of S[t] Peter, Paul's Wharf, Lond, S Married by Licence and consent of Thomas Ivory, the Father of the said Minor, by John Gibbons, Curate Wit · Mark White Seager [?], Thomas Ivory

Dec 12 Matthew Allen of Watford, co Hertford, W, and Rebecca Saint of this parish, W; by John Gibbons, Curate Licence Wit Edward Cross, Margaret Cross

1781

Jan 23 William Chapman of S[t] Botolph in the town of Cambridge, B, and Ann Hamilton of S[t] Peter near Paul's Wharf, Lond, S, by John Gibbons, Curate Licence Wit Catherine Hamilton, Latitia Tomlinson

Feb 27 William Shaw of Romford, Essex, W, and Sarah Britton† of S[t] Bennet, Paul's Wharf, Lond, S, by Edmund Gibson, Rector Licence. Wit : Mary Hastings, Ann Mott

April 11 Charles Moore of this parish, W, and Sarah Dickman* of S[t] Stephen, Coleman St, Lond, W., by John Gibbons, Curate Licence Wit Robert Richards & Mary Dickman

15 John Undutch of S[t] Peter, Paul's Wharf, B, and Elizabeth Briant* of S[t] Botolph without Aldgate, W, by John Gibbons, Curate Licence Wit John Ohlson & Mary Jones

17 Sampson Coysgarne of this parish, W, and Rebecca Willcox of the same, S, by John Gibbons, Curate Banns Wit Watton Willcox & Elizabeth Willcox

20 Benjamin Beamont of this parish, B, and Sarah Ding of the same, S, by John Gibbons, Curate Licence Wit Mary Ding & Ann Finch

29 William Brewer of this parish, B, and Susannah Cooke of the same, S., by John Gibbons, Curate. Banns. Wit : Mary Luff & Joseph Jones.

* Signs by mark —ED. † Signs "Sarah Brittain otherwise Britton"—ED

1781-2

May 8 George Smith of this parish, B., and Dorothy Richards* of the same, S.; by John Gibbons, Curate. Licence. Wit.: Charles Horne & John Mears.

20 John Poole of St Dionis Backchurch, Lond., B., and Jane Bewley of this parish, S.; by John Gibbons, Curate. Licence. Wit.: Samuel Welchor, Ann Bewley.

June 2 William Finch of St Mary le Strand, Midx., B., and Frances Elizabeth Rogers of this parish, S.; by Edmund Gibson, Rector. Licence. Wit.: J. Rogers & George Chapman.

3 Edward Lewis of this parish, B., and Charlotte Childs of the same, S.; by John Gibbons, Curate. Banns. Wit.: Charles Horne & John Mears.

Oct. 1 John Morris* of this parish, W., and Mary Hughes* of the same, W.; by J. Ward, Min^r. Banns. Wit.: Charles Horne & John Mears.

25 George Mason of this parish, B., and Elizabeth Devonshire of the same, S.; by John Gibbons, Curate. Banns. Wit.: James Shrives, Jenny Shrives.

Nov. 4 Joseph Ireland of this parish, W., and Ann Jones* of the same, W.; by John Gibbons, Curate. Banns. Wit.: Richard Ireland, Charles Horne.

6 John Hughes of this parish, B., and Ann Emery of the same, W.; by Edmund Gibson, Rector. Banns. Wit.: Benjamin Cardery, Charles Horne.

Dec. 21 Ambrose Nicholls of this parish, B., and Mary Kemp of the same, S.; by John Gibbons, Curate. Banns. Wit.: William Kemp, James Hayward.

22 Peter Theobald of St George, Bloomsbury, Midx., B., and Anna Maria Rogers of St Peter's, Paul's Wharf, Lond., S.; by Edmund Gibson, Rector. Licence. Wit.: John Rogers, George Chapman.

23 John Monks* of this parish, W., and Martha Horne of the same, W.; by G. Potts, Off. Min^r. Banns. Wit.: Sarah Dancer, John Cornish.

1782.

Jan. 1 Richard Ward of this parish, W., and Mildred Jackson of the same, S.; by John Gibbons, Curate. Licence. Wit.: Richard James Macquillin, Charles Horne.

14 John Edwards of St Peter, Paul's Wharf, B., and Mary Greaves of the same, S.; by John Gibbons, Curate. Banns. Wit.: John Jebb, Ann Setty.

Feb. 4 Henry Spillard of this parish, B., and Sarah Chambers* of the same, S.; by John Gibbons, Curate. Banns. Wit.: Peter Bell, Charles Horne.

7 William Tuck of Broxburn, co. Hertford, W., and Ann Shadbolt* of this parish, S.; by John Gibbons, Curate. Licence. Wit.: William Barham, Charles Horne.

10 Hugh Vallance of this parish, B., and Ann Blake of the same, S.; by John Gibbons, Curate. Licence. Wit.: Robert Blake, Edward Horne.

18 Richard Jago of this parish, W., and Elizabeth Howlett of the same, S.; by John Gibbons, Curate. Banns. Wit.: William Clarke, John Mears.

26 James Lovell of this parish, B., and Elizabeth Collier of the same, S.; by John Gibbons, Curate. Banns. Wit.: R. Adems & Mary Adems.

* Signs by mark.—Ed.

1782-3

April 14 William Bruin of S[t] George the Martyr, Surry, B., and Mary Butcher of this parish, S.; by John Gibbons, Curate. Licence. Wit.: Robert Harrison, Charles Horne.

May 21 The Reverend Lewis Southcomb, clerk of this parish, B., and Margaret Dodwell of the same, S.; by Arthur Dodwell, Minister of S[t] Thomas, Sarum. Banns. Wit.: Elizabeth Dodwell, Robert Dodwell.

Aug. 13 Joseph Froud of this parish, B., and Susanna Smith of the same, S.; by John Sanders, Curate. Banns. Wit.: Philip Williams, Catherine London.

19 Thomas Stringer of this parish, B., and Elizabeth Bascum of the same, S.; by John Sanders, Curate. Banns. Wit.: Philip Williams, Joyce Yeomans.

25 Richard Cowley of this parish, B., and Mary Rogers of the same, S.; by John Sanders, curate. Banns. Wit.: Philip Williams, H. E. Church.

Sept. 1 John Swift Saxelbye of this parish, B., and Elizabeth Cobb of Milton in Kent, S.; by John Sanders, curate. Lic. Wit.: Charles Horne, John Mears.

1 Thomas Mayhew of Camberwell, Surry, B., and Mary Hastings of this parish, S., a minor, by consent of her mother, Mary Hastings; by John Sanders, curate. Lic. Wit.: Mary Hastings, Richard Read.

19 Archibald Wilson of this parish, W., and Jane Horne* of the same, W.; by John Sanders, curate. Banns. Wit.: Rich[d] Hopkins, Charles Horne.

Oct. 14 William Payne of this parish, B., and Ann Hockes* of the same, S.; by John Sanders. Banns. Wit.: Charles Horne, Prudence + Hockes, her mark.

Dec. 3 John Sanders of this parish, B., and Sarah Mullett of the same, S.; by John Pridden, B.A., of Queen's Coll., Oxon. Banns. Wit.: John Sanders, Sarah Mullett.†

1783.

Feb. 9 William Robson of this parish, B., and Mary Clarke of the same, S.; by John Sanders. Banns. Wit.: John James, Susanna James, Charles Horne.

Mar. 2 Henry Watkins* of this parish, B., and Sarah Fillery* of the same, W.; by John Sanders. Banns. Wit.: Charles Horne, John Mears.

4 Jonathan Drew of Woodford, Essex, B., and Jane Murril* of S[t] Bennetts, Paul's Wharf, London, S.; by John Sanders, curate. Lic. Wit.: Samuel Shepherd, Charles Horne.

April 28 Samuel Rose of this parish, B., and Ann Carrett of the same, S.; by John Sanders. Banns. Wit.: William Quinton, John Carrett.

May 11 Fedde Miyer of S[t] Peter, Pauls Wharf, London, B., and Grace Maysmore of S[t] Gabriel, Fenchurch, London, S.; by John Sanders. Lic. Wit.: Hauman Moyer, Charles Horne.

July 6 John Adams of this parish, B., and Susanna Booth* of the same, S.; by John Sanders. Banns. Wit.: Charles Horne, John Mears.

Sept. 1 David Davies of S[t] Ann, Westminster, Middx., W., and Margaret Davis of S[t] Peter, Pauls Wharf, London, S.; by John Sanders. Lic. Wit.: George Vasey, A. Dalkin.

1 Daniel Godfrey of this parish, B., and Mary Hunt* of the same, S.; by John Sanders. Banns. Wit.: William Quinton, Mary Quinton.

* Signs by mark.—ED.

† Signed in the wrong place, the contracting parties signing as witnesses, and Mary Mayhew and John Hyde signing as contracting parties.—ED.

1783-4

Sept. 2 Richard Steel of this parish, B., and Rebecca Wilder* of S[t] Luke, Middx., S.; by J. Maidmun, minister. Lic. Wit.: James Bent, Edw. Carpenter.

Stamp Act on Marriages commenced 2nd October 1783.

Oct. 12 Thomas Brock of this parish, B., and Elizabeth Prat* of the same, S.; by James Roy, Curate pro hac vice. Banns. Wit.: Ann Peace, Charles Horne.

Nov. 17 Edward Millard* of this parish, W., and Sarah Showns* of the same, S.; by John Sanders, curate. Banns. Wit.: Susanna Webb, Charles Horne.

20 John Drew of this parish, B., and Mary Cole Akid of the same, S.; by John Sanders, Curate. Banns. Wit.: W. Hewett, Elizabeth Drew.

30 John Reading* of this parish, W., and Hannah Astle of the same, S.; by John Sanders, curate. Banns. Wit.: John Mears, William Cunningham.

Dec. 9 William Hughes of this parish, W., and Jane Williams* of S[t] Andrew, Holborn, London, W.; by John Sanders, curate. Lic. Wit.: Charles Horne, Ann Mendlove.

Inspect[d] to 31 Dec. by J. Dalton, D[y] Insp[r].

1784.

Jan. 1 John Maxted of this parish, B., and Ann Millington of the same, S.; by John Butler Sanders, curate. Banns. Wit.: Martha Millington, Charles Horne.

11 William Kneller of this parish, B., and Elizabeth Wildman of the same, S.; by John Butler Sanders, curate. Lic. Wit: Ann Wildman, Edward Wildman.

12 Samuel Walker of this parish, W., and Elizabeth Vaughan of the same, W.; by John Butler Sanders, curate. Banns. Wit.: Hannah Fornnan, Mary Parris.

Mar. 16 Thomas Jackson of this parish, B., and Jane Watson of the same, S.; by J. B. Sanders, curate. Banns. Wit.: Rebecca Thompson, Charles Horne.

April 14 William Gore of this parish, W., and Ann Burney* of the same, W.; by J. B. Sanders. Banns. Wit.: Charles Horne, John Mears.

May 9 John Wheeler of S[t] Peter, Pauls Wharf, London, B., and Mary Frank of the same, S.; by John Sanders, curate. Banns. Wit.: Charles Horne, John Mears.

July 12 William Chambers* of this parish, B., and Mary Brown* of the same, S.; by Richard Edwards, curate. Banns. Wit.: Richard Winter, Christian Crinckshaw (meant for Cruickshank) [*sic*].

Aug. 14 Henry Garlick of Frocester, co. Gloucester, B., and Mary Stodart of S[t] Benedict, Pauls Wharf, London, S.; by M. Davies, pro hac vice. Licence from the Faculty Office. Wit.: Isaac Heard, Gr. Rich[d] Bigland, Ralph Bigland.

Sept. 12 Adams Alsop of S[t] Peter, Pauls Wharf, London, B., and Sarah Kitchin of S[t] Mary Magdalen, Old Fish Street, W.; by Richard Edwards, curate. Lic. from the Bishop of London. Wit.: James Carey, Ann Carey, Charles Horne.

23 Robert Death of this parish, B., and Margaret Fells* of the same, S.; by Rich[d] Edwards, curate. Banns. Wit.: Charles Horne, James Godfrey.

Inspected and Duty received to y[e] 30th Sept. 1784.—R. Keene, Reg. & Inspector.

* Signs by mark.—Ed.

1784-5

Nov. 3 Samuel Fall of this parish, W., and Mary Sherwood of the same, W.; by Edm. Gibson, Rector. Banns. Wit.: Richard Wiseman, James Bradley.

18 James Waller of S[t] Peter, Pauls Wharf, London, B., and Ann Baggshaw of the same, S.; by Richard Edwards, curate. Banns. Wit.: William Blackett, James Godfrey.

1785.

Jan. 11 William Smith of this parish, B., and Sarah Jesup of the same, S.; by Rich[d] Edwards, curate. Banns. Wit.: J. Birkwood, Peter Jesup.

Feb. 8 Francis Newman of S[t] Peter, Pauls Wharf, London, B., and Lydia Smith of the same, S.; by Rich[d] Edwards, curate. Banns. Wit.: John Know, Cha[s] Horne.

Mar. 14 Gilbert Paterson of this parish, B., and Nancy Marsh of the same, S.; by Rich[d] Edwards, curate. Banns. Wit.: George Marsh, Margery Mackintosh.

16 Thomas Johnson of this parish, B., and Mary Eggleston* of the same, S.; by Rich[d] Edwards, Curate. Banns. Wit.: Charles Horne, James Godfrey.

24 Aaron Hale of this parish, W., and Sarah Hughes of S[t] Andrew Wardrobe, London, W.; by Rich[d] Edwards, curate. Lic. Wit.: C. Mellor, Charles Horne.

Inspected & Duty received to the 31st March 1785.—R. Keene, Register & Inspec[r].

May 16 Robert Hughes* of this parish, B., and Ellen Davis* of the same, W.; by Rich[d] Edwards, curate. Banns. Wit.: Richard Hopkins, Evan Jinkin.

June 21 Thomas Burrows of this parish, B., and Mary Wayman of the same, S.; by W. E. Faulkner, curate of S[t] Mildred's. Lic. Wit.: Rebekah Birkwood, William Birkwood.

July 3 Joseph Morrison of S[t] Peter, Pauls Wharf, London, B., and Harriott Atkinson of the same, S.; by Tho[s] Woods, minister. Banns. Wit.: Samuel Heckford, Elizabeth Billton.

7 Henry Foljembe† of Chatham, Kent, B., and Eleanor Jones of S[t] Benedict, Pauls Wharf, London, S.; by Tho. Woods, minister. Lic. Wit.: John Langhelt, Mary Langhelt.

12 John Baker of Beddinton, Kent, B., and Ann Baker* of S[t] Benedict, Pauls Wharf, London, W.; by Rich[d] Edwards, curate. Lic. Wit.: Jane Bleke, Samuel Shepherd.

16 William Dye* of this parish, B., and Jane Filewood* of the same, W.; by Rich[d] Edwards, curate. Banns. Wit.: Eleanor Baker, James Godfrey.

Aug. 2 Thomas Riley of this parish, B., and Mary Friday of Chipstead, Surry, S.; by Rich. Edwards, curate. Lic. Wit.: William Fryday, Susanna Fryday.

19 Robert Glave of this parish, W., and Martha Davies of S[t] Mary Magdalen, Bermondsey, Surry, S.; by Rich[d] Edwards, curate. Lic. Wit.: William Barham, Charles Horne.

Sept. 10 John Lane of S[t] Clement Danes, Middx., B., and Elizabeth Evans of this parish, S.; by Theophilus Lane. Lic. Wit.: John Wiggin, Ab[m] Raguineau.

26 William Sorrell of this parish, B., and Elizabeth Sorrell of the same, W.; by Rich[d] Edwards, curate. Banns. Wit.: John Williams, Elizabeth Dawson.

* Signs by mark.—Ed. † Signs "Henry Foljambe otherwise Foljembe."—Ed.

1785-6

Sept. 29 Daniel Smith of New Windsor, co. Berks, B., and Jane Smith of St Peter, Pauls Wharf, London, S.; by Richard Edwards, curate. Lic. Wit.: Samuel Smith, Geo. Smith, Junr.

Inspected & Duty received to September 30th.—R. Keene, Inspec^r.

Oct. 2 Joseph Hardy of this parish, B., and Lydia Kemp of the same, S.; by Richd Edwards, curate. Banns. Wit.: James Hayward, Charles Horne.

2 Charles Smith* of this parish, B., and Mary Tombling of the same, W.; by Richd Edwards, curate. Banns. Wit.: Ann Westbrook, John Castle.

Nov. 24 Thomas Coare of this parish, W., and Mary Shout [signature Shoot] of the same, W.; by Richd Edwards, curate. Banns. Wit.: John Nowell, Mary Weedon.

Dec. 26 Minard Carkett of this parish, W., and Mary Crowther of the same, S.; by Richd Edwards, curate. Banns. Wit.: Charles Bott, Charles Horne.

Inspected & Duty received to March 31, 1786.—R. Keene, Inspec^r.

1786.

April 19 Thomas Sandford of this parish, W., and Mary Bull of the same, S.; by Richd Edwards, curate. Banns. Wit.: John Miller, Mary Judkin.

23 Richard Jones of this parish, B., and Mary Owen of the same, S.; by Richd Edwards, curate. Banns. Wit.: R. Davis, D. Lewis.

May 3 James Currie of Luton, co. Beds, B., and Mary Alsop of St Benedict, Pauls Wharf, S.; by Richd Edwards, curate. Lic. Wit.: A. Alsop, Thomas Thornton.

24 James Blackman* of Endfield, Middx., B., and Sarah Rackett* of this parish, S.; by Richd Edwards, curate. Lic. Wit.: Sarah Bannester, Charles Horne.

25 John Dobson of Twickenham, Middx., B., and Elizabeth Bent of this parish, S.; by Richd Edwards, curate. Lic. Wit.: Mary Jones, George Dobson.

June 4 Thomas Hilbery of this parish, B., and Mary Goddard of the same, S.; by Richd Edwards, curate. Banns. Wit.: Sarah Plush, John Plush.

15 George Dawes of this parish, B., and Mary Sargood of the same, S.; by Richd Edwards, curate. Banns. Wit.: C. Jons, Tho. Barett, James De Winser, A. Nash, Anne Hanson.

Aug. 17 George Monday* of this parish, B., and Martha Pritchard* of the same, S.; by Richd Edwards, Curate. Banns. Wit.: Hen^y Parsons, Fanny Pickwick [? Kekwick].

Sept. 9 John Bellin of this parish, B., and Ann Mott of the same, S., by Licence from the Archbishop of Canterbury; by Henry Fly, officiating minister. Wit.: John Mott, Elizabeth Lavender, Mary Mayhew, Thomas Jones.

Inspected & Duty paid to Sep^t 30th, 1786.—R. Keene, Inspc^r.

Oct. 8 Benjamin Prosser of this parish, B., and Elizabeth Powis of the same, S.; by Richd Edwards, curate. Banns. Wit.: Wm Prosser, Elizabeth Powis, Lucy Breggen.

12 Charles Randall Bloxham of this parish, B., and Elizabeth Catharine Horne of the same, S.; by Richd Edwards, curate. Banns. Wit.: Henry Styles, Chas Horne.

* Signs by mark.—Ed.

1786-7

Oct. 22 Thomas Wales of this parish, B., and Henrietta Parsons of the same, S.; by Rich[d] Edwards, curate. Lic. Wit.: Ja[s] Collins, Cha[s] Horne.

Nov. 17 Richard Goodhew of this parish, B., and Grace Basset* of the same, S.; by Rich[d] Edwards, Curate. Lic. Wit.: John Jelly, James Godfrey.

20 George Drummond* of S[t] Mary, Islington, Middx., B., and Elizabeth Brown* of this parish, S.; by Rich[d] Edwards, curate. Lic. Wit.: Tho[s] Cutler, James Godfrey.

Dec. 3 Robert Hawkes of this parish, B., and Sarah Perry* of the same, S.; by Rich[d] Edwards, curate. Banns. Wit.: William Payne, Edw[d] Lewis.

1787.

Jan. 21 John Isaac of this parish, B., and Sarah Williams of the same, S.; by Rich[d] Edwards, curate. Banns. Wit.: Sarah Baker, Cha[s] Horne.

23 John Shave of this parish, B., and Rebecca Carter of S[t] Albans, co. Herts, W.; by Rich[d] Edwards, curate. Lic. Wit.: John Wyles, W[m] Shave.

30 John Nourse of this parish, B., and Sarah Armstrong of the same, S.; by Rich[d] Edwards, curate. Banns. Wit.: Samuel Armstrong, A. A. Chamber, Edw[d] Edwards.

Mar. 11 Thomas Lancey of Greenwich, Kent, B., and Anne Coxill of S[t] Bennett, Pauls Wharf, London, S.; by Rich[d] Edwards, curate. Licence from the Archbishop of Canterbury. By Rich[d] Edwards, curate. Wit.: W[m] Barham, Cha[s] Horne.

Inspected.—B. K., Insp[r]. Insp[d] & Duty paid.—J. Dalton.

May 5 Samuel Roberts of S[t] Bride, London, W., and Ann Cutler of S[t] Bennett, Paul's Wharf, S.; by Rich[d] Edwards, curate. Lic. Wit.: Marg[t] Milne, Thomas Thornton.

June 3 George Goodey of this parish, B., and Alice Lathom of the same, S.; by W. Lucas, curate. Banns. Wit.: George Lewis, Cha[s] Horne. "The erasement on which the witnesses names are wrote were done at the time of ther marriage the Parties married having signed their names in the wrong place. C. Horne, Parish Clerk, James Godfrey, Sexton."

10 Joseph Munday of this parish, B., and Ann Howard of the same, S.; by Hen. Fly, officiating Minister. Banns. Wit.: Cha[s] Horne, James Godfrey.

July 15 James Canwell of this parish, W., and Elizabeth Barrie alias Barreic of the same, W.; by Rich[d] Edwards, curate. Banns. Wit.: Henry Roche, Cha[s] Horne.

31 William Nash of Wandsworth, Surry, B., and Frances Wight of S[t] Bennett, Pauls Wharf, London, S.; by Rich[d] Edwards, curate. Licence from the Archbishop of Canterbury. Wit.: Miles Hill, Daniel Hill.

Aug. 6 David Dundas M[c]Douall of this parish, B., and Catherine Layton of the same, S.; by Rich[d] Edwards, curate. Banns. Wit.: John Dyson, Mary Horne.

19 Robert Carter of S[t] Peter's, B., and Mary Betts* of the same, S.; by Rich[d] Edwards, curate. Banns. Wit.: Tho[s] Rudkin, James Godfrey.

27 John Nickolson* of this parish, B., and Mary Ransom* of the same, S.; by Rich[d] Edwards, curate. Banns. Wit.: E. Horne, Martha Smith, John Smith, Thomas Nicklinson (?).

* Signs by mark.—Ed.

1787-8

Sept. 18 John Maud Wright of St George, Middx., B., and Sarah Consett of St Bennett, Pauls Wharf, London, S.; by Richd Edwards, Curate. Lic. Wit.: Joseph Consett, W. Wright.

30 William Shave of this parish, B., and Phillis Sealey* of the same, S.; by Richd Edwards, curate. Banns. Wit.: John Staples, Ann Nicoll.

Inspected & Duty paid to Sept. 30, 1787.—B. K., Inspr.

Oct. 11 James Brown of this parish, B., and Martha Edmanston of the same, S.; by Richd Edwards, curate. Banns. Wit.: James Atkins, Mary Edwards.

28 Jonathan Bennett of St Peter's, B., and Mary Vaughan* of the same, S.; by Richd Edwards, curate. Banns. Wit.: James Bennett, Chs Horne.

Nov. 5 Henry Meriton of this parish, B., and Jane Richardson of the same, S.; by Richd Edwards, curate. Banns. Wit.: Luke Meriton, Elizabeth Richardson.

27 James Hammerton of this parish, W., and Louisa Bolton of the same, S.; by Tho. Woods, Minister. Banns. Wit.: Chas Horne, James Godfrey.

Dec. 2 William Warby of this parish, B., and Sarah Tyler* of the same, S.; by Richd Edwards, curate. Banns. Wit.: Chas Horne, James Godfrey.

25 John Hood of this parish, B., and Hannah Jones of the same, S.; by Richd Edwards, curate. Banns. Wit.: Richd Ireland, W. Hawkins.

Inspd & Duty paid.—J. Dalton.

1788.

Feb. 24 Robert Hill of this parish, W., and Sarah Reeves* of St James, Garlickhithe, London, W.; by Richd Edwards, curate. Lic. Wit.: John Wotton, E. Wheadon.

Mar. 29 George Harrison, Esq., Norroy King of Arms, of St Benedict, Pauls Wharf, B., and Ann Bishop of St John, Hackney, Middx., W.; by Richd Edwards, curate. Lic. Wit.: J. Banger, Alice Fenwick.

Inspected & Duty paid to March 31, 1788.—B. K., Inspr.

April 20 William Fowler of this parish, B., and Rose Brimmer of the same, S.; by Richd Edwards, curate. Banns. Wit.: Wm Fowler, Chas Horne.

June 5 Lutye Blancken of this parish, B., and Elizabeth Ohlrogh* of the same, W.; by Richd Edwards, curate. Banns. Wit.: George Dearberg, Ann Dearberg, Elizabeth Starcke.

17 Peter Groves of St Peter, Pauls Wharf, B., and Elizabeth Bavin of the same, S.; by W. Lucas, minr. Banns. Wit.: Benjamin Watson, Chas Horne.

22 Thomas Horn of this parish, W., and Ann Gravat* of the same, S.; by Richd Edwards, curate. Banns. Wit.: William Owers, Jane Jubb.

Inspected & Duty paid to Sept. 30, 1788.—B. K., Inspr.

Oct. 13 Thomas Huke of this parish, B., and Mary Elizabeth Pipes of the same, S.; by Richd Edwards, curate. Banns. Wit.: Tho. Whywall, Ann Jordan.

Nov. 5 John Thompson of this parish, B., and Sarah Felkin of the same, S.; by Richd Edwards, curate. Banns. Wit.: Chas Horne, James Godfrey.

Dec. 16 George Gould of this parish, W., and Elizabeth Johnson* of the same, W.; by Richd Edwards, curate. Banns. Wit.: Charles Horne, James Godfrey.

* Signs by mark.—Ed.

1788-9

Dec. 18 Joseph Lewis* of this parish, W., and Elizabeth Cutter* of the same, W.; by Richd Edwards, curate. Banns. Wit.: Chas Horne, James Godfrey.

1789.

Jan. 10 William Buck of St Andrew, Holborn, B., and Sarah Rubery of St Bennetts, Pauls Wharf, London, S.; by Richd Edwards, curate. Lic. Wit.: R. Wheadon, Ed. Horne.

13 John Adamson of St Peter, Pauls Wharf, London, W., and Sarah Martin of St Faith, London, S.; by Richd Edwards, curate. Lic. Wit.: Thos Letts, Mary Martin.

Feb. 19 William Burn of St Mary le Bow, London, W., and Sarah Steel* of St Bennett, Pauls Wharf, London, W.; by Richd Edwards, curate. Lic. Wit.: Chas Horne, James Godfrey.

Mar. 24 John Geere of St Martin in the Fields, Middx., B., and Elizabeth Suffolk of this parish, S., a minor, by consent of Sarah Hale and Charles Horne, two of her guardians; by Richd Edwards, curate. Lic. Wit.: Aaron Hale, William Binfield, Chas Horne.

26 William Douglass of this parish, B., and Sarah Prichet of the same, S.; by Richd Edwards, curate. Banns. Wit.: Thomas Heritage, Daniel Pritchard.

Inspected & Duty paid to March 31st, 1789.—B. K., Insp^r.

April 5 Edward Wildman of this parish, B., and Jane Pond of the same, S.; by Richd Edwards, curate. Banns. Wit.: Eliz. Kneller, Chas Horne.

15 William Jones of this parish, W., and Jane Jones of the same, W.; by W. Lucas, Min^r. Banns. Wit.: Edward Jones, Eliz^th Weeden.

15 Stephen Horne of this parish, B., and Martha Almes† of the same, S.; by W. Lucas, min^r. Banns. Wit.: Stephen Reynolds, Charles Horne.

20 John Ives of this parish, B., and Rachael Ealey of the same, S.; by W. Lucas, min^r. Banns. Wit.: William Berry, Ann Gascoigne.

May 11 William Phillips* of this parish, B., and Mary King of the same, S.; by Richd Edwards, curate. Banns. Wit.: Thomas Walton, George King, Ann Wright.

June 24 William Thompson of this parish, B., and Margaret Taylor of the same, S.; by W. Lucas, Min^r. Banns. Wit.: Chas Horne, James Godfrey.

July 6 William Cowin of St George, Hanover Square, Middx., B., and Mary Taylor of St Benedict, Pauls Wharf, London, S.; by Richd Edwards, curate. Lic. Wit.: Samuel Shepherd, Chas Horne.

Aug. 13 William Lawrence of this parish, B., and Mary Amory of the same, S.; by Richd Edwards, curate. Banns. Wit.: Jacob Bown, Elizabeth Noon.

Inspected & Duty paid to Sep. 30th, 1789.—B. K., Insp^r.

Nov. 5 Andrew Timbrill of this parish, B., and Elizabeth Richardson of the same, S.; by Richd Edwards, curate. Banns. Wit.: Sarah Richardson, E. Horne.

Dec. 3 Robert Woodward of St Andrew by the Wardrobe, London, W., and Elizabeth Lewis of St Benedict, Pauls Wharf, London, S.; by Richd Edwards, curate. Lic. Wit.: James Godfrey, Agnes + Clark, her mark.

28 Richard Price of St Peter, Pauls Wharf, London, B., and Mary Butcher* of the same, S.; by Richd Edwards, curate. Lic. Wit.: Chas Horne, James Godfrey, Hugh + Roberts, his mark.

* Signs by mark.—Ed.

† Signs "M. Elmes, otherwise Eemes" (?).—Ed.

1790-91

1790.

Jan. 26 John Baker of this parish, B., and Ann Jackson* of the same, S.; by Richd Edwards, Curate. Banns. Wit.: John Jackson, John Jackson.

Feb. 1 Edward Pain of this parish, B., and Rebecca Raymond of the same, S.; by Richd Edwards, curate. Banns. Wit.: Wm Raymond, Chas Horne.

5 Nathaniel Gash of this parish, B., and Mary Dod of the same, S.; by Richd Edwards, curate. Banns. Wit.: Richd Gash, John Dod.

14 John Weatherhead of St Peter, Pauls Wharf, London, B., and Mary Ashby of the same, S.; by Richd Edwards, curate. Banns. Wit.: Saml Ballard, Sarah [?] Ballard, Chas Horne.

21 Robert Spence of this parish, B., and Ann Barlow of the same, S.; by Richd Edwards, curate. Banns. Wit.: James Robson, J. Birkwood, Hannah Callcutt.

Inspected & Duty paid to March 31st, 1790.—B. K., Inspr.

April 20 Richard Readwin of this parish, B., and Mary Cork of the same, S.; by Richd Edwards, curate. Banns. Wit.: Chas Horne, James Godfrey, James Miller [by mark].

May 5 Joseph Higinbottom of this parish, B., and Sarah Davis* of the same, S.; by Richd Edwards, curate. Banns. Wit.: William Storey, James Godfrey.

20 William Durdell of this parish, W., and Elizabeth Carlton of the same, W.; by Richd Edwards, curate. Banns. Wit.: Martin Bulmer, Chas Horne.

June 8 Samuel Holman of this parish, B., and Ann Archer of the same, S.; by W. Lucas. Banns. Wit.: Mary Cooper, Chas Horne.

15 Thomas Grace of this parish, B., and Martha Markham of the same, S.; by W. Lucas, Minr. Banns. Wit.: Thos Markham, Martha Markham.

20 William Birchmore of St Peter, Pauls Wharf, B., and Sarah Dunn* of the same, S.; by W. Lucas, Minr. Banns. Wit.: John Odwell, James Godfrey.

24 Francis Norwood of Watford, co. Herts, B., and Mary Mace of St Bennett, Paul's Wharf, London, S.; by W. Lucas, Minr. Married in the church of St Mary Magdalen, St Bennett's being under repair. Lic. Wit.: Elizabeth Mace, Joseph Tapp.

28 Samuel Fisher of St Bennett, Paul's Wharf, London, B., and Sarah Pestil* of the same, S.; by W. Lucas, Minr. Married at St Mary Magdalen, Old Fish Street, St Bennett's being under repair. Banns. Wit.: Charles Surety, Chas Horne.

Aug. 19 Matthew Kemp of St Bennett, Pauls Wharf, London, B., and Mary Hutchinson of the same, S.; by Richd Edwards, curate, at St Mary Magdalen, Old Fish Street, St Bennett's being under repair. Banns. Wit.: Chas Horne, James Godfrey.

Oct. 25 James Good of St Bennett, Pauls Wharf, London, B., and Sarah Early of the same, S.; by W. Lucas, Minr, at St Mary Magdalen, Old Fish Street, St Bennett's being under repair. Banns. Wit.: John Early, Edward Early.

Dec. 5 George Wallan* of St Bennett, Pauls Wharf, B., and Elizabeth Sell* of the same, S.; by Tho. Woods, at St Mary Magdalen, Old Fish Street. Banns. Wit.: William Birchmore, James Godfrey.

1791.

Jan. 6 John Slemon of St Peter, Pauls Wharf, W., and Elizabeth Bellington of the same, S.; by Richd Edwards, curate. Lic. Wit.: James Byrn, Mary King.

* Signs by mark.—Ed.

1791-2

Feb. 3 William Cook of Taplow, co. Bucks, B., and Elizabeth Smith of S[t] Peter, Paul's Wharf, London, S.; by Rich[d] Edwards, curate. Lic. Wit.: Sam[l] Smith, Sarah Simmonds.

20 Thomas Rathbon of this parish, B., and Sarah Mills* of the same, S.; by Rich[d] Edwards, curate. Banns. Wit.: Richard Readwin, Mary Readwin.

21 William Calvert Price of S[t] Sepulchre, Middx., B., and Elizabeth Barker of S[t] Peter, Pauls Wharf, London, S.; by Rich[d] Edwards, curate. Lic. Wit.: George Ridiford, John Adamson.

Inspected and Duty paid to 31 March 1791.—W. Goodwin.

May 18 Thomas Ivery* of S[t] Bennett, Pauls Wharf, London, B., and Sarah Tyhurst of Eltham, Kent, S.; by Rich[d] Edwards, curate. Lic. Wit.: Cha[s] Horne, James Godfrey.

22 John Andrew Rider of this parish, B., and Margaret Kent of the same, S.; by Rich[d] Edwards, curate. Banns. Wit.: George Kent, Cha[s] Horne.

22 Richard Baker of the Precinct of White Friers, London, W., and Elizabeth Needham of this parish, S.; by Rich[d] Edwards, curate. Lic. Wit.: Henry Smith, Rob[t] Needham.

June 12 Thomas Chapman of this parish, B., and Mary Dray* of the same, S.; by Rich[d] Edwards, curate. Banns. Wit.: Elizabeth Levens, Cha[s] Horne.

July 3 George Williams of this parish, B., and Elizabeth Harris* of the same, S.; by W. Lucas, Min[r]. Banns. Wit.: Tho[s] Harris, Cha[s] Horne.

Sept. 13 James Austin of Hounslow, Middx., W., and Hannah Pocock* of S[t] Bennett, Pauls Wharf, London, W.; by Rich[d] Edwards, curate. Lic. Wit.: Mary Wright, James Godfrey.

Inspected and Duty paid to 29 Sept. 91.—W. Goodwin.

Oct. 21 John Oliver of this parish, B., and Mary Howell of the same, S.; by W. Lucas, Min[r]. Banns. Wit.: George Bywater, Mary Prosser.

30 Joseph Ewers of this parish, W., and Ann Vere* of the same, S.; by Rich[d] Edwards, curate. Banns. Wit.: E[d] Horne, James Godfrey.

Nov. 12 William Barmore of S[t] Peter's, Pauls Wharf, B., and Mary Williamson of Christ Church, Middx., S.; by Rich[d] Edwards, curate. Lic. Wit.: Ed. Horne, James Godfrey.

Dec. 6 John Langley of Great Marlow, co. Bucks, B., and Mary Briggs* of S[t] Peter, Pauls Wharf, S.; by Rich[d] Edwards, curate. Lic. Wit.: Sarah Adamson, Ed. Horne.

30 John Haig of this parish, B., and Jane Sturdy of the same, S.; by Rich[d] Edwards, curate. Lic. Wit.: W. Highman, James Godfrey.

1792.

Feb. 2 Daniel Nathaniel Weeden of this parish, B., and Mary Dixon of the same, S.; by Rich[d] Edwards, curate. Banns. Wit.: James Godfrey, Ed. Horne.

20 Samuel Thornhill of this parish, B., and Martha Hill* of the same, S.; by Rich[d] Edwards, curate. Banns. Wit.: John Hill, Ed. Horne.

Inspected to 31 March 1792.—W. Goodwin.

April 8 Richard Taylor of this parish, B., and Rachael Aspray† of the same, S.; by Rich[d] Edwards, curate. Banns. Wit.: Stephen Taylor, Eliz[th] Boughton.

* Signs by mark.—Ed.

† Signs "Asprey."—Ed.

1792-3

April 9 William Ellis* of this parish, B., and Elizabeth Hills* of the same, W.; by Richd Edwards, curate. Banns. Wit.: Samuel Shepherd, James Godfrey.

29 Philip Norgrove of this parish, B., and Hannah Dellahay of the same, S.; by Richd Edwards, Curate. Banns. Wit.: George Williams, James Godfrey.

May 20 Robert Evans of this parish, B., and Ann Haines of the same, S.; by Richd Edwards, curate. Banns. Wit.: James Brown, Ed. Horne.

28 Henry Thomas of this parish, B., and Mary Mills of the same, S.; by Richd Edwards, curate. Banns. Wit.: Thomas Rathbon, Ed. Horne.

June 17 William West* of this parish, W., and Mary Harle* of the same, W.; by W. Lucas, Min^r. Banns. Wit.: Robert Finn, Thos Wm Harle.

27 Thomas Fuller of this parish, B., and Mary Barnes of the same, S.; by W. Lucas, Min^r. Banns. Wit.: J. Stanynought, S. Stanynought.

July 30 John Stockwell of this parish, B., and Jane Hollyoake of the same, S.; by Richd Edwards, curate. Banns. Wit.: Thos Brigg, Eliz. Barker.

Sept. 2 Thomas Lockwood of this parish, B., and Margaret Chesshem of the same, S.; by Thos Woods, Min^r. Banns. Wit.: John Bates, Ed. Horne.

Dec. 20 Thomas Pearson of this parish, B., and Sarah Parrack of St George, Hanover Square, Middx., S.; by Richd Edwards, curate. Lic. Wit.: Jane + Godfrey, her mark, Ed. Horne.

1793.

Jan. 11 John Nevile of Messing, Essex, B., and Hannah Townsend* of St Bennett, Pauls Wharf, S.; by Richd Edwards, curate. Lic. Wit.: Ed. Horne, James Godfrey.

Mar. 29 Richard Cullern of this parish, B., and Mary Cock of Burnham, co. Bucks, S.; by Richd Edwards, curate. Lic. Wit.: Susale, Ed. Horne, Robert Hill.

Inspected to 31 March 1793.—W. Goodwin, Insp^r.

April 1 Thomas Horme* of this parish, B., and Mary Element* of the same, S.; by Richd Edwards, curate. Banns. Wit.: Ed. Horne, James Godfrey.

11 Christian Lohman* of this parish, B., and Jane Nancken of St Mary, White Chaple, W.; by Richd Edwards, curate. Lic. Wit.: Christopher Ludewig Mauer, Elizabeth Ercks.

17 John Healy of this parish, B., and Esther Livermore of the same, S.; by Richd Edwards, curate. Banns. Wit.: John Mascall, Elizabeth Smith.

May 5 James Jordan of this parish, W., and Mary Weatherhead of the same, W.; by Richd Edwards, curate. Banns. Wit.: John Wyles, Ed. Horne.

7 Thomas Burton of Egham, Surry, B., and Ann Brumbridge of St Benedict, Paul's Wharf, S.; by Richd Edwards, curate. Lic. Wit.: Trew Jegon, sen^r, Ann Jegon, Trew Jegon, jun^r, Elizabeth Jegon.

20 William Baldwin of this parish, B., and Sarah Turner of the same, S.; by W. Lucas, Min^r. Banns. Wit.: James Godfrey, Ed. Horne.

June 3 William Johnson of this parish, B., and Mary Keyess of the same, S.; by Richd Edwards, curate. Banns. Wit.: Ed. Horne, Robert Evans.

* Signs by mark.—Ed.

1793-4
June 10 William Peach of this parish, B., and Susanna Allen of the same, S.; by Rich[d] Edwards, curate. Banns. Wit.: George Lewis, Ed. Horne.

July 7 William Bridges* of this parish, B., and Hannah Turner of the same, S.; by W. Lucas, Min[r]. Banns. Wit.: Sarah Balwen, Ed. Horne.

19 Christopher Staplefield of this parish, W., and Ann Dickhout of S[t] Botolph, Aldgate, W.; by Rich[d] Edwards, curate. Lic. Wit.: James Fandam, Ed. Horne.

Aug. 3 David Williams of this parish, B., and Elphar Harris of S[t] Giles in the Fields, Middx., S.; by Rich[d] Edwards, curate. Lic. Wit.: Catherine Harris, Ed. Horne.

Sept. 7 William Absalom of New Windsor, co. Berks, B., and Elizabeth Smith of S[t] Bennett's, Pauls Wharf, S.; by Rich[d] Edwards, curate. Lic. Wit.: Mary Wheadon, Katherine Wootton, Joseph Wootton.

8 Thomas William Elkins of this parish, B., and Ann Horne of the same, S.; by Rich[d] Edwards, curate. Banns. Wit.: Tho. Horne, Elizabeth Rachel Elkins.

16 William Stanley of this parish, B., and Martha Jesset of the same, S.; by Rich[d] Edwards, curate. Banns. Wit.: George Hodges, Charlotte Jesset.

17 Joseph Hudson of this parish, W., and Mary Cole* of the same, S.; by Rich[d] Edwards, curate. Banns. Wit.: Ed. Horne, James Godfrey.

28 William Jones of this parish, B., and Mary Wagner of Wraysbury, co. Bucks, S.; by James Grant, A.M., Min[r]. Lic. Wit.: James Godfrey, Ed. Horne.

Inspected to 30th Sept. 1793.—J. Baillie.

Nov. 1 Thomas Nicholson of S[t] Peter's, B., and Fanny Skeffington of the same, S.; by Rich[d] Edwards, curate. Lic. Wit.: Mary Ludlam, James Ludlam.

21 George Bych of this parish, B., and Elizabeth Hatton of the same, S.; by Rich[d] Edwards, curate. Banns. Wit.: Samuel Perrens, Hannah Hall.

Dec. 5 George Harris of this parish, B., and Charlotte Gilbert of the same, S.; by Rich[d] Edwards, curate. Banns. Wit.: James Godfrey, Ed. Horne.

1794.

Jan. 2 Henry Dawson of this parish, B., and Ann Elliott of the same, S.; by W. Lucas, Min[r]. Banns. Wit.: James Godfrey, Ed. Horne.

6 Thomas Ives of this parish, W., and Betty Bostock of the same, W.; by Rich[d] Edwards, curate. Banns. Wit.: Jane [?] Thompson, Tho[s] Ives.

Mar. 4 John Pinchard of S[t] Mary Magdalen, Taunton, Somerset, B., and Elizabeth Sibthorpe of this parish, S.; by Arthur Iredell, min[r]. Lic. Wit.: Elizabeth Townsend, A. R. Pinchard, Tho. Sibthorpe.

April 21 William Howard of this parish, B., and Fanny Burr* of the same, S.; by Rich[d] Edwards, curate. Banns. Wit.: Ann Howard, Robert Lewis.

May 13 John M[c]Farlan of this parish, B., and Elizabeth Kightley of the same, S.; by Rich[d] Edwards, curate. Banns. Wit.: Ed. Horne, James Godfrey.

18 William Lloyd of S[t] Peter's, B., and Ann Day of the same, S.; by Rich[d] Edwards, curate. Banns. Wit.: Elizabeth Cottrell, Ed. Horne.

June 14 John Pinfold of this parish, B., and Elizabeth Wade* of the same, S.; by Rich[d] Edwards, curate. Banns. Wit.: William Jones, Hannah Maria Hoal, Ed. Horne.

* Signs by mark.—Ed.

1794-6

Aug. 10 William Price of this parish, B., and Susannah Newell of the same, S.; by Rich[d] Edwards, curate. Banns. Wit.: Ed. Horne, James Godfrey.

Sept. 28 Joseph Stanton of this parish, B., and Elizabeth Warren* of S[t] Peter, Cornhill, London, S.; by Rich[d] Edwards, curate. Lic. Wit.: Ed. Horne, James Godfrey.

Dec. 7 Joseph Holland of this parish, B., and Ann Slater of the same, W.; by Rich[d] Edwards, curate. Banns. Wit.: William Styles Jones, William Slater.

17 Thomas Gregory of this parish, B., and Elizabeth Cook of the same, S.; by Rich[d] Edwards, curate. Banns. Wit.: Adam Gawin, William Styles Jones.

30 Richard Tomkies† of this parish, B., and Ann Murphy of the same, S.; by W. Lucas, min[r]. Banns. Wit.: Will[m] Murphy, Ed. Horne.

1795.

Feb. 15 John Baty of S[t] Dunstan in the West, B., and Elizabeth Virgoe of this parish, W.; by Rich[d] Edwards, curate. Lic. Wit.: James Godfrey, E. Horne.

Mar. 24 John Atkinson Wardell of S[t] Ann, Blackfriars, London, B., and Ann Jegon of S[t] Bennett, Pauls Wharf, London, S.; by Rich[d] Edwards, curate. Lic. Wit.: Trew Jegon, sen[r], Elizabeth Jegon, Mary Brumbridge, Thomas Burton, James Wardell, Trew Jegon, jun[r].

April 9 James Collins of this parish, B., and Elizabeth Armsworth* of the same, S.; by Rich[d] Edwards, curate. Banns. Wit.: J. Collins, Elizabeth Hammond, E. Horne.

May 21 John Armitage of this parish, B., and Ursula Ann Prestage of S[t] Andrew, Holborn, London, S.; by Rich[d] Edwards, curate. Lic. Wit.: Christ[r] Swithen Sheldon, Mary Horne.

Aug. 15 Joseph Spence of S[t] Mary, Rotherhithe, B., and Ann Lewis of S[t] Bennett, Pauls Wharf, S.; by W. Lucas, Min[r]. Lic. Wit.: Thomas Worthy, Mary Nicholson.

17 Richard Davies* of this parish, B., and Mary Eddowes of the same, S.; by Rich[d] Edwards, curate. Banns. Wit.: James Tovey, E. Horne.

Sept. 14 Thomas Egan of this parish, B., and Mary Marah of the same, S.; by Rich[d] Edwards, Curate. Banns. Wit.: Mary Mullarky, James Corney, Luke M[c]Gann.

Nov. 8 Henry Holmes of S[t] Peter, Pauls Wharf, B., and Grace Bruce of the same, S.; by Rich[d] Edwards, curate. Lic. Wit.: Thomas Nicholson, E. Horne.

Dec. 12 Jeremiah Thompson of this parish, B., and Mary Wiseman of the same, S.; by Rich[d] Edwards, curate. Banns. Wit.: James Godfrey, E. Horne.

1796.

Jan. 6 John Hill of S[t] Stephens in S[t] Albans, co. Herts, W., and Sarah Ellis of S[t] Bennett, Paul's Wharf, S.; by W. Lucas, Min[r]. Lic. Wit.: E. Horne, Jane Godfrey [by mark].

26 George Lawrence of this parish, B., and Sarah Fawcett of Christ Church, Surry, a minor, by consent of Richard Fawcett, her father; by Rich[d] Edwards, curate. Lic. Wit.: Richard Fawcett, Sarah Stewardson, E. Horne.

Feb. 14 John Morrell of this parish, B., and Sarah Smith of the same, W.; by Rich[d] Edwards, curate. Banns. Wit.: W[m] Edwards, E. Horne.

* Signs by mark.—Ed. † Signs "R[d] Tomkins."—Ed.

1796

Feb. 21 Thomas Beverly Humpleby of this parish, B., and Sarah French* of the same, S.; by Rich[d] Edwards, curate. Banns. Wit.: E. Horne, James Godfrey.

Mar. 14 Thomas Evans of this parish, B., and Sarah Wetherhead* of the same, S.; by Rich[d] Edwards, curate. Banns. Wit.: James Godfrey, E. Horne.

April 19 George Crothall of this parish, B., and Elizabeth Webb of the same, S.; by Rich[d] Edwards, curate. Banns. Wit.: Maria Sewell, John Bristow.

June 27 William Pearce of this parish, W., and Ann Easton* of the same, W.; by Rich[d] Edwards, curate. Banns. Wit.: Tho. Carey, E. Horne, James Godfrey.

July 1 William Thackara of this parish, W., and Mary Bassett of S[t] George, Southwark, Surry, W.; by Rich[d] Edwards, curate. Lic. Wit.: John Thackara, Mary Horne, E. Horne.

6 Thomas Mead of this parish, B., and Jane Strangman of the same, S.; by W. Lucas, Min[r]. Banns. Wit.: Thomas Strangman, Sarah Armstrong.

25 Richard Jobson of this parish, B., and Jane Chamberlain* of S[t] Thomas, Southwark, Surry, S.; by Rich[d] Edwards, curate. Lic. Wit.: James Godfrey, E[d] Horne.

Aug. 16 William Quarterman of New Windsor, co. Berks, B., and Mary Rogers of S[t] Bennett's, Paul's Wharf, London, S.; by Rich[d] Edwards, curate. Lic. Wit.: William Taylor, C. Smith.

Sept. 12 Joseph Carr of this parish, B., and Abigail Raymond of the same, S.; by Rich[d] Edwards, curate. Banns. Wit.: Tho[s] Carey, E. Horne.

13 George Cathrow of this parish, B., and Elizabeth Lawless of S[t] Augustine, London, S.; by Rich[d] Edwards, curate. Lic. Wit.: R. Briand, S. Briand, K. Briand, J. Cathrow, Amy Briand.

Oct. 2 William Fraile of this parish, W., and Mary Fenno of S[t] Botolph, Aldersgate, S.; by Rich[d] Edwards, curate. Lic. Wit.: James Godfrey, E. Horne.

4 William Walker of this parish, B., and Margaret Wells of the same, S.; by Tho. Woods, Min[r]. Banns. Wit.: George Crothall, Elizabeth Jeffry, E. Horne.

6 Samuel Pashler of this parish, B., and Elizabeth Baker of the same, W.; by Tho. Woods, Min[r]. Banns. Wit.: Philip Hustwait, Jane Warby, Frances Baker.

12 William Lane of this parish, B., and Maria Medler* of the same, S.; by W. Lucas, Min[r]. Banns. Wit.: Christ[r] Sheldon, E. Horne.

Nov. 7 Thomas Olivers of this parish, W., and Ann Ellis of the same, S.; by Rich[d] Edwards, curate. Banns. Wit.: E. Bebbington, Tho. Symons.

21 Edward Murrell of this parish, B., and Betsy Johnson of the same, S.; by Rich[d] Edwards, curate. Banns. Wit.: C. Sheldon, E. Horne.

Dec. 4 Benjamin Porter of this parish, B., and Jane Bee of the same, S.; by Rich[d] Edwards, curate. Banns. Wit.: Tho[s] Carey, E. Horne.

8 George Groves of this parish, B., and Elizabeth Brierhurst of the same, W.; by Rich[d] Edwards, curate. Banns. Wit.: Peter Powell, Elizabeth Powell, E. Horne.

15 Thomas Marlton of Brentwood in Essex, W., and Ann Riddley* of S[t] Benedict, Pauls Wharf, London, S.; by Rich[d] Edwards, curate. Lic. Wit.: Samuel Liggins, Elizabeth Wilson, Mary Gibbon.

[End of Volume H.]

* Signs by mark.—ED.

BOOK I.

St. Benet & St. Peter.

MARRIAGES FROM 1ST JANY 1797 TO 3RD NOVR 1812.

1797 — 1797.

Jan. 1 Robert Livermore of this parish, B., and Susan Richardson of the same, S.; by Richard Edwards, Curate. Banns. Wit.: John Healy & Daniel Richardson.

Feb. 24 William Foy of this parish, B., and Elizabeth Barrs* of the same, S.; by Richard Edwards, Curate. Banns. Wit.: Benjamin Moore and E. Horne.

April 20 John Edwards* of this parish, B., and Sarah Wells* of the same, S.; by Manley Wood, Curate of St Bride. Banns. Wit.: John Gildersleve, James Godfrey, & E. Horne.

27 Azariah Drage of this parish, B., and Sarah Ann Woodward of St Saviour, Southwark, Surry, S.; by Richard Edwards, Curate. Licence. Wit.: John Wheadon, E. Horne, & Samuel Wheadon.

28 William Armitage of this parish, B., and Sarah Curties of the same, S.; by Richard Edwards, Curate. Banns. Wit.: Charles Thame, Ann Thame, & E. Horne.

May 1 Joseph Burch of Tottenham, Midx., B., and Mary Burton of St Bennett's, Paul's Wharf, Lond., S.; by Richard Edwards, Curate. Licence. Wit.: Thomas Richards & E. Horne.

1 Charles Sanders of Eltham, Kent, B., and Mary Russell of St Bennett's, Paul's Wharf, Lond., S.; by Richard Edwards, Curate. Licence. Wit.: Thomas Richards, E. Horne.

19 Thomas Skeffington of St John the Baptist, Lond., B., and Jane Dodds of St Bennett's, Paul's Wharf, Lond., S.; by Richard Edwards, Curate. Licence. Wit.: Hope Innes, Ann Skeffington, & Edward Cruse.

June 10 Thomas Ensom of this parish, B., and Jane Kemp of the same, S.; by Richard Edwards, Curate. Banns. Wit.: E. Horne & James Godfrey.

July 31 John Wilkins of this parish, B., and Mary Jackson of the same, S.; by Richard Edwards, Curate. Banns. Wit.: James Godfrey & E. Horne.

Aug. 12 John Rollins of this parish, B., and Ann Steel of the same, S.; by Richard Edwards, Curate. Licence. Wit.: C. Smith, William Lane, & E. Horne.

14 John Flack of this parish, B., and Susannah Livermore* of the same, S.; by Richard Edwards, Curate. Banns. Wit.: John Healy & E. Horne.

Sept. 19 George White of St Peter's, Paul's Wharf, W., and Elizabeth Humphries* of the same, W.; by Richard Edwards, Curate. Banns. Wit.: David Roberts & James Yates.

21 George Coulton of this parish, W., and Sarah Sharman* of Thundridge, Hertford, S.; by Richard Edwards, Curate. Licence. Wit.: John Wheadon & E. Horne.

Oct. 9 John Trainer† of this parish, B., and Eleanor Byrne* of the same, W.; by Richard Edwards, Curate. Banns. Wit.: The mark of Andrew Welch, E. Horne.

* Signs by mark.—ED. † Signs "John Trenor."—ED.

1797-8

Oct. 11 William Richardson of S[t] Benedict, Paul's Wharf, Lond., B., and Rebecca Wyatt of Twickenham, Midx., S.; by Richard Edwards, Curate. Licence. Wit.: John Jones & John Wheadon.

Nov. 15 John Mortimer of this parish, B., and Mary Satcher of the same, S.; by Richard Edwards, Curate. Banns. Wit.: John Mortimer & E. Horne.

1798.

Jan. 25 John Rushton of this parish, B., and Maria Cox of S[t] George, Hanover Square, S.; by Richard Edwards, Curate. Licence. Wit.: W. Cliff, Ann Cliff, & E. Horne.

April 10 Leonard Ferosh of this parish, B., and Elizabeth Tilley of the same, S.; by Richard Edwards, Curate. Banns. Wit.: William Wilson & James Godfrey.

30 James Kelly of this parish, B., and Mary Knight of the same, S.; by Richard Edwards, Curate. Banns. Wit.: Ann Finch & E. Horne.

May 27 George Phare of this parish, B., and Sarah Paris of S[t] Thomas, Southwark, Surry, S.; by Richard Edwards, Curate. Licence. Wit.: Samuell Meadows, Richard Barjorge [? Bayorge], Frances Browne.

Sept. 19 Raphael Lamar West of S[t] Mary le Bone, Midx., B., and Maria Siltso of this parish, S.; by W. Holmes, Rector. Licence. Wit.: John Wheadon & E. Horne.

22 Charles Sharp of S[t] Matthew, Friday Street, Lond., B., and Maria Tovey of this parish, S.; by W. Holmes, Rector. Licence. Wit.: James Tovey, Mary Crutcher, Anna Maria Tovey, Elizabeth Tovey, H. Warren, & James Dawson.

25 Peter Sers of Gedney, co. Lincoln, W., and Frances Nayler of this parish, S.; by W. Holmes, Rector. Licence. Wit.: Mary Nayler & Eliza Sers.

Oct. 4 William Brett Quinton of this parish, W., and Elizabeth Connor of the same, S.; by W. Holmes, Rector. Banns. Wit.: The mark of Catherine Bradley, E. Horne.

18 Nicholas Stevens of this parish, B., and Esther Murphy of the same, S.; by W. Holmes, Rector. Banns. Wit.: The mark of Jane Godfrey, E. Horne.

Nov. 5 Thomas Fleming of this parish, B., and Harriott Bee of the same, S.; by W. Holmes, Rector. Banns. Wit.: Mary Palmer, Mary Bee, E. Horne.

8 John Watson of Wingfield, Berks, W., and Ann Raynor of this parish, W.; by W. Holmes, Rector. Licence. Wit.: J. Jackson, J. Shaftoe, E. Horne.

13 Henry Brumbridge of Thorpe, Surry, B., and Elizabeth Hughes of this parish, S. Licence. By W. Holmes, Rector. Wit.: John Hughes, Elizabeth Jegon, Thomas Burton, Susanna Brumbridge, Trew Jegon, jun[r].

13 John Guyer of this parish, B., and Sophia Saunders of the same, S.; by W. Holmes, Rector. Banns. Wit.: The mark of Jane Godfrey, E. Horne.

28 Thomas Satcher of this parish, B., and Mary Leball of S[t] Luke, Midx., S.; by W. Clarke, Off. Min[r]. Licence. Wit.: Mortimer, Mary Mortimer, & E. Horne.

Dec. 11 Peter Mazell Faulkner of this parish, B., and Elizabeth Veazey of the same, S.; by W. Holmes, Rector. Banns. Wit.: Nath. Veazey, Mary Ann Browne, Mary Browne.

1799.

1799-1800

Feb. 3 Bryan Fitzpatrick of this parish, B., and Mary Withit* of the same, W.; by W. Holmes, Rector. Banns. Wit.: Elizabeth Tovey, Samuel Shepherd.

17 William Eynott of this parish, B., and Mary Statem† of the same, W.; by W. Holmes, Rector. Banns. Wit.: Wm Aston & E. Horne.

Mar. 25 William Dunkley of this parish, B., and Elizabeth Hudson of the Chapelry of Norwood, Midx., W.; by W. Holmes, Rector. Licence. Wit.: John Wheadon & John Bender.

28 James Cathrow of this parish, B., and Elizabeth Ann Ellen Wyatt of St Olave, Hart Street, Lond., S.; by Richard Edwards, Curate. Licence. Wit.: George Cathrow, Joseph Wyatt, & John Brazier.

April 28 Francis Robert Cooper of this parish, W., and Martha Holloway of the same, S.; by Richard Edwards, Curate. Banns. Wit.: Isaac Mallyon & E. Horne.

May 12 Edward Akam of this parish, B., and Sarah Mottram† of the same, S.; by Richard Edwards, curate. Banns. Wit.: Samuel Akam & Mary Read.

15 John Wootton of this parish, B., and Sarah Ringers† of the same, S.; by Richard Edwards, Curate. Banns. Wit.: Christopher West & E. Horne.

June 2 Joseph Langrish of this parish, B., and Jane Dunn of the same, S.; by Richard Edwards, Curate. Banns. Wit.: Ann Finch & E. Horne.

July 1 Henry Carrington of this parish, B., and Ann Craig† of the same, W.; by Richard Edwards, Curate. Banns. Wit.: Joseph Langham & E. Horne.

6 Billy Babb of this parish, B., and Elizabeth James of the same, S.; by Richard Edwards, Curate. Banns. Wit.: Peter Jackson & Sarah James.

Aug. 7 Thomas Reynolds of this parish, B., and Sophia Parish‡ of Epping, Essex, S.; by Richard Edwards, Curate. Licence. Wit.: Thomas Spencer & N. Buckerfiel.

11 William Jones of St Michael, Cornhill, Lond., B., and Mary Purcell of this parish, S.; by Richard Edwards, Curate. Licence. Wit.: James Humphreys & N. Humphrys.

Nov. 3 Andrew White of this parish, B., and Ann Wells† of the same, W.; by Richard Edwards, Curate. Banns. Wit.: Thomas Carey and William Wilson.

1800.

Jan. 15 James Barry of St Clement in the Town & Port of Hastings, Sussex, W., and Charlotte Walters of this parish, S.; by Thomas Townsend of Pirbright, Surry. Licence. Wit.: Francis Townsend, Windsor Herald, & Margaret Thomas.

16 Henry Hoskins of St Clement Danes, Midx., W., and Mary Meekens of this parish, S.; by Richard Edwards, Curate. Licence. Wit.: John Mellish & John Wheadon.

20 John Ives of this parish, W., and Eleanor Harold of the same, W.; by W. Lucas, Min^r^. Banns. Wit.: Bethel Goodwyn & Thomas Ives.

July 22 Richard Lake of this parish, B., and Ann Freeman of the same, W.; by Richard Edwards, Curate. Licence. Wit.: W. Lake & S. Lake.

27 William Charles Le Gay of this parish, B., and Elizabeth Bennett of the same, W.; by Richard Edwards, Curate. Banns. Wit.: Elizabeth Slark & William Wilson.

* Signs "Mary Witheat."—Ed. † Signs by mark.—Ed. ‡ Signs "Parrish."—Ed.

1800-01

Aug 3 Thomas Sansom of this parish, B, and Mary Coleman of the same, W; by Richard Edwards, Curate Banns Wit George Boore, J Martin, & S Everett

4 John Haynes* of this parish, B, and Elizabeth Parsons* of the same, W, by Richard Edwards, Curate Banns Wit James Hunter Gray & William Wilson

Sept 1 Isaac Hamaway* of this parish, W, and Susanna Dunkin of the same, W, by Richard Edwards, Curate Banns Wit Alexander Gardiner, Margaret Gardiner, her mark

4 Edward Kelsey of S[t] George the Martyr, Midx, B, and Harriet Sophia Street of S[t] Bennet, Paul's Wharf, S, by Richard Edwards, Curate Licence Wit Frances Street, A. H. Kelsey, & James Cathrow

Nov 23 Thomas Bowen of this parish, B, and Susannah Parry of the same, S; by Richard Edwards, Curate Banns Wit Henry Morgan & Louisa Linton

Dec 11 John Cottingham of Laxfield, Suffolk, W, and Jemima Balls of S[t] Peter, Paul's Wharf, Lond, W., by Richard Edwards, Curate Licence Wit Joseph Orlibar Cottingham, Elizabeth Cottingham, & Benjamin Carden

1801

Jan. 1 Thomas Sage of this parish, B, and Margaret Edwards of the same, S, by Richard Edwards, Curate Banns William Garn & William Wilson, Par[h] Clerk

6 Edward Thomas of this parish, B, and Ann Clark of the same, W, by Richard Edwards, Curate Banns Wit William Wilson & Elizabeth Slark.

23 George Whitmell of this parish, W, and Elizabeth Hodge of the same, S, by Richard Edwards, Curate Banns Wit George West & William Wilson

Feb 16 Thomas Mason of this parish, B, and Mary Hambling of the same, S, by Richard Edwards, Curate Banns Wit Thomas Wake & Mary Wake, William Wilson

28 Peter James Hillary of S[t] George, Bloomsbury, Midx, B, and Mary Ann Horder of S[t] Peter, Paul's Wharf, S, by Richard Edwards, Curate Licence Wit V T Horder & T W. Horder

April 5 Thomas Hall of this parish, B, and Maria Roberts of the same, S, by W Holmes, Rector Banns Wit Samuel Cannon & William Wilson

18 Sir John Arundel, Knight of Huntingdon, co Huntingdon, W, and Sarah Anne Sharpe of S[t] Benedict, Paul's Wharf, S, by Richard Edwards, Lecturer Licence Wit Sarah Freeman, William Sharpe, & Mary Freeman

May 3 Joseph Smart of S[t] Clement Danes, Midx, B, and Elizabeth Tovey of S[t] Bennet, Paul's Wharf, S, by W. Holmes, Rector Licence Wit Maria Sharp, Thomas Hubbard, & James Tovey

June 4 George Weatherstone of S[t] Savior, Southwark, Surry, B, and Sarah Vernon Duffill of S[t] Bennet, Paul's Wharf, S, by W Holmes, Rector Licence Wit G Weatherstone, senior, & Rebecca Gainsford

18 Henry Green of S[t] Benet, Paul's Wharf, B, and Ann Daykin of the same, S.; by W Holmes, Rector Banns Wit John Humphrys & Hannah Rice

July 12 William Lincoln* of S[t] Benet, Paul's Wharf, B, and Abigail Wells* of the same, S, by W Clarke, Off Min[r] Banns Wit John Gildersleve & William Wilson

* Signs by mark —Ed

1801-3

Sept. 1 William Carden of S[t] Bennet, Pauls Wharf, B., and Ann Kendall of the same, W.; by Richard Edwards, Lecturer. Banns. Wit.: James Carden & Rosomond Carden.

22 Joseph Harris of S[t] Albans, co. Hertford, B., and Mary Ann Mayhew of S[t] Bennet, Paul's Wharf, S.; by W. Holmes, Rector. Banns. Wit.: Robert Caldwell, Eliza Arnett, & William Sanders.

Nov. 26 Thomas Brady of S[t] Mary, Lambeth, Surry, W., and Mary Ann Aubrey of S[t] Bennet, Pauls Wharf, S.; by W. Holmes, Rector. Licence. Wit.: R. Wackrill & William Wilson.

Dec. 8 Theophilus Norman of S[t] Bennet, Paul's Wharf, B., and Jane Foster of S[t] Paul, Shadwell, Midx., S.; by W. Holmes, Rector. Licence. Wit.: Priscilla Guteridge & John Jones.

1802.

Jan. 18 John Walters of S[t] Bennet, Paul's Wharf, Lond., B., and Margaret Hogg* of S[t] Paul, Deptford, Kent, S.; by W. Holmes, Rector. Licence. Wit.: Isabella Hogg & William Wilson.

April 4 Benjamin Parton of S[t] Bennet, Paul's Wharf, Lond., B., and Sophia Maund of the same, S.; by John Owen, Rector. Banns. Wit.: John Scott & William Meacher.

4 William Jones of S[t] Bennet, Paul's Wharf, Lond., B., and Mary Parton of the same, S.; by John Owen, Rector. Banns. Wit.: William Meacher & John Scott.

June 29 Francis Lavender of S[t] Peter, Paul's Wharf, Lond., B., and Mary Ann Chatterley* of S[t] Michael, Crooked Lane, Lond., S.; by W. Lucas, Min[r]. Licence. Wit.: Ralph Tittensor, Hugh Humphrys.

Aug. 23 Thomas Jeff* of S[t] Bennet, Paul's Wharf, Lond., B., and Eleanor Talbot of the same, S.; by Richard Edwards, Lecturer. Banns. Wit.: Robert Higgins & Elizabeth Worrall.

26 William Watts of S[t] Bennet, Paul's Wharf, Lond., B., and Sarah Mattress of the same, S.; by Richard Edwards, Lecturer. Licence. Wit.: John Mattress & William Wilson.

Sept. 13 Richard Bennett of S[t] Bennet, Paul's Wharf, B., and Jane Law of the same, W.; by Richard Edwards, Lecturer. Licence. Wit.: S. Shepherd & William Wilson.

Nov. 14 Thomas Friend Robinson of S[t] Saviour, Southwark, Surry, B., and Elizabeth Armstrong* of S[t] Bennet, S.; by W. Lucas, Min[r]. Licence. Wit.: Martha Tomkins & Charlotte Tomkins.

1803.

Jan. 1 James Richardson* of this parish, B., and Etheldray Andrews of the same, S.; by W. Lucas, Min[r]. Banns. Wit.: Sarah Wotton & Edward Stratton.

Feb. 26 Thomas Best of this parish, W., and Ann Bineham of the same, W.; by W. Lucas, Min[r]. Banns. Wit.: Thomas Child and William Wilson.

June 16 Benjamin Smith of S[t] Bennet, Paul's Wharf, B., and Mary Bishop of the same, S.; by W. Lucas, Min[r]. Banns. Wit.: Hannah Smith & William Willson.

20 William Evans of S[t] Bennet, Paul's Wharf, B., and Sarah Rose of the same, S.; by W. Lucas, Min[r]. Banns. Wit.: Rose & Ann White.

July 3 Samuel Joseph Bird of S[t] Bennet, Paul's Wharf, London, B., and Mary Phœbe Smith of the same, S.; by W. Lucas, Min[r]. Banns. Wit.: Peter Potter & William Wilson.

* Signs by mark.—Ed.

1803-6

Aug. 20 Charles Geeves of S[t] Bennet, Paul's Wharf, B., and Lucy Edwards of the same, S.; by W. Lucas, Min[r]. Banns. Wit.: David Porter & Edde Porter.

Sept. 21 Benjamin Evan Jones of S[t] Bennet, Paul's Wharf, Lond., B., and Eliza Hawes of the same, S.; by W. Lucas, Min[r]. Banns. Wit.: Owen Jones & William Wilson.

Oct. 11 George Smith of S[t] Bennet, Paul's Wharf, Lond., B., and Sarah Howell of the same, S.; by W. Lucas, Min[r]. Licence. Wit.: Richard Howell & Mary Howell.

1804.

Jan. 28 James Didcock of S[t] Bennet, Paul's Wharf, B., and Ann Knight of the same, S.; by John Owen, Rector. Banns. Wit.: Thomas Meager & William Wilson.

Feb. 19 John Bumpstead of S[t] Bennet, Paul's Wharf, Lond., B., and Sarah Woodhouse of the same, S.; by W. Lucas, Min[r]. Banns. Wit.: John Batchelor & Margaret Batchelour.

Aug. 21 Daniel Desormeaux of S[t] Bennet, Paul's Wharf, Lond., B., and Elizabeth Mayhew of the same, S.; by John Owen, Rector. Banns. Wit.: James Harris, Hastings John Mayhew, David Evans, & William Alcock.

1805.

May 13 Nicholas Whitehouse of S[t] Peter, Paul's Wharf, Lond., B., and Ann Ashmore of the same, S.; by John Owen, Rector. Banns. Wit.: Joyce N. Whitehouse & William Wilson, Parish Clerk.

July 7 William Nicholas of S[t] Margaret Patten, Lond., B., and Margaret Tittley of S[t] Bennet, Paul's Wharf, S.; by John Owen, Rector. Licence. Wit.: James Humphreys, H. Humphreys, & William Wilson.

Aug. 19 Owen Owens of S[t] Bennet, Paul's Wharf, Lond., B., and Catherine Daniel of the same, S.; by John Owen, Rector. Banns. Wit.: Hinrich Krute & E. Edwards.

1806.

May 13 Thomas Meager of S[t] Bennet, Paul's Wharf, Lond., B., and Jane Cadwalder of the same, S.; by John Owen, Rector. Banns. Wit.: Elizabeth Markwick & William Blunden.

24 Ralph Bigland, Esquire, Norroy King of Arms, of S[t] Bennet, Paul's Wharf, Lond., W., and Charlotte Mary Lorimer of the same, S.; by Richard Edwards, Lecturer. Licence. Wit.: Isaac Heard, Garter, Rose [?] Bigland, & James Cathrow, Rouge Dragon.

July 20 James Thomas Hayward of this parish, B., and Lucy Collibee of the same, S.; by John Owen, Rector. Banns. Wit.: James Hayward & Elizabeth Collibee.

22 John Barnes of the town and county of Bedford, B., and Charlotte Maxey of S[t] Peter, Paul's Wharf, Lond., S.; by W. Lucas, Min[r]. Licence. Wit.: Charles Maxey and Richard Maxey.

Sept. 27 Henry White of S[t] Bennet, Paul's Wharf, Lond., B., and Ruth Hagar Field of the same, S.; by John Owen, Rector. Banns. Wit.: Mary Wood & Jane Feild.

Dec. 1 William Wilson* of S[t] Bennet, Paul's Wharf, Lond., B., and Ann Edwards of the same, S.; by John Owen, Rector. Banns. Wit.: Charles Geeves, Lucy Geeves, & Mary Clagget.

* Signs by mark.—Ed.

1807.

1807-8

Jan. 15 Edward Cope of this parish, B., and Mary Rawlins of the same, S.; by John Owen, Rector. Banns. Wit.: James Cope & Elenor Rawlins.

April 3 William Barrett of Christ Church, Surrey, B., and Mary Greenwich Bailey of St Bennet, Paul's Wharf, S.; by John Owen, Rector. Licence. Wit.: Joseph Burrowes & William Wilson.

May 14 Samuel Smith of St Mary, Rotherhithe, Surry, B., and Mary Frances Elizabeth Campbell of St Peter, Paul's Wharf, Lond., S., a minor, by and with the consent of Hector Campbell, the natural and lawful Father of the said Minor; by John Owen, Rector. Licence. Wit.: Hector Campbell, Sinai Catherine Winter, Frances Campbell, & William Wilson.

June 24 Thomas Jones of St Benet, Paul's Wharf, B., and Elizabeth Reynole of the same, S.; by John Owen, Rector. Banns. Wit.: James Bernard & William Wilson.

July 19 William Pearce of St Benet, Paul's Wharf, W., and Rebecca Cooper* of the same, W.; by John Owen, Rector. Banns. Wit.: William Wilson & James Alford.

Aug. 4 William Cran of St Benet, Paul's Wharf, B., and Elizabeth Platt of the same, S; by John Owen. Banns. Wit.: Mary Ann Platt & William Wilson.

Oct. 4 Thomas Dauncey of St Peter, Paul's Wharf, Lond., [*blank*], and Sarah Edwards of the same, S., a Minor, by & with the consent of George Edwards, the natural and lawful Father of the said minor; by John Owen, Rector. Licence. Wit.: George Edwards, Mary Giles, & Mary Clark.

Nov. 8 Adam Burnett of St Bennet, Paul's Wharf, W., and Sarah Jameson of the same, W.; by John Owen, Rector. Banns. Wit.: Thomas Mullins, An Corn, & William Wilson.

Dec. 21 William Houlton of St Benet, Paul's Wharf, B., and Rebecca Randell* of the same, S.; by John Owen, Rector. Banns. Wit.: Sarah Miller & James Alford.

1808.

Feb. 3 Charles White of St Benet, Paul's Wharf, B., and Mary Stainton of the same, S.; by John Owen, Rector. Licence. Wit.: James Maclaren, Anne Maclaren, Charlotte Maclaren.

7 Samuel Plume* of St Benet, Paul's Wharf, B., and Margaret Davis of the same, S.; by John Owen, Rector. Banns. Wit.: Elizabeth Griffiths, Daniel Carr, Thomas Tanner, & Elizabeth Butterfield.

10 William Cann of St Peter, Paul's Wharf, Lond., B., and Mary Brooker of the same, W.; by William Pace, Minr. Licence. Wit.: Jane Lee, Emma Pace, Jessy Pace, John Cann, Mary Cann.

Mar. 21 William Howes of St Bennet, Paul's Wharf, B., and Margaret Batchelour of the same, W.; by John Owen, Rector. Banns. Wit.: John Bumpstead & Sarah Bumpstead.

May 29 Thomas Cockhead of St Benet, Paul's Wharf, Lond., W., and Martha Lagden of the same, S.; by John Owen, Rector. Banns. Wit.: James Smith, Mary Smith, her mark.

June 19 Michael Harbron of St Benet, Paul's Wharf, Lond., B., and Sally Gough of the same, S.; by John Owen, Rector. Banns. Wit.: William Wilson & James Alford.

July 10 Daniel Orphin of St Peter, Paul's Wharf, Lond., B., and Helena Kie of the same, S.; by John Owen, Rector. Banns. Wit.: Thomas Hickman & William Wilson.

* Signs by mark.—Ed.

1808-10

July 12 Gasper Warner of St Peter, Paul's Wharf, Lond, B, and Sarah Luff of the same, S, by John Owen, Rector Banns Wit Thomas Bennett and Elizabeth Jones

Dec 1 Robert Yarker of St Peter, Paul's Wharf, Lond, B, and Louisa Euinsford of the Chapelry of Laleham in the parish of Staines, Midx, S, by W Lucas, Minr Licence Wit Lydia Watts & Thomas Wilson

22 James White of St Peter, Paul's Wharf, Lond, B, and Elizabeth Nyst of the same, S., by W Lucas, Minr Banns Wit Henry Blatch & Martha Blatch

26 Charles Johnson of St Bennet, Paul's Wharf, Lond, W, and Ann Baudon of the same, S, W Lucas, Minr Banns Wit Henry Johnson, Elizabeth Johnson

31 John Newton of St Bennet, Paul's Wharf, B, and Elizabeth Edwards of the same, S, by W. Lucas, Minr Banns Wit Abraham Frankland & Lucy Geeves

1809

April 2 Joseph Ashelford of St Bennet, Paul's Wharf, W, & Elizabeth Cox* of the same, W, by W Lucas, Minr Banns Wit Richard Blackmore & William Wilson

3 Thomas Chapman of St Bennet, Paul's Wharf, B, and Elizabeth Woodhams of the same, S, by W Lucas, Minr Banns Wit. George Frankes and Sally Mandy.

11 William Grenfell Peyton of St Bennet, Paul's Wharf, Lond, B, and Mary Lane of Croydon, Surry, S, by John Lane, A M, Rector of Little Widgborow, Essex Licence Wit R F Peyton, Pascoe Grenfell, William Lane, M J Peyton, & Susanna Lane

May 1 William Edwards of St Bennet, Paul's Wharf, Lond, W, and Mary Manser of the same, S, by W Lucas, Minr Banns Wit William Manser & Elizabeth Manser

June 10 Thomas Leach of St Matthew, Friday Street, Lond, B, and Mary Howell of St Benedict, Paul's Wharf, S, by W Lucas, Minr. Licence Wit Richard Howell, Catherine Howell, Harriet Tenton, & Henry Schaaf.

July 23 Thomas Jennings of St Benet, Paul's Wharf, Lond, B, and Ann Jane Bloxham* of the same, S, by John Owen, Rector Banns Wit. Charles Randell Bloxham, Ann Dulley

Sept 15 Ezekiel Delight of St Benedict near Paul's Wharf, Lond, W, & Hannah Tooley of St James, Clerkenwell, Midx, W, by W Lucas, Minr Licence Wit William Wilson, Mary [?] Elfud

21 John McCoy of St Benet, Paul's Wharf, B, and Mary Ann Ford of the same, S, by John Owen, Rector Banns Wit Charles Smith, Mary Elfud

Oct 22 William Gower of St Benet, Paul's Wharf, Lond, B, and Ann Jacobs* of the same, S, by John Owen, Rector Banns Wit James Alford, Hannah Jacob, & Henry Hopwaft [?]

Nov. 28 Frederick Adolphus Butt of St Benet, Paul's Wharf, Lond, B, and Elizabeth Abigail Jones of the same, S, by John Owen, Rector. Banns. Wit. Ann Davison [?] & Sarrah Alford

1810.

June 11 James Hildred of St Peter, Paul's Wharf, Lond, B, and Charlotte Ellis of the same, S; by John Owen, Rector Banns Wit W Grey & J Stewart

* Signs by mark.—Ed

1810-14

Aug. 10 William Lewis* of S[t] Benet, Paul's Wharf, Lond., W., and Hannah Nunn* of the same, S.; by W. Lucas, Min[r]. Licence. Wit.: Jonathan Bull & William Wilson.

26 William Aldrich of S[t] Benet, Paul's Wharf, Lond., B., and Ann Cole of the same, S.; by John Owen, Rector. Banns. Wit.: William Cole, Thomas Cole, & James Aldrich.

Nov. 19 Richard Strubell of S[t] Benet, Paul's Wharf, B., and Mary Ann Davis of the same, S.; by W. Lucas, Min[r]. Banns. Wit.: Giles Davis, William Davis, & Sarah Davis.

1811.

May 23 The Reverend Charles Laprimaudaye, Clerk of Leyton, Essex, B., and Jane Lee of S[t] Peter, Paul's Wharf, Lond., S.; by William Pace, Min[r]. Licence. Wit.: Cath. Laprimaudaye, J. H. Randell, Richard E. N. Lee, & Sarah Randell.

June 17 Mark Burn of S[t] Benet, Paul's Wharf, Lond., W., and Mary Day* of the same, S.; by John Owen, Rector. Banns. Wit.: John Williams & Ann Williams.

23 Robert Lloyd* of S[t] Peter, Paul's Wharf, Lond., B., and Louisa Goodjohn* of the same, S.; by John Owen, Rector. Banns. Wit.: Martin Alexander & Charles Smith.

1812.

July 21 John Power of S[t] Andrew, Holborn, B., and Ann Elizabeth Evans of S[t] Bennet, Paul's Wharf, S.; by John Owen, Rector. Banns. Wit.: Maria Evans & William Wilson.

Nov. 30 William Clark of S[t] Benet, Paul's Wharf, Lond., B., and Mary Ann Searle of the same, S.; by John Owen, Rector. Banns. Wit.: William Murray & Margaret Rogers.

See Register Book of Marriages agreeably to Act of Parliament.

[The rest of this volume is blank paper.]

BOOK L.

Register of Marriages in the Parish of St. Benet, Paul's Wharf, in the City of London.

MARRIAGES SOLEMNIZED IN THE PARISH OF S[T] BENET, PAUL'S WHARF, IN THE CITY OF LONDON, IN THE YEAR 1813.

1813.

Aug. 2 John Ford Jones of this parish, B., and Catherine Smith of the same, S.; by Richard Edwards, Lecturer. Banns. Wit.: Eleanor Tripp & James Alford.

1814.

Mar. 27 William Holder of this parish, B., and Hannah Maria Hood of the same, S.; by John Owen, Rector. Banns. Wit.: Charles Smith & James Alford.

* Signs by mark.—ED.

1814-20

June 16 Perrot Fenton the younger of St Gregory, Lond, Esq, and Catharine Howell of St Benet, Paul's Wharf, Lond, S, with consent of their parents, being both of age, by John Owen, Rector Licence Wit P Fenton, Harriot Walker, Thomas Leach, & Mary Leach

Nov 27 Henry Freshwater of this parish, B, and Louisa Griffiths of the same, S, by Richard Edwards, Lecturer Banns Wit Mary Harrison & Richard Bliss

1815

June 7 John Alford of this parish, B, and Ann Eastaugh of Ealing, Midx, S, by Richard Edwards, Lecturer Licence Wit John Thomas Denny & Sarah Ann Alford

11 James Edwards of this parish, W, and Sarah Rouse of the same, W, by John Owen, Banns Wit Penelope Eames & James Alford

[NOTE.—This marriage, from a cancelled entry, took place on the 15th of May previous By a note in the Rector's hand the woman's name in the banns was Rouch, but she signed "Rouse" The banns were therefore republished & they were remarried as above]

June 25 Tobias Michell of St Benet, Paul's Wharf, W, and Jane Gillham, S, of St Bartholomew by the Royal Exchange, Lond, by John Owen, Rector Licence Wit Hannah Watson and Charles Smith

25 William Fletcher* of St Benet, Paul's Wharf, [*blank*], and Frances Shrimpton* of the same, S, by John Owen, Rector. Banns Wit Sarah Giles & Charles Smith

27 William Dixon of Portsmouth, Hants, B, and Mary Sansom of this parish, W, by Richard Edwards, Lecturer Licence Wit William Brooks & Ann Brooks

Oct 23 John Cousins of St Benet, Paul's Wharf, W, and Margaret Robson of the same, W., by John Owen, Rector Banns Wit. William Coventry & Alexander Cuthbert

There are no entries in 1816 —ED

1817.

April 6 Robert Snell of St Benet, Paul's Wharf, B, and Sarah Bloxham* of the same, S., by John Owen, Rector Banns Wit Thomas Jennings & Timothy Smith

May 20 Henry Stainton, St Benet, Paul's Wharf, B, and Sarah Tomkison of Lewisham, Kent, S, by John Owen, Rector. Licence Wit Charles White, Anne Maclaren, William Maclaren, & Charlotte Maclaren

26 Joseph Roberts of St Benet, Paul's Wharf, B, and Elizabeth Bower of St James, Clerkenwell, S, by John Owen, Rector Licence Wit Jane Burstall & Timothy Smith

June 23 Florence [*sic*] M'Carthy of St Peter's, Paul's Wharf, B, and Helen Coffee* of the same, S, by John Owen, Rector Banns Wit Michael Connor & Timothy Smith

There are no entries in 1818 *or* 1819 —ED

1820

May 13 Joseph Coward of St Benet, Paul's Wharf, W, and Ann Pasco of St Giles, Camberwell, Surrey, S, by John Owen, Rector Licence Wit Thomas Hood & Susannah Hood

Sept 24 George Thomas Dean of St Benet, Paul's Whart, B, and Jane Wentworth of the same, S., by Richard Edwards, Lecturer Banns Wit Richard Smith & Timothy Smith

* Signs by mark.—ED

1821-6

1821.

Mar. 18 John Wheeler of S[t] Peter, Paul's Wharf, B., and Maria Everett of the same, S.; by John Owen, Rector. Banns. Wit.: The marke of William Martin, Timothy Smith.

Sept. 9 Charles Deacon of S[t] Benet, Paul's Wharf, B., and Caroline Smith of the same, S.; by Richard Edwards, Lecturer. Licence. Wit.: Robert Davis & Timothy Smith.

Nov. 11 Samuel Smith of S[t] Benet, Paul's Wharf, B., and Sarah Ann Churcher of the same, S.; by John Owen, Rector. Banns. Wit.: Robert Girling & Timothy Smith.

1822.

Mar. 31 Joseph Thompson of S[t] Luke, Old Street, B., and Harriot Smethurst of S[t] Benet, Paul's Wharf, S.; by John Owen, Rector. Licence. Wit.: John Thompson & Timothy Smith.

June 2 George Roberts of S[t] Benet, Paul's Wharf, B., and Elizabeth Lyon of London Stone, London, S.; by John Owen, Rector. Licence. Wit.: Hawks Lyon & Priscilla Roberts.

2 John Hassall of S[t] Peter, Paul's Wharf, B., and Elizabeth Dixon* of the same, S.; by John Owen, Rector. Banns. Wit.: James Alford, Timothy Smith.

July 7 Michael Clunan of S[t] Benet, Paul's Wharf, B., and Rachel Shepherd of the same, S.; by John Owen, Rector. Banns. Wit.: Paul Stepney & George Smith.

1823.

Feb. 16 Carl Setzer of this parish, W.,† and Maria Vergles of S[t] Mary, Lambeth, S.; by John Owen, Rector. Banns. Wit.: George Krause & Caroline Cokoe [?].

1824.

Jan. 14 Thomas Baker of S[t] Benet, Paul's Wharf, W., and Rebecca Martin of Epsom, Surrey, W.; by John Owen, Rector. Licence. Wit.: William Evans & Mary Evans.

Sept. 19 Henry Welford of S[t] Benet, Paul's Wharf, B., and Sarah Mary Ayre of the same, S.; by Richard Edwards, Lecturer. Banns. Wit.: Timothy Smith & James Alford.

Dec. 9 John Gordon of Endfield, Midx., B., and Martha Butler of S[t] Benet, Paul's Wharf, Lond., S.; by Richard Edwards, Lecturer. Licence. Wit.: Timothy Smith & Mary Scrivenor Bartlet.

1825.

July 19- Charles Rattee of this parish, W., and Elizabeth Lake of the same, S.; by Henry Du Cane, Rector. Banns. Wit.: Timothy Smith, Henry Man [?].

Dec. 12 Thomas Moss Dimmock of this parish, W., and Jane Brereton of the same, S.; by Richard Edwards, Lecturer. Banns. Wit.: Timothy Smith & James Alford.

1826.

Feb. 2 Joseph Nunn of S[t] Pancras, Midx., B., & Eliza Flint of S[t] Peter, Paul's Wharf, Lond., S.; by Richard Edwards, Lecturer. Banns. Wit.: Joshua Nunn & Martha Dallen.

* Signs by mark.—Ed.

† Altered from "Bachelor" and same noted by the Rector on the same day.—Ed.

1826-30
Mar. 24 William Martin of this parish, W., and Margaret Jones of the same, W.; by Richard Edwards, Lecturer. Banns. Wit.: Timothy Smith & James Alford.

Aug. 24 Edget Jones of this parish, B., and Margaret Giles of the same, W.; by W. J. Hall, M.A., Curate. Banns. Wit.: Timothy Smith & James Alford.

Nov. 7 William Morris of this parish, B., and Sarah Rittangall Woolnough of the same, S.; by W. J. Hall, M.A., Curate. Banns. Wit.: John Walters & Timothy Smith.

1827.

Mar. 31 Furnell Bolden of S[t] Peter, Paul's Wharf, B., and Harriot Emma Wiskon of Bishop Stortford, S.; by W. J. Hall, M.A., Curate. Banns. Wit.: John Hughes, Ann Bolden, & Helen Bolden.

April 30 Samuel Ramsay of this parish, B., and Mary Haynes of this parish, S.; by W. J. Hall, M.A., Curate. Banns. Wit.: Thomas Ramsay, Ann Ramsay, & Jn. Ramsay.

Sept. 24 Peter Sandys of this parish, B., and Isabella Morton of the same, S.; by W. J. Hall, M.A., Curate. Banns. Wit.: William Beard & T. Smith.

Oct. 22 James Frederick Walker of this parish, B., and Anna Maria Short of the same, S.; by W. J. Hall, M.A., Curate. Banns. Wit.: Timothy Smith & James Alford.

1828.

Jan. 27 Benjamin Smith Fairbrother of this parish, B., and Catherine Coward of the same, W.; by W. J. Hall, M.A., Curate. Banns. Wit.: Joseph Coward, T. Smith, & Rachael Coward.

Feb. 17 John Robinson of this parish, B., and Phoebe Tizzard of the same, S.; by Richard Edwards, Lecturer. Banns. Wit.: Elizabeth Robinson, John Robinson, & James Cattenden.

July 30 Thomas Delves Atkinson of this parish, B., and Maria Davis of the same, W.; by J. T. Bennett, Off. Min[r]. Banns. Wit.: T. Smith & Ann Williams.

Oct. 19 Henry Henderson of this parish, B., and Charlotte Stratton* of the same, S.; by J. T. Bennett, Off. Min[r]. Banns. Wit.: Richard Weller & Sarah Bowen.

1829.

Jan. 24 Frederic Caldecott of this parish, B., and Anna Fiske of the same, S.; by W. J. Hall, M.A., Curate. Licence. Wit.: J. Smith & T. Smith.

June 14 William Welch of this parish, B., and Charlotte Cornhill of the same, S.; by W. J. Hall, M.A., Curate. Banns. Wit.: Ann Hudson & Timothy Smith.

Aug. 12 John Philip Burnaby of S[t] Michael Bassishaw, Lond., B., and Jemima Savage of this parish, S.; by G. A. Burnaby, Off. Min[r]. Licence. Wit.: S. B. Burnaby, Mary Taylor, Will. Dyott Burnaby, K. Hotham.

1830.

Sept. 6 Henry Freeman of this parish, B., and Caroline Belbin of this parish, S.; by W. J. Hall, M.A., Curate. Banns. Wit.: The mark of Charles Higgins & The mark of Elizabeth Higgins.

Oct. 19 William Wilmot George Norman of this parish, B., and Mary Ann Hollister of the same, S.; by W. J. Hall, M.A., Curate. Banns. Wit.: Theophilus Norman & Mary Ann Norman.

* Signs by mark.—Ed.

1831-7

1831.

July 17 John Rayment of this parish, B., and Harriet Lincoln of the same, S.; by W. J. Hall, M.A., Curate. Banns. Wit.: James Nihell [?] & Sarah Miller.

Oct. 29 George Caswell of this parish, B., and Martha Sarah Buller of the same, S.; by J. T. Bennett, M.A., Off. Minr. Banns. Wit.: Timothy Smith & James Alford.

There are no entries in 1832.—Ed.

1833.

Mar. 28 George Macilwain of Ely Place, Holborn, W., and Elizabeth Daubeny of this parish, S.; by John Hewlett, B.D., Rector of Hilgay. Licence. Wit.: C. C. Raper, Anne Sladen, F. Raper, C. M. Kingston, H. Sikes, W. Sikes, Peter Nugent Kingston.

July 30 William George Cave of St Benet, Paul's Wharf, Lond., B., and Harriette Elizabeth Wood of St Dionis Backchurch, Lond., S.; by J. T. Bennett, M.A., Off. Minr. Licence. Wit.: James Hayward & James Alford.

Oct. 25 John Lee of this parish, B., and Celia Rutter of the same, S.; by W. J. Hall, M.A., Curate. Licence. Wit.: Philip Gavey & Hannah Gavey.

1834.

May 12 George Tregarthen of St Marys, Scilly, in the Island of Scilly, B., and Jane Colenso of this parish, S.; by R. H. Barham, Rector of St Mary Magdalene, Old Fish Street. Licence. Wit.: James Gardiner & Ann Bramble.

Aug. 3 William Smith of this parish, B., and Eliza Gillman of the same, S.; by W. J. Hall, M.A., Curate. Banns. W. S. Alford and J. Alford.

Dec. 2 John Masters of this parish, B., and Anna Stone of Bexley, Kent, S., a Minor, married by licence, with consent of William Stone, the natural and lawful Father; by W. J. Hall, M.A., Curate. Wit.: Mary Ann Stone & James Alford.

1835.

April 28 John Harding Cook Gregory of this parish, B., and Phœbe Collingridge of this parish, S.; by W. J. Hall, M.A., Rector. Banns. Wit.: James Richardson & Timothy Smith.

Aug. 22 Matthew Seymour Jonn* of this parish, W., and Mary Ann Barnes of this parish, W.; by J. C. Haden, M.A., St Paul's Cathedral. Banns. Wit.: William Sackville Alford & Eliza Sophia Larnder.

There are no entries in 1836.—Ed.

1837.

Mar. 23 Frederick Augustus De Wilde of this parish, B., and Harriet Harrison of St George, Bloomsbury, S., a Minor; by W. J. Hall, M.A., Rector. By Licence, with consent of Parent. Wit.: James Hayward, James Alford.

†June 1 William Sheldrick of this parish, B., and Sarah King of the same, S.; by J. T. Bennett, M.A., Off. Minr. Banns. Wit.: Richard Ball & Caroline King.

* Altered from "Inn," with a note signed J. C. Haden that the alteration was made by him at the time the entry was made.—Ed.

† This entry is on form No. 59; the remaining forms in the book are all blank.—Ed.

The Registers
OF
St. Peter, Paul's Wharf.

BOOK A.

MARRIADGES.

Begone the ffirst daie of Aprill, Anno Dñi 1607 Annoq; regni Regis Jacobi &c Quinto, John Kinde, Parson, Mathewe Gwyn, and David Griffithe, Churchwardeins

1607

April 6 William Simson, blacksmith, of London, and Marye Chambers Lic from Faculty

May 3 George Congrave, Carman, and Abigall Somers Lic from Faculty

4 William Burton of St Stephens, Coleman Street, and Elizabeth Buttones of St Botolph, Aldersgate Lic from Fac

4 Thomas Burton of Finchley, Middx, gent, and Winefrid Malwerth Lic from Fac

7 Richard Maye of the Inner Temple, gent, and Audreye Hebden of St Anne by Aldersgate, W Lic from Fac

9 Erasmus Page of Hendon, Middx, husbandman, and Elizabeth Fletcher of the same Lic. from Fac

9 William Wisse of Capgrave* in Yorkshire, gent, and Kathern Hicchinson of York Lic Fac

19 Walter Lowman of St Sepulchres, mucisbener, and Anne Hetfalt of St Giles, Cripplegate

19 Roger Coondy of Bevenger in Essex, husbandman, and Mary Gooddin Lic Fac

June 18 Richard Armsted of Mims, co Herts, and Joane Stanbrought of the same Lic Fac

24 Edward Patesonne of St Dunstans and Annes Gawshawke

July 6 John Greener of Bary in Hampshire, husbandman, and Anne Whittead Lic Fac

10 William Leithe, s'vant to Rouland Rutt, Innholder, Bredstreet, and Frances Dent Lic Fac

13 Eggremont Thinne of the Middle Temple, gent, and Barbery Colthrop. Lic Fac

18 Humffrey Kenniston of St James, Garlickhithe, merchant tayler, and Luce Barreys Lic Fac

21 Roger Pottes and Cristian Burgesse, W Lic Fac

26 Thomas Browne of St Michael, Queen hive, and John Phillipes. Lic Fac

27 Thomas Kente of St Thomas the Apostle, clothworker, and Avisse Davis, W

* Copgrove —ED

1607

July 27 John Haweed of the parish of Honey Lane, mercer, and Frauncis Dilline. Lic. Fac.

29 William Hide and Sislie Colher, S. Lic. Fac.

Aug. 1 Ambrose Birde of Ufford, co. Northampton, gent., and Parnell Browne. Lic. Fac.

1 John Swinscoe of St Andrew, Holborne, haberdasher, and Margrat Slacke. Lic. Fac.

10 Humffrey Hunt of St Michael, Queenhithe, vintner, and Allis Hunt. Lic. Fac.

17 John Knight, vitler, and Faith Ince, W. Lic. Fac.

27 Richard Steventone of Layton and Elizabeth Lydiatt. Lic. Fac.

30 William Blackburne of St Catheren Cree church, tayller, and Sussan Fosset. Lic. Fac.

Sept. 8 John Clarke of St Olave, Southwark, currier, and Rebecka Dodd. Lic. Fac.

10 Overington Jayle of Charlwood, Surry, Yeoman, and Dennis Cronport. Lic. Fac.

16 Nicolas Booden of Reading, co. Berks, gent., and Mary Mercer. Lic. Fac.

16 William Jonnes of Deptford, tayller, and Rebecka Howell, W. Lic. Fac.

18 John Nelsson of Low Lawton, Essex, husbandman, and Magdaline Mynsse. Lic. Fac.

23 Abraham Fisher of All Hallows the Great, brewer, and Anne Hayly. Lic. Fac.

27 Robert Elford of St Mary Aldermary, tayler, and Elizabeth Rashbrooke. Lic. Fac.

28 John Langton of Felton, Middx., yeoman, and Kathern Blaunche. Lic. Fac.

Oct. 16 Moris Davis of Hodson [*sic*], husbandman, and Anne Hodson. Lic. Fac.

25 John Coo and Margarett Lickman, W. Banns.

26 Gorge Sealye of St Clement without Temple Bar, butcher, and Allis Shelley, W.

26 William Griffine and Sehell Kinge. Banns.

Nov. 1 Richard Ginn of Anstry, co. Hertford, yeoman, and Mary Dinley. Lic. Fac.

5 Water Davis, brewer, and Margaret Hickson. Lic. Fac.

5 William Blake, merchant tayler, and Alles Maye. Lic. Fac.

5 Olyver Moodye of St Giles wthout Cripplegate, yeoman, and Margaret Weakley. Lic. Fac.

13 John Fletcher of St Giles wthout Cripplegate, cook, and Elizabeth Flambathe, W. Lic. Fac.

15 Thomas Washlin of St Andrew, Holborne, gent., and Sara Brewer. Lic. Fac.

17 Gorge Johnson of St Margaret, Westminster, and Elizabeth Flecknall, W. Lic. Fac.

19 Richard Buckerstaffe of St Martin, silk weaver, and Jonne Marchall, W. Lic. Fac.

23 Richard Millinge of St Andrew, Holborne, gent., and Joysse Rice. Lic. Fac.

30 John Savage of Islington, Yoeman, and Sussand Greye, W.

30 William Broadstachc of Appleford, co. Berks, yeoman, and Mabell Wichelawe, W. Lic. Fac.

Dec. 1 Walter Eastwood of Lewisham, butcher, and Janne Carlesse. Lic.

8 John Kelley and Margaret Fredericke, W. Lic. out of Mr Coston's Office.

1607-9
Dec. 10 Edward Reynolds and Mary Hobson, both of Greenwich, by certifficat under Mr Kinds hand or P'son that they have bine three tymes axte in his pish Church at Grenwiche and that noe impediment was found that myght hinder there maiage
Jan 6 Hughe Moris and Margratt Yeavones, W Banns
13 Edward Sheward of St Botulph, Aldersgate, London, smith, and Jane Swyne, mayden Lic Fac
17 John Adams of St Sepulchres, London, chandler, and Urssula Hoode, mayden Lic Fac
21 William Agasse of Oxsted, Surrey, miller, and Alsse Richell, mayden Lic Fac
Feb 2 William Lacke of Horton, co Berks, yeoman, and Jonne Nutmaker, W Lic Fac
2 John Horichett of St Dunstan in the East, and Margaret Bulbrige, W. Lic Fac
2 John Nashe of St John Zacharye, London, and Elizabeth Lenton, W. Lic Fac
2 Thomas and Margrat . Lic Fac
3 Peeter Newport of Thissellworth, yeoman, and Margratt Paffeeld, mayden Lic Fac
10 Henry Cole of Heston, Middx, yeoman, and Margrat Baringer Lic Fac
10 John Deverex of St Michaell's and Elizabeth Bussher Lic Fac
12 John Walter of Limehouse in Stepney, mariner, and Judeth Hilles, W. Lic Fac.

1608

April 3 John Monke of Bridewell precinct, woodmonger, and Mary Mascoll, mayden. Lic. Fac
24 Nicholas Hudson of Stabell In, London, gent, and Brygett Sarvay, W. Lic Fac
May 9 Thomas Browne of Meinster, shoemaker, and Jayne Birrlls, mayden Lic Fac
June 2 Mr Anthony Bennett of East Greenwich, Esquier, and Elyzabethe Goudrithe, mayden Lic Fac

Da Deo Gloria, Amen

19 Henry Tabor of Hackney, husbandman, and Anne Snape Lic Fac
July 7 James Lambe, gent, and Amy Noxton Lic Fac.
Aug 11 Thomas Hide, grocer, and Annes Collier Lic Fac.
24 Harry Milburne and Margarett Palmer Lic Fac
Oct 9 John Crewe, smith, and Alles Byggins Banns
Nov 2 Richard Glascoke, tayler, and Elizabeth Walker. Lic Fac
24 William Winnye and Johan Jones Lic Fac
Jan 15 Adam Denton and Elyzabeth Roche Lic. Fac
26 Thomas Bolte and Mary Byggs Lic Fac
Feb 20 Harry Bosom and Anne Gersey Lic. Fac

1609

May 29 John Donne and Alles Hooker. Lic Fac
July 25 Fraunces Rookes and Margarett Jarvis Lic Fac.

Thomas David, clarke

Sept. 3 Thomas Owen and Gayno Williams Banns.
17 Edward Squier and Grace Witcom. Banns
27 Thomas Gyrton and Johann Atwode.
Oct. 22 Thomas Lupford and Sara Bodde Lic Fac.
Nov. 8 William Hall and Elyzabethe Vachell Lic. Fac.

1609-13
Nov. 23 Fraunces Braunche and Alles Odeham. Lic. Fac.
Dec. 12 Thomas Miller and Anne Nokes. Lic. Mr Coston's office.
Jan. 8 Thomas Gowldwin and Katherin Waren. Three tymes axed.
Feb. 10 Richard Ferry and Anne Clarke. Lic. Fac.
15 James Wamsley and Catherin Clarke. Lic. Fac.
19 David Powell and Annes Spyney. Lic. Fac.

1610.

April 10 Salamon Gravenor and Elyzabethe Harper. Lic. Fac.
May 1 William Hoor and Johan Sayvadge. Lic. Fac.
16 John Fowler and Margarett Ryvers. Lic. Fac.
29 Thomas Ive and Ellen Watkins. Lic. Fac.
June 18 John Waby and Margery Gurney. Lic. Fac.
July 21 Josephe Iniver and Johan Kent. Lic. Fac.
Aug. 11 Robert Dunninge and Alles Dune. Lic. Mr Coston's office.
Sept. 3 Robert Cole and Mary Nightingall. Lic. Fac.
20 John Stocker and Judithe Wright. Lic. Fac.
Oct. 11 William Sage and Mary Bamfrid. Lic. Fac.
31 Andrewe Kempe and Susan Goodwin. Lic. Fac.
Nov. 13 Thomas Huddelstone and Lucy Crayne, mayden. Lic. Fac.
22* John Careless and Anne Jackson, mayden. Lic. out of Mr Coston's office.
26* James Tootinge of Mortlake, husbandman, and Mary Fisher, W. Lic.
30* George Grace, waterman, and Alles Furneu, W. Lic. Fac.
Dec. 2* Ralphe Davye, taylor, and Elyzabethe Dunscombe, mayden. Lic.
Jan. 14* Richard Davis, fleatcher, and Joyse Chaddocke, W. Lic. Fac.
20* Edward Eavanes, laborer, and Susan Hughes. 3 tymes axed.
23 Richard Wimpe of Windsor, co. Berks, labourer, and Johanne Durdant.
Feb. 4* John Barnes of Rygate, Surrey, gent., and Jane Carleton, mayden. Lic. Fac.
16* John Ware als. Weare of Chiswick, husbandman, and Elyzabeth Mills, mayden. Lic. Fac.
17* John Crookedecke of St Katherine by Tower Hill, mariner, and Annes Walker, mayden. Lic. Fac.
Mar. 6* Richard Fuller of Mayfeild in Sussex, gent., and Elyzabeth Alcharne, W.

1611.

Mar. 29* Thomas Graye of Stepney, mariner, and Annes Valentine. Lic. Fac.
April 8* Thomas Graye of Melton, co. Cambridge, yeoman, and Mary Cooke, mayden. Lic. Fac.

1613.

Mr JOHN KYNDE, P'son. Davye Griffithe, William Whitt } Church Wardens.
Thomas David, clarke.

1613.

Mar. 28* William Cowarne, taylor, and Dorothy Wooddc. Lic. Fac.
April 8* Rice Griffithe of St Giles in the Fields, gent., and Anne Yates. Lic.
15* John Kersterson of St Leonard, Shoreditch, musicioner, and Magdalen Austen.
20* Henry Strugnell, taylor, and Elyzabeth Simson. 3 tymes axed.
22* Nicolas Ayleworthe, gent., and Constance Richardson. Lic. Fac.

* The entries about this period are not always consecutive. Some seem to have been copied from slips, and those indicated with an asterisk are repeated. Inasmuch as the repeated entries do not always exactly correspond with the earlier entries, it has been thought best to follow the original and give both.—ED.

1613
April 24* John Banes, pewterer, and Alles Hitchmough, mayden. Lic.
May 20* Ambrose Randolphe, gent., and Dorethy Wilson. Lic.
June 8* Edward Coypse and Jane Stonne.
July 15* Edward Lewis and Anne Beverey.

1610.

Nov. 22 John Carlesse of S[t] Andrew, Holborne, and Anne Jacksonne, S. Lic. out of M[r] Coston's Office.
26 Jeames Tolinge of Matclacke, Surry, and Mary Fisher, W. Lic. Fac.
30 Gorge Grace of the parish of Savoy, waterman, and Alls Furner, W. Lic. Fac.
Dec. 2 Raphe Davie of S[t] Mildred, Bread Street, taylor, and Elizabeth Dunscome, puella. Lic. out of Coson's office.
18 Henry Tomsonne of Cavdishe in Suffolk, Yeoman, and Margreat Page, mayden. Lic. Fac.
Jan. 12 Renolls Broker of Worth in Sussex, farrier, and Marye Mugge, mayden. Lic. Fac.
14 Richard Davis of S[t] Margaret, Westminster, fletcher, and Joyse Chaddocke, W. Lic. Fac.
20 Edward Evanes, laborer, and Susane Hughes. Three tymes axed.
Feb. 4 John Barenes of Rigate, Surrey, gent., and Jayne Carelltone, mayden. Lic. Fac.
16 John Ware of Chiswicke, husbandman, and Elizabeth Mills, mayden. Lic. Fac.
17 John Crookdecke of S[t] Katherine's, Mariner, and Annes Wallker, mayden. Lic. Fac.
Mar. 6 Richard Fuller of Mayfeelde, Sussex, gent., and Elizabeth Alcharne, wid. Lic. Fac.

1611.

Mar. 29 Thomas Gray of Stepney, Mariner, and Annes Valleutine, wid. Lic. Fac.
April 8 Thomas Graye of Mellton in Cambridgeshire, yeoman, and Marye Cooke, mayden. Lic. Fac.
May 6 Thomas Wood of S[t] Andrew, Holborn, yeoman, and Alles Willsonne, wid. Lic. Fac.
12 William Adlingtonne of London, grocer, and Anne Prockter, wid. Lic. Fac.
23 Richard Hall of S[t] Thomas the Apostle, fruterer, and Margret Loocke, mayden. Lic. Fac.
27 Harrye Graye of S[t] Edmund, Lumbard Street, taylor, and Alles Brewster, wid. Lic. Fac.
29 Edward Bunnie of S[t] Lawrence, Reading, gent., and Annes Hellier, wid. Lic. Fac.
29 John Relfe of S[t] Andrew, Holborne, taylor, and Phillipe Longe, mayden. Lic. out of M[r] Coston's office.
30 Peter Cadwallader of Stoke Newington, Middx., yeoman, and Alles Jones, mayden. Lic. Fac.
June 8 Nickolas Alworth of Morenton in Dorset, gent., and Elizabeth Langtone, mayden. Lic. Fac.
12 Thomas Wilkes of Bedforton, co. Worcester, yeoman, and Anne Morrise, Wid. Lic. Fac.
18 Blase Snowe of Greenwich, Kent, Yeoman, and Elizabethe Hurmane. Lic. Fac.
24 John Brabye of S[t] Brides, haberdasher, and Alles Moren, W. Lic. Fac.

* See note on previous page.—ED.

1611-12

July 7 Vallentine Jeames of Stratforde Bowe, gent., and Johan Kinge, W. Lic. Fac.

7 Hughe Jones and Rebecka Davis, sent by Mr Kynde from Greenwich.

Aug. 15 Edward Trote, gentell, and Jayne Kinder, mayden. Lic. Fac.

Sept. 24 John Prateyer and Isaball Harman, mayden. Lic. Fac.

Oct. 17 Richarde Clarke of Twicknam, Fisherman, and Dorothy Brewer, mayden. Lic. Fac.

31 Thomas Nickellsonne of Westminster, shoemaker, and Elline Hall, W. Lic. Fac.

29 Williame Baker of St Thomas the Apostle, embrother, and Anne Rucke, mayden. Lic. Fac.

Nov. 7 Hughe Cranfeyld of Clarkenwell, yeoman, and Elizabeth Medburne, mayden. Lic. Fac.

7 William Tarry and Anne Page. Three tymes axed.

9 William Felle of Clarkenwell, taylor, and Anne Bettensonne, mayden. Lic. Fac.

28 Robarte Millner, haberdasher, and Anne Simsonne, mayden. Lic. Fac.

Dec. 12 Nickolas Archer, leatherseller, and Elizabethe Risbye, mayden. Lic. Fac.

12 Tucher Carter of Great Marlow and Beatrice Collier, W. Lic. Fac.

19 John Castell of St Peter, Paul's Wharfe, gent., and Judith Raynallds, mayden. Lic. Fac.

19 William Berrye of St Mary at Hill, tallow chandler, and Elizabethe Walline, W. Lic. Fac.

30 John Lawrance, farrier, and Margreat Fristfilde, mayden. Lic. Fac.

Jan. 9 John Mathews of Maribone, Middx., baker, and Elizabeth Smalwode. Lic. Fac.

9 Edward Hollforde of Dounstones, taylor, and Mary Hynde, mayden. Lic. Fac.

14 John Preistney of St Andrew Wardrobe, yeoman, and Katherine Wallis, mayden. Lic. Fac.

16 Gabreill Siderse of the city of Parris, gentell, and Isabelle Knowles, mayden. Lic. Fac.

16 Edward Baylie, servant to my Lord Harry Nevell, and Alles Crampe, mayden. Lic. Fac.

30 Roger Gaye of Aldermanbury, taylor, and Jayne Strutte, mayden. Lic. Fac.

30 Roger Birde of St Peter's, vintner, and Dorcas Bathe, mayden. Licence out of my Lord of London's Court.

Feb. 5 Robarte Forde of St Botolph, Bishopsgate, Woodmonger, and Anne Gillborne, W. Lic. Fac.

Jan. 16 Humphrey Bell, skinner, and Hellen Warden, mayden. Lic. Fac.

Feb. 18 John Tenaunte of Cambridge, haberdasher, and Elizabethe Prind, mayden. Lic. Fac.

24 Robart Pertis of St Brides, taylor, and Anne Goughe, mayden. Lic. Fac.

18 Mr George Smythe, gentell, and Judyth Litton, mayden. Lic. Fac.

1612.

April 13 Henry Coulethirste of St Clements, Temple Bar, haberdasher, and Marye Crouche, W. Lic. Fac.

May 1 Henry Mansell, haberdasher, and Rachelle Cransbye, mayden. Lic. Fac.

10 William Wattsone of Walbrook, merchant, and Ursule Pearse, mayden. Lic. Fac.

12 Thomas Sandhame of Wouing, Sussex, yeoman, and Elizabeth Tayler, mayden. Lic. Fac.

22 John Loade of West Hame, yeoman, and Dorothye Finche, mayden. Lic. out of Mr Coston's office.

1612-13
May 28 Fellix Holloway of Dartford, gent., and Alles Hobbes, W. Lic. Fac.
28 Richard Mutten of North-hall, yeoman, and Grace Finche, mayden. Lic. Fac.
June 5 John Bachalar of St Clements, Temple Bar, joyner, and Elizabeth Hunter, mayden. Lic. Fac.
12 John Hayne, servingman, and Juliane Picke, mayden. Lic. Fac.
18 Edmonte Fawne of St Dounstones, London, gent., and Lettice Colles, W.* Lic. Fac.
18 Thomas Gatewarde of London, grocer, and Anne Halleye, mayden. Lic. Fac.
22 Barthellmew Massey, weaver, and Hellen Munus, W. Lic. Fac.
July 13 Thomas Batte of Harrow Hill, husbandman, and Anne Evanes, mayden. Lic. Fac.
16 Robarte Dimocke of Bartway, yeoman, and Marthae Carlle, mayden. Lic. Fac.
19 Thomas Thornetone of St George, Southwark, leatherseller, and Ellen Blackwaye, mayden. Lic. Fac.
19 Henry Morgan of St Mary Overys and Marye Davis. Three tymes axed.
29 Roger Turtlle of St Andrew, Holborne, gent., and Mary Crose, W. Lic. Fac.
Aug. 18 Edmont Neadhurst, yeoman, and Johan Miller, S. Lic. Fac.
23 Ambrose Gibbynes of Allgat, joiner, and Elizabeth Potter. Lic. Fac.
28 John Childe of Langley Abbots, yeoman, and Johane Warner, mayden. Lic. Fac.
Sept. 7 Thomas Hollines of St Brides, taylor, and Marye Wattsone, mayden. Lic. Fac.
14 John Cartwright, gent., and Anne Bigge, W. Lic. Fac.
20 Davide Astberye and Elizabeth Barker. 3 tymes axed.
Oct. 8 Milles Hickes, haberdasher, and Abigall Hawes, W. Lic. Fac.
22 Robart Allen, draper, and Elizabeth Wottone, mayden. Lic. Fac.
Nov. 10 Morrice Brasell, fruterer, and Sarae Spurling, mayden. Lic. Fac.
10 Timothy Hopper, tanner, and Susane Ashe, mayden. Lic. Fac.
12 Thomas Cowper of Stepney and Jayne Willowby of this parish. 3 tymes axed.
15 John Vickars of Chastehe, Schoolmaster, and Edeth Masland.
16 Edward Hurste, yeoman, and Alles Brouse, mayden. Lic. Fac.
24 John Martine of Sussex, yeoman, and Elizabeth Davye, W. Lic. Fac.
30 William Norris of Cornhill, boxmaker, and Lettice Colle, mayden. Lic. Fac.
Dec. 14 Gilbarde Bushe of Savoy in the Strand, taylor, and Rebecka Hall. Lic. Fac.
23 William Pricharde of St Margaret, Westminster, and Anne Whit, mayden. Lic. Fac.
29 Williame Ipwell, butcher, and Grace Kilbye, mayden. Lic. Fac.
30 Samuel Atkines, malster, and Isabell Dalling, mayden. Lic. Fac.
Jan. 8 John Comes, butcher, and Johan Evans, mayden. Lic. Fac.
Feb. 3 Thomas Roptsone and Elizabeth Powell. 3 tymes axed.
7 John Hall and Ellen Olliver. 3 tymes axed.
10 William Sutten, painter-stacioner, and Dorethye Lee, W. Lic. Fac.
Mar. 21 Henry Dichfeyld of St Katherine's and Elizabeth Vanicksonne, W.

1613.

Mar. 28 William Cowarne, taylor, and Dorethy Woode, mayden. Lic.
April 8 Rice Gryffith, gentellman, and Anne Yattes. Lic. Fac.
12 John Kerstersone, musicioner, and Magdlen Austen, mayden. Lic.

* "Mayden" struck out and "Weddow" written above.—ED.

1613-14
April 20 Henry Strugnell, taylor, and Elizabeth Simsonne. 3 tymes axed.
22 Nickolas Aylworth, gent., and Constance Richardsonne, mayden. Lic.
24 John Banes, pewterer, and Alles Hichmough, mayden. Lic.
May 20 Ambrose Randolphe, gent., and Dorethy Willson, mayden. Lic.
June 8 Edward Coyfe, taylor, and Jeane Stonne, mayden. Lic.
20 Daniell Cooke, gowldsmith, and Elizabeth Marsom, mayden. Lic.
29 Thomas Ratlife and Mary Bayte. 3 tymes axed.
July 15 Edward Lewes, gent., and Anne Teverye, mayden. Lic.
Aug. 14 Thomas Coped, shomaker, and Elizabeth Bodhame, mayden. Lic.
Sept. 23 Richard Webley, yeoman, and Dorethy Boxe. Lic.
23 Edwarde Burrose and Ellizabeth Frenche. 3 tymes axed.
Oct. 11 Josias Cocke of Chessen, co. Bucks, yeoman, and Elizabethe Sextin. Lic. Fac.
12 Phillipe Garland of Maudlens, Milk street, weaver, and Marye Bodley. Lic. Fac.
19 Henrye Ingraham and Annes Edwardes, mayden. Lic. Fac.
28 John Smithe of St Ollives, Southwark, grocer, and Elizabeth Pettye. Lic. Fac.
Nov. 4 Richard Bragge and Johanne Percevall. Lic. Fac.
11 William Wallascott and Susane Fryer, mayden. Lic. Fac.
16 Michell Ewbancke, gent., and Marye Bull, mayden. Lic. Fac.
24 John Alline, cordwainer, and Jayne More, mayden. Lic. Fac.
Dec. 8 Jarvis Combers and Elizabeth Dovie. 3 tymes axed.
9 Peter Batty and Marye Beare. Lic. Fac.
18 John Bovles and Katherine Wyamor, both of this parish. 3 tymes axed.
20 Josuae Blacke, dyer, and Briscilla Yattes, mayden. Lic.
28 Thomas Stylle and Elizabeth Chesbye, W. Lic. Fac.
Jan. 15 Harrye Legge, shomaker, and Margret Procter. Lic. Fac.
18 Thomas Weste and Johan Rolphe, W. Lic. Fac.
24 John Mountford, carpenter, and Audrey Knowles, W. Lic.
30 Josephe Dennis, taylor, and Elizabeth Symones. Lic. Fac.
Feb. 7 Thomas Babtine, vintner, and Hellen Bassett, mayden. Lic. Fac.
10 Allexander Dunsier, gent., and Katherine Holline, mayden. Lic. Fac.
10 Henrye Wattes, husbandman, and Dorethe Pye, mayden. Lic. Fac.
18 William Ruffine, gent., and Margreat Martine. Lic.
18 Phillipe Yourthe, dyer, and Elizabeth Rogers, mayden. Lic.
23 George Rith, gent., and Clacye Clitter, mayden.
Mar. 3 Erasmus Grenway, grocer, and Barbarae Hornblowe, W. Lic. Fac.
9 Robarte Amerye, taylor, and Dorethy Lilliman, mayden. Lic.
9 John Saunders, gouldsmith, and Emme Marberye. Lic.

1614.

Mar. 25 John Tayler, yeoman, and Briggit Hill, mayden. Lic.
April 4 George Ravenscrofte, gent., and Mary Stevens, mayden. Lic.
18 John Hallybread, brewer, and Elizabeth Kent.
27 Jeames Durdant, gent., and Allice Worth, W. Lic.
30 Thomas Yate, Stationer, and Mary Curten, mayden. Lic.
May 4 John Toogood, vintner, and Mary Eves, mayden. Lic. Fac.
5 Thomas Girton, vintner, and Elizabeth Dawsone. Lic. Fac.
5 Richard Fillpote and Anne Raven, both of this parish. 3 tymes axed.
12 Richard Sheldon, gent., and Anne Wallcote, mayden. Lic. Fac.
15 William Fawilt, bricklayer, and Elizabeth Price, W. Lic.
30 Edward Savage, yeoman, and Johan Jhones, W. Lic. Fac.
June 1 Thomas Lannowaye, yeoman, and Annes Napper. Lic. Fac.
5 William Audley, scrivener, and Allse Bowles, mayden. Lic.
23 Jonathan Stockwood and Francis [*sic*] Draples. Lic. Fac.

1614-15
July 13 Richard Messinger, yeoman, and Joane Hammond Lic Fac
23 Oliver Godfrey and Mary Terlinge Lic Fac
25 William Heminges and Joyse Wetherall Lic
25 Richard Alldersone and Elizabeth Dane, W Lic Fac
26 Robeart Breares and Grace Lathame Lic Fac.
Aug 1 Jeames Hyeate, Preacher, and Cicely Craforde
4 Jefferye Prescote, merchant taylor and Margret Foster, W Lic Fac
4 Henry Smith and Katherine Peake Sent by Mr Kynde
7 John Kofford and Blanch Redman 3 tymes axed

The bottom of the page is signed John Davis, August 1614

Mr John Kynd, P'sone
William Whit } Churchwardens
William Anslow }

8 Robearte Callingame, carpenter, and Anne Richardsonne, W Lic. Fac
10 Mathew Putnume, yeoman, and Marye Humphreys, W. Lic Fac
17 Roger Rowley, sallter, and Anne Grenlefe, mayden Lic Fac
17 William Wayte, carpenter, and Anne Marchante, mayden Lic Fac
22 Richard Prise, vintner, and Margreat Tuncke, mayden Lic Fac
Sept 15 Jacobe Flower, gentellman, and Margroat More, mayden Lic Fac
26 John Bowes, gente, and Maudlen Phillipes, mayden Lic Fac
Oct 5 Charlles Carrolle, haberdasher and Blanch Foster, W Lic. Fac
15 Pillgrime Johnsone, Ingraver and Elizabeth Wood, W Lic Fac
Nov 3 Williame Edwardes and Marthae Brigges 3 tymes axed
3 Arthur Astone, gent, and Marye Bignoll, mayden Lic Fac
12 John Burchet, husbandman, and Anne Jeninges, mayden Lic. Fac
24 Simon Wisman gent, and Annes Smith, W Lic Fac
30 Francis Peirsone and Francis [*sic*] Harrise Lic Fac
Dec 8 Edward Harvill, husbandman, and Alse Siblye, mayden Lic Fac
Jan. 10 Richarde Frobusher and Johan Bayley Lic out of Mr Drackes office
19 Henrye Lockley, yeoman, and Anne Ridley, mayden Lic Fac
31 Thomas Frewine, yeoman, and Sarae Jonsonn, mayden Lic Fac
Feb 8 Robart Harris, yeoman, and Elizabeth Stansell, mayden
9 Edwarde Archer, brewer, and Jhon Wall, W
17 Robarte Chstonne of Windsor, mercer, and Katherine Weaste, W Lic Fac
25 William Jolly and Anne Waters. Came from Greenwich

1615

April 8 Agustine Wells, bargman, and Alice Joyse, W Lic Fac
19 Lewes Hughes, gent, and Jhon Davis, mayden Lic Fac
23 Robarte Benfeyld, player, and Marye Bugge, mayden Lic Fac
30 John Browne, clothworker, and Margret Hayden Lic Fac
May 4 Jacobe Cattley, haberdasher, and Isbell Morris Lic Fac
June 12 Henry Cossenes, vintner, and Lipse Comber, mayden Lic Fac
12 Richard Austen, husbandman, and Margret Gamon, mayden. Lic. Fac
13 John Gray, mercatorye, and Anne Pallmer, W Lic. Fac
15 Richarde Androwes of Erithe, husbandman and Clement Jemson, W Lic Fac
July 10 Henrye Bure, yeoman and Ursley Fosset, W Lic Fac
20 Williame Lowme, silkweaver, and Elizabeth Foster, W Lic Fac
30 Richarde Halleley, tayler, and Margreat Edwardes, mayden Lic Fac
Aug 18 John Mickellfeild, clothier, and Sarae Scothmur, mayden Lic Fac.

1615-16

Aug. 24 Williame Shrinptone, Genellmann, and Marian Newingtone, W. Lic. Fac.
24 Thomas Tyrell and Marye Noblle. 3 tymes axed.
29 Robarte Trode, waterman, and Katherine Rithe. Lic. Fac.
29 John Gates, yeoman, and Jone Tayler, W. Lic. Fac.
Sept. 20 Williame Luter, yeoman, and Elizabeth Prate, mayden. Lic. Fac.
21 Allexander Cotterell, mircator, and Annes Rawling, mayden. Lic. Fac.
Oct. 5 Richarde Samforde, mariner, and Joane Perry, W. Lic. Fac.
10 Henrye Newman and Penellope Snell, celebye. Lic. Fac.
16 Gregorye Hilliard, yeoman, and Margreat Radforde, mayden. Lic. Fac.
29 Francis Walker, merchant, and Elizabeth Willde, mayden. Lic. Fac.
Nov. 1 Nickolase Bude, husbandman, and Joane Holden, W. Lic. Fac.
2 Gabriell Fisher of S[t] Mildred, Breadstreet, haberdasher, and Mary Marshe.

M[r] Hyaete, minister, 21 Dec. 1615.

Dec. 28 Henrye Whalley of S[t] Lawrence Powntiny, clothworker, and Margret Coven, mayden. Lic. Fac.
29 Christopher Theaker, gentellman, and Friswid Hill, mayden. Lic. Fac.
Jan. 4 Henrye Lee, yeoman, and Joan Barthellmew, mayden. Lic. Fac.
5 Charlles Rowe, gent., and Elizabeth Wilkinsone, W. Lic.
5 Richard Pember, Aurifaber, and Anne Tewe, W. Lic. Fac.
10 Ralphe Gren, blacksmith, and Margerye Gardner. Lic. Fac.
13 Lawrance Hopkins, gentellman, and Margreat Salter, mayden. Lic. Fac.
16 Richarde Smith, gentellman, and Anne Smith, W. Lic. Fac.
24 Owen Davis, husbandman, and Anne Pricklow, W. Lic. Fac.
27 Hughe Bachus, tayler, and Mary Hayes, mayden. Lic. from M[r] Drackes office.
Feb. 2 Calebe Whitfeild, scrivener, and Marthae Jenkine, mayden. Lic. Fac.
3 William Husher, tayler, and Wandsworth [*sic*], mayden. Lic. Fac.
8 Thomas Garnet, yeoman, and Elizabeth Turner. Lic. out of M[r] Drackes office.
10 Thomas Butler, yeoman, and Patience Wigge, mayden. Lic. from M[r] Drackes office.
13 Robeart Hawleye, clothworker, and Elizabeth Ballet, W. Lic. Fac.
21 Gorge Worringtone, carpenter, and Alls Grene. Lic. from M[r] Drackes office.
21 Rogger Collines, cutler, and Mary Harvie, W. Lic. from M[r] Drackes office.

M[r] John Kynd, P'sonne, 1616.
Robarte Smith, Williame Rutter } Churchwardens.

1616.

Mar. 25 John Wellder of Buckingham, yeoman, and Elizabeth Brittridge, W. Lic. out of M[r] Drackes Office.
28 John Burlacye of S[t] Thomas the Apostle, tayler, and Elizabeth Rogers, mayden. Lic. Fac.
April 8 James Clether, tayler, and Marye Luddendend, mayden. By Lic. out of Drackes Office.
13 John Scotte, weaver, and Jhoan Holly, W. Lic. Fac.
21 John Banckes, yeoman, and Margery Dune, W. Lic. Fac.
May 3 William Hardye, yeoman, and Rebecka Munsun, W. Lic. Fac.
6 Samuel Stanbourroe, husbandman, and Venice Harrisone, mayden. Lic. Fac.
6 Edmund Forsset, gentell., and Phebe Hutchinsone. By Lic. out of Drackes Office.

1616
May 10 Thomas Meason, taylor, and Margreat Ludgalle, S. Lic. Fac.
12 John Hardwick, yeoman, and Joyse Brace, mayden. Lic. Fac.
14 Thomas Browne, yeoman, and Margreat Cowper. By Lic. out of Drackes office.
17 Christopher Plumley, gent., and Briggit Terry, W. Lic. Fac.
27 John Price, yeoman, and Marthae Harrisone, mayden. Lic. Fac.
27 George Elliott, clothworker, and Margreat Archer. 3 tymes axed.
June 4 Anthony Duell of Kingston and Prudence Buckmaster, W. By Lic. out of Drakes Office.
7 Christopher Battesone, yeoman, and Frauncis [*sic*] Sellman, mayden. Lic. Fac.
9 Wallter Chamberline, gent., and Elizabeth Russell, S. Lic. Fac.
13 John Mackinder, yeoman, and Dorothie Underwood, mayden. Lic. Fac.
24 William Blunte, yeoman, and Jane Sharpe, mayden. Lic. Fac.
27 Elias Glover, mircator,* and Dine Bowle, S. Lic. Fac.
July 3 Edward Lewes, gent., and Elizabeth Awbery, W. Lic. Fac.
14 Nicholas Belcher, silkweaver, and Anne Smith, W. Lic. Fac.
19 Roger Wright, armorer, and Anne Meridith, W. Lic. Fac.
27 William Butler, yeoman, and Florance Keye. Lic. out of Drackes office.
Aug. 18 Christopher Wyell and Margreat Cage. Lic. Fac.
28 Rafe Crofte, yeoman, and Eme Logey, singellwoman. Lic. Fac.
31 Gregorye Weeden and Alce Burges, mayden. Lic. Fac.
Sept. 4 Josephe Beade, grocer, and Marye Tayler, mayden. Lic. Fac.
6 John Nickolles, gent., and Jane Drurye, genellwoman. Lic. Fac.
15 James Cowper, tayler, and Jean Price. Lic. out of M[r] Drackes office.
15 Thomas Woode, yeoman, and Margreat Huchens, W. Lic. Fac.

Da Domino Gloria. Amen.

18 Richarde Warde and Jhoan Kirbye. A Licence from my Lorde of Londone.
18 Clare Hayard and Mary Cooke, mayden. Lic. Fac.
23 John Erridge, brickmaker, and Francis [*sic*] Maddox, S. Lic. Fac.
23 Stephen Arnold, yeoman, and Dorethy Addames, W. Lic. Fac.
27 Edward Severall, turner, and Jane Price, mayden. Lic. Fac.
28 Thomas Shaw, taylor, and Rose Trowell, mayden. By Lic. out of Drackes office.
Oct. 4 David Edwardes and Mary Phillips. Lic. from M[r] Drackes office.
5 James Pease and Sarae Ockley. Lic. Fac.
5 Edmund Englishe, Tayler, and Marye Fairchild. Lic. Fac.
17 John Markland, grocer, and Elizabeth Prestone, S. Lic. Fac.
24 Water Powell, brewer, and Helline Lewis. Lic. Fac.
25 Robart Cleyton, haberdasher, and Joan Jacksone, puelle. Lic. Fac.
25 John Beast, gent., and Mary Ramsey, mayden. Lic. Fac.
31 Francis Harrison, farried, and Susan Ladd. Lic. Fac.
Nov. 4 Henrye Rich, husbandman, and Elizabeth Lightfoot. Lic. Fac.

John Davis, claricem.

5 Francis Pigott, taylor, and Anne Penvind, mayden. Lic. Fac.
15 Leonarde Nedhame, stationer, and Anne Rowe, W. Lic. Fac.
21 Michalle Bellfoure and Susane Lee, W. Lic. Fac.
31 Thomas Parrat, yeoman, and Alce Goldsmith, mayden. Lic. Fac.
Dec. 3 William Coop, Ironmonger, and Judith Wilkinsone, mayden. Lic. out of Drackes office.
7 Williame Savage, broker, and Margreat Dorset, mayden. Lic. Fac.
8 Ralphe Rawlinsone, yeoman, and Margreat Steele, mayden. Lic. Fac.
10 Griffine Jones and Basset Eyre, puelle. Lic. Fac.
14 Gallfrid Baunce, yeoman, and Margreat Langstone, mayden. Lic. Fac.

* "Mircator" written over "taylor" struck out.—ED.

1616-17

Dec. 16 John Haunsell, cordwainer, and Phillipe Baker, mayden. Lic. Fac.
18 John Standish and Hester Ruband, W. Lic. out of Mr Drackes office.
26 John Frybery of Barkinge and Prudence Leddall of this parish, beinge thryce asked.

Jan. 9 John Dixone of Edmontone, Middx., yeoman, and Allice Northe, mayden. Lic. Fac.
23 Simone Mumforde of St Gregory by Paul's, orrice worker, and Dorothye Welch, mayden. Lic. Fac.
23 John Wright of St Dunstan in the West, sadler, and Marye Yorke, singellwoman. Lic. Fac.
24 Mathew Conney of Gowthurst, weaver, and Johanne Wattes, W. Lic. Fac.
28 John Downes of Collney Hatch, Middx., yeom., and Anne Heyes, S. Lic. Fac.

Feb. 19 Michalle Swane of St Martin in the Fields, gentellmane, and Annes Westcote, mayden. Lic. Fac.
23 Edwarde Strowd of Reddinge, co. Berks, yeoman, and Johane Langforde, singellwoman. Lic. Fac.
24 John Smith of St Martin in the Fields, barber, and Elizabeth Marston, mayden. Lic. out of Mr Drakes office.
26 Gedeon Amondesha als. Awnsham of Isleworth, Middx., Esq., Armigery, and Jayne Wyatte, gentellwoman. Lic. Fac.

Mar. 2 Richard Bonde of St Mary Somerset and Elizabeth Birte of this parish, beinge three tymes asked.
7 Allexander Bradley of St Clement, Temple Bar, vitulear, and Dorothie Jennete, mayden. Lic. Fac.
19 Eaustacio Hanwaye, gentellman, and Elizabeth Hoke, mayden. Lic. Fac.
20 Williame Wigffalle of St Mary Magdalen, feltmaker, and Lidie Elltone, mayden. Lic. out of Drackes office.
21 John Cranmer of St Michael in the Querne, clothworker, and Anne Gravner, mayden. Lic. out of Mr Drackes office.

MR JOHN KYNDE, P'sonne.
William Rutter, John Squire } Churchwardens.

1617.

April 21 Isacke Finche of St Botolph, Billingsgate, dier, and Anne Shaler, mayden. Lic. Fac.
21 Armell Gould of St Saviour, Southwark, yeoman, and Mary Jones, mayden. Lic. Fac.

May 6 William Curtice of Oaking, Surrey, yeoman, and Mary Haward, mayden. Lic. Fac.
23 Thomas Bucke of St Giles, Cripplegate, yeoman, and Jayne Davorell, mayden. Lic. Fac.
25 Nicholasc Milltone of Barling in the county of Canterbury and Edith Frees, mayden. Lic. Drackes office.

June 9 Thomas Thomas of St Clements, Temple Bar, taylor, and Anne Hollman, mayden. Lic. Fac.
15 Williame Tayler of Heningtone, yeoman, and Barbarae Hardinge, mayden. Lic. Fac.
17 John Evanes of Stepney, Sayler, and Francise Boddilow, mayden. Lic. Fac.
17 John Bristow, yeoman, and Elizabeth Whit, mayden. Lic. out of Mr Drackes office.
31 [*sic*] John Bartram of Maullden, yeoman, and Mary Warren, mayden. Lic. Fac.

July 8 Jeames Marchant of St Martin in the Fields, Taylor, and Jhane Kent, gentellwoman. Lic. Fac,

1617-18

July 16 Williame Droney, silkweaver, and Johane Wheeler, puelle. Lic. Fac.

Aug. 7 *Phillipe Rowbery and Ellen Helligrowe, both of Greenwich. Sent by Mr Kynde.

9 Ellice Combe of Alldermanbury, draper, and Judith Bargar, puelle. Lic. Fac.

12 Nickolase Chester, dier, and Francis [*sic*] Lamberte. Lic. Fac.

14 John Thorner, gent., and Eme Kisbye, puelle. Lic. Fac.

19 Thomas Bury, leatherseller, and Jayn Stoughton, mayden. Wth a licence from my lord of London.

Oct. 3 Larance Royll, smith, and Christian Howell, W. Lic. Fac.

2 John Gallaway of Grays Inn, gent., and Elizabeth Beetes.† Lic. Fac.

19 Christopher Colle of St Giles, Cripplegate, yeoman, and Anne Knightley, W. Lic. Fac.

27 John Denley of St Magnus and Elizabeth Butler, W. Lic. Fac.

Nov. 17 Richard Banam of Alldermanbury, clothworker, and Elizabethe Parker, mayden. Lic. Fac.

Dec. 2 Roger Archer of St Brides, fishmonger, and Mary Okleye, puelle. Lic. Fac.

2 Thomas Perrine, gentellman, and Katherine Dawtre, puelle. Lic. Fac.

3 Henry March, chapman, and Elizabeth Powell, W. Lic. Fac.

John Davis, clarke.

Jan. 27 Thomas Howse, silkweaver, and Mary Wattes, puelle. Lic. Fac.

Feb. 17 Richarde Kentish, yeoman, and Johane Foxe, mayden. Lic. Fac.

17 Richarde Grene, haberdasher, and Ellen Griffine, puelle. Lic. Fac.

17 William Steedman, gent., and Susane Checke, mayden. Lic. Fac.

21 John Sealy, barber Surgion, and Annes Noke, W. Lic. Fac.

Mar. 4 Richarde Wapshote, coachman, and Mary Wilsher, W. Lic. Fac.

21 Richard Strudder, whit baker, and Elizabeth Ursley. Lic. Fac.

1618.

Mar. 25 John Severall, turner, and Margreat Jaumpe, W. Lic.

31 John Warde, yeoman, and Mary Humphrie, puelle. Lic. Fac.

April 2 Robarte Fleminge, haberdasher, and Anne Langworthe. Lic. out of Drackes office.

5 Richarde Dorringetone of Stow, gent., and Anne Chare, puelle. Lic. Fac.

13 Allexander Dennet, gent., and Francis Forreste, mayden. Lic. Fac.

14 John Hill, generoso, and Audrie Lenarde, mayden. Lic. out of Drackes office.

16 Edward Flude of Waltham and Helinor Peacoke, W. Lic. Fac.

16 Machelle Sponley of St Stephen, Coleman Street, blacksmith, and Anne Johnsone. Lic. Fac.

MR JOHN KYNDE, P'son.

John Squire } Churchwardens.
Robartt Tomson }

May 12 Thomas Jearman of Whitchappell, mariner, and Abigalle Edwardes, W. Lic. Fac.

26 Francis Bovette of St John Zacharye, taylore, and Ann Simes, mayden. Lic. Fac.

June 2 Edwarde Pryer of St Mildred, Bread street, clothworker, and Katherine Wightman, mayden. Lic. Fac.

9 John Hamond of St Martin in the Fields, coachman, and Ellenor Neeler, W. Lic. Fac.

24 Israell Wildbludd of St Christopher by the Stockes, clothworker, and Ursule Foster, mayden. Lic. Fac.

* This entry has been interlined.—ED.

† "Elizabeth Beetes" is written over an erasure.—ED.

1618

June 25 Andrew Turley of St Andrews, Holborne, taylor, and Margreat Starling, singellwoman. Lic. Fac.

25 Daniell Lee of St Martin's in the Vintre, bricklayer, and Susan Bulgare. Lic. Fac.

28 Robarte Smyth of Christ church parish, butcher, and Elizabeth Grave, mayden. Lic. Fac.

July 8 Robarte Munday of St Larance in Redding, co. Berks, lanio [butcher], and Alicie Brinckwell, mayden. Lic. Fac.

16 Thomas Smyth of St Botolph, Bishopsgate, grocer, and Johane Nevill, mayden. Lic. Fac.

22 John Crosse of St Andrewes, Holborne, yeoman, and Elizabeth Jones, W. Lic. Fac.

26 Philipe Burbidge of St Anne, Aldersgate, taylor, and Anne Clearke, mayden. Lic. Fac.

Aug. 20 Thomas Rushe of Springfeild in Essex, gent., and Thomasine Stanstead, mayden. Lic. Fac.

9 Gorge Man of St Pancridg in the Fields, tanner, and Francis [*sic*] Hyncone, mayden. Lic. Fac.

10 Thomas Fisher of St Clement, Temple Bar, vituler, and Lidie Tanner, puelle. Lic. Fac.

13 Thomas Payne, vicar, and Johane Crowder, W. Lic. Fac.

26 Robarte Allen of St Margaret, Westminster, vintner, and Elizabeth Claye, puelle. Lic. Fac.

Sept. 12 Williame Whittorne of St Michalls, Cornhill, uphoulster, and Marye Whitfeyld, puelle. Lic. Fac.

16 Isacke Ashe of St Botolph, Aldgate, cutler, and Barbara Simpsone, W. Lic. Fac.

21 Robarte Cleer of Fulham, yeoman, and Elizabeth Kent, singellwoman. Lic. Fac.

24 John Bigge of Whitchappell, chandler, and Johane Loadye, W. Lic. Fac.

24 Nickolas Williames of Stepney, mariner, and Rebecka Jones, puelle. Lic. Fac.

30 Robarte Dickines of St Brides, aurifaber [goldsmith], and Elizabeth Rickards, S. Lic. Fac.

Oct. 6 John Lucas of St Dunstan in the East, skinner, and Anne Ponsenbye, puelle. Lic. Fac.

28 John Thurgood of Maudlen Laver, Essex, yeoman, and Mary Kinke, puelle. Lic. Fac.

29 Thomas Weston of Stratfield, Hants, yeoman, and Elizabethe Catten, puelle. Lic. Fac.

Nov. 4 Thomas Gardner, gentell, and Francis [*sic*] Gardner, gentellwoman. Lic. Fac.

9 Peter Gravner of St Anne, Blackfryers, fethermaker, and Sarae Jones, puelle. Lic. out of Mr Drackes office.

15 Henry Clemson, husbandman, and Johane Waters, puelle. Lic. Fac.

15 Richard Whitehead of St Swithines, London Stone, merchant taylor, and Elizabeth Burell, W. Lic. Fac.

22 John Lakines of St Martin in the Feilds, sadler, and Elizabeth More. Lic. Fac.

29 Francis Halles of St Dionis Backchurch, grocer, and Margreat Benione, mayden. Lic. out of Mr Drackes office.

Dec. 1 Jacobe Bennet, gardner, and Sarae Nevard, mayden. Lic. Fac.

17 John Forrest, vintner, and Grace Quinton, mayden. By licence out of Drackes office.

17 Thomas Roffe, yeoman, and Margreat Hayward, puelle. Lic. Fac.

29 Samuel Nealand of St Martin, Ludgate, stationer, and Rebecka Gwyn. Lic. Fac.

1618-19
Jan. 6 Thomas Rogers, blacksmith, and Elizabeth Haver, mayden Lic Fac
12 Henry Weabstear, yeoman, and Margreat Machett, mayden Lic. Fac.
12 John Hallsey, taylor, and Ursulee Haye, mayden Lic Fac
22 John Eames, yeoman, and Mary Marston, mayden Lic Fac.
29 Henry Sherman, haberdasher, and Brigitte Needes, mayden Lic Fac
Feb. 6 William Heath, taylor, and Sarae Smith, mayden Lic Fac
10 Perce Edwardes, merchant Taylor, and Elizabeth Savell, mayden Lic Fac
Mar 6 Barnard Feverell, yeoman, and Prissillee Polleard Lic Fac
12 Martine Becket, yeoman, and Elizabeth Higgines, mayden Lic Fac.

1619.

April 4 John Edwardes, gent, and Sarae Clemvell, mayden Lic Fac
7 Randollphe Grube, yeoman, and Brigitt Winstanley, mayden. Lic Fac.
30 Lewes Monoux, Esquir, and Jane Birch, gent'woman Lic. Fac.
4 John Hayward, yeoman, and Susan Sweether, mayden. Lic Fac
14 William Rowman, yeoman, and Elizabeth Beets, mayden Lic. Fac
May 6 Thomas Cowling, clothworker, and Allce Alway, W Lic Fac

M[R] John Kynd, P son
Mathew Gwyn } Churchwardens.
Thomas Finche }

June 12 Henry Bagley, vicar of Iver, co. Bucks, and Hellene Welleer, mayden Lic out of M[r] Drakes Office.
15 Edwarde Warden of S[t] Andrews, Holborne, barber, and Mary Fyfe, W. Lic Fac
16 Henry Clapham of Westminster, cordwayner, and Mary Hoper, mayden Lic. Fac.
26 Thomas Budd of Hendon, husbandman, and Jhon Long, W Lic Fac
July 30 John Mallet, feltmaker, and Elizabeth Weast, W By Licence from Drakes Office
Sept 13 Huge Evanes of S[t] Dunstan, vintner, and Katherin Ball, W Lic Fac.
13 Edwarde Owsley, taylor, and Marie Jacksone, mayden Lic Fac
14 Richarde Hullse of S[t] Dunstan, gen[t], and Hellenor Probine, puelle. Lic. Fac
28 Thomas Willmott, yeoman, and Dorothy Gyn, mayden Lic Fac
Oct 4 Rafe Foster, yeoman, and Elizabeth Weomell, puelle. Lic. Fac
13 Nightom May, tayler, and Jeane Bayley, W By Licence out of M[r] Drackes office.
13 William Ishame and Marye Harding, mayden Lic Fac
21 William Pywall, vintner, and Janne Hullines Lic out of Drackes office
22 Henrye Short of S[t] Giles, Cripplegate, gent, and Charity Spillmane, mayden Lic Fac
Nov 2 Thomas Canter, taylor, and Francis [sic] Steer, W. Lic Fac.
3 Arthur Levet, gent, and Mary Hall, mayden Lic Fac
10* Robarte Saxen, gent, and Marye Hall, mayden. Lic. Fac
14 Richard Robarts and Elizabeth Jarvis, W Lic Fac
19 Stephen Hollingrucke, brewer, and Sarae Richmond, puelle Lic Fac
24 John Callverly and Elizabeth Freboddy, W Lic Fac
30 Gorge Mathewes, gent, and Jane Smith, mayden Lic Fac
Dec. 8 John Gowld, gent, and Sarae Tredway, mayden Lic Fac
Jan 4 Larance Dudley, stationer, and Elizabeth Hollingworth. Lic Fac
16 Richard Browne and Grace Catline, mayden Lic Fac
24 Richard Brown, coqus [cook], and Mary Phillipes, mayden Lic Fac.
24 Humphrey Willsone, grocer, and Elizabeth Nickollsone, mayden. By licence out of Drackes office

* The entries from 10 Nov. to 13 March 1619 are written on one side of a loose parchment leaf, which has been pinned into its place The other side of the leaf has entries for the year 1625 —Ed

1619-22
Jan. 30 Thomas Potter, pewterer, and Anne Stutfeld, W. Lic. Fac.
Feb. 15 Thomas Prestone, coqus [cook], and Joane Durbrig, W. Lic. Fac.
20 Edward Archbold, gent., and Mercy Jerman, puelle. Lic. Fac.
29 Roger Corham, generosus, and Sarae Broksey, puelle. By licence out of Drackes office.
Mar. 7 Wallter Bird, clothworker, and Cicilie Deiose, puelle. Lic. Fac.
13 Benjamine Parsone, mercer, and Anne Burvesley, mayden. Lic. Fac.

[On four leaves of paper, about half the size of the leaves of the book, and pinned to the next parchment leaf, are the following marriage entries in Latin for the year 1622.]

" Nuptiæ p licentiâ celebratæ in ecclesia parochiali St Petri juxta ripā paulinā a mense Junii A[o] Dñi 1622."

June 29 Richardus Hincksman, cœlebs, & Anna Newberry, puella.
July 9 Edwardus Norris, generosus, & Elizabetha Dewell, vidua.
9 Richardus Crompton, cœlebs, & Katharina Mathewes, puella.
9 Raudallus Taylor, cœlebs, & Jane Whaly, vidua.
15 Johannes Baptista Parkes, Italus [Italian], & Margareta Leeth, puella.
29 Jacobus Goffe, cœlebs, & Alicia Powell, puella.
29 Guiliel: Taylor, cœlebs, & Joanna Powell, puella.
Aug. 1 Laurentius Phillips, viduus, & Sybella Tomlyn, vidua.
17 Richardus Floud, cœlebs, & Maria Price, innupta.
21 Amramus Stucky, generosus, & Maria Howson, puella.
23 Georgius Fleming, generosus, & Anna Eives, puella.
24 Guiliel: Web, cœlebs, & Elizabetha Rogers, puella.
Sept. 3 Johannes Briscoe, generosus, & Anna Taylor, puella.
19 Richardus Vaughan, scissor [tailor], & Maria Baker, vidua.
30 Edwardus Davis, scissor [tailor], & Elizabetha Farrow, puella.
Oct. 1 Johannes Tedderton, scissor [tailor], & Anna Colley, vidua.
1 Robertus Holman, scissor [tailor], & Anna Whitakere, puella.
5 Willihelmus Crocklow, lanius [butcher], & Alicia Anderson, vidua.
9 Odienus Griffith, plebeius, & Juditha Bayly, puella.
10 Rodulphus Barnes, crevisiarius [brewer], & Elizabetha Crowch, puella.
14 Thomas Awsyter, laterarius [brickmaker or bricklayer], & Francisca Nayler, puella.
22 Jacobus Buny, scissor [tailor], & Maria Browne, puella.
23 Rodulphus Eve, pannicularius [draper], & Rebecca Wympe, puella.
30 Johannes Snax, agricola [husbandman], & Johanna Butt, puella.
27 [*sic*] Johannes Fisher, lanius [butcher], & Blancha Butler, puella.
29 [*sic*] Johannes Dynne, plebeius, & Elizabetha Stowe, vidua.
Nov. 8 Robertus Friar, operarius [labourer], & Susanna Streete, puella.
13 Charolus Thekerton, generosus, & Maria Webster, puella.
14 Johannes Wiles, xilini textor [linen weaver], & Alicia Butler, lanifria [woollen spinner].
14 Thomas Whiting, pannificus [clothier], & Elizabetha Stocke, puella.
19 Johannes Mayney, pilio [hatter], & Elizabetha Paradine, puella.
19 Arthurus Coles, generosus, & Margareta Risby, puella.
25 Thomas Halfaker, pictor [painter], & Hanna Aldridg, puella.
27 Andrew Harbell, tinctor [dyer], & Alicia Lawrence, puella.
Dec. 2 Georgius Harber, agricola [husbandman], & Johanna Page, vidua.
7 Petrus Murrey, textor [weaver], & Maria Feury, puella.
9 Thomas Smarthwaite, cœlebs, & Alicia Abbots, vidua.
14 Johannes Chapman, generosus, & Francisca Bagnall, vidua.
19 Guliel: Pilgrim, generosus, & Elizabetha Lilly, puella.
20 Robertus Sheralock, coquus [cook], & Johanna Hewes, vidua.
23 Johannes Whale, sclopifactor [gunmaker], & Elizabetha Coxe, vidua.
28 Guliel: Morgan, generosus, & Maria Creed, puella.

1622-3

Jan. 6 Johannes Bosworth, sutor crepidarius [shoemaker], & Janna Hertwell, vidua.

13 Guiliel: Johnson, cœlebs, & Anna Smith, puella.

15 Adamus Crosby, plebeius, & Ellen Salter, puella.

31 Thomas Smithwood, cœlebs, & Johanna Sherly, puella.

Feb. 24 Guliel: Hide, aromotarius [spice merchant], & Katharina Occold, vidua.

Mar. 19 Marmadux Mayers, viduus, & Margareta Williamus, puella.

1623.

Mar. 26 Amos Pricklop & Maria Hodgkins.

April 5 Johannes Goodwin & Diner Hasting.

11 Henricus Bartlet & Elizabetha Windoe.

17 Johannes Coxe & Maria Godfrey.

22 Edwardus Okely & Susanna Randall.

26 Guliel: Wheeler & Elizabetha Croome.

May 1 Charolus Cottle & Dorothea Fenne.

1 Johannes Carpenter & Margareta Weston.

1 Michaell Tarrer & Maria Gardner.

6 Georgius Cole & Francisca Darby.

11 Johannes Sympson & Catherina Edsall.

22 Guliel: Mullet & Alicia Diat.

25 Thomas Simons & Cicilea Peterson.

25 Guliel: Price & Maria Dorkenoll.

June 9 Thomas Willoby & Sarah Kingsall.

2 Johannes Caplin & Catherina Banes.

10 Edwardus Hatfeild & Johanna Bartlet.

11 Simon Boys & Alicia Cole.

14 Thomas Sprat & Alicia Lacy.

23 Johannes Braham & Elizab. Roane.

24 Robertus Goodall & Emme North.

July 8 Richardus Wise & Margareta Mathew.

10 Thomas Hume & Catherina Castlin.

13 Johannes Snell & Ellen Bedford.

21 Andradius Corney & Margareta Lansdale.

27 Johannes Addington & Magdalena Randall.

30 Richardus Higgs & Johanna Butler.

Aug. 1 Guliel: Witherington & Anna Mason.

2 Jonas Fraunce & Dorothea Ithell.

4 Guliel: Robinson & Maria Wolnoth.

8 Petrus Hursan & Anna Brend.

18 Johannes Saluck & Margareta Orton.

25 Johannes Relion & Margareta Hannes.

26 Thomas Poole & Maria Aylet.

Sept. 9 Thomas Batt & Maria Badham.

10 Johannes Friar & Alicia Warner.

15 Johannes Stocker & Janna Parrey.

17 Thomas Gaskin & Juditha Clifford.

25 Stephanus Atkinson & Janna Munne.

25 Thomas Spencer & Penelope Filiall.

Oct. 4 Nicholas Cole & Maria Williams.

8 Guliel: Michel & Elizabetha Chawkewell.

8 Franciscus Benning & Johanna Langly.

8 Johannes Flayle & Catherina Packer.

16 Alexandrus Auchtmontie & Elizabetha Naper.

19 Robertus Lawrence & Maria Rogers.

19 Nicholas Dolby & Anna Harrison.

1623-4

Oct. 27 Thomas Hill & Elizabetha Davis.
29 Thomas Page & Elizabetha Symons.
29 Robertus Spykin & Margareta Mathew.
Nov. 1 Edwardus Say & Margareta Tooting.
5 Robertus Cholmeley & Johanna Cason.
6 Thomas Browse & Clare Skipwith.
11 Thomas Solley & Elizab. Musgrave.
14 Joshuah Faunt & Maria Atkinson.
16 Robertus Shasted & Grace Osbond.
20 Robertus Gasker & Aglandby Williams.
30 Johannes Reynolds & Dorothea Dent.
Dec. 8 Henricus Harrison & Martha Osmold.
18 Edmundus Brett & Anna Gulson.
22 Guliel: Steeper & Maria Newdygate.
23 Samuel Savedg & Juditha Kiplyn.
31 Richardus Booth & Maria Davis.
Jan. 1 Johannes Kempton & Johanna Goble.
3 Samuel Nichols & Elizab. Foster.
26 Rogerus Price & Alicia Bostock.
28 Edwardus Osborne & Catherina Dixon.
Feb. 3 Edmundus Walker & Sarah Durrant.
8 Thomas Buckmayster & Eliz. Dopsly.
9 Guliel: Bab & Elizab. Broin.
12 Johannes Rowly & Anna Hickes.
14 Guliel: Overberry & Gertrude Gee.
17 Johannes Coe & Mariana Chandeler.
Mar. 9 Edwardus Smith & Margareta Winckfeild.
23 Johannes Hudson & Alicia Johnson.

1624.

Mar. 29 Anthonius Ballet & Francisca Bartlet.
April 5 Edwardus Amwood & Joanna Mosely.
13 Edwardus Hopkins & Cycilia Perce.
15 Edwardus Salter & Debora Osmond.
17 Thomas Miller & Catherina Nelham.
15 Mathias Joanes & Hellena Downing.
19 Rowland Pes [? Res] of St Andrew Undershaft & Maria Dickinson. [Altered by another hand from "Andradius Undershaft."]
27 Abrahamus Sea & Margareta Spicer.
27 Richardus Hopkins & Elizab. Morgan.
27 Stephanus Hills & Sarah Parsons.
21 Thomas Cooke & Maria Jones.
29 Richardus Robbins & Elizab. Lyddyes.
May 5 Georgius Woodson & Susanna Langar.
19 Christopher Creery & Margareta Sherly.
20 John Holles [" Hobbes " in another hand] & Maria Cole.
22 Guill: Peichare & Elizabeth Davis [added in another hand].
21 Christopher Silcock & Maria Rixon.
19 Johannes Griffin & Johanna Questonbury.
27 Rogerus Prosser & Catherina Richardson.
27 Thomas Carter & Catherina Harling.
27 Rogerus Scarre & Maria Normivill.
June 5 Robertus Davie & Elizab. Tate.
18 Guliel: Bulckly & Margareta Spaine.
14 Guliel: Joanes & Alicia Ebbe.
14 Richardus Heydon & Anna Underwood.

1624-5
June 5 Johannes Mascall & Janne Owin.
16 Radulphus Worthington & Milicenta Ward.
30 Guliel: Morris & Anna Chittum.
1 Mathias Hewet & Juditha Denton.
28 Guiliel: Perkings & Elizab. Perce.
29 Michael Hemsley & Hellena Carter.
29 Rodolphus Heely & Elizab. Lasenby.
July 3 Thomas Hugbon & Dorothea Sharow.
8 Richardus Poole & Joanna Browne.
26 Richardus Perrey & Maria Seward.
Aug. 2 Edwardus Wilson & Margeria Cooper.
4 Guliel: Nott & Elizab. Bonus [? Good].
8 Nathaniel Rowe & Sarah Browne.
9 Petrus Raye & Anna Waterer.
26 Richardus Guy of S[t] Clement & Priscilla Meadowes.
Sept. 7 Michael Ginger & Elizabetha Inward.
22 Rowlandus Bevan & Eliz. Robinson.
Oct. 5 Thomas Beedan & Catherina Webster.
6 Phinias Andrews & Mildreda Fanshaw.
14 Daniell Gell & Janna Lake.
13 Edmundus Paine & Rosamunda Southworth.
28 Georgius May & Susanna Johnson.
Nov. 5 Johannes Bolt & Margareta Allen.
20 Lucas Maney & Maria Herriman.
Dec. — Jacobus Browne & Thomasis Restrix.
11 Stephanus Scandret & Catherina Gardner.
Jan. 5 Guliel: Glover & Margeria Cuddington.
6 Gregorius Moone & Junia Georg.
17 Johannes Morris & Catherina Jones.
20 Jacobus French & Margareta Chesheere.
25 Alexandrus Hill & Anna Jones.
28 Johannes Miles & Elizabetha Davis.
29 Ludovicus Williams & Maria Katharines.
Feb. 6 Guliel: Ridg & Martha Ginger.
7 Guliel: Sleigh & Sybilla King.
7 Johannes Crosier & Elizab. Nichols.
5 Richardus Sheepeherd & Maria Paine.
17 Richardus Tanson & Blancha Williams.
19 Arthurus Dier & Elizab. Crowch.
12 Richardus Sleigh & Anna Hubbard.
25 Johannes Harris & Susanna Paramore.
26 Edmundus Kelham & Maria Smith.
Mar. 24 Robertus Vaus & Elizabetha Upham.
1 Henricus Lache & Priscilla Cawdell.
23 Johannes Handley & Rachell Shaw.
29 Johannes Hunter & Elizabetha Strandbridg.
3 Richardus Reynolds & Alicia Taylor.

1625.

Mar. 31 Rowlandus Paine & Isabella Grannaway.
31 Edmundus Leutner & Sarah Richardson.
April 13 Robertus Shawe & Magdalena Stanger.
15 Johannes Udy & Susanna Frisby.
26 Johannes Dendy & Elizab. Imge.
3 Anselmus Read & Janna Manning.
20 Guliel: Rush & Janna Brian.
May 5 Josephus Guarinovo & Alicia Stiff,

1625-40

May 12 Edwardus Reynolds & Rosa Claxon.
30 Thomas Dee & Sarah Wels.
24 Francisus Robson & Wilsia Harbert.
28 Henricus Felkes & Joyce Bullock.
20 Robertus Smith & Johanna Provert.
29 Guliel: Scot & Brigetta Kelham.

[The rest of this paper page is blank, but on the other side, partly obliterated, can be read:—]

.... Homes, Skine^r^, of this pish.
ward Higginbothem.
John Hoykin de les, St Marie P .... alls Burmodes et Margarete Buller fil. Johannes (?) Buller de Scti Dunston oriente, London, 27 May 1622.
George Burnam de Scti Sepulcker, London, generosus, et Juditho Davis filie W^m^ (?) Davis nup. pro Scti Andrea, Holburne, 19 daie of June 1622.

May 8 George Lashly, talar, and Rose Underhill, widdoe.

[NOTE.—This last entry in the original is on fol. 51 of the parchment book, and is the only entry on that side.]

1625.

[Marages seince Hugh Jones was addmitted clark.]

June 6 Thomas Steeple of St Giles, Cripplegate, and Mary Waterhowse, s'vent to Mr Cotchet of this parish, puella. Banns.
3 George Hickman of Bushey, co. Herts, yeoman, and Elizabeth Felles of the same, puella, dau. of William Fells also of Bushey, maltman.
20 William Thurston of St Dunstan, London, Salter, and Alice Death, puella, dau. of Thomas Death of Dartford, Kent, generosus. Lic. from Cha. Ceasar.
23 Randolfe Andrewes of St Katherine Creechurch, London, pewterer, and Elizabeth Brewninge, dau. of William Brewninge of St Andrewes in the Wardrobe. By licence from Rog. Christian.
July 20 Thomas How of Chipping Barnet, co. Herts, and Ann Ansteed, W., of South Mims, Middx. Lic. from Rog. Christian. [This entry has been crossed out.]
Oct. 13 Richard Kempe of St Clement, Temple Bar, Joyner, and Rebecca Glover of St Martin in the Fields, W. Nic. Weston, p. lic.
Nov. 13 John Redinge of this parish, W., and Elizabeth Burras of the same, W. Banns.
16 Hugh Jones and Elizabeth Chandler, W., both of this parish. Lic.
17 .... Wiggins of St Andrew Undershaft, bricklayer, and Mrs Parker, W., of this parish. Lic.

MR MARBROW, Parson, January 27th, 1639.
Simon Turges } Churchwardens.
John Madox }
Thomas French, Clarke.

1639.

Mar. 10 James Willson, cordwaynder, and Elizabeth Crispe, maide. Lic.

1640.

April 29 James Beard, cordwaynder, and Mary Graves, W.
June 8 Robert Neeld of Greenwich, gardner, and Parnella Russell of St James, Garlickhithe, virgin; mar. in this church by James Eglesfeild.

1640-4

June 12 John Russell of Cullumpton, Devon, gent., and Elizabeth Duell of Ickham, Kent, mayden; by James Eglesfeild. Lic. Fac.

11 Robert Shaw of S[t] Sepulchre and Sara King, puella, of the same parish. Lic. from D[r] Arthur Duck.

10 John Burrowes of S[t] Andrew, Holborne, London, yeoman, and Ann Swale, puella, of S[t] Sepulchre. Lic. from D[r] Arthur Duck. [The last two entries are in Latin.]

Aug. 1 Edward Baynton and Mary Bowells; by James Eglesfeild.

The entry next above written was shewed to James Eglesfeild, clerk, & Thomas French p'ish clerk att the tyme of theire s'rall examinations taken in Chancery on the p[te] of Dame Mary Baynton widd. and Robert Baynton Comp[lts] ag[t] Edward Baynton Esq[r] and others defend[ts].—Reyton. . . .

Jan. 1 Roger Twist . . . . and Jane Floyd, mayde. By Lic. from Arthur Duck.

15 Gorge Coollman of S[t] Andrew Wardrobe, porter, and Ann Buckston, W., of this parish. Banns.

1641.

April 23 Robert Poyns and Ciesley Smith.

[Rest of this page blank.]

June 16 Francis Winter and Iszabell Kitte.

July 18 Richard Nickes and Debera Morgan.

Aug. 3 Walter Crooke and Marie Archbold.

15 Walter Baker, fishmonger, and Anne Graye.

16 John Deckcom, B., and Mary Hudson.

Oct. 10 William Baitts and Marye Lisut, both of this parish.

Nov. 2 Hennery Fleming and Frances Halford.

Dec. 2 Francis Neale and Ruth Smith.

Mar. 12 Samuell Grayham and Bridgett Reede.

1642.

May 19 Gaberill Tomlinson and Dorithey Wilson.

Aug. 25 William Callow and Ann Cooke.

Dec. 1 Robert Stockeham and Chathern Kindder.

11 Richard Brooks and Margeritt Oare.

Jan. 18 George Parslye and Elin Oswell.

Mar. 16 John Clarke and Ellen Boughton, W.

16 John Nutbroune and Grace Lassome.

1643.

May 23 Arthur Bingles and Sara Evans.

June 6 William Harden and Ann Samon.

27 William Stoddeard and Phebee Osborn.

Oct. 5 Charles Collard, groser, and Suzan Anderus.

22 Richard Gibbes and Barbere Baker.

26 Authurne Isemunger, carpinter, and Ann Tasker.

Dec. 24 Richard Churchis and Ann Doe.

Jan. 16 Steven Stronge and Marye Fullwood.

16 Thomas Lare and Frances Smith.

1644.

April 3 Phillipp Leversuch and Abigall Woodstock.

5 Thomas Efelyn and Jane Bennett.

24 Richard Hill and Ann Worten.

May 18 Robert Trevellan and Catharne [*blank*].

20 Thomas Woodhouse and Margerie Keyes.

1647, 1644-5

1647.

Aug. 12* Thomas Wills and Anne Morgan, both of Chiswick, were marryeed according to the forme and institution of the church & kingdome of England. John Williams, Clerk.

1644.

May 23 Nicolas Strelle and Ann Tillman.
June 18 Thomas Beech and Ann Griffith.
24 Richard Allin and Sara [*blank*].
July 4 Thomas Harris and Sara Dallam.
4 Benjamin Goulden and Mary Lee.
30 Thomas Walter and Ann Morrise.
Aug. 25 John Biszaker and Dorothey More.
Oct. 8 John Bradley and Elizabeth Gitthings.
Sept. 29 Hircewlas Cozer and Isabell Boulten.
Nov. 3 William Cooper and Ann Boase.
5 John Anderus and Ann Greene.
20 John [*blank*] and Ann [*blank*].
Dec. 1 Peter Moris and Rebecka Mounford.
22 Joseph Gater and Elizabeth Kitthersonn.
26 Nicolas Burnesley and Cothedcrall Bailes.
27 William Kinge and Eam [*blank*].
Jan. 14 Bassell Wright and Elizabeth [*blank*].
16 Thomas Morill and Ann Bludworth.
23 Robert Brookehurst and Sarath Blew.
26 Thomas Hamton and Damerus Parchett.
28 John Perse and Sara Hollister.
Feb. 6 Edward Cleeten and Ann Lake.
Mar. 23 Thomas Hogdkins and Elizabeth Cordwell.

1645.

Mar. 25 John Pim and Elizabeth Williams.
May 15 Richard Deacon and Elizabeth Pickersgill.
June 17 Arthur Colthourpe and Ann Witteker.
18 Nicolas Nickcols and Mary Hersent.
Aug. 1 Humfry Kelin and Jane Vinson.
21 John Thomas and Cissell Popley.
21 Henry Gaile and Ann Harte.
26 Edward Cooper and Marthay [*blank*].
Sept. 5 William Parson and Sussana Anthony.
21 Moris Jones and Elizabeth Precher.
26 John Coker and Amee Hawes.
29 Jeffery Collins and Alce Juddin.
Dec. 2 Henry Some and Ann Idle.
12 Thomas Weekes and Mary Beckcomb.
20 Francis Corye and Elizabeth Seakrye.
28 Robert Hume and Mary Cundall.
Nov. 1 Thomas Horten and Ann Midleton.
2 John Skidmor and Jone Shaw.
16 Christopher Clarke and Mary Bell.
24 William Laxson and Isarill Peckeffer.
Dec. 28 Robert Hume and Mary Cundall [entered previously].
30 John Campe and Jone Pattifer.
Jan. 1 William Dakers and Margarett Wayger.

* This entry is written on the top of the page, and is in a different handwriting to the previous and subsequent entries.—Ed.

1645-7
Feb. 1 Richard Woollye and Margeritt Williams.
6 Robert Petefer and Jone Coxshed.

1646.

April 2 Edmond Bryan and Rachell Hickes.
12 James Audoire and Susan Meservy.
28 Thomas Smith and Elizabeth Warner.
30 John Stevens and Elizabeth Bowinn.
May 13 Charles Fitch and Ann Shires.
21 James Norman and Judeth Greene.
27 Walter Madther and Elizabeth Newcomb.
28 William Adames and Susan Cockshead.
28 Thomas Ronne and Elizabeth Etton.
July 2 William Weetherell and Charitie Courtnye.
13 Fulke Gouldsmith and Ruchorde Filkin.
17 Francis Mandy and Elizabeth Watters.
17 Ralfe Forde and Susan Ryding.
Aug. 3 James Harbert, Esq., and Jane Spiller.
9 Thomas Baker and Alce Smith.
12 Robert [*blank*] and Elizabeth [*blank*].
13 Henry [*blank*] and Margerye [*blank*].
Oct. 4 John Dandye and Elizabeth [*blank*].
4 Samuell Pilington and Katherin Fisher.
22 Walter Baker and Alce Row.
22 John Evins and Margerett Roberts.
Nov. 5 John Smith and Anne Bliss.
17 John Balliard and Mathee Withrinton.
Dec. 1 Joseph James and Frances Taler.
15 John Gill and Dorothye Okee.
20 Thomas Thomas als. Fuller and Margaritt Powell.
30 Thomas Hern and Winnifret Cherrye.
Mar. 4 Arthur Coullcock and Marye Whittwell.
Dec. 22 John Goddard and Elizabeth Gibbs.
31 Thomas Hareland and Jane Haris.
Feb. 7 Thomas Hayvad and Katherin Paris.
9 Samuell Flowerdew and Elizabeth Pullin.
13 Arthur Hemingham and Jane Mynne.
19 Richard Worall and Anne Banister.
27 William Turner and Elizabeth Wilmott.
28 James Wilcocks and Margerett Hill.
Mar. 1 William Woolfe and Anne Nablet.

1647.

April 4 Robert Boulton and Alce Teag.
4 George White and Frances Edwards.
12 John Fisher and Marye Dunn.
15 Nicolas Boucher and Dorothye Caring.
May 24 Gregory Peake and Anne Colt.
25 Henry Counstable and Marye Archdeale.
28 William Johnson and Anne Hayward.
June 25 Stephen Agge and Anne Tounge.
29 Danell Masson and Susan Morton.
15 George Regnell and Anne Capper.
July 26 Anthony Judd and Margerett Peach.
28 Thomas Gibbson and Frances Eldredge.
29 Edward Duke and Elizabeth Tollemach.
Aug. 3 William Tuke and Elizabeth Hancock.
25 John Hilliard and Susan Day.

1647
Aug. 25 Thomas Pew and Anne Lovell.
26 Adrianus Wazzoone and Margery Jennings.
31 Thomas Spur and Anne Phillips.
Sept. 2 William Elsmore and Elinor Abell.
4 Robert Conway and Elizabeth Morton.
5 Richard Quale and Susana Smith.
9 Henry Gasstill and Margery Surtuse.
12 Edward White and Susana Butlin.
21 Charles Gataker and Anne Jones.
21 Thomas Goodman and Elizabeth Younge.
22 Thomas Richardson and Anne Gurney.
28 Michall Robinson and Sara Graygouse.
Oct. 19 Walter Price and Anne Stephens.
19 John Lee and Elizabeth Wattson.
19 Thomas Dewce and Marcye Martin.
26 James Guy and Elizabeth Day.
26 James Easland and Elizabeth Easland.
26 Richard Whitlock and Mary Lawrants.
Nov. 3 Henry Huchins and Mary Price.
4 Richard Sheritt and Jone Mathews.
7 Thomas Bunnyes and Elizabeth Eden.
14 Edward Rollisson and Charitye Chapple.
18 William Langlye and Marye Sherbrook.
18 Samuell Skelton and Katherine Calmodye.
23 Joseph Pidgeon and Elizabeth Rogers.
Dec. 4 Isaac Odell and Anne Allin.
6 Thomas Hooke and Elizabeth Gleede.
7 John Cryer and Anne Hatch.
9 William Abram and Anne Cross.
12 Thomas Lavander and Jone Penington.
15 John Weritt and Sarah Edlin.
25 John Price and Elin Tommas.
28 Thomas Slaynett and Frances Bouser.
29 John Tareman and Sarah Gilbert.
Jan. 3 Samuell Harvy and Elinor Hopkins.
10 Mathew Pickayes and Hester Evans.
13 John Jeffaryes and Margery Garman.
18 Jonathan Tucke and Elizabeth Winne.
20 Henry Numan and Anne Toung.
Feb. 1 Peyton Meres and Mary Right.
2 Henry Annekey and Katherin Keeton.
8 Richard Catesby and Hana Roper.
10 John Burnell and Bridgett Thornbugh.
10 John Henley and Priscilla Floyd.
11 George Pickering and Susan Evans.
12 Christopher Treweike and Winifrid Allen.
14 William Younge and Alce Nicolson.
14 John Norton and Mary Slingsby.
14 John White and Ursula Loveking.
14 Carey Sprige and Anne Gilsland.
15 John Pesstill and Anne Night.
17 William West and Susan [*blank*].
22 Thomas Betts and Elizabeth Nettlefould.
22 Edward Sisson and Anna Atkins.
25 Tristram Gilsland and Grace Nicolson.
27 William Hantley and Katherin Johnson.
27 John Morgan and Mary Peeston.
29 Rice Evans and Mary Cockeyne.

1647-8
Mar. 9 John Roberts and Dorothy Whitley.
16 Edward Goulden and Elizabeth Prosser
21 Richard Clackston and Jane Dice.

1648

Mar. 26 George Bodinton and Philepra Heath.
26 Thomas Kent and Mary Ayres
April 3 Richard Bialy and Jane Chadderton
3 Richard Bateman and Iditha Pinkaman
4 Abraham Fluyd and Jane Coulte
6 Phillip Hollybury and Grace Blackmurre
6 Arthur Webb and Thomisine James
10 Thomas Wood and Katherin Lutgall
23 Edward Carpinter and Jone Jarman
23 Edmund Adkinson and Elizabeth Slingett
23 Christopher Marshall and Elizabeth Marshall.
28 Alexander Courthorp and Susana Browne
30 Jervayse Ansley and Mary Wateress
May 11 John Fosster and Elizabeth Lewis
14 Edmon Cradge and Elizabeth Meares
14 Thomas Walden and Mary Watsee
15 John Boycott and Elizabeth Ball
16 Samuell Barwicke and Margeretta Blake.
18 Richard Taylor and Katharine Bosdon
21 Richard Chrischan and Sara [*blank*]
24 Elizear Fletcher and Jane Cale
25 Henry Lord and Mathay Curtis
26 Winston Churchill and Elizabeth Drake
June 8 Robert Whitting and Martha Tilldeun
8 John Tomkins and Anne Merry
15 Humphrey Edmonds and Margarett Blech
15 William Baker and Elizabeth Rennalls
25 Walter Davis and Grace Julson
26 Edward Williams and Alce Richardson
27 Edmond Paxton and Elizabeth Smith
29 Edward Spillman and Frances Reeve
July 3 Thomas Eustris and Anne Barker
14 Michaell Baker and Mary Benson
15 Anthony Bradshawe and Martha Newton
24 Henry Boulton and Judeth Dobson
24 Anthony Hallett and Mary Harte
26 John Lacoure and Elizabeth Raines
27 Thomas Walley and Mary Whitle
27 Henry Barnhard and Katherin Thornton
27 Thomas Wood and Rebecka Gisby
28 John Jackson and Ann Low
Aug 3 Paule Knell and Anne Powell
3 Roger Howse and Katherin Greeneburgh
10 James Howle and Isabell Care
13 Gabriell Key and Anne Stanford
13 George Brewmer and Martha Larkin
16 Steven Mixon and Anne Lislie
17 Thomas Jeffres and Jone Edlin
17 Samuell Fowle and Mary Wibers
21 Robert Hall and Margarett Shattowe
22 John Wade and Elizabeth Dane,

1648

Aug. 24 Alexander Charley and Juliae Pargrave.
24 Nicolas Besley and Joane Balduck.
29 Henry Wallis and Jone Crooke.
30 Henry Stiles and Martha Smith.
Sept. 3 William Pitt and Katherin Helding.
14 John West and Joane Roberts.
15 William Lurtin and Elizabeth Fox.
21 Edward Terill and Anne Northes.
24 John Drapter and Rose Tibballs.
27 James Mills and Margarett Hardy.
27 Richard Powdich and Alce Geary.
27 Thomas Bolten and Mary Boswell.
28 Sir John Dingley, Knt., and Elizabeth Butler.
Oct. 3 Richard Stevens and Elinor Underwood.
4 Jasper Lucus and Elizabeth Lane.
8 Thomas Dickinson and Anne Charlton.
17 Henry Gauton and Sarath Ashwynn.
17 Thomas Hawkins and Hana Stevens.
17 Benjaman Dun and Anne Paine.
22 Thomas Watis and Jane Robinson.
Nov. 2 John Bradley and Winifret Newman.
2 John Vitell and Mary Sentelow.
2 William Kingsly and Margarett Courthop.
5 Henry Poderish and Alce Parker.
9 Samuell Birwnrigg and Elinor Hall.
12 Thomas Thornton and Joyce Clarke.
14 Henry Rayner and Alce Allen.
15 Charles Evelyn and Jane Evelyn.
20 John Priss and Lettis Tyssen.
21 William Spunner and Dorothy Fox.
23 Robert Ducy and Anne Baldwin.
26 Adrian Person and Alice Spratling.
26 Robert Denten and Elizabeth Braydway.
29 Thomas Clarke and Martha Phillips.
Dec. 2 Thomas Switte and Mary Eccleston.
11 Alabaster Fludd and Mary Maplisden.
14 John Nash and Tomissen Epslee.
17 Francis Raband and Jane Baugh.
19 Samuell Mosse and Anne Elsworth.
20 John Whistler and Elizabeth Typpinge.
27 William Steele and Judith Crowde.
28 Henry Upsheir and Elizabeth James.
Jan. 1 Ralph Tomlinson and Sarah Cutts.
1 Robert Whiting and Elizabeth Stanley.
3 William Beverlee and Lucye Dobbinson.
9 Humfry Charme and Joane Robson.
10 Thomas Page and Elinor Bennett.
11 John Upshan and Alice Don Bavian.
14 Roger Byston and Anne [*blank*].
15 Thomas Lion and Jane Coveredge.
16 Robert Colborne and Anne Hornebee.
16 Hugh Owen and Jane Bowen.
21 Edward Phipps and Sarah Dance.
21 Hugh Buckston and Alice Ellis.
25 John Boughton and Bridgett Coopper.
25 Robert Walter and Katherine Parsons.
25 Richard Stoakes and Jane Baddiley.

1648-9
Feb. 1 Edward Eaton and Anne Glover.
5 Thomas [*blank*] and Susanna Witteker.
6 George Rogers and Anne Crockford.
7 William [*blank*] and Winnefritt Chamberlin.
8 Ambrose Beverscombe and Mary Jeffers.
9 Francis Kinge and Katherine Hall.
11 Stephen Squire and Elizabeth Day.
13 Soloman Sharpe and Joanna Kendall.
20 Jonas Hopkins and Elizabeth Mayne.
21 John Newporte and Jullian Murrey.
Mar. 1 Francis Astey and Honora Brumskell.
1 John Smith and Margeritt Wright.
6 George Cuthburt and Susana Edrydge.
7 Thomas Gnash and Anne Ward.
8 William Spencer and Sarah Rivington.
16 John Hilliard and Grace Godwinn.
22 Joseph Whiston and Elizabeth Travell.

1649.

Mar. 26 John Dermer and Elizabeth Bishop.
26 Richard Johnson and Patience Wellard.
26 Richard Lewes and Margere Goff.
26 Richard Baker and Marye Shaw.
26 John Walmesley and Tabitha Gumley.
27 Bartholomew Roberts and Katherine Semour.
28 Edmund Perss and Joan Crover.
April 2 Thomas Graham and Alce Clarke.
2 Thomas Russell and Susana Whaylsbee.
4 William Howard and Elizabeth Dandasee.
6 John Shepkmine and Joyce Rowe.
6 John Gisbye and Susana Cole.
10 William Kilburne and Damaris Beanmont.
10 Thomas Partington and Gweltha Gough.
12 Robert Neue and Susana Thicknes.
13 Samuel Jenkinson and Anne Ludby.
15 Mallyca Whutten and Alce Roberts.
17 Benjamine Hodylow and Joane Peck.
19 James Paveley and Mary Loveland.
20 John Tute and Mary Foxon.
24 John Lukener and Anne Minn.
26 Thomas Line and Elizabeth Archer.
26 James Mills and Margeritt Hardee.
May 1 Simon Fowler and Sarah Floyd.
1 Nicholas Bennett and Elizabeth Currer.
3 William Allen and Anne Bird.
6 Thomas Spatchhurst and Martha Forth.
8 William Townley and Mary Kimbould.
10 John Cole and Anne Farnybee.
13 Thomas Rainndenn and Elizabeth Sledge.
13 Thomas Fleshmonger and Anne Sebett.
13 Samuell Stillingstrete and Elizabeth French.
14 John Fullilove and Anne Reve.
14 Edward Fisher and Anne Crukefild.
14 George Burleigh and Alice Bacon.
14 Robert Filmer and Dorothy Tuke.
14 Anthony Harding and Anne Gullivell.

1649

May 14 Henry Wilson and Elizabeth Saunders.
15 Henry Neale and Clements Harte.
15 William Darkenoll and Rebecca Rawleigh.
16 Isaac Swift and Margerett Hill.
21 William Bristow and Anne Waldren.
22 William Blincowe and Dorothy Kirton.
22 Edmond Browne and Frances Richardson.
24 John Caryll and Hester Mushamp.
24 Francis Swift and Anne Berry.
31 James Pratten and Margeritt Meakemes.
31 Thomas Jones and Katherine Dew.
31 Hugh Chanell and Anne Bryres.
June 2 Henry Brassey and Elizabeth Snelling.
2 William Young and Rebecca Shephard.
7 Christopher Pope and Anne Pope.
10 Jeffarry Jones and Elizabeth Allin.
10 John Bumsted and Mary Dennis.
11 James Hope and Jane Murrey.
12 Christian Tayler and Judith Jermin.
15 Richard Mead and Jane Carvill.
15 Charles Branfeild and Alles Noxson.
19 Richard Lamb and Ellinor Vahan.
19 Edmund Smith and Elizabeth Scudamore.
20 William Wilder and Jane Greeneway.
21 Isaac Letelle and Ursula Jerrers.
24 Mathew Browne and Mary Deane.
27 Edward Tuffnell and Rachell Hickman.
July 2 William Trewlocke and Lettis Digby.
4 Thomas Brookes and Mary Bell.
4 Robert Sparrow and Dorothy Goodall.
8 Joseph Semonds and Bridget Woodward.
12 Angelo Stonher and Anne Homes.
12 Samuell Glover and Anne Coleman.
12 Edward Leigh and Mary Eywe.
14 John Bord and Jane Fabian.
15 Daniell Hensey and Jone Bigan.
17 John Punter and Elizabeth Darnett.
17 Henry Rampton and Anne Wright.
30 Henry Georye and Mary Knight.
30 Francis Radcliffe and Anne Betts.
Aug. 1 Thomas Bradbury and Bridget Phillips.
2 William Wright and Mary Paradine.
3 Thomas Lee and Dorothy Eldred.
9 John Browne and Rebecca Marson.
11 James Rawlinson and Deborah Jones.
12 Thomas Wills and Anne Morgan.
13 Roger Parris and Elizabeth Shepard.
14 Thomas Scott and Alce Griffes.

[The marriages end suddenly in this volume with this entry, although followed by fourteen blank folios.]

BOOK B.

For the title of this book see Baptisms; the marriages commence at the other end of the book It will be seen there is a hiatus between the end of the marriages in book A and their commencement in this book

MARRIAGES

Begun since the Twentie Ninth daie of September Anno D'ni 1653 and brought in by Richard Aldridge and Richard Heydon, Churchwardens

1653

Nov 23 Richard Rooke and Sarah Bromhall
Dec 1 William Waxhill and Susanna Bird
6 John Ridgway, bricklar, and Mary Chart, widdow, according to a Act of Parliment baringe date the 24th of August 1653, was three severall times Publissed in the Market Place and afterwarde maried by mee upon tuesday the six of December 1653 —Tho Atkin

[NOTE —This entry will be found in the original at the commencement of the Christenings in 1758, to which a reference in the Marriages directs one —ED]

Dec 25 Richard White and Elizabeth Turner
27 Robert Lee and Joane Paulfreeman
29 Thomas Tomson and Elizabeth Neave
29 Hugh Hicks and Katherine Hall
29 Samuell Wilson and Ann Wallis
Jan 5 Emanwell Billings and Mary Collings
7 Marke Graves and Ursula Yates
10 Thomas Binckes and Susanna Hood
12 Isaac Boyse and Rebecca Perry
16 Richard Davis and Elizabeth Clarke
16 Sadrach Furnes and Grace Watts
19 Robert Scutter and Mary [*blank*]
19 Humphry Humphry and Elizabeth Crauncinford
19 Henry Webster and Elizabeth Tayler
24 Rowland Morris and Magdaylin Harlow
25 Rowland Buffett and Elizabeth Munck
26 Hugh Harris and [*blank*] Roberts
29 Roger Toogood and Ann Williams
Feb 2 William Davis and Mary Edwards
2 Thomas Croydon and Ann Loutton
2 Robert Carr and Elizabeth Commens
2 Henry Wilson and Sara Powell
4 Thomas Downbell and Hellen Barker
4 John Chapman and Hanna King
6 John Barnes and Margaret Pembrock
7 John Evelyn, Esq , and Mary Farmer
7 Henry Clarke and Jone Greene
9 Richard Furnis and Ann Hastinges
9 John Whetston and Ann Reynolds
13 Mathew Nelson and Elizabeth Goddard
14 John Fox and Ann Booker
16 Robert Sanderson and Margarett Harle
16 John Cawbacke and Susanna Element
19 Richard Flude and Amye Gibson

1653-4
Feb. 23 Elyas Payne and Susan Godfrey.
26 Francis Turver and Edith Steeven.
26 William Fox and Susan Hale.
28 Samuell Harris and Judith Rich.
Mar. 2 John Butler and Margarett Youle.
9 Robert Harris and Anne Frime.
12 Edward Stayse and Elizabeth Milborn.
12 Lawrance Mayne and Mary Burchall.
13 Francis Royley and Ann Corbin.
14 James Asnoll and Martha Good.
14 Robert Morris and Mary Kimberley.
18 Andrew Davis and Grivell Tomson.
19 Solomon Ward and Joane Simons.
20 Thomas Finch and Alice Phillips.
21 James Sedden and Hester Portman.
22 John Sammon and Prudence Underwood.

1654.

Mar. 25 William Meares and Senesh Watts.
27 Francis Bishop and Abigal Feild.
27 Francis Keepe and Elizabeth Colston.
27 Robert Squire and Grissell Wilson.
28 John Hebb and Jane Long.
28 John Lane and Amy Berry.
28 John Thatcher and Mary Pymme.
29 Edward Hudson and Anne Heds.
29 Thomas Hunt and Alice Berrisfoord.
30 Richard Pyne and Elizabeth Gallant.
30 Robert Driver and Anne Newton.
April 2 Richard Foukes and Dorothie Heywood.
13 Richard Custerfild and Abigall Jenny.
17 Walter Vaughan and Alice Bond.
16 Richard Fryer and Frances Roe.
16 Thomas Hayre and Anne Woodall.
19 John Hill and Jone Millett.
23 Daniell Hossack and Elizabeth Hales.
27 Roger Busbe and Dorothy Jenninges.
30 William Webb and Elizabeth Tue.
May 4 Richard Cleufley and Sara Oram.
4 Robert Peat and Elizabeth Miles.
5 Richard Darwell and Christian Pechee.
4 Valentine Roosse and Anne Dyneley.
9 Charles Martyn and Elizabeth Bishopp.
July 4 Thomas Ellyott and Sarah Rosse.
4 Thomas Stretten and Priscilla Perkyns.
4 Jacob Humphrye and Elizabeth Symon.
6 Edward Harrison and Mary Dowson.
8 Matthias Smyth and Margarett Lovejoy.
13 Joseph Draywer and Mary Nimlaw.
13 Thomas Hyne and Margery Fancutt.
17 John Perry and Ann Brome.
17 Mr Thomas Salkeld and Mrs Elizabeth Wharton.
18 Robert Vaughan and Mary Jackson.
25 John Fribbins and Mary Beardsley.
25 Marke Allexander and Elizabeth Tracie.
25 Richard Field and Judith Nutley.

1654
July 26 Thomas Oliver and Ann Lyddall
30 Richard Smyth and Alice Allin
Oct. 5 Edward Nugent, gent, and Elizabeth Rose, spinster.
5 John Palhill and Frances Wheeler.
6 Thomas Keyle and Mary Mestoe
9 Daniell Frone and Elizabeth Collins
16 William Farrey and Ann Cooper.
16 Francis Phillipps and Elizabeth Beale
17 Hugh Ethersay and Elizabeth Teare.
19 Willyam Joye and Lucye Turner.
27 M[r] John Fox and M[rs] Sara Cooke
29 Thomas Dew and Margarett Hazard.
29 Thomas Perkyns and Ann Rogers.
31 Samuell Rundoll and Ann [*blank*]
Nov. 7 John Allen and Margarett Hicks.
9 Edward Blackabee and Alice Edgerley
10 John Stokes and Joan Darling
Jan 1 Edward Woolward and Mary Paule
1 John Blake and Elizabeth Johnson
1 Thomas Fortune and Joyce Bridges
2 Henry Squibb and Ellenor Edwards
2 John Holder and Mary Sargeant
2 John Duke and Grace Johnston
7 William Tomlinson and Isabell Thorowgood
9 John Clayton and Suzan Perrye.
10 Richard Skarman and Mary Reavett
15 William Gardiner and Abigail Foreman
17 Samuell Simkins and Susan Boothsbye
17 Edward Woodcocke and Mary Ratcliffe.
17 Charles Wheeler and Mary Tatton
18 William Hickes and Latina Barnell
18 Andrew Carter and Naomi Warner
18 Richard Armestrong and Sith Porter
22 Walter Duning and Ann Harwood
25 William Harrison and Ellen Wood
27 Christopher Williams and Winnifrido Powell
29 Thomas Steevens and Margery Light
29 Thomas Summerell and Jane Bottomley.
29 William Floyd and Sarah Chapman
30 John Pull and Hannah Pratt.
30 Oliver Ramsbottome and Elizabeth Thew
30 Henry Middlemore and Elizabeth Pennyston
30 Richard Odber and Sarah Helme
30 Ferdinando Draycott and Elizabeth Fox.
Feb. 3 Henry Morris and Jone Gidney.
4 John Duprey and Elizabeth Weedinge
5 Henry Smyth and Sarah Beale.
5 Robert Morecock and Sarah Dudley
7 Walter Trotter and Sarah Thomas
8 Isaiah Domvill and Jone Dickins.
5 Josepth Sole and Mary Cooke
8 George Baker and Elizabeth Mills
8 Richard Hill and Ann Pattison
8 Everard Febus and Joyce Fortune
8 John Hilton and Anne Burgis
8 James Margetson and Anne Antturne.
8 Thomas Playford and Mary Bragge

1654-5
Feb. 13 Thomas Daynes and Elizabeth Richardson.
13 Thomas Woolmer and Sarah Pluckington.
14 Thomas Fisher and Mary Huse.
15 John Stansbee and Mary Challice.
15 William Burgin and Ann Bellinger.
19 Thomas Batkett and Elizabeth Carlton.
18 John Jackson and Margarett Smyth.
20 John Tailor and Elinor Newton.
20 Richard Gdell and Elizabeth Rowson.
24 Edward Norwood and Alice Badcock.
26 Giles Bolton and Anne Browne.
27 John Higgons and Mary Fellow.
27 Samuell Williams and Thomasine Payne.
28 Stephen Phesant and Mary Staunton.
27 Stephen James and Mary Parrett.
Mar. 1 Nathaniell Buckooke and Alice Floyd.
1 Robert Stone and Jane Gray.
4 Richard Akers and Elizabeth Brooke.
4 John Snatt and Jane Hind.
4 George Roberts and Barbarah Ivitt.
4 Nicholas Driwood and Jane Snell.
5 John Ireland and Jane Blackfell.
5 Thomas Hogg and Jone Harris.
6 John Wicker and Constance Bartram.
7 Robert Hawkinges and Hester Haynes.
7 George Southern and Jane Feeild.
8 Francis Newman and Alice Humpbach.
10 Francis Mayhew and Barbara Leggin.
11 Robert Reade and Ann Hendrick.
12 Court Helderman and Rebecca Hawker.
13 John Coxton and Elizabeth Barthwicke.
19 Richard Hawkesworth and Ann Hanchick.
23 Robert Bowley and Margarett Ballard.
23 John Bullard and Alice Speakeman.

1655.

Mar. 27 Anthony Locksmith and Rose Clarke.
27 Henry Mabb and Ann King.
June 3 William Adams and Katherine Frost.
3 William Andrewes and Anne Longstaffe.
4 Thomas Allman and Thomazin Ogle.
4 Robert Beardsley and Ann Spicer.
4 Nicholas Newman and Judith Poore.
5 Richard Harding and Elizabeth Ekins.
11 Christopher Monkton and Martha Diman.
12 Roger Upton and Ann Barker.
13 Richard Hopton and Susanna Hurvy.
17 Thomas Tarlington and Mary Chadwick.
21 Robert Welch and Suzan Justice.
22 William Howes and Winifrid Greene.
28 John Clift and Ellen Howgrave.
29 Andrew Townsend and Jone Jenks.
July 1 John Banks and Jane Tiballs.
5 Henry Barrowe and Dorothy Barnard.
3 Allixander Robinson and Ann Simmons.
5 Thomas Clarke and Mary Gooddin.

1655
July 5 George Rossiter and Jone Woolhowse.
7 John Allen and Deborah Bryan.
8 Richard Marryott and Margarett Wilde.
12 Richard Knight and Frances Leighton.
14 Daniell Brothers and Mary Foote.
15 William Maslyn and Rose Orton.
15 Mathew Fry and Mary Craftes.
24 Richard Whinyard and Frireth Laneere.
24 Henry Bowyer and Elizabeth Gill.
25 Josepth Hammond and Dulsabella Strudwick.
29 William Coulson and Sarah Jordan.
31 William Harker and Ann Burgis.
Aug. 1 John Briscoe and Sarah Gurnell.
6 Richard Keene and Jone Rickitt.
6 Thomas Dunn and Martha Hassall.
8 John Noate and Margarett Champion.
8 George Bowyer and Jone Lovell.
9 Robert Milton and Alice Dogwell.
9 William Dearmer and Sidney Hodges.
11 George Franck and Sarah Jarvis.
13 John Palne [? Palmer] and Martha Saunders.
14 Robert Fuller and Katherine Ballestone.
14 Richard Hudson and Mary Rest.
15 John Cropley and Isabell Wheeler.
16 James Dodderidge and Mary Wadley.
16 Lawrance Evins and Jane Ladds.
17 Thomas Valentyne and Mary Plaisterer.
20 Robert Mehewe and Jane Mallard.
21 John Sherwyn and Alice Jackson.
21 Edward Vernon and Margarett Favell.
23 William Davis and Katherine Morris.
24 John Cherry and Margery Moudy.
27 Hugh Vaughan and Elizabeth Cooke.
27 William Cash and Bridgett Bottome.
28 Thomas Norton and Katherin Wilkins.
29 Samuell Newton and Mary Day.
30 William Gibson and Elizabeth Leake.
Sept. 3 Francis Wigginton and Elizabeth Bennett.
3 John Potton and Margarett Wright.
6 Thomas Bynum and Mary Bacon.
6 George Boulgton and Bridgett Holborough.
10 Thomas Rose and Mary Hudson.
10 Thomas Griffin and Mary Oakes.
16 Stephen Brookes and Mary Brunman.
16 Clement Gage and Ann Jackson.
24 Richard Pulver and Katherine Hewes.
27 Thomas Harler and Dorothie Morrall.
30 John Smedley and Mary Pearlys.
Oct. 3 Samuell Hunt and Hanna Bottom.
3 Reynald Marriott and Barbara Tucke.
4 Charles Meredith and Lucy Finett.
8 John Johnson and Joanna Tompson.
9 Robert Dillack and Katherine Jones.
9 John Sutton and Elizabeth Porter.
9 John Woodhall and Elizabeth Fletcher.
10 Charles Dickenson and Ellynor Chambers.
11 John Rich and Anne White.

1655-6

Oct. 17 William Fellow and Jane Robjohn.
18 John Sex and Mary Feake.
21 John Beaumond and Alice Beacon.
24 George Price and Mary Kempe.
25 George Teage and Jane Higgins.
26 Josuah Saunders and Elizabeth Gray.
26 Henry Taylor and Mary Sallis.
27 Anthony Sarreson and Katherine Fibins.
29 Richard Humphryes and Margarett Sapsfoord.
31 Edward Dubber and Alice Harding.
Nov. 5 John Hulett and Elizabeth Heaton.
5 George Howard and Alice Keisar.
8 John Peck and Frances Wheeler.
20 Charles Pomery and Anne Pomeroy.
13 Thomas Tilcock and Susan Bigg.
13 Thomas Marsh and Elizabeth Hales.
15 William Leaver and Margarett Brigham.
18 John Knight and Ann Greenebury.
21 Thomas Smyth and Sarah Scott.
27 Thedias Mathewes and Christian Norton.
27 Nicholas Morris and Ellen Cason.
30 Theophilus Linch and Jane Reynell.
Dec. 1 Cornelius Simpson and Judith Hafins.
3 Josepth Browne and Anne Brasbye.
5 William Inglebirt and Elizabeth Turner.
8 Ralph Bannister and Katherin Beale.
18 David Clyatt and Hanna Baits.
18 William Franckish and Elizabeth Floyd.
17 Henry Winne and Elizabeth Kilby.
17 John Willson and Margarett Hillyard.
20 John Tretheney and Margarett Stocker.
20 William Gay and Mary Jennings.
26 Edmund Fary and Elizabeth Sprafford.
Feb. 7 William Wells and Anne Powell.
8 John Gettinges and Susan Hunt.
10 Mr Richard Ely and Mrs Elizabeth Haviland.
13 John Willey and Alice Lewys.
14 Francis Ellis and Jane Dixon.
20 William Sprattbury and Alice Howe.
21 Nicholas Greene and Elizabeth Gaskell.
21 Richard Gathorne and Mary Frummond.
22 John Underwood and Elizabeth Walles.
23 John Boles and Mary Marden.
23 John Topham and Jeane Stoughton.
25 Thomas Gould and Frances Cole.
Mar. 4 Stephen Wells and Katherine Blanye.
5 William Wood and Elizabeth Twittye.
7 Luke Mumford and Hanna Heart.
19 William Stiles and Mary Gray.
23 Charles Colbett and Ann Dibbeell.
23 Richard Goodhew and Ann Child.

1656.

Mar. 27 Robert Scales and Alice Ransume.
29 Barnabee Whitwell and Michall Hall.
April 1 Ralph Ferryman and Mary Johnson.

1656
April 2 Thomas Bishopp and Suzan Moore.
3 Ralph Gray and Mary Starky.
5 Robart Ballard and Martha Roberts.
7 George Roberts and Elizabeth Norton.
7 William Russell and Thomasin Foukner.
8 Edmund Geree and Elizabeth Chapman.
10 Richard Bush and Mary Barren.
10 Robert Stevenson and Margarett Heath.
10 Robert Johnson and Elizabeth Lee.
14 Ranere Hilson and Katherine Lwert.
16 Henry Penn and Ann Denham.
17 William Cox and Elizabeth West.
21 John Smyth and Mary Smyth.
27 Thomas Harwood and Susanna Gunston.
28 Roger Cosborne and Sarah Watson.
28 George Beeson and Katherine Turgis.
May 1 Thomas Mekins and Ann Neve.
3 William Diaper and Ann Lambert.
7 John Perne and Ann Callison.
8 Nicholas Hoockes and Elizabeth Swayne.
10 George Rogers and Sarah Humfryes.
12 Thomas Clutton and Frances Bull.
13 Thomas Maddocks and Frances Wuccles.
13 Henry Hargrave and Magdalin Smyth.
15 John White and Elizabeth Haddon.
15 Valentyne Clarke and Jone Goodwyn.
17 John Boult and Ann Corney.
24 William Coundley and Judith Meade.
24 Thomas Manley and Margarett Eksyngs.
25 John Baldwyn and Mary Woossiter.
25 Patrick Ruthen and Sarah Head.
25 John Webber and Mary [*blank*].
26 John Lambert and Katherine Hide.
27 Roger James and Jane Bull.
27 Gandy Brampton and Dorothie Bristoe.
27 James Rivers and Margarett Goord.
28 William Adams and Suzan Porter.
29 Ralph Eve and Dorothy Ramme.
29 Reinale Fulgason and Mary Burgett.
30* John Stallford and Hester Freewell.
June 2 Henry Longe and Amye Burstow.
3 Richard Hinde and Dorothy West.
3 John Constable and Sarah Perrye.
3 Thomas Aldin and Mary Wigham.
6 James Mumford and Ellinor Williams.
7 John Stalford and Hester Freewell.
7 Edward Bayley and Grezell Covell.
10 Robert Wells and Ann Smyth.
10 Richard Bowles and Alice Parker.
10 Humfry Buckner and Darcus Linch.
11 Christopher Monckton and Martha Dyman.
12 Walter Dalton and Jone Parsons.
12 George Senior and Mary Hunt.
12 Robert Minors and Mary Haviland.
12 William Wells and Alice Webb.
13 Roger Norton and Ellinor Hulkers.

* Repeated on 7th June *infra*.—ED

1656
June 14 Milliscent Colquitt and Susanna Rich.
14 Griffith Davis and Rebecca Rogers.
16 Elisha Ellett and Ann Early.
16 Symon Beale and Margarett Sawell.
16 John [*blank*] and Elizabeth [*blank*].
22 James French and Sarah Wheeler.
24 Thomas Frence and Jane Lawe.
24 Edward Sheppard and Lyddiah Clinch.
25 Francis Lee and Amye Marryner.
25 Arthur Header and Sarah Dawson.
27 James Wilcox and Lidia Mayger.
July 3 William Owen and Mary Garth.
3 Gilbert Marshall and Elizabeth Moorey.
4 George Ware and Elizabeth Wiborne.
6 John Aldridg and Hester Gwilliams.
7 Oneley Mathew and Joice Sired.
8 John Hicks and Ann Hill.
14 Andrew Freeman and Ann Bent.
20 John Barrett and Mary White.
22 Thomas Chamberlaine and Frances Scott.
22 John Lincolne and Alice Gadsbye.
24 John Watson and Grace Evans.
28 John Cartwrite and Katherine Loveton.
Aug. 3 Thomas West and Katherin Cousens.
5 John Davis and Bennett Goulding.
5 Henry Smyth and Grace Briggs.
6 Richard Medcafe and Elizabeth Urwinn.
7 Edward Shaw and Ann Mainnard.
8 Richard Retorick and Margaret Raine.
8 Richard Jones and Mary Ransom.
12 Thomas Clutton and Frances Bull.
13 Thomas Browneing and Frances Symonds.
19 William Sheld and Meriall Adworth.
18 Edward Clouch and Elizabeth Corbett.
20 Peeter Price and Julian Phillipps.
27 John Crowch and Elizabeth Hughes.
Sept. 1 John Haynes and Rebecca Bashford.
2 Edman Kent and Martha Gibbs.
3 Christopher Ashcoll and Mary Carpenter.
8 Roger Fowler and Temperance Treinmer.
8 Oliver Tredwell and Margarett Melton.
6 Nicholas Duckett and Phillis Hill.
9 William Wakeley and Mary Bingley.
11 John Bray and Johane Payne.
20 Symon Perkins and Magdalen Shackleton.
18 William Hide and Ann Dynn.
21 Edward Waterhouse and Elizabeth Wilmott.
18 Robert Crosby and Mary Smyth.
30 Lawrance Hall and Jeminey Tayler.
Oct. 1 Lawrance Bateman and Alice Loveday.
9 Edward Cooper and Mary Adcock.
9 Thomas Collier and Frances Bannister.
10 William Allen and Elizabeth Cartwright.
13 Thomas Gillibrand and Dorothy Manley.
13 Francis Hippisley and Frances Reywell.
14 Thomas Hall and Ann Peepes.
16 Obydia Emons and Alice Sharpe.
16 Henry Baldwyn and Ann Baldwynn.

1656
Oct. 18 Nicholas Mason and Judith Duncomb.
22 Thomas Meades and Elizabeth Capes.
26 Richard Panton and Alice Kingsland.
29 Michaell Parr and Rossaman Downes.
30 Phillipp Richards and Mary Leach.
Nov. 2 Samuell Brookes and Alice Smyth.
4 Henry Turner and Ann Chapman.
6 John Elmes and Lillicia Smyth.
12 Henry Fortescue and Jone Lewys.
27 George Beare and Grizeld Spottswood.
Dec. 4 Nathaniell Lee and Tomisson Mallin.
2 Thomas Cage and Mary Wight.
2 John Browne and Elizabeth Fowler.
4 John Allyn and Margarett Godden.
7 Francis Cheyney and Ann Munden.
9 Thomas Bulfell and Ann Clappam.
9 William Ladson and Jane Warren.
18 Charles Roberts and Penelope Streete.
25 John Moore and Mary Goodyeare.
25 Richard Roberts and Elizabeth Standish.
26 Andrew French and Ann Atkin.
26 Edward Woodroffe and Mary Cane.
30 William Mullinder and Elizabeth Day.
Jan. 1 Edward Hewson and Hester Davis.
4 John Farley and Christiann Shrimpton.
6 Robert Russell and Elizabeth Lowe.
7 John Gaskynge and Ellyn Weane.
9 George Melton and Ann Higgison.
22 Samuell Hounsfeeild and Jone Staresmore.
22 Thomas Levingston and Jane Richardson.
22 Charles Fathingham and Lucie Shutter.
22 John Sandford and Mary Peyton.
26 Francis Platt and Tabitha Austin.
26 Richard Wise and Elizabeth Fowler.
Feb. 2 Henry Baker and Barbara Sydenham.
2 Richard Ruddiard and Elizabeth Burnell.
5 Thomas Fanshaw, Esq., and Margaritt Heath.
5 John Garrard and Susanna Bowsell.
8 Thomas Fitzwater and Jone Cummings.
8 Thomas Jones and Mary Mathewes.
9 Giles Bridgwater and Mary Gardner.
10 John Gunn and Catherine Benge.
12 Thomas Clarke and Jane Hill.
19 George Medborn and Elizabeth Lambert.
19 Walter Downton and Ann Burton.
23 Thomas Hawkswell and Sarah Godfrey.
21 Tobias Oven and Ann Huse.
28 John Harding and Mary Cramer.
Mar. 1 David Williams and Katherina Jones.
2 Robert Farley and Prudence Hughes.
7 Joseepth Wassington and Jane Jones.
10 Widdup Waterhouse and Elizabeth Rand.
11 Francis Mitchell and Mary Lawrance.
13 Mr John Bernard and Mrs Elizabeth St John.
14 Thomas Southwell and Elinor Grice.
15 Charles Moore and Alice Dowce.
18 Robert Pitty and Jane Stockes.

1656-7
Mar. 19 Valentine Robinson and Ann Hurt.
24 Thomas Beale and Barbarah Egerton.

1657.

Mar. 30 John Kingham and Edith French.
30 John Darbye and Katherine Webb.
30 Willyam Tayler and Ann Goodfall.
April 2 Richard Bowles and Elizabeth Heyborne.
2 Francis Streywey and Jane Hough.
3 James Barnett and Ellen Morgan.
4 Edward Connick and Ann Evans.
6 William Ellett and Hannah Roberts.
7 Richard Hammond and Jane King.
9 Thomas Ricoe and Elizabeth Buckley.
12 John Hampton and Mary Couch.
14 William Norcoate and Mary Kirbye.
19 Arthur Murrye and Margarett Hams.
20 Gabriell Price and Mary Powell.
20 Edward Nottingham and Sarah Waller.
27 John King and Suzan Ward.
May 6 Edward Foster and Susan Newth.
8 Robert Jenkyn and Elizabeth Robins.
11 Thomas Cooke and Mary Holloway.
12 Francis Vernon and Mary Steele.
12 Henry Langton and Elizabeth Bludworth.
12 Josepth Steevens and Barbarah Powle.
12 Henry Shearing and Mary Hill.
14 William Burlegh and Mary Sayer.
18 John Yeates and Sarah Pendred.
18 William Grismound and Elizabeth Roston.
18 Nicholas Briddon and Barbarah Hill.
19 Peter Hayes and Jane Evans.
19 Richard Chase and Bridgett Munday.
21 John Webb and Mary Owen.
25 Abraham Scott and Mary Tayler.
25 Anthony Highway and Catherine Allen.
26 Richard Martyn and Martha Tucker.
26 Anthony Brudnell and Elizabeth May.
June 1 William Heyward and Frances Curtise.
2 Jonathan Stiles and Frances Masters.
5 John Norris and Ellynor North.
9 Edmund Coleright and Ann Rogers.
9 Francis Shellay and Jone Greenoway.
11 Hugh Phillipps and Martha Asnold.
12 Rowland Robinson and Jane Collins.
12 Thomas Fairefall and Margery Till.
15 Samuell Ricketts and Sarah King.
16 John Deane and Ann Wilson.
17 William Spencer and Elizabeth Maynard.
18 Sir James Wittlock and Mary Pricher.
24 John Seare and Jane Cleafe.
July 5 William Page and Mary Ward.
6 Bartholomew Hurlebatt and Ann Younge.
6 John Sherwood and Ellinor Clarke.
7 John Weekes and Elizabeth Scott.
7 Richard Woornall and Gartrude Foord.

1657
July 8 John Grove and Protasie Jefford
9 Nicholas White and Frances Bedell
9 Mathew Taylor and Katherin Sytbry.
9 Ralfe Massey, gent, and Judith Cornell.
9 John Draper and Clase Gill
13 John Stonhill and Ann Lawrants
14 Edward Weeton and Sarah Farley
15 Francis Hodgson and Mary Bridg
16 Humfry Gore and Precissus England
17 John Bromyard and Elizabeth Carr
18 Emanuell Toomes and Mary Larkyn.
19 Thomas Symmondes and Margarett Phillipps
19 Edward Stretch and Ann Holmes
19 Arthur Hayler and Rebeccah Pennock
20 Robert Collyns and Mary Cooper
20 Charles Toungue and Elizabeth Penlered
26 James Fox and Joane Vintner
28 John Combes and Damaris Collett
28 William Jackson and Elizabeth Godfry.
28 William Twisden and Elizabeth Atkins
30 Edward Terrick and Ann Edgeley
30 Mathew Dun and Elizabeth Tissoe
Aug. 3 John Butler and Mary Fossell
4 William Swadling and Ann Darling
6 Roger Marshall and Fortune Wallis.
10 Thomas Allen and Ann Jones
11 George Hay and Jane Spootswood.
13 John Payne and Ann Dalton
20 Samuell Warde and Margarett Lenthall
20 Nicholas Douthwaite and Elizabeth Law
20 Marke Cottle and Frances Clemants
24 George Penn and Katherin Palmer
24 Richard Smyth and Elizabeth Conyers
25 William Wallis and Katherine Sole
26 John Feeild and Katherine Alden.
27 Henry Thomas and Elizabeth Corkin
27 John Duncombe and Calleberry Bulstrode
30 Peter Withers and Elizabeth Corney
31 William Emerye and Jane Lambert
31 Samuell Warde and Jane Lawson
27 William Weekes and Martha Crowde
Sept. 1 William Guy and Martha Nowell
1 Ralph Johnson and Elizabeth Hughes
2 John Wells alias Otwell and Mary Williams
3 Thomas Powell and Grace Foulkes
4 John Chester and Anne Mitten
8 John Slunn and Jane Cowell
9 Ambrose Harris and Ann Merrefeeild.
13 Edward Batt and Ann Robinson
15 Gelbard Chetwind and Ellyn Floud
16 Robert Tucker and Susana Turner.
16 Timothy Jones and Ann Hamer
17 William Yates and Elizabeth Wilcotts.
17 John Sherwyn and Elizabeth Greene
17 Thomas Albery and Jone Woodyere.
19 Robert Nash and Judeth Woollee
20 John Taylor and Dorothy Warner.

1657

Sept. 21 John Boughton and Bridgett Bassett.
22 Edmund Scott and Frances Smyth.
22 John Yarling and Barbara Wilson.
23 Christopher Cooke and Isabell Smyth.
23 Daniell Wayte and Ann Bradford.
24 Benjamyn Tanner and Edith Marriatt.
24 Thomas Hewett and Jane Stevens.
25 John Langley and Thomasin Moore.
28 Richard Tredwell and Bridgett Wright.
29 Thomas Perkyns and Elizabeth Martin.
30 Richard Shooter and Mary Fowler.
30 George Maldon and Elizabeth Horsenaile.
Oct. 1 Morgan Price and Jone Edwardes.
1 Edward James and Mary Rande.
5 Edward Fewster and Hannah Hoggs.
5 Tymothy Edgerton and Elizabeth Henshaw.
6 Edward Stanthwaite and Ann Attye.
6 Nicholas Harman and Rose Lovett.
6 George Todd and Mary Coddrington.
7 Robert Abbis and Ann Corey.
10 John Mill and Jone Braborne.
12 Henry Bolton and Ann Chambers.
14 Nicholas Wheatley and Elizabeth Walker.
15 Josepth Harrupp and Penelope Hayes.
15 William Todmartyn and Elizabeth Stone.
15 Ralph Page and Jane Battman.
15 Arthur Meantis and Elizabeth Eldridg.
16 William Donning and Jane Sutton.
18 George Harper and Lyddia Meares.
21 Robert Harris and Judith Bloome.
22 Joshua Martyn and Martha Rawlett.
25 Michaell Swift and Frances Neave.
27 Samuell Smyth and Frances Colton.
29 Thomas Pagett and Sarah Pickering.
30 John Vinyare and Sarah Greenehall.
Nov. 2 Nicholas Gilpin and Alice Glynn.
5 John Ruslyn and Margarett Blundell.
5 Robert Udall and Anne Browne.
5 Edward Floyd and Sarah Pym.
8 William Baylye and Dorothie Ride.
9 Benjamyn Pickering and Jane Flloyd.
9 John Bigg and Elizabeth Wall.
10 John Morris and Elizabeth Seavokle.
12 Allexander Briggs and Sarah Gill.
12 Thomas Johnson and Dorcas Cussey.
18 John Wilkins and Katherine Richards.
19 William Jones and Cecilie Jordan.
19 Thomas Heather and Elizabeth Tappin.
25 William Britan and Elizabeth Walker.
26 John Papworth and Frances Gray.
Dec. 2 William Jefferis and Elleanor Exton.
3 Thomas Bucknall and Martha Garnell.
3 Richard Caryll and Kinborough Wescombe.
6 John Browne and Ann Whetstone.
7 Thomas Hine and Rebeccah Deane.
8 Robert Marshall and Sarah Smalepeice.
8 John Cooke and Mary Hussey.

1657
Dec 8 John Burye and Jane Mawlinge
10 Samuell Babbett and Ann Fewtrell
10 William Hewson and Joyce Blankley
10 Samuell Lester and Elizabeth Birch
13 John Vaughan and Alice Edwardes
13 John Hotchkin and Jane Lewis
15 John Boulton and Elizabeth Peirsall.
15 John Eldridg and Elizabeth Wyvan
17 Emanuell Decritz and Ann Oglby
26 George Andrewes and Elizabeth Atye
27 Francis Dowsing and Margarett Vinson
29 Abraham Bletsaund and Grace Chamberlaine
29 Richard Annins and Mary Mathewes
Jan 1 John Mitton and Susanna Gough
1 John Luckett and Alice Worthing
1 Edmund Clarke and Katherine Evans
9 Hugh Philpotts and Jone Mousley
11 Edward Alcock and Mary Jones
14 Thomas Cocking and Rachell Stury
14 Robert Reynoldes and Hannah Widdens
15 William Sergood and Mary Harrison
21 John Hardcastle and Elizabeth Aborve
23 John Cocklinge and Ann Mascall
23 William Russell and Sarah Hutton
24 Thomas Spencer and Patience Hampton
24 Jenver Lane and Elizabeth Bright
25 Thomas Davis and Susan Toler
26 Thomas Martyn and Ursula Bradshaw
28 John Towne and Alice Browne
31 Samuell Sandford and Jane Lewellyn
Feb 1 Robert Houghton and Elizabeth Sedley
1 Robert Nicholson and Margery Wilcocks
2 Thomas Robinson and Phillis Baxter
4 Robert Lee and Margarett Whittin
4 John Hollis and Elizabeth Gibbs
8 Abraham Eades and Joyce Wilcox
9 John Bradbury and Jane Fowkes
10 James Button and Sarah Alleyn
11 Lawrance Bathurst and Susan Cooke
12 John Cox and Susan Smale.
14 Samuell John Write and Ann Symmons
16 Henry Marshall and Elizabeth Allen
15 Roger Pedley and Elizabeth Harwood
17 Thomas Saunderson and Ann Bishopp
15 Richard Chase and Ealkenah Chillinworth.
16 John Spackman and Elizabeth Smyth
18 Thomas Saunders and Alice Day
18 Henry Johnson and Mary Palmer
23 Michal Hicker and Jone Woodtall
22 John Trewman and Mary Birch
23 William Wilmott and Mary Ansell.
23 Michael Knight and Jone Outram
23 William Morris and Jane Hilliard
26 William Ollowrenshaw and Elizabeth Bradbury
26 Samuell Britwell, Esq , and Susana Loftus.
Mar 1 John Carter and Rose Burman
4 John Whatman and Mary Murrall

1657-8
Mar. 10 Henry Tuke and Elizabeth Barrett.
10 John Dove, Esq., and Ann Aurstin.
18 John Darby and Ann Shaw.
20 Leonard Scott and Elizabeth Wright.
23 Benjamyn Dollowfeild and Ann Miles.
23 John Port and Anne Sandye.

1658.

Mar. 28 John Catlin and Jane Ayllett.
30 Thomas Wats and Mary Wilkinson.
April 2 Henry Burkenhead and Mary Osbond.
6 William Corker and Mary Bery.
7 Robert Chennell and Sara Towese.
11 Thomas Griffith and Susanna Parker.
11 Andrew Lawrance and Frances Dickinson.
11 Thomas Fookes and Lucy Taylor.
12 John Browne and Mary Osborne.
12 William Bingley and Alice Holt.
12 Thomas Goodridg and Elizabeth Dibdall.
12 John Stanbridg and Elizabeth Coale.
12 Daniell Gunberd and Mary Hinderson.
13 Edmund Riches and Jone Bushnell.
13 Robert White, gent., and Margaritt Tayler.
13 John Clarke and Ann Drurye.
13 Robert Dixon and Mary Blagiter.
13 John Draper and Elizabeth Robinson.
13 Richard Chadwick and Ellen Hawley.
15 William Saltmarsh and Phebe Cakebread.
13 Samuel Handy and Frances Puckeringe.
15 Thomas Hamond and Hannah Newth.
14 Robert White and Elizabeth Tayler.
15 Thomas Mountgomery and Dorothy Hawley.
21 John Hickson and Jane Nocke.
19 Henry Vallett and Elizabeth Vallett.
22 Thomas Vaughan and Mary Malby.
24 Michaell Fowler and Ellen Carr.
25 Edward Powell and Jane Smyth.
29 Thomas Cooke and Mary Bugbery.
29 Allexander Smyth and Margery Herrell.
May 1 Walter White and Sarah Hitching.
3 James Coleman and Elizabeth Wenstone.
4 Tobell Acton and Charity Symmons.
5 William Cutbirth and Mary Ireland.
6 John Jones and Elizabeth Richardes.
9 John Roberts and Ann Knowlton.
11 William Bury and Frances Cooke.
11 Thomas Denne and Ann Coningsby.
14 Josepth Locke and Anne Bacey.
16 Thomas Aldridg and Katherin Maior.
18 Henry Morgan and Jone Bartlett.
19 William Games and Rebecca Ward.
20 William Wilkinson and Anne Kensley.
21 Henry Parker and Mary Martyn.
22 Ralph Gerrard and Margarett Pullen.
22 Edward Bibey and Elizabeth Cole.
23 Nicholas Hassellwood and Heaster Parsons.

1658
May 25 Martyn Gardner and Mary Low.
27 William Thornhill and Katherin Ramsford.
30 William Blincoe and Jane Yates.
30 John Dunsdon and Ellen Hake.
30 John Grove and Jane Hunt.
30 Nicholas Isgar and Anne Reason.
31 Henry Curstertine and Ellen Packe.
June 1 George Hubberne and Elizabeth Hall.
1 Thomas Hillman and Margaritt Broddrick.
2 Thomas Robinson and Elizabeth Willson.
3 Francis Hurd and Jane Powell.
3 John Preston and Alice Davis.
5 Mathew Bullock and Barbarah Ditton.
7 William Orpin and Sarah Knight.
8 Richard Baylsfoord and Rachell Barker.
8 John Cooper and Jane Tapper.
8 Samuell Laddington, Esq., and Dame Mary Chestar.
13 Richard Hoy and Frances Deane.
14 John Smyth and Elizabeth Wilson.
17 John Smyth [*sic*] and Martha Gwynn.
18 John Owen and Jone Wolter.
18 Henry Atkinson and Dorothie Cotes.
20 Allexander Tayes and Dorothie Trowell.
22 William Seares and Katherin Rayner.
23 William Pope and Audre James.
24 Edward Hill and Mary Squibb.
24 Bartholomew Rigg and Dinah Butt.
24 Richard Chilton and Ann Davis.
26 William Bury and Jane Pledg.
26 Thomas Davis and Margarett Rogers.
26 Richard Early and Elizabeth Doobey.
July 2 John Giles and Elizabeth Medcalfe.
4 Thomas Spencer and Elizabeth Johnson.
5 William Hayse and Dorothy Fry.
6 John Barnes and Martha Bish.
17 James Fullwood and Elizabeth Chestar.
20 William Bryand and Frances Stroude.
22 George Nicholls and Elizabeth Palmer.
26 George Holton and Margarett Williams.
26 Thomas Heather and Elizabeth Widmere.
26 William Redding and Jane Widmere.
27 Richard Keynsham and Mary Peppiat.
28 William Copeland and Unas Atkinson.
Aug. 1 Richard Powell and Susanna Collyns.
1 John Bunnyon and Sophia Sheppard.
4 Thomas Wood and Elizabeth Higgins.
5 Symon Radford and Rebecca Skuddamamore.
8 Robert Eaton and Elisha Allen.
8 John Mackly and Elizabeth Watson.
9 Robert Meakyn and Mary Dike.
10 William Rolfe and Elizabeth Mouse.
12 Stephen Carter and Mary Whooton.
12 William Burrowes and Dorothie Burges.
17 Samuell Bradwell and Katherine Skuell.
18 Tobias Knowles and Jane Helyn.
19 Henry Hope and Elizabeth Nevill.
23 John Ash and Ann Wilkinson.

1658
Aug. 24 John Webster and Mary Cracke.
25 Josepth Trundey and Ann Bray.
26 William George and Mary Francis.
26 John Nevis and Mary Ball.
29 William Clarke and Mary Holmes.
30 Jefferye Tibballs and Alice Gardiner.
Sept. 2 Ascanis Hinde and Mary Boord.
3 William Price and Katherine Frost.
7 John Lever and Ann Bishopp.
8 John Rafes and Ann Bishopp [*sic*].
10 Josepth Milward and Dorothy Wigginton.
12 John Barrett and Lucy Dodderidg.
15 William Hawkes and Awdrey Lawson.
16 Robert Redway and Elizabeth Colthust.
19 Robert Gale and Ann Floyd.
20 William Westwood and Mary Cosbrooke.
22 Thomas Owen and Katherine Peere.
23 Mathias Harrison and Anna Hellum.
23 Robert Hilton and Mary Randoll.
27 Thomas Scott and Mary Watson.
27 Edward Williams and Mary Peircye.
29 Samuell Hanham and Mary Seele.
30 Richard Reade and Mary Milton.
Oct. 2 Jonas Charton and Jone James.
3 John May and Bridgett Heart.
4 Robert Douglas and Mary Hayes.
6 John Turner and Sarah Ruckwood.
7 John Hubberd and Grace Chitham.
10 Nicholas Page and Mary Charles.
10 Allexander Siddall and Ann Deacon.
11 George Lane and Elizabeth Davenport.
12 Daniell Flaunders and Alice Scant.
12 James Scant and Sarah Richford.
12 William Morke and Martha Browne.
18 William Davis and Ann Tilley.
18 Richard Evans and Elizabeth Gosnell.
19 Samuell Bodle and Mary Harman.
19 Thomas Biddle and Elizabeth Prime.
19 Josepth Smyth and Camelia Konnell.
21 John Macro and Mary Soper.
21 Richard Lawes and Martha Broomer.
21 Thomas Stone and Ellinor Jarvis.
21 John Burton and Rebecca Stiles.
22 Mathew Giles and Katherin Watts.
26 Allexander Tapsell alias Tapshar and Ann Date.
28 William Clunn and Mary Ellis.
28 John Tombes and Mary Crutchfeeild.
28 William Rolfe and Elizabeth Mouse.
28 Nicholas Waite and Elizabeth Ceires.
Nov. 1 William Roome and Sarah Newmarch.
1 George Lovedaie and Elizabeth Gilett.
2 James Milner and Ann Strange.
2 Josepth Owen and Elizabeth Kelloway.
2 Samuell Brooks and Alice Smyth.
7 Thomas Powell and Tomasin Hafeild.
8 Rosament Hitchins and Jane Lane.
10 Thomas Freeman, gent., and Elizabeth Wilkes.

1658
Nov 11 Richard Richardes and Elizabeth Medlebur.
11 Thomas Masson and Abigall Bailey
14 Ralffe Foord and Susan Riding
15 John Rogers and Frances Gibson
16 George Leeson and Frances Gully.
16 William Pearse and Mary Jones.
16 Henry Duck and Ellynor Elton
18 Robert Pardoe and Ann Dunn
18 John Spicer and Ruth Dove
18 William Sherman and Martha Cooke
23 Thomas Awdrey and Elizabeth Blissett
23 Richard Pellett and Jone Rombell
23 Thomas Rhodes and Elizabeth Morgan
23 Francis Hall and Mary Boys.
25 George Cliffoord and Elizabeth Price
25 William Mathewes and Mary Wall
25 Robert Burdon and Priscilla Pratt
28 Humphery Edmundes and Alis [*blank*]
30 Bartholomew Marsh and Mary Countrey
30 Roger Pitkin and Margarett Marston
30 Pellam Yates and Willmott Cranbrie
Dec 1 Richard Lowe and Ellenor Probert
1 Charles Jackson and Jone Crosse.
1 Henry Lawrance and Elizabeth Johnson
1 Edmund Hall and Katherin Finch
2 Edward Lawrence and Ann Horne
3 John Paule and Mary Sarjeant
7 John Gosling and Elizabeth Wood.
9 Robert Deane and Edy Bamford
14 Richard Whisom and Mary Andrewes
14 Edmund Scott and Elizabeth Worth
14 Thomas Wilson and Elizabeth Chusin
14 Evan Bottom and Phillis Ayliffe
14 Thomas Vaughan and Ann Wolfe
16 Stephen Briggs and Frances Smyth
17 James Wilson and Ann Partridge
18 Stephen Galloway and Elizabeth Newman.
20 John Marshall and Martha Scott
21 Henry Pym and Margaret Forse
21 Robert Miller and Elizabeth Freeman.
22 William Danby and Margery Raymar
23 William Roberts and Mary Crant
26 Richard Wilcox and Ann Fisher
27 Thomas Keymer and Dorothie Hughes
27 Willyam Crayle and Elizabeth Alkyn
28 Richard Worrall and Margarett Lidwidge
29 Robert Barker and Frances Williams
30 Richard Foster and Jane Moore
30 Patrick Hogg and Mary Shoreditch
Jan. 1 John Seelue and Isabell Randoll
1 Richard Ethersey and Mary Witcom
1 Francis Ramsford and Mary Juxon
2 William Skwington and Mary Symmons
4 Richard Evans and Susan Cowslipp
4 Edward Winston and Mary Welmore
6 William Peere and Mary Nettles
7 John Rummyns and Katherin Coke.

1658-9

Jan. 10 John Reade and Mary Adgoe.
11 John Moore and Ann Cooper.
13 George Wight and Elizabeth Hawtyn.
13 John Beverley and Elizabeth Crabtree.
13 Walter Williams and Margarett Davis.
13 Richard Staffoord and Frances Shaw.
15 William Iver and Frances Wilmer.
16 Thomas Powle and Elizabeth Wallis.
20 Edward Golding and Ann Langley.
20 Edward Johnson and Thomasin Burwarsh.
23 John Holmes and Wiberry Perkyns.
24 Richard Lillington and Elizabeth Harding.
25 Robert Greenefecild and Ellyonor Agborough.
26 Thomas Amos and Mabell Ward.
26 John Ekills and Mary Floyd.
27 Christopher Goddard and Martha Waters.
31 John Allen and Elizabeth Wright.
31 Edward Steevenson and Katherin Nuby.
Feb. 2 John Heardy and Dorothy Piggott.
5 John Hodges and Sarah Reignolds.
6 William Homes and Ann Creswell.
9 John Tateham and Elizabeth Varney.
10 Bryan Kenniston and Elizabeth Pedley.
10 Thomas Edwards and Elizabeth Hough.
11 Lewys Meakyn and Mary Glynn.
13 Thomas Candler and Alice Rudd.
14 Gilbert Pickering and Alice Hobkins.
14 Richard Fletcher and Rebeccah Scarrett.
14 William Appleton and Suzanna West.
16 John Farrington and Susan Oakesbutt.
16 Henry Payne and Gartrud Marshall.
22 Richard Duning and Sarah Browes.
24 George Heeler and Elizabeth Croxfoord.
24 John Philpott and Ann Wainwrite.
26 Josepth Lloyd and Mary Heather.
28 Mathew Collyns and Frances Widmere.
Mar. 14 William Bishopp and Elizabeth Pasfeeild.
14 Samuell Smyth and Katherin Measey.
16 William Hadsley and Lyddia Boreham.
16 Andrew Wormewood and Elizabeth Symmons.
19 Nathaniell Staynes and Elizabeth Grigg.
22 George Dashwood and Margarett Percy.

1659.

Mar. 25 Robert Woodward and Katherin Clarke.
26 John Wyatt and Alice Barsley.
29 Thomas Bridges and Sara Spencer.
April 4 William Dodson and Frances Tayler.
4 John Goodchild and Elizabeth Creswell.
4 Thomas Man and Sarah Wilton.
4 William Fairebrother and Margery Lee.
5 Grevell Powell and Jane Titchmarsh.
5 Edmund Kevell and Elizabeth Paylor.
5 Thomas Boorer and Elizabeth Grambridg.
5 John Stanton and Mary Tinsley.
6 Nicholas Peasley and Rebeccah Power.

1659
April 7 James Chowning and Jane Waker.
8 William Butcher and Martha Rogers.
11 Barnard Chittey and Jone Goare.
14 Jeremiah Bates and Elizabeth Wade.
14 Thomas Crosse and Margarett Freeman.
14 Walter Piper and Ursula Best.
14 Humphrey Morris and Frances Carey.
14 Samuell Watson and Mary Barksted.
14 John Harris and Alice Banester.
16 Michaell Wandsfoord and Jane Waindright.
17 Jeffery Church and Margarett Beddosse.
18 George Johnson and Elizabeth Bing.
20 Oliff Richmond and Jane Archer.
24 James Huckle and Judith Singleton.
25 Thomas Osland and Jane Price.
26 John Cuttee and Dasee Jones.
28 Robert Lee and Jane Arnell.
May 2 Nicholas Carellis and Elizabeth Wickes.
5 Thomas Moore and Alice Blackabee.
5 William Thorpe and Joane Scarfe.
5 George Vaughan and Elizabeth Carrington.
16 Thomas Webb and Elizabeth Tompson.
17 Richard Eades and Barbara Powell.
17 Thomas Russon and Dorothie Loveland.
19 William Wiseman and Sarah Jackson.
21 John Oder and Ann Lambe.
22 Walter Latty and Mary Holte.
23 Jenkyn Kempe and Elizabeth Yockney.
23 Nicholas Rochford and Mary Yeat.
23 William Jolly and Martha Folley.
24 Thomas Stanthwaite and Elizabeth Pettibones.
24 Samuell French and Elizabeth Walker.
25 Henry Foster and Ann Alsopp.
June 2 Thomas Collyns and Susan Follye.
2 Francis Tidcome and Elizabeth Kingstone.
2 Richard Morley and Sarah Edwardes.
2 Leonard Hoockham and Margery Booth.
2 Richard Taylor and Dorothy Browne.
12 John Hince and Rebeccah Lenthall.
12 Thomas Lane and Elizabeth Snooke.
14 Phillipp Gery and Elizabeth Leaper.
15 Edward Trestean and Mary Hinman.
17 Charles Frye and Margarett Stronge.
19 James Pipes and Ellen Duffell.
21 William Prescott and Elizabeth Hawkyns.
23 Thomas Softley and Katherin Hudson.
23 John Whaley and Mary Mason.
23 Nicholas Thatcher and Ann Parsons.
27 Lancelott Robins and Jemima Hope.
30 Christopher Rose and Elizabeth South.
30 Bryan Dale and Dorothy Payley.
30 Thomas Neale and Debora Best.
July 3 John Moody and Mary Weeden.
4 James Porter and Ann Payler.
5 George Baxter and Mary Knowles.
7 Henry Wickham and Mary Warren.
7 Augustyne Weed and Mary James.

1659
July 10 James Cocom and Jone Cooke.
17 Josepth Cooke and Margarett Bradey.
18 William Ward and Mary Day.
19 John Alcott and Jane Vye.
19 William Yates and Jane Foster.
20 John Salace and Ann Goodwyn.
21 Symon Lloyd and Jone Sevill.
28 Thomas Lingard and Elizabeth Burnell.
28 William Sachwell and Ann Cranway.
28 William Whetley and Dorothy Punsonbey.
30 Francis Ronwell and Ellyn Munford.
Aug. 2 Richard Smyth and Sarah Gillinges.
3 Henry Pett and Martha Crabtree.
4 Thomas Moore and Katherin Gardiner.
9 Richard Lloyd and Elizabeth Colton.
14 Edward Sartyn and Mary Adkins.
16 Thomas Mell and Elizabeth Pale.
16 John Ruffin and Helyn Waters.
21 Thomas Grey and Elizabeth Spencer.
28 Robert Stanley and Ann Fookes.
30 William Haffecild and Dorcus Obee.
Sept. 5 Rubin Barker and Ann Haydon.
6 John Russell and Julyan Beadle.
7 George Briggs and Elizabeth White.
8 James Andrewes and Elizabeth Wyar.
8 John Poole and Rachell Masson.
8 Robert Birkitt and Susan Williams.
13 John Ayscagh and Susanna Ashburne.
19 Greegory Clement and Frances Sedley.
20 Rice Saunders and Elizabeth Grove.
22 Josepth Wheeler and Ann Cooper.
22 Benjamyn Wescom and Ann Wormewell.
24 Edmund Johnson and Alice Spurr.
25 William Rickabey and Jane Reade.
27 John Alcock and Ann Woodfall.
28 Nicholas Bartlett and Margarett Holliberry.
28 George James and Rebecca Cobham.
29 Andrew Tayler and Ellyn Williams.
Oct. 3 Edward Upton and Abigall King.
3 Richard Bragg and Ann Maynnard.
6 George Clifford and Elizabeth Price.
6 Richard Ryle and Elizabeth Holloway.
10 Robert Wilde and Ann Whetstone.
11 John Homes and Sybill Tompson.
11 Theoder Fenwick and Avis Banbury.
13 Richard Payne and Margarett Sedgwick.
13 William Sympson and Katherin Harvey.
14 George Stamper and Elizabeth Puttenham.
16 Richard Nottingham and Elizabeth Elderton.
16 Humphry Symmons and Margarett Cocker.
17 John Taylor and Elizabeth Bell.
17 Richard Earnley and Elizabeth Birt.
20 Richard Garrett and Sarah Block.
20 Edward Walker and Elizabeth Pickett.
20 Thomas Magson and Elizabeth Knight.
20 William Allyn and Elizabeth Hampher.
20 Henry Littlebury and Winifrid Cluffe.

1659
Oct. 25 John Luddington and Mary Luddington.
27 Edward Birch and Margaret Seaseley.
27 John Keating and Grace Shugburgh.
Nov. 1 Francis Sawyer and Jane Osbourne.
1 Richard Pollett and Alice Adcock.
1 John Thoroton and Mary Rowson.
6 Justinian Phipps and Sara Hull.
6 Thomas Bradshaw and Rebecca Perry.
10 Benjamyn Marriot and Martha Greene.
10 William Laurants and Margarett Siggins.
14 Robert Holmes and Dorcas Foster.
17 Ralfe Silverton and Martha Peake.
20 Roger Hopkins and Ann Roberts.
22 Benjamin Gurnell and Sarah Blyett.
22 William Sawkett and Deborah Doggett.
24 James Leving and Joanna Weekes.
Dec. 3 Robert Lettice and Frances Frale.
8 Peeter Kemsall and Mary Jordan.
11 Henry Spencer and Suzan Roberts.
15 Arise Jones and Judith Nicholls.
15 William Bridgges and Isabell Wake.
18 William Barker and Abigall Browne.
19 Phillipp Valentyne and Elizabeth Goodridg.
26 John Wiggins and Ann Johnson.
27 William Fosse and Frances Barnaby.
27 Thomas Jones and Ann Graine.
28 John Beamond and Sarah Martyn.
Jan. 1 William Hull and Emm Harman.
1 Marke Lawne and Joyce Garritt.
2 William Freeman and Alice Randall.
3 William Mawbey and Ann Huett.
5 Andrew Cooke and Jane Mosley.
7 James Wington and Mary Hawkyns.
8 Robert Punnock and Margaret Raner.
12 Dudley Mathew and Ann Ash.
15 Humpheric Barnes and Ann Cope.
16 John Cressey and Mary Bolter.
19 Andrew Thorne and Mary Sompner.
19 Richard Waters and Ann Robinson.
19 Francis Higginson and Elizabeth Rogers.
22 William Cooke and Ann Smyth.
24 Anthony Collett and Margery Greene.
25 Alexander Holbrooke and Suzan Vidler.
26 Richard Mundy and Mary Morgan.
29 George Parke and Ellynor Hill.
31 Ralph Clarke and Mary Cole.
Feb. 1 John Miles and Katherine Hunt.
2 Edward Parker and Alice Holland.
7 Thomas Bray and Mary Lee.
9 Henry Vaughan and Alice Moore.
21 Richard Hilliard and Mary Veron.
25 Bazill Moore and Ann Humble.
28 John Isaac and Elizabeth Watson.
Mar. 5 John Podell and Mary Copeland.
5 Rowland Simpson and Hannah Limburey.
6 Thomas Marshall and Ann Conesby.
18 William Neve and Elizabeth Purston.

1660 1660.

Mar. 26 [*blank*].
27 Stephen Naw and Ann Bennett.
29 Christopher Roper and Margaret Fitzmorris.
31 Henry Ashfeeild and Joane Slye.
April 5 William Kinsey and Elinor Kneebone.
17 Thomas Walley and Jone Farley.
23 William Coles and Ann Knowles.
23 John Payne and Ann Greene.
24 Robert Walkden and Mary Magdalen.
24 Ralph Brampton and Elizabeth Holloway.
25 Edward Clarke and Elizabeath Perkins.
26 Benjamyn Ladd and Mary Stanborn.
29* Jarvis Anslowe and Elizabeth Browne.
15 John Lucar and Mary Hurst.
May 1 Samuell Clay and Judith Greene.
1 Arthur Maber and Bddoe [*sic*].
1 Thomas Salter and Katherine Carter.
1 Edward Yallopp and Ann Crosse.
1 Thomas Frith and Sarah Hammon.
3 John Hansard and Mary Coulstock.
6 Richard Maydwell and Suzan Carswell.
14 Nathaniel Day and Nicholette Marre.
7 John Cordrey and Jone Phillipps.
24 William Mitchell and Mary Novell.
24 William Frith and Ann Hodgson.
27 William Dennis and Elizabeth Driver.
28 Henry Osborn and Mary Alford.
28 John Dalby and Martha Jaques.
31 Christopher Musgrave and Mary Cogan.
31 Cecill Tufton and Mary Lloyd.
June 3 Thomas Hones and Elizabeth Gould.
4 Charles Holmes and Ann Bowlter.
4 George Bradford and Dorothy Braner.
5 Richard Astrey and Mary Pert.
10 Bryan Thomas Orton and Thomasin Haynes.
12 William Bridgman and Ann Calthrope.
16 Richard Holgrave and Susan Stowers.
17 Henry Coney and Elizabeth Spicer.
17 Richard Gascott and Dorothy Rogers.
19 John Morrey and Elizabeth Boynes.
21 James Wilson and Mary Allyn.
26 William Ruskin and Mary Pew.
27 Francis Betts and Elizabeth Butcher.
26 Nicholas Ward and Martha Hale.
29 Christopher Tommas and Mary Pryer.
July 5† Thomas Woolson and Anne Newman.
10 John Fouller and Elizabeth Hewes.
13 John Salisbury and Jane Cowell.
13 Sir John Talbott and Barbera Slingsby.
15 Thomas Carter and Ann Wilkinson.
15 Marmaduke Iles and Mary Hayes.
17 William Parkham and Anna Maria Dobozy.

* This and several other entries on this page of the Register appear to have been interpolated.—ED.

† Repeated *infra*.—ED.

1660
July 5 Thomas Winter and Elizabeth Meare
5 Thomas Woolson and Anne Newman
20 Michaell Yong and Jone Hutchins
22 Richard Williams and Elizabeth Shorter
22 John Turner and Ellynor Phelpes
23 John Varnam and Ellen Pootth
24 Jeremy Blackman and Bridgett Wake
24 John Bentley and Jane Revell
25 Thomas Collyns and Elizabeth Wheeler
26 Ralph Cardiffe and Elizabeth Mabbes
29 Thomas Butterfeeild and Mary Wardner.
*29 Thomas Ball and Mary Forroll
30 William Lucas and Tabitha Gant
Aug 1 Norrys Fynes and Margarett Rayngs
6 Josepth Clarke and Jone Rowe
6 William Body and Precilla Adkyns
10 Richard Sanders and Jane Crewes
10 Humphrye Selwood and Ann Collyton
*13 John Salsbury and Joane Cowell
16 John Mew and Isabell Betteridg
16 Robert Evans and Elizabeth Gill
19 Josepth Lee and Elizabeth Dennys
20 Thomas Browne and Martha Man
23 Peter Salway and Matilda Blundell
26 Edmund Turner and Isabell Lapton
28 Edward Boswele and Margarett Calvert
30 Robert Goodwyn and Ann Hayes
Sept 2 Henry Avery and Ellyn Houlton
3 John Etheridg and Elizabeth Wisdom
6 Edmund Reade and Garthwrit Davis.
6 Robert Law and Amy Clare
6 George Ellis and Mary Freeman
6 Edward Wade and Mary Tippin
16 Randolph Emerson and Elizabeth Watts
20 William Maior and Elizabeth Erpe
23 John Bustian and Gwyn Watkyns
25 John Carter and Mary Balliard
30 Thomas Beckley and Ann Deakins
30 James Bastard and Ann Northam
Oct 1 Edward Lloyd and Frances Hales
13 James Camber and Hannah Harper
16 Henry Petit and Katherine Sterpin
23 Thomas Watkins and Jane Saunders
24 Peter Gunning and Elizabeth Estry
25 John Lewys and Jone Phillipps
25 James Staart and Mary Greene
30 Walter Croxton and Mary Maplesden
Nov. 1 Richard Wells and Mary Edmondes
1 Andrew Yateman and Mary Miles
3 William Boucee and Ann Tyndall.
4 Francis Allen and Frances Turner
5 Francis Smyth and Ann Palin
7 Marke Garrett and Jane Bankes.
11 Michaell Pack and Alice Exon
13 William Allen and Anna Legatt.

* Entry interpolated —ED.

1660
Nov. 13 Anthony Sadler and Hellen Tweyford.
13 Salomon Winch and Joan Weller.
15 Nicholas Potter and Margarett Jones.
17 George Denton and Hester Hutchins.
27 Josepth Thorbun and Jone Key.
Dec. 2 James Seddon and Alice Lawton.
2 Isaack Browne and Elizabeth Hinch.
3 Richard Onyons and Mary Hayman.
4 John Rothton and Ann Plummer.
4 Bartholomew Fowke and Katherine Vine.
6 James de Aillon and Marthe de Cartigney.
12 Edward Sutton and Sarah Higdon.
13 Edward Barnes and Jane Collinwood.
16 George Hedges and Rachell Bent.
23 Robert Smyth and Ann Luckas.
24 Sir William Beetcher and Elizabeth Hillarsden.
25 Thomas Price and Sarah Stansbee.
27 Roger Dubbleday and Ann Duckett.
27 Edward Richman and Mary Darnell.
30 William Ancell and Percilla Barker.
Jan. 1 William Mannell and Alice Mills.
3 Thomas Searin and Elizabeth Chanler.
4 John Bastine and Mary Williams.
8 John Chamberlaine and Margaret Lloyd.
13 Humphery Norman and Alice Jones.
16 John Darsden and Elizabeth Pritchard.
17 Thomas Parrett and Mary Causby.
21 John Hartry and May Bee.
22 Samuell Cotton and Mary Pavett.
23 John Morley and Mary Wilmott.
27 Alexander Adams and Katherin Saunder.
31 John Stiles and Dorothy Ashly.

The Marriages in Vol. B. end here, but the following single entry occurs on a loose sheet of parchment pinned to the last page of the Marriages :—

1684 June 9 Nathaniel Rider and Anne Bard.

St. Peter, Paul's Wharf.

Book C. has Burials only; Book D., a long narrow book (16 ins. by 7½ ins.), with twenty-five paper pages, is evidently the Day Book. With the exception of a register of Births, which has been collated with the register of Baptisms, and the following Marriages, it has only entries of Burials in woollen, which have also been collated with the Burials in Book C.

MARRIAGES IN BOOK D.

1698.

Aug. 24 Nicholas Normond . . . . boo man married.
Nov. 27 Henary Man, labourer, and Eliz. Freman, both of St Peters.

1699.

June 1 Richard Sedden, seaman, and Anne Brockway, both of this parish.
28 William Harrison, waterman of St Peter's, and Mary Jues [? Ives] of St Anne, Blackfryers.
Nov. 26 James Homes, B., weebster, and Mary Gutteridg, both of this parish, mar. at St Bennett, Pauls Wharfe. Banns. "See St Benet book A, 1699."

1700.

May 28 James Weekes, B. and collermaker, and Elizabeth Burstow, both of this parish, on St Peter's Hill near Theames Street, married at St Bennett, Pauls Wharfe.

1701.

May 13* Mark Frost, W. and baker of this parish over against the Katherin wheel in Theames Street, and Bridget Meddowes of St Mary, Whit Chappel, married at St Olave, Southwark.
19 Nevel Simmond, B. and printer at sine of too Brewers at the corner of St Peter Hill in Theames Street, and Alce Doman of St Saviour, Southwark, married at St Saviour, Southwark.
Feb. 14 John Baker, B. and Silk Dyer in Black Boy Alle in Theames Street, and Tabitha Jonson of St Mary Sumaset.

1704.

June 29 George Holden, B. and late sarving man to the Duke of Ormond, and Jane Hawkins, both of this parish.
Feb. 6 Richard Box, B. and faryer of this parish in Theames Street, and Susanna Barnett of St Bennett, Pauls Wharfe. Banns. (See St Benets, Book A. 1704.)

End of Marriages in Book D.

* Date altered from April 13th.—ED.

In a thin book of printed forms marked at the back, "S. P. 1828-1834 marriages," and on the side, "St Peter" marriages, are the following three entries, the remainder of the book being blank.

1828.

Dec. 15 Thomas Martin of this parish, B., and Hannah Pope of the same, S. Witnesses: Felicia Turner, Tim. J. Smith. Married by W. J. Hall, M.A., Curate. Banns.

1834.

Nov. 15 Reginald Easton of this parish, B., and Julia Tatum of the same, S. Witnesses: Alfred Easton, Clara Tatum, John Easton. Married by W. J. Hall, M.A., Curate. Lic.

Dec. 27 John Easton of this parish, B., and Clara Sophia Tatum of the same, S. Witnesses: Reginald Easton, Julia Easton. Married by W. J. Hall, M.A., Curate. Lic.

END OF VOLUME III.

INDEX NOMINUM.

An asterisk (*) indicates that the name occurs more than once on the page.

A

Abbis (Abbiss), Ann, 302; Robert, 162, 302; Sarah, 162.
Abbot (Abbut), Ann, 59, 147, 182; Hannah, 47; John, 47, 182; Sarah, 100.
Abbots, Alice, 272.
Abdy, Millicent, 219.
Abell, Abraham, 1; Eleanor, 286; Elizabeth, 1.
Abercrombie, Sarah, 75; William, 75.
Abraham, Ann, 286; Edward, 212, 207; Martha, 207; Mary, 110; William, 286.
Absalom, Elizabeth, 247; William, 247.
Abson, Sarah, 137; William, 137.
Achison, James, 101; Mary, 101.
Acland (Ackland), Charles, 230; Elizabeth, 141, 230.
Acors, Hannah, 181; John, 181.
Acton, Ann, 156; Edward, 156; Martha, 10; Richard, 50; Sarah, 50.
Adams (Adames, Addames, Addams, Adems), Abraham, 101; Alexander, 314; Ann, 31, 55, 110, 111, 172; Betty, 139; Diana, 73; Dorothy, 42, 273; Edward, 11, 192; Elizabeth, 23, 120, 138; George, 169; Hester, 234; Humphrey, 31; Rev. James, 214*, 216; Jane, 169; John, 100, 237, 265; Katherine, 294, 314; Kerenhappuch, 140; Letitia, 11, 50; Mary, 40, 46, 153, 162, 192, 236; Nancy, 224; Peter, 40; Richard, 42; Robert, 73, 162; R., 236; Sarah, 4, 101, 116; Shute, 140; Susan, 285, 297; Susanna, 100, 237; Thomas, 224; Ursula, 265; William, 110, 153, 172, 285, 294, 297.
Adamson, Ann, 205; John, 243, 245; Robert, 205; Sarah, 243, 245.
Adcock, Alice, 311; Elizabeth, 160; Mary, 126, 298; Thomas, 126.
Addames, **Addams**, *see* Adams.
Addington, John, 279; Magdalen, 279.
Addis, Henry, 94; Susanna, 94.
A'Dean, James, 171; Mary, 171.
Adems, *see* Adams.
Adgoe, Mary, 308.
Adkins (Adykins), Mary, 310; Precilla, 313.
Adkinson, Edmund, 287; Elizabeth, 287.
Adlam, Sarah, 168.
Adlingtoune, Ann, 267; William, 267.
Adnett, Ann, 160; William, 160.
Adson, Philippa, 2.
Adworth, Meriall, 298.
Adye, Susanna, 103.
Aeiry, Elizabeth, 185.
Affleck, Ann, 103; James, 103.
Agar, Edward, 113; Elizabeth, 113.
Agasse (Agace, Agas), Alsse, 265; Elizabeth, 83; Henry, 83; Leah, 12; William, 265.
Agborough, Eleanor, 308.
Agge, Ann, 285; Stephen, 285.
Agnew, Catherine, 45; James, 45.
Ahlam, Christopher, 219; Mary, 219.
Aingworth, James, 217.
Ainsworth (Answorth), Ann, 63; Elizabeth, 86; Samuel, 63.
Aiskell, Ann, 111.
Aiton, Mary, 108; Robert, 108.
Akam, Edward, 252; Joseph, 221; Samuel, 252; Sarah, 221, 252.
Akers, Elizabeth, 294; Mary, 152; Richard, 294; Thomas, 152.
Akid, Mary Cole, 238.
Albery, Joan, 301.
Alchorne (Alcharne), Elizabeth, 266, 267; Mary, 86.
Alcock (Allcock), Ann, 310; George, 188; John, 310; Mary, 173, 188; William, 255.
Alcott, Jane, 310; John, 310.
Alden (Aldin), Elizabeth, 202; Katherine, 301; Mary, 297; Thomas, 297.
Alder, Mary, 143.
Alderman, Beatrice, 121; John, 121.
Alders, Dorothy, 46; Gabriel, 46.
Alderton, Ann, 43; Joel, 43.
Aldin, *see* Alden.
Aldridge (Aldrich, Aldridg, Alldridge), Abel, 57; Anna Maria, 53; Ann, 258; Elizabeth, 17; Hannah, 278; Hester, 298; James, 258; John, 53, 298; Richard, 291; Robert, 17; Sarah, 57, 128; William, 128, 258.
Aldwin, Martha, 10.
Alesbery, Sarah, 53.
Alexander (Allexander), Alexander, 140; Cordelia, 193; Elizabeth, 199, 292; Grace, 177; Hannah, 171; Hester, 55; Isabella, 140; Jane, 124; Mark, 292; Martin, 258; Mary, 186; William, 186.
Alford, Ann, 259; Elizabeth, 53; James, 256*, 257, 258*, 260*, 261*, 262*; John, 259; J., 262; Mary, 312; Sarah, 257, 259; Sarah Ann, 259; William Sackville, 262; W. S., 262.
Alkyn, Elizabeth, 307.
Allanson, Michael, 194; Sarah, 194.
Allatt, Mary, 38; Parker, 38.
Allchin, Sarah, 116; William, 116.
Allcock, *see* Alcock.
Alldersone, Elizabeth, 271; Richard, 271.
Alldridge, *see* Aldridge.
Allen (Aleyn, Alin, Alleen, Allin, Alline, Allyn), Alice, 27, 293; Anna, 313; Anne, 20, 24, 71*, 130, 220, 286, 289, 301; Benjamin, 193; Benn, 187; Catherine, 303; Daniel, 224, 228; Deborah, 295; Dorothy, 26; Eli-

B

Bayeux, Ann, 115; Mary, 129.
Bayford, Mary, 11; Samuel, 11.
Baylesfoord, Rachael, 305; Richard, 305.
Bayley (Baylie, Baylye), *see* Bailey.
Bayliss (Baylis), Eleanor, 150, 161; Robert, 161; Thomas, 150.
Baynard, John, 61; Mary, 61.
Bayne, Ann, 100.
Baynes (Baines, Banes), Alice, 59, 267, 270; Arthur, 198; Catherine, 279; Dorothea, 3; Elizabeth, 225; James, 97; John, 267, 270; Judith, 198; Lucy, 13; Martha, 25; Rachael, 97; Richard, 13; Thomas, 59.
Baynham, Richard Rowden, 174; Sophia, 174.
Baynton, Edward, 283*; Elizabeth, 14; Frances, 26; Josias, 14; Mary, 283*; Robert, 26, 283.
Bayte, *see* Bate.
Bazson, Mary, 82.
Bddoe, —, 312.
Beach, *see* Beech.
Beacham (Beecham), James, 40; Joseph, 225; Mary, 40.
Beachcroft, Rev. Mr., occurs from 47 to 89.
Beade, Joseph, 273; Mary, 273.
Beadle, *see* Bedell.
Beake (Beek), Sarah, 151; Rebecca 165.
Beakley, Margaret, 102; William, 102.
Beale, Anne, 129; Barbara, 300; Eleanor, 159; Elizabeth, 158, 293; Grace, 141; Isaac, 159; James, 59; Joanna, 59; John, 158; Judith, 74; Katherine, 296; Margaret, 298; Richard, 77, 129; Sarah, 77, 177, 293; Symon, 298; Thomas, 300.
Beales (Beilles), Elizabeth, 13; Mary, 94; William, 94.
Bealey, Elizabeth, 144.
Bealing, Benjamin, 70; Elizabeth, 70.
Beaman, Bridget, 70; Elizabeth, 169; John, 70; William, 169.
Beamish, Charles, 225; Mary, 225; Susanna, 128; William, 128.
Beamont, *see* Beaumont.
Bean, Margaret, 39; Thomas, 39.
Beanmont, Damaris, 289.
Bearcroft, Arabella, 24.
Beard, Elizabeth, 92; James, 282; Mary, 232; Richard, 92; William, 261.
Beardshaw, John, 125; Mary, 125.
Beardsley, Ann, 294; Mary, 292; Robert, 294.
Beare, George, 299; Grizel, 299; Mary, 270.
Beart, Thomas, 227.
Beast (Beest), John, 273; Mary, 90, 273.
Beauchamp, Elizabeth, 138; Mary, 85, 178; Robert, 138.
Beaumont (Beamont, Beaumond), Alice, 296; Benjamin, 235; John, 296, 311; Sarah, 22, 141, 235, 311.
Beaver, Elizabeth, 168.
Beazer, Susanna, 9.
Beazley (Beezly), Margaret, 171; Sarah, 151.
Bebb, Elizabeth, 193.
Bebbington, E., 249.
Beck, Elizabeth, 148, 152; Katherine, 200; Joshua, 148; Mary, 37, 175; Rachael, 9; Roger, 110, 200; Sarah, 110.
Beckcomb, Mary, 284.
Beckett, Ann, 43, 117; Elizabeth, 115, 277; Esther, 127; Martin, 277; Mary, 21; Thomas, 21; William, 43, 115.
Beckley, Ann, 313; Thomas, 313.
Beckwith, Elizabeth, 70.
Beckworth, Elizabeth, 137.
Bedder, Dorothy, 99.
Beddosse, Margaret, 309.
Bedell (Beadle, Beedell), Frances, 301; John, 232; Julyan, 310; Mary, 171; Rosanna, 232.
Bedford, Elizabeth, 127; Ellen, 279; Dinah, 192; Hanuah, 65; Henry, 206; Joshua, 214; Martha, 214; Mary, 206; Matthew, 192.
Bedingfield, Sarah, 90.
Bedwell, Mary, 67.
Bee, Harriet, 251; Jane, 249; Mary, 251, 314.
Beech (Beach), Ann, 284; Anthony, 203; Elizabeth, 130; Esther, 203; James, 132; Jane, 98; John, 39, 165; Joseph, 3; Margaret, 132; Martha, 3; Mary, 39, 165; Thomas, 130, 284; William, 98.
Beecher (Beetcher), Elizabeth, 314; Sir William, 314.
Beedan, Catherine, 281; Thomas, 281.
Beedell, *see* Bedell.
Beedells, Mary, 25.
Beek, *see* Beake.
Beeson, George, 297; Katherine, 297.
Beest, *see* Beast.
Beete, Jane, 20; Joseph, 20.
Beetes (Beets), Elizabeth, 275, 275*n*., 277.
Beetham, Elizabeth, 184.
Beevor, Catherine, 30; Henry, 30.
Beezly, *see* Beazley.
Beezon, Ann, 113.
Beilles, *see* Beales.
Belbin, Caroline, 261.
Belch, Amy, 26; Thomas, 26.
Belchcoben, Sarah, 120.
Belcher (Belchier), Anne, 273; Elizabeth, 42; Samuel, 42; Sarah, 71; Nicholas, 273.
Belfour (Bellfoure), Caroline, 140; John, 140; Michael, 273; Susan, 273.
Belitha, Hannah, 198.
Bell, Agnes, 136; Alexander, 142; Ann, 68, 123, 137; Catherine, 61, 192; Dorothy, 23; Elizabeth, 8, 64, 66, 199*, 217, 310; Helen, 268; Henry, 27; Humphrey, 268; Isabella, 117; John, 64, 102, 217; Margaret, 20; Martha, 7, 87; Mary, 23, 27, 79, 93, 208, 284, 290; Michael, 199; Peter, 236; Philip Henry, 20; Priscilla, 122; Robert, 7, 122, 137; Sarah, 102, 142; Stephen, 136; Susanna, 73; Thomas, 61, 79; Tibal, 87; William, 73, 93, 199, 208.
Bellamy, Daniel, 11; Eleanor, 11.
Belldom, Mary, 77.
Belles, Ann, 92.
Bellin, Ann, 240; John, 240.
Bellinger, Ann, 294.
Bellington, Elizabeth, 244.
Bellman, John, 4; Judith, 4.
Bellow, Elizabeth, 92.
Belson, Anne, 204.
Bence, Abraham, 201; Susanna, 201.
Bendall, Elizabeth, 167; William, 167.
Bender, John, 252.
Benfeyld, Mary, 271; Robert, 271.
Benge, Catherine, 299.
Bengerfield, Rebecca, 165.
Benham, Edward, 171; Johanna, 171; Robert, 234.
Benione, Margaret, 276.
Benn, Margaret, 91.
Bennett (Benett, Bennet), Ann, 16, 51, 74, 152, 312; Anthony, 265; Bridget, 41; Cary, 87; Catherine, 205; Dinah, 26; Eleanor,

288 ; Elizabeth, 74, 92, 157, 252, 265, 289, 295 ; Emm, 74 ; Francis, 74 ; Jacob, 276 ; James, 57, 157, 188, 242 ; Jane, 205, 254, 283 ; Jonathan, 242 ; John, 74, 92, 172, 209 ; Martha, 37 ; Mary, 15, 57, 176, 188, 242 ; Nicholas, 289 ; Peter, 62 ; Priscilla, 62 ; Rev. F. G., 222 ; Rev. J. T., 261*, 262* ; Rev. Richard Hannot, 211*, 214, 215 ; Richard, 254 ; Robert, 205 ; Samuel, 16 ; Sarah, 162, 172, 209, 276 ; Thomas, 87, 257 ; William, 152, 205 ; Rev. Mr., 192*, 193.*
Benning, Francis, 279 ; Johanna, 279.
Benson, Ann, 97 ; Catherine, 5 ; Elizabeth, 69, 71 ; John, 5, 71 ; Joseph, 71 ; Mary, 19, 71, 79, 287 ; Richard, 19.
Bent, Ann, 298 ; Elizabeth, 240 ; James, 238 ; Magdalen, 8 ; Mary, 101 ; Rachael, 314.
Bentinck, Lord George, 208 ; Lady Mary, 208.
Bentley (Bently), Ann, 95 ; Edward, 23 ; Jane, 163, 313 ; John, 313 ; Mary, 23, 215.
Benton, Edward, 190 ; Mary, 190 ; Sarah, 76, 187.
Berkeley (Barkley, Bearkley), Ann, 153 ; Catherine, 43 ; Elizabeth, 156 ; Hannah, 63 ; Jane, 124 ; John, 156 ; Rowland, 153.
Berland, Anne, 38 ; Paul, 38.
Berley, *see* Burleigh.
Bermingham, Mary, 24 ; Thomas, 24.
Bernard, Bartholomew, 123 ; Elizabeth, 123, 299 ; Frederick, 186 ; James, 190, 256 ; John, 299 ; Magdalen, 186 ; Mary, 177, 186, 190 ; Susanna, 53.
Berner, Lucy, 233.
Berridge, Lydia, 122 ; Thomas, 122.
Berrisford, Alice, 292.
Berron, Rev. Mr., 152, 162.*
Berry, Amy, 292 ; Ann, 191, 290 ; Catherine, 11 ; Elizabeth, 164, 201, 268 ; Grace, 85 ; John, 201 ; Margaret, 64 ; Mary, 41, 125, 193 ; Rebecca, 235 ; Sarah, 3 ; William, 243, 268.
Bertell, William, 220.
Bertie, Elizabeth, 76 ; Peregrine, 76.
Bertrand, Mary, 16.
Besgrove, Ann, 38.
Besley, Isaac, 177 ; Joane, 288 ; Mary, 177 ; Nicholas, 288.
Best, Ann, 254 ; Arthur, 125 ; Deborah, 309 ; Elizabeth, 153, 183 ; Francis, 35 ; John, 132 ; Mary, 125, 132 ; Sarah, 35 ; Thomas, 254 ; Ursula, 309 ; Rev. Dr., 41, 48*, 70, 94, 121.
Beswell, Elizabeth, 79 ; James, 79.
Beswick, Elizabeth, 98 ; John, 49 ; Silence, 49.
Bethell, Elizabeth, 118, 226 ; Mary, 183 ; Thomas, 183 ; William, 226.
Bethwin, Grace, 21.
Bettenham, Charles, 194 ; Elizabeth, 194.
Bettensonne, Ann, 268.
Betteridg, Isabel, 313.
Bettew, Elizabeth, 16.
Betton, Susanna, 124.
Betts, Ann, 290 ; Elizabeth, 286, 312 ; Francis, 312 ; Joseph, 25 ; Mary, 149, 241 ; Sarah, 25 ; Thomas, 286.
Bettsworth, Ann, 228 ; Elizabeth, 152 ; Mary, 92, 202 ; William, 152, 202.
Betty, Jane, 23.
Beucon, Alice, 296.
Bevan (Beven), Ann, 85, 194 ; Elizabeth, 281 ; Rowland, 281 ; Sarah, 11 ; Thomas, 11.
Bevens, Mary, 156.
Beverey, Ann, 267.
Beveridge, John, 230 ; Mary, 230.
Beverley (Beverlee), Ann, 22 ; Elizabeth, 308 ; John, 308 ; Lucy, 288 ; Robert, 22 ; William, 288.
Beverscombe, Ambrose, 289 ; Mary, 289.
Bevis, Hannah, 161 ; Robert, 161.
Bew, Ann, 196.
Bewley, Ann, 236 ; Jane, 236.
Beyellin, Edward, 56 ; Mary, 56.
Bialy, Jane, 287 ; Richard, 287.
Bibben, Elizabeth, 199.
Biby, Catherine, 58.
Bick, Edmund, 232.
Bickerton, Charles, 34 ; Jane, 11 ; John, 123 ; Mary, 123 ; Sarah, 34.
Bickford, Mary, 170.
Bickham, Sarah, 133 ; Thomas, 133.
Bickley, George, 137 ; Jane, 137.
Bickseall, Mary, 189.
Biddelcome, Elizabeth, 12 ; William, 12.
Biddle (Biddell), Ann, 75 ; Bliss, 173 ; Catherine, 75 ; Elizabeth, 306 ; Martha, 61 ; Richard, 156 ; Sarah, 156, 192 ; Thomas, 306 ; William, 75.
Biford, Elizabeth, 97 ; John, 97.
Bigan, Joan, 290.
Bigge (Bigg), Anne, 62, 235, 269 ; Bartholomew, 165 ; Elizabeth, 165, 302 ; Johan, 276 ; John, 62, 276, 302 ; Susan, 296.
Biggs (Byggs), Charles, 212 ; Elizabeth, 171, 206 ; Henry, 69 ; John, 206 ; Margaret, 39 ; Mary, 18, 58, 211, 227, 265 ; Matthew, 171 ; Susanna, 69.
Bigland, Charlotte Mary, 255 ; Gr. Richard, 238 ; Ralph, Norroy King of Arms, 255 ; Ralph, 238 ; Rose, 255.
Bignall (Bignell, Bignoll), Ann, 183 ; James, 226 ; Margaret, 38 ; Mary, 271 ; William, 38, 183.
Bigsby, Abigail, 8 ; Nelson, 8.
Billby (Bilby), Margaret, 171 ; Roger, 156, 171 ; Sarah, 156.
Billings, Emanuel, 291 ; Mary, 291.
Billington, Mary, 181.
Bilson, Eleanor, 121.
Bilton (Billton), Andrew, 234* ; Elizabeth, 190, 239 ; Joseph, 190.
Binder, Elizabeth, 93 ; Martha, 58 ; Thomas, 93.
Bineham, Ann, 254.
Binfield, Martha, 171 ; Robert, 171 ; William, 243.
Binford, Elizabeth, 101 ; William, 101.
Bing, *see* Byng.
Bingham, Edward, 106 ; Eleanor, 82 ; Elizabeth, 106 ; Leonora, 129 ; Robert, 153 ; Sarah, 153 ; William, 82.
Bingles, Arthur, 283 ; Sarah, 283.
Bingley, Dorothy, 208 ; Elizabeth, 46 ; John, 208 ; Mary, 298 ; Matthew, 138 ; Sarah, 138 ; William, 46.
Binks (Bincks), Elizabeth, 87 ; Susanna, 291 ; Thomas, 291.
Binney, Ann, 36.
Binon, Hannah, 76 ; Thomas, 76.
Birbeck, Margaret, 17.
Birch, *see* Burch.
Birchmore, *see* Burchmore.
Bird, Ambrose, 264 ; Anne, 132, 158, 289 ; Cicely, 278 ; Dorcas, 268 ; Edward, 132 ; Elizabeth, 28, 66, 92, 149 ; Frances, 109 ; Hannah, 79, 179 ; Jane, 91 ; John, 92 ; Lydia, 179 ; Martin, 117, 179 ; Mary, 7, 117, 135 ; Mary Phebe, 254 ; Parnell, 264 ; Roger, 268 ; Samuel Joseph, 254 ; Sarah, 57, 208, 291 ; Thomas, 66 ; Walter, 278 ; William, 109.

Birdwhissell, Isaac, 88; Sophia, 88.
Bire, Mary, 185.
Birkett (Burkitt), Charles, 133; Elizabeth, 133; Margaret, 30; Robert, 310; Susan, 310.
Birks, Ann, 50; John, 50; Mary, 54; Robert, 54.
Birkwood, J., 239, 244; Rebecca, 229, 239; William, 229, 239.
Birrlls, Jane, 265.
Birt, *see* Burt.
Birwnrigg, Eleanor, 288; Samuel, 288.
Bisenden, Jane, 23; Thomas, 23.
Bish, Martha, 305.
Bishop (Bishopp, Büshop), Abigail, 292; Amy, 51; Ann, 54, 76, 183, 242, 306*; Deborah, 35; Edward, 149; Elizabeth, 92, 105, 289, 292, 308; Frances, 292; Henry, 6; Joan, 198; John, 183, 198, 216, 217; Maria, 76; Martha, 93; Mary, 6, 149, 217, 254; Sarah, 109, 194; Susan, 297; Susanna, 1; Thomas, 297; William, 51, 308.
Bisse (Biss), Mary, 159; Samuel, 159; Rev. Mr., 52*, 57.*
Bissell, Mary, 83.
Biston, Margaret, 15.
Biszaker, Dorothy, 284; John, 284.
Bithell, Mary, 200; William, 200.
Bitton, John Claudius, 67; Marianne, 67.
Black (Blacke), Abigail, 157; Isabella, 155; James, 157; Joshua, 270; Priscilla, 270; Robert, 216; William, 155.
Blackabee, Alice, 293, 309; Edward, 293.
Blackburn (Blackbourn), Ann, 94; Elizabeth, 17; Esther, 5; Frances, 129; Ralph, 5; Sarah, 50; Quince, 94; Susan, 264; William, 264.
Blackett, Edward, 1; Margaret, 1; William, 239.
Blackfell, Jane, 294.
Blackford, John, 151; Mary, 151.
Blackham, Letitia, 82.
Blacklook, Elizabeth, 95.
Blackman, Bridget, 313; James, 240; Jeremy, 313; Sarah, 240.
Blackmore (Blackmurre), Grace, 287; Richard, 257.
Blacknell, Margaret, 144.
Blackshaw, Frances, 11.
Blackwaye, Ellen, 269.
Blackwell, Ann, 157, 197; Elizabeth, 119; Joseph, 157; Mary, 16; William, 197.
Bladen, Ann, 23.
Blagrave, Charles, 156; Hannah, 156.
Blagrove, Elizabeth, 13; Robert, 13.
Blair, Sarah, 161.
Blake, Alles, 264; Ann, 236; Archer, 219; Bridget, 61; Elizabeth, 89, 184, 293; James, 188; Jane, 188; John, 89, 90, 216, 293; Margaretta, 287; Mary, 216; Phillis, 219; Robert, 236; Sarah, 90; William, 264.
Blakes, Rebecca, 143; William, 143.
Blamyre, Ann, 164; Mary, 161.
Blanch (Blaunche), Charles, 201; Elizabeth, 201; Katherine, 264.
Blanchard, Mary, 34.
Blancken, Elizabeth, 242; Lutye, 242.
Bland, Ann, 22, 181; Elizabeth, 160; James, 22; Michael, 61; Patience, 61; Sarah, 194; Susanna, 25, 73; William, 160.
Blandy (Blandye), Ann, 118; Elizabeth, 17; Katherine, 296.
Blanks, John, 74; Mary, 74.
Blastock (Blasstock), Esther, 104; Mary, 128.
Blatch, Henry, 257; Martha, 257.
Blaunche, *see* Blanch.
Blease, Catherine, 18.
Bleathman, Benjamin, 100; Mary, 100.
Blech, Margaret, 287.
Bleke, Jane, 239.
Blencow (Blencoe, Blincowe), Dorothy, 290; Elizabeth, 47; Jane, 305; William, 290, 305.
Blenkinsopp, Margaret, 64.
Bletso, Elizabeth, 116.
Blew, Sarah, 284.
Blinckhorn (Blinkarne), Catherine, 206; Sarah, 123.
Blincoe, Blincowe, *see* Blencow.
Blinston, Elizabeth, 61, 77; John, 61.
Bliss, Ann, 285; Jane, 94; Richard, 259.
Blissett, Elizabeth, 8, 82, 307.
Blizzard (Blizard), Ann, 135; Susanna, 108.
Block, Sarah, 310.
Blondell, Ann, 32, 161; John, 80; Susanna, 80; William, 32.
Bloome (Bloume), Judith, 302; Susan, 72.
Bloor, James, 215; Susanna, 215.
Blowen, Ann, 73.
Blower, John, 22; Sarah, 22, 220.
Bloxham, Ann Jane, 257; Charles Randell, 240, 257; Elizabeth Catherine, 240; Sarah, 259.
Bludworth, Ann, 284; Elizabeth, 300.
Bluett, Susan, 41.
Blundell, Ann, 37; Margaret, 302; Matilda, 313; Mildred Stevenson, 135.
Blunden, William, 255.
Blunt, Jane, 273; Joseph, 229; Sarah, 4, 218; William, 273.
Bly, Sarah, 96.
Blyett, Sarah, 311.
Blyth, Mary, 228; Thomas, 228.
Boaird, Margaret, 221.
Boan, Lucy, 154.
Boar, *see* Boore.
Boarum, Sarah, 85.
Boase, Ann, 284.
Boatswain, Elizabeth, 58; Thomas, 58.
Bocksell, Sarah, 101.
Bocock, Elizabeth, 131; James, 131.
Bodde, Sarah, 265.
Boddilow, Frances, 274.
Boddington (Bodinton), Edmund, 99; Elizabeth, 99; George, 287; Philippa, 287.
Bodhame, Elizabeth, 270.
Bodicoat (Bodicoate), James, 139; Martha, 143; Mary, 139.
Bodley (Bodle), Mary, 207, 306; Samuel, 306.
Body, Martha, 19; Mary, 62; Priscilla, 313; William, 19, 313.
Boffly, Elizabeth, 12; William, 12.
Boffree, Charles, 212; Elizabeth, 212.
Boggis, Elizabeth, 232; Joseph Allen, 232.
Boiton, Mary, 158.
Bolas, Catherine, 77; Thomas, 77.
Bold, Bridget, 102.
Bolden, Ann, 261; Furnell, 261; Harriet Emma, 261; Helen, 261.
Boldrow, Elizabeth, 54.
Boles, *see* Bowles.
Bolland, Ann, 100; Elizabeth, 114; Joseph, 100; Thomas, 114.
Bolney, Mary, 161; Thomas, 161.
Bolsford, Sarah, 153.
Bolt (Boult), Ann, 297; Elizabeth, 17, 212; John, 281, 297; Margaret, 281; Mary, 265; Richard, 212; Susanna, 228; Thomas, 265.

C

119 ; Mary Frances Elizabeth, 256 ; Rev. Mr., 132*, 172, 195.
Campe. Elizabeth, 231 ; Joan, 284 ; John, 284 ; Joseph, 231.
Camper, Ann, 34 ; Edmund, 34 ; James, 139 ; Sarah, 139.
Campin, Mary, 196.
Campion, Jane, 97.
Candler, Alice, 308 ; Thomas, 308.
Candy, Susanna. 31 ; Thomas. 31.
Cane (Cain. Kane), Mary, 155. 156, 299.
Canham, Henry, 122 ; Mary, 122.
Cann, John, 256 ; Mary, 256* ; William, 256.
Cannaway. Alice, 130 ; Mary, 85 ; Robert, 130.
Cannell, Mary, 57.
Cannon (Cannan), Elizabeth, 187 ; Frances, 13 ; Mary, 153 ; Patrick, 69 ; Samuel. 253 ; Susanna, 69.
Cannon *alias* Weeks, *see* Weeks *alias* Cannon.
Cannum. Elizabeth. 198 ; James, 199 ; Mary. 199.
Canter, Frances. 277 ; Thomas, 277.
Cantrell (Cantrill), Jane, 147 ; John, 147 ; Mary, 47 ; William, 47.
Canwell, Elizabeth, 241 ; James, 241.
Capes, Elizabeth, 299.
Caplin, Catherine, 279 ; John, 279.
Capon, Sarah, 159.
Capper, Anne, 285 ; Avice, 127.
Capps, Elizabeth, 126 ; John, 126.
Capstack, James, 65 ; Sarah, 65.
Carbarey, Sarah, 228.
Card, Susanna, 59 ; Thomas, 59.
Carden, Ann, 254 ; Benjamin, 253 ; Isabella, 79 ; James, 254 ; Judith, 207 ; Rosamond, 254 ; William, 254.
Cardery, Benjamin, 236.
Cardiffe, Elizabeth, 313 ; Ralph, 313.
Cardman, Martha, 102.
Cardonnell, Charlotte, 33.
Care, Isabel, 287.
Careless, Carelesse, *see* Carless.
Carellis, Elizabeth, 309 ; Nicholas, 309.
Carellton, Carelton, *see* Carlton.
Carey (Cary), Ann, 238 ; Elizabeth, 62 ; Frances, 309 ; George, 220 ; James, 238 ; Mary, 155, 220 ; Sarah, 211 ; Thomas, 249*, 252.
Caridus, Phillis, 99.
Caring, Dorothy, 285.
Caripell, Elizabeth, 64.
Carkett, Mary, 240 ; Minard, 240.
Carless (Careless, Carlesse, Carloss), Ann, 266, 267 ; Augustine, 52, 160 ; Elizabeth, 52, 160 ; Frideswade, 135 ; Jane, 264 ; John, 266, 267 ; Robert, 135.
Carlle, Martha, 269.
Carloss, *see* Carless.
Carltou (Carelltone, Carelton, Carleton), Barbara. 57 ; Elizabeth, 50, 244, 294 ; Jane, 266, 267 ; Mary, 151 ; Thomas, 50, 294.
Carlyle. Joseph, 53 ; Sarah, 53.
Carpenter, Edward, 238, 287 ; Eleanor, 52 ; Elizabeth, 117 ; Henry, 117 ; Joan, 287 ; John, 279 ; Margaret, 279 ; Mary, 298 ; Susanna, 25 ; Thomas, 52 ; William, 220.
Carr, Abigail, 249 ; Ann, 179 ; Catherine, 184 ; Christian, 23 ; Daniel, 256 ; Dorothy, 105, 110 ; Elizabeth, 32, 71, 178, 200, 291, 301 ; Francis, 23 ; Jane, 160 ; Joseph, 110, 249 ; Martin, 200 ; Richard, 204 ; Rev. Robert, 71 ; Robert, 291 ; Susanna, 204.
Carrell, *see* Carroll.
Carrett, Ann, 237 ; John, 237.
Carrew, George, 50 ; Martha, 50.
Carrig, Margaret, 145.
Carrington, Ann, 252 ; Elizabeth, 309 ; Henry, 252.
Carroll (Carrell, Carrolle), Alice, 51 ; Ann, 215 ; Blanch, 271 ; Charles, 271 ; John, 215 ; Margaret, 17.
Carroway, Jeremiah, 178 ; Mary, 178.
Carson. Mary, 91 ; William, 91.
Carswell, Susan, 312.
Carter, Andrew, 293 ; Ann, 80, 88, 109, 157, 312 ; Beatrice, 268 ; Benjamin, 32 ; Carah, 196 ; Catherine, 63, 280 ; Charles, 153 ; Dorothy, 211 ; Elizabeth. 15, 17, 41, 119, 121, 166 ; George. 33 ; Helen, 281 ; Henry, 160 ; Jane, 32, 44, 78 ; John. 27, 104, 313 ; Joyce, 233 ; Katherine, 312 ; Margaret, 38, 73 ; Martha, 73, 99 ; Mary, 33, 104, 166, 176, 212, 241, 305, 313 ; Moses, 121 ; Naomi, 293 ; Philadelphia, 56 ; Rebecca, 27, 207, 241 ; Richard, 41, 109 ; Robert, 88, 211, 241 ; Samuel, 73 ; Sarah, 2, 121, 153, 160 ; Stephen, 305 ; Thomas, 176, 280, 312 ; Tucker, 268 ; William, 73.
Cartlitch, Elizabeth, 92 ; John, 92.
Cartwright, Ann, 269 ; Charles, 193 ; Elizabeth, 298 ; John, 125, 269, 298 ; Katherine, 298 ; Lucy, 191 ; Martha, 59 ; Mary, 97, 125 ; Newman, 59 ; Rebecca, 193 ; Richard, 191 ; Susanna, 186 ; Thomas, 97.
Carvill, Jane, 290.
Cary, *see* Carey.
Caryll, Hester, 290 ; John, 290 ; Kinborough, 302 ; Richard, 302.
Casberd (Casbard), Sarah, 67 ; William, 67 ; Rev. Mr., 40.
Casebroock, Anne, 143.
Casemore, Betty, 52.
Casey, Anne, 227 ; John, 227.
Cash, Bridget, 295 ; William, 295.
Caslin, Catherine, 279.
Cason, Ellen, 296 ; Johanna, 280 ; Mary, 105.
Cass, Ann, 31.
Cassal, Abraham, 17 ; Eleanor, 17.
Castell (Castel), John, 268 ; Judith, 268 ; Sarah, 175.
Castle, John, 240.
Castleman, Thomas, 214.
Castlow, Sarah, 225.
Castolow, John, 84 ; Susanna, 84.
Caswell, George, 262 ; Martha Sarah, 262.
Caten, Elizabeth, 93.
Cater, Mary, 84 ; Sarah, 142.
Cates, Grace, 102 ; Kezia, 75 ; Moses, 102.
Catesby, Hannah, 286 ; Richard, 286.
Cathrall, Ann, 66 ; Hugh, 66.
Cathrow, Elizabeth, 249 ; Elizabeth Ann Ellen, 252 ; George, 249, 252 ; James (Rouge Dragon), 255 ; James, 252, 253 ; J., 249.
Catliff, Edward, 225 ; Mary, 225.
Catline (Catlen), Elizabeth, 276 ; Grace, 277.
Cattenden, James, 261.
Catterns, James, 95 ; Mary, 101 ; Susanna, 95.
Cattley, Isabel, 271 ; Jacob, 271.
Causby, Mary, 314.
Causton, Elizabeth, 119.
Cauvin, Mary Bayeux, 111.
Cave, Anne, 132 ; Harriet Elizabeth, 262 ; William George, 262.
Cavel, Elizabeth, 180.
Cawbacke, John, 291 ; Susanna, 291.

Chitham, Grace, 306.
Chitley, Ann, 32.
Chittenden, Anne Maynard, 149 ; John, 149.
Chittey, *see* Chitty.
Chittick, Ann, 103 ; Walter, 103.
Chittington, Rebecca, 27.
Chittum, Ann, 281.
Chitty (Chittey), Avice, 127 ; Barnard, 309 ; Elizabeth, 42 ; Frances, 59 ; Joan, 309 ; John, 127 ; Thomas, 59.
Chivers, Ann, 75 ; Christian, 39 ; Hannah, 163 ; John, 163.
Choell, Mary, 66 ; Samuel, 66.
Choice, Dorothy, 150.
Cholmeley (Chomley, Chumley), Johanna, 280 ; Martha, 19 ; Mary, 180 ; Robert, 280 ; William, 180.
Chown, Elizabeth, 204 ; Thomas, 204.
Chowning, James, 309 ; Jane, 309.
Christian (Chrischen), Ann, 84 ; Charles, 58, 61 ; Jane, 58 ; Martha, 61 ; Richard, 287 ; Rog., 282* ; Sarah, 287.
Christopher, Barbara, 84 ; Esther, 36 ; Joan, 198 ; Sarah, 82.
Christy, Agnes, 2.
Chrutchley, John, 8 ; Martha, 8.
Chubb, Ann, 182 ; William, 182.
Chumley, *see* Cholmeley.
Chumm, Rebecca, 30.
Church, Ann, 95, 219 ; Benjamin, 217 ; Elizabeth, 183, 219 ; H. E., 237 ; Jeffery, 309 ; John, 30 ; Margaret, 30, 309 ; Mary, 53, 78, 217 ; Sarah, 219 ; Susanna, 143 ; Thomas, 53 ; Rev. Mr., 77, 114.
Churcher, Elizabeth, 32 ; Sarah Ann, 260 ; Thomas, 32.
Churchey, Ann, 105 ; George, 94, 105 ; Mary, 94.
Churchill, Ann, 216 ; Eleanor, 168 ; Elizabeth, 287 ; Mary, 87 ; George, 216 ; Thomas, 168 ; William, 87 ; Winston, 287.
Churchis, Ann, 283 ; Richard, 283.
Chusin, Elizabeth, 307.
Clackston, Jane, 287 ; Joseph, 42 ; Phœbe, 42 ; Richard, 287.
Clagget, Mary, 255.
Clanfield, Elizabeth, 230 ; William, 230.
Clann, Catherine, 87.
Clapham (Clappam), Ann, 299 ; George, 229 ; Henrietta Clarentia, 189 ; Henry, 277 ; James, 165 ; Jane, 166 ; John, 189 ; Mary, 277 ; Sarah, 165, 229 ; William, 166.
Clapp, John, 231.
Clapshaw, Benjamin, 55 ; Catherine, 55.
Clare, Amy, 313 ; Ann, 20 ; Elizabeth, 193 ; Joseph, 193 ; Mary, 233 ; Sarah, 24 ; Rev. Mr., 137.
Claridge, Mary, 40.
Clarke (Clark, Clearke), Agnes, 243 ; Alexander, 214 ; Alice, 289 ; Amy, 93 ; Ann, 35, 39, 44, 131, 133, 145, 184, 187, 197, 201, 231, 253, 266, 276 ; Benjamin, 143 ; Burges, 11 ; Catherine, 135, 218, 266 ; Christopher, 284 ; Dorothy, 48, 268 ; Edward, 78, 220, 312 ; Eleanor, 300 ; Elijah, 12 ; Elizabeth, 14, 21, 63, 76, 78, 110, 121, 122, 135, 140, 173, 193, 203, 214, 291, 312 ; Ellen, 283 ; Ester, 121 ; Ferdinando, 193 ; Frances, 52 ; Grace, 220 ; Hannah, 152, 220 ; Henrietta, 182 ; Henry, 52, 291 ; Katherine, 308 ; James, 191 ; Jane, 24, 121, 299 ; Joan, 291, 297, 313 ; John, 48, 63, 133, 173, 187, 201, 264, 283 ; Joseph, 81, 313 ; Joyce, 288 ; Leah, 12 ; Lucy, 230 ; Margaret, 70, 83, 149, 221 ; Martha, 128 ; Martin, 83 ; Mary, 3, 8, 34, 53, 63, 102, 103, 108, 143, 149, 158, 169, 175, 185, 191, 233, 234, 237, 256, 284, 294, 306, 311 ; Mary Ann, 258 ; Penelope, 81 ; Peter, 121 ; Ralph, 311 ; Rebecca, 55, 264 ; Richard, 203, 268 ; Robert, 131 ; Rose, 294 ; Ruth, 7, 198 ; Salome, 8 ; Rev. Samuel, A.M., 48 ; Samuel, 158 ; Sarah, 11, 25, 130, 172, 192 ; Sibella, 231 ; Tanneguy, 182 ; Thomas, 21, 39, 175, 233, 299 ; Valentine, 297 ; William, 44, 121, 130, 145, 214, 231, 236, 258, 306 ; Rev. W., 251, 253.
Clarkson, Christian, 64 ; Isabella, 5 ; James, 195 ; Mary, 191 ; Sarah, 195.
Clason, John, 31 ; Mary, 31.
Clater, Sarah, 57.
Claudius, Elizabeth, 89.
Claus, Ann, 165.
Claussen, Caspar, 115 ; Sarah, 115.
Clavering, Eleanor, 228 ; Robert, 228.
Claverley, Jane, 34.
Claxon, Elizabeth, 146 ; Rose, 282.
Clay, Charles, 39 ; Elizabeth, 195, 276 ; Judith, 312 ; Mary, 39, 81 ; Samuel, 312 ; Sarah, 209 ; William, 209.
Clayton, Elizabeth, 26, 180 ; John, 293 ; Margaret, 112 ; Mary, 68 ; Sarah, 196 ; Susan, 293.
Cleafe, Jane, 300.
Clear, Mary, 82.
Clearke, *see* Clarke.
Cleaveland, Edward, 39 ; Elizabeth, 39 ; Mary, 73.
Cleaver, Jane, 141, 174 ; Robert, 141.
Cleer, Elizabeth, 276 ; Robert, 276.
Cleeten, Ann, 284 ; Edward, 284.
Clegg, Ellen, 136 ; John, 136 ; Joseph, 151 ; Mary, 90, 151.
Clemens, Elizabeth, 123 ; Isaac, 176 ; Margaret, 86 ; Sarah, 176.
Clement, Elizabeth, 62 ; Frances, 310 ; Gregory, 310 ; Sarah, 197.
Clements, Elizabeth, 167 ; Frances, 301 ; Lucy, 91 ; Repentance, 33 ; William, 33.
Clempson, Frances, 203 ; George, 182, 203 ; Sarah, 182.
Clemson, Ann, 107 ; Dorothy, 54 ; Henry, 276 ; Johane, 276.
Clemvell, Sarah, 277.
Clench, Hannah, 31 ; Stephen, 31.
Cleufley, Richard, 292 ; Sarah, 292.
Clevell, Mary, 154.
Cleyton, Joan, 273 ; Robert, 273.
Cliff, Ann, 251 ; W., 251.
Clifford (Cliffoord), Elizabeth, 34, 307, 310 ; George, 307, 310 ; Judith, 279 ; Mary, 46 ; Susanna, 203 ; Thomas, 46.
Clift, Ellen, 294 ; John, 294.
Clifton, Ann, 218 ; Elizabeth, 231, 233 ; Simeon, 218, 231.
Clinch, Lydia, 298.
Clinkard, Elizabeth, 47.
Clisbee, Elizabeth, 5 ; William, 5.
Clistonne, Katherine, 271 ; Robert, 271.
Clither, James, 272 ; Mary, 272.
Clitter, Clacye, 270.
Cloak (Cloake), Alice, 224, 224*n*.
Clocner, Martha, 128 ; Michael, 128.
Clouch, Edward, 298 ; Elizabeth, 298.
Clousinger, Ann, 182.
Clowes, Eleanor, 72 ; Hannah, 19 ; Peter, 19.

Cluffe, Winifred, 310
Clunan, Michael, 260 , Rachael, 260
Clunn, Elizabeth, 165 , Mary, 306 , William, 165, 306
Clutton, Frances, 297, 298 , Thomas, 297 298
Clyatt, David 296 , Hannah, 296
Coales, *see* Coles
Coare (Coar, Cooar, Coore), Ann, 228 , Jane, 222, 228 , Mary, 240 , Sarah, 22, 224 , Susanna, 218, 218*n* , Thomas, 228 240
Coates (Cotes), Ann 116 , Dorothy, 305 , Hannah, 196, 199 , Margaret 189 Mary, 92 , Ruth, 190 , Thomas, 92, 190 , William, 196
Coatham *see* Cotham
Cobb, Elizabeth, 210, 237 , Grace 170 , Mary, 44 , Samuel, 44, 170 , Sarah, 44
Cobbet, Mary 53
Cobden, Joanna, 120
Cobham, Jane, 168, 179 , John, 122 Mary, 122 , Rebecca, 310 , Sarah, 192 , Stockley, 192 , Thomas, 168
Cobus, Mary, 104
Coby Mary, 71 , Peter, 71
Cock (Cocke), Abia, 147 , Abraham 10 Ann, 10 , Elizabeth, 156, 270 , Frances, 216 , John, 17, 147, 151 Josias, 270 , Mary, 17, 151 246 , Prudence, 188 , Rachael, 110 , Susanna, 175 , Thomas 110 , William, 188
Cockayne (Cockeyne), Elizabeth, 103 , Mary, 28 286 , William, 28
Cocker, Margaret, 310
Cockerill, Jane, 4 , William, 4
Cockett, Elizabeth, 24 , Richard, 24
Cockeyne, *see* Cockayne
Cockhead, Martha, 256 , Thomas, 256
Cockin, Margaret, 165 , Mary, 176
Cockram, Elizabeth, 14 , Hannah, 107
Cockshead, *see* Coxshed
Cocom, James 310 , Joan 310
Coddrington, Mary, 302
Codgell, Abigail, 54 , William, 54
Coe, John, 280 , Mariana, 280
Coffee, Helen, 259
Cogan, Mary, 312
Cogger, Hannah, 142 , John, 142
Coggin, Frances, 88
Coghell, Martha 110 , Thomas, 110
Coke Ann 183 , Edith 205 , John 205 , Katherine 307 , Thomas, 183
Coker, Amee, 284 , Ebenezer, 106 , Elizabeth, 106 , John, 284
Cokoe Caroline, 260
Colbatch, Ann, 14
Colbett, Anne, 296 , Charles 296
Colborne Anne, 288 , Robert 288
Colbron, Anne, 103 , William, 103
Colchin (Collchen), Elizabeth 153 , John, 152 , Mary, 152 Samuel, 153
Cole, Alice, 279 , Ann, 107, 110, 137 258, 289 David 37 , Edward, 205 , Elizabeth, 46, 95 109, 135 195, 234 , Frances, 279, 296 , George, 279 , Harriet, 85 119 , Henry, 125, 265 , Job, 95 , John, 109, 135, 289 , Margaret, 265 , Martha 37, 214 , Mary, 28, 39, 72, 164, 223, 247, 266, 279 280, 311 , Nicholas, 279 Robert, 266 , Sarah, 205 , Susanna, 125, 289 , Thomas, 83, 258 , William, 46, 223, 258
Colebrook, Anne, 2 , Samuel, 2
Coleby, Ann, 93.
Colegrave, Ann, 201.
Coleman, Ann, 90, 124, 144 161, 290 , Frances, 142 , Hannah, 22 , James, 90 , John, 79 , Mary, 84, 145, 199, 253 , Sarah, 111 , Susanna, 79, 159 , Thomas, 22, 124 , William, 144
Colenso, Jane, 262
Coleright, Ann 300 , Edmund 300
Coles (Coales), Ann, 213, 222, 312 , Arthur, 278 , Edward, 63 , Elizabeth 63 , Frances, 12 , James 221, 223 , Jane, 99, 217 John, 12 Margaret, 278 Michael, between 213 and 225* , William, 312
Coleston, Catherine, 129 William 129
Colher, Cicley, 264
Colhown Elizabeth, 18 , Jane, 20
Coliere *see* Collier
Colins, *see* Collins
Colishaw, Mary 123
Collard, Charles, 283 , Susan, 283
Collas, *see* Collis
Colle Anne, 275 , Christopher, 275 , Lettice, 269
Collen, *see* Collin
Colless, Colles, *see* Collis
Colleton (Collyton) Lady Ann 1 , Ann, 313 , Edward, 1.
Collett, Anne, 162 211 Anthony, 311 , Damaris, 301 , Lucy, 191 , Margery, 311 , Mary, 135 , Sarah, 96 , Thomas, 135
Colley, Ann, 158 278 , Elizabeth 60 Mary, 139 , Richard, 158 , Robert, 139 , Thomas, 60
Collibee, Elizabeth 255 , Lucy, 255
Colliber, Hannah, 102 , John, 102 Mary, 213
Collier (Coliere, Collyer), Anne, 54, 157 , Annes 265 , Beatrice, 268 , Bethiah 205 Catherine 85 , Dorothy, 105 , Elizabeth, 200, 201, 236 , Frances 78, 150, 298 , John, 40, 105 150 Margaret, 189 Mary 180 , Patience, 40 Richard, 54 , Samuel, 204 , Susanna, 204 , Thomas, 298 , Rev Mr , 71
Collin (Collen, Collyn), Ann 202 , Frances, 91 , Hannah, 188 , John, 188, 202
Colling Isabella, 130
Collingridge, Phœbe 262
Collins (Colins, Collines Collyns), Agnes, 77 , Alice 284 , Ann, 232 , Elizabeth 38, 187, 225, 248, 293, 313 Frances, 308 , George, 10 James 241, 248 , Jane, 300 , Jeffery 284 Jemima, 125 , Jeremiah, 112 , J , 248 , Margaret 31, 112 , Martha, 121 , Mary, 10, 133, 137 161, 218 272, 301 Matthew, 308 , Robert, 301 Roger 272 , Sarah 162 182 , Susan 309 , Susanna 305 Thomas, 31, 309, 313 , Timothy, 187 , Tristram, 77 Rev William 214 217 , William, 133
Collinson, Mary, 22
Collinwood Jane, 314
Collis (Collas Colles Colless), Alice, 57 , John, 96 , Lettice, 269 , Margaret, 10 , Mary, 96, 218 , Thomas, 218
Collison John 204 Sarah 204
Colly, Elizabeth, 131
Collyer, *see* Collier
Collyn, *see* Collin
Collyns, *see* Collins
Collyton, *see* Colleton
Colman, Charles 160 , Elizabeth, 119 , Jeremiah, 119 , Sarah, 160
Colnett, Ann, 50
Colquitt, Millicent, 298 , Susanna, 298
Colston, Elizabeth, 292
Colt, Ann, 285
Colthourpe, Ann, 284 Arthur, 284
Colthrop, Barbery, 263.

187; Elizabeth, 16; John, 1; Martha Matilda, 187; Mary, 214.
Crawshay, Elizabeth, 227; Richard, 227.
Cray, Susanna, 197.
Crayford (Craforde), Cecily, 271; Mary, 4; Peter, 4.
Crayle, Elizabeth, 307; William, 307.
Crayne, Lucy, 266.
Crease, Cloe, 11.
Credocke, Elizabeth, 107.
Creed, Amme, 111; Christopher, 141; Elizabeth, 6, 48; George, 15; John, 48; Mary, 15, 141, 278.
Creery, Christopher, 280; Margaret, 280.
Cremer, Ann, 116; Elizabeth, 68; Francis, 51, 116; Mary, 51; Robert, 68.
Cress, Mary, 169.
Cressell, Ann, 126.
Cressey, John, 311; Mary, 311.
Cresswell, Ann, 308; Elizabeth, 308; Lucy, 213.
Crewe, Alles, 265; John, 265.*
Crewes, Jane, 313.
Criche, Frances, 26.
Crichlowe, Christian, 18; John, 18.
Cripple, Mary, 64.
Cripps, Mary, 67.
Crispe, Catherine, 226; Elizabeth, 282; James, 226; Mary, 136.
Critchett, Edmund, 198; Sarah, 198.
Crittall, Mary, 90.
Croasdell, John, 186; Katherine, 186.
Crockford, Anne, 289.
Crocklow, Alice, 278; William, 278.
Crofte, Ann, 150; Eme, 273; Rafe, 273; Thomas, 150.
Cromp, James, 171; Mary, 171.
Crompton, Katherine, 278; Martha, 204; Richard, 278.
Cromwell, Ann, 70, 78; John, 70.
Cronkshaw, Rev. Mr., between 184 and 207.*
Cronport, Dennis, 264.
Crook (Crooke), Elizabeth, 122; Eutrisha, 46; James, 162; Joane, 288; John, 116; Jonathan, 122; Marie, 283; Mary, 76, 116, 162; Richard, 46; Susanna, 195; Walter, 283.
Crookdecke, Annes, 266; John, 266.
Crookenden, Jane, 171; Thomas, 171.
Crooks, Hannah, 42; Henry, 42.
Crookshank, Hannah, 234; William, 234.
Crookshanks, Jane, 161; John, 161.
Croome, Elizabeth, 279.
Cropley, Elizabeth, 195; Isabel, 295; John, 295; Joseph, 195.
Cropp, Elizabeth, 201.
Crosby (Crosbie, Crossby), Adam, 279; Anne, 129; Ellen, 279; James, 10; Jane, 10, 110; Mary, 170, 298; Robert, 129, 298; Sibella, 196.
Crosfield, Alice, 54.
Crosier, Elizabeth, 281; John, 81, 281; Mary, 81.
Crosley (Crossleey), Hannah, 44; Peter, 44; Sarah, 86.
Cross (Crosse), Abraham, 15; Ann, 15, 45, 75, 111, 286, 312; Catherine, 97; Edward, 235; Elizabeth, 105, 276; Joan, 307; John, 105, 276; Margaret, 235, 309; Mary, 139, 269; Robert, 139; Sarah, 70; Theophilus, 97; Thomas, 309; William, 111.
Crossby, *see* Crosby.
Crossleey, *see* Crosley.
Crossman, Elizabeth, 28; Mary, 182.
Crothall, Elizabeth, 249; George, 249.*
Crouch (Crowch), Elizabeth, 76, 112, 278, 281, 298; John, 298; Mary, 32, 268; Sarah, 192; William, 112.
Crousdon, John, 82; Mary, 82.
Crover, Joan, 289.
Crow, Bridget, 102; Isabella, 4; Mary, 141; Philip, 195; Sarah, 88, 195; Susanna, 54; William, 102.
Crowch, *see* Crouch.
Crowcher, Sarah, 151.
Crowde, Judith, 288; Martha, 301.
Crowder, Alice, 213; Elizabeth, 194; Johane, 276; John, 194.
Crowhurst, Mary, 119.
Crowley, Jane, 170.
Crown, James, 114; Phillis, 114, 141.
Crowther, Esther, 182; Henry, 37; Mary, 37, 240.
Croxen, John, 132; Susanna, 132.
Croxfoord, Elizabeth, 308.
Croxton, Mary, 313; Walter, 313.
Croydon, Ann, 291; Thomas, 291.
Crozer, Ann, 54; Richard, 54.
Crucefix, Ann, 8; Robert, 8.
Crudge, Martha, 204.
Cruickshank, Christian, 238.
Crukefild, Ann, 289.
Crump, Elizabeth, 17, 97; Sarah, 206.
Crumpton, Henrietta, 23.
Crunden, Jane, 83; Samuel, 83.
Cruse, Edward, 250; John, 234.
Crutcher, Mary, 251.
Crutchfeeild, Mary, 306.
Crutchley, Alice, 213; Elizabeth, 70; Joseph, 70.
Cruthwell, W., 230.
Cryer, Ann, 286; John, 286.
Cubbidge, Ann, 197; William, 197.
Cuddington, Margery, 281.
Cullen, Jane, 23.
Cullerne, Martha, 189; Mary, 246; Richard, 246; William, 189.
Cullinfor, John, 202; Sarah, 202.
Culling, Arthur, 65; Susanna, 65.
Cullingworth, Ann, 14.
Culpeper, Jane, 24.
Culver, Elizabeth, 209; John, 209.
Cumber, Robert, 91; Martha, 91.
Cumberlidge, Mary, 146.
Cumenge, Esther, 190.
Cumlyn, Mary, 133, 164; William, 164.
Cummings, Joan, 299.
Cundall, Elizabeth, 153; Mary, 284.*
Cunningham, David, 66; Elizabeth, 214; Jane, 60; John, 214; Mary, 66, 107; William, 238.
Cureton, Ann, 209; Thomas, 209.
Curle, Mary, 150.
Curn, Mary, 107; Robert, 107.
Currant, James, 155; Jane, 155.
Currer, Elizabeth, 289.
Currie, Hannah, 193; James, 193, 240; Mary, 240.
Curstertine, Ellen, 305; Henry, 305.
Curten, Mary, 270.
Curthberthson, *see* Cuthbertson.
Curtis (Courtis, Curtice, Curties, Curtise, Curtiss), Ann, 143, 184; Charles, 234; Elizabeth, 164, 170, 189, 234; Frances, 129, 300; George, 101; Jane, 101; Joan, 146; John, 129, 184; Mary, 89, 111, 142, 163, 274; Mathay, 287;

128; Clement, 4; Elizabeth, 82, 148, 184, 239, 270; Frances, 183; Hannah, 92, 153, 166; Henry, 158, 247; James, 82, 224, 251; John, 9, 107, 128; Mary, 4, 140; Moses, 183; Rebecca, 224; Robert, 148; Sarah, 298; Ursula, 125; William, 166, 216, 222.
Dawtre, Katherine, 275.
Day, Ann, 41, 71, 73, 137, 192, 247, 286, 289; Bridget, 30; Charles, 2, 43; Deborah, 62; Elizabeth, 2, 41, 86, 299; Elizabeth Mary, 132; Henrietta, 216; Henry, 73; Johanna, 203; John, 203; Mary, 6, 106, 258, 295, 310; Mary Ann, 207; Nathaniel, 312; Nickolette, 312; Samuel, 207; Sarah, 43, 156, 168, 211; Susan, 285; William, 132.
Daykin, *see* Dakin.
Daynes, Elizabeth, 294; Thomas, 294.
Deacon, Ann, 306; Caroline, 260; Charles, 260; Elizabeth, 43, 284; Richard, 284.
De Aillon, James, 314; Martha, 314.
Deakins, Ann, 313.
Dean (Deane), Ann, 29, 124, 156, 300; Edy, 307; Eleanor, 212; Elizabeth, 20, 77; Frances, 305; George Thomas, 259; Grace, 139; Jane, 23, 259, 300; Martha, 73; Mary, 128, 165; Phineas, 29; Rebecca, 302; Robert, 124, 307; Sarah, 169; Thomas, 77, 139, 227; William, 165.
Dear (Deire), Ann, 226; Cary, 87; John Halsted, 226.
Dearberg, Ann, 242; George, 242.
Dearmer (Dearmor), Martha, 207; Sidney, 295; William, 295.
Deasley, Thomas, 202; Thomasine, 202.
Death, Alice, 282; Margaret, 238; Robert, 238; Thomas, 282.
Debank, Sarah, 157.
Debart, Abraham, 153; Elizabeth, 153.
Debatt, Mary, 85.
Debbit, Susanna, 216.
Debble, Elizabeth, 30.
De Bela, Mary, 145; Peter, 145.
De Berdt, Jane, 9.
De Bissye, Catherine, 221; Stephano Barow, 221.
Deboust, Joseph, 139; Mary, 139.
De Cartigney, Martha, 314.
De Caux, Mary, 120.
Deckeom, John, 283; Mary, 283.
Dee, Mary, 44; Sarah, 282; Thomas, 282.
Deely, Ann, 233.
Deeping, Sarah, 40.
Degrave, Edward, 202; Hannah, 202.
Deiose, Cicely, 278.
Deire, *see* Dear.
Delaballe, Francis, 111; Mary Bayeux, 111.
Delabertauche, Elizabeth, 180; Mary, 139.
Delaferte, Mary, 206.
De la Forte, Benjamin Picart, 88; Mary, 88.
Delahay (De La Haie, Dellahay), Benjamin, 86; Elizabeth, 123; Hannah, 246; Mary, 86.
Delajaille, Mary Easter, 108.
Delany, Ann, 66; Sarah, 208.
Delarne (Delarene), Elizabeth, 152; Susanna, 154.
Delemar, Ann, 138.
Delight, Ezekiel, 257; Hannah, 257.
Deliot (Deliott), Elizabeth, 109; Frances, 169; Frances Ann, 190; Gaspar, 109; James, 169.
Dell, Elizabeth, 152; John, 103, 152; Sarah, 28; Susanna, 103.
Dellow, Susanna, 124.
Delzanne, Susanna, 101.
Dempey, Elizabeth, 199; James, 199.
Dench, Margaret, 122.
Dendy, Elizabeth, 281; John, 281.
Denham, Ann, 297; Sarah, 68.
Deniord, Mary, 162.
Denley, Elizabeth, 275; John, 275.
Dennet, Alexander, 275; Frances, 275.
Dennis (Dennys), Ann, 11, 12, 167; Edward, 9; Elizabeth, 192, 270, 312, 313; James, 79*; Joseph, 270; Martha, 46; Mary, 10, 290; Sarah, 9, 79*, 195; Thomas, 12, 46; William, 312.
Dennison (Denison), Abraham, 225; Ann, 28; Frances, 60; John, 60; Mary, 185.
Denny, John Thomas, 259.
Denson, Catherine, 101.
Dent, Christopher, 92; Dorothy, 280; Elizabeth, 92; Frances, 263.
Denton (Denten), Adam, 265; Ann, 137; Elizabeth, 265, 288; George, 314; Hester, 314; Judith, 281; Ruth, 18; Thomas, 288.
Denyer, Mary, 210; Richard, 210.
Denzer, Sarah, 179.
Depear, Elizabeth, 231.
De Ponthieu, Josiah, 218; Mary, 218.
De Prado, Lea, 174.
Derby, Ann, 173; Robert, 173.
Derigo, Mary, 189.
De Roche (De Roach), James Chatine, 163; Martha, 16; Susanna, 163.
Derry, Elizabeth, 83; Mary, 66.
Desborough, Mary, 126.
D'Esgens, Ann, 97; John Anthony, 97.
Desormeaux, Daniel, 255; Elizabeth, 255.
Detton, Margaret, 152.
Devallee, Magdeline, 130; Peter, 130.
Devenport, Charles, 129; Eleanor, 110; Phillis, 129.
Devereux (Deverex), Elizabeth, 265; John, 265; Mary, 33.
Deverill (Deveral), Ann, 230; George, 217.
Devey, Eleanor, 173.
Devonish, Elizabeth, 145; Silvester, 145.
Devonshire, Elizabeth, 236.
Dew, Katherine, 290; Margaret, 293; Thomas, 293.
Dewberry, Joseph, 162; Mary, 162.
Dewce, Mercy, 286; Thomas, 286.
Dewell, Elizabeth, 278; Mary, 104; Sarah, 223; Timothy, 104.
Dewes, John, 41, 178; Mary, 178; Sarah, 41.
Dewiche, Anne, 95; Thomas, 95.
De Wilde, Frederick Augustus, 262; Harriet, 262.
De Winser, James, 240.
Dexter, Enos, 158; Frances, 158.
Diaper, Mary, 98; Samuel, 98.
Diat, Alice, 279.
Dibbil (Dibbeel), Ann, 119, 296.
Dibley, John, 66; Mary, 66.
Dicas, Sarah, 75.
Dice, Jane, 287.
Dichfeyld, *see* Ditchfield.
Dick, Mary, 148; William, 148.
Dicker, Dinah, 176; Hannah, 228; John, 228.
Dickers, Eleanor, 164.
Dickhout, Ann, 247.
Dickins (Dickines), Elizabeth, 276; Joan, 293; Robert, 276.
Dickinson (Dickenson), Ann, 288; Charles,

295; Eleanor, 295; Elizabeth, 5; Henry, 63; James, 195; Martha, 63; Mary, 76, 101, 171, 210, 280; Susanna, 195; Thomas, 288.
Dickman, Mary, 235; Sarah, 235.
Dickson, *see* Dixon.
Didcock, Ann, 255; James, 255.
Didelsfold, Grace, 6; John, 6.
Didier, Jane, 155; Mary, 4; Peter, 155.
Dier, *see* Dyer.
Digby, Lettice, 290.
Diggs, Elizabeth, 20; Robert, 20.
Dighton, Elizabeth, 7; John, 7; Mary, 205.
Dignell, Catherine, 111.
Digweed, Joanna, 45; Samuel, 45.
Dike, Mary, 305.
Dilkes, Mary, 85.
Dillack, Katherine, 295; Robert, 295.
Dilley, Ann, 135; Isabella, 114; John, 135, 158, 203; Margaret, 203; Mary, 158.
Dilline, Frances, 264.
Dillingham, Benjamin, 153; Jane, 199; John, 199; Susan, 153.
Dillo, Alice, 197.
Diman, Martha, 294.
Dimmock (Dimocke), Jane, 190, 260; Martha, 269; Robert, 269; Thomas Moses, 260.
Ding, Mary, 235; Sarah, 235.
Dingley, Elizabeth, 288; Sir John, 288.
Dinley, Mary, 264.
Dinsdale, Elizabeth, 198; Jeffry, 198; Joshua, 101; Mary, 101, 102; Thomas, 102.
Dinton, Penelope, 156; William, 156.
Dirixon, Elizabeth, 39.
Ditchfield (Dichfeyld), Elizabeth, 269; Henry, 269; Martha, 163.
Ditton, Barbara, 305; Elizabeth, 144; John, 144.
Divett, Margery, 126.
Dix, John, 231; Mary, 231.
Dixon (Dickson), Alice, 274; Ann, 16; Catherine, 280; Elizabeth, 24, 136, 149, 171, 214, 260; James, 157; Jane, 179, 296; John, 179, 274; Margaret, 64; Mary, 40, 64, 132, 157, 245, 259; Stanhope, 132; Susanna, 65; Thomas, 16; William, 259.
Dobbins, Elizabeth, 143; Frances, 88; George, 88; John, 143.
Dobbinson, *see* Dobinson.
Dobbs, Avis, 29.
Dobey, Rev. John, 215.*
Dobinson (Dobbinson), Ann, 46; Lucy, 288; William, 46.
Dobney, Alice, 20.
Dobozy, Anna Maria, 312.
Dobson, Ann, 51, 109, 148, 222; Eleanor, 140; Elizabeth, 142, 240; George, 240; Isaac, 142; John, 148, 240; Judith, 287; Mary, 137; Richard, 137.
Dockin, Susanna, 53; William, 53.
Dockwray, Ann, 28; William, 28.
Dodd (Dod), Ann, 89; Charles, 136; Edward, 190; Elizabeth, 39, 136, 190; James, 70; Jane, 70; John, 244; Mary, 187, 244; Rebecca, 264; Samuel, 71; Sarah, 71.
Dodderidge, James, 295; Lucy, 306; Mary, 295.
Dodds, Jane, 250.
Dodemead, Elizabeth, 114.
Dodson, Frances, 308; William, 108.
Dodwell, Rev. Arthur, 237; Elizabeth, 137, 157; Margaret, 237; Robert, 237.
Doe, Ann, 283; Ursula, 102.
Doggett, Deborah, 311.
Dogwell, Alice, 295.
Doig, James Alexander, 208; Joan, 208.
Dolben, Rev. Mr., 90.
Dolby, Ann, 279; Nicholas, 279.
Dolley, Maurice, 224.
Dolling, Rev. Robert, 234.
Dolman, Elizabeth, 120; William, 120.
Dolton, William, 234.
Doman, Alice, 315.
Domine, Ann, 61; Benjamin, 61.
Domivell, Isaiah, 293; Joan, 293.
Domvile, Mary, 125; Richard, 125.
Donaldson, Frances, 34, 117; Margaret, 134; Mark, 34.
Donde, Ann, 133.
Dongworth, Anne, 107.
Donnall, Anne, 170; Francis, 170.
Donne, Alles, 265; Mary, 113; John, 265.
Donning, Jane, 302; William, 302.
Dontoun, Elizabeth, 13.
Dooby, Elizabeth, 305.
Doody, Elizabeth, 140; Richard, 140.
Doolin, Elizabeth, 135; Patrick, 135.
Door, Samuel, 200; Sarah, 200.
Dopsly, Elizabeth, 280.
Dorkenoll, Mary, 279.
Dorkin, Mary, 56.
Dormer, Catherine, 115; Hannah, 94; William, 115.
Dorrell, Dorcas, 106; Elizabeth, 94; Francis, 94.
Dorringetone, Ann, 275; Richard, 275.
Dorset (Dorsett), Anne, 145; John, 101; Margaret, 273; Mary, 101.
Dossett (Doset), Benjamin, 168; Elizabeth, 168; Mary, 42.
Doughty, Catherine, 49; Elizabeth, 54; Hannah, 68; Margaret, 110; Robert, 68, 110; Thomas, 54; Rev. Mr., 193.
Douglas (Douglass), Elizabeth, 25, 79; George, 10; John, 3, 223; Lewis, 13; Margaret, 10; Mary, 3, 13, 306; Robert, 306; Sarah, 243; Seabra, 223; William, 243.
Doury, Anna, 71.
Douthwaite, Elizabeth, 210, 301; John, 210; Nicholas, 301.
Dove, Elizabeth, 192, 228; Hester, 121; Margaret, 48; Nicholas, 228; Ruth, 307; William, 48, 192.
Dovie, Elizabeth, 270.
Dowbiggin, Dorrington, 111.
Dowce, *see* Dowse.
Dowd, Jemima, 215.
Dowding, Anne, 79; James, 79.
Dowell (Dowle), Ann, 139; Grace, 113; Richard, 139.
Dowling, James, 226, 227.
Downbell, Helen, 291; Thomas, 291.
Downer, Mary, 149.
Downes (Downs), Ann, 49, 274; John, 274; Joseph, 114; Mary, 15; Richard, 15; Rossaman, 299; Sarah, 114.
Downham, Dorothy, 60.
Downing, Charles, 48; Elizabeth, 22; Frances, 106; Helena, 280; Henrietta Sara Margaretta, 48.
Downton, Ann, 299; Walter, 299.
Dowse (Dowce), Alice, 299; Amy, 77.
Dowson, Mary, 292.
Dowthat, Ann, 3; Elizabeth, 50.
Doyle, Dennis, 127; Isabella, 127.
Doyly, Peregrine, 36; Prudence, 36.

Drage, Azariah, 250 ; Sarah Ann, 250.
Drake, Edmund, 43 ; Edward, 50 ; Elizabeth, 50, 52, 287 ; Mary, 43 ; Samuel, 52 ; Sarah, 135 ; William, 225 ; Mr., 275, 276, 277, 278.
Drakes (Drackes), Mr., 271, 272, 273, 274.
Draper, Ann, 297 ; Clase, 301 ; Daniel, 68 ; Frances, 215 ; Hannah, 67 ; John, 43, 301 ; Joseph, 67 ; Mary, 15, 43, 68 ; Samuel, 68 ; Susanna, 68 ; Thomas, 15 ; William, 297.
Draples, Frances, 270.
Drapter, John, 288 ; Rose, 288.
Dray, Elizabeth, 210 ; John Henry, 210 ; Mary, 245.
Draycott, Elizabeth, 293 ; Ferdinando, 293.
Draywer, Joseph, 292 ; Mary, 292.
Dredge, Martha, 276 ; William, 276.
Drew, Ann, 32 ; Elizabeth, 117, 238 ; Jane, 237 ; John, 32, 238 ; Jonathan, 237 ; Mary, 85 ; Mary Cole, 238 ; Sarah, 219 ; William, 117, 219.
Drewry, *see* Drury.
Drinkwater, Elizabeth, 123, 128 ; George, 225 ; John, 128 ; Richard, 123.
Driver, Ann, 89, 189, 212, 292 ; Elizabeth, 312 ; John, 212 ; Robert, 292 ; William, 89.
Driwood, Jane, 294 ; Nicholas, 294.
Droney, Johane, 275 ; William, 275.
Drucee, Mary, 112.
Drummond, Elizabeth, 241 ; George, 241.
Drury (Drewry, Drurye), Catherine, 51 ; Elizabeth, 114 ; Jane, 273 ; Joseph, 134 ; Lettice, 105 ; Mary, 80, 134, 225 ; Michael, 77 ; Samuel, 77 ; Susanna, 122 ; Thomas, 114, 122.
Dryer, Sarah, 156.
Dryhurst, Ann, 29 ; James, 29.
Dubber, Alice, 296 ; Edward, 296.
Dubbleday, Ann, 314 ; Roger, 314.
Du Bec, Ann, 154.
Du Cane, Rev. Henry, 260.
Ducar, Ann, 191.
Duce, Catherine, 65.
Duck, Dr. Arthur, 283 ; Eleanor, 307 ; Henry, 307.
Ducker, Eleanor, 180.
Duckett (Duckitt), Ann, 51, 314 ; Mark, 51 ; Mary, 50 ; Nicholas, 298 ; Phillis, 298.
Ducy, Anne, 288 ; Robert, 288.
Dudenee, Ann, 19.
Dudfield, Mary, 60 ; Thomas, 60.
Dudley, Ann, 175 ; Elizabeth, 277 ; Hannah, 70 ; Lawrence, 277 ; Margaret, 179 ; Sarah, 293 ; Thomas, 179.
Dudman, Elizabeth, 160.
Duell, Anthony, 273 ; Elizabeth, 283 ; Prudence, 273.
Duffield (Duffell), Ann, 207 ; Catherine, 108 ; Ellen, 309 ; Sarah Vernon, 253 ; Thomas, 207.
Du-Hamel, Ann, 144 ; Isaac, 144.
Duke, Ann, 85 ; Edward, 285 ; Elizabeth, 285 ; Grace, 293 ; John, 293 ; Mary, 63, 186.
Dulley, Ann, 257.
Dumas, John, 115 ; Mary, 115.
Dummer, Mary, 206.
Dunbar, Jane, 52 ; Mary, 121 ; Robert, 121 ; William, 52.
Duncan (Dunkun), Andrew, 114 ; Catherine, 166 ; Elizabeth, 114 ; George, 166 ; Mary, 156.
Duncombe, Callaberry, 301 ; David, 86, 161 ; Elizabeth, 161 ; John, 301 ; Judith, 299 ; Margaret, 86 ; Mary Ann, 16.
Dundas, Alexander, 68 ; Catherine, 21 ; Mary, 68.
Dune, Alles, 266 ; Margery, 272.
Dungate, Elizabeth, 84.
Dungitt, Jane, 22 ; John, 22.
Dunkarton, Elizabeth, 97 ; John, 97.
Dunkin, Mary, 72 ; Susanna, 253.
Dunkley, Elizabeth, 252 ; William, 252.
Dunkun, *see* Duncan.
Dunn (Dun), Anne, 288, 307 ; Benjamin, 288 ; Daniel, 59 ; Easter, 34 ; Eleanor, 5 ; Elizabeth, 166, 301 ; James, 5 ; Jane, 252 ; John, 34 ; Jonathan, 202 ; Martha, 295 ; Mary, 215, 235, 285 ; Matthew, 301 ; Sarah, 59, 202, 214, 244 ; Susan, 41 ; Thomas, 41, 295.
Dunnam, Mary, 16.
Dunning (Duning), Alles, 266 ; Ann, 218, 293 ; Richard, 308 ; Robert, 266 ; Sarah, 308 ; Walter, 293.
Dunscombe (Dunscome), Elizabeth, 266, 267.
Dunsdon, Ellen, 305 ; John, 305.
Dunsier, Alexander, 270 ; Katherine, 270.
Dunstan, Elizabeth, 84.
Dunster, Jane, 118.
Dunton, James, 56 ; Mary, 56.
Duplessy, Hannah, 178 ; William, 178.
Dupont, Sarah, 32 ; Peter, 32.
Dupree (Duprey), Ann, 205 ; Elizabeth, 293 ; John, 205, 293.
Duran, Charles, 49 ; Mary, 49.
Durand, Mary, 163.
Durbrig, Joane, 278.
Durdant, Alice, 270 ; Joan, 266 ; James, 270.
Durdell, Elizabeth, 244 ; William, 244.
Durham, Elizabeth, 128 ; John, 128.
Durin, Rachael, 10.
Durnford, Mary, 85 ; Philip, 85.
Durrant, Sarah, 280.
Duston, Henrietta Maria, 39.
Dutens, Elizabeth, 70 ; Peter, 70.
Dutton, Anna, 77.
Dwight, Lydia, 87.
Dyas, Elizabeth, 30.
Dye, Ann, 47 ; Jane, 239 ; William, 239.
Dyer (Dier), Arthur, 281 ; Elizabeth, 281 ; Hannah, 47 ; James, 29 ; Mary, 302 ; Sarah, 29.
Dykes, John, 40, 207 ; Mary, 207 ; Sarah, 40.
Dyman, Martha, 297.
Dyment, Betty, 220.
Dyne, Elizabeth, 208.
Dyneley, Ann, 292.
Dynne (Dynn), Ann, 298 ; Elizabeth, 278 ; John, 278.
Dyson, John, 241.

E

Eades (Eadds, Edes), Alice, 112 ; Barbara, 309 ; Elizabeth, 48 ; Mary, 40 ; Richard, 309.
Eagle, James, 156 ; Mary, 156.
Eaglesfield, Ann, 49 ; George, 49.
Eagleton, Edward, 153 ; Martha, 153.
Eakman, Lawrence, 115 ; Mary, 115.
Eales (Eels), Lucretia, 22 ; Lucy, 144 ; Margaret, 206 ; Mary, 72 ; Thomas, 144.
Ealey (Ealy), Henry, 98 ; Rachael, 243 ; Sarah, 98.
Ealing, Mary, 16.
Eames (Eemes, Emes), Elizabeth, 66 ; Frances 168 ; John, 277 ; Martha, 25, 243*n.* ; Mary 277 ; Penelope, 259 ; Richard, 25 ; William, 66.
Eardley, Nathaniel, 194 ; Susanna, 194.

F

Filber, Ambrose, 150; Ann, 150.
Fildie, Mary, 20.
Filewood, Jane, 239.
Filial, Penelope, 279.
Filkin, Ruchorde, 285; Sarah, 242.
Fillby, Hannah, 134; John, 134.
Fillery, Sarah, 237.
Filley, George, 221; Margaret, 221.
Fillingham, Jane, 186; William, 186.
Fillon, John, 37; Mary, 37.
Fillpot, *see* Philpott.
Filmer, Dorothy, 289; Robert, 289.
Finch, Alice, 292; Ann, 9, 235, 251, 252, 274; Anna Maria, 154; Catherine, 26; Dorothy, 268; Elizabeth, 87, 182, 187; Frances Elizabeth, 236; Grace, 269; Isaac, 274; Jerehjah, 154; John, 175; John Ewer, 87; Katherine, 307; Mary, 175; Richard, 182; Rev. R. P., 222; Samuel, 9, 187; Thomas, 277, 292; William, 236.
Finchett, Arnold, 40; Mary, 40.
Finck, Frederick, 162; Jane, 162.
Findall, Amelia, 163; Jeffery, 163.
Finett, Lucy, 295.
Finn, Robert, 246.
Finton, Dorothy, 39; Francis, 39.
Firebrace, Ann, 195.
Firmin, Easter, 63.
Fish, John, 53; Joseph, 62; Mary, 167; Rose, 62; Susanna, 53.
Fisher, Abraham, 264; Ann, 23, 264, 289, 307; Anna Maria, 154; Blanch, 278; Catherine, 4, 29, 75; Charlotte, 154; Edward, 74, 289; Emm, 74; Gabriel, 272; Hannah, 48; John, 75, 278, 285; Joseph, 159; Katherine, 285; Lidie, 276; Mary, 22, 57, 70, 75, 144, 171, 266, 267, 272, 285, 294; Mary Magdalen, 159; Richard, 22; Samuel, 244; Sarah, 96, 244; Thomas, 23, 48, 276, 294; Rev. Mr., 152.
Fishley, Elizabeth, 213; Mary, 232; Walter, 213, 282.
Fiske, Anna, 261.
Fist, Sarah, 133.
Fitch, Ann, 285; Charles, 285.
Fitchall *alias* Fitsall, James, 209; Jane, 209.
Fitter, Henrietta, 23; Jasper, 23.
Fitzer (Fitzor), Anne, 67; Dorothy, 103.
Fitzgerald, Catherine, 169, 175; Edward, 56; Elizabeth, 28; Hannah, 56, 124; Mary, 21, 99, 228; Richard, 21.
Fitzherbert, Sarah, 120; Thomas, 120.
Fitzmorris, Margaret, 311.
Fitzpatrick, Bryan, 252; John, 215; Mary, 252; Richard, 179; Susanna, 179.
Fitzwater, Elizabeth, 32; Joan, 299; Mary, 189; Thomas, 299.
Flack, John, 250; Susanna, 250.
Flambathe, Elizabeth, 264.
Flather, Elizabeth, 167; James, 167.
Flaunders, Alice, 306; Daniel, 306.
Flawn, Lydia, 122.
Flayle, Catherine, 279; John, 279.
Flecknall, Elizabeth, 264; Mary, 22; William, 22.
Fleetwood, Carr, 101; Hannah, 135; Joseph, 135; Thomas, 101.
Fleming (Flemming, Flemingc), Ann, 275, 278; Christian, 46; Elizabeth, 136; Frances, 283; Gabriel, 56; George, 278; Hannah, 193; Harriet, 251; Henry, 283; John, 23; Mary, 23, 56; Robert, 275; Susanna, 46, 155; Thomas, 251.
Fleshmonger, Anne, 289; Thomas, 289.
Fletcher (Fletchar), Elizabeth, 219, 263, 264, 295; Elizear, 287; Frances, 259; George, 137; Jane, 200, 287; John, 264; Louisa, 117; Margaret, 20; Mary, 12, 138, 157, 220; Rebecca, 308; Richard, 308; Sarah, 102, 137; Thomas, 12; William, 259; Rev. Mr., 108, 146.
Fletchet, Elizabeth, 190; Francis, 190.
Flewster, Margaret, 136.
Flexman, Elizabeth, 54; Joseph, 54.
Flexney, Mary, 180.
Flight, Francis, 15; Margaret, 15.
Fling, Elizabeth, 172; John, 172.
Flint, Alexander, 22; Elza, 260; Frances, 106; Lucretia, 22; Mary, 127.
Flood, Joseph, 44; Mary, 81; Sarah, 44.
Flude, *see* Fluyd.
Floud, Ellen, 301; Mary, 278; Richard, 278.
Flower, Deborah, 211; Jacob, 271; Jane, 68; Margaret, 271; Susanna, 84; Thomas, 68.
Flowerdew, Elizabeth, 285; Samuel, 285.
Flowers, Elizabeth Willby, 171.
Floyd (Flloyd), Alice, 294; Ann, 306; Edward, 302; Elizabeth, 296; Jane, 283, 302; Joyce, 201; Mary, 308; Priscilla, 286; Sarah, 289, 293, 302; William, 293.
Fluse, Elizabeth, 9.
Fluyd (Fludd, Flude), Abraham, 287; Alabaster, 288; Amy, 291; Edward, 275; Helena, 275; Jane, 287; Mary, 288; Richard, 291.
Fly, Rev. Henry, 240, 241.
Foath, Eleanor, 60.
Fobing, Elizabeth, 131*n*.
Foddy, Elizabeth, 210; Richard, 210.
Fogg, Catherine, 110.
Foggs, George, 178; Judith, 178.
Folder, Ann, 35; William, 35.
Foljambe (Foljembe), Eleanor, 239; Henry, 239, 239*n*.
Follett, Sarah, 16.
Folley (Follye), Martha, 309; Susan, 309.
Fontanan, Lucy Elizabeth, 84; Peter, 84.
Foo, Mary, 201.
Fookes, Ann, 310.
Foord, *see* Ford.
Foot (Foote), Ann, 53, 70; Rev. Edward G., 226; Mary, 295; Robert, 53.
Foots, Jane, 137.
Forbes, Martha, 130; Thomas, 130.
Forces, Ann, 229.
Ford (Foord), Ann, 75, 149, 195, 268; Cornelius, 88; Corn., M.A., 1; Gertrude, 300; James, 230; John, 59; Joseph, 53, 213; Lucy, 213; Mary, 38, 88, 194; Mary Ann, 257; Rachael, 53; Ralph, 285, 307; Robert, 268; Samuel, 218; Sarah, 59, 230; Susan, 285, 307; William, 39, 75, 149, 211, 218.
Forman, Ann, 93; Hannah, 238; Henrietta, 207; John, 93.
Forrest, Eleanor, 103; Frances, 275; Grace, 276; Jane, 213, 235, 276; Kerenhappuch, 140; Martha, 4; Sarah, 235.
Forrester, Mary, 196.
Forroll, Mary, 313.
Forse, Margaret, 307.
Forsset, Edmund, 272; Phebe, 272.
Forster, Alice, 82; Charles, 115; Elizabeth, 218; Jane, 149; Margaret, 190; Mary, 54, 56, 115, 171; Thomas, 218.

G

Grigg, Alexander, 150; Elizabeth, 150, 308; Joseph, 149, 198; Margaret, 60; Mary, 198; Susanna, 149.
Griggs, George, 194; Hannah, 94; Mary, 194; Patience, 194; Raby, 94; Thomas, 194.
Grillier, *see* Grellier.
Grilliet, Rene, 166; Susanna, 166.
Grimault, Ann, 108; Esther, 112; James, 108.
Grimes, Mary, 68.
Grimmit, Elizabeth, 191.
Grimsdell, Elizabeth, 30; John, 30.
Grimsmound, Elizabeth, 300; William, 300.
Grimward, Margery, 73; Thomas, 73.
Grindall, Hannah, 72.
Grindley, John, 229; Mary, 229.
Grinwell, Esther, 129; James, 129.
Griszel, Mary, 115.
Grolmen, Elizabeth, 159; John, 159.
Groney, Christian, 40; Robert, 40.
Gronlow, Mary, 123.
Groom, Agnes, 99; Ann, 161; Esther, 94; George, 99; Henry, 155; Jemima, 155; Martha, 139; Sarah, 57; Thomas, 94; William, 57, 139.
Gross, George, 35; Mary, 35.
Grosvenor, Elizabeth, 102; Stephen, 102.
Grout, Mary, 17.
Grove, Alice, 200; Anne, 123; Elizabeth, 164, 310; Honor, 176; Jane, 305; John, 200, 301, 305; Protasie, 301; Thomas, 216; William, 123.
Grover, John, 3; Silence, 3.
Groves, Elizabeth, 133, 151, 242, 249; George, 249; Hannah, 92; Peter, 242; Rachal, 227.
Grubb (Grube), Bridget, 277; John, 165, 185; Martha, 185; Mary, 165; Randolph, 277.
Grumbald, Elizabeth, 141; Susanna, 65.
Grumein, Ann, 5.
Grundy, Bridget, 118; Eleanor, 53; Elizabeth, 34; John, 34; Richard, 118.
Gryffith, *see* Griffith.
Guarinovo, Alice, 281; Joseph, 281.
Guest, Ann, 134; Jane, 124; Richard, 124.
Guidot, Priscilla, 173.
Guillman, Elizabeth, 200.
Gullivell, Anne, 289.
Gulliver, Anne, 82; Elizabeth, 137; Thomas, 137.
Gully, Frances, 307.
Gulson, Ann, 280.
Gumley, Tabitha, 289.
Gundry, Mary, 150; Robert, 150.
Gunn, Catherine, 299; Jane, 220; John, 140, 299; Mary, 135, 140.
Gunner, Ann, 33; Dorothy, 186; Henry, 186; Richard, 33.
Gunning, Elizabeth, 313; Peter, 313.
Gunston, Susanna, 297.
Gunter, Elizabeth, 59.
Gunthorpe, Frances, 8.
Guppey, Elizabeth, 136.
Gurnell (Gurnall), Benjamin, 311; Sarah, 85, 295, 311.
Gurney, Ann, 286; Jane, 168; Margery, 266.
Gusthart, Adiliza, 155; Robert, 155.
Gutteridge, Ann, 180; Rev. Benjamin, 180; Mary, 315; Priscilla, 254.
Guy, Ann, 113; Elizabeth, 286; James, 286; John, 113; Judith, 178; Martha, 301; Mary, 214; Priscilla, 281; Richard, 281; Robert, 230; Theodora, 230; William, 301.
Guyer, John, 251; Sophia, 251.
Gwilliams, Hester, 298.
Gwillim, Edward, 222.
Gwilt, Charles, 149; Mary, 149.
Gwyn (Gwynn), David, 35; Martha, 305; Mary, 35; Mathew, 263, 277; Rebecca, 276.
Gyles, *see* Giles.
Gyn, *see* Ginn.
Gynander, Anne Catherine, 149; Henry Jacob, 149.

H

Hack, Elizabeth, 89; Mary, 120.
Haddon, Elizabeth, 297.
Haden, *see* Hayden.
Hadley, Anne, 93; Bridget, 167; Elizabeth, 59.
Hadsley, Lydia, 308; William, 308.
Hadwin, Eleanor, 162.
Hafeild (Haffeeild), Dorcas, 310; Thomasin, 306; William, 310.
Hafins, Judith, 296.
Hagg, Mary, 55.
Hagger, George, 12; Sarah, 12.
Haig, Jane, 245; John, 245.
Haile, *see* Hale.
Haines, *see* Haynes.
Hake, Ellen, 305.
Hakewell (Hakewill), Catherine, 29; Elizabeth, 66; John, 29, 66; Mary, 145.
Halaway, *see* Halloway.
Halbert, Jane, 190; John, 190.
Hale (Haile), Aaron, 235, 239, 243; Elizabeth, 91; Margaret, 291; Mary, 90; Matthew, 132; Sarah, 239, 243; Susan, 132, 292; Thomas, 90.
Hales, Ann, 95; Edith, 74; Edward, 74, 162; Elizabeth, 292, 296; Frances, 313; Mary, 162; Sarah, 178; William, 95.
Haley (Halleye), Ann, 231, 269; Diana, 189.
Halfaker, Hannah, 278; Thomas, 278.
Halfhead, John, 72; Mary, 72.
Halfhide, Elizabeth, 54; Hannah, 66; John, 54, 161; Susanna, 161.
Halford (Hallford), Ann, 44; Elizabeth, 88; Frances, 283.
Halifax, Rev. James, 226.
Halker, Charles, 70; Hannah, 70.
Hall, Ann, 53, 86, 201, 298; Catherine, 31; Edmund, 307; Eleanor, 288; Elizabeth, 11, 19, 24, 52, 76, 126, 128, 148, 176, 192, 211, 265, 305; Ellen, 60, 268, 269; Francis, 307; George, 135; Grace, 187; Hannah, 107, 138, 174, 247; Henry, 52, 202; Jacob, 138; James, 60; Jeminey, 298; John, 28, 126, 148, 176, 269; Jonathan, 46; Joseph, 107; Judith, 160; Katherine, 289, 291, 307; Lawrence, 298; Margaret, 267, 287; Maria, 253; Mark, 46; Mary, 23, 28, 35, 39, 46*, 56, 65, 70, 135, 155, 162*, 169, 181, 277*, 307; Michael, 296; Nicholas, 211; Philip, 18; Rachael, 18, 56; Ralph, 70; Rebecca, 269; Richard, 267; Robert, 287; Samuel, 56; Sarah, 41, 47, 126, 131, 202; Thomas, 76, 253, 298; Walter, 187; William, 24, 56, 155, 201, 265; Rev. W. J., 261* to 316.*
Hallcley, Margaret, 271; Richard, 271.
Halles, *see* Halls.
Hallett, Ann, 171; Anthony, 287; Henry, 18,

Heritage (Herritage), Hannah, 145; Thomas, 243; William, 145.
Herly, *see* Hurley.
Herne, *see* Hearn.
Heron, Elizabeth, 164; Jane, 166; Peter, 164.
Herrell, Margery, 304.
Herriman, Mary, 281.
Herring, Jane, 160.
Herriott, Selenia, 6.
Hersent, Mary, 284.
Hertwell, Jane, 279.
Heskey, Elizabeth, 221; John, 221.
Hessey, Hesther, 78; James, 78.
Hester, James, 56; Sarah, 56, 202.
Hetfalt, Ann, 263.
Hethwell, Elizabeth, 121.
Heude, Andrew, 138; Mary, 138.
Hewes, *see* Hughes.
Hewitt (Hewet, Hewett, Huett), Ann, 311; Catherine, 155; Edward, 121; Elizabeth, 18, 84; Jane, 302; Judith, 281; Mary, 121; Matthias, 281; Thomas, 155, 302; W., 288.
Hewke, Elizabeth, 47; John, 47.
Hewkin, Sarah, 115.
Hewland, Ann, 28.
Hewlett, Rev. John, B.D., 262.
Hewson, Edward, 299; George, 91; Hester, 299; Joyce, 303; Mary, 91; William, 303.
Heyborne, Elizabeth, 300.
Heycock, *see* Haycock.
Heydon, *see* Haydon.
Heyes, *see* Hays.
Heylin, John, 227; Rebecca, 227.
Heyward, *see* Hayward.
Heywood, *see* Haywood.
Hicchenson, Katherine, 263.
Hichmough, *see* Hitchmough.
Hicker, Jone, 303; Michael, 303.
Hickes, *see* Hicks.
Hickleton, George, 109; Mary, 109.
Hickman, Ann, 99; Eleanor, 72; Elizabeth, 282; George, 282; Rachael, 290; Thomas, 256.
Hicks (Hickes), Abigail, 269; Alie, 1; Ann, 280, 298; Dorothy, 75; Effery, 18; Elizabeth, 24, 73; Emanuel, 1; Hugh, 291; Jane, 141; Joanna, 59; John, 183, 298; Katherine, 291; Litina, 293; Margaret, 293; Milles, 269; Rachael, 285; Sarah, 59, 183; William, 59, 293.
Hickson (Hixon), Jane, 304; John, 304; Margaret, 264; Mary, 19, 133; Phillis, 198.
Hide, *see* Hyde.
Hieatt, *see* Hyatt.
Hier, Christian, 48; John Henry, 48.
Higdon, Sarah, 314.
Higginbothem, (Higinbottom), Joseph, 244; Sarah, 244; —, 282.
Higgins (Higgines, Higgons), Ann, 89, 98, 210, 299; Charles, 261; Elizabeth, 121, 261, 277, 305, 311; Francis, 311; Hannah, 213; James, 98; Jane, 296; John, 294; Joyce, 200; Mary, 21, 129, 294; Rebecca, 27; Richard, 214; Robert, 254; Rev. Thomas, 221* to 226.
Higgs, Edward, 230; Elizabeth, 127; George, 127; Johanna, 279; Mary, 181; Richard, 279; Samuel, 181; Sarah, 230.
Higham, Richard, 146; Sarah, 146.
Highman, W., 245.
Highway, Anthony, 300; Catherine, 300.
Higinbottom, *see* Higginbotham.
Higley, Mary, 25; Walter, 25.
Hignon, Judith, 63.
Hilbert, Barbara, 165.
Hilbery, Mary, 240; Thomas, 240.
Hildred, Charlotte, 257; James, 257.
Hildyard, Francis, 57; Sarah, 57.
Hill, Adam, 178; Alexander, 281; Ann, 61, 111, 140, 152, 202, 281, 283, 293, 298; Audrie, 275; Barbara, 300; Bridget, 270; Charlotte, 226; Daniel, 241; Edward, 305; Eleanor, 48, 311; Elizabeth, 38, 43, 47, 98, 122, 162, 178, 280; Frances, 130; Friswid, 272; Hannah, 152; James, 111; Jane, 6, 299; Joan, 292; John, 38, 50, 106, 217, 224, 245, 248, 275, 292; Joseph, 130; Joyce, 63; Judith, 45, 224; Littleton, 169; Margaret, 114, 169, 285; Martha, 245; Mary, 19, 67, 105, 106, 112, 114, 174, 190, 198, 208, 300, 305; Michael, 63; Miles, 241; Phillis, 298; Phœbe, 108; Rachael, 29; Richard, 283, 293; Robert, 61, 67, 242, 246; Rose, 191; Samuel, 45, 202; Sarah, 50, 111, 123, 168, 224, 242, 248; Susanna, 38, 156; Thomas, 111, 224, 280; William, 98, 105, 112, 162, 198.
Hillam, Elizabeth, 139.
Hillarsden, Elizabeth, 314.
Hillary, Mary Ann, 253; Peter James, 253.
Hilldreth, Elizabeth, 170; John, 170.
Hiller, Ann, 158; Elizabeth, 29, 83; Mary Ann, 106; Maurice, 158; Thomas, 106.
Hilles, *see* Hills.
Hilliar (Helliar, Hellier, Hillier, Hillyear), Annes, 267; Elizabeth, 25, 43, 44; Grace, 289; Henry, 43; John, 289; Mary, 191, 198; Prudence, 232.
Hilliard, Gregory, 272; John, 285; Margaret, 272; Mary, 229, 311; Richard, 311; Susan, 285; Thomas, 229.
Hillier, *see* Hilliar.
Hillman, Margaret, 305; Thomas, 305; Rev. Mr. Thomas, 14; Rev. Mr., 34* to 149.*
Hills (Hilles), Anne, 24; Elizabeth, 246; Hannah, 76; James, 234; John, 24; Judith, 265; Sarah, 280; Silence, 37; Stephen, 280.
Hillton, *see* Hilton.
Hillyard, John, 94; Margaret, 296; Mary, 94.
Hillyear, *see* Hilliar.
Hilson, Katherine, 297; Ranere, 297.
Hilton (Hillton), Ann, 57, 293; Elizabeth, 124; Esther, 189; Jane, 124; John, 225, 293; Mary, 306; Robert, 124, 306.
Hince, John, 309; Rebecca, 309.
Hinch, Elizabeth, 314.
Hinchliff, Margaret, 84.
Hincksman, Anna, 278; Richard, 278.
Hinde (Hind, Hynde), Ann, 114; Ascanis, 306; Dorothy, 297; James, 114; Jane, 294; Mary, 185, 268, 306; Richard, 297.
Hinderson, *see* Henderson.
Hindmarsh, Jane, 95.
Hindson, David, 79; Hannah, 79.
Hine, Rebecca, 302; Thomas, 302.
Hines, Elizabeth, 163; Roger, 163.
Hingston, Christian, 31; John, 31.
Hinket, Elizabeth, 201.
Hinman, Mary, 309.
Hinsoll, Elizabeth, 183.
Hinton, Ann, 120, 162; Catherine, 137; David, 218; Edward, 11; Elizabeth, 16, 119, 191; Frances, 11; John, 137; Martha, 73; Mary, 218; Richard, 120; Robert, 162, 191; Vincent, 119; Rev. Mr., 166.
Hiorn, Hester, 77; John, 77.

Honore (Honor), Deborah, 184 ; Elizabeth, 65 ; Peter, 65.
Honyborne, Constance, 24.
Honychurch, John, 192 ; Mary, 192.
Honyman, Mary, 3, 28 ; Richard, 3.
Hoockes, Elizabeth, 297 ; Nicholas, 297.
Hoockham, Leonard, 309 ; Margery, 309.
Hood (Hoode), Allison, 192 ; Ann, 122 ; Elizabeth Maria, 235 ; Hannah, 242 ; Hannah Maria, 258 ; John, 192, 242 ; Susanna, 259, 291 ; Thomas, 259 ; Ursula, 265 ; William, 235.
Hooke (Hook), Ann, 73, 138 ; Elizabeth, 286 ; Jane, 25 ; Sarah, 69 ; Thomas, 73, 286.
Hooker, Alles, 265 ; Ann, 20, 168 ; Elizabeth, 129 ; John, 129 ; Margaret, 132 ; Mary, 163 ; Sarah, 166 ; Thomas, 20.
Hoole, Margery, 233.
Hooper, Elizabeth, 103, 135, 147 ; Frances, 73 ; Grundy, 127 ; John, 73 ; Mary, 57, 127 ; Robert, 147 ; Sarah, 54.
Hoor, *see* Hoar.
Hooton, Charles, 199 ; Mary, 199.
Hope, Elizabeth, 305 ; Ely, 109 ; Henry, 305 ; James, 290 ; Jane, 290 ; Jemima, 309 ; Judith, 139.
Hopegood, Elizabeth, 84.
Hoper, Mary, 277.
Hopkin, Elizabeth, 17.
Hopkins (Hobkins), Alice, 308 ; Ann, 123, 163, 215, 311 ; Cicelia, 280 ; Edward, 143, 215, 280 ; Eleanor, 286 ; Elizabeth, 88, 115, 192, 280, 289 ; Haddon, 163, 202 ; Jonas, 289 ; Lawrence, 272 ; Margaret, 272 ; Mary, 121, 143, 174, 201, 202 ; Richard, 237, 289, 280 ; Roger, 311 ; Thomas, 192.
Hopper, Susan, 269 ; Timothy, 269.
Hopperton, Elizabeth, 162 ; Samuel, 162.
Hoppey, Hannah, 230.
Hopton, Richard, 294 ; Susanna, 294.
Hopwaft, Henry, 257.
Hopwood, Ephraim, 137 ; John, 160 ; Mary, 137 ; Sarah, 160.
Horbutt, Elizabeth, 56.
Hord, Eleanor, 17.
Horder, Mary Ann, 253 ; T. W., 253 ; V. T., 253.
Horichett, John, 265 ; Margaret, 265.
Hornblowe, Barbara, 270.
Hornblower, Ann, 179 ; William, 179.
Hornby (Hornebee), Ann, 288 ; Daniel, 25 ; Elizabeth, 25.
Horne (Horn), Ann, 88, 242, 247, 307 ; Charles, 226* to 245* ; Dorothy, 234 ; Edward, 98, 236 ; Elizabeth, 14, 63, 77 ; Elizabeth Catherine, 240 ; E., 228 to 252 ; Grace, 72 ; James, 14 ; Jane, 237 ; Joyce, 111 ; Marsba, 236, 243 ; Mary, 241, 246, 248, 249 ; Parnell, 98 ; Stephen, 243 ; Thomas, 242, 246, 247.
Horner, Anne, 56 ; Frederick, 144 ; George, 74 ; Isabella, 74 ; Rev. John, 235 ; Mary, 144 ; William, 56.
Hornsby (Hornsboe), Ann, 71, 169 ; Edward, 71 ; Jonathan, 169 ; Sarah, 216.
Horrocks, Priscilla, 107.
Horsenaile (Horsnaile), Christopher, 127 ; Elizabeth, 302 ; Mary, 127.
Horsey, Sarah, 230.*
Horsfield, Ann, 134.
Horskins, Esther, 72.
Horsley, Hannah, 174 ; Sarah, 35.
Horsman, Mary, 152 ; Samuel, 152.
Horton (Horten), Alice, 151 ; Ann, 281 ; John, 1, 151 ; Mary, 1 ; Sarah, 38 ; Thomas, 284 ; Rev. Mr., 14.
Horwell, Frances, 84.
Hose, Elizabeth, 132 ; Thomas, 132.
Hosey, John, 96 ; Sarah, 96.
Hosier, Ann, 200 ; John, 200.
Hoskins, George, 184 ; Henry, 252 ; Mary, 252 ; Sarah, 184.
Hoskinson, Jane, 108.
Hosley, Mary, 210.
Hossack, Daniel, 292 ; Elizabeth, 292.
Host, Elizabeth, 167 ; Joseph, 167.
Hotchin, Ann, 146 ; Henry, 146.
Hotchkin, Jane, 303 ; John, 303.
Hotchkiss, Anna Christiana, 97 ; Vincent, 97.
Hotham, K., 261.
Houchett, Justinian, 66 ; Mary, 66.
Houdten *alias* Houdetn, Andrew, 73 ; Elizabeth, 73.
Hough, Elizabeth, 308 ; Jane, 300 ; John, 106 ; Susanna, 106.
Houghton, Elizabeth, 79, 303 ; Robert, 303.
Houldsworth, Grace, 64 ; William, 64.
Houlton, Elizabeth, 208 ; Ellen, 313 ; Isabella, 225 ; John, 225 ; Mary Ann, 206 ; Rebecca, 256 ; Robert, 206 ; William, 256.
Hounsfeeild, Joan, 299 ; Samuel, 299.
Houseman (Housman), Ann, 115 ; Joyce, 78.
Housson, *see* Howson.
Hovell, Elizabeth, 68 ; William, 68.
Hovord, Ann, 169 ; Philo, 169.
How, *see* Howe.
Howard, Alice, 296 ; Anne, 73, 156, 241, 247 ; Elizabeth, 31, 41, 52, 73, 121, 148, 289 ; Fanny, 247 ; George, 296 ; Grace, 11 ; Hannah, 205 ; Harriet, 85 ; Henry, 11, 121 ; Jane, 114 ; John, 52 ; Joseph, 73 ; Josiah, 200 ; Mary, 4, 162, 200 ; Prudence, 98 ; Richard, 41 ; Sarah, 106 ; William, 31, 247, 289.
Howdell, Rev. John, 206 ; Patience, 206.
Howe (How), Abigail, 37 ; Alice, 296 ; Ann, 223, 282 ; Barbara, 148 ; Elizabeth, 32, 87 ; George, 34 ; Henry, 32 ; John, 223 ; Martha, 34 ; Mary, 41, 145, 150 ; Richard, 148 ; Sarab, 2 ; Thomas, 282.
Howell (Howle), Alice, 134 ; Catherine, 257, 259 ; Charles, 13 ; Christian, 275 ; Edward, 180 ; Isabel, 287 ; James, 287 ; Jane, 160, 180 ; John, 134 ; Martha, 183 ; Mary, 92, 138, 245, 255, 257 ; Rebecca, 261 ; Richard, 183, 255, 257 ; Sarah, 13, 255 ; Thomas, 92, 138.
Howes, Litchfield, 168 ; Margaret, 256 ; Penelope, 168 ; Rev. Thomas, 222 ; William, 256, 294 ; Winnifred, 294.
Howgrave, Ellen, 294.
Howit, Lydia, 68.
Howland, Ann, 54 ; Augustin, 54 ; Elizabeth, 163 ; Frances, 75 ; Joseph, 186 ; Mary, 186.
Howle, *see* Howell.
Howlett, Elizabeth, 67, 236 ; John, 219 ; Joseph, 166 ; Mary, 166, 174 ; Robert, 174 ; William, 67.
Howse, Katherine, 287 ; Mary, 275 ; Roger, 287 ; Thomas, 275.
Howsell, Jane, 27.
Howson (Housson), Ann, 56 ; Eleanor, 110 ; Elizabeth, 29 ; Hannah, 70 ; Henry, 110 ; Mary, 107, 278 ; Ralph, 56 ; Sarah, 134 ; Thomas, 107.
Hoxley, Mary, 138.
Hoy (Hoye), Frances, 305 ; Jenny, 15 ; John, 15 ; Mary, 149 ; Richard, 305 ; Samuel, 149.
Hoyken, John, 282 ; Margaret, 282.

I

J

Timothy, 301; Tudor, 222; Vincent, 61; William, 11, 15, 63, 185, 214, 217, 243, 247, 252, 254, 280, 302; William Styles, 248*; Rev. Dr., 33; Rev. Mr., 70 to 168.
Jonn, *see* John.
Jope, Caleb, 119; Elizabeth, 119.
Jordan (Jordine, Jourdain, Jourdan), Anne, 72, 183, 242; Benjamin, 77; Catherine, 77; Cecilia, 302; Elizabeth, 66, 121, 145, 153, 199; Emery, 121; Hannah, 69; James, 246; Joanna, 144; John, 72; Mark, 153; Mary, 18, 42, 58, 246, 311; Nicholas, 58; Rachael, 6; Richard, 216; Sarah, 21, 295; William, 121.*
Joselyn (Joslin), Elizabeth, 209, 218.
Joseph, Mary, 27.
Jourquet, Jane, 142.
Joyce, Alice, 271; Ann, 48, 56; Eleanor, 120; John, 56; Joseph, 120; Sarah, 131.
Joye, Lucy, 293; William, 293.
Jubb, Jane, 242; Sarah, 191.
Jubber, Barbara, 177.
Juck, Jane, 90.
Jucks, Susanna, 204.
Juda, Mary, 175.
Judd, Anthony, 285; Margaret, 285; Rolana, 69.
Juddin, Alice, 284.
Judery, Mary, 68.
Judge, Elizabeth, 195; Frances, 154; Joanna, 210; William, 154.
Judgson, Sarah, 13.
Judkin, Mary, 240.
Juer, Henry, 3; Mary, 15; Sarah, 3.
Jues, Mary, 315.
Jull, Elizabeth, 207.
Julson, Grace, 287.
Jump, Ruth, 72.
Jury, Elizabeth, 58.
Justice, Susan, 294.
Juxon, Mary, 307; Susanna, 183.

K

Kam, Mary, 13.
Kamp, Jane, 143.
Kañ, Francis Jockim Gram, 38; Mary, 38.
Kane, *see* Cane.
Karby, Ann, 9.
Kaslar, Ann, 217; Christopher, 217.
Katharines, Mary, 281.
Katterns, Elizabeth, 46.
Kay (Kaye), Ann, 4; John, 4, 191; Mary, 174; Rose, 191; Sarah, 48; William, 48.
Keate (Keet), Edward, 219; Elizabeth, 219; John, 110; Sarah, 110.
Keating, Grace, 311; John, 311.
Kebal, Beata, 193.
Keddey, George, 193; Martha, 193.
Keech, Elizabeth, 25.
Keele (Keil), Elizabeth, 171; Jane, 156.
Keeling (Kelin), Ann, 71, 186; Humphrey, 284; Jane, 284; John, 186; Mary, 44.
Keene (Keen), Elizabeth, 73, 98, 178; Grace, 33; Henry, 175; Joan, 295; John, 178; Joseph, 73; Martha, 64; Mary, 159; Morgan, 33; Richard, 159, 295; R., 238 to 244; Sarah, 137, 175.
Keep (Keepe), Ann, 184; Elizabeth, 292; Francis, 292; George, 75; Isabel, 126; John, 126; Mary, 75; Susanna, 5.
Keet, *see* Keate.
Keeton, Katherine, 286.
Kefford, Blanch, 271; John, 271.
Keighley (Keighly), Rev. Mr., 94 to 206.
Keightly, Charles, 104; Elizabeth, 104.
Keil, *see* Keele.
Keinsey, Mary, 48.
Keisar, Alice, 296.
Keith, Elizabeth, 12.
Kekwick, Fanny, 240.
Kelham, Bridget, 282; Edmund, 281; Mary, 281.
Kelin, *see* Keeling.
Kelk, Ann, 158.
Kell, Sarah, 60; Tabitha, 194.
Kellfull, Ann, 210.
Kellock, *see* Killock.
Kelloway (Kellaway), Elizabeth, 306; Robert, 105; Susanna, 105.
Kelly (Kelley), Affabilea, 142; Elizabeth, 186; Henry, 142; James, 251; Jane, 18; John, 264; Margaret, 196, 264; Mary, 251.
Kelse, James, 64; Mary, 64.
Kelsey, A. H., 253; Edward, 253; Harriet Sophia, 253.
Kember, Elizabeth, 167.
Kempe (Kemp), Andrew, 266; Ann, 55, 110, 231; Daniel, 172; Elizabeth, 172, 203, 309; Jane, 250; Jenkyn, 309; John, 110; Lydia, 240; Mary, 59, 231, 236, 244, 296; Matthew, 244; Nicholas, 64; Rebecca, 282; Richard, 282; Sarah, 64; Susan, 266; William, 55, 231, 236.
Kempton, Johanna, 280; John, 280.
Kemsall, Mary, 311; Peter, 311.
Kendall, Ann, 254; Benjamin, 136; Elizabeth, 219, 229; Henry, 219; Joanna, 289; Mary, 33, 136; Sarah, 88.
Kendrick, Amy, 6; Esther, 36; Hannah, 134; William, 36.
Kennedy (Kenedy, Kennady), Ann, 29, 70; Augustus, 221; James, 152; Rebecca, 152.
Kennett, Frances, 212; Thomas, 212.
Kenniston, Bryan, 308; Elizabeth, 308; Humphrey, 263; Lucy, 263.
Kensett, Elizabeth, 119; John, 119.
Kensley, Anne, 304.
Kent, Anna Maria, 130; Ann, 145; Avis, 263; Edman, 298; Elizabeth, 96, 111, 138, 270, 276; George, 245; Isaac, 14; James, 96; Jane, 205, 274; Joan, 266; John, 103, 130, 161; Margaret, 103, 245; Martha, 161, 298; Mary, 132, 166, 287; Sarah, 14; Thomas, 111, 263, 287; William, 166.
Kentish, Elizabeth, 169; Jane, 44; Johan, 275; Mary, 5; Richard, 275.
Kenwrick, Rev. Mr., 42.
Kenyon, Charles, 119; Mary, 119.
Kerby, *see* Kirby.
Kerly, Sarah, 202.
Kerr (Ker), Elizabeth, 67, 86; Mary, 23; Thomas, 67; William, 86.
Kerry, Ann, 112.
Kerstersou, John, 266, 269; Magdalen, 266, 269.
Kerton, *see* Kirton.
Kerwell, Susanna, 95.
Kettle, Ann, 71; Elizabeth, 61; Grace, 132; James, 61; Joseph, 71, 132; Margaret, 183.
Kevell, Edmund, 308; Elizabeth, 308.
Kevets, Frances, 26.
Kewell, John, 65; Mary, 65.
Key, Anne, 287; Florence, 273; Gabriel, 287; Joan, 314.
Keyess, Mary, 246.
Keyle, Mary, 293; Thomas, 293.

L

M

Mackay, Alexander, 155; Elizabeth, 155.
Mackcullach, David, 140; Margaret, 140.
Mackee, *see* Mackie.
Mackelean, Ann, 206; Nicholas, 206.
Mackenzie (Mackenzey), Alexander, 203; Jane, 83; Mary, 139, 203.
Mackett, Anne, 109.
Mackie (Mackee), John, 80; Mary, 128; Sarah, 80.
Mackinder, Dorothy, 273; John, 273.
Mackintosh, Charles, 141; Margery, 239; Mary, 141.
Macklane, Elizabeth, 71; John, 71.
Macklaren, Anne, 256, 259; Charlotte, 256, 259; James, 256; William, 259.
Macklin, Jane, 210.
Mackly, Elizabeth, 305; John, 305.
Mackoy, Margaret, 221.
Mackrell, Deborah, 211; Richard, 211.
Macleod, Alexandrina Anna, 127; Jane, 83; John, 83.
Maclery, Sarah, 96; Thomas, 96.
Macquillin, Richard James, 236.
Macro, John, 306; Mary, 306.
Maddock, Martha, 90.
Maddocks (Maddox, Madox), Elizabeth, 38; Frances, 273, 297; James, 28; John, 282; Mary, 28; Thomas, 297.
Madham, Sarah, 51.
Madther, Elizabeth, 285; Walter, 285.
Magdalen, Mary, 312.
Maggott, Elizabeth, 144; Jane, 26.
Magrath, Frances, 117; James, 117.
Magson, Elizabeth, 40, 310; Frances Ann, 190; Robert, 190; Thomas, 310.
Maid, Simon, 211.
Maidment, James, 214; Martha, 214.
Maidmun, Rev. J., 238.
Maidstone, Sarah, 54.
Mailes, Elizabeth, 138; Thomas, 138, 213.
Maillard, *see* Maylard.
Mainard, *see* Maynard.
Maine, *see* Mayne.
Maingett, Daniel, 138; Elizabeth, 109; Jane, 138.
Mainstone, Esther, 20.
Maior, *see* Mayor.
Maitland, Ann, 123; William, 123.
Major, Ellen, 26; Thomas, 26;
Makemault, James, 130; Martha, 130.
Makepeace, Jane, 179; Samuel, 179.
Makins, Ann, 51; William, 51.
Malby, Mary, 304.
Malcher, Elizabeth, 103; Mary, 39; William, 103.
Maldon, Elizabeth, 302; George, 302.
Maldus, Rev. Mr., 135.
Malin, *see* Mallin.
Malkin, Elizabeth, 152; Richard, 152.
Mallandain, James, 70; Rachael Susanna, 70.
Mallard, Anne, 121; Jane, 295.
Mallet (Mallett), Alice, 279; Elizabeth, 277; John, 277; Rebecca, 185; William, 185, 279.
Mallick, Robert, 21; Susanna, 21.
Mallin (Malin), Penelope, 68; Sarah, 10; Tomisson, 299.
Mallory, Charles, 96; Elizabeth, 96.
Mallyon, Isaac, 252.
Maltus (Maltas), Ann, 51; Rev. Mr. F., 178.
Malwerth, Winifred, 263.
Manby, Ann, 100; Edward, 100; Elizabeth, 235; William, 235.
Manchester, Elizabeth, 90.
Mandevill, Isabella, 9; William, 9.
Mandy, Elizabeth, 285; Francis, 285; Sally, 257.
Maner, Christopher Ludewig, 246.
Maney, Lucas, 281; Mary, 281.
Manley (Manle, Manly), Ann, 40; Berry, 105; Dorothy, 298; Henry, 38; Johanna, 229; John, 40; John Henry, 229; Margaret, 297; Mary, 39, 105, 167; Sarah, 38; Thomas, 297.
Mann (Man), Elizabeth, 315; George, 276; Frances, 276; Henry, 260, 315; James, 207; Martha, 313; Penelope, 163; Samuel, 211; Sarah, 207, 308; Thomas, 308.
Mannell, Alice, 314; William, 314.
Manners, Lord Robert, 217.
Manning, Daniel, 209; Eleanor, 120; Elizabeth, 22, 209; Jane, 281; Mary, 49; Richard, 22; William, 120.
Mannister, Elizabeth, 43; Nathaniel, 43.
Mannooch, Elizabeth, 83; Philip, 83.
Manoury, Esther, 112; John, 112.
Mansbridge, Ann, 226; Richard, 226.
Mansell, Henry, 268; Rachael, 268; Sarah, 93.
Manser, Elizabeth, 257; Mary, 257; William, 257.
Manslow, Jane, 21.
Manson, Mary, 124.
Mantle, Martha, 91; Susanna, 1.
Manton, Susanna, 164.
Manwaring (Mannering, Maynwaring), Ann, 117; Arthur, 102; Catherine, 102; Martha, 113.
Maperley, Ann, 211; Walter, 211* to 215.*
Maples, Christiana, 198; Elizabeth, 138; Hannah, 117; John, 117.
Maplesden (Maplisden), Mary, 288, 313.
Mapleton, Mary, 26.
Marah (Mara), Edward, 208; Hannah, 208; Rev. John, A.B., 208; Mary, 248.
Marbery, Emme, 270.
Marbrow, Rev. Mr., 282.
Marcellus, Mary, 229.
March, Ann, 29, 176; Charles, 16; Elizabeth, 275; Henry, 275; Mary, 16; William, 225.
Marchall, *see* Marshall.
Marcham, Elizabeth, 209; Simon, 209.
Marchant (Marchante), Anne, 271; James, 274; Jane, 274.
Marchegay, Catherine, 125.
Marcy, Sarah, 59.
Marden, Mary, 296.
Margetson, Ann, 293; James, 293.
Margett, Ann, 201; Susanna, 173.
Margetts, Anne, 129; Sarah, 114.
Marham, John, 191; Mary, 191.
Mariner, Amy, 298.
Maris, Mary, 103.
Mark, Catherine, 1.
Markey, Ann, 46.
Markham, Ann, 144; George, 232; Martha, 244*; Thomas, 244.
Markinfield, Elizabeth, 141; William, 141.
Markland, Elizabeth, 273; John, 273.
Marks, Ann, 224; William, 224.
Marle, Anthony, 108; Margaret, 108.
Marlow, Elizabeth, 227.
Marlton, Ann, 249; Thomas, 249.
Marpole, Ann, 225; George, 225; Mary, 225.
Marr (Marre), Henry, 109; Martha, 109; Mary, 130; Nicholette, 312.
Marriott (Marriatt, Marryott, Maryat), Bar-

10, 300; Frances, 77; Henry, 87; Martha, 144, 212; Mary, 219; Rebecca, 191; Samuel, 212; Sarah, 87; William, 212, 215, 219; Mrs., 215.
Mayne (Main, Maine), Ann, 64; Elizabeth, 14, 35, 60, 289; George, 35; Lawrence, 292; Martha, 220; Mary, 172, 292; Philip, 220.
Mayney, Elizabeth, 278; John, 278.
Maynwaring, *see* Manwaring.
Mayo, Ann, 220; Daniel, 220; Joseph, 220; Susanna, 187.
Mayor (Maior), Ann, 217; Christopher, 106; Elizabeth, 313; Hannah, 106; Katherine, 304; Mary, 58; William, 313.
Mays, Elizabeth, 222; Grace, 170; John, 222.
Maysmore, Grace, 237.
McCarthy, Florence, 259; Helen, 259.
McCarty (MacCarty), Catherine, 118; James, 222; Mark, 118; Mary, 222.
McClye, John, 107; Mary, 107.
McCoy, John, 257; Mary Ann, 257.
McDonald (Mackdonell, McDonall), Deborah Catherine, 158; Elizabeth, 87; William, 87.
McDouall, Catherine, 241; David Dundas, 241.
McFarlan, Elizabeth, 247; John, 247.
McGann, Luke, 248.
McGilchrist, Rev. Mr., 157*, 164*, 165.*
McKaine, James, 226.
McLean, Daniel, 76; Elizabeth, 76, 218; James, 218; Mary, 29; Michael, 29.
Meacham, Sarah, 80.
Meacher, William, 254.*
Meade, Elizabeth, 98; Jane, 249, 290; Judith, 297; Richard, 290; Thomas, 249; Tomlinson, 74; Rev. Mr., 123, 145.
Meader, Elizabeth, 185.
Meades (Meads), Edward, 119; Elizabeth, 299; Mary, 62, 119; Thomas, 62, 299.
Meadows (Meddowes), Bridget, 315; Elizabeth, 63, 127; John, 63; Priscilla, 281; Samuel, 251.
Meadwell, Catherine, 133; John, 133.
Meager, Jane, 255; Thomas, 255.*
Meakin (Meakyn), Lewis, 308; Margaret, 146; Mary, 305, 308; Robert, 305.
Meale, Ann, 173.
Meantis, Arthur, 302; Elizabeth, 302.
Meare (Meere), Catherine, 25; Elizabeth, 313; Richard, 25.
Meares (Mears, Meres), Elizabeth, 287; John, 226*, 227*, 228*, 229*, 230*, 231*, 232*, 233, 234*, 235*, 236*, 237*; Lydia, 302; Mary, 234, 286; Peyton, 286; Senesh, 292; William, 292.
Measey, Katherine, 308.
Meason, Margaret, 273; Thomas, 273.
Medborn, Elizabeth, 299; George, 299.
Medburne, Elizabeth, 268.
Medcalfe (Medcafe), Elizabeth, 298, 305; Richard, 298.
Meddowes, *see* Meadowes.
Medlebur, Elizabeth, 307.
Medler, Maria, 249.
Medley, Samuel, 199; Sarah, 199.
Meebourne, George, 154; Sarah, 154.
Meek, Ann, 53; Mary, 60; Richard, 53.
Meekins (Meakemes, Meekens, Mekins), Ann, 176, 297; Godin, 176; Margaret, 290; Mary, 252; Thomas, 297.
Meere, *see* Meare.
Meierhoff, John, 170; Sarah, 170.
Meirvin, Henrietta, 152.
Meldrum, Elizabeth, 148; Robert, 148.
Mell, Elizabeth, 310; Thomas, 310.
Meller, Elizabeth, 165.
Mellichamp, Kezia, 80; Lewin, 80.
Mellish, John, 252.
Mellone, Jane, 52.
Mellor, C., 239.
Meloy, Elizabeth, 59; John, 59.
Melton, Ann, 299; George, 299; Margaret, 298.
Melven, Dinah, 26; John, 26.
Memberry, Mary Ann, 106.
Mendez, Abraham, 144; Margaret, 144.
Mendlove, Ann, 238.
Mercer (Merser), James, 26; Mary, 14, 264; Rhoda, 96; Sarah, 26.
Meredith, Ann, 273; Charles, 295; Elizabeth, 138; Frances, 3; Lucy, 295; Susanna, 202; William, 138, 202.
Meres, *see* Meares.
Merigeot, Elizabeth, 132; John, 132.
Meriton, Elizabeth, 142; Henry, 242; Jane, 242; Luke, 242.
Merle, Mary Ann, 197.
Merrefield (Merryfield), Ann, 301; Jane, 62; Thomas, 62.
Merrick, Elizabeth, 93; Frances, 150; George, 10; Jane, 10; Mary, 117; Rev. M., 228; William, 93.
Merrill, Elizabeth, 10; John, 10.
Merriman, Ann, 208.
Merrin, Judith, 26; Richard, 26.
Merriott, Mary, 130; Richard, 130.
Merritt (Merrit), Diana, 59; Francis, 41; John, 227; Mary, 13; Sarah, 41.
Merry, Ann, 287; Elizabeth, 115; Joseph, 115.
Merryweather, John, 138; Martha, 138.
Merser, *see* Mercer.
Mertins, Mary, 201; William, 201.
Meservy, Susan, 285.
Meslier, Maria Ann, 188; Paul, 188.
Messenger (Messinger), Joane, 271; Lucy, 154; Richard, 271.
Messiter, Ann, 201.
Mestoe, Mary, 293.
Metcalfe, Ann, 107, 112; Diana, 26; Jemima, 155; Margaret, 142; Richard, 26; Sarah, 229; William, 142.
Methuen, Mary, 118; William, 118.
Methwold, Mary, 163.
Mew, Isabel, 313; John, 313.
Mewburne, Elizabeth, 121.
Meyer, Paul, 20; Sarah, 20.
Meymac, Ann, 59; Anthony, 59.
Meyrick, Ann, 96.
Michell (Michel), Ann, 183; Elizabeth, 198, 279; Jane, 259; Mary, 26; Peter, 198; Philip, 26, 183; Tobias, 259; William, 279.
Michellett, Mary Ann, 23.
Michie, Mary, 151.
Michilson, Barbara, 48.
Mickelfield, Elizabeth, 120; John, 271; Joshiah, 120; Sarah, 271.
Middlebrook, Mary, 45, 190; Robert, 45.
Middleditch, Elizabeth, 99; Rebecca, 137; William, 137.
Middlehurst, James, 167; Mary, 167.
Middlemore, Elizabeth, 293; Henry, 293.
Middleton, Alice, 65; Ann, 284; Elizabeth, 190, 204; John, 222; Loyd, 135; Richard, 220; Sarah, 119, 135; Susanna, 48; William, 119.
Midgley, Margaret, 184.

 B B B

Musgrove, Fanny, 198 ; Martha, 116 ; William, 116.
Mushamp, Hester, 290.
Muskett, Mary, 152.
Mutten, Grace, 269 ; Richard, 269.
Myers, Elizabeth, 48.
Myhill, Elizabeth, 58 ; George, 58.
Mylett, *see* Millett.
Mynatt, Elizabeth, 38 ; John, 38.
Mynne (Minn), Ann, 289 ; Elizabeth, 220 ; Jane, 285.
Mynnes, Samuel, 182 ; Sarah, 182.
Mynsse, Magdalen, 264.
Mynton, *see* Minton.
Myon, Ferdinand, 169 ; Mary, 169.

N

Nablet, Ann, 285.
Nadall, Peter, 223.
Naden, Martha, 209.
Naish, *see* Nash.
Nancken, Jane, 246.
Napper (Naper), Annes, 270 ; Elizabeth, 128, 279.
Narwell, Ralph, 223.
Nash (Naish), Alice, 9 ; Ann, 32, 118, 289 ; A., 240 ; Charlotte, 194 ; Dorothy, 8 ; Elizabeth, 39, 74, 265 ; Ferrers, 194 ; Frances, 241 ; Rev. John, 227 ; John, 39, 93, 118, 265, 288 ; Joshua, 141 ; Judith, 301 ; Lydia, 141 ; Mary, 72, 163, 174 ; Robert, 301 ; Ruth, 111 ; Sarah, 93, 130, 156 ; Thomas, 72, 289 ; Tomisson, 288 ; William, 111, 241.
Nassau, Hon. Lady Frances, 81.
Naw, Ann, 312 ; Stephen, 312.
Nay, Ann, 100.
Naylor (Nayler), Ann, 12 ; Catherine, 52, 127 ; Frances, 251, 278 ; James, 127 ; John, 12 ; Margaret, 206 ; Mary, 251 ; Sarah, 137, 214 ; Thomas, 206, 214.
Neadhurst, Edmond, 269 ; Joan, 269.
Nealand, Rebecca, 276 ; Samuel, 276.
Neale, Alice, 13 ; Clements, 290 ; Deborah, 309 ; Elizabeth, 3, 181, 206 ; Esther, 16 ; Francis, 283 ; Gervas, 13 ; Henry, 290 ; Mary, 103, 164 ; Matthias, 206 ; Peter, 43 ; Rachael, 43 ; Ruth, 283 ; Thomas, 103, 309.
Neate, Jenny, 202.
Neave (Neve), Ann, 297 ; Elizabeth, 291, 311 ; Frances, 302 ; Robert, 289 ; Susanna, 289 ; William, 311.
Neazer, Elizabeth, 41.
Nedel, Ann, 183.
Needes, Bridget, 277.
Needham (Nedhame), Ann, 167, 273 ; Elizabeth, 70, 245 ; George, 167 ; Leonard, 273 ; Mary, 90 ; Robert, 245 ; Sarah, 32.
Needler, Elizabeth, 73 ; William, 73.
Neeld, Parnella, 282 ; Robert, 282.
Neeler, Eleanor, 275.
Neep, Cornelius, 202 ; Sarah, 202.
Neeves, Ann, 59 ; Corbett, 59.
Negus, Rev. Mr., 200.
Nehring, Frances, 8 ; John, 8.
Neilson, Allison, 192 ; Elizabeth, 101.
Nelham, Catherine, 280.
Nell, Beneria, 111 ; Daniel, 111 ; Elizabeth, 145 ; Henry, 125 ; Joan, 208 ; Ursula, 125.
Nelson, Alexander, 205 ; Ann, 44, 189 ; Anna, 207 ; Elizabeth, 83, 291 ; Hannah, 173 ; Henrietta Maria, 94 ; John, 173, 189, 233, 264 ; Magdalene, 264 ; Mary, 55, 205 ; Matthew, 291 ; Richard, 55 ; Robert, 94 ; Sarah, 233 ; Seth, 207 ; Susanna, 199 ; Tobitha, 194 ; Zachary, 194 ; Rev. Mr., 207.
Nepucie, Mary, 15 ; Peter, 15.
Nethaway, Elizabeth, 17 ; Richard, 17.
Nethercoat, Martha, 128.
Nettlefould, Elizabeth, 286.
Nettles, Mary, 307.
Nettleship, Mary, 160.
Neuenburchg, Ann, 47 ; John, 47.
Nevard, Sarah, 276.
Neverson, Ann, 112 ; Thomas, 112.
Nevill (Nevile), Elizabeth, 204, 305 ; Hannah, 246 ; Lord Harry, 263 ; Jane, 164 ; Johane, 276 ; John, 246 ; Mary, 144, 145 ; Richard, 145 ; Titus, 164.
Nevin, Margery, 73.
Nevis, John, 306 ; Mary, 306.
New, Mary, 172.
Newberry, Anna, 278 ; Elizabeth, 78 ; Isaac, 78.
Newbon, Elizabeth, 199.
Newbould, Elizabeth, 93.
Newbourne, Elizabeth, 75.
Newby (Newbee), Ann, 99, 184 ; Mary, 173 ; Thomas, 99.
Newcomb (Newcome), Elizabeth, 44, 285 ; Hannah, 221 ; John, 23 ; Lydia, 43 ; Richard, 43 ; Thomas, 44 ; Usle, 23.
Newdegate (Newdygate), Mary, 280 ; Sarah, 174.
Newell, Ann, 180 ; Elizabeth, 199 ; Hephzibah, 195 ; Mary, 110 ; Susanna, 248 ; William, 195.
Newham, Ann, 19.
Newhouse, Mary, 211.
Newingtone, Marian, 272.
Newland, Andrew, 231 ; Earl, 9 ; Elizabeth, 101 ; Susanna, 9.
Newman, Alice, 294 ; Ann, 36, 58, 286, 312, 313 ; Bridget, 118 ; Charles, 148 ; Diana, 59 ; Elizabeth, 17, 83, 307 ; Francis, 239, 294 ; Hannah, 178 ; Henry, 272, 286 ; Joanna, 148 ; Judith, 294 ; Leonard, 59 ; Lydia, 239 ; Margaret, 188 ; Nicholas, 294 ; Penelope, 272 ; Rose, 2 ; Samuel, 58 ; Susanna, 9 ; Winifred, 288.
Newmarch, Sarah, 306.
Newport, Ann, 34 ; Charles, 145 ; Elizabeth, 3 ; Frances, 145 ; John, 289 ; Juliana, 289 ; Margaret, 265 ; Peter, 265.
Newsham, Esther, 154.
Newstead, Dorothy Elizabeth, 171 ; Elizabetha Sophia, 120 ; George, 171 ; Theophilus, 120.
Newth, Hannah, 304 ; Susan, 300.
Newton, Ann, 61, 292 ; Anna Maria, 110 ; Charles, 193 ; Eleanor, 294 ; Elizabeth, 52, 151, 257 ; John, 58, 257 ; Martha, 116, 287 ; Mary, 58, 88, 181, 295 ; Penelope, 58 ; Robert, 88 ; Samuel, 295 ; Sarah, 66, 193 ; Thomas, 52, 110.
Niblett, John, 134 ; Susanna, 134.
Nice, Fanny, 160.
Nicholas, Ann, 69, 208 ; Edward, 202 ; Eleanor, 138 ; Jenny, 202 ; John, 69 ; Margaret, 255 ; Mary, 233 ; William, 255.
Nicholl (Niccoll, Nicoll), Ann, 242 ; Rebecca, 197 ; Samuel, 174 ; Sarah, 174 ; Rev. Mr., 82.
Nicholls (Nicholles), Ambrose, 236 ; Anthony, 106 ; Catherine, 80 ; Eleanor, 193 ; Elizabeth, 4, 24, 54, 106, 207, 280, 281, 305 ; George, 305 ; Hannah, 35 ; James, 60 ; Jane, 273 ; John, 4,

273; Judith, 311; Mary, 4, 60, 82, 131, 140, 236, 284; Nicholas, 284; Phœbe, 71; Sarah, 99, 200; Thomas, 80; William, 24.
Nicholson (Nickellsone, Nickollsone), Alice, 286; Ann, 188; Catherine, 62; Elizabeth, 28, 89, 95, 114, 277; Ellen, 268; Fanny, 247; Grace, 286; Hannah, 70; James, 28, 95; John, 185, 241, 286; Joyce, 201; Lewis, 188; Margery, 303; Mary, 241, 248, 286; Rebecca, 185; Richard, 70; Robert, 303; Sarah, 95; Susanna, 200; Thomas, 201, 247, 248, 268.
Nickes, Deborah, 283; Richard, 283.
Nicklinson, Thomas, 241.
Night, *see* Knight.
Nightingale (Nightingall), Edith, 196; Mary, 154, 266; Thacker, 154; Thomas, 196.
Nihell, James, 262; Sarah, 262.
Nimlaw, Mary, 292.
Nind, Elizabeth, 200; James, 200.
Nisbett (Nisbitt), Francis, 149; John, 18, 213; Lucy, 18, 213; Mary, 149.
Nitten, Sarah, 138.
Nixon, Elizabeth, 73, 153; Hannah, 107; Jane, 224; Kimble, 144; Mary, 18; Sarah, 119; Susanna, 144; William, 18.
Noate, John, 295; Margaret, 295.
Nobbs (Nobs), Mary, 178; Robert, 93; Sarah, 93.
Noble, Agnes, 136; Ann, 28; Elizabeth, 64; Joshua, 133; Margaret, 49; Mary, 15, 133, 272; Richard, 49; Thomas, 15.
Nocke, Jane, 304.
Nodes, Elizabeth, 73.
Nodrum, Hendrick, 218.
Nokes, Ann, 266.
Noon, Edward, 56; Elizabeth, 243; Hannah, 56.
Noots, Susannah, 147; Thomas, 147.
Norbury, Sarah, 79.
Norcott (Norcoate, Norcutt), Alexander, 140; Elizabeth, 140, 208; John, 97; Mary, 97, 300; William, 300.
Norcross, Ann, 176.
Norgate, Ann Huffam, 226; Christian, 226.
Norgrove, Hannah, 246; Philip, 246; Sarah, 113.
Norley, Elizabeth, 31; Richard, 31; William, 31*n*.
Norman, Alice, 314; Grissell, 125; Henry, 69, 125; Humphrey, 314; Jane, 254; Margaret, 159; Mary, 124, 148; Mary Ann, 261*; Susanna, 69; Theophilus, 254, 261; William, 124; William Wilmot George, 261.
Normand, Nicholas, 315; —, 315.
Normivill, Mary, 280.
Norrington, Elizabeth, 222; James, 222; Martha, 45; Timothy, 45.
Norris, Agatha, 88; Ann, 18, 85; Dorothy, 24; Edward, 278; Eleanor, 300; Elizabeth, 65, 100, 193, 278; Hannah, 118; James, 50; Jane, 182; John, 100, 300; Letitia, 50; Lettice, 269; Mary, 32, 70; Philip, 65; Randle, 158, 182; Sarah, 36, 158, 220; Sophia, 161; Susan, 105; Susanna, 30; Thomas, 70, 85, 105; William, 32, 269.
North, Alice, 274; Clement, 214; Eleanor, 300; Elizabeth, 133, 170; Emme, 279; Margaret, 206; Mary, 69, 150.
Northall, Mary, 96.
Northam, Ann, 313.
Northes, Ann, 288.
Northridge, Phillis, 185.
Norton, Ann, 179; Christian, 296; Duke, 18; Effery, 18; Eleanor, 297; Elizabeth, 201, 297; Jane, 51; John, 201; Katherine, 295; Mary, 103, 203; Roger, 297; Sarah, 85, 204; Susanna, 3; Thomas, 295; William, 3, 203.
Nortrop, Ann, 125; John, 125.
Norwood, Alice, 294; Edward, 294; Francis, 244; Mary, 149, 244; Rachael, 76; Thomas, 149; William, 76.
Nossiter, John, 3; Mary, 3.
Nott, Elizabeth, 3, 281; John, 3; William, 281.
Nottingham, Edward, 300; Elizabeth, 310; Richard, 310; Sarah, 300.
Nourse, Charles, 136; John, 241; Margaret, 136; Sarah, 241.
Novell, Mary, 312.
Nowell, Alice, 196; John, 240; Martha, 301; Rev. Mr., 208.
Nowers, Mary, 153.
Noxson, Alice, 290.
Noxton, Amy, 265.
Noyce, Robert, 24; Sarah, 24.
Noyes, Catherine, 143; Elizabeth, 180; William, 143.
Nuby, Katherine, 308.
Nugent, Edward, 293; Elizabeth, 293; Grace, 26; Nicholas, 26.
Nunn, Eliza, 260; Elizabeth, 157; Hannah, 258; Joseph, 260; Joshua, 260; Sarah, 217.
Nunns, Elizabeth, 93.
Nurse, Ann, 176; Prudence, 22.
Nutbrowne, Grace, 283; John, 283.
Nuthall, Charles, 44; Mary, 44.
Nutkins, Elizabeth, 183; Robert, 183.
Nutley, Judith, 292.
Nutmaker, Joan, 265.
Nutt, Bartholomew, 187; Catherine, 143; Susanna, 187.
Nuttal, Elizabeth, 17.
Nutter, Alice, 214.
Nynn, Rachael, 131.
Nyst, Elizabeth, 257.

O

Oaker, Joacim, 93; Mary, 93.
Oakes (Okes), Lucy, 20; Mary, 140, 295; Thomas, 20, 140.
Oakesbutt, Susan, 308.
Oakey, Eleanor, 104; John, 104.
Oakley (Oakeley, Okely, Okleye), Edward, 279; Mary, 93, 275; Susanna, 279; Rev. Mr., 159.
Oare, *see* Ore.
Oates, Elizabeth, 8.
Obee, Dorcas, 310.
Obrian, Sarah, 189.
Occold, Katherine, 279.
Ockford, Mary, 34; William, 34.
Ockley, Eleanor, 11; Sarah, 273.
Odber, Ann, 193; Richard, 293; Sarah, 293; William, 193.
Oddy, Hannah, 89; Michael, 89.
Odeham, Alice, 266.
Odell, Ann, 286; David, 55; Elizabeth, 37; Frances, 55; Isaac, 286.
Oder, Ann, 309; John, 309; Mary, 15; William, 15.
Odin, Mary, 36; Peter, 36.
Odling, Benjamin, 83; Ursula, 83.

P

Penury, Mary, 131.
Penus, Marianne, 67.
Penvind. Anne, 273.
Peplow (Peploe), Margaret, 89; Rebecca, 79; Thomas, 79.
Pepper, Elizabeth, 138.
Peppering, Susanna, 58; Thomas, 58.
Peppiat, Mary, 305.
Perbrite, Eleanor, 225; John, 225, 225*n*.
Perce, Cecila, 280; Elizabeth, 281; John, 281; Sarah, 284.
Percey, Sarah, 11.
Percival (Percivall), Elizabeth, 74, 102, 169, 195, 196; Isaac, 74; Joan, 270; Mary, 208; Nathaniel, 169.
Perdue, Mary, 194.
Percy, *see* Perry.
Perham, John, 157; Rebecca, 157.
Perkin, Elizabeth, 206; James, 206.
Perkins (Perkings, Perkyns), Ann, 142, 293; Arthur, 52; Elizabeth, 58, 62, 201, 281, 302, 312; Felix, 58; Hannah, 104; Henry, 104; Hutton, 133; Jane, 52; John, 192; Magdalen, 298; Martha, 187; Mary, 130, 149; Priscilla, 292; Samuel, 62; Sarah, 133, 192; Symon, 298; Thomas, 130, 201, 293, 302; Wiberry, 308; William, 281.
Perks, Ann, 168; Elizabeth, 84.
Perlour, Elizabeth, 114.
Perne, Ann, 297; John, 297.
Pero, Isabella, 75; John, 75.
Perrens, Samuel, 247.
Perrett, Elizabeth, 77.
Perrin (Perrine), Catherine, 31, 133; Elizabeth, 119; Francis, 119; Honor, 97; Katherine, 275; Thomas, 275; William, 97.
Perry (Percy), Alice, 127; Ann, 4, 23, 165, 209, 234, 292; Elizabeth, 5, 77, 85, 91, 134, 138, 197; Frances, 21; Hills, 23; Isabella, 227; James, 91; Joan, 272; John, 4, 165, 292; Margaret, 308; Mary, 74, 190, 222, 281; Rebecca, 291, 311; Richard, 281; Samuel, 234; Sarah, 48, 241, 297; Susan, 293.
Person, Adrian, 288; Alice, 288.
Perss, Edmund, 289; Joan, 289.
Pert (Purt), Joseph, 81; Margaret, 112; Mary, 312; Sarah, 81.
Pertis, Ann, 268; Robert, 268.
Pes, Mary, 280; Rowland, 280.
Pescot, Elizabeth, 3; John, 3.
Pestil (Pesstil), Ann, 286; John, 286; Sarah, 244.
Petefer, *see* Pettifer.
Peters (Petters), Catherine, 208; Elizabeth, 164; Hannah, 107; John, 107; Rebecca, 233, 233*n*.; Thomas, 208; Rev. Mr., 81.
Peterson (Petterson), Cicelia, 279; Elizabeth, 39; Frances, 50; John, 39; Mary, 130.
Pether, Mary, 60; Nicholas, 60.
Petit, *see* Pettit.
Petley, John, 192; Sarah, 192; Thomas, 226.
Petor, John, 40; Ruth, 40.
Petre (Petrie, Pettre, Pettrie), Anna Maria, 17; David, 169; Elizabeth, 161; George, 17; Jennet, 169; Philip, 161.
Pett, Ann, 112; Henry, 310; Martha, 310; Samuel, 112.
Pettener, Rev. John, 2; Sarah, 2.
Petters, *see* Peters.
Petterson, *see* Peterson.
Pettibones, 309.
Pettifer (Petefer, Pettiver), Alice, 103; Ann, 158; Joan, 285; Robert, 285; William, 158.
Pettit (Petit, Pettyt), Alice, 193; Elizabeth, 218; George, 218; Henry, 313; Katherine, 313; Martha, 125; Mary, 4; Sarah, 18; Ursula, 83; William, 4, 125.
Pettre, *see* Petre.
Petty (Pety), Elizabeth, 12, 270; Joan, 270; Stephen, 12.
Pevey, Isaac, 140; Mary, 140.
Pew, Ann, 285; Elizabeth, 312; Jane, 74; Thomas, 285.
Pewtress, Benjamin, 144; Mary, 144.
Peyton, Mary, 257, 299; M. J., 257; R. F., 257; William Grenfell, 257.
Phare, George, 251; Sarah, 251.
Phelps, Ann, 138, 148, 164; Eleanor, 313; Elizabeth, 44; John, 138, 211; Maria, 86, 211; Samuel, 86; William, 148.
Phesant, Mary, 294; Stephen, 294.
Phillip, Elizabeth, 125; John, 125.
Phillips (Philipps, Phillips), Alice, 292; Ann, 2, 100, 286; Bridget, 13, 290; Catherine, 50; Daniel, 76; Elizabeth, 43, 47, 66, 117, 168, 192, 211, 293; Frances, 191; Francis, 293; George, 45, 180; Grace, 106; Hannah, 33, 45, 212; Hugh, 300; Jacob, 161; James, 128; Joan, 52, 312, 313; John, 7, 19, 33, 106, 211, 212, 263; Julian, 298; J., 216; Lawrence, 278; Margaret, 186, 301; Martha, 288, 300; Mary, 64, 83, 94, 128, 152, 213, 273; Maudlen, 271; Sarah, 7, 19, 26, 76, 95; Sibilla, 278; Sophia, 161; Susanna, 180, 182; Theodosia, 23; Thomas, 52, 191; William, 13, 64, 100, 243.
Phillipshill, Elizabeth, 142; Robert, 142.
Phillipson, Edward, 223; Sarah, 223.
Phillis, Mary, 128.
Philotts, Hugh, 303; Joan, 303.
Philpot (Fillpote, Philpott), Ann, 270, 308; Elizabeth, 34; John, 308; Mary, 19; Richard, 270; Sabrine, 174; Stephen, 34.
Phipps, Ann, 158; Edward, 288; Elizabeth, 10, 140; Jane, 188; Jonas, 188; Justinian, 311; Sarah, 288, 311.
Phithion, Catherine, 137; John, 137.
Picherd, Mary, 181.
Pick, Julian, 269; Sarah, 11.
Pickance, Alice, 196; Daniel, 196.
Pickard, Dorothy, 146.
Pickayes, Hester, 286; Matthew, 286.
Pickering, Alice, 308; Ann, 92; Benjamin, 302; George, 286; Gilbert, 308; Jane, 302; John, 212; Mary, 197; Sarah, 302; Susan, 286; Ursula, 102; William, 102, 197.
Pickersgill, Elizabeth, 284.
Pickett (Picket), Ann, 72; Anthony, 63; Barbara, 48; Elizabeth, 310; Jane, 212; John, 48; Martha, 77; Sarah, 63.
Pickman, Mary, 137.
Pickwick, Fanny, 240.
Piddington, Rev. Mr., 30*, 31*, 42, 48.*
Pidgeon (Pigeon), Elizabeth, 286; Jane, 95, 99; John, 95; Joseph, 286; Mary, 42; William, 99.
Piers, Rebecca, 152.
Pignet, Mary, 141.
Pigott (Piggott), Ann, 15, 115, 273; Catherine, 67; Dorothy, 308; Francis, 273; Joanna, 24; John, 15; Sarah, 37.

Potticary, Christopher, 80; Elizabeth, 80.
Pottinger, Ann, 108; George, 108; Mary, 74.
Potton, Jane, 2; John, 295; Margaret, 295; William, 2.
Potts (Pottes), Alice, 20; Christian, 263; Elizabeth, 87, 126; Rev. G., 236; Mary, 38; Roger, 263; Thomas, 20; William, 126.
Pouchet, Ann, 150.
Poulter (Powlter), Ann, 87, 206; John, 87; Thomas, 206.
Poulton, Blackburn, 113; Mary, 113; Sarah, 196; William, 196.
Poundleficks, Joanna, 28; Thomas, 28.
Poupard, Peter, 155; Sarah, 155.
Povey, Ann, 177; Sarah, 2; William, 177.
Powdich, Alice, 288; Richard, 288.
Powell (Powle), Alice, 278; Ann, 17, 164, 165, 266, 287, 296; Barbara, 300, 309; David, 266; Ebenezer, 32; Edward, 147, 304; Elizabeth, 210, 224, 249, 269, 275, 308; Ellen, 136; Giles, 164, 210; Grace, 301; Grevell, 308; Hellen, 273; Henry, 132; Jane, 304, 305, 308; Joanna, 278; John, 127, 188; Jonas, 16; Margaret, 181, 285; Mary, 16, 84, 127, 132, 147, 209, 224, 300; Peter, 224, 249; Richard, 305; Sarah, 32, 168, 188, 291; Stephen, 168; Susanna, 305; Thomas, 301, 306, 308; Thomasin, 306; Walter, 273; Winifred, 293.
Power, Ann Elizabeth, 258; John, 210, 258; Mary, 174, 210; Rebecca, 308; Thomas, 174.
Powis, Elizabeth, 240*; Sarah, 116; Thomas, 235.
Powle, *see* Powell.
Powlter, *see* Poulter.
Powney, Elizabeth, 134; Penyston, 134; Robert, 118; Susanna, 118.
Poyns, Cicely, 283; Robert, 283.
Poynter, Charles, 227; Christian, 64; Elizabeth, 227; Joseph, 64.
Poynton (Pointon), Ann, 120; Sarah, 140.
Praed, Frances, 77; William, 77.
Prance, Ann, 58; Richard, 58.
Prate, Elizabeth, 272.
Prateyer, Isabel, 268; John, 268.
Pratt (Prat), Amy, 105; Ann, 26; Edward, 124; Elizabeth, 238; George, 162; Hannah, 293; James, 290; John, 58, 105, 167; Lydia, 12; Margaret, 5, 290; Margery, 124; Mary, 58, 162, 167; Priscilla, 307; Thomas, 5.
Precher, Elizabeth, 284.
Preist (Priest), Ann, 43; Catherine, 34; Elizabeth, 53; Francis, 43; Martin, 34; Mary, 217.
Preistley, Mary, 206.
Preistney, John, 268; Katherine, 268.
Prentice, Hannah, 117; John, 117.
Prescott (Prescote), Elizabeth, 309; Jeffery, 271; Margaret, 271; William, 309.
Prestage, Ursula Ann, 248.
Preston, Alice, 305; Catherine, 30; Elizabeth, 225, 273; Fanny, 198; Hannah, 117; James, 185; Joan, 278; John, 305; Martha, 211; Mary, 185; Samuel, 211; Thomas, 198, 278.
Preswick, John, 162; Sarah, 162.
Pretty, Christian, 209; Sarah, 198.
Pricar, Elizabeth, 106; Joseph, 106.
Price (Pryce), Alice, 280; Ann, 33, 121, 161, 192, 286; Anna Maria, 172; Rev. David, 213*; Elizabeth, 30, 59, 60, 142, 145, 212, 245, 270, 307, 310; Esther, 42, 126; Frances, 212; Gabriel, 300; George, 296; Grace, 142; Hannah, 212; James, 60; Jane, 147, 273, 309; Jean, 273; Jeremiah, 42; Joan, 302; John, 30, 124, 145, 226, 233, 273, 286; Julian, 298; Katherine, 306; Littleton, 96; Margaret, 48, 233, 271; Mary, 26, 96, 190, 248, 278, 279, 296, 300; Morgan, 302; Peter, 298; Richard, 248, 271; Roger, 280; Sarah, 40, 314; Shaw, 126; Susanna, 106, 248; Thomas, 161, 314; Walter, 286; William, 248, 279, 306; William Calvert, 245.
Pricher, Mary, 300.
Pricklop, Amos, 279; Mary, 279.
Pricklow, Ann, 272.
Pricquett, John, 123; Winifred, 123.
Pridden, Rev. John, 237.
Pride, Alice, 108.
Prideaux, Ann, 10; Richard, 10.
Pridgeon, Elizabeth, 74.
Pridham, Frances, 189; John, 189.
Priest, *see* Preist.
Prignan, John, 102; Mary, 102.
Prime, Elizabeth, 306; Frances, 129; Hephzibah, 38; Mary, 208; Priscilla, 122.
Primrose, Hannah, 22.
Prince, Elizabeth, 78; Sarah, 186.
Prind, Elizabeth, 268.
Prior (Pryar, Pryer), Edward, 190, 275; Elizabeth, 190; John, 61; Katherine, 275; Mary, 50, 207, 312; Sarah, 61.
Prisley (Prisly), Esther, 105; Jane, 118; William, 118.
Priss, John, 288.
Prissick, John, 69; Mary, 69.
Pritchard, Ann, 115, 133, 269; Daniel, 243; Elizabeth, 161, 191, 314; Margaret, 112; Martha, 240; Mary, 216; Rebecca, 104; Richard, 133; Sarah, 111, 243; Thomas, 115; William, 269.
Pritham, Elizabeth, 26.
Probert (Probort), Eleanor, 307; Hugh, 66; Jane, 154; Mary, 66; William, 154.
Proberts, Mary, 226; Richard, 226.
Probine, Eleanor, 277.
Procter (Prockter), Ann, 36, 267; John, 36; Margaret, 270; Mary, 59, 207; Thomas, 59.
Promfritt, James, 84; Mary, 84.
Prophet, Margaret, 126.
Prompy, Sarah, 65.
Prosser, Benjamin, 240; Catherine, 185, 280; Daniel, 84; Edward, 68; Elizabeth, 240, 287; Jane, 84, 205; John, 167, 173; Margaret, 173; Martha, 167; Mary, 21, 68, 214, 245; Nevill, 48; Philip, 21; Roger, 280; Sarah, 48; Susanna, 99; William, 214, 240.
Proudman, John, 23; Sarah, 23.
Provert, Johanna, 282.
Provey, Elizabeth, 178.
Proview, Elizabeth, 182.
Prowse, Ann, 35; Roger, 35.
Pruce, John, 95; Mary, 95.
Prudence, Ann, 63.
Prudom, Hester, 201.
Pryar, Pryer, *see* Prior.
Pryce, *see* Price.
Puckeringe, Frances, 304.
Puckridge, Charles, 230; Mary, 65, 230; William, 65, 230.*
Puddefort, Faustin, 90; Mary, 90.
Pugh, Edward, 184; Hester, 206; James, 206;

Q

R

Rauthmall, Catherine, 2.
Raven, Ann, 270; Hannah, 56.
Ravenell, Abraham, 120; Lucy, 53; Mary, 120.
Ravenfirth, Jane, 21; John, 21.
Ravenscrofte, George, 270; Mary, 270; Sarah, 50.
Ravis, Mary, 33; Sarah, 92; Thomas, 92.
Rawdon, Marmaduke, 186; Rebecca, 186.
Rawleigh, Rebecca, 290.
Rawlett, Martha, 302.
Rawling, Annes, 272.
Rawlings (Rawlins), Ann, 222; Deborah, 206; Eleanor, 256; Elizabeth, 71, 105, 164; John, 105; Mary, 68, 194, 256; Richard, 222.
Rawlinson, Deborah, 290; Elizabeth, 27, 132; Honor, 125; James, 290; Joseph, 132; Margaret, 273; Ralph, 273; Sarah, 116.
Raworth, Amy, 51; Ann, 165; Charles, 173; Mary, 173.
Rawson, Amy, 6; Jervis, 6.
Ray (Raye), Ann, 87, 281; Bethiah, 148; Dorothy, 174; Elizabeth, 75, 92; Frances, 106; Matthew, 75; Peter, 281; Rachael, 131; Walter, 131; William, 106.
Ray *alias* Holdsworth, Mary, 4.
Rayman, Christian, 217.
Raymar, Margery, 307.
Raymen, Mary, 217.
Rayment, Harriet, 262; John, 262.
Raymond (Ramond), Abigail, 249; Elizabeth, 30, 64; Francis, 64; James, 18; Rebecca, 244; Sarah, 18; William, 244.
Raynallds, *see* Reynolds.
Rayndolls, Jane, 90.
Rayner, Adam, 137; Alice, 288; Anne, 81, 251; Henry, 288; Jonathan, 81; Katherine, 305; Mary, 137; Sarah, 225; William, 225.
Raynes, Martha, 94; Susanna, 129; William, 94.
Rayngs, Margaret, 313.
Rayson, Alicia, 147.
Razer, James, 59; Mary, 59.
Read (Reade), Ann, 31, 294; Anselm, 281; Catherine, 155; Edmund, 313; Elizabeth, 113, 172; Frances, 34; Garthwrit, 313; James, 36; Jane, 281, 310; Jonathan, 31; John, 221, 308; Margaret, 41; Mary, 115, 252, 306, 308; Richard, 231, 237, 306; Robert 294; Sarah, 36; Susanna 2.
Reader, Philip, 79; Mary, 79.
Reading (Redding, Redinge), Elizabeth, 189, 282; Hannah, 238; Jane, 305; John, 187, 238, 282; Mary, 80; Susanna, 187; William, 305.
Readwin, Mary, 244, 245; Richard, 244, 245.
Ready, Alexander, 75; Sophia, 75.
Reamy, Jane, 42.
Reason, Ann, 305.
Reavett, Mary, 293.
Reay, Margaret, 103.
Rebend, Catherine, 115.
Record, Mary, 104.
Redborn, Ann, 21.
Redding, Redinge, *see* Reading.
Reddish, Margaret, 140; Mary, 234; Thomas, 140.
Rederup, Elizabeth, 29; John, 29.
Redford, Ann, 178; Catherine, 230; John, 230.
Redfurn, Lydia, 43.
Redhead, Alice, 30; Ann, 133; Rebecca, 77.
Redman, Blanch, 271; Elizabeth, 209.
Redway, Elizabeth, 306; Robert, 306.
Reece, Elizabeth, 85; Francis, 85; Phillis, 219.
Reed, Andrew, 202; Ann, 109, 158; Bridget, 283; Catherine, 1; Daniel, 32; Dinah, 6; Mary, 32, 202, 212; Nathaniel, 6; Rachael, 110; Richard, 158; Theodosius, 109; Thomas, 1.
Rees, Mary, 179; William, 179.
Reeve (Reve), Anne, 289; Frances, 287; Jarvis, 135; John, 104; Margaret, 135; Mary, 75, 175, 188; Nathaniel, 75; Rachael, 104.
Reeves, Ann, 18; Elizabeth, 63, 93; James, 63; Jane, 6; John, 18, 68, 93; Linstead, 6; Margaret, 83; Mary, 187; Sarah, 68, 162, 242.
Regnell, Ann, 285; George, 285.
Reid, Elizabeth, 113; George, 200; John, 9; Rachael, 9; Sarah, 200; Thomas, 113.
Reignolds, Sarah, 308.
Relfe (Relph), Catherine, 48; Edmund, 48; John, 267; Phillipe, 267.
Relion, John, 279; Margaret, 279.
Remington (Rementon, Remington), Hester, 40; Isaac, 179; Sarah, 160, 179, 205; William, 40.
Renaux, Ann, 35; Peter, 35.
Reneuf, Christian, 159; James, 159.
Renshaw, Ann, 157.
Res, Maria, 280; Rowland, 280.
Rest, Mary, 295.
Restrix, Thomasin, 281.
Retorick, Margaret, 298; Richard, 298.
Reull, Isabella, 124.
Reve, *see* Reeve.
Revell, Jane, 313; John, 209; Mary, 209.
Revett, Hannah, 17.
Reviss, Sarah, 108.
Rewse, Martha, 56; William, 56.
Reynell (Reynal), Elizabeth, 141; Jane, 296; Thomas, 141.
Reyner (Reynier), Jane, 62; John, 62; Rev. Mr., 62 to 134.
Reynolds (Raynallds, Renalds, Rennalls, Rennells), Alice, 281; Ann, 20, 95, 113, 186, 188, 205, 291; Dorothy, 280; Edward, 265, 282; Elizabeth, 40, 201, 221, 287; Hannah, 303; James, 20, 193; Jane, 53, 159; John, 280; Judith, 268; Margaret, 89; Mary, 71, 95, 96, 134, 152, 159, 175, 193, 265; Mary Ann, 16; Richard, 134, 281; Robert, 303; Rose, 282; Rowland, 16; Sarah, 60, 139; Sophia, 252; Stephen, 243; Thomas, 40, 71, 89, 188, 252; William, 139, 175.
Reynole, Elizabeth, 256.
Reywell, Frances, 298.
Rhodes (Rodes), Ann, 140; Charles, 140; Elizabeth, 114, 219, 307; Francis, 176; John, 60; Jonas, 114; Margaret, 60; Mary, 17, 93, 176; Thomas, 307.
Rice, Ann, 69; Benjamin, 58; David, 55; Elizabeth, 55, 79, 196; Hannah, 253; James, 191; John, 69; Joyce, 264; Martha, 55; Mary, 58, 191, 194; Morgan, 194; Sarah, 58; Thomas, 58, 79.
Rich, Ann, 33, 191, 295; Cordelia, 193; Elizabeth, 273; Henry, 191, 273; John, 295; Judith, 292; Mary, 52; Nicholas, 193; Susanna, 298.
Richard, Henry, 41; Mary, 41.
Richards (Richardes), Ann, 62, 166, 206; Daniel, 62; David, 218; Dorothy, 236; Elizabeth, 43, 49, 155, 304, 307; Frances, 73; Henry, 233; Jane, 26, 164; John, 26, 166; Joseph, 43; Katherine, 302; Mary, 9, 126, 130, 219, 234, 299; Nicholas Sweeting, 219; Philip, 299; Rachael, 198; Richard, 307; Robert,

Rocher, Ann Gabriel, 173.
Rochford, Mary, 309; Nicholas, 309.
Rock, Daniel, 159; Sarah, 12, 159.
Rocket, Edward, 234; Elizabeth, 234.
Rocque, Ann, 196; John, 196.
Rodburn, Sarah, 46.
Rodes, *see* Rhodes.
Rodgers, *see* Rogers.
Roe, Christopher, 106; Dianna, 59; Elizabeth, 1; Frances, 292; John, 59; Rev. Stephen, 217; Susanna, 106.
Roebuck (Robuck), Hannah, 51, 62; John, 62; Sibilla, 76.
Roffe (Rofe), Ann, 230; John, 230; Margaret, 276; Thomas, 276.
Roffey, George, 85; Margaret, 145; Patience, 206; Richard, 206; Robert, 145; Sarah, 85.
Rogers (Rodgers), Abraham, 41; Amy, 176; Ann, 112, 289, 293, 300; Anna Maria, 236; Catherine, 26; Daniel, 81; Dorothy, 312; Elizabeth, 15, 44, 49, 81, 92, 138, 193, 270, 272, 277, 278, 286, 311; Esther, 227; Frances, 156, 307; Frances Elizabeth, 236; George, 289, 297; Hanameel, 193; Hannah, 134; Henrietta, 222; Jane, 33; John, 26, 98, 112, 134, 154, 176, 201, 227, 236, 307; J., 236; Margaret, 56, 258, 305; Martha, 98, 309; Mary, 42, 68, 98, 105, 138, 154, 201, 213, 237, 249, 279; Miriam, 39; Osmun, 56; Rebecca, 298; Robert, 44, 156; Samuel, 116; Sarah, 41, 116, 181, 297; Solomon, 39; Thomas, 49, 277; William, 33, 213.
Rogerson, Mary, 39; Samuel, 39.
Rokeby, Elizabeth, 16.
Rokes, Esther, 104; James, 104.
Rolfe (Rolphe), Ann, 11, 22; Elizabeth, 305, 306; Joan, 270; Phœbe, 165; Rev. Waters, 165; William, 11, 305, 306.
Rollins, Ann, 250; John, 250.
Rollisson, Charity, 286; Edward, 286.
Rollo, Frances, 78; Joseph, 78; Rachael, 15; Thomas, 15.
Rolston, Catherine, 34.
Rolt, Elizabeth, 44; Samuel, 44.
Romaine, Ann, 118; Phillis, 128.
Roman, John, 128; Priscilla, 128.
Rombell, Joan, 307.
Rone, Michael, 47; Sarah, 47.
Ronne, Elizabeth, 285; Thomas, 285.
Ronsom, Sarah, 1.
Ronwell, Ellen, 310; Francis, 310.
Rood, Andrew, 218.
Rooding, Mary, 111.
Rooke, Ann, 187; Anna Maria, 53; Richard, 291; Sarah, 291; William, 187.
Rookes, Frances, 265; Margaret, 14, 265.
Roome, Martha, 73; Samuel, 73; Sarah, 306; William, 306.
Roosse, Ann, 292; Valentine, 292.
Root, Elizabeth, 178; Samuel, 178.
Roper, Christopher, 312; Hannah, 286; Margaret, 312; Mary, 227.
Roptsone, Elizabeth, 269; Thomas, 269.
Rose, Alice, 187; Ann, 237; Christopher, 309; Elizabeth, 113, 293, 309; Hannah, 31; John, 187; Martha, 13; Mary, 13, 44, 61, 220, 295; Richard, 13; Robert, 13; Samuel, 237; Sarah, 79, 254; Thomas, 220, 295.
Ross, Ann, 123, 150; Eleanor, 194; John, 150; Sarah, 292; William, 123.
Rosser, Margaret, 183.
Rossiter, George, 127, 295; Joan, 295; Mary, 127.
Roston, Elizabeth, 300.
Roswell, Ann, 6.
Rotherford, John, 112; Mary, 112.
Rothton, Ann, 314; John, 314.
Roubel, Catherine, 25; John, 25.
Rouby, Ann, 59.
Rouge, Elizabeth, 95.
Rouin, David, 23; Eleanor, 23.
Roules, Elizabeth, 54.
Roullet, Lucy Elizabeth, 84.
Round, Daniel, 34; Elizabeth, 34; Sarah, 76.
Rounsivell, Elizabeth, 114; John, 114.
Rous, Benjamin, 66; Elizabeth, 7; George, 224; James, 7; Margaret, 66.
Rouse, Mary, 219, 227; Sarah, 259, 259*n*.
Roussell, *see* Russell.
Roussoa, Mary, 67.
Rowberry (Rubery), Ellen, 275; Phillipe, 275; Sarah, 243;
Rowe (Row), Alice, 285; Ann, 273; Charles, 272; Eleanor, 210; Elizabeth, 272; Joan, 313; Joyce, 289; Nathaniel, 281; Sarah, 281.
Rowed, Susanna, 121.
Rowland, Evan, 220.
Rowlands, Elizabeth, 310.
Rowlandson, Elizabeth, 84; Jonas, 84;
Rowlatt, Ann, 231; William, 231.
Rowles, Elizabeth, 122; William, 122.
Rowley, Ann, 271, 280; Anna, 132; Elizabeth, 7; John, 280; Mary, 11; Roger, 271; Sarah, 76; William, 76.
Rowlings, Sarah, 31.
Rowlls, Mary, 108.
Rowlstone, Mary, 28; Rebecca, 23.
Rowman, Elizabeth, 277; William, 277.
Rown, Diana, 88.
Rowson, Elizabeth, 294; Mari Ann, 188; Mary, 311.
Rowth, Dorothy, 147.
Roxby, Deborah, 143.
Roy, Rev. James, 238.
Royall (Royle, Royll), Ann, 189; Christian, 275; Gertrude, 80; Lawrence, 275; Samuel, 80; Sarah, 113; William, 189.
Royley, Ann, 292; Francis, 292.
Royston, Elizabeth, 86; John, 86.
Ruband, Hester, 274.
Rubery, *see* Rowberry.
Rubidge, Mary, 111; William, 111.
Rucke, Ann, 268.
Ruckwood, Sarah, 306.
Rudd, Alice, 308; Rachael, 28.
Ruddiard, *see* Rudyerd.
Ruddock, Mary, 99.
Rudgley, Mary, 206.
Rudkin, Thomas, 241.
Rudyerd (Ruddiard), Elizabeth, 299; Jane, 117; Laurence, 117; Richard, 299.
Ruffe, Henrietta, 73.
Ruffin, Helen, 310; John, 310; Margaret, 270; William, 270.
Rufford, Mary, 132.
Rugeiro, Bridget, 140.
Rugeley, George, 45; Hannah, 51, 159; Mary, 45; Rowland, 51.
Rugg, Mary, 159; Patience, 206; Richard, 159.
Ruler, Martha, 66.
Rumball, John, 108; Susanna, 108.
Rumbold, Sarah, 83; Thomas, 83.

S

Shield, Adliena, 134.
Shilbeck, Elizabeth, 142.
Shilford, Hannah, 120.
Shillecorne, Sarah, 41.
Shilling, Christian, 48.
Shillingford, Elizabeth, 190; Jonathan, 190.
Shilton, Dorothy, 155.
Shingle, Mary, 91.
Shipley, Edward, 116; Elizabeth, 116; Hannah, 46; Mary, 203.
Shipman, Elizabeth, 64; John, 64.
Shippin, Mary, 66.
Shipton, Sarah, 206; Thomas, 206.
Shires, Ann, 285.
Shireson, Catherine, 25; John, 25.
Shirley (Sherley, Sherly, Shurley), Arabella, 34; Elizabeth, 11; Johanna, 279; Joseph, 24; Margaret, 280; Mary, 24, 97; Sarah, 92; Thomas, 11, 34; William, 92.
Shirres, Ann, 29; William, 29.
Shirt, Ann, 45; Margaret, 37.
Shonorey, Gabriel, 73; Henrietta, 73.
Shonsey, Hannah, 224.
Shoot, Mary, 240.
Shooter, Mary, 302; Richard, 302.
Shore, Sarah, 143.
Shoreditch, Mary, 307.
Short, Ann, 84; Anna Maria, 261; Charity, 277; Hannah, 166; Henry, 277; James, 181; Lucy, 21; Mary, 44, 181; Richard, 166; Thomas, 84.
Shorter, Elizabeth, 313.
Shott, Ann, 155.
Shotton, Mary, 71.
Shout, Mary, 240.
Shove, Anne, 24.
Showell, Anne, 112; James, 112.
Shower, Frances, 163; John, 163.
Showns, Sarah, 238.
Shrimpton, Amy, 97; Christian, 299; Frances, 259; Marian, 272; William, 272.
Shrives, James, 236; Jenny, 236.
Shugburgh, Grace, 311.
Shugg, Mary, 5.
Shurley, *see* Shirley.
Shute, Ann, 29, 111.
Shutter, Lucy, 299; Mary, 136.
Shuttlewood, Ann, 53; Nathaniel, 53.
Shuttleworth, Ann, 221; Barbara, 1; Elizabeth, 111.
Siant, Alice, 30.
Sible, Elizabeth, 135.
Sibley (Siblye), Alse, 271; Ann, 170; Thomas, 29; Winifred, 29.
Sibson, Thomas, 213.
Sibthorpe, Elizabeth, 159, 247; John, 159; Mary, 209; Thomas, 209, 247.
Siddall (Siddell), Alexander, 306; Ann, 215, 306; Mary, 35, 169; Samuel, 35.
Sicker, Phebe, 106.
Siderse, Gabriel, 268; Isabel, 268.
Sidey (Sidy), Benjamin, 116; Elizabeth, 116, 118.
Sidney, Hannah, 76; James, 76.
Sidwey, Anne, 29.
Sifford, Elizabeth, 126.
Siggins, Elizabeth, 183; Margaret, 311; Thomas, 183.
Sikes, *see* Sykes.
Silcock, Christopher, 280; Mary, 280.
Silk, Elizabeth, 8; Robert, 8.
Silkwood, Elizabeth, 219.
Sills, Elizabeth, 56; Mary, 221; Richard, 221.
Siltso, Maria, 251.
Silver, Jacob, 53; Jane, 53.
Silverthorne, Oliver, 32; —, 32.
Silverton, Martha, 311; Ralph, 311.
Silvertop, Mary, 42.
Silvey, Ann, 39; Emanuel Francis, 39.
Simes, *see* Simms.
Simkins, Elizabeth, 115; Margaret, 202; Samuel, 293; Susan, 293; Thomas, 115.
Simmond, Alice, 315; Nevel, 315.
Simmonds (Simmons, Symmons), Alice, 315; Ann, 38, 70, 172, 187, 294, 303; Anna, 120; Caleb, 2; Charity, 304; Christiana, 56; Elizabeth, 14, 29, 55, 169, 308; Frances, 142; Humphrey, 310; John, 142, 172; Joseph Bell, 120; Josias, 14; Judith, 2; Margaret, 6, 310; Mary, 83, 85, 128, 228, 307; Guested, 83; Ruth, 131; Samuel, 85; Sarah, 37, 97, 245; Thomas, 6; William, 38, 128.
Simms (Simes, Sims, Symes), Ann, 275; Elizabeth, 95, 183; Hannah, 192, 212; Isaac, 48; John, 27; Mary, 7, 48, 198; Mary Ann, 108; Rachael, 206; Rebecca, 27; Richard, 7; Thomas, 212; William, 108.
Simnell, Anne, 129.
Simpson (Simpsone, Simson, Simsonne, Sympson, Symson), Ann, 174, 179, 268; Barbara, 276; Catherine, 279; Cornelius, 296; Edward, 150; Elizabeth, 12, 98, 121, 150, 185, 266, 270; Hannah, 44, 118, 311; James, 118; John, 121, 185, 279; Judith, 296; Katherine, 310; Martha, 29; Mary, 12, 263; Richard, 174; Robert, 98; Rowland, 311; Stephen, 224; William, 12, 263, 310.
Sims, *see* Simms.
Sinfield, Elizabeth, 63; Joyce, 63; Lydia, 211.
Singer, Edith, 74; Elizabeth, 184; Hannah, 16; Thomas, 16.
Singler, Elizabeth, 151.
Singleton, Anne, 108; Esther, 142; John, 108, 221; Judith, 309; Mary, 221; Sarah, 195.
Sink, Ann, 30; John, 30.
Sinnett, Margaret, 235.
Sired, Joyce, 298.
Sisson (Sison), Ann, 10, 146; Anna, 286; Edward, 286; Elizabeth, 199; James, 199.
Sisum, John, 27; Judith, 186; Rebecca, 27, 148; Thomas, 148, 186.
Sixe, Diana, 59.
Sizemor, Elizabeth, 171.
Skaines, John, 149; Sarah, 149.
Skarman, Mary, 293; Richard, 293.
Skeff, Winifred, 108.
Skeffington, Ann, 250; Fanny, 247; Jane, 250; Thomas, 250.
Skegg, Abraham, 120; Elizabeth, 122; Hannah, 120.
Skeggs (Skiggs), Ann, 210; Elizabeth, 204; Thomas, 210.
Skelding, Joseph, 175; Mary, 175.
Skelton (Skilton, Skillton), Elizabeth, 33; Hannah, 132; Jane, 23; Katherine, 286; Samuel, 286; Thomas, 33; William, 132.
Skemp, Susanna, 171.
Skerrett, Margaret, 201; Thomas, 201.
Skerry, Elizabeth, 7; John, 7.
Skey, Hester, 200; Margaret, 81; William Stephen, 81.

Snell, Ellen, 279; Jane, 294; John, 279; Penelope, 272; Robert, 259; Sarah, 259.
Snelling, Elizabeth, 87; John, 87; Mary, 71.
Snook (Snooke), Elizabeth, 309; Mary, 148; Susanna, 139; William, 139, 148.
Snow (Snowe), Blase, 267; Elizabeth, 267; Jane, 94; Mary, 62; Samuel, 62; Sarah, 223; William, 94, 223.
Snowden (Snowdin), Edward, 120; Elizabeth, 120, 170; John, 170; Mary, 50.
Snowsell, Elizabeth, 50; Herbert, 50.
Soane (Soan), Barbara, 21; Catherine, 159; William, 21.
Soaper, *see* Soper.
Softley, Carah, 196; Cuthbert, 196; Katherine, 309; Thomas, 309.
Sole, Joseph, 293; Katherine, 301; Mary, 293.
Solinus, Andrew, 34; Susanna, 34.
Solley (Solie), Elizabeth, 280; John, 96; Rebecca, 96; Thomas, 280.
Some, Ann, 284; Henry, 284; Mary, 5.
Somers, Abigail, 263.
Sompner, Mary, 311.
Soper (Soaper), Ann Thomas, 228; Jane, 98; Mary, 18, 306.
Sopp, Elizabeth, 122; John, 137; Robert, 122; Sarah, 99, 137; William, 99.
Sore, John, 117; Mary, 117.
Sorletta, Baston, 166; Mary, 166.
Sorrell, Elizabeth, 239; Johanna, 171; William, 239.
Soubier, Elizabeth, 67.
South, Elizabeth, 309; Hannah, 118; Henry, 34; Jane, 34; Mary, 181, 207; Nicholas, 181.
Southall, Elizabeth, 71.
Southcomb, Rev. Lewis, 237; Margaret, 237.
Southern (Southen), Ann, 43; George, 294; Hannah, 22; Jane, 294; John, 22.
Southgate, James, 213.*
Southwell, Eleanor, 299; Hannah, 177; Thomas, 299; William, 177.
Southwood, Sarah, 176; William, 176.
Southworth, Rosamond, 281.
Sowerby, Arabella, 125; John, 125.
Sowter, Elizabeth, 146; Joseph, 146.
Spackman, *see* Spakeman.
Spaine, Margaret, 280.
Spakeman (Spackman), Abigail, 72; Elizabeth, 303; John, 303; Sarah, 184.
Spalding (Spaldin), Elizabeth, 63; John, 41; Mary, 41, 124, 190.
Sparepoint, Deborah, 206; Thomas, 206.
Sparke, Deborah, 184.
Sparks (Sparkes), Esther, 72; George, 24; Jane, 24, 232; Johannah, 120; Thomas, 72; Rev. Mr., 122.
Sparrow, Ann, 88; Dorothy, 290; Elizabeth, 126; Grace, 6; Robert, 290; Sarah, 14, 37; Thomas, 126.
Spatchhurst, Martha, 289; Thomas, 289.
Speakeman, Alice, 294.
Speaks, Elizabeth, 91; Robert, 91.
Spearing, Mary, 61; Richard, 61.
Spearman, Ann, 163; Body, 163.
Spedding, Thomas, 228, 229.
Speed, Elizabeth, 225.
Speke, Elizabeth, 98; Henry, 98.
Spence, Ann, 244, 248; Dorothy, 174; James, 174; Jane, 10; Joseph, 248; Mary, 57; Robert, 244; William, 57.
Spencer, Alice, 187; Ann, 140, 169, 225; Catherine, 194; Dorothy, 110; Edward, 45; Elizabeth, 100, 105, 141, 300, 305, 310; George, 62, 100; Henry, 311; Isabella, 5; Jane, 62; Jarvis, 145; Jasper, 91; John, 5; Judith, 151; Margaret, 15, 145; Mary, 38, 45, 91, 175, 218; Patience, 303; Patrick, 173; Penelope, 279; Richard, 105, 194; Samuel, 140; Sarah, 289, 308; Susan, 311; Susanna, 173; Thomas, 175, 252, 279, 303, 305; William, 289, 300.
Spendelow, Charles, 112; Hannah, 112, 206.
Spender, Ann, 16.
Sperin, Ann, 134; Isaac, 134.
Sperinck, John, 209; Mary, 209.
Spetigue, Jane, 172; Solomon, 172.
Spicer, Ann, 294; Elizabeth, 312; John, 307; Margaret, 280; Martha, 175; Ruth, 307; William, 175.
Spier (Spire), Hannah, 17; James, 17; Sarah, 107.
Spillard, Henry, 236; Sarah, 236.
Spiller, Jane, 285; Rebecca, 185.
Spillman (Spillmane), Charity, 277; Edward, 287; Frances, 287.
Spindler, Jane, 54.
Spink, Ann, 57; Edward, 57.
Spire, *see* Spier.
Spong, Mary, 191; William, 191.
Sponley, Ann, 275; Machelle, 275.
Spooner, Dorothy, 83.
Spootswood, Jane, 301.
Spottswood, Grizeld, 299.
Spradbery, Margaret, 136; John, 136.
Sprafford, Elizabeth, 296.
Spragg, Mary, 213; Samuel, 213.
Sprat, Alice, 279; Grissell, 125; Thomas, 279.
Spratling, Alice, 288.
Spratly, James, 127; Martha, 127.
Sprattbury, Alice, 296; William, 296.
Spreakley, Anne, 72.
Sprigg (Sprige), Ann, 95, 286; Carey, 286.
Spriggins, Sarah, 32.
Spriggs, Mary, 97; Mildred Stevenson, 135; Thomas, 135.
Spring, Catherine, 11; Sarah, 134.
Sprong, Benjamin, 182; Elizabeth, 182.
Sprules, Mary, 174; William, 174.
Spry, Amelia, 216; William, 216.
Spunner, Dorothy, 288; William, 288.
Spurgen, Sarah, 170.
Spurling, Alexander, 95; Edward, 79; Isabella, 79; Mary, 95; Sarah, 269.
Spurr (Spur), Alice, 310; Ann, 286; Deborah, 62; Edward, 62; Thomas, 286.
Spurrier, James, 211; Mary, 144.
Spyers, Lowdey, 101; Thomas, 101.
Spykin, Margaret, 280; Robert, 280.
Spyney, Annes, 266.
Squibb, Eleanor, 293; Henry, 293; Mary, 305.
Squire (Squier), Alice, 30; Catherine, 67; Edward, 265; Elizabeth, 116, 289; Grace, 265; Grissell, 292; Jane, 68, 156; John, 30, 67, 274, 275; Richard, 68; Robert, 292; Stephen, 289; Thomas, 116, 156.
Srayton, Sarah, 108.
Staart, James, 313; Mary, 313.
Stables, Benjamin, 122; Martha, 131; Mary, 41, 122; Thomas, 131.
Stace, Ann, 91; John, 155; Martha, 155.
Stacey (Stacy, Stayse), Ann, 202; Edward, 292; Elizabeth, 142, 292; Mary, 54, 77, 127, 224;

T

George, 298; James, 184; Jane, 57; John, 57, 267; Margaret, 113.
Ware *alias* Weare, Elizabeth, 266; John, 266.
Warfield, Dennis, 157; Thomas, 157.
Waring, Mary, 38.
Warland, Lydia, 87; Thomas, 87.
Warner, Alice, 279; Charles, 131; Dorothy, 301; Elizabeth, 79, 131, 285; Gasper, 257; James, 79; Johan, 269; Mary, 63, 159, 215; Naomi, 293; Rachael, 97; Sarah, 257; Susanna, 138; Vere, 159.
Warnich, Joachim Johan Lodewick, 186; Joanna, 186.
Warr, John, 215.
Warray, Mary, 74.
Warren, Ann, 33, 55; Catherine, 55; Christopher, 222; Edward, 55; Eleanor, 184; Elizabeth, 30, 59, 222, 248; H., 251; James, 166; Jane, 191, 299; John, 174; Katherine, 266; Mary, 88, 96, 166, 174, 274, 309; Samuel, 227; Sarah, 46, 182; Susanna, 114; Thomas, 59, 184; William, 30, 191.
Warrener, Frances, 109.
Wartham, Martha, 202; Thomas, 202.
Warwick, Edward, 10; Hannah, 178; John, 153; Lucy, 106; Martha, 10; Mary, 153; Richard, 178.
Washington, Martha, 37; William, 37.
Washlin, Sarah, 264; Thomas, 264.
Wass, Mary, 148, 149.
Wassell, Elizabeth, 193; George, 193.
Wassington, Jane, 299; Joseph, 299.
Waterer, Ann, 281.
Wateress, Mary, 287.
Waterhouse, Ann, 169; Benjamin, 169; Edward, 298; Elizabeth, 298, 299; Mary, 282; Widdup, 299.
Waterman, Ann, 194; James, 194; Jane, 217; Susanna, 97; Thomas, 217.
Waters (Watters), Alexander, 221; Ann, 102, 221, 271, 311; Christian, 23; Elizabeth, 285; Helen, 310; Johane, 276; Martha, 308; Mary, 164; Richard, 311.
Waterson, Sarah, 129.
Watford, Mary, 26.
Watis, *see* Watts.
Watkins (Watkyns), Ann, 47, 56, 59, 68, 99; Christopher, 30; Eleanor, 30; Elizabeth, 216; Ellen, 266; Esther, 91; George, 99; Gwyn, 313; Henry, 237; Rev. James, 233; Jane, 313; Margaret, 128; Mary, 50; Ruth, 190; Sarah, 237; Thomas, 313; William, 68.
Watkinson, Jane, 95; Rev. Dr., 1 to 131.
Watkis, Mary, 118; Richard, 118.
Watkyns, *see* Watkins.
Watlington, Elizabeth, 193.
Watmore, Rebecca, 23; Thomas, 23.
Wats, *see* Watts.
Watsee, Mary, 287.
Watson (Wattsone), Ann, 42, 49, 251; Arabella, 34; Bartholomew, 3; Bathsheba, 212; Benjamin, 242; Dorothea, 3; Edward, 42; Eleanor, 61; Elizabeth, 3*, 143, 286, 305, 311; Grace, 298; Hannah, 66, 196, 259; Jane, 68, 199, 221, 238; Joanna, 17; John, 3, 68, 251, 298; Martha, 97, 209; Martin, 97, 143; Mary, 15, 269, 306, 309; Samuel, 309; Sarah, 138, 297; Simon, 66; Thomas, 138, 221; Ursula, 268; William, 268.
Watters, *see* Waters.
Watton, Lydia, 69.
Watts (Watis, Wats, Wattes), Alice, 92; Ann, 15, 26, 29, 182, 206, 223, 226; Barbara, 165; Dorothy, 270; Elizabeth, 89, 147, 173, 191, 313; Francis, 191; George, 147; Grace, 291; Henrietta Clarentia, 189; Henry, 165, 270; Jane, 288; Johanne, 274; John, 26, 89; Katherine, 306; Lydia, 257; Mary, 27, 275, 304; Samuel, 206; Sarah, 35, 254; Senesh, 292; Thomas, 288, 304; William, 27, 35, 254.
Wattsone, *see* Watson.
Waving, Isabella, 196.
Waxam, Sarah, 22.
Waxhill, Susanna, 291; William, 291.
Wayger, Margaret, 284.
Waylett, Ann, 226; James, 226.
Wayman, Ann, 124; Elizabeth, 155; Mary, 239.
Waymark, Elias, 108; Elizabeth, 53; John, 53; Susanna, 108.
Wayte, *see* Waite.
Wazzoone, Adrian, 286; Margery, 286.
Weakley, Margaret, 264.
Weane, Ellen, 299.
Weare *alias* Ware, *see* Ware *alias* Weare.
Weaste, Katherine, 271.
Weatherhead, Elizabeth, 216; John, 244; Mary, 104, 244, 246; William, 104.
Weatherstone, George, 253; G., 253; Sarah Vernon, 253.
Weaver, Ann, 184; Barbara, 158; Francis, 184; John, 39; Mary, 39, 82; Milbrow, 91; Sarah, 98; William, 158.
Webb, Adam, 54; Alice, 54, 297; Amy, 206; Ann, 40, 41, 49, 109, 124, 150, 205, 232; Arthur, 287; Daniel, 179; Diana, 209; Edmund, 37; Elizabeth, 22, 37, 39, 58, 93, 101, 249, 278, 292, 309; Frances, 179; George, 101; Hannah, 41; Henry, 206; Isaac, 109; James, 161; John, 220, 300; Joseph, 205; Judith, 3; Katherine, 300; Martha, 158, 161; Mary, 9, 23, 26, 53, 101, 173, 220, 224, 225, 300; Priscilla, 128; Rebecca, 185; Richard, 93, 218, 232; Robert, 49; Sarah, 31, 161, 181, 220, 233; Susanna, 219, 238; Thomas, 220, 309; Thomasine, 287; William, 173, 224, 225, 278, 292.
Webber, Elizabeth, 53, 183; John, 297; Mary, 297; Thomas, 183.
Webley, Dorothy, 270; Richard, 270.
Webster, Catherine, 281; Elizabeth, 179, 291; Godfrey, 179; Henry, 277, 291; John, 306; Margaret, 277; Mary, 153, 175, 278, 306; Saince, 207; Sarah, 148, 218; William, 218.
Wedd, Mercy, 146; Nathaniel, 146.
Weddell, Samuel, 231; Sibella, 231.
Weed, Augustine, 309; Elizabeth, 134; Mary, 309; William, 134.
Weedon (Weeden), Alice, 94, 273; Ann, 6; Daniel, 6; Daniel Nathaniel, 245; Elizabeth, 6, 243; Gregorye, 273; Henry, 18; John, 165; Martha, 110; Mary, 240, 245, 309; Nathaniel, 6; Rebecca, 165; Sarah, 32; Susanna, 18.
Weedinge, Elizabeth, 293.
Week, Susanna, 48.
Week *alias* Cannon, Susanna, 54, 65; William, 54, 65.
Weekes (Weeks), Elizabeth, 300, 315; Hannah, 28; James, 315; Joanna, 311; John, 206, 300; Margaret, 206; Martha, 301; Mary, 284; Thomas, 284; William, 301.

Wiles, Alice, 278 ; John, 278.

Wilkey, Joanna, 78.

Wilkins. Alice, 2, 197 ; Elizabeth. 148. 178 ; John, 197. 250, 302 ; Katherine, 295, 302 ; Margaret, 8 ; Mary, 250 ; —, 32.

Wilkinson, Agnes, 125 ; Ann, 51. 111. 172. 197, 214. 304, 305, 312 ; Charles, 185 ; Elizabeth, 84. 108. 183, 272 ; George. 17, 197 ; Jane, 170, 190 ; John. 84, 94, 190 ; Judith, 273 ; Margaret, 220 ; Mary, 94. 173. 185, 304 : Peter. 170 : Ralph, 111, 172 ; Sarah, 17, 28, 51 ; Susanna, 69 ; Thomas, 125, 227* ; William, 304.

Wilks (Wilkes), Ann, 143. 267 ; Eleanor, 223 ; Elizabeth. 306 ; James, 180 ; Jane. 95 : John, 143 ; Margaret, 180 ; Mary, 62, 102, 123 ; Thomas, 267 ; William, 123.

Willan. Rosanna, 232.

Willard, Mary, 206, 221, 222 ; Robert, 206 ; Sarah, 221.

Willcockson, Ann, 207 ; Joseph, 207.

Willdon, Judith, 19.

Willes, *see* Willis.

Willett, Ann. 65 ; Edward, 65.

Willey, Alice, 296 ; John, 296.

Williams, Aglandby, 280 : Alice, 287 ; Ann, 88, 109, 133, 140, 196, 202, 220, 258, 261, 291 ; Anna Maria, 173 ; Blanche, 123, 231 ; Catherine, 18, 139, 237 ; Charles, 217 ; Christopher, 293 ; Daniel, 117 ; David, 247, 299 ; Diana. 70 ; Edward, 287, 306 ; Eleanor, 61, 184, 297 ; Ellen, 310 ; Elizabeth, 5, 31, 72. 85, 88, 120, 163, 245, 284, 313 ; Elphar, 247 ; Frances. 198, 307 ; Francis, 203 ; Gayno. 265 ; George, 166, 245, 246 ; Hannah, 103 ; Henry, 18 ; Honor, 97 : Jane, 91, 117, 149, 193, 238 ; Joanna, 120 ; John, 31, 81, 154, 239, 258, 284 ; John Tilbury, 228 ; Katherine, 299 ; Lewis, 281 ; Lucy, 21 ; Lydia, 203 ; Margaret, 165, 181, 221, 233, 279, 285, 305, 308 ; Mary, 57, 81, 89, 102, 152, 166, 279. 281, 301, 306, 314 ; Mary Ann, 108, 207 ; Moses, 82 ; Nicholas, 276 ; Phœbe, 76 ; Philip, 227, 237* ; Rachael, 209, 217 ; Ralph, 181 ; Rebecca, 276 ; Rev. Rice, 27 ; Richard, 133, 196, 313 ; Robert, 76 ; Samuel, 294 ; Sarah, 82, 128, 196, 220, 241 ; Simon, 120 ; Susan, 310 ; Susanna, 115, 154 ; Thomas, 21, 61, 149, 173, 193, 233 ; Thomasine, 294 ; Walter, 308 ; William, 57 ; Winifred, 293 ; Rev. Mr., 156, 157, 163, 168.

Williamson, Ann, 140 ; Catherine, 165 ; Elizabeth, 6 ; John, 6 ; Mary, 38, 69, 82, 245 ; Rev. Mr., 163, 166.

Willioc. Blaise, 163 ; Mary, 163.

Willis (Willes). Abraham, 194 ; Alice, 144 ; Ann, 73 ; Edward. 5 ; Elizabeth. 101 ; Jane, 15 ; John. 202 ; Margaret, 129 ; Mary. 5*, 6, 19, 110, 194, 202 ; Robert, 15 ; Thomas, 73, 101 ; William. 5.

Willmott, *see* Wilmot.

Willoughby (Willoby, Willowby). Elizabeth, 83 : Jane, 269 : John, 167 ; Mary, 112, 146, 167 ; Sarah, 279 ; Thomas, 279.

Wills, Anne. 114, 186, 284, 290 ; George, 114 ; Jane, 66 ; John, 66, 110, 186 ; Margaret, 110 ; Thomas, 284. 290 ; Rev. J., 18 ; Rev. Mr., 176* to 191.*

Willson, *see* Wilson.

Wilmer, Frances, 308 ; Mary, 78 ; Thomas, 78.

Wilmot (Willimot, Willmott, Wilmott), Ann, 188 ; Dorothy, 277 ; Elizabeth, 43, 199, 285, 298 ; Hannah, 12 ; Judith, 89 ; Martha, 125 ; Mary, 18, 303, 314 ; Rev. Samuel, 199 ; Thomas, 277 ; William, 303 ; Zaccheus, 43 ; Rev. Mr., 158.

Wilsher, Mary, 275.

Wilson (Willsone). Adam, 48 ; Alice, 267 ; Ann, 9, 119, 124, 177, 255, 291, 300, 307 ; Archibald, 237 ; Barbara, 97, 302 ; Catherine, 49 ; Cornelius, 56 ; Daniel, 119 ; Dorothy, 60, 267, 270, 283 ; Edward, 145, 281 ; Elizabeth, 6. 62, 95*. 114, 145, 157, 185, 200, 249, 277, 282, 290, 305, 307 ; Felice, 7 ; Forbes, 46 ; Frances, 106, 157 ; Francis, 4 ; Grissell, 292 ; Hannah, 218 ; Hellena, 142 ; Henry, 2, 189, 290, 291 ; Humphrey, 277 ; Isabella, 4, 74, 140 ; James, 9, 193, 232, 282, 307, 312 ; Jane, 34, 136, 225, 232, 237 ; John, 6, 42, 49, 114, 232, 296 ; Margaret, 126, 189, 296 ; Margery, 281 ; Martha, 66, 99 ; Mary, 7, 13, 42, 57, 75, 86. 143, 193*, 219, 222, 312 ; Matthew, 95 ; Michael, 126 ; Peace, 48 ; Rebecca, 48, 109 ; Robert, 61, 106 ; Rose, 33 ; Ruth, 61 ; Samuel, 62, 291 ; Sarah, 2. 27, 46, 187. 222, 232, 291 ; Susanna, 56 ; Thomas, 48, 57, 97, 99, 257, 307 ; Rev. Mr. William, 65 ; William, 33, 251, 252*, 253*, 254*, 255*, 256*, 257, 258.*

Wilton (Whilton), David, 204 ; Elizabeth, 204 ; Sarah, 308.

Wiltshire. Joanna, 124.

Wimbush. Elizabeth, 19 ; John, 19.

Wimpe (Wympe), Joan, 266 ; Rebecca, 278 ; Richard, 266.

Wimpey, Anne, 127.

Winbush, Anne, 46.

Winch, Elizabeth, 162 ; Henry, 44 ; Joan, 314 ; Salomon, 314 ; Sarah, 44.

Winchcombe, Catherine, 34.

Winchester, Elizabeth, 83 ; John, 83.

Winckfield, Margaret. 280.

Winckles, Ann, 182 ; John, 182.

Winckley, Myrtilla, 129 ; Richard, 129.

Wind, Bridget, 7 ; William, 7.

Windell, John, 159 ; Susanna, 159.

Winder, Eleanor, 116 ; Humphrey, 117 ; Mary, 177 ; Rebecca, 117 ; Samuel, 177.

Windham, Sarah, 188 ; William, 188.

Windley, Rachael, 209 ; Thomas, 209.

Windoe, Elizabeth, 279.

Windred, Jane, 218 ; Joseph, 218.

Winfield. John, 2 ; Mary, 4 ; Sarah, 2 ; Susanna. 3.

Wing, Mary, 55.

Wingate, Sarah, 131.

Wingfield, Richard, 219 ; Susanna, 219 ; Thomas, 228.

Wingrove, Ann, 207 ; Hannah, 160 ; Jane, 90 ; Moses, 207 ; Thomas, 160 ; William, 90.

Wington, James, 311 ; Mary. 311.

Winkin, Joanna, 24 ; William, 24.

Winkworth, Francis, 20 ; Mary. 20.

Winnye, Joan, 265 ; William, 265.

Winpenny. Rolana, 69 ; Thomas, 69.

Winslow, Elizabeth, 214.

Winsmore, Frances, 185.

Winson, Elizabeth, 55.

Winspear, Edward, 215 ; Mary, 22.

Winstanley, Bridget, 277 ; Rev. Mr., 182.

Winston, Edward, 307 ; Mary, 307.

Winter, Elizabeth, 21, 163, 183, 216, 313 ; E.,

X

Y

ADDENDA.

INDEX LOCORUM.

* Signifies that a place or parish occurs more than once on the page.

C

D

E

M

N

O

Oxford, St. Aldate's in, 181.
St. Ebb's in, 157.
St. Michael's in, 17.
Oxted, Surrey, 11, 15, 24, 66, 140, 190, 265.

P

Packwood, Warwickshire, 36.
Paddington, Middx., 46, 95, 96, 206.
Pancras, Middx., 182.
Papworth, Huntingdonshire, 199.
Paris, France, 268.
Pauler's Pury, Northampton, 42, 88.
Peckham, Surrey, 73.
Penham, Essex, 13.
Penn, Bucks, 110.
Penryn, Cornwall, 96.
Penshurst, Kent, 129, 140, 207.
Penzance, Cornwall, 192.
Pershore, Worcestershire, 55.
Petersfield, Hants, 119.
Petersham, Surrey, 33.
Petworth, Sussex, 8, 169.
Pickenham, North, Norfolk, 165.
Pickhilt, Denbighshire, 50.
Piddleton, Northants, 35.
Pinner, Middx., 108.
Pirbright, Surrey, 252.
Playstead, Essex, 126.
Plumstead, Kent, 7.
Plymouth, Devon, 114, 130, 158.
Plymouth, St. Andrew's in, 218.
Poplar, Stepney, Middx., 12, 17, 26, 49, 136, 154.
Portsmouth, Hants, 58, 98, 119, 172, 178, 179, 180, 196, 200, 259.
Potton, Beds., 45, 206.
Presteign, Herefordshire, 180.
Preston, Cape, Northants, 26.
Preston, Lancashire, 196.
Purfleet, Essex, 55.
Putney, Surrey, 14, 27, 48, 49, 62, 83, 100, 105, 106, 119*, 132, 161, 171, 177, 179*, 197, 205.

Q

Quatford, Shropshire, 4.
Queenborough, Kent, 72, 205.
Queenby, Leicestershire, 184.
Quorndon, Leicestershire, 105.

R

Radnor, Old, Radnorshire, 12.
Ramsden, Essex, 207.
Rayleigh, Essex, 62.
Raynham, Essex, 157.
Reading, Berks, 31, 74, 114, 130, 146, 185, 198, 199, 264, 274.
Reading, St. Lawrence in, 24, 267, 276.
Reading, St. Mary's in, 16, 20.
Redbourn, Herts, 33, 90, 137.
Redgrave, Suffolk, 43, 44.
Reigate, Surrey, 24, 81, 84.
Rendlesham, Suffolk, 44.
Restbury, Cheshire, 174.
Richmond, Surrey, 3, 4, 5, 7, 49, 59, 70, 71, 74, 79, 80, 81, 84, 101, 105, 108, 111, 112*, 115, 117, 121, 126, 134, 138, 140, 141, 151, 160, 161, 163, 169, 179, 183, 190, 197, 201, 204, 206.
Richmond, Yorkshire, 14.
Rickenhall, Suffolk, 189.
Rickmansworth, Herts, 3, 10, 18, 20, 32, 62, 202.
Ripley, Surrey, 50.
Ripon, Yorkshire, 156.
Risborough, Bucks, 12.
Rislip, Middx., 40, 41, 52, 56, 119, 151, 231.
Rochester, Kent, 39, 60, 104, 153, 163.
Rochester, St. Margaret's in, 26, 123, 191.
Rochester, St. Nicholas in, 152, 191.
Rochford, Essex, 139.
Rocliff (Rockcliffe), Cumberland, 6.
Romford in Hornchurch, Essex, 4, 39, 50, 64, 68, 85, 108*, 146, 166, 172, 235.
Romney, Kent, 34.
Romney, New, Kent, 53.
Romsey, Hants, 100.
Roxwell, Essex, 154.
Ross, Herefordshire, 81.
Rotherham, Yorkshire, 80.
Rotherhithe, Surrey, 19, 42, 65, 70, 84, 94, 175.
Rotherhithe, St. Mary, Surrey, 4, 18, 19, 21, 25*, 29, 30, 31, 35*, 36, 41, 42, 49, 54, 56, 58*, 65, 70, 77, 82, 83, 88, 95, 98, 109, 112, 114, 118, 122, 123, 134, 135, 136, 137, 145, 151, 152, 161*, 166, 169, 170, 174, 180, 182, 183, 187, 193, 198, 200, 201*, 203, 206, 208, 209, 248, 256.
Rowndway (Rowde), Wilts, 202.
Roydon, Essex, 35.
Royston, Herts, 41, 172.
Rudgwick, Sussex, 149*.
Runwell, Essex, 62.
Rushden, Northants, 199.

S

Saffron Walden, Essex, 11, 196.
St. Albans, Herts, 2, 4, 6, 36, 87, 183, 191, 200, 241, 254.
St. Albans, St. Stephen's in, 55, 119, 248.
St. George in the East, Middx., 4, 15, 16, 18, 24, 28, 38, 48, 51, 62*, 78, 89*, 101, 110, 111, 114, 116, 120, 124, 127, 130, 134, 137, 156, 184, 187, 217.
St. George the Martyr, Middx., 1, 2, 5, 7, 10, 11, 12, 16, 19, 20*, 21, 23*, 25, 30, 32, 38, 39, 40, 42, 43*, 44, 46, 48, 49*, 52, 53*, 55*, 59, 60, 62, 64*, 66*, 71, 72, 79, 81, 90*, 91*, 92, 93, 95*, 96, 97, 99, 100, 103, 104, 106, 107, 108, 109, 112, 114, 115, 116, 117, 124, 125, 126, 128, 131, 133, 136, 137, 138*, 150, 151, 153, 156, 158, 159, 160, 162*, 163, 164, 165, 166, 167, 170*, 171, 172, 174, 175*, 178*, 179, 180, 181, 188, 190, 191*, 192*, 198, 205*, 207, 208*, 209, 212, 213, 225, 234, 242, 253.
St. George the Martyr, Queen's Square, Bloomsbury, 6, 7, 11, 13, 14, 15, 16, 17, 18, 20*, 21*, 22, 27, 30*, 31, 32, 35, 38, 40, 42*, 44, 45, 46, 53, 55, 56, 57*, 62, 66, 68, 69*, 71, 73*, 74, 77, 80, 82*, 84, 85, 88, 94, 99, 100, 101, 105, 109*, 111, 112, 114, 115, 121, 127, 128, 131, 135, 136, 137, 140, 143, 146*, 154, 157, 158*, 159*, 163, 167, 174, 182, 184*, 185, 188, 191, 191, 201, 202, 205, 207*, 209, 217, 229, 236, 253, 262.
St. Giles, Dorset, 18, 195.
St. Hilary in Jersey, 159.
St. Ives, Huntingdonshire, 149.

T

U

W

Y

London: Mitchell Hughes and Clarke, Printers, 140 Wardour Street, W.

Lightning Source UK Ltd.
Milton Keynes UK
UKHW020644190722
406066UK00005B/578

9 781376 941937